TO Jon
"my little aircraft
love from   fanatic
  XXX   sisha

D1141252

GREAT AIRCRAFT
—OF THE WORLD—

An illustrated
history of the
most famous
civil and military planes

Colour Library Books

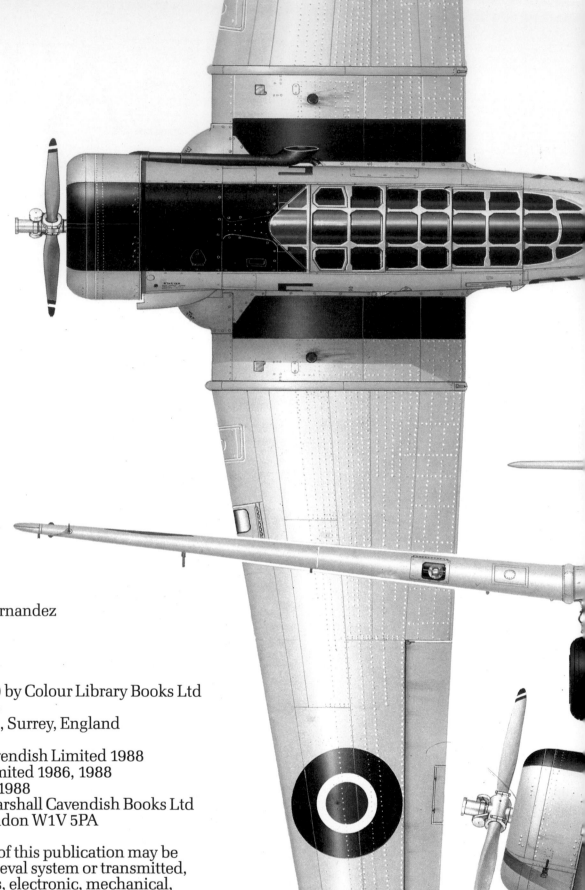

Series Editor: Peter Allez-Fernandez
Book Editor: Len Cacutt

CLB 2203

This edition published 1989 by Colour Library Books Ltd
Godalming Business Centre
Catteshall Lane, Godalming, Surrey, England

This edition prepared by Marshall Cavendish Books Ltd
58 Old Compton Street, London W1V 5PA

Typeset by J&L Compositions Ltd, Filey, North Yorkshire
Printed in Italy

ISBN 0-86283-627-1

Contents

Contents

Introduction

Deciding on a choice of the world's most famous aircraft is no easy matter. There is no objective yardstick that can be used to decide on how famous an aircraft is. But there are some criteria which help make the choice easier. Manfred von Richthofen with his triplane was a legend even in his own lifetime. The Messerschmitt Bf 109 worked its way into the history books through the sheer numbers in which it was built, and in Britain the Spitfire became a symbol of an entire nation's war effort. The indestructible DC-3 survived not only the war, but is still being used all over the world today, more than half a century after its maiden flight. In contrast, there are virtually no working Junkers Ju 52s left, but they were known to a generation of Germans as the 'Tante Ju'. Nor is being famous necessarily the same as being successful. The tragic series of crashes involving Comets and Starfighters has made more headlines than the technical innovations they embodied, and Concorde's record-breaking performances rapidly eclipsed the financial disaster this ambitious project represented. But more successful from an economic point of view have been two of the undisputed stars of the world of modern aviation, the Airbus and the Tornado, both of which reflect the upturn experienced by the European aircraft industry during the past few decades. All the aircraft described here represent an epoch, a country, a design team and outstanding technical performance. All of them have become celebrities of the air.

Peter Alles-Fernandez

Avro 504

Efficient product of Britain's great pioneering aircraft designer, Alliott Verdon Roe, the Avro 504 became the most widely-used British trainer during World War 1, and laid the foundations of formal flying training that were to persist for more than 30 years; it went on to become the sporting pilot's favourite mount during the 'barnstorming years' of the 1920s.

During the first decade of this century, when many major young talents were at work on the construction of aircraft, A. V. Roe was championing the idea of Britain having its own aircraft industry. In 1907 he built his first prototype, the Roe I biplane. But his first success in powered flight was not until 1909 when, on 13 July, twelve days before Louis Blériot's historic flight across the English Channel, he became the first British pilot successfully to fly an all-British powered aircraft, the Roe II triplane.

After considerable experimenting and the production of further triplanes and biplanes, Roe produced several examples of his two-seat E500 biplane, and in 1912 three such aircraft, fitted with dual controls, were ordered by the War Office, nine others being ordered by early 1913. This business made possible the formation of the private company of A. V. Roe and Co. Ltd.

The construction of a direct development, the Avro 504, was started in April 1913; this was completed within 12 weeks and started flying at Brooklands in July. On 20 September it was flown into fourth place in the Second Aerial Derby by Fred Raynham at a speed of 66.5 mph (107 km/h). The aeroplane was a well-proportioned biplane with two-bay, equal-span wings and wire-braced wooden box-girder fuselage. The engine originally fitted was an 80-hp (60-kW) Gnome rotary attached to a nose bearing mounting in a square cross-section cowling. A float version was also produced for sporting customers.

In the months immediately preceding the outbreak of World War 1 the War Office ordered 12 Avro 504s and the Admiralty one, and these were delivered between July and September 1914. However, although further orders quickly followed the declaration of war, Avro 504s did not feature in any numbers in RFC squadrons in France. It was an Avro of No. 5 Squadron that became the first British aircraft to be shot down when on 22 August the aircraft flown by Lieutenant V. Waterfall was brought down by infantry fire over Belgium. Avro 504s were also flown in a small number of audacious bombing raids, of which the most famous was the attack by RNAS aircraft on the Zeppelin sheds at Friedrichshafen, Lake Constance, on 21 November 1914, led by Squadron Commander E. F. Briggs. Aerial attacks were also made on Zeppelins in their own element by dropping 20-lb (9-kg) bombs on them from above.

The Avro 504A appeared early in 1915, retaining the 80-hp (60-kW) Gnome but with shorter and broader ailerons; some aircraft had the lower wing roots left uncovered so as to improve the downward field of vision. This was the main version produced during the years 1915–6. The Avro 504B, of which 240 were built by Avro, Parnall, Sunbeam and Regent Carriage for the Admiralty, reverted to the long ailerons and featured a large unbalanced rudder hinged to a prominent, low aspect ratio fin. The RNAS also insisted on wing spars of increased cross section, and the Avro 504B introduced a big ash tailskid, sprung with rubber cord and hinged to a pylon under the rear fuselage, a feature retained on all subsequent Avro 504s. Some Avro 504Bs served operationally at Dunkirk, at least two being fitted with a forward-firing gun with interrupter gear and an upward-firing Lewis gun. Later aircraft were powered by 80-hp (60-kW) Le Rhône engines.

This superb replica was built by Vivian Bellamy for an abandoned film and snapped up by Cole Palen for his Old Rhinebeck (New York State) airfield. It is a copy of E2939, an Avro 504K built by Morgan & Co. of Leighton Buzzard. The replica regularly shoots down von Richthofen's Fokker Dr.I with 'Le Prieur' rockets.

Avro 504

Specification

Avro 504K

Type: two-seat ab initio elementary trainer

Powerplant: one 110-hp (82-kW) Le Rhône rotary piston engine

Performance: maximum speed 95 mph (153 km/h) at sea level; climb to 3,500 ft (1065 m) in 5 minutes; service ceiling 16,000 ft (4875 m); range 250 miles (402 km)

Weights: empty 1,230 lb (558 kg); maximum take-off 1,829 lb (830 kg)

Dimensions: span 36 ft 0 in (10.97 m); length 29 ft 5 in (8.97 m); height 10 ft 5 in (3.17 m); wing area 330.0 sq ft (30.66 m²)

Armament: none

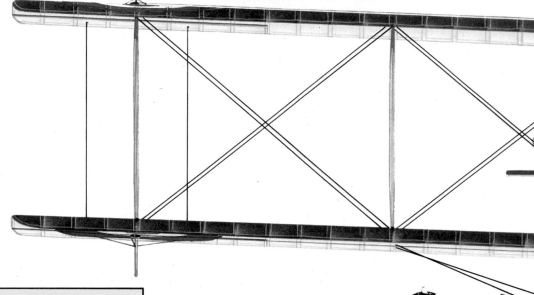

The Avro 504K shown here in pristine factory finish, E3785, was a wartime product of A. V. Roe's own Miles Platting works at Manchester. The small company logo was applied to almost all aircraft before delivery but was usually overpainted on arrival at the service aircraft parks. Although much is made of the Avro 504's suitability for the barnstorming 'work' it performed in the 1920s, it was unforgiving of slipshod maintenance, and many aircraft, purchased by shoestring companies run by enthusiastic ex-wartime pilots, came to grief as the result of inadequate servicing.

Avro 504 variants

Avro 504: prototype first flown in summer 1913; 80-hp (60-kW) Gnome, and later Gnome Monosoupape engine

Avro 504: first production, four commercial aircraft and 63 for RNAS and RFC, 80-hp (60-kW) Gnome or Le Rhône engines (Avro-built)

Avro 504A: production by Avro, Saunders, Humber, Biériot & Spad, Parnall and Eastbourne; total uncertain but seen under 540J, short ailerons; 80-hp (60-kW) Gnome or Le Rhône engines

Avro 504B: 240 built by Avro, Parnall, Sunbeam, and Regent in 1915–6, 80-hp (60-kW) Gnome or Le Rhône engines; RNAS version with long fin and long ailerons

Avro 504C: 80 built by Avro and Brush Electric, 80-hp (60-kW); Gnome engines, single-seaters for RNAS

Avro 504D: six built by Avro, as 504C but for RFC;

Avro 504E: 10 built by Avro; 100-hp (75-kW) Gnome Monosoupape engines; straight top longerons and long fin; served with RNAS

Avro 504F: one 504C (8603) with 75-hp (56-kW) Rolls-Royce Hawk engine

Avro 504G: unknown number of 504Bs modified as gunnery trainers for RNAS with two guns; 80-hp (60-kW) Gnome engines

Avro 504H: one 504C modified for catapult trials

Avro 504J: first major production variant built by Avro, Harland & Wolff, Sunbeam and Brush in 1917–18; introduced Gosport communication; 80-hp (60-kW) Le Rhône or 100-hp (75-kW) Gnome Monosoupape engine (unknown number built, but said to be about 1,050; total number of 504As and 504Js computed as 1,455)

Avro 504K: main production variant, total of 6,350 built by Avro, Sage, Henderson, Scottish, Hewlett & Blondeau, Grahame-White, Parnall, Harland & Wolff, Morgan, Savage, Humber, Eastbourne, Brush and Sunbeam (plus one built by RAF from spares); engines included 90-hp (67-kW) RAF 1A and Thulin; 100-hp (75-kW) Gnome Monosoupape, Curtiss K6 and Sunbeam Dyak; 110-hp (82-kW) Le Rhône, 130-hp (97-kW) Clerget; 150-hp (112-kW) Bentley B.R.1; 170-hp (127-kW) A.B.C. Wasp and 220-hp (164-kW) Hispano-Suiza; many sold to civilian customers, including 51 new-built; unknown number also privately built from spares; licence

production of 20 in Australia by Broadsmith and AAEC, 27 in Belgium by SABCA, two by CAL in Canada, 74 by Nakajima in Japan; others were presented or exported to Argentina, Australia, Belgium, Brazil, Canada, Chile, Denmark, Estonia, Finland, Guatemala, India, Ireland, Japan, Malaya, Mexico, Netherlands, Indies, New Zealand, Norway, Peru, Portugal, South Africa, Spain, Sweden, Switzerland, USA and Uruguay

Avro 504L: six aircraft (three-seat floatplanes), new built with 150-hp (112-kW) Bentley B.R.1 engines plus numerous conversions from 504K; imperial gifts of five conversions to Canada, two to Australia and two to New Zealand, some converted in Japan

Avro 504M: single conversion (G-EACX) of 504K as three-seat cabin aircraft by Avro (Hamble) for Avro Transport Co.; 100-hp (75-kW) Gnome Monosoupape

Avro 504N: principal peacetime production variant; engines included 100-hp (75-kW) Bristol Lucifer, 115-hp (86-kW) Lucifer IV; 150-hp (112-kW) Armstrong Siddeley Mongoose IIIA or Lynx; 180-hp (134-kW) Lynx IVC; 200-hp (149-kW) Wright Whirlwind; six prototypes and eight development aircraft, plus four interim aircraft for Armstrong Whitworth; 512 new-built plus 78 504K conversions for RAF; licence production in and export to; 17 to Belgium (plus 31 licence), four to Brazil (including 504Os), six to the Netherlands (including 504Os), six to Chile (including 504Os), one to Denmark (plus five licence), one to Japan, unknown number to South Africa, 20 to Thailand, one to Sweden

Avro 504P: unbuilt version of 504N with side-by-side seating

Avro 504Q: one three-seat aircraft (G-EBJD) with enclosed cabin for Oxford University Arctic Expedition; 160-hp (119-kW) Lynx engine

Avro 504R Gosport: six prototype and development aircraft, engines included 90-hp (67-kW) Avro Alpha; 100-hp (75-kW) Gnome Monosoupape; 150-hp (112-kW) Mongoose; 180-hp (134-kW) Lynx; 10 sold to Argentina (and 100 built under licence); about six to Estonia and an unknown number to Peru

U-1: copy of 504K mass-produced in USSR; NU-1 seaplane version

A Sunbeam-built Avro 504K, F2623, possibly belonging to the Central Flying School, Upavon, on a training flight over Salisbury Plain shortly after the end of the war. At the time of the Armistice the RAF held 2,999 504Js and Ks on charge, of which 2,267 were serving with flying schools.

Nostalgia abounds in this inter-war scene showing Avro 504Ks and their ground personnel awaiting an inspection at an RAF station. With huge quantities of war-surplus spares available at virtually no cost, the 504 was probably the most cost-effective military trainer of all time.

Early variants

Eighty Avro 504Cs were built by Avro and Brush Electrical Engineering: this model was a single-seat version produced for the RNAS with a big cylindrical fuel tank in place of the front cockpit to increase the aircraft's endurance to 8 hours 30 minutes. A gap in the top-wing centre section allowed a Lewis gun to fire upwards at an angle of 45°. Six examples of an equivalent RFC version, the Avro 504D, were ordered but doubt remains that they were ever delivered.

Ten Avro 504Es were produced for the RNAS with the 100-hp (75-kW) Gnome Monosoupape; the rear cockpit was moved aft to allow space for a fuel tank behind the front cockpit, and the resulting centre of gravity change was countered by reducing the wing stagger from 24 to 9 in (61 to 23 cm). These aircraft served at Chingford, Cranwell and Fairlop. Only one Avro 504F was produced, this being a converted Avro 504C with 75-hp (56-kW) Rolls-Royce Hawk six-cylinder inline engine, but for some reason nothing came of this version.

Some uncertainty surrounds the Avro 504G, said to have been an RFC gunnery trainer with 130-hp (97-kW) Clerget engine, and with a synchronized Vickers at the front and a Lewis gun in the rear; 10 such aircraft were produced, but the designation was also used to cover conversions of the Avro 504B for the RNAS with 80-hp (60-kW) Gnome and two guns. One Avro 504H was produced by converting an Avro 504C for catapult trials by Flight Commander R. E. Penny in 1917; the aircraft was specially strengthened and featured catapult pick-up points.

It may be said that the A to H versions of the Avro 504 were exploratory variants, undertaken before large-scale wartime production got under way of the widely used Avro 504J and Avro 504K. The Avro 504J, otherwise externally identical to the Avro 504A, was powered by a 100-hp (75-kW) Gnome Monosoupape in a characteristic lobed cowling; indeed many aircraft originally ordered as Avro 504As were completed as Avro 504Js, thus making it impossible to determine the exact production of each version; manufacture was undertaken by Avro, S.E. Saunders, Humber, Parnall, Sunbeam and Brush Electrical in 1916–8. The model was significant in introducing the 'Gosport' speaking tube which enabled the flying instructor to communicate with his pupil, thereby allowing the system of demonstration and explanation, a system that persisted in biplane training to the end of the Tiger Moth era in the Royal Air Force. The Avro 504J was also fully aerobatic, joining the School of Special Flying at Gosport and almost every other training establishment in the UK as well as many overseas. Some Avro Js were also fitted with surplus 80-hp (60-kW) Le Rhônes but without change of designation.

Best-remembered of all is the Avro 504K, which introduced a new type of universal engine mounting, designed by H. E. Broadsmith; consisting of two bearer plates which would accept any suitable engine, the mounting allowed the

use of a smooth, open-fronted cowling, and the standardization of the airframe gave rise to a considerable increase in production. Forthwith Avro planned to produce 100 aircraft per week, plus spares; 20 further sets of parts were also despatched to Egypt for assembly at Aboukir. Fifty-two Avro 504Ks were purchased by the USA, and these were flown for advanced training by the American Expeditionary Forces in France in 1918, the survivors being shipped to the USA after

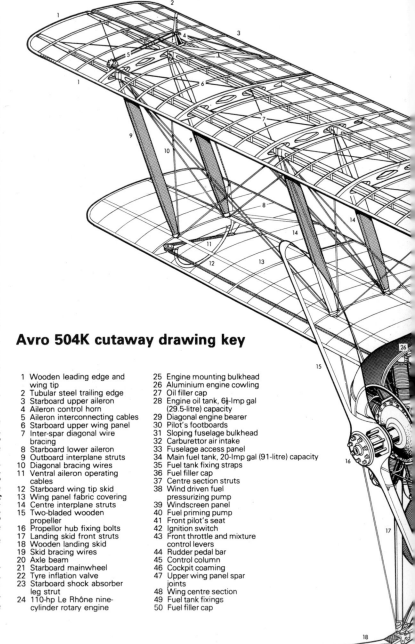

Avro 504K cutaway drawing key

1 Wooden leading edge and wing tip
2 Tubular steel trailing edge
3 Starboard upper aileron
4 Aileron control horn
5 Aileron interconnecting cables
6 Starboard upper wing panel
7 Inter-spar diagonal wire bracing
8 Starboard lower aileron
9 Outboard interplane struts
10 Diagonal bracing wires
11 Ventral aileron operating cables
12 Starboard wing tip skid
13 Wing panel fabric covering
14 Centre interplane struts
15 Two-bladed wooden propeller
16 Propeller hub fixing bolts
17 Landing skid front struts
18 Wooden landing skid
19 Skid bracing wires
20 Axle beam
21 Starboard mainwheel
22 Tyre inflation valve
23 Starboard shock absorber leg strut
24 110-hp Le Rhône nine-cylinder rotary engine
25 Engine mounting bulkhead
26 Aluminium engine cowling
27 Oil filler cap
28 Engine oil tank, 6½-Imp gal (29.5-litre) capacity
29 Diagonal engine bearer
30 Pilot's footboards
31 Sloping fuselage bulkhead
32 Carburettor air intake
33 Fuselage access panel
34 Main fuel tank, 20-Imp gal (91-litre) capacity
35 Fuel tank fixing straps
36 Fuel filler cap
37 Centre section struts
38 Wind driven fuel pressurizing pump
39 Windscreen panel
40 Fuel priming pump
41 Front pilot's seat
42 Ignition switch
43 Front throttle and mixture control levers
44 Rudder pedal bar
45 Control column
46 Cockpit coaming
47 Upper wing panel spar joints
48 Wing centre section
49 Fuel tank fixings
50 Fuel filler cap

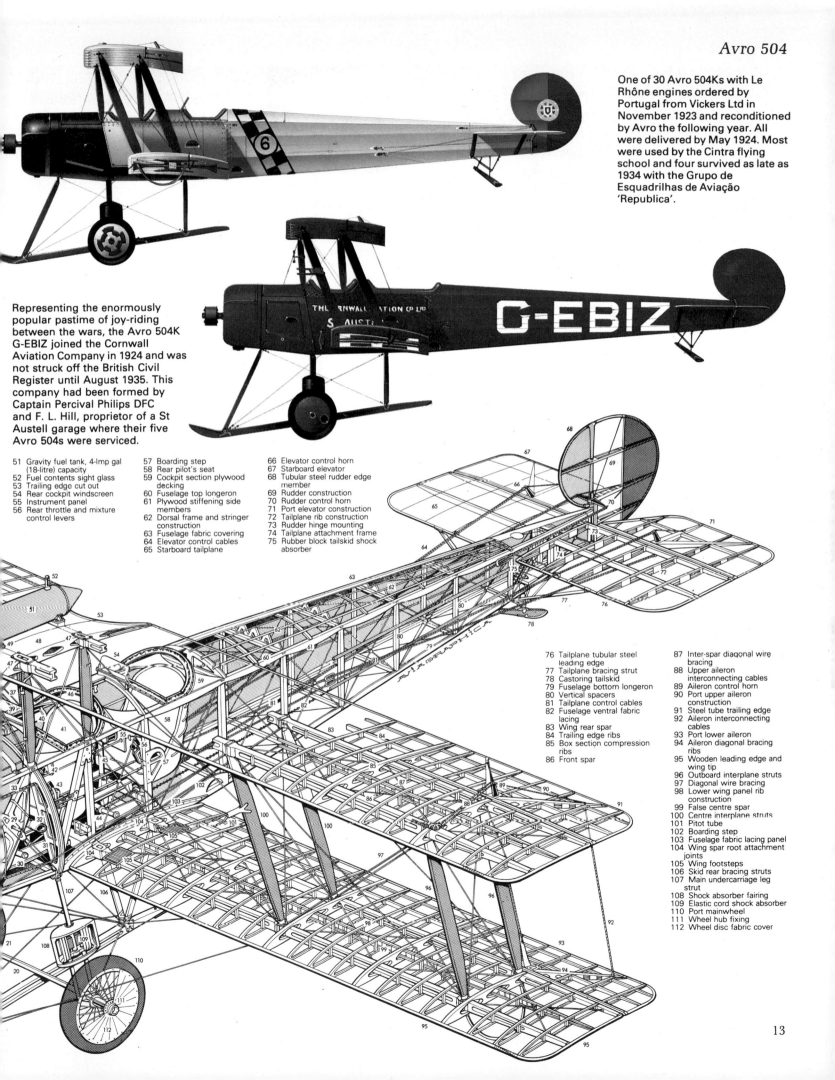

One of 30 Avro 504Ks with Le Rhône engines ordered by Portugal from Vickers Ltd in November 1923 and reconditioned by Avro the following year. All were delivered by May 1924. Most were used by the Cintra flying school and four survived as late as 1934 with the Grupo de Esquadrilhas de Aviação 'Republica'.

Representing the enormously popular pastime of joy-riding between the wars, the Avro 504K G-EBIZ joined the Cornwall Aviation Company in 1924 and was not struck off the British Civil Register until August 1935. This company had been formed by Captain Percival Philips DFC and F. L. Hill, proprietor of a St Austell garage where their five Avro 504s were serviced.

51 Gravity fuel tank, 4-Imp gal (18-litre) capacity
52 Fuel contents sight glass
53 Trailing edge cut out
54 Rear cockpit windscreen
55 Instrument panel
56 Rear throttle and mixture control levers
57 Boarding step
58 Rear pilot's seat
59 Cockpit section plywood decking
60 Fuselage top longeron
61 Plywood stiffening side members
62 Dorsal frame and stringer construction
63 Fuselage fabric covering
64 Elevator control cables
65 Starboard tailplane
66 Elevator control horn
67 Starboard elevator
68 Tubular steel rudder edge member
69 Rudder construction
70 Rudder control horn
71 Port elevator construction
72 Tailplane rib construction
73 Rudder hinge mounting
74 Tailplane attachment frame
75 Rubber block tailskid shock absorber

76 Tailplane tubular steel leading edge
77 Tailplane bracing strut
78 Castoring tailskid
79 Fuselage bottom longeron
80 Vertical spacers
81 Tailplane control cables
82 Fuselage ventral fabric lacing
83 Wing rear spar
84 Trailing edge ribs
85 Box section compression ribs
86 Front spar
87 Inter-spar diagonal wire bracing
88 Upper aileron interconnecting cables
89 Aileron control horn
90 Port upper aileron construction
91 Steel tube trailing edge
92 Aileron interconnecting cables
93 Port lower aileron
94 Aileron diagonal bracing ribs
95 Wooden leading edge and wing tip
96 Outboard interplane struts
97 Diagonal wire bracing
98 Lower wing panel rib construction
99 False centre spar
100 Centre interplane struts
101 Pitot tube
102 Boarding step
103 Fuselage fabric lacing panel
104 Wing spar root attachment joints
105 Wing footsteps
106 Skid rear bracing struts
107 Main undercarriage leg strut
108 Shock absorber fairing
109 Elastic cord shock absorber
110 Port mainwheel
111 Wheel hub fixing
112 Wheel disc fabric cover

Production of the Avro 504K continued long after the Armistice of 1918, this example being produced by the Henderson Scottish Aviation Factory of Aberdeen in 1919 or 1920.

The post-war Avro 504K joy-riding phenomenon was inaugurated by the Avro Company at Easter 1919 with three aircraft, including E4360 (later G-EABM), on Blackpool sands.

the war. Total wartime production of the Avro 504 exceeded that of any other British aircraft. The figure of 3,696 built by Avro and 4,644 by sub-contractors has frequently been quoted but the total of 8,340 appears to be an overstatement by about 236. By far the greater proportion was flown by training units (more than 4,800 in the United Kingdom and some 320 overseas).

Peacetime production

With so many war-time pilots being trained on the Avro 504 and such enormous stocks of the aircraft being declared surplus, it was not surprising that the type should survive well into the years of peace. There were, moreover, huge stocks (some estimates put them at almost 3,000) of un-delivered aircraft at storage parks and at the factories. Aircraft were sold at public auction at Hendon, until in 1920 Handley Page purchased all stocks and thereafter sold them through its subsidiary the Aircraft Disposal Co. at Croydon. New price of an Avro 504K, without engine, was £868, and a 130-hp Clerget cost £907; average price paid by civilian buyers in 1920 was around £650 for a Clerget-powered Avro 504K.

Among the multitude of popular flying events at which civil-registered Avro 504Ks appeared were the Aerial Derbies, the Wakes Weeks and Air Traffic Exhibitions, not to mention the countless displays mounted by the fast-growing numbers of local flying clubs up and down the country. Alan Cobham was among the newly demobilized service pilots who started the famous 'barnstorming' tours with Avro 504Ks in the 1920s, and persisted until the 1930s. One of his pilots, Captain Percival Philips DFC, carried more than 91,000 passengers, almost all of them in one famous aeroplane, G-EBIZ, over a period of about 15 years.

The RAF continued to use the Avro 504K, aircraft of this type serving with Nos 1, 2, 3 and 5 FTS in the UK and with No. 4 FTS at Abu Sueir, and at East Retford, Throwley and Newmarket; others flew at the CFS at Upavon, and the Royal Air Force College, Cranwell, as well as the newly-created Auxiliary Air Force in the late 1920s. The Fleet Air Arm used Avro 504Ks at Leuchars and Netheravon.

Avro 504Ks enjoyed a brisk trade in the export market and some ex-Australian Flying Corps aircraft served with the RAAF until 1928. Others included 63 Imperial Gift Avro 504Ks to Canada and 20 to New Zealand. The largest overseas licence manufacturer of the Avro 504K was Nakajima of Japan. Far greater numbers were built without a licence in the USSR in 1922–8 as the U-1 and sea-plane NU-1, powered by the M-2 copy of the 100-hp (75-kW) Gnome.

The Avro 504L was a peacetime development employing two wooden pontoon-type floats and a 130-hp Clerget driving a four-blade propeller, The aircraft was not adopted by the RAF and new production was confined to six aircraft produced by Avro at Hamble, although numerous float conversions were carried out in the UK and overseas. The single Avro 504M (G-EACX) was a standard Avro 504K modified to feature enclosed accommodation for two passengers, and a similar version was put into licence

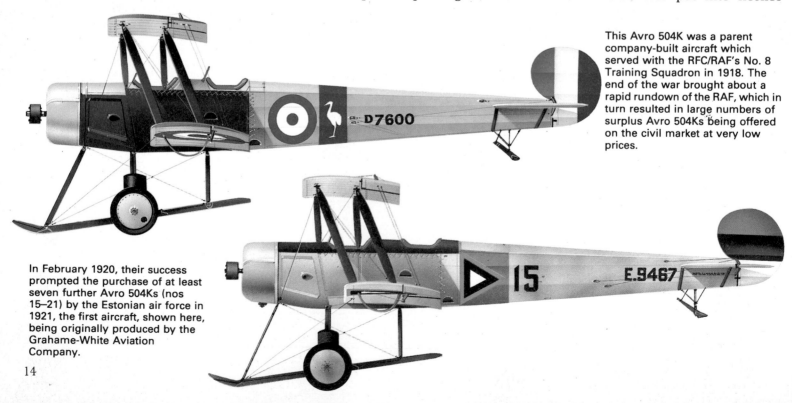

This Avro 504K was a parent company-built aircraft which served with the RFC/RAF's No. 8 Training Squadron in 1918. The end of the war brought about a rapid rundown of the RAF, which in turn resulted in large numbers of surplus Avro 504Ks being offered on the civil market at very low prices.

In February 1920, their success prompted the purchase of at least seven further Avro 504Ks (nos 15–21) by the Estonian air force in 1921, the first aircraft, shown here, being originally produced by the Grahame-White Aviation Company.

This Avro 504K was built in 1918 and has a 100-hp (75 kW) Avro Le Rhône nine-cylinder engine. It is now owned by the Shuttleworth Collection and occasionally still appears in flying displays. (*Photo: Air Portraits*)

Originally purchased as an Avro 504K (no. 104, previously H2021) by the Danish navy in 1920, this aircraft was converted to an Avro 504N (no. 112) in 1928 in Denmark as OY-DEL. It was sold in July 1936 to Czechoslovakia and in 1940 was seized by the Germans. The aircraft is shown with its blind-flying hood closed over the rear cockpit.

The Avro 504R was not adopted by the RAF, but a small number was sold abroad to Argentina, Estonia and Peru. At least six went to the Estonian air force for service at Tallinn in November 1928, including the example depicted here, and some of them survived into the 1940s.

production in Japan as the Aiba Tsubami IV with 150-hp (112-kW) Gasden Jimpu engine.

The Avro 540N was the main production variant introduced after the end of World War 1. Prototypes and development aircraft were largely produced by converting Avro 504Ks, but six new-built aircraft appeared after 1924. The new version featured a wholly revised landing gear, comprising two main legs attached to the axle which in turn was hinged to two horizontal tubes by two rear Vee-struts behind and in line with the main legs. In this characteristic 'N-type' landing gear the central skid (for so long a feature of the Avro 504) was discarded. Production orders for the RAF, placed between 1927 and 1933, amounted to 512 aircraft, plus 78 conversions from Avro 504Ks, and these aircraft gave yeoman service with Nos 1, 2, 3, 4 and 5 FTS, No. 23 ERFTS, the RAF College, the Oxford and Cambridge University Air Squadrons, and Nos 500, 501, 502, 601, 602, 603, 604 and 607 Squadrons of the Auxiliary Air Force. In due course many of these Avro 504Ns were replaced by the Avro Tutor and Hawker Tomtit, and eventually found their way on to the commercial market. Among the modified versions of the Avro 504N was a single-float aircraft with Wright Whirlwind J-4 engine, produced by Canadian Vickers in 1926, and a light glider-tug version. Seven of the latter were produced in 1940 (as conversions) to equip a Special Duty Flight at Christchurch, towing Hotspur gliders 40 miles (66 km) out to sea to test radar reflection of wooden aircraft; other Avro

One of the many Avro 504 derivatives was the Avro 548, with Renault engine, for example, produced by Surrey Flying Services from ex-E3043 in 1921–2, was used in radio telegraphy work by Marconi Wireless Telegraph Co. in the early 1920s and sold to the Henderson School of Flying in 1926.

504N glider tugs were used during World War 2 at Ringway to develop towing techniques for the airborne forces.

The single Avro 504Q was a three-seat enclosed-cabin floatplane produced at Avro's Hamble works for the Oxford University Arctic Expedition; powered by a 160-hp (119-kW) Armstrong Siddeley Lynx and registered G-EBJD, this aeroplane sported a large dorsal fin and carried extra fuel tanks under the upper wing. During the course of an exciting voyage via Spitzbergen (on which G-EBJD was all but wrecked several times but repaired), it reached latitude 80° 15' on 8 August 1924, the farthest north yet reached by an aeroplane. G-EBJD was eventually abandoned to test the effect of Arctic exposure on wooden aircraft, but when examined in the 1930s it was found to have been partly devoured by polar bears!

The last version of the Avro 504 was the Gosport or Avro 504R. This was an attempt to produce a version which could emulate the performance of the RAF's Avro 504N, despite having a cheaper, lower-power engine than the Lynx. Various engines were tested, but most proved not to be powerful enough. Finally, the manufacturers came to the conclusion that a 150-hp (112-kW) Mongoose would give the best performance. Six test aircraft were built, and a few exported to Argentina, Estonia and Peru. The Fábrica Militar de Aviones, in Cordoba, Argentina, built 100 of these machines under licence. As far as is known, when SABCA in Belgium ordered ten Avro 504s in October 1937, it was the last time any of these aircraft were ordered.

Most celebrated RAF unit to fly the Avro 504N was the Central Flying School, Upavon, the aircraft shown here serving with the school from 1931 onwards. Just visible is the blind-flying hood for the student's cockpit, shown here folded down. When covering the rear cockpit the u/t pilot had to fly solely on instruments.

Handley Page O/100 and O/400

No other aircraft manufacturer achieved sufficient fame as to grace the pages of the Concise Oxford Dictionary with the definition 'Type of large aeroplane', and it was the impression created by Frederick Handley Page's O/100 and O/400 bombers of World War 1 which caused the name Handley Page to become a generic title for large aircraft

Two events shortly after World War 1 gave a definite boost to the development of these two great aircraft types. When the Royal Flying Corps and other Air Forces realised how useful aircraft could be for reconnaissance purposes they set off falteringly into the skies using BE2a biplanes, Blériot and Taube monoplanes and various other unsafe aircraft. But the Royal Navy, or at least a few keen young officers, notably the redoubtable Commander C. R. Samson, already had other ideas. Although Samson commanded the No. 1 Wing of the Royal Naval Air Service in France, in between flying missions he would wage war using a column of armoured vehicles. For him, war was synonymous with attack, and two weeks after World War 1 began he sent two of his tiny biplanes off to bomb Zeppelin hangars. Lieutenant Marix managed to blow up a hangar, and the Zeppelin it contained, with two 20-lb (9-kg) bombs, and shortly afterwards four Avro 504s attacked the Zeppelin factory on Lake Constance, causing considerable destruction.

Front-line service as RAF No. 214 Sqn (previously RNAS No. 14) ready their O/100s for another night raid into Germany from Coudekerke, which in early 1917 had been one of the first bases for naval Handleys. Note the wide but shallow fin flash, and long nacelles for the 266-hp (198-kW) Eagle IIs. The serial is probably on the extreme tail.

'A bloody paralyser to stop the Hun in his tracks' was the urgent signal sent by Commander Charles Rumney Samson in 1914 which led to the Handley Page O/100 and O/400 being developed. The O/400 had a 100-ft (30.48-m) wing span and exposed positions for gunners and pilots. Thankfully for the pilots and nose gunner, their positions ahead of the propellers spared them from most of the effects of turbulence, but nevertheless conditions were difficult. Note the wing folding joints immediately above the engine nacelles.

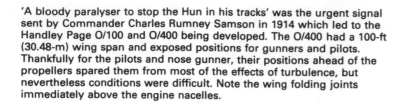

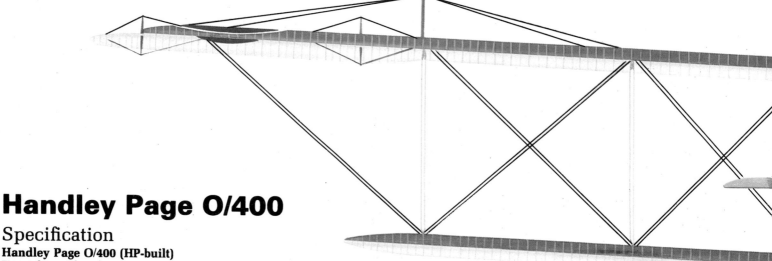

Handley Page O/400

Specification

Handley Page O/400 (HP-built)
Type: heavy bomber with crew three to five
Powerplant: two 360-hp (268-kW) Rolls-Royce Eagle VIII water-cooled Vee-12 piston engines
Performance: maximum speed (with full bomb load) 97.5 mph (157 km/h) at sea level; cruising speed at 10,000 ft (3048 m) 74 mph (119 km/h); time to reach 10,000 ft (3048 m) 40 min; endurance 8 hours
Weights: empty 8,502 lb (3857 kg); loaded 13,360 lb (6060 kg)
Dimensions: span 100 ft (30.48 m); length 62 ft 10¼ in (19.17 m); height 22 ft 0¾ in (6.72 m); wing area 1,648 sq ft (153.1 m²)
Armament: bombload varied but usually 16 of 112-lb (50.8-kg) size, with single 1,650-lb (748 kg) an alternative; defensive guns also varied but usually one or two 0.303-in (7.7-mm) Lewis guns on Scarff ring in nose, two single Lewis guns on side posts at mid-upper position, and single pin-mounted Lewis gun firing through lower rear trapdoor

Handley Page O/100 and O/400

Britain made a present of one of the first Handley Pages to the enemy. O/100, No. 1463, was landed by its RNAS crew on the first good field they saw after breaking cloud on their flight to France on 1 January 1917; it was 12 miles inside enemy territory, near Laon. Among the German evaluation pilots was Manfred von Richthofen.

Before 1914 was out Captain Murray Sueter at the Admiralty Air Department had asked Handley Page to build four production prototypes of a bomber of vast size to comply with Samson's signal to build 'a bloody paralyser of an aeroplane'. The fact that Handley Page had only built a few, rather unconventional, aircraft to this date deterred neither Sueter nor 'H.P.' himself, and 1915 saw work steadily progressing on the first of the aircraft, known as the O/100 — the Handley Page Type O with a 100-ft (30.48-m) span, at Cricklewood. As the parts emerged they were incorporated in the final assembly at Kingsbury, whence the completed aircraft was towed to Hendon. With the serial number 1455 this first machine arrived there on 10 December and took to the air on 17 December 1915 with Lieutenant Commander John Babington at the controls. Within a year of the Admiralty's decision this vast step forward in British bombing aircraft had emerged and flown.

The three subsequent prototypes had several different features, with an amidships gun position and extended nose, features later incorporated in the production aircraft, a batch of eight of which had already been ordered to follow the first four off the production lines. A RN Training Flight was established at Manston in the spring of 1916, receiving the second prototype and the first production machines (serial numbers were 1459 to 1466). An initial and potentially disastrous problem with tail flutter was soon cured with a new elevator.

Then the War Office looked with envy at the Royal Navy's new possession and ordered a batch of 12 for the Royal Flying Corps, to take their place after the next batch of 28 for the Royal Naval Air Service.

Two O/100s were delivered to the 3rd Wing at Luxeuil in

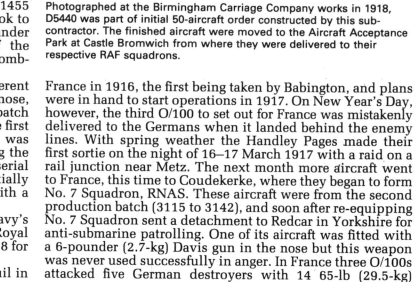

Photographed at the Birmingham Carriage Company works in 1918, D5440 was part of initial 50-aircraft order constructed by this sub-contractor. The finished aircraft were moved to the Aircraft Acceptance Park at Castle Bromwich from where they were delivered to their respective RAF squadrons.

France in 1916, the first being taken by Babington, and plans were in hand to start operations in 1917. On New Year's Day, however, the third O/100 to set out for France was mistakenly delivered to the Germans when it landed behind the enemy lines. With spring weather the Handley Pages made their first sortie on the night of 16–17 March 1917 with a raid on a rail junction near Metz. The next month more aircraft went to France, this time to Coudekerke, where they began to form No. 7 Squadron, RNAS. These aircraft were from the second production batch (3115 to 3142), and soon after re-equipping No. 7 Squadron sent a detachment to Redcar in Yorkshire for anti-submarine patrolling. One of its aircraft was fitted with a 6-pounder (2.7-kg) Davis gun in the nose but this weapon was never used successfully in anger. In France three O/100s attacked five German destroyers with 14 65-lb (29.5-kg)

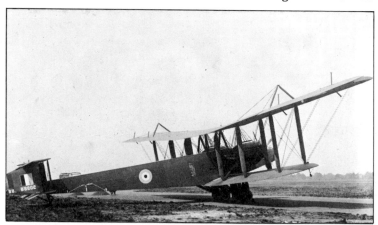

Pictured on a rare apron of concrete at Farnborough in early 1918, B8802 was the first of a batch of O/400s built by the Royal Aircraft Factory. The serials had originally been assigned to the first War Office (as distinct from RN) contract for Handley Pages, with RAF 3a engines.

F5417 was one of the standard Eagle VIII-powered O/400s assembled by National Aircraft Factory No. 1, at Waddon (Croydon). This was run by Cubitts to build bombers from parts fed in from hundreds of furniture and building firms in the London area. The markings are non-standard.

At the time the RAF was formed, the RFC's standard day bomber was the O/400, an aircraft from No. 207 Sqn at Ligescourt, France, in 1918 being shown here. This was the first British squadron used solely for long-range night bombing, and the first to operate Handley Page bombers.

G-EATN was one of the last O/400s built, as HP-built J2261 in 1918. It was then rebuilt as one of nine O/10 12-passenger airliners for Handley Page Air Transport, operating between Croydon and Paris in 1920. This particular O/10 was used for trials with the Aveline Stabilizer, an early two-axis automatic pilot.

bombs each and severely disabled one of them. A similar attack resulted in the loss of one of the bombers. Meanwhile one of the Manston aircraft (3124) flew out to Mudros in the Aegean in May 1917 for attacks on two German cruisers there. It succeeded in bombing the battle-cruiser *Goeben* and in carrying out some other raids before being forced to ditch in the Gulf of Xeros.

From O/100 to O/400

One of the problems at the time was the lack of Rolls-Royce Eagle engines for these giants, so 3117 became an engine test-bed at Farnborough, where no fewer than four different engine configurations were tried, including one with four Hispano-Suizas in tandem pairs. By September 1917, however, an aircraft powered by later Eagle engines and refined in many ways was flying at the Aeroplane & Armament Experimental Establishment at Martlesham Heath as the prototype O/400. This version had much increased fuel tankage, Eagle VIIIs and an increased bomb load. All sub-

sequent production was to this standard. No. 7 Squadron and its offshoot, No. 7A Squadron, were now keeping up a steady bombing offensive, having gone over to night bombing, and were joined by another RNAS unit, 'A' Squadron, later numbered No. 16 Squadron, which was based at Ochey from 17 October onwards.

The success of this giant aircraft resulted in quantity production orders for the RFC and RNAS and, when the Royal Air Force was formed on 1 April 1918, the naval units were renumbered Nos 207, 214 (ex-7A) and 216 Squadrons, RAF. These units were split, the first two supporting the army in the north, the latter being used for strategic bombing in the Nancy area. The RAF soon expanded these two groupings, adding No. 58 Squadron, now re-equipped with Handley Pages, to Nos 207 and 214 Squadrons in August and building up the strategic force with Nos 97, 100, 115 and 215 Squadrons, forming the 83rd Wing. This was part of the revolutionary Independent Force tasked with bombing industrial installations. This force, which was conceptually ahead of its time, showed to the rest of the world the possibilities of aerial bombardment inherent in an air force independent of the army and navy. Valuable lessons were learnt and digested by those involved in the force in the few short months of strategic bombing before the Armistice

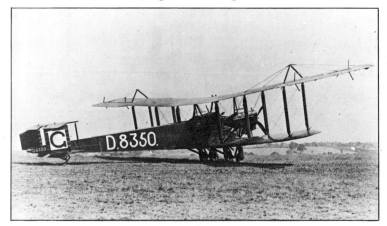

In the impoverished post-war RAF the O/400 soldiered on in overseas theatres, and this example with No. 70 Sqn was photographed in 1921, at Heliopolis. The ladder strapped to the landing gear was often carried for crew exit at desert strips, and even a bicycle was an occasional adjunct.

D8350 was the last of a batch of O/400s assembled by Handley Page from British Caudron parts. She is pictured at Cricklewood (on which houses were now visible) after becoming a civil aircraft, *Vulture*; on 4 May 1919 Lt.Cdr Sholto Douglas took the first passengers from Cricklewood to Manchester.

This Handley Page O/100 was captured by the Germans on New Year's Day 1917; here it is shown still in its English markings shortly before its ill-fated landing on enemy territory to the obvious delight of German aviation experts.

of November 1918. Although the Independent Force flew several other types of bombers, there was no doubt in anybody's mind that the big Handley Pages set the pattern for the future. Despite the initial disbelief of the new Air Board in the effectiveness of night bombing the exploits of the Handley Page squadrons during 1918 gave them proof they could not ignore. Up to 40 of the big bombers would be airborne on good nights, ranging over German industrial areas, attacking factories, railway junctions and docks. Up until this time the biggest bombs normally carried were 112-lb (51-kg) weapons, but now the O/100s and O/400s were carrying 520- and 550-lb (236- and 250-kg) bombs, having a profound effect on the recipients. The farthest the squadrons reached was Mannheim, which was attacked on 25 August 1918 by two aircraft of No. 215 Squadron. The offensive was maintained right until the Armistice, and by then 1,650-lb (748-kg) bombs were being used. This all seems 'small beer' compared with the weapons of World War 2, but for those times it was formidable indeed.

Mention of 3124's exploit outside the Western Front has already been made. Two other O/400s set out for Egypt before the Armistice, one arriving in time to serve in the successful campaign through Palestine. This was C9681 which after arriving at Heliopolis, was attached to No. 1

The O/100 serial number 3124 belonged to the Royal Navy and was stationed in Manston, Kent. This bomber eventually made its name far from the Western Front, leading several attacks in the Aegean Sea, and in May 1917 by bombing the German battle-cruiser *Goeben*.

Handley Page O/400 cutaway drawing key

1 Twin 0.303-in (7.7-mm) Lewis guns
2 Rotatable Scarff ring
3 Gunner's cockpit (plywood construction)
4 Folding seat
5 Slat flooring
6 Entry hatch to gunner's cockpit
7 ASI pitot tube
8 Negative lens
9 Rudder pedals
10 Control wheel
11 Clear Pyralin windshield
12 Padded cockpit coaming
13 Pilot's seat
14 Observer's seat
15 Slat flooring
16 Light-bomb rack (manual)
17 Batteries
18 Trap-type forward entry door
19 Fabric lacing
20 Transparent panel
21 Plywood turtle-deck

22 Aluminium fairing
23 Steel propeller hub
24 Brass tip sheathing
25 Four-blade walnut propeller
26 Radiator filler cap
27 Radiator
28 360 hp Rolls-Royce Eagle VIII engine
29 Exhaust manifold
30 Nacelle bracing strut/control spar
31 Oil tank, 15 Imp gal (68 litres) in each nacelle
32 Rigging lines
33 Streamlined steel struts
34 Double flying cable braces
35 Spruce/plywood inner strut
36 Double flying cable braces
37 Single landing cable brace
38 Single stagger cables
39 Spruce/plywood outer strut
40 Double flying braces
41 Outer aileron control horn
42 Cabane braces (four point)
43 Steel cabane
44 Inner aileron control horn
45 Solid end ribs
46 Wing dihedral break-line
47 Gravity-feed fuel tanks in leading edge, two of 12-Imp gal (54.5-litre) capacity
48 Centre-section streamlined forward cabane strut
49 Centre-section streamlined aft cabane strut

50 Forward cylindrical fuel tank (held by web straps), capacity 130 Imp gal (591 litre)
51 Filler cap
52 Cross member
53 Engine control pulley cluster
54 Centre-section main bomb-bay
55 Six volt wind-driven generator (port and starboard)
56 Perforated baffle plate
57 Air-driven fuel pumps
58 Aft fuel tank, capacity 130 Imp gal (591 litres)
59 Solid rib at dihedral break-line
60 Upper gunner's seat
61 Transparent panels
62 Ammunition racks
63 Ventral gunner's hatch
64 Clear Pyralin panels
65 Gunner's slatted flooring
66 Plywood bulkheads
67 Single dorsal 0.303-in (7.7-mm) Lewis gun
68 Fabric lacing
69 Control cable pulleys
70 Fuselage frame
71 Multi-strand cable bracing
72 Elevator control cable
73 Interplane streamlined spruce strut
74 Starboard rudder
75 Fabric-covered upper tailplane
76 Elevator control horn
77 Fixed surface centre-section
78 Fabric-covered elevator
79 Port rudder spruce frame
80 Port lower elevator frame
81 Fabric-covered lower tailplane
82 Rudder hinge spar
83 Plywood tail covering
84 Rear navigation light
85 Interplane strut
86 Vertical stabilizer
87 Steel attachment point
88 Faired struts
89 Tailskid
90 Removable fabric panel
91 Lifting points (stations 10 and 12)
92 Port steel cabane
93 Rear upper mainplane spar
94 Forward upper mainplane spar
95 Plywood covering

Though Standard Aircraft, of Elizabeth, NJ, were under contract to supply parts for assembly in England, seven O/400s with Liberty engines were assembled in the USA. This was the first, given the name *Langley*. In 'Billy' Mitchell's trials to show that bombers could destroy warships, no. 62448 hit *Ostfriesland* and later dropped a 4,000-lb (1814-kg) bomb.

Believed to have been taken at Langley Field, the heart of today's vast NASA research centre, this photograph shows the first of the seven Liberty-engined O/400s assembled in the USA for the US Army, from parts off the British production by Standard Aircraft. It made its first flight, as no. 62445, on 6 July 1918. Many O/400s were stored by the US Army Air Service.

96 Steel fitting
97 Solid drag strut
98 Wing structure
99 Port aileron structure
100 Port outer interplane struts (plywood-covered spruce)
101 Lower mainplane end rib
102 Wing structure
103 Leading-edge rib construction
104 Port inner interplane struts (plywood-covered spruce)
105 Hinge strut
106 Lower mainplane dihedral break-line
107 Steel tube engine nacelle support struts
108 Wing/fuselage attachment points
109 Wing root walkway
110 Fire extinguisher
111 Starboard undercarriage
112 Undercarriage forward strut
113 Port twinmain wheels
114 Faired rubber chord shock strut
115 Aft strut

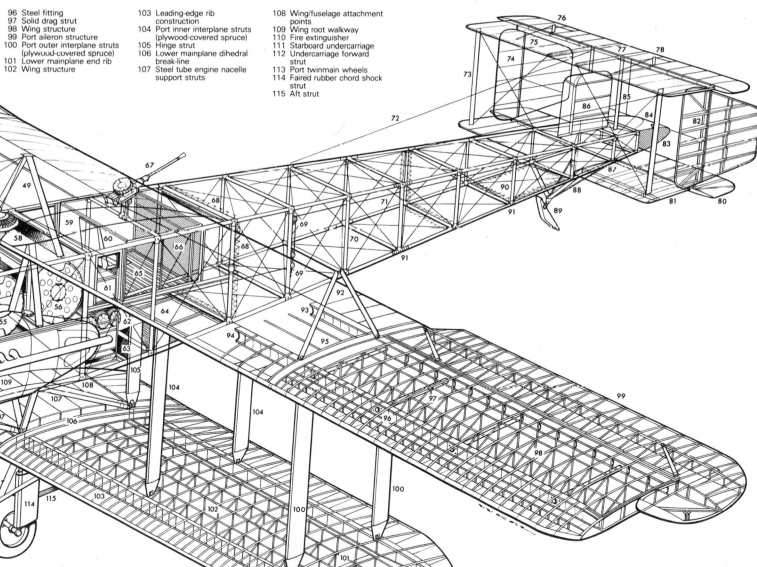

Squadron, Australian Flying Corps. From Heliopolis it set out on 19 September to attack the Turkish HQ, a successful raid destroying the enemy's means of communications with its 7th and 8th Armies and hastening their demise. But its principal task in the Middle East was as a transport to take supplies and fuel to the advanced airstrip at Azrak, where Lawrence of Arabia centred his activities. The second machine, C9700, was too late for the war in Egypt but flew on east to Calcutta, pioneering what was eventually to become the air mail route. It ended its days in India, being wrecked at Lahore.

Post-war duties

As well as the bomber squadrons mentioned, the big Handley Pages also served as navigation trainers, at Andover and Stonehenge, and after the armistice these aircraft came to the fore. An imperial air mail service had already been considered a possibility, and with the war over O/400s from Andover began expanding their activities into longer-distance navigational exercises to prepare crews, experienced in navigation, for the long-awaited civil air transports. Long-distance navigation of a different kind took place when it was decided to move three of the Independent Force units to Egypt and to take them by air. It was an expensive expedition, for of the 51 aircraft of Nos 58, 214 and 216 Squadrons which set out from France 25 never made it. The survivors were used in Egypt into the early 1920s, flying operationally against troublesome Arab tribes amongst other tasks. The squadrons were regrouped into Nos 70 and 216 Squadrons, two units which formed the bomber-transport force in the Middle East until 1940.

The first genuine transport schedules on which this type flew were those run by No. 86 Wing RAF, which provided a link between London and Versailles during the peace treaty negotiations in 1919; the wing was based at Hendon. Nearby, at Handley Page's Cricklewood airfield, the company had acquired surplus aircraft and decked them out as 16-seat airliners. Here they flew familiarization flights for the joy-riding public and more serious routes to Paris, Brussels and Amsterdam (Handley Page Air Transport being one of the founder British air lines), sporting civil registration in place of roundels and serial numbers. Altogether about 25 served

Handley Page O/100 and O/400 variants

O/100 no. 1455: first prototype, initially with 250-hp (186-kg) Rolls-Royce engines (later called Eagle) in armoured nacelles, with armoured and glazed nose for crew; later several times modified
O/100 nos. 1456/1458: prototypes with various detail improvements and 266-hp (198-kg) Eagle II engines
O/100 production, nos. 1459/1466 and 3115/3142: Eagle II engines, except (because of shortage of engines) 3117 flown with two RAF 3a and then four 200-hp (149-kW) Hispano Hs 8b engines; no. 3142 flown with two 300-hp (223-kW) Fiat A. 12 engines
O/100 production B9446/9451: powered by two 320-hp (238-kW) Sunbeam Cossack engines
O/400 prototype: in effect O/100 no. 3138 rebuilt with new fuel system with tanks in fuselage, air-driven pumps, and short nacelles for 275-hp (205-kW) Eagle II engines
O/400 production: by Handley Page. C3381/3480, C9636/9785 and F3748/3767, all with either 284-hp (212-

kW) Eagle IV, 360-hp (268-kW) Eagle VIII (Standard), 275-hp (205-kW) Sunbeam Maori or 350-hp (261-kW) Liberty 12; by RAF Farnborough, B8802/8813 and C3487/3498 (latter from HP-build parts) with Eagle VIII; by British Caudron Co. for erection at HP Cricklewood, D8301/8350; by Birmingham Carriage Co. D5401/5450, F301/320 and J2242/2291 (only 2242/2274 completed by Armistice) with Eagle VIII; by Metropolitan Wagon Co., D4561/4660 and J3542/3616 (none of last batch delivered); by Clayton & Shuttleworth, D9681/9730; by National Aircraft Factory No. 1 at Waddon, F5349/5448 (at least 70 delivered with Liberty 12, later re-engined with Eagle VIII)
O/400 US production: 1,500 ordered from Standard Aircraft for final assembly in England and 100 sets accepted in UK by Armistice, plus seven assembled at Langley Field with Liberty 12 engines as US Army Aviation Service Nos. 62445/62451, remainder cancelled
Total production: 46 O/100 plus 554 O/400 excluding US production

in this way until 1924 and the advent of civil airliner derivatives of the O/400 put them out of service. Others of the breed found their way to South Africa and to China, where they formed the basis for an early air mail service and also, in one case, reverted to the military role.

As early as 1917 the Americans had been showing a great interest in the Handley Page. They were impressed with the considerable success it had experienced. A licence agreement was signed with the Standard Aircraft Corporation to manufacture the aircraft in the USA, but with Liberty 12 engines. A British aircraft (B9449) was sent to the United States to be used as a model, and complete sets of parts were shipped across the Atlantic. But only one-seventh of these ever reached the USA, and production took a long time to get off the ground. The Armistice brought the highly ambitious production schedule to a premature end. The US Army took only 13 of these aircraft, and a further 20 were put into storage. One of these was used for General 'Billy' Mitchell's experiments to persuade the US Navy that airborne bombers could be used to sink warships. At the beginning of the 1920s the Handley Page O/100 and O/400 bombers gradually disappeared from the scene, to be replaced by newer and more effective bombers and transport planes.

This O/400, registration number D8350, is one of the machines which was converted to civil use and made pleasure trips and commercial flights.

SPAD S.VII

When it appeared in 1916, the SPAD S.VII was a remarkable fighter: in comparison with its contemporaries, it was heavier and considerably faster; and while it lacked something of their agility, it also dispensed with their alarming tendency to break up in the air during prolonged manoeuvres. Successful in its own right, the S.VII also gave birth to the great S.XIII fighter.

During the critical months of 1917, French and Italian newspapers were also reporting on a great new brand of fliers: Charles Nungesser, Georges Guynemer and René Fonck in France, and Francesco Baracca in Italy.

Each gallant aviator was pictured with his unit or personal insignia in striking resemblance to medieval and renaissance knights with their colourful shields or pennants. World War 1 newspaper cuttings reveal Nungesser and his macabre skull and candles, Guynemer with the beautifully designed Stork badge of the Cigognes, and Baracca's finely outlined 91a Squadriglia 'Cavallino Rampante' (prancing horse). But there was scarce mention made of the aircraft which bore the insignia. Yet in most instances it was the same reliable design – the tough, highly stable little SPAD biplane which did so much to wrest aerial supremacy over the Western Front for precious months from the ever-threatening Albatros and Fokker single-seaters, presenting a threat to which the Germans did not react for several costly months.

The S.VII owed its conception to the successful development of a new aero engine. The Allied air arms had relied heavily during the first two years of war on Gnome, Le Rhône and Clerget rotary engines, which possessed limited development potential. It was hardly surprising, then, that the French and British air staffs showed great interest in the new water-cooled stationary engine developed by the famed Hispano-Suiza company under the direction of a talented Swiss designer, Marc Birkigt. The first examples of his new V-8 engine, the Hispano-Suiza 8Aa, delivering 150 hp (112 kW), were available early in 1916. The task of producing an airframe to be married to the new engine so as to achieve a world-beating single-seat fighter was allotted to the chief

engineer of SPAD (the Société Anonyme pour l'Aviation et ses Dérivés), a subsidiary of the famous Blériot company. This decision might have seemed foolhardy since the chief engineer was a certain Louis Béchereau, notorious for his Type A two-seaters, whose major design feature was the mounting of the engine and propeller in the fuselage, separating the observer-gunner in the nose from the pilot in the rear. French and Russian aircrew operating the A-2 production version had little good to say for it, since any nose-over on landing tended to kill the gunner.

Yet several features of the A-2 design, including the wing construction, were excellent and were retained by Béchereau for his new fighter. When the SPAD Type V prototype appeared in the spring of 1916, it was revealed as a neat and powerful tractor biplane. Flying initially in April 1916, it performed well in subsequent company and service trials. With a maximum level speed of over 130 mph (210 km/h), it promised a substantial performance improvement over the Nieuport sesquiplane scouts currently in Allied service. The French authorities were quick to order the new fighter into production, awarding the SPAD company a contract for 268 aircraft on 10 May 1916.

Strong and sure

Series aircraft incorporated a number of minor modifications, but the basic design of the prototype remained unchanged. The service designation S.VII was applied to the new fighter, although it was often described as the S.7 or Spa 7. The wings were of remarkably thin aerofoil section, a feature which became the hallmark of all derivatives of the basic

The detachable panel marked 'PHOTO' on this SPAD S.VII indicates that it was one of a limited number adapted to carry a camera for photographic reconnaissance work, a role in which the S.VII's speed and flight steadiness were important assets to survival and good photography. The technique of aerial photographic reconnaisance was new.

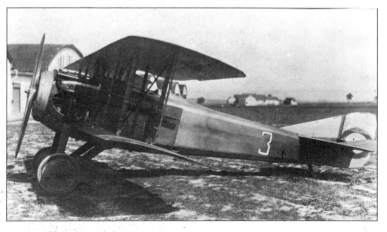

This SPAD S.VII is in the markings adopted by the air arm of the newly created state of Czechoslovakia in 1919. The concentric circles of the insignia were white (in the centre), blue and red. The roundels just visible on the rudder were replaced by a facsimile of the Czech national flag two years later. S.VII No. 3 was photographed at Cheb.

design. There were ailerons on the upper wing only. Although a single-bay biplane, with a pair of bracing struts on each side, the S.VII had the superficial appearance of a two-bay aircraft, since it had inboard intermediate articulated struts, which served as tie struts for the flying and bracing wires and thus gave added structural strength. As with the wings, the fuselage was of wooden construction: built up on four longerons, it had curved top and bottom decking and was fabric covered. The landing gear was of cross-axle Vee-type, with the axle articulated at the centre. Shock absorbers were of the then indispensable 'bungee' elastic cord.

Great care was taken to give the S.VII smooth contours. Attempts to fit a large propeller spinner were abandoned at an early stage, but the engine had curved metal cowlings formed round the circular shutter for the frontal engine radiator and extending back to a position just in front of the pilot's open cockpit. A single Vickers 0.303-in (7.7-mm) machine-gun was mounted on top of the engine cowling. Engine designer Marc Birkigt himself had developed the ingenious mechanical interrupter gear, which was driven off the rear of the starboard cam shaft.

The S.VII soon proved itself a nimble and rugged fighter, able to hold its own in dogfights. It had a respectable rate of climb and an ability to make sudden extended dives, which could be repeated without risk to the structure, features which gave it an ability to manoeuvre vertically in a way unequalled by any contemporary aircraft, Allied or German, in 1916. Above all the SPAD provided a stable gun platform.

The first SPAD S.VII to reach the front line was issued to Lieutenant Armand Pinsard of Escadrille N.26, and it was he who scored the first recorded victory by an S.VII on 23 August 1916. From then on the SPAD opened the road to glory and honour for a galaxy of French fliers whose names became household words. By the summer of 1917 the S.VII equipped more than 50 *escadrilles de chasse* (fighter squadrons) on the Western Front. This pre-eminence was achieved despite the failure of the grandiose production plans of the French high command, which relied on licence manufacture by a whole range of companies. That output was little more than half that anticipated was hardly surprising, since apart from a few experienced manufacturers, such as Blériot, the parent company of the SPAD firm, the bulk of contractors had negligible experience in building aircraft. Nevertheless, in the hands of veterans such as Georges Félix Madon, Marcel Noguès and Armand de Turenne, the S.VII continued to make its mark.

Ahead of the Germans

Efforts to improve the performance of the S.VII, always in danger of being overtaken by newer German types, were vigorously pursued. From April 1917 all S.VIIs leaving the

In this particular photograph of the SPAD the grill covering the lower part of the 180-hp (134-kW) Hispano-Suiza 8Ab engine has been removed, possibly as an aid to cooling. Engine cooling was a perpetual problem with SPADs, and this and other contemporary photographs reveal a wide diversity of louvring and even of radiator configuration.

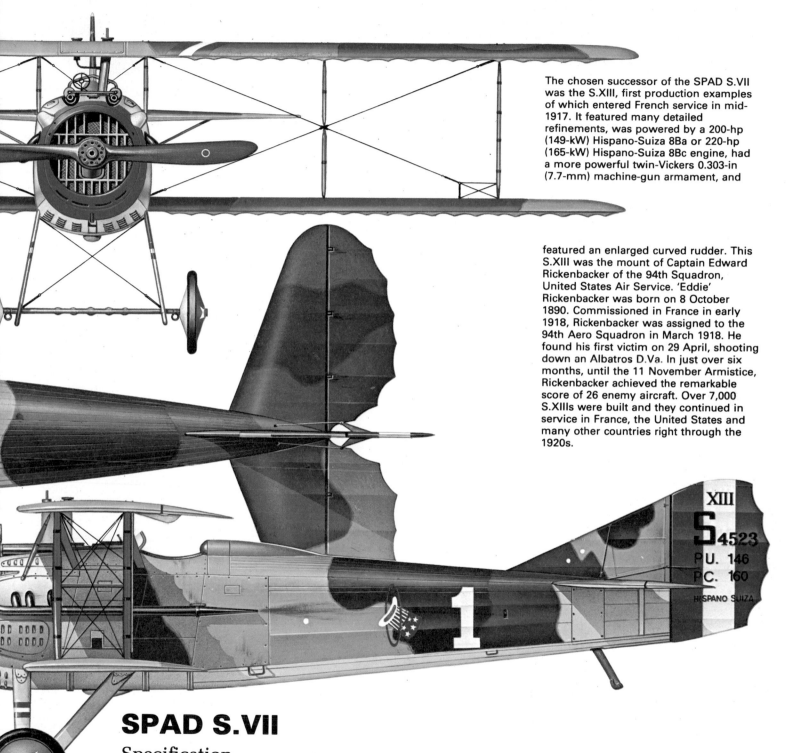

The chosen successor of the SPAD S.VII was the S.XIII, first production examples of which entered French service in mid-1917. It featured many detailed refinements, was powered by a 200-hp (149-kW) Hispano-Suiza 8Ba or 220-hp (165-kW) Hispano-Suiza 8Bc engine, had a more powerful twin-Vickers 0.303-in (7.7-mm) machine-gun armament, and

featured an enlarged curved rudder. This S.XIII was the mount of Captain Edward Rickenbacker of the 94th Squadron, United States Air Service. 'Eddie' Rickenbacker was born on 8 October 1890. Commissioned in France in early 1918, Rickenbacker was assigned to the 94th Aero Squadron in March 1918. He found his first victim on 29 April, shooting down an Albatros D.Va. In just over six months, until the 11 November Armistice, Rickenbacker achieved the remarkable score of 26 enemy aircraft. Over 7,000 S.XIIIs were built and they continued in service in France, the United States and many other countries right through the 1920s.

SPAD S.VII

Specification

SPAD S.VII
Type: single-seat fighting scout
Powerplant: one 180-hp (134-KW) Hispano-Suiza 8Ab inline piston engine
Performance: maximum speed 132 mph (212 km/h) at sea level, and 124 mph (200 km/h) at 13,125 ft (4000 m); climb to 6,560 ft (2000 m) in 4 minutes 40 seconds; service ceiling 21,490 ft (6550 m); range 217 miles (350 km); endurance 1 hour 30 minutes

Weights: empty 1,102 lb (500 kg); maximum take-off 1,554 lb (705 kg)
Dimensions: span, upper 25 ft 8 in (7.82 m), lower 24 ft 10¼ in (7.57 m); length 19 ft 11¼ in (6.08 m); height 7 ft 2½ in (2.20 m); wing area 192.14 sq ft (17.85 m²)
Armament: one fixed forward-firing 0.303-in (7.7-mm) Vickers machine-gun with 500 rounds

factories had the new Hispano-Suiza 8Ab engine, developed from the original powerplant and offering 180 hp (134 kW). This kept the type ahead of the opposition, but other experiments, with a wing of revised aerofoil section, and with the temperamental 200-hp (149-kW) Hispano-Suiza 8B engine, were soon abandoned. With the personal encouragement of Georges Guynemer, Louis Béchereau designed the SPAD S.XII Ca.1, powered by a 200-hp (134-kW) Hispano-Suiza 8C engine and armed with the powerful 37-mm Hotchkiss gun, fitted between the cylinder blocks and firing through the hollow airscrew shaft. Guynemer received his S.XII in July 1917, promptly scoring four of his victories with it, but the type did not become popular, no more than 100 of the original order for 300 being completed.

The hopes of the French and their allies, however, were pinned on the SPAD S.XIII, natural successor to the S.VII. Retaining the good qualities of the S.VII, it had the more powerful 220-hp (165-kW) Hispano-Suiza 8Ba engine fitted with reduction gear, was armed with twin Vickers guns and had a number of other modifications, including increased rudder area, which rendered it a more manoeuvrable and formidable fighting machine. The prototype flew in April 1917, but production got under way only very slowly. Although eventually over 7,000 S.XIIIs were built, at the time of the last great German offensives in March 1918, only seven months before the war was to end, the S.VIIs in first-line service still exceeded the S.XIIIs. Thus the S.VII soldiered on past its prime, outclassed by the new Fokker D.VII in the fast-changing fortunes of war.

Precise figures for French production of the S.VII are not known, but at least 3,500 were completed. From French-built

An aircraft of the famed French 'Cigognes', Groupe de Chasse 12, commanded by Capitaine Armand Brocard. In this view the flying stork insignia can be clearly seen on the fuselage side next to the coloured stripe. The French ace Georges Guynemer was also a member of this *Group de Chasse*.

SPAD S.VII variants

Type V: prototype of S.VII; one built, flew spring 1916; designated with letter V under SPAD company alphabetical system

SPAD S.VII (initial French production): powered by Hispano-Suiza 8Aa engine 150 hp (112 kW), estimated 500 built May 1916–March 1917

SPAD S.VII (Renault-powered): one-off 1916 experimental variant with 150-hp (122-kW) Renault 8G engine, back-up in event of difficulties with Hispano-Suiza engine

SPAD S.VII (main French production): powered by 180-hp (134-kW) Hispano-Suiza 8Ab engine, some 3,000 constructed by following French companies from March 1917: SPAD, Blériot, Janair, Kellner, de Marçay, Regy Frères and Sommer, wartime foreign sales to Italy (214) USA (189), UK (185 to RFC), Russia (43) and Belgium (15), post-war surplus French aircraft widely exported to countries that included Brazil, Czechoslovakia, Greece, Peru, Poland, Portugal, Romania, Thailand and Yugoslavia

SPAD S.VII (200-hp (149-kW) variants): only two S.VIIs have been identified as built with experimental 200-hp (149-kW) Hispano-Suiza 8B engine

SPAD S.VII (Russian production): 100 constructed by Duks Company, Moscow; specification identical with French aircraft, powered by imported engines

SPAD S.VII (British production): 100 built by British-based Blériot and SPAD company, serialled A8794 to A8893. 120 built by Mann, Egerton Company, serialled A9100 to A9161, B1351 to B1388 and B9911 to B9930; British-built SPADs mostly powered by British development of Hispano-Suiza, Wolseley W.4A Python engine. Python 1 of 150 hp (112 kW) succeeded by Python II of 180 hp (134 kW)

Total production was at least 3,500

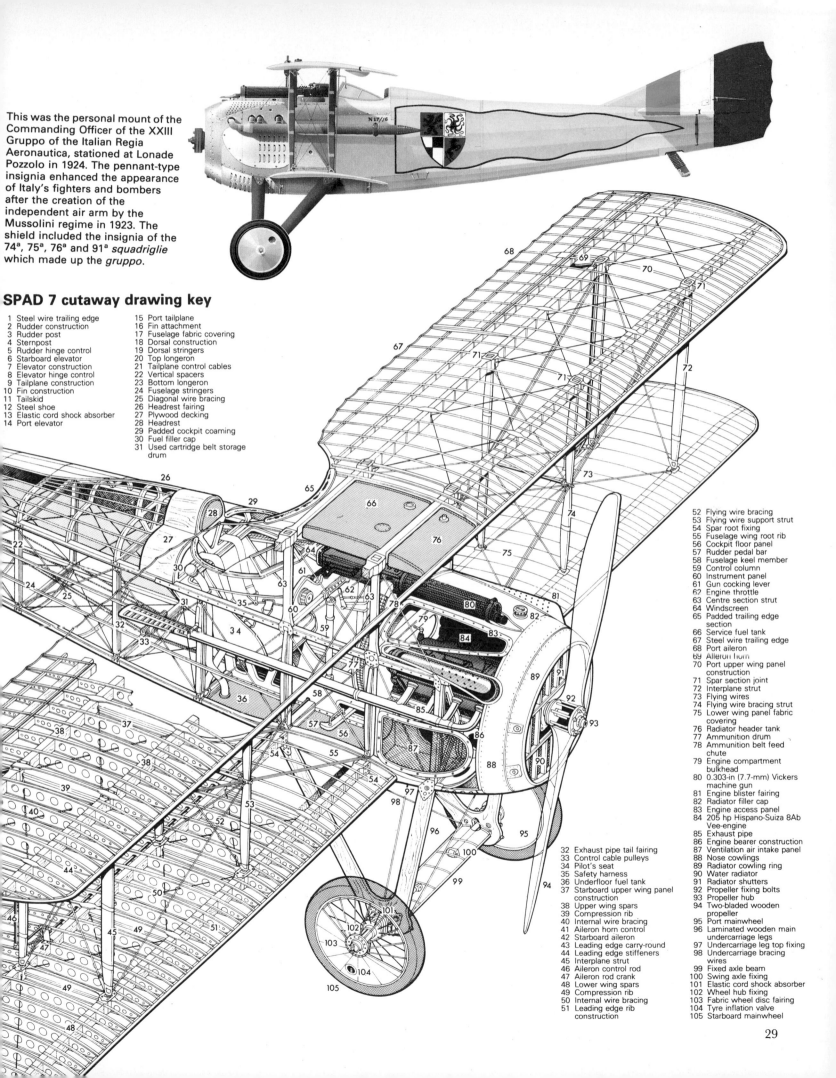

This was the personal mount of the Commanding Officer of the XXIII Gruppo of the Italian Regia Aeronautica, stationed at Lonade Pozzolo in 1924. The pennant-type insignia enhanced the appearance of Italy's fighters and bombers after the creation of the independent air arm by the Mussolini regime in 1923. The shield included the insignia of the 74ª, 75ª, 76ª and 91ª *squadriglie* which made up the *gruppo*.

SPAD 7 cutaway drawing key

1 Steel wire trailing edge
2 Rudder construction
3 Rudder post
4 Sternpost
5 Rudder hinge control
6 Starboard elevator
7 Elevator construction
8 Elevator hinge control
9 Tailplane construction
10 Fin construction
11 Tailskid
12 Steel shoe
13 Elastic cord shock absorber
14 Port elevator
15 Port tailplane
16 Fin attachment
17 Fuselage fabric covering
18 Dorsal construction
19 Dorsal stringers
20 Top longeron
21 Tailplane control cables
22 Vertical spacers
23 Bottom longeron
24 Fuselage stringers
25 Diagonal wire bracing
26 Headrest fairing
27 Plywood decking
28 Headrest
29 Padded cockpit coaming
30 Fuel filler cap
31 Used cartridge belt storage drum
32 Exhaust pipe tail fairing
33 Control cable pulleys
34 Pilot's seat
35 Safety harness
36 Underfloor fuel tank
37 Starboard upper wing panel construction
38 Upper wing spars
39 Compression rib
40 Internal wire bracing
41 Aileron horn control
42 Starboard aileron
43 Leading edge carry-round
44 Leading edge stiffeners
45 Interplane strut
46 Aileron control rod
47 Aileron rod crank
48 Lower wing spars
49 Compression rib
50 Internal wire bracing
51 Leading edge rib construction
52 Flying wire bracing
53 Flying wire support strut
54 Spar root fixing
55 Fuselage wing root rib
56 Cockpit floor panel
57 Rudder pedal bar
58 Fuselage keel member
59 Control column
60 Instrument panel
61 Gun cocking lever
62 Engine throttle
63 Centre section strut
64 Windscreen
65 Padded trailing edge section
66 Service fuel tank
67 Steel wire trailing edge
68 Port aileron
69 Aileron horn
70 Port upper wing panel construction
71 Spar section joint
72 Interplane strut
73 Flying wires
74 Flying wire bracing strut
75 Lower wing panel fabric covering
76 Radiator header tank
77 Ammunition drum
78 Ammunition belt feed chute
79 Engine compartment bulkhead
80 0.303-in (7.7-mm) Vickers machine gun
81 Engine blister fairing
82 Radiator filler cap
83 Engine access panel
84 205 hp Hispano-Suiza 8Ab Vee-engine
85 Exhaust pipe
86 Engine bearer construction
87 Ventilation air intake panel
88 Nose cowlings
89 Radiator cowling ring
90 Water radiator
91 Radiator shutters
92 Propeller fixing bolts
93 Propeller hub
94 Two-bladed wooden propeller
95 Port mainwheel
96 Laminated wooden main undercarriage legs
97 Undercarriage leg top fixing
98 Undercarriage bracing wires
99 Fixed axle beam
100 Swing axle fixing
101 Elastic cord shock absorber
102 Wheel hub fixing
103 Fabric wheel disc fairing
104 Tyre inflation valve
105 Starboard mainwheel

Bearing the insignia of Escadrille SPA 48 — the crowing cockerel — which went with the escadrille motto *Chante et Combat*, this SPAD had clear doped finish and the aircraft-in-squadron number '2' on the upper decking as well as on the sides of the rear fuselage. This was the aircraft of Lieutenant de Turenne.

A French-built S.VII bought by the British government and flown by the Royal Flying Corps during 1917 with the serial B1524. It belonged to No. 23 Sqn RFC flying from La Lovie aerodrome, France, summer 1917. Apart from the forward fuselage panelling, the entire finish was in natural doped fabric.

aircraft 185 were supplied to the Royal Flying Corps, 214 to the Aeronautica Militare Italiana, 43 to Russia, 15 to Belgian units and 189, mostly for training, to the US Air Service operating with the American Expeditionary Force in France.

In addition, at least 100 S.VIIs were licence-built by the Duks company in Moscow, and 220 in the UK. British-produced SPADs suffered many vicissitudes. Mann, Egerton & Co. of Norwich eventually built 120 examples, most of which revealed structural weakness and often varied considerably from specification. After several fatal crashes, acceptance was refused by the RFC until August 1917, by which time considerable strengthening had been undertaken. The British 'Bleriot and SPAD' company, based at Brooklands in Surrey, constructed the remaining 100 British SPAD S.VIIs.

SPAD S.VIIs began to reach Italy in March 1917, going first to the 77a Squadriglia and then to the 91a Squadriglia, whose commanding officer from May 1917 was Maggiore Francesco Baracca. In October 1917, when the Italian army and nation were reeling under the crisis created by the disastrous defeat at Caporetto, public morale was raised by news that 91a Squadriglia pilots had shot down 14 Austro-Hungarian aircraft within a few days. Baracca himself had destroyed two aircraft in a single skirmish on 21 October

1917. The Italian ace's affection for the S.VII was such that he retained his aircraft for some months in preference to the later S.XIII. He had 34 confirmed victories when he was shot down and killed on 19 June 1918, a high proportion of them achieved with the S.VII.

Although the S.VII was tested by the Royal Naval Air Service, an agreement was made whereby all Sopwith Triplane fighters went to the RNAS and all S.VIIs to the RFC, where they equipped Nos 19 and 23 Squadrons in France. Operational use was restricted to French-built aircraft, RFC pilots having a justified mistrust of British-built machines. The S.VII also flew in the Middle East with Nos 30, 63 and 72 Squadrons, RFC.

Several Russian SPADs survived the revolution to fly with the Red air arm during the Russian Civil War. Others operated with Polish units in the immediate post-revolution period. The American Expeditionary Force in France received its first S.VIIs in the summer of 1917, but they served mainly to train pilots for the S.XIII, supplied in large numbers to the USAS.

Post-war the S.VII remained in French service as an advanced trainer for nearly a decade. In 1924 eight Italian fighter *squadriglie* still had the S.VII on strength. Other countries to utilize the type included Greece, Portugal and Romania, together with the newly independent states of Czechoslovakia, Finland, Poland and Yugoslavia, as well as several countries in Latin America and the Far East.

Today the SPAD S.VII is remembered with affection and gratitude in its native country, where the *Vieux Charles* of Guynemer is preserved to remind pupil pilots at the Academy of the Armée de l'Air at Salon-de-Provence of the great traditions they have to uphold. Of the handful of remaining SPAD S.VIIs in Europe and North America, the most renowned is the aircraft flown by Baracca, now exhibited at Lugo di Romagna in a Museum dedicated to Italy's foremost World War 1 ace.

In the history of French flight, the SPAD fighter was inextricably linked to the famous Cigognes of the Aviation Militaire. Initially only one flight of aircraft (SPA.3) bore the coveted stork symbol, but as the number of S.VIIs gradually increased, the Cigognes were extended to the five flights of the Groupe de Chasse 12, commanded by Captain Armand Brocard. The French public soon took to these heroes of the air, pilots such as René Dorme of SPA.3 (23 Siège), Armand Pinsard (27 Siège) of SPA.26, and Bernard de Romanet of SPA.167 (18 kills), René Fonck (a record 75 kills), and the great Guynemer, who finally fell on 11 September 1917 after 54 victories, many of them in the S.VII. Their fame was due in no small measure to that small but remarkable fighter, the SPAD S.VII.

A number of S.VIIs have been beautifully restored and preserved by American private owners. Notable on this example is the star decoration on the landing gear wheels.

Sopwith Camel

Joining the Royal Flying Corps just too late to avert the 'Bloody April' slaughter of Allied aircraft in 1917 over the Western Front, the Sopwith Camel was a tricky aeroplane to fly but, once mastered, was the most successful and popular of the fighting scouts of what was popularly known as the 'Kaiser's War'.

Not a particularly easy aircraft to fly, the little Sopwith Pup wrought a considerable amount of damage on German fighters over the Western Front during the second half of 1916, even after the appearance on the scene of the Albatros D.I, with its twin machine guns. But it was soon apparent that the Albatros D.I and other German aircraft types were merely precursors of an aircraft technology that was rapidly gathering momentum. The chief designer for Sopwith, Herbert Smith, realised this at an early stage. In the late summer of 1916 he was busy designing a successor to the Pup. The first prototype, known as Sopwith F.1, was cleared to fly by the company on 22 December of the same year.

Although an obvious descendant of the Pup, the F.1 was a compact and purposeful-looking little aircraft with a deeper fuselage, accentuated by a humped fairing forward of the cockpit which covered the breeches of a pair of synchronized Vickers guns. Structurally the new aeroplane was conventional, the fuselage being a wire-braced wooden box girder with rounded top decking; immediately aft of the engine the structure was aluminium covered, then plywood covered as far as the rear of the cockpit, and fabric covered on the rear fuselage. Smith originally intended that both upper and lower wings should have equal dihedral, but Fred Sigrist, the chief engineer, favoured a flat upper wing to facilitate production by permitting construction as a single continuous unit. In compensation the dihedral of the lower

wing was arbitrarily doubled. Even when it was later decided to produce the top wing in three parts to assist maintenance and repair in the field, the top wing dihedral was not restored, and the Camel's 'tapered gap' remained one of its best-known characteristics.

The most important design feature was the concentration of propeller, engine, fuel tank, armament and pilot's cockpit within the front 7 ft (2.1 m) of the front fuselage; such a concentration of mass contributed to the extraordinary manoeuvrability of the new fighter, but also led to its tricky turning habits. On account of the considerable torque and its small inertia about the centre of gravity and marked gyroscopic movement, the Camel could be turned very tightly, but in a turn to the left the nose rose sharply, and to the right it dropped – demanding coarse use of rudder – without which the aircraft would rapidly spin without warning.

Company records suggest that three (or possibly four) F.1 prototypes were built at private expense (the F.1, F.1/1, F.1/2 and F.1/3, although the F.1/2 has never been authoritatively identified). The F.1/1 'Taper Wing Camel' featured tapered wings and single broad-chord interplane struts on each side; the F.1 was powered by a 110-hp (82-kW) Clerget 9Z rotary, and the F.1/3 by a 130-hp (97-kW) Clerget 9B; it has been suggested that the F.1/2 was identifiable by a cut-out panel in the top wing to increase pilot view.

First flown by Harry Hawker, probably at Brooklands early

Sopwith Camel

Specification

Sopwith F.1 Camel (Clerget)
Type: single-seat fighting scout
Powerplant: one 130-hp (97-kW) Clerget 9-cylinder air-cooled rotary piston engine
Performance: maximum speed 117 mph (188 km/h) at sea level;
climb to 10,000 ft (3050 m) in 10 minutes 35 seconds; service ceiling 19,000 ft
(5790 m); endurance 2 hours 30 minutes
Weights: empty 929 lb (421 kg); maximum take-off 1,453 lb
(659 kg)
Dimensions: span 28 ft 0 in (8.53 m); length 18 ft 9 in (5.72 m);
height 8 ft 6 in (2.60 m); wing area 231.0 sq ft (21.46 m²)
Armament: two 0.303-in (7.7-mm) Vickers machine-guns on nose and synchronized
to fire through the propeller, plus four 25-lb (11.35-kg) bombs carried on external racks
below the fuselage

A Sopwith-built 2F.1 Camel flown by the high-scoring Canadian pilot William Alexander with 'A' Flight, No. 10 (Naval) Sqn, RNAS, at Treizennes, a squadron that was to become No. 210 Sqn, RAF, on amalgamation of the RFC and RNAS on 1 April 1918.

in January 1917, the F.1 was quickly followed by the above prototypes plus two aircraft (N517 and N518) ordered by the Admiralty. The F.1/3 was tested at Martlesham Heath in March, and this was adopted as standard for production, although it returned in May with a 110-hp (82-kW) Le Rhône 9J and in July with a 130-hp (97-kW) Clerget.

Meanwhile the second Admiralty prototype was flown at Martlesham with the new AR.1 (Admiralty Rotary) of 150 hp (112 kW); designed by Lieutenant W. O. Bentley (later of motor car fame), this engine was the first production aero engine to employ aluminium as an air-cooled cylinder material and soon entered production as the BR.1, and was ready for the first production Camels for the Admiralty which started delivery from Sopwith on 7 May. They joined No. 4 Naval Squadron (commanded by Squadron Commander B. L. Huskisson) and were in action for the first time on 4 July when five attacked 16 Gothas north of Ostend, destroying at least one of the large German 'heavy' bombers. By the end of the month Nos 3, 4, 6, 8 and 9 Naval Squadrons had received Sopwith Camels.

The Camel was the private-venture stablemate to the S.E.5. It served with great distinction on the Western Front. Originally bought by the RNAS, it is seen here in service with a naval squadron which became No. 208 Sqn when the RAF was formed.

An anonymous Gnome Monosoupape-powered F.1 Camel without nose Vickers guns fitted; this may indeed be the Boulton & Paul-built aircraft, B9278, which was later equipped with two downward-firing Lewis guns (not fitted here) and which became the Sopwith TF.1 trenchfighter.

The first War Office contracts for Camels were given to Ruston Proctor & Co. at Lincoln for 250 aircraft on 22 May 1917 and to Portholme Aerodrome Ltd at Huntingdon for 50 aircraft on 2 June. The former contract specified the 130-hp (97-kW) Le Rhône 9J. A contract placed with Sopwith on 7 June specified the Clerget 9B as an alternative. Contract prices included £874 for the unequipped Camel airframe, and engine prices ranged from £907 for a 130-hp (97-kW) Clerget down to £643 for the 150-hp (112-kW) BR.1.

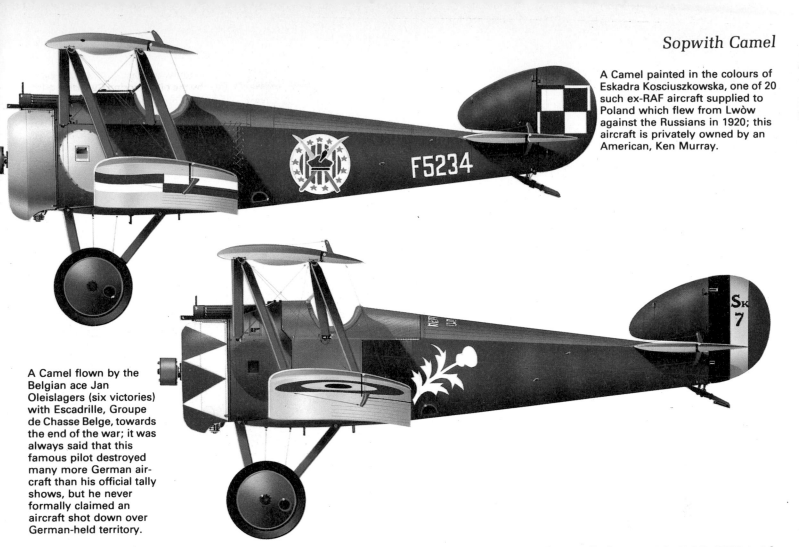

A Camel painted in the colours of Eskadra Kosciuszkowska, one of 20 such ex-RAF aircraft supplied to Poland which flew from Lwòw against the Russians in 1920; this aircraft is privately owned by an American, Ken Murray.

A Camel flown by the Belgian ace Jan Oleislagers (six victories) with Escadrille, Groupe de Chasse Belge, towards the end of the war; it was always said that this famous pilot destroyed many more German aircraft than his official tally shows, but he never formally claimed an aircraft shot down over German-held territory.

Fighting scout supreme

Between 4 July 1917 and 11 November 1918 the Sopwith Camel destroyed 1,294 enemy aircraft, more victories than achieved by any other type of aircraft in the war. Only the Fokker Dr.I triplane could match its manoeuvrability.

The first RFC unit to receive the F.1 was No. 70 Squadron at Boisdinghem in July 1917, in time to take part in the Battle of Ypres which opened on 31 July. It was followed quickly in France by No. 45 (also in July), and No. 43 with Clerget Camels; in October No. 28 Squadron took Camels from the UK to France. At the end of August three pilots of No. 44 Squadron, Major (later Group Captain) G. W. Murlis Green, Captain (later Air Vice-Marshal Sir Quentin) C. J. Q. Brand and Lieutenant C. C. Banks flew Camels at night against raiding Gothas proving that, though tricky, the little fighter could be flown in darkness.

In the great Battle of Cambrai in March 1918 the Camel squadrons played a conspicuous part, many being equipped with a rack for four 20-lb (9-kg) Cooper bombs. Nos 3 and 46 Squadrons were particularly prominent in their ground-attack work, such famous names as Bourlon Wood, Flesquières and Lateau featuring among their targets. In air combat individual Camel pilots were already becoming well-known. During the Cambrai battle Captain J. L. Trollope of No. 43 Squadron shot down six enemy aircraft in one day, 24 March, an RFC record. On 12 April, when the new Royal Air Force was but 12 days old, Captain H. W. Woollett, also of No. 43 Squadron, equalled the achievement.

On 21 April a Canadian pilot, Captain A. R. Brown of No. 209 Squadron (previously No. 9 Naval Squadron), flying a Bentley Camel, was credited with shooting down Rittmeister Manfred, Freiherr von Richthofen, the victor of 80 air combats and scourge of the Western Front. Indeed many of the RFC's and RAF's most illustrious pilots flew Camels, including Lieutenant Colonel R. Collishaw, DSO, DSC, DFC (with 60 victories), Major D. R. MacLaren, DSO, MC, DFC (54 victories) and Major W. G. Barker VC, DSO, MC (53 victories).

The Camel itself had undergone some development. A total of 1,325 aircraft was completed during 1917 powered by Clerget, Le Rhône and Bentley rotaries (although the last were in a minority). However, with America now in the war not even the 3,450 Camels ordered by the end of that year appeared likely to meet the demand, and new contracts were placed with Boulton & Paul Ltd, British Caudron Co. Ltd, Clayton & Shuttleworth Ltd, Hooper & Co. Ltd, March, Jones & Cribb Ltd, Nieuport & General Aircraft Co. Ltd, Wm

Flown by Lieutenant J. A. Myers of the US Air Service, this F.1 Camel was one of a large batch built by March, Jones & Cribb Ltd, Leeds, and which flew with the 17th Aero Squadron on the Western Front in 1918. Its 'donor' – Thomas Carlyle – has his name at the rear.

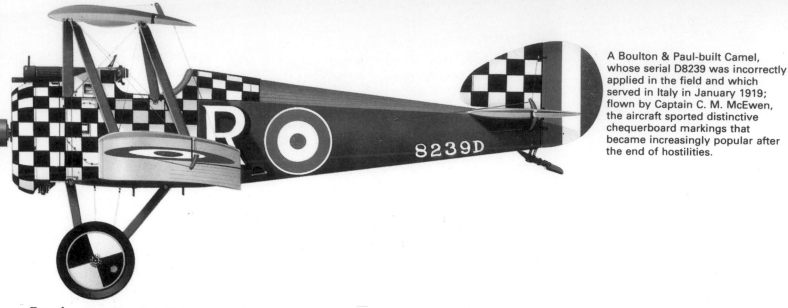

A Boulton & Paul-built Camel, whose serial D8239 was incorrectly applied in the field and which served in Italy in January 1919; flown by Captain C. M. McEwen, the aircraft sported distinctive chequerboard markings that became increasingly popular after the end of hostilities.

Beardmore & Co. Ltd, Fairey Aviation Co. Ltd, and Pegler & Co. Ltd.

Numerous different rotary engines were flown in Camels, among them the 150-hp (112-kW) Gnome Monosoupape which featured an adjustable ignition switch which enabled the pilot to run the engine on one, three, five, seven or nine cylinders; a witness recalls seeing the Camel being flown near the ground on one cylinder only, when, accompanied by a blast of flame, the pilot cut in all nine cylinders. The name Camel, incidentally, was never used officially (the name being quite unofficially, but universally, adopted by

Sopwith F.1 Camel cutaway drawing key

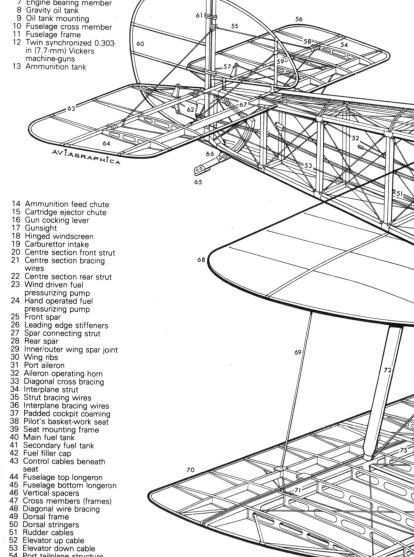

1 Two-blade wooden propeller
2 Propeller attachment plate
3 Attaching bolts
4 Engine cowling
5 130 hp Clerget nine-cylinder rotary engine
6 Engine mounting bulkhead
7 Engine bearing member
8 Gravity oil tank
9 Oil tank mounting
10 Fuselage cross member
11 Fuselage frame
12 Twin synchronized 0.303-in (7.7-mm) Vickers machine-guns
13 Ammunition tank
14 Ammunition feed chute
15 Cartridge ejector chute
16 Gun cocking lever
17 Gunsight
18 Hinged windscreen
19 Carburettor intake
20 Centre section front strut
21 Centre section bracing wires
22 Centre section rear strut
23 Wind driven fuel pressurizing pump
24 Hand operated fuel pressurizing pump
25 Front spar
26 Leading edge stiffeners
27 Spar connecting strut
28 Rear spar
29 Inner/outer wing spar joint
30 Wing ribs
31 Port aileron
32 Aileron operating horn
33 Diagonal cross bracing
34 Interplane strut
35 Strut bracing wires
36 Interplane bracing wires
37 Padded cockpit coaming
38 Pilot's basket-work seat
39 Seat mounting frame
40 Main fuel tank
41 Secondary fuel tank
42 Fuel filler cap
43 Control cables beneath seat
44 Fuselage top longeron
45 Fuselage bottom longeron
46 Vertical spacers
47 Cross members (frames)
48 Diagonal wire bracing
49 Dorsal frame
50 Dorsal stringers
51 Rudder cables
52 Elevator up cable
53 Elevator down cable
54 Port tailplane structure
55 Tailplane stay (upper)
56 Port elevator
57 Elevator operating horn
58 Elevator hinge
59 Fixed fin structure
60 Rudder
61 Rudder hinge
62 Rudder operating horn
63 Starboard elevator
64 Starboard tailplane structure
65 Tailskid
66 Tailskid pivot mounting
67 Elastic cord shock absorber
68 Starboard aileron (top)

As part of a series of experiments to provide British airships with their own fighter defence, two F.1 Camels (N6622 and N6814) were modified for trials by No. 212 Sqn, RAF, with the airship R.23; N6814 is seen here, probably at Pulham, Norfolk. The first live release was made by Lieutenant R. E. Keys DFC.

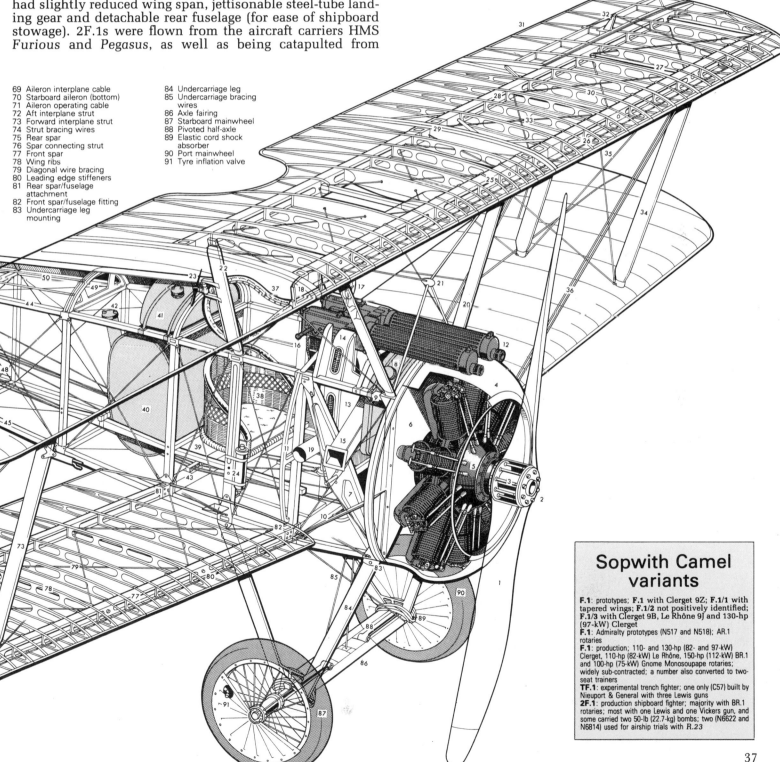

the flying services), F.1 being the formal designation. This also covered a night-fighter version, introduced with Home Defence units, which featured a pair of Lewis guns on a double Foster mounting above the top-wing centre section, and the cockpit moved about 12 in (30 cm) aft to allow the pilot to operate the guns; navigation lights and flare brackets were also included.

Camels at sea

Two versions did, however, merit a change of designation, the TF.1 and the 2F.1. The former, a trench fighter with two down-firing Lewis guns and a third on the upper wing centre section did not enter production but paved the way for the Sopwith Salamander. The latter, the 2F.1 shipboard fighter, had slightly reduced wing span, jettisonable steel-tube landing gear and detachable rear fuselage (for ease of shipboard stowage). 2F.1s were flown from the aircraft carriers HMS *Furious* and *Pegasus*, as well as being catapulted from

platforms erected on the gun turrets and forecastles of many other warships. These Camels accompanied sweeps by the Harwich Force in the Heligoland Bight in 1918 and shot down a number of German seaplanes. Perhaps the most spectacular use of Camels at sea involved those that took off from towed lighters, a procedure pioneered by that extraordinary pilot Commander C. R. Samson; however, it was Lieutenant Stuart Culley who, flying from a lighter towed by the destroyer HMS *Redoubt*, shot down the last German airship, *L.53* (Kapitänleutnant Prölss), to fall during the war on 11 August near Terschelling. Other 2F.1 Camels were employed in trials to provide defence for the UK's own airships, the aircraft being suspended below the airship *R.23* flying from Pulham; Lieutenant R. E. Keys DFC of No. 212

69 Aileron interplane cable
70 Starboard aileron (bottom)
71 Aileron operating cable
72 Aft interplane strut
73 Forward interplane strut
74 Strut bracing wires
75 Rear spar
76 Spar connecting strut
77 Front spar
78 Wing ribs
79 Diagonal wire bracing
80 Leading edge stiffeners
81 Rear spar/fuselage attachment
82 Front spar/fuselage fitting
83 Undercarriage leg mounting
84 Undercarriage leg
85 Undercarriage bracing wires
86 Axle fairing
87 Starboard mainwheel
88 Pivoted half-axle
89 Elastic cord shock absorber
90 Port mainwheel
91 Tyre inflation valve

Sopwith Camel variants

F.1: prototypes; **F.1** with Clerget 9Z; **F.1/1** with tapered wings; **F.1/2** not positively identified; **F.1/3** with Clerget 9B, Le Rhône 9J and 130-hp (97-kW) Clerget
F.1: Admiralty prototypes (N517 and N518); AR.1 rotaries
F.1: production; 110- and 130-hp (82- and 97-kW) Clerget, 110-hp (82-kW) Le Rhône, 150-hp (112-kW) BR.1 and 100-hp (75-kW) Gnome Monosoupape rotaries; widely sub-contracted; a number also converted to two-seat trainers
TF.1: experimental trench fighter; one only (C57) built by Nieuport & General with three Lewis guns
2F.1: production shipboard fighter; majority with BR.1 rotaries; most with one Lewis and one Vickers gun, and some carried two 50-lb (22.7-kg) bombs; two (N6622 and N6814) used for airship trials with R.23

This Camel, N6616, was flown by Captain Claude Emery, who was seconded to the Estonian Aviation Company in 1919. The aircraft was obtained from HMS *Vindictive*, and served alongside other British aircraft such as the Avro 504K, D.H.9 and Short 184, which had been supplied by the British government.

Squadron made the first live release, but the rapid end to the war eclipsed his achievement and the trials were eventually ended in 1925.

In all, 48 squadrons of the RFC and RNAS (and RAF) flew Camels and, apart from those that served in the UK and France, Camels took part in the campaigns in Italy, the Aegean, Macedonia, Greece, Russia and Mesopotamia. At the time of the Armistice the RAF had on charge a total of 2,519 F.1s and 129 2F.1s, including 802 with the Expeditionary Force in France and 112 2F.1s with units of the Grand Fleet. Total Camel production was 5,490, comprising 1,325 produced in 1917 and 4,165 in 1918.

Flown by the famous Canadian pilot, 'Billy' Barker, originally with No. 28 Squadron, RAF, in France, who, took his Camel with him when posted to command No. 66 Squadron in Italy, and kept it with him when given command of a Bristol Fighter Squadron, No. 139. In all, while flying his faithful B6313, Barker destroyed 48 enemy aircraft before his epic fight in which he destroyed four German aircraft while flying a Snipe, and for which he was awarded the Victoria Cross. It is now generally believed that no other single aeroplane has ever matched the achievement of B6313.

Camels also served with several foreign air forces. About 36 were supplied to Belgium in 1918, remaining in service until 1922, and one of these has been preserved to this day. Six were delivered to Greece and were flown by pilots of the Royal Hellenic naval air service.

In June 1918 143 Clerget Camels were purchased for use by the American Expeditionary Force in France, and these served with the 17th, 27th, 37th and 41st Aero Squadrons. As a result of their unforgiving handling characteristics they were never very popular with the Americans and few were ever flown in combat; instead they were used as trainers to acclimatize pilots arriving at the front. A well-known American pilot declared 'I don't want to fly Camels and certainly not Clerget Camels ... those little popping firecrackers'.

At the end of the war most of the American Camels were left in France or the UK; six which had flown with the US Navy in France were shipped to the United States where they underwent shipboard trials, being flown from platforms erected on the warships USS *Texas* and *Arkansas*. A small number of Camels also went to Canada after the war,

and about 20 were supplied to Poland whose Eskadra Kosciuszkowska flew them from Lwòw against the Russians in 1920.

In 1918 Camels accompanied the Slavo-British Aviation Group to Russia, flying from Archangelsk, with 'B' Flight, No. 47 Squadron, RAF, at Beketovka in 1919 and No. 221 Squadron at Petrovsk until 1920. In 1919 a Sopwith 2F.1 Camel was operating from HMS *Vindictive* against the Bolsheviks in the Baltic.

For all its magnificent exploits the Camel would have completely disappeared from combat service with the RAF had the war continued to rage for three or four months longer – replaced by the Sopwith Snipe, an excellent fighter without the vicissitudes of what Captain Norman Macmillan described as 'a fierce little beast'.

A preserved Camel, displaying spurious markings. This view nevertheless emphasizes the compact concentration of engine, guns and cockpit in a very short length of fuselage nose, as well as the cut-out in the top wing to improve the pilot's field of vision.

British pilots scored more successes with the Sopwith Camel than with any other type of aircraft during World War 1. This Camel is an accurate replica. (*Photo: Air Portraits*)

Royal Aircraft Factory S.E.5

'It's a bloody awful machine!' With these words to General Trenchard, rising 'ace' Albert Ball, finally victor in 44 combats and prejudiced in favour of the rotary-engined Nieuports, dismissed the Royal Aircraft Factory's new S.E.5 fighter.

Left: The first prototype of the S.E.5 (A4561), which flew for the first time towards the end of 1916. It had no weapons and was powered by a 150 hp (111.9 kW) Hispano-Suiza engine with no reduction gears.

The S.E.5 was designed around the Hispano Suiza engine in 1915, with the aircraft itself being designed by H. P. Folland and J. Kenworthy. The unarmed prototype with its direct-drive propeller appeared in November of the following year, although the choice of a gearless engine obviously meant that the original plan to have a Lewis machine gun installed between the rows of cylinders would have to be abandoned.

Only seven days later a second prototype appeared. In all essentials this was identical to its predecessor, but an early test flight resulted in damage that was not put right until the end of the month. During repairs the opportunity had been taken to fit a new landing gear and the armament which was later to become standard, namely an offset Vickers gun on the fuselage and a Lewis gun on a Foster mounting above the upper wing centre-section alongside an external gravity tank.

The middle of the following month saw the maiden flight of a third prototype, which was very similar to the first except for details of the tanks and a somewhat different radiator occasioned by the geared 200-hp (149.1-kW) Hispano-Suiza. It also carried the centre-section and port upper wing of the first machine, and when these were replaced an enlarged cut-out was incorporated, as were a centre-section gravity tank, armament, and a windscreen with such large side panels that it in effect formed a hood which severely obstructed the pilot's forward vision. Meanwhile the second prototype was lost when it broke up in the air, killing its pilot, so that ply webs were subsequently added to the compression struts and standardized strut fittings were introduced. The only other major modification took the form of less acutely raked wing tips to cure the claim by some pilots that the S.E.5 was 'almost uncontrollable' below 70 mph (112.7 km/h) if conditions were gusty.

First production S.E.5s equipped No. 56 Squadron, RFC, but to the dismay of the pilots these were fitted with even larger 'greenhouses' than before, so that their removal was ordered before the unit, which accounted for most of the machines built, was declared operational for service in France. Meanwhile a handful each went to Nos 24, 60 and 85 Squadrons.

Delayed in taking the new machines into action by the windscreen modifications, No. 56 carried out its first offensive patrol only late in April 1917, and Ball, together with other pilots, soon came to appreciate the strength and firepower of the type. However, a forgotten exponent of the S.E.5 with No. 56 Squadron was Lieutenant L. M. Barlow of B Flight, who finally brought down 18 of the enemy and won for himself three Military Crosses while flying these aircraft.

Typical of Barlow's actions was the special mission on the afternoon of 7 June when he shot up the sheds at Bisseghem which he identified by the adjacent mineral water factory. A few moments later a train was attacked twice from a height of only 20 ft (6.1 m), while another was left in a blanket of smoke and steam. The next targets were the troops in Wevelghem streets, as well as the railway station where a train was stopped. From an altitude of only 50 ft (15.2 m) Barlow then strafed Reckem aerodrome off the Menin road, a troublesome ground gunner being silenced, though not before he had succeeded in shooting away the port elevator of the S.E.5 while Barlow was flying below the level of the nearby roofs to make sure of his aim.

Meanwhile production of the fighter had got into its stride and models were no longer being delivered with the modified wing tips, although it is recorded that at least the first delivery of this fresh batch retained the large windscreen and boasted the external gravity tank of the prototypes. The total of all 150-hp (111.9-kW) S.E.5s built was probably fewer than 59, and it was soon replaced by the S.E.5a when there were available sufficient 200-hp (149.1-kW) Hispano-Suizas such as powered the third prototype S.E.5.

As might be expected, it was one of the prototype S.E.5s that later became the first version of what was to become known as the S.E.5a, a fact that was proven even by its external appearance. The historic machine in question was the third S.E.5 (A4563), but in a modified form as it appeared

A direct development of the third S.E.5 prototype (A4563) was the S.E.5a *(left and below)*, which itself had been considerably modified by the time it first appeared in May 1917.

Royal Aircraft Factory S.E.5a

Specification
S.E.5a (Royal Aircraft Factory)

Type: single-seat fighting scout

Powerplant: one Hispano-derived V-8 water-cooled engine, usually a 200-hp (149-kW) Wolseley Viper

Performance: (Viper) maximum speed 138 mph (222 km/h) at sea level, falling to 123 mph (198 km/h) at 15,000 ft (4572 m); time to climb to 5,000 ft (1524 m) 4.9 minutes; endurance 2.5 hours

Weights: empty about 1,430 lb (649 kg); maximum loaded 1,940 lb (880 kg)

Dimensions: span 26 ft 7.5 in (8.12 m); length 20 ft 11 in (6.38 m); height 9 ft 6 in (2.90 m); wing area 244 sq ft (22.67 m²)

Armament: usually one 0.303-in (7.7-mm) Vickers machine-gun fixed in top of fuselage to left of centre, firing through propeller disc, with 400-round belt; plus one 0.303-in (7.7-mm) Lewis machine-gun on Foster mount, with four 97-round drum magazines; provision for four 25-lb (11.3-kg) Cooper bombs carried under fuselage

An RAF squadron that was to see outstanding success with the S.E.5a during World War 1 was No. 74. Receiving its first aircraft in March 1918, the squadron quickly moved to France where, on its first dogfight, five enemy aircraft were downed for no losses to the squadron. The majority of operations were of an offensive nature, often with

25-lb (11-kg) bombs for low-level attacks on retreating German forces, though by Armistice Day the squadron had a total of 140 aerial combat 'kills'. One of the unit's most deadly pilots was Major E. 'Mick' Mannock VC, who, despite having sight in only one eye, scored over 70 kills before his death. This is one of the aircraft he flew in achieving that figure.

Plans for mass production of the S.E.5a by the Curtiss company in America did not come to fruition, other than the assembly of 56 British-built airframes. In 1922–3 50 of these were rebuilt by the Eberhart Steel Company as advanced trainers.

This Royal Aircraft Factory S.E.5a replica was used, as were all modern rebuilds or copies, for sky writing before World War 2.

E5808 was one of a large batch of S.E.5as made by the Austin Motor Company at Birmingham, close to the Wolseley engine factory. It was assigned around the time of the Armistice to No. 56 Squadron, RAF, the original S.E.5 user in March 1917 (with large wrap-round windscreens). Note the long Aldis optical sight, an alternative to the ring-and-bead system.

at Martlesham Heath testing establishment in May 1917, its alterations including a head fairing behind the cockpit, gravity fuel and water tanks in the centre section, short-span wings and L-shaped exhausts. But more importantly, a 200-hp (149.1-kW) Hispano-Suiza engine had been retained, driving a four-blade propeller so that superior performance was assured.

Contracts for the new machine, designated S.E.5a, were placed as early as February 1917 with Martinsyde and Vickers, only a small number being manufactured by the Royal Aircraft Establishment itself, the resultant models differing little from the final form of the prototype. Some of these first variants were fitted with Wolseley-built engines despite the troubles associated with engines of the type from this source, and some of the first batch of new scouts again went to No. 56 Squadron, these even retaining the L-shaped exhausts of the prototype, although these were later replaced by a long horizontal type; any of this pattern which went to No. 56, however, were promptly cut down to mere extensions of the manifold.

As the year progressed, not only did the production tempo increase, but so too did the orders placed with other builders until the total expected was 3,600 by the end of the year, although only about 900 had been delivered at this time, a number which included S.E.5s which were still being manufactured.

Production problems

December found the S.E.5a in service with only five front-line squadrons, with a further one expecting re-equipment in the coming year. The reason for such a poor state of affairs lay in the fact that production of airframes had outstripped that of engines. In part this was due to the defective nature of the Wolseley products already mentioned, but added to this was the fact that those of French manufacture had in some instances shafts and gears manufactured poorly by the Brasier company, and although these were in some cases replaced by similar components of British make, demand eventually exceeded supply to the extent that faulty parts had knowingly to be passed and used. It was not until this

had been going on for some time that relief came in the form of a supply of engines which had been ordered on the advice of the Admiralty from other French companies.

A further precautionary measure was an order placed with the Wolseley company for Hispano engines of the earlier 150-hp (111.9-kW) type, but insufficient clarity of instruction resulted in the organization developing a 220-hp (164-kW) high-compression motor, and although this was eventually to prove a blessing in disguise (since this Viper power unit was to be specified for all 1918 contracts), the immediate result was a mere trickle of engines where a flood had been expected.

In combat the S.E.5a soon proved a formidable fighting machine, and its name was quickly to become associated with the foremost British pilots of the day, as well as those of

Almost without exception the aircraft of the US American Expeditionary Force in France rivalled those of the German circuses for bright colour schemes. Still bearing British serial F8010, this Austin-built S.E.5a wears the 'black executioner' badge of the 25th Squadron (which kept the badge, as a bomber unit, into the 1930s).

At least 20 ex-RAF S.E.5as were shipped to Poland as that newly-formed country's first fighters. Soon after their arrival, in 1920, they became hotly engaged in the war with the Russian Bolsheviks, mainly on the Ukrainian front. Photographs are known of a captured machine in Red Star markings.

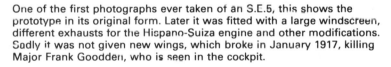

the single Australian unit (No. 2 Squadron, AFC) and two from the United States (the 25th and 148th Aero Squadrons) which flew the type, not only on the Western Front, but in Macedonia (Nos 17, 47 and 150 Squadrons), Mesopotamia (No. 72 Squadron), Palestine (Nos 111 and 145 Squadrons), plus the units using the type on Home Defence (Nos 37, 50, 61 and 143 Squadrons of the RFC and RAF). These were the 'aces' of the war years, the top-scorers who seemed to live charmed lives, and they included not only Albert Ball who had become reconciled to the design he had been at first swift to condemn, but also those with comparatively modest claims of kills, such as Longton (12), Clayson (21), Shields (24) and Maxwell (27). However, at the opposite end of the list of famous S.E.5a pilots are the names of Mannock (with a total of 73 victims) and McCudden, who not only raised his

One of the first photographs ever taken of an S.E.5, this shows the prototype in its original form. Later it was fitted with a large windscreen, different exhausts for the Hispano-Suiza engine and other modifications. Sadly it was not given new wings, which broke in January 1917, killing Major Frank Goodden, who is seen in the cockpit.

total to 57 while flying the type but was also one of those who flew specially-modified machines, his B4891 having narrow-chord elevators when he took it over on 3 December 1917; factory workers responsible for this machine later recalled that they already knew to whom it was going, although the modification was by no means unique, B4890 also being on record as being thus modified.

Indeed, the S.E.5a was the subject of continuous change and refinement so that towards the end of 1917 a stronger landing gear became standard with substantially tapered forward legs, while other modifications included additional braces to the leading edge of the fin, which was itself revised; strengthened trailing edges; and improved oil tankage.

This was not all, for trials were conducted with a view to improving the armament: thus twin Lewis guns were experimentally fitted over the centre-section to augment the fixed Vickers gun below, and another triple-gun arrangement for Home Defence application included three Lewis guns on an Eeman fuselage mounting that carried the armament arranged to fire forwards and upwards at an angle of 45° through slots in the centre-section. Neither of these installations was adopted officially.

Modifications of a more academic nature were the fitting

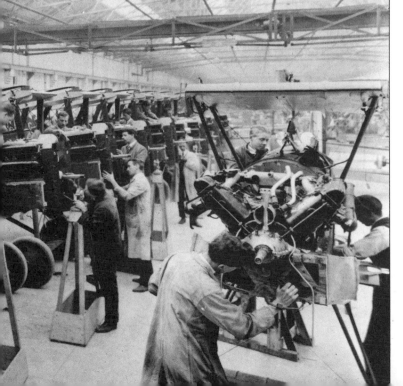

The assembly lines at Wolseley Motors, where the radiators and other components were produced, and other parts were checked.

45

Royal Aircraft Factory S.E.5

Hundreds of S.E.5as were given to the fledgeling air forces in countries of the British Empire after the Armistice. One batch went to what was then the Union of South Africa, and No. 320 is pictured at the headquarters at Pretoria in early 1920. Finish was silver, and markings blue/white/orange.

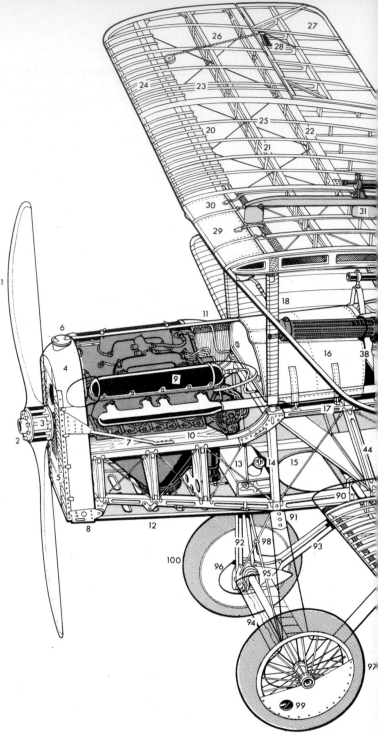

of newly designed fins and rudders, underslung radiators and even a variable-pitch propeller, while there also existed the modifications necessary to produce two-seat S.E.5a aircraft, and although these did yeoman service for instructional purposes, the resultant flying qualities left much to be desired; meanwhile another series of test programmes was conducted to explore the question of stowage of both the Calthrop Guardian Angel and Mears parachutes.

Before the comparatively sudden termination of World War 1, plans were made for construction of the S.E.5a by the Curtiss company for use by the US Air Service. One thousand were ordered, and although 56 were assembled from British parts, only one (SC43153) was completed with a Wright-Martin (Hispano-Suiza derived) engine of 180 hp (134.2 kW), the designation of this variant being S.E.5E. More radical had been the changes in June 1917 resulting in the S.E.5b at Farnborough: this type emerged with unequal-span wings and a considerably cleaner nose with an underslung radiator, and although there were no plans to develop an operational version it is of interest to note that such was the improvement in performance that the single example

The S.E.5a registered as F904 is the only original machine still flying today (here with a Wolseley Viper engine).

survived the war by at least two years, being finally flown with standard wing panels. Total production of the S.E.5 and S.E.5a was 5,205.

With the end of the war, the S.E.5a vanished from military use fairly rapidly, although small numbers lingered on in Australia, Canada and South Africa, but as unwanted fighters became available to the civil market, they were quickly bought and pressed into use in some unexpected roles: included among these were experiments in fire prevention, while one went to Japan with the British Aviation Mission of 1921 and exerted some considerable influence on future single-seat design in that country.

Civil conversions

A number of S.E.5a aircraft came onto the civil register from May 1920, the first being G-EATE. Not all of the privately-owned machines were fitted with the original engines, G-EAZT for example having an RAF 1A motor, while G-EBCA had a Renault which offered a maximum speed of only 65 mph (104.6 km/h).

Royal Aircraft Factory S.E.5a cutaway drawing key

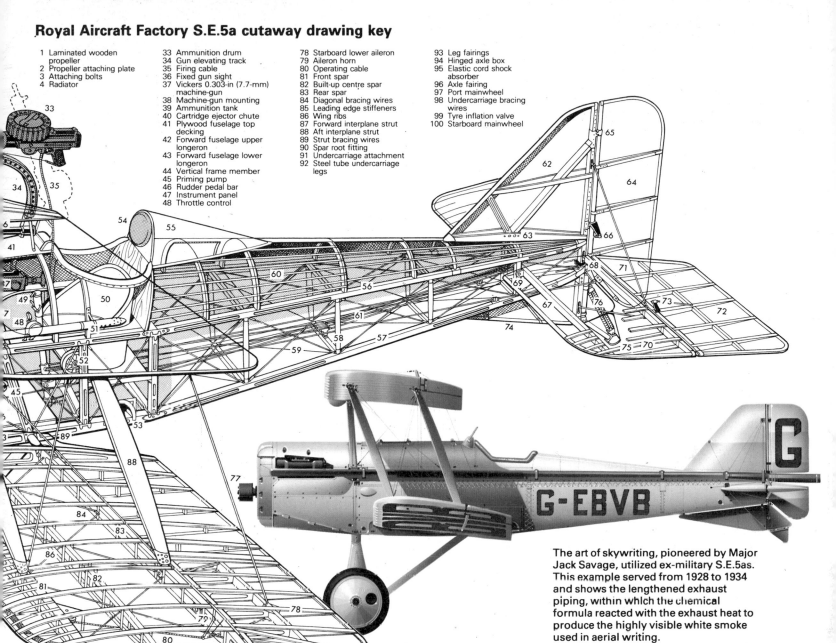

1 Laminated wooden propeller
2 Propeller attaching plate
3 Attaching bolts
4 Radiator

33 Ammunition drum
34 Gun elevating track
35 Firing cable
36 Fixed gun sight
37 Vickers 0.303-in (7.7-mm) machine-gun
38 Machine-gun mounting
39 Ammunition tank
40 Cartridge ejector chute
41 Plywood fuselage top decking
42 Forward fuselage upper longeron
43 Forward fuselage lower longeron
44 Vertical frame member
45 Priming pump
46 Rudder pedal bar
47 Instrument panel
48 Throttle control

78 Starboard lower aileron
79 Aileron horn
80 Operating cable
81 Front spar
82 Built-up centre spar
83 Rear spar
84 Diagonal bracing wires
85 Leading edge stiffeners
86 Wing ribs
87 Forward interplane strut
88 Aft interplane strut
89 Strut bracing wires
90 Spar root fitting
91 Undercarriage attachment
92 Steel tube undercarriage legs

93 Leg fairings
94 Hinged axle box
95 Elastic cord shock absorber
96 Axle fairing
97 Port mainwheel
98 Undercarriage bracing wires
99 Tyre inflation valve
100 Starboard mainwheel

The art of skywriting, pioneered by Major Jack Savage, utilized ex-military S.E.5as. This example served from 1928 to 1934 and shows the lengthened exhaust piping, within which the chemical formula reacted with the exhaust heat to produce the highly visible white smoke used in aerial writing.

5 Radiator shutter plates
6 Filler cap
7 Radiator mounting strut
8 Bottom fitting
9 200-hp (149-kW) Wolseley Viper V-8 engine
10 Engine mounting structure
11 Top cowling
12 Hinged bottom cowling
13 Oil tank
14 Oil filler cap
15 Engine cooling air duct
16 Main fuel tank
17 Fuel tank fixing
18 Centre section forward strut
19 Centre section aft strut
20 Front spar
21 Built-up centre spar
22 Rear spar
23 Wing ribs
24 Leading edge stiffeners
25 Diagonal wire bracing
26 Aileron connecting cable
27 Starboard upper aileron
28 Aileron horn
29 Auxiliary fuel tank
30 Radiator header tank
31 Lewis gun mounting
32 0.303-in (7.7-mm) calibre Lewis gun

49 Control column
50 Pilot's seat
51 Exhaust pipe
52 Tailplane incidence control
53 Access step
54 Headrest
55 Headrest fairing
56 Aft fuselage top longeron
57 Aft fuselage bottom longeron
58 Vertical spacers
59 Diagonal wire bracing
60 Dorsal structure
61 Rudder and elevator cables
62 Fin structure
63 Fin attachment
64 Rudder structure
65 Rudder hinge
66 Operating horn
67 Variable incidence tailplane
68 Tailplane actuator
69 Hinge point
70 Tailplane structure
71 Tailplane bracing wire
72 Elevator structure
73 Elevator horn
74 Ventral fin
75 Steerable tail-skid
76 Tail-skid shock absorber
77 Aileron interconnecting wire

Royal Aircraft Factory S.E.5 variants

S.E.5 prototypes: three built, A4561 unarmed and powered by a direct-drive 150-hp (111.9-kW) French-built Hispano-Suiza motor with a gravity tank in the leading edge of the upper, port wing; A4562 which was similar but later armed and fitted with an enlarged windshield and centre-section gravity tank mounted externally, and A4563 powered by a 200-hp (149.1-kW) geared Hispano-Suiza; armed, this last became in effect the prototype S.E.5a.
S.E.5 production: originally fitted with extra-large windshields, these were soon discarded as was the armoured seat of the prototypes; flown with or without headrests, span of later versions reduced by 1 ft 3.6 in (0.40 m) by reducing rake of wing-tips; 150-hp (111.9-kW) Hispano-Suiza engine.
S.E.5a prototype: modified A4563 fitted with four-blade propeller and having L-shaped exhausts.
S.E.5a production: powered by 200-hp (149.1-kW),

220-hp (164.1-kW) or 240-hp (179.0-kW) Hispano-Suiza, some of the early units of French manufacture, or (final standard) 200-hp (149.1-kW) Wolseley W.4a Viper, an underslung radiator being tried on one such; various trials conducted with different tail assemblies or a version armed with three upward-firing Lewis guns; also some flown with reduced dihedral and steel or wooden landing gears, narrow-chord ailerons etc; some modified as two-seaters, or as civil smoke-writers.
S.E.5b: only one (A8947) produced with 200-hp (149.1-kW) motor, underslung radiator and sesquiplane configuration at one time; original armament retained
S.E.5E: designation for USA Curtiss-assembled variant with 180-hp (134.2-kW) Wright-Martin Hispano Suiza; only one (SC43153) completed, fuselage covered in ply
S.E.6: uncompleted project to be fitted with 275-hp (205.1-kW) Rolls-Royce Falcon water-cooled motor

Royal Aircraft Factory S.E.5

The average cost of these machines offered for disposal was £700 each, and eight were procured for a unique race by the Royal Aero Club in 1921, the contest being a proposed speed trial between Oxford and Cambridge Universities on 16 July. Civil registrations on the fuselage apart, the six competing aircraft (one was held in reserve by each team) were to fly in their old military dope scheme relieved only by the appropriate shade of blue on the rear fuselage and tail assembly.

The race finally took place on one of the hottest afternoons of the summer and it was undoubtedly the choice by the Cambridge pilots to fly in the cooler conditions of the upper air that contributed to their taking the first three places and an accumulated prize of more than £400. All the competing aircraft were Viper-powered.

Perhaps better known than the privately owned or racing S.E.5a aircraft were the few that might be seen on a summer's day skywriting in white smoke trails the words of advertisements such as *Buick* or *Persil*. The S.E.5 aircraft used for this purpose were piloted by M. L. Bramson or Sidney St Barbe, or alternatively Major Jack Savage who invented the art of skywriting and was at the time the proprietor of the company formed for its exploitation.

The aircraft were in all essentials standard machines powered by 200-hp (149.1-kW) Wolseley Vipers but with a special modification to the exhaust pipes: these were lengthened down the fuselage to accommodate this. Into this the smoke-producing substance was introduced from a tank

D5995 was built by Vickers at Weybridge, and is depicted while serving with No. 143 Sqn, RFC, at Throwley on home defence duties. The Lewis gun on its Foster mounting can be seen clearly, in its upper position for firing. This looks as 'standard' an S.E.5a as one could find (there were hundreds of minor variations).

inside the fuselage, the flow being controlled by means of a cock inside the cockpit. The pilot had only to turn this cock to allow the entry of the chemical, the formula for which was always a closely kept secret, the heat of the pipes then transforming it into dense white smoke. Thus it was that astonished spectators lifted their eyes on 30 May 1922 to read the single word *Vim* against the backdrop of the sky, a word chosen for its simplicity.

Perhaps unintentionally, and possibly due in part to the Skywriter's Union, we still have a few examples of the S.E.5a around today. This is partly shown by the fact that all the museum models still extant in Britain today were used for skywriting at some stage in their lives. Perhaps the best example of these aircraft is in the Science Museum in London. With the exception of its headrest, former G-EBIB has been restored to its original military configuration.

Left: A replica S.E.5a built by trainees at the Royal Aircraft Establishment at Farnborough. *Below:* In this photo the additional Lewis machine-gun can be clearly seen on top of the wing.

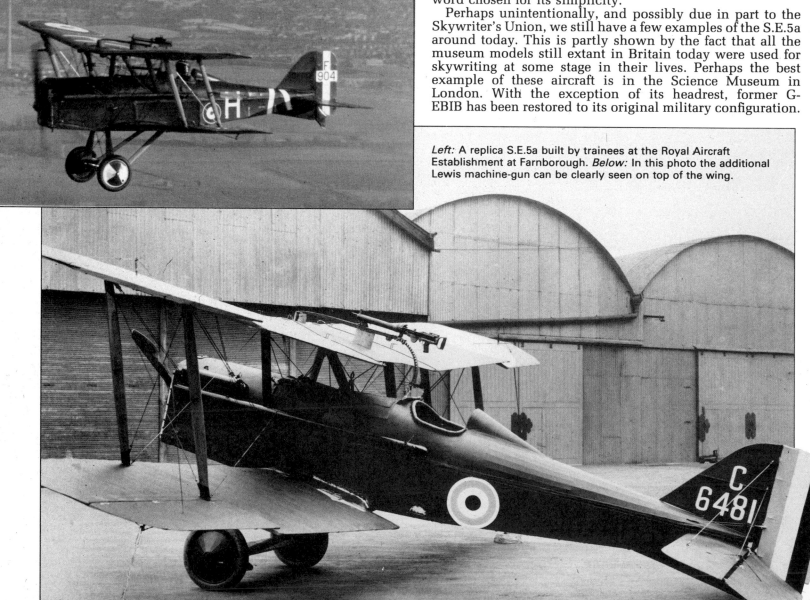

Fokker Dr.I Triplane

Conceived as a counter to the Sopwith Triplane, the Fokker Dr.I was one of the most agile combat aircraft in history. Flown by such men as Manfred von Richthofen, the small number built shot down many times their own number of enemy aircraft on the Western Front. It was in one of these aircraft that von Richthofen, the legendary Red Baron, met his death.

Manfred von Richthofen and his scarlet Fokker Dr.I triplane have become a legend in their own right. This is despite the fact that Leutnant Werner Voss shot down many more aircraft from his Fokker triplane, and von Richthofen's kills were mostly achieved with other aircraft. What is more, the number of these aircraft flying in World War 1 was comparatively small, and it was only designed as an answer to, and built along the same lines as, the British Sopwith Triplane. But the renown of the Fokker Dr.I still eclipses that of any other aircraft which flew in this war.

Released by the Sopwith Experimental Department on 28 May 1916, the first Triplane was a very neat fighting scout with a fuselage and tail almost identical to those of the Sopwith Pup, perhaps the most agile and well-loved aircraft of its day. Sopwith designed the Triplane for several reasons. Its three wings were much narrower (smaller chord) than the biplane wings of the Pup, so that though span remained unchanged the wing area actually was reduced. The more powerful (130-hp/97-kW) instead of 80- or 100-hp/60- or 75-kW) engine made the Triplane significantly faster. The narrower wings gave the pilot a better view, especially as the

middle wing was on the same level as his eyes. The narrow chord also meant that the centre of pressure (the point through which the resultant lift force acts) did not move so far from front to rear, or vice versa, as in a normal broad-winged machine during violent manoeuvres, and as this meant the fuselage could be short it enhanced manoeuvrability. Manoeuvrability was also assisted by keeping the span short, which with three wings was simple.

Frightening example

All the Triplanes went to the Royal Naval Air Service and, in no small measure because of the tremendous aggressiveness and skill of the pilots, soon struck a chill into the hearts of German flyers. The Triplanes really got into action during the Battle of Arras in April 1917. So great was their success that an official historian wrote: 'The sight of a Triplane

A replica of the Fokker Dr.I painted to represent von Richthofen's famous aircraft, though the face painted upon the engine cowling simulates that of the aircraft flown by Werner Voss.

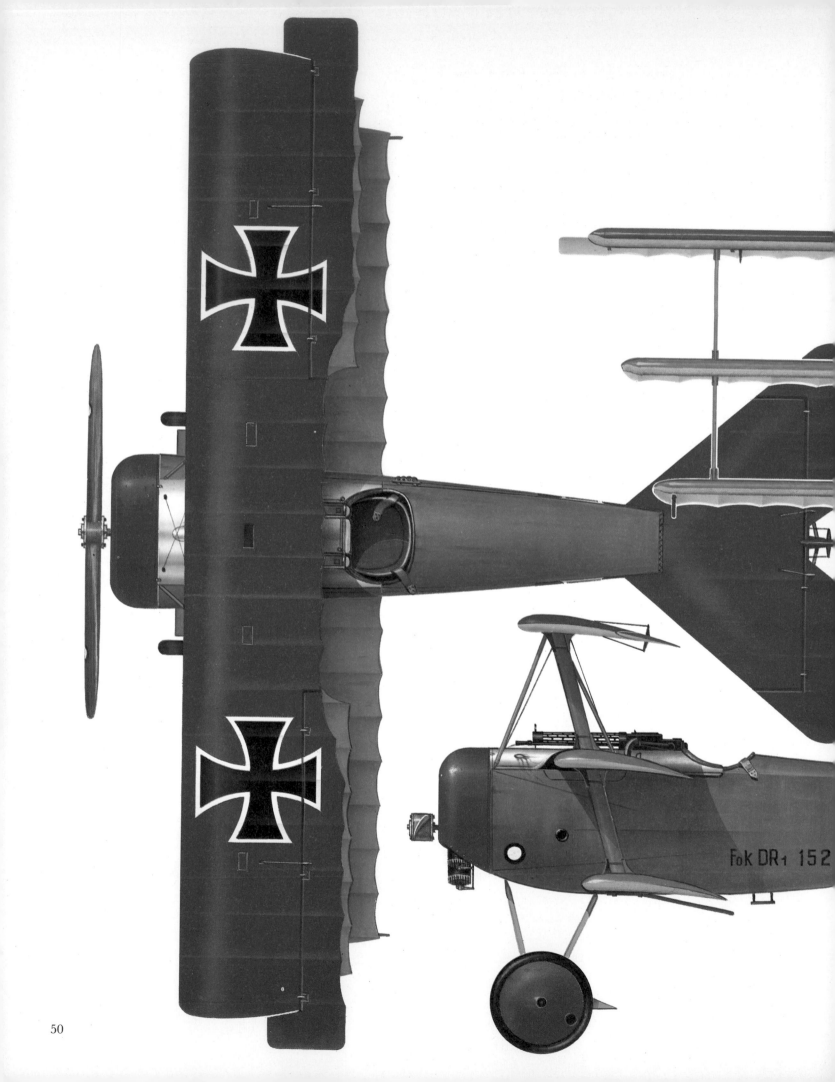

The Fokker Dr.I serialled 152/17 (construction no. 1864) was one of a batch of 30 from early in the type's production run. Allocated to Jasta 11, this aircraft was on occasion flown by Manfred von Richthofen, and survived the war to go on display in a Berlin museum in an all-red scheme.

Fokker Dr.I

Specification

Type: single-seat fighting scout

Powerplant: one 110-hp (82-kW) Oberursel Ur.II nine-cylinder rotary piston engine

Peformance: maximum speed 115 mph (185 km/h) at sea level, and 103 mph (165 km/h) at 13,125 ft (4000 m); climb to 3,280 ft (1000 m) in 2 minutes 55 seconds; service ceiling 20,015 ft (6100 m); range 186 miles (300 km); endurance 1 hour 30 minutes

Weights: empty 894 lb (406 kg); maximum take-off 1,291 lb (586 kg)

Dimensions: span, upper 23 ft 7 in (7.19 m), centre 20 ft 5¼ in (6.23 m) and lower 18 ft 8½ in (5.70 m); length 18 ft 11 in (5.77 m); height 9 ft 8 in (2.95 m); wing area, including axle fairing 200.85 sq ft (18.66 m²)

Armament: two 7.92-mm (0.31-in) LMG 08/15 machine-guns with 500 rounds per gun

Fokker Dr.I

This all-black Dr.I had unusual white crosses on its fuselage and wings (it is believed other black German machines had white-outlined black crosses). It was the aircraft of Leutnant Josef Jacobs of Jasta 7, who finally gained 41 confirmed victories. This put him level with Hauptmann Bruno Loerzer in eighth place in Germany.

Perhaps the most famous fighter of all time, the triplane number 425/17 was the last mount of the 'Red Baron', Rittmeister Manfred, Freiherr von Richthofen, the top-scoring ace of World War 1 with 80 confirmed kills. He was shot down on 21 April 1918. Here the old cross can just be seen under the new one.

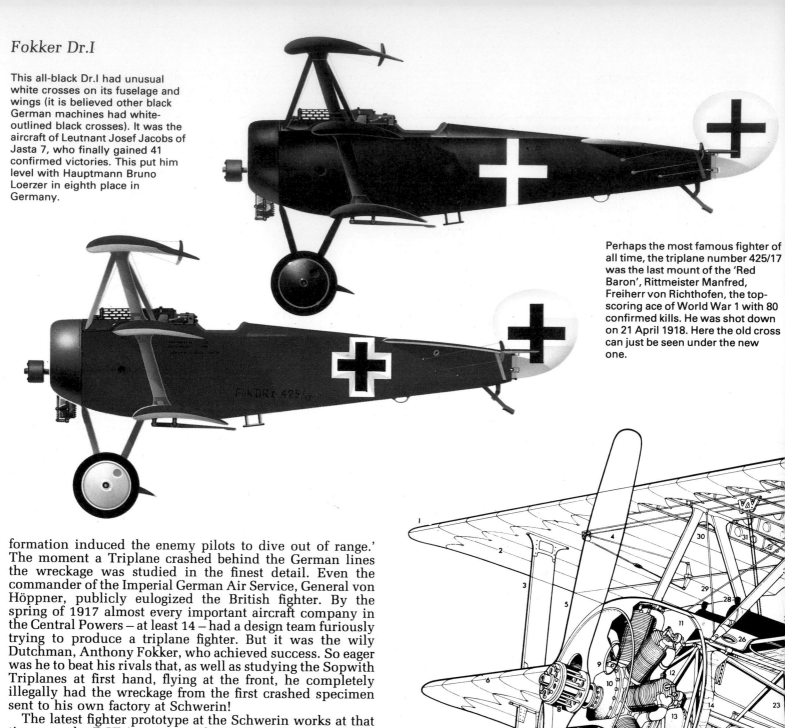

formation induced the enemy pilots to dive out of range.' The moment a Triplane crashed behind the German lines the wreckage was studied in the finest detail. Even the commander of the Imperial German Air Service, General von Höppner, publicly eulogized the British fighter. By the spring of 1917 almost every important aircraft company in the Central Powers – at least 14 – had a design team furiously trying to produce a triplane fighter. But it was the wily Dutchman, Anthony Fokker, who achieved success. So eager was he to beat his rivals that, as well as studying the Sopwith Triplanes at first hand, flying at the front, he completely illegally had the wreckage from the first crashed specimen sent to his own factory at Schwerin!

The latest fighter prototype at the Schwerin works at that time was the D.VI (a company designation unrelated to the later production D.VI), intended for the Luftfahrttruppe (air force) of Austro-Hungary. In June 1917 chief designer Reinold Platz quickly re-drew the drawings and the D.VI emerged round 1 July 1917 as the first triplane to fly in Germany. It was immediately tested by Lt Werner Voss, already a famed ace. Platz had already designed extremely advanced biplane fighters with completely cantilever wings, and he made the D.VI the same way, unbraced wings being easier on a short-span triplane. The two lower wings were attached to the top and bottom of the fuselage, and the only struts were long steel-tube inverted-Vee cabane struts carrying the top wing high above the fuselage. This wing was the only one with ailerons, whereas the Sopwith Triplane had had ailerons on all three wings, linked by light rods. Powered by a 110-hp (82-kW) Oberursel Ur.II rotary engine, the D.VI flew excellently, though before being sent to Hungary in August the upper wing, with its ailerons, was increased in span. To eliminate slight wing vibration, light wooden streamline I-type struts were added linking the wings near their tips. Armament was two synchronized 0.31-in (7.29-mm) LMG 08/15 guns.

Further developments

The D.VI, often incorrectly called the V 3, was succeeded by the first of the Fokkers to have a *Versuchs* (experimental) number, the V 4. Two V 4 triplanes, with balanced ailerons squared-off at the wingtips, were ordered on 11 July 1917. In August a number of V 7 triplanes were ordered with more powerful engines, such as the 160-hp (119-kW) Siemens-Halske Sh.III, 160-hp (119-kW) Ur.III, 145-hp (108-kW) Steyr-built Le Rhône and 170-hp (127-kW) Goebel Goe.III. These introduced modified wings with span increasing in equal steps from bottom to top. They retained the I-strut linking the wings, and all had horn balances on the ailerons and elevators, those on the ailerons projecting beyond the tips of the wings. No data survive, but because of their power the V fighter prototypes were probably more formidable than the eventual production fighter triplane.

Action at the Front

Lt Voss spent over 20 hours testing the two V 4 prototype triplanes in August 1917, and by the end of that month had them to his satisfaction. Both had by that time seen action at the front, and Fokker himself had also done a lot of active flying in them (previously he had had to don the uniform of a German officer and fly on active operational missions to test his synchronizing gear, despite the fact he was a Dutch civilian!).

Voss made the first operational flight in Fok.103/17 (Fokker No.103 for year 1917), the second V 4 prototype, on 30 August 1917. He claimed a victory on this mission. Two days later, on 1 September, von Richthofen flew the original V 4 (102/ 17) and scored his 60th victory. Flying with von Richthofen's *Jagdgeschwader* 1 (JG1) the two prototypes scored success after success. Voss monopolized the second Dr.I (103/17) scoring a remarkable 20 confirmed victories in it in 24 days before being killed in a classic fight on 23 September with no fewer than six S.E.5a fighters.

Structurally it was typical Fokker and Platz, with very strong mixed construction. The wings were almost wholly wood, with steel at the main joints and the attachments of bracing wires. Each wing had a single built-up box spar with main longerons of spindled (machined away for lightness on a router) hardwood, carrying built-up plywood ribs. Trailing edges were wire, resulting in the characteristic scalloped appearance when the fabric covering was doped and tightened.

Fokker Dr.I cutaway drawing key

1 Starboard upper wing tip
2 Wing panel fabric covering
3 Starboard upper interplane strut
4 Aileron cable run
5 Two-blade wooden propeller
6 Starboard centre wing
7 Lower interplane strut
8 Propeller hub fixing bolts
9 Ventilated engine cowling
10 Oberursel Ur.II (le Rhône) nine-cylinder rotary engine
11 Engine compartment fireproof bulkhead
12 Engine bearer struts
13 Reduction gearbox
14 Plywood side fairing panel
15 Carburettor
16 Rudder pedal bar
17 Pilot's footboards
18 Compass mounting
19 Control column
20 Control column-mounted secondary throttle control
21 Gun firing cables
22 Ammunition boxes
23 Fuel tank (20-Imp gal/91-litre capacity)
24 Wing spar box construction
25 Centre wing/fuselage attachments
26 Fuel filler cap
27 Twin 7.92-mm (0.31-in) LMG 08/15 machine guns
28 Ring-and-bead gunsight
29 Diagonal wire bracing

30 Centre section V-struts
31 Aileron cables
32 V-strut attachment
33 Plywood covered leading edge
34 Upper wing spar box
35 Wing ribs
36 Port upper interplane strut
37 Wing tip construction
38 Rib bracing tapes
39 Aileron horn balance
40 Welded steel tube aileron construction
41 Aileron control horn
42 Wire trailing edge
43 Port centre wing construction
44 Interplane strut attachment
45 Wing root cut-out, forward and downward visibility
46 Machine gun breeches
47 Padded cockpit coaming
48 Engine instruments
49 Engine throttle and fuel cock controls
50 Pilot's seat
51 Sliding seat adjustment
52 Welded steel-tube fuselage construction
53 Aft end of plywood side fairing panel
54 Plywood top decking
55 Port lower interplane strut
56 Fuselage top longeron
57 Horizontal spacers
58 Port lower wing tip
59 Wing tip skid
60 Tailplane centre section mounting
61 Welded steel tube tailplane construction
62 Rudder horn balance
63 Steel tube leading edge
64 Elevator horn balance
65 Steel tube elevator construction

66 Rudder fabric covering
67 Sternpost
68 Rudder control horn
69 Elevator control horn
70 Tailskid hinge mounting
71 Steel-shod tailskid
72 Elastic cord shock absorbers
73 Fuselage vertical spacers
74 Lifting handles
75 Fuselage fabric covering
76 Diagonal wire bracing (double wires)
77 Tailplane control cables
78 Fuselage bottom longeron
79 Control cable guides
80 Mounting step
81 Seat support frame
82 Dust proof fabric bulkhead
83 Pilot's floor
84 Control column mounting shaft
85 Lower wing centre section spar box
86 Undercarriage strut attachments
87 Main undercarriage V-struts
88 Port mainwheel
89 Wheel disc fabric covering
90 Wheel spokes
91 Pivoted half-axle
92 Axle fairing construction
93 Axle spar box
94 Elastic cord shock absorbers
95 Starboard mainwheel
96 Tyre valve access
97 Starboard lower wing tip skid

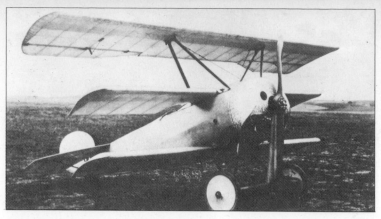

First of the Fokker triplanes, this neat prototype is commonly (but incorrectly) known as the V 3. Its true designation was D.VI, in an early-1917 series of D designations unrelated to the official series which included the famed D.VII. Powered by a 110-hp (82-kW) Ur.II rotary, it was flown by Leutnant Werner Voss in mid-1917.

One of the best surviving photographs of a genuine Dr.I. This aircraft provided the basis for the restored triplane N864DR which, after a busy flying career, was donated to the Australian War Memorial at Canberra. Numerous replicas of this famous fighter have been built in recent years, powered by non-rotary engines.

The small fuselage and tail were accurately welded in jigs from pre-shaped steel tubes, the fuselage then having light wooden fairings added prior to being covered in fabric. The traditional rubber-sprung main landing gears had an axle faired by a small wing, a feature of many Fokker fighters. Again a common feature of the day was the absence of a fin, the only vertical tail surface being the simple rounded rudder pivoted to the fuselage sternpost. The small riveted fuel tank was immediately behind the spinning engine, and beneath the guns; the usual armament, seldom altered in practice, comprised two LMG 08/15 (commonly called 'Spandau') machine-guns with belt magazines inside the fuselage behind the tank and the breeches immediately in front of the pilot inside the cockpit.

It added up to a simple, relatively cheap and fairly agile fighter, which with the standard 110-hp (82-kW) engine could climb faster than many more powerful aircraft and also turn inside them, a factor which in a dogfight was vital. But the speed was unimpressive by late 1917 standards and the range and endurance were exceptionally poor – only a skilled pilot could keep a Dr.I airborne longer than 80 minutes whereas 2 (if not 3) hours was easily within the grasp of all Allied fighter pilots.

Richthofen's Flying Circus

But for the brief period from October 1917 the 318 Fokker Dr.I triplanes, plus the two prototypes, were to carve out a niche in the hall of fame of military aviation. As with the Sopwith which inspired it, this was to some extent because of the brilliant flyers who went to war in it. No more famous flying unit has ever existed than von Richthofen's JG1, often called 'Richthofen's Flying Circus' because of the large number of fighters under one command, their carefully planned and organized combat techniques and, not least, their brilliant and often highly personal colour schemes. Of

course, the 318 production Dr.Is equipped not just the four *Jagdstaffeln* (fighter squadrons) of JG1 but several other *Jagdgeschwäder*, notably JG2 and JG3.

The successful service career of the Dr.I was briefly marred by a spate of crashes in the first two weeks of combat duty by production aircraft. The cause was eventually traced to shockingly bad workmanship at the Schwerin factory, and all Dr.Is were at once grounded until their wings had been stripped of fabric and inspected. In many cases properly made wing spars had to be produced, and the factory spent almost the whole of November 1917 urgently repairing or rebuilding the wings of Dr.Is. Thus it was not really until late November that the Dr.I became effective in numbers on the Western Front, and it is remarkable that such a relatively small number of a basically outdated design should have acquired so great a reputation.

This reputation is, of course, inextricably interwoven with the great Red Baron himself, Rittmeister Manfred, Freiherr von Richthofen, a German aristocrat who was the top-scoring ace of World War 1 and perhaps the most famous fighter pilot of all time. Though most of his victories had been gained on other types, such as the Albatros D.III, he favoured the Dr.I over faster biplanes and continued to fly one almost exclusively on combat missions in 1918. It was in one of two Dr.Is regularly flown by him that he met his death on 21 April 1918 – probably at the hands of Roy Brown, a Canadian captain with No. 209 Squadron, RAF (the RAF was then just 20 days old). The Freiherr (not actually a baron) died from a single bullet that went diagonally through his body, penetrating the heart.

The last Dr.I was delivered in May 1918, at a time when this type was rapidly being taken out of service in favour of the considerably superior Fokker D.VII. At no time were there more than 171 Dr.Is in active service – the maximum was reached in May 1918 – and by the middle of June this had fallen to 125. During the summer, most of them had been transferred back to Germany to defend their home territory. Other famous Dr.I pilots apart from Richthofen were Kurt Wolff, with 33 aircraft shot down, Voss with 48, Erich Löwenhardt with 53, and Ernst Udet with 62. Richthofen himself had 80 kills to his credit.

This Dr.I was on the strength of Jasta 18 in the final year of the war. After the Armistice it was acquired by France and preserved. The interplane strut linked the single spars of the three wings. Not all Dr.Is were fitted with the ash skid attached under the tips of the lowest wing to prevent damage.

Vickers Vimy

Just too late to fight in World War 1, the Vimy bomber gained immortal fame when Alcock and Brown succeeded in flying the Atlantic nonstop for the first time. The Vimy gave long service with the Royal Air Force and made several outstanding long-range flights to distant destinations in the British Empire.

When one thinks that 'strategic' bombing began as early as 1915, especially on the Italian and Russian fronts, it is perhaps surprising that the British Air Board did not begin developing a heavy bomber until 1917, particularly since Britain had regularly been overflown by German aircraft. It is even more surprising that on 23 July of that year (only two months after a daylight attack on London by 30 Gotha G.IV bombers which left 162 people dead and 432 wounded), the Board cancelled its order for heavy bombers for the Royal Flying Corps. In the face of heated protests this decision was reversed, and in addition to a new order for more than 100 Handley Page O/400s, prototypes for new aircraft were ordered from Handley Page and Vickers.

Designed by Reginald Kirshaw Pierson, the Vickers F.B.27 project of which three prototypes were ordered, was in-

tended to feature two 200-hp (149-kW) RAF 4d air-cooled Vee-12 engines, but these were not ready in time and when first flown at Joyce Green by Captain Gordon Bell on 30 November 1917 the first aircraft (B9952) was powered by a pair of 200-hp (149-kW) Hispano-Suiza engines.

With a crew of three (pilot, nose gunner/bomb-aimer and mid-ships gunner) the Vimy (named after the famous battlefield of World War 1) was a three-bay biplane with upper and lower wings of equal span, the engines being strut-mounted between the wings, and had a twin-finned biplane tail unit and four-wheel landing gear with central nose-

Fine in-flight study of F9147, an Eagle-powered Vimy of No. 9 Sqn, one of a batch of 50 aircraft (F9146–F9295) produced by Vickers. No. 9 Sqn flew Vimys from Manston between April 1924 and June 1925.

Vickers Vimy variants

F.B.27: three prototypes (B9952–B9954) with Hispano-Suiza, Sunbeam Maori and Fiat A-12bis engines; first flight 30 November 1917

Vimy Mk I: 12 (F701–F712) built by Vickers, Crayford, 1918–9 with Fiat, BHP or Liberty engines specified; at least seven completed with Fiat A-12bis

Vimy Mk I: six (F2915–F2910) built by RAE, Farnborough; probably all with Fiat engines; F2915 with central fin and rudder for RAE trials

Vimy Mk I: 40 (F3146–F3185) built by Morgans, Leighton Buzzard with Rolls-Royce Eagle VIII; some reconditioned and re-engined in mid-1920s as trainers

Vimy Mk I: 50 (F8596–F8645) built by Vickers, Weybridge, all probably with Eagle VIIIs; F8625 became G-EAOL and flown to Spain; F8630 became G-EAOU for England–Australia flight by Smith brothers

Vimy Mk I: 50 (F9146–F9195) built by Vickers, Weybridge, all with Eagle VIIIs; 26 later reconditioned, 17 converted to dual-control trainers and four re-engined with Jupiter radials

F.B.27a Vimy Mk II: one prototype (F9569) with Rolls-Royce Eagle VIIIs

Vimy Mk III: 10 (H651–H660) built by RAE, Farnborough; Fiat engines specified but Eagles fitted; H651 used in automatic landing trials by RAE; redesignated Vimy Mk II

Vimy Mk IV: 25 (H5065–H5089) built by Westland, Yeovil, with Eagle engines; redesignated Vimy Mk II

Vimy Special: one prototype (H9963); believed used for torpedo trials in 1920; probably Vickers-built

Vimy Mk II: 10 (J7238–J7247) built by Vickers, Weybridge; these were first Vimys ordered post-war (in 1923), and at some time referred to as Vimy Mk IV

Vimy Mk II: 15 (J7440–J7454) built by Vickers, 1923–4, with Eagle VIII engines; some re-engined with Jupiter and Jaguar radials in 1926; J7451 with smoke-laying gear

Vimy Mk III: five (J7701–J7705) built by Vickers, 1924–5; most reconditioned and re-engined in 1927

Vimy Transatlantic: one aircraft, Vickers-built; no registration; flown by Alcock and Brown, April–June 1919, Eagle VIIIs, increased fuel

Vimy (Civil): one company-owned trials aircraft (G-EAAR allocated)

Vimy (Cape Flight): *Silver Queen*, one aircraft (G-UABA) flown by Van Ryneveld and Brand but crashed at Korosko, Upper Egypt, 11 February 1920; *Silver Queen II* was standard RAF aircraft

Type 66 Vimy Commercial: one prototype (K-107, later G-EAAV); used in flight attempt to Cape by Broome and Cockerell but crashed 27 February 1920

Vimy Commercial: Chinese aircraft; 40 built by Vickers between April 1920 and February 1921 and shipped out to fly Peking–Tsinan air post; not all flown

Vimy Commercial: two aircraft, namely G-EASI *City of London* flown by Instone and Imperial Airways, and F-ADER flown by Grands Express Aériens

Vimy Commercial: one aircraft with Lion engines and high-lift wings; employed as Vernon prototype; sold to USSR in 1922

Vimy Ambulance: five aircraft (J6855, J6904, J6905, J7143 and J7144) with Lion engines; later converted to Vernons

Vernon Mk I: 20 aircraft (J6864–J6883) with Eagle VIII engines

Vernon Mk II: 25 aircraft (J6884–J6893, J6976–J6980 and J7133–J7142) with Lion engines

Vernon Mk III: 10 aircraft (J7539–J7548) with Lion III engines and extra wing tanks

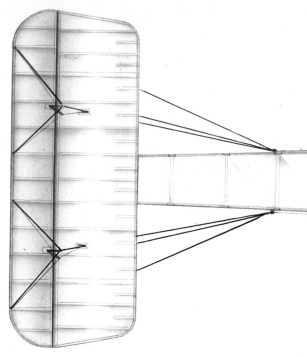

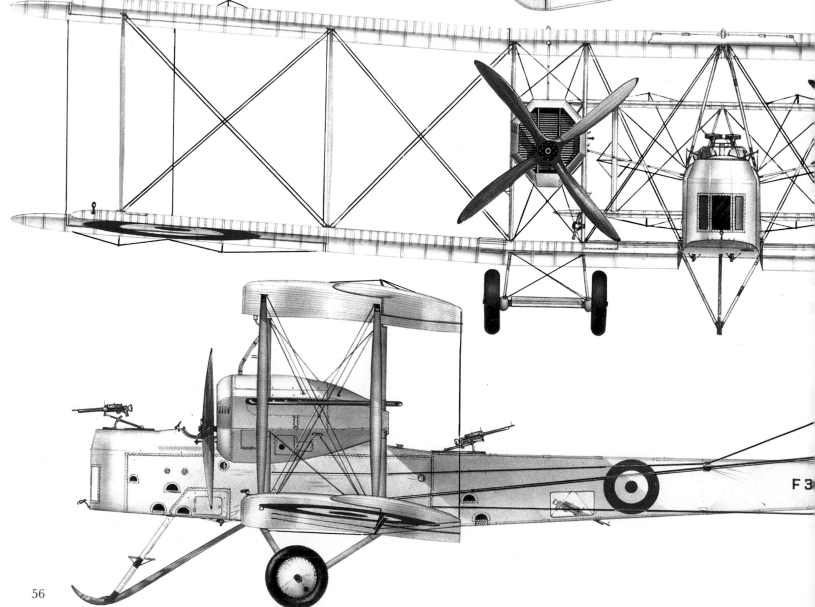

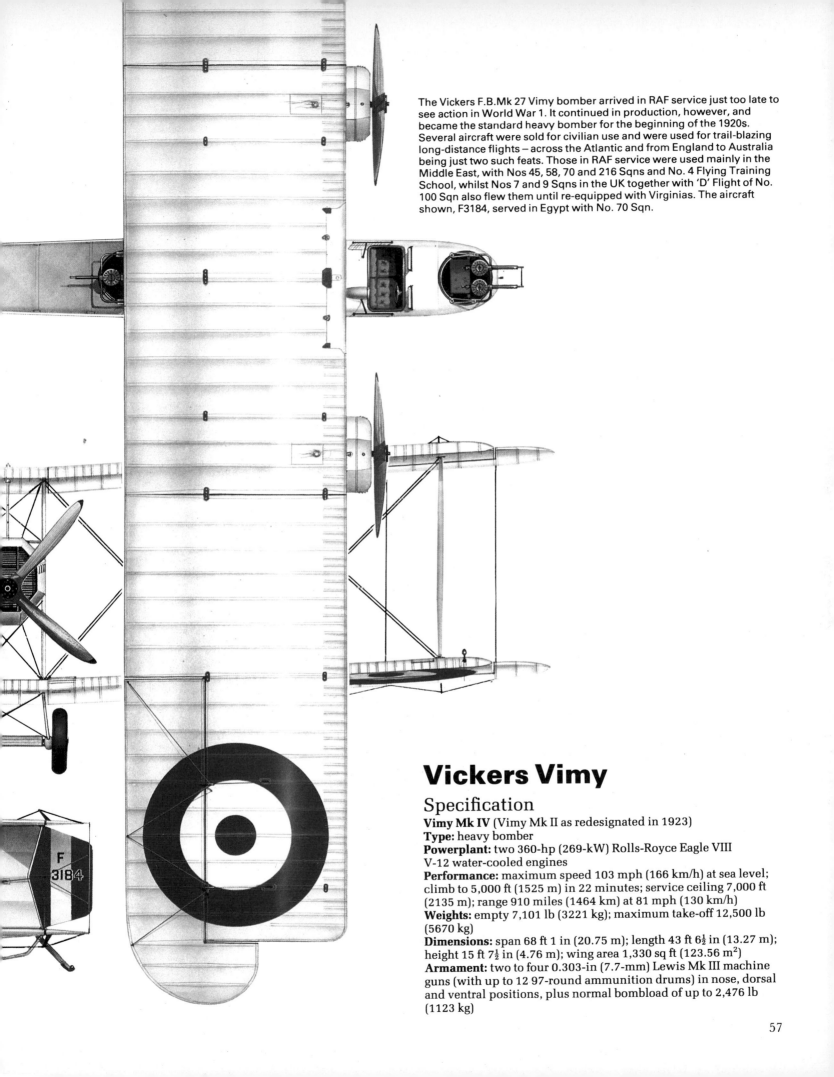

The Vickers F.B.Mk 27 Vimy bomber arrived in RAF service just too late to see action in World War 1. It continued in production, however, and became the standard heavy bomber for the beginning of the 1920s. Several aircraft were sold for civilian use and were used for trail-blazing long-distance flights – across the Atlantic and from England to Australia being just two such feats. Those in RAF service were used mainly in the Middle East, with Nos 45, 58, 70 and 216 Sqns and No. 4 Flying Training School, whilst Nos 7 and 9 Sqns in the UK together with 'D' Flight of No. 100 Sqn also flew them until re-equipped with Virginias. The aircraft shown, F3184, served in Egypt with No. 70 Sqn.

Vickers Vimy

Specification

Vimy Mk IV (Vimy Mk II as redesignated in 1923)
Type: heavy bomber
Powerplant: two 360-hp (269-kW) Rolls-Royce Eagle VIII V-12 water-cooled engines
Performance: maximum speed 103 mph (166 km/h) at sea level; climb to 5,000 ft (1525 m) in 22 minutes; service ceiling 7,000 ft (2135 m); range 910 miles (1464 km) at 81 mph (130 km/h)
Weights: empty 7,101 lb (3221 kg); maximum take-off 12,500 lb (5670 kg)
Dimensions: span 68 ft 1 in (20.75 m); length 43 ft 6½ in (13.27 m); height 15 ft 7½ in (4.76 m); wing area 1,330 sq ft (123.56 m²)
Armament: two to four 0.303-in (7.7-mm) Lewis Mk III machine guns (with up to 12 97-round ammunition drums) in nose, dorsal and ventral positions, plus normal bombload of up to 2,476 lb (1123 kg)

Vickers Vimy

Purchased by the RAF for £6,300, Vickers Vimy ambulance J7143 displays the prominent Red Cross markings incorporated in the national insignia. Note the uncowled Napier Lion engines and deletion of the nosewheel.

mounted skid. The internal bombload comprised twelve 112-lb (51-kg) bombs stowed vertically in the centre fuselage; this was later increased to eight 250-lb (113-kg) and four 112-lb (51-kg) bombs, plus two 250-lb (113-kg) bombs under the fuselage and four 230-lb (104-kg) bombs under the wing centre sections. Indeed the Vimy astonished spectators at Martlesham Heath when it lifted a greater load than the O/400 on half the power. Fuel capacity was 92 Imp gal (418 litres) and armament four 0.303-in (7.7-mm) Lewis Mk III machine-guns with 12 97-round ammunition drums.

After trials at Martlesham Heath in 1918, during which the Hispano-Suiza engines gave persistent trouble as a result of over-heating, B9952 returned to Joyce Green to be re-engined with two 260-hp (194-kW) Salmson water-cooled radials; the wing dihedral was also increased from 1° to 2°. The second prototype was flown in February 1918 and featured plain elevators and ailerons in place of the first aircraft's horn-balanced surfaces; it was powered by 260-hp (194-kW) Sunbeam Maori engines driving four-blade propellers, each engine nacelle featuring its own instruments on the inboard side, where they were visible from the cockpit. This aircraft also introduced a ventral gun position.

The second Vimy (B9953) crashed in May following engine failure, and was followed in June by B9954 with 300-hp (224-kW) Fiat A-12bis engines in octagonal-section nacelles similar to those adopted in production aircraft. The rear upper gun mounting was a twin-Lewis Scarff ring, and the fuel capacity was increased to 226 Imp gal (1027 litres). This aircraft also crashed, at Martlesham on 11 September when the pilot stalled after take-off with a full load of bombs, which exploded. A fourth prototype, which appeared somewhat later, was powered by two 360-hp (269-kW) Rolls-Royce Eagle VIII V-12 engines.

Production was widely subcontracted by Vickers, but the end of the war brought cancellation of most orders. However, Vickers built 12 aircraft at Crayford and 132 at Weybridge (production continuing until about 1924); Morgan & Co, Leighton Buzzard, produced about 40 aircraft, and Westland Aircraft, Yeovil, a further 25. The Royal Aircraft Establishment at Farnborough also completed 10.

At the end of October 1918 the RAF had taken delivery of only three aircraft, of which one was on charge with the Independent (Bombing) Force, and none is known to have taken part in war operations. The Vimy only reached full service status in July 1919 when it replaced Handley Page O/400s with No. 58 (Bomber) Squadron at Heliopolis, Egypt, followed by No. 70 (Bomber) Squadron, also at Heliopolis, in February the following year.

Subsequent service with the RAF continued with deliveries to No. 45 (Bomber) Squadron at Almaza, Egypt, in November 1921; to 'D' Flight, No. 100 (Bomber) Squadron at Spitalgate, Lincolnshire, in March 1922; to No. 216 Squadron (a general bomber-transport unit) at Heliopolis in June 1922; to No. 7 (Bomber) Squadron at Bircham Newton in June 1923; to No.

9 (Bomber) Squadron at Upavon (and later Manston) in March 1924; and to No. 99 (Bomber) Squadron at Netheravon in April 1924. Also in April 1924 No. 58 Squadron, which had been renumbered No. 70 Squadron in February 1920 and had then given up its Vimys, was re-formed with Vimy Mk IVs at Worthy Down under the command of Wing Commander A. T. (later Marshal of the Royal Air Force Sir Arthur) Harris, perhaps the greatest advocate of strategic bombing in the history of the RAF. Finally, No. 502 (Ulster) Squadron, first of the Special Reserve Units to be incorporated in the new Auxiliary Air Force, received Vimys as initial equipment in June 1925 at Aldergrove in Northern Ireland.

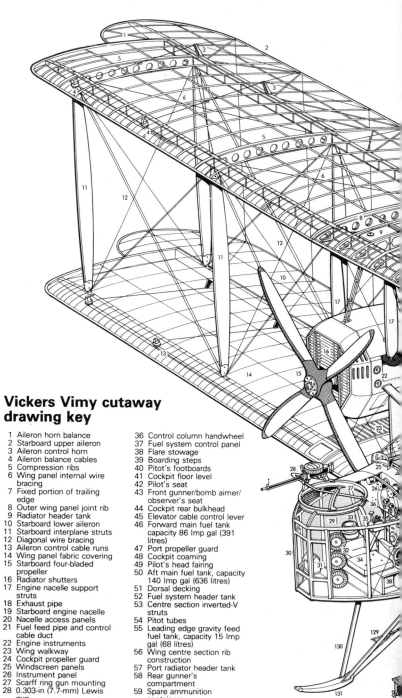

Vickers Vimy cutaway drawing key

1 Aileron horn balance
2 Starboard upper aileron
3 Aileron control horn
4 Aileron balance cables
5 Compression ribs
6 Wing panel internal wire bracing
7 Fixed portion of trailing edge
8 Outer wing panel joint rib
9 Radiator header tank
10 Starboard lower aileron
11 Starboard interplane struts
12 Diagonal wire bracing
13 Aileron control cable runs
14 Wing panel fabric covering
15 Starboard four-bladed propeller
16 Radiator shutters
17 Engine nacelle support struts
18 Exhaust pipe
19 Starboard engine nacelle
20 Nacelle access panels
21 Fuel feed pipe and control cable duct
22 Engine instruments
23 Wing walkway
24 Cockpit propeller guard
25 Windscreen panels
26 Instrument panel
27 Scarff ring gun mounting
28 0.303-in (7.7-mm) Lewis gun
29 Front gunner/bomb aimer's compartment
30 Nose compartment glazing
31 Drift sight
32 Spare ammunition containers
33 Compass
34 Gunner/bomb aimer's seat
35 Engine throttle and mixture control levers

36 Control column handwheel
37 Fuel system control panel
38 Flare stowage
39 Boarding steps
40 Pitot's footboards
41 Cockpit floor level
42 Pilot's seat
43 Front gunner/bomb aimer/observer's seat
44 Cockpit rear bulkhead
45 Elevator cable control lever
46 Forward main fuel tank capacity 86 Imp gal (391 litres)
47 Port propeller guard
48 Cockpit coaming
49 Pilot's head fairing
50 Aft main fuel tank, capacity 140 Imp gal (636 litres)
51 Dorsal decking
52 Fuel system header tank
53 Centre section inverted-V struts
54 Pitot tubes
55 Leading edge gravity feed fuel tank, capacity 15 Imp gal (68 litres)
56 Wing centre section rib construction
57 Port radiator header tank
58 Rear gunner's compartment
59 Spare ammunition containers
60 Scarff ring gun mounting
61 0.303-in (7.7-mm) Lewis gun
62 Wing rear spar
63 Trailing edge ribs
64 Fuselage top longerons
65 Horizontal spacers
66 Tail control cables
67 Starboard fixed tailfin
68 Starboard rudder

69 Fabric covered tailplane
70 Elevator control horn
71 Upper elevator
72 Tailplane rib construction
73 Port rudder construction
74 Rudder control horn
75 Elevator interconnecting cables

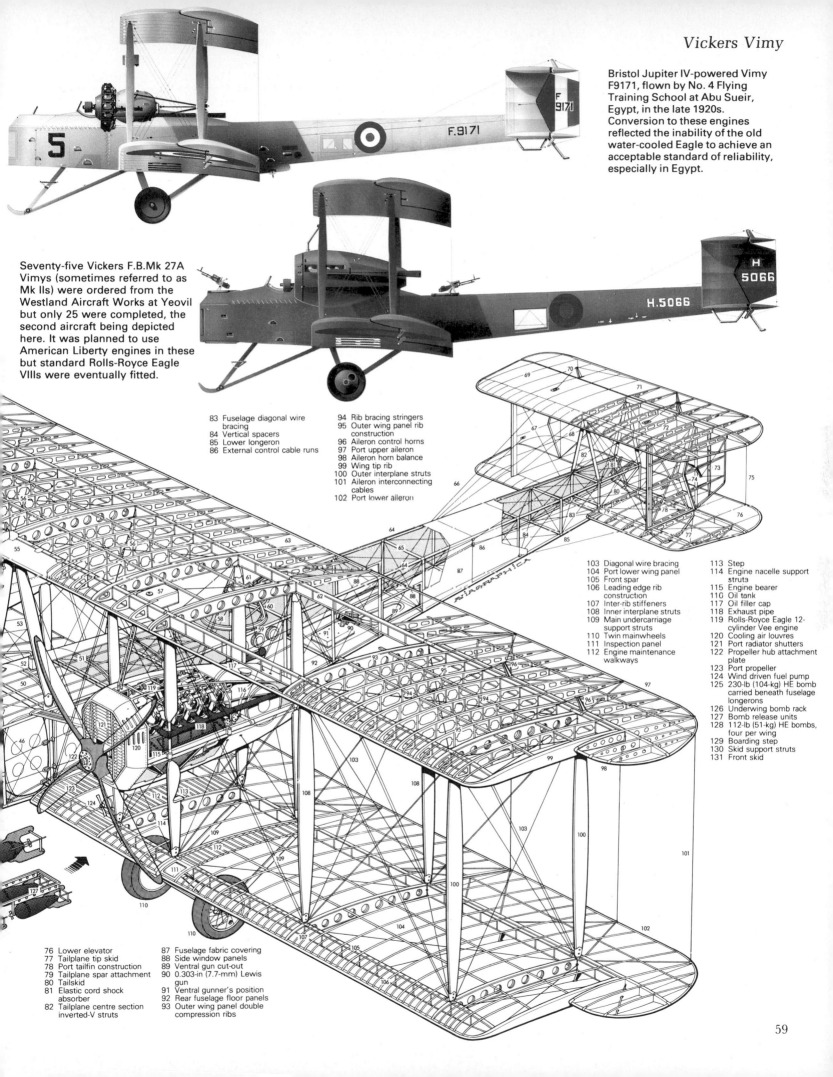

Vickers Vimy

Bristol Jupiter IV-powered Vimy F9171, flown by No. 4 Flying Training School at Abu Sueir, Egypt, in the late 1920s. Conversion to these engines reflected the inability of the old water-cooled Eagle to achieve an acceptable standard of reliability, especially in Egypt.

Seventy-five Vickers F.B.Mk 27A Vimys (sometimes referred to as Mk IIs) were ordered from the Westland Aircraft Works at Yeovil but only 25 were completed, the second aircraft being depicted here. It was planned to use American Liberty engines in these but standard Rolls-Royce Eagle VIIIs were eventually fitted.

83 Fuselage diagonal wire bracing
84 Vertical spacers
85 Lower longeron
86 External control cable runs
94 Rib bracing stringers
95 Outer wing panel rib construction
96 Aileron control horns
97 Port upper aileron
98 Aileron horn balance
99 Wing tip rib
100 Outer interplane struts
101 Aileron interconnecting cables
102 Port lower aileron

103 Diagonal wire bracing
104 Port lower wing panel
105 Front spar
106 Leading edge rib construction
107 Inter-rib stiffeners
108 Inner interplane struts
109 Main undercarriage support struts
110 Twin mainwheels
111 Inspection panel
112 Engine maintenance walkways
113 Step
114 Engine nacelle support struts
115 Engine bearer
116 Oil tank
117 Oil filler cap
118 Exhaust pipe
119 Rolls-Royce Eagle 12-cylinder Vee engine
120 Cooling air louvres
121 Port radiator shutters
122 Propeller hub attachment plate
123 Port propeller
124 Wind driven fuel pump
125 230-lb (104-kg) HE bomb carried beneath fuselage longerons
126 Underwing bomb rack
127 Bomb release units
128 112-lb (51-kg) HE bombs, four per wing
129 Boarding step
130 Skid support struts
131 Front skid

76 Lower elevator
77 Tailplane tip skid
78 Port tailfin construction
79 Tailplane spar attachment
80 Tailskid
81 Elastic cord shock absorber
82 Tailplane centre section inverted-V struts
87 Fuselage fabric covering
88 Side window panels
89 Ventral gun cut-out
90 0.303-in (7.7-mm) Lewis gun
91 Ventral gunner's position
92 Rear fuselage floor panels
93 Outer wing panel double compression ribs

Production versions of the Vimy included the Vimy Mk II with 280-hp (209-kW) Sunbeam Maori engines, the Vimy Mk III with 310-hp (231-kW) Fiat A-12bis V-12 engines and the Vimy Mk IV with 360-hp (269-kW) Rolls-Royce Eagle VIIIs. Post-war trainers were fitted with 420-hp (313-kW) Bristol Jupiter IV radials, 450-hp (336-kW) Jupiter VIs or 420-hp (313-kW) Armstrong Siddeley Jaguar IV radials. Three ambulance aircraft were also produced for service with No. 216 Squadron in the Middle East.

RAF Vimys gave long and sterling service. The standard aircraft of No. 216 Squadron operated the air mail service between Cairo and Baghdad from 1923 until August 1926, reducing the service time from 16 days to two, while at home the Vimys of No. 7 Squadron constituted the RAF's entire home-based heavy bomber force from June 1923 until March 1924.

Three Vimys also served with the Night-Flying Flight at Biggin Hill from 1923 onwards for co-operation with search-light and gun defences, and during the General Strike of 1926 they were employed to distribute the government's emergency news sheet, the *British Gazette*. The Jupiter- and Jaguar-powered versions were aircraft re-engined for use by flying training schools and as parachute trainers at Henlow. The Vimys with No. 502 Squadron remained in service until 1929, when they were replaced by Handley Page Hyderabads; those with FTS at home remained in service until 1931, and the last aircraft (H657) continued with No. 4 FTS at Abu Sueir, Egypt, until 1933 and its pilots averred that it still was as robust and reliable as ever.

Designation of Vimy versions was complicated indeed, despite attempts to rationalize it in 1923, and by 1925 semi-official designations had again proliferated, being further complicated by such appellations as the Vimy Reconditioned Mk I, Vimy Reconditioned Mk II, Vimy Reconditioned Mk III School, and Vimy Production School.

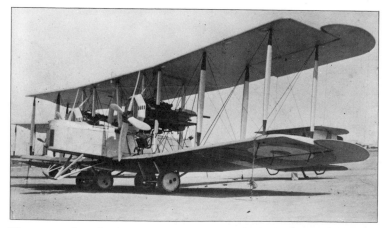

Vimys were found to be the best available aircraft for training purposes in the Middle East, and served for some years with No. 4 FTS at Abu Sueir, Egypt. Though shown here with Eagle engines, wear and tear in the hot dusty environment eventually caused most Vimys to be re-engined with air-cooled Jupiter or Jaguar engines.

A Westland-built Vimy H5089, serving with No.216 Sqn at Heliopolis, Egypt, in the early 1920s. Later re-registered HR5089, it underwent rebuilding at Abu Sueir for issue as a trainer to No. 4 FTS, probably with Jupiter radials.

Finally among the proposed versions there was the Liberty-powered Vimy, an aircraft re-engined with 400-hp (298-kW) Liberty 12 V-12 engines at the request in 1918 of the United States government in preparation for possible production in the USA (Liberty engines had also been specified for some RAF aircraft); however, when being prepared for flight at Joyce Green the aircraft caught fire and was destroyed, and the proposal was abandoned in 1919.

The great flights

Before World War 1 the *Daily Mail* had put up a prize of £10,000 to be awarded to the first airman to fly an aeroplane across the Atlantic nonstop, with anywhere in the British Isles as the destination achieved. Although some preparations had been made by various pilots (notably Fred Raynham) the war intervened, so that after the Armistice the prize remained unwon. Then in May 1919 the American Curtiss NC-4 was flown from New York to Plymouth (with intermediate landings at the Azores and Lisbon) by Lieutenant Commander A. C. Read of the US Navy. And at about the same time an attempt to make the flight nonstop failed when Harry Hawker and Lieutenant Commander K. F. Mackenzie-Grieve were forced down in a Sopwith biplane in mid-ocean (and were miraculously rescued).

Meanwhile in the UK Captain John Alcock DSC, RNAS and Lieutenant Arthur Whitten-Brown RFC had been testing a specially-prepared and company-owned Vimy; all its military equipment had been removed and extra fuel tankage installed, increasing its capacity to 865 Imp gal (3932 litres). Standard Eagle VIII engines were retained. After a few trial flights the Vimy was dismantled and shipped to Newfoundland where it was erected at Quidi Vidi airfield near St John's; this airfield was found to be unsuitable for take-off by the heavily-laden aircraft, which was moved to Lester's Field. At 16.13 (GMT) on 14 June 1919 Alcock and Brown took off, crossing out over the Newfoundland coast 15 minutes later. Most of the 1,890-mile (3042-km) flight was made during the hours of darkness, and at 08.40 on the following morning the Vimy landed in Derrygimla Bog, Clifden, Co. Galway in Ireland. The two naval officers were

A wry sense of humour was reflected by the name bestowed by the Australians Ross and Keith Smith, 'God 'elp all of us', on their Vimy G-EAOU for the first-ever England–Australia flight during November–December 1919.

given a tumultuous welcome in London, and received the *Daily Mail* prize of £10,000. The Vimy, which had nosed over in the ground on landing, was repaired and presented to the Science Museum, South Kensington.

Although overshadowed by this 'Blue Riband' achievement, the flight by the Australian brothers, Captain Ross Smith and Lieutenant Keith Smith, with Sergeants W. H. Shiers and J. M. Bennett (all of the Australian Air Force), from the UK to Australia must rank as one of the greatest of all feats in long-distance flying. Their aircraft, a Weybridge-built Vimy (F8630) was registered G-EAOU (and dubbed 'God 'elp all of us') and prepared for the flight which was undertaken in response to an offer by the Australian government of £A10,000 for the first flight by Australians from the UK to Australia within 30 days before the end of 1919. Pre-flight planning demanded the provision of fuel and stores at the various landing points.

Taking off from Hounslow, Middlesex, at 08.00 on 12 November, the Vimy eventually reached Darwin at 16.00 on 10 December, having successfully battled its way through tropical storms and undergone running repairs skilfully performed by the two flight mechanics en route. The 11,130-mile (17912-km) flight had been completed in just under 28 days, in 135 hours 55 minutes elapsed flying time, G-EAOU was presented to the Australian government by Vickers and was preserved in a special memorial hall at Adelaide airport.

Third of the great flights was that undertaken by Lieutenant Colonel Pierre Van Ryneveld and Major Christopher Quintin (later Air Vice-Marshal Sir Quintin) Brand from England to Cape Town, including a flight from Cairo to the Cape for a *Daily Mail* prize of £10,000. In a Vimy (G-UABA) named *Silver Queen*, Van Ryneveld and Brand left Brooklands on 4 February 1920 and landed safely at Heliopolis, setting off again after dark on 10 February; on the following day, when still 80 miles (130 km) short of Wadi Halfa, the aircraft was wrecked in a forced landing following engine over-heating.

A second Vimy was loaned by the RAF at Heliopolis (and named *Silver Queen II*), and this aircraft reached Bulawayo, Southern Rhodesia, before being badly damaged when it failed to get airborne in a 'hot-and-high' take-off. The two pilots eventually reached Cape Town in a borrowed de Havilland D.H.9, and were subsequently awarded £5,000 each by the South African government. In recognition of these three great pioneering flights, Alcock, Brown, the Smith brothers, Van Ryneveld and Brand all received knighthoods from HM King George V.

The Vimy Commercial and Vernon

Built in the Vickers factory at Bexleyheath, a considerably modified version of the Vimy made its first flight at Joyce Green on 13 April 1919 in the hands of Stan Cockerell. Originally known as the Monocoque, this crystallized as the Vimy Commercial with much enlarged fuselage of generous oval cross section capable of accommodating 10 passengers in padded-leather or wicker chairs. A rear freight hold of 300 cu ft (8.5 m³) could accommodate 2,500 lb (1134 kg) of baggage. Originally registered K-107, and later G-EAAV, the prototype was followed by three production aircraft, of which one (with 450-hp/336-kW Napier Lions, and later 400-hp/298-kW Lorraine Dietrich engines) was purchased by the French airline, Grands Express Aériens. The Chinese government also ordered 40 Commercials to establish civil air travel in that country, but it seems that not all these aircraft were ever flown, some remaining in their crates. The other two British-registered aircraft G-EASI and G-EAUL, undertook some early route flying work with the pioneer airline S. Instone & Co. in Europe, the former being handed on to Imperial Airways and the latter shipped to China.

The last Vimy Commercial to be produced featured high-lift wings and Lion engines, and was effectively the prototype of a transport version being developed for the RAF; it was eventually sold to the USSR in September 1922, thereafter being loaned to the Russian airline Dobrolet in 1924.

The Atlantic Vimy of Alcock and Brown was specially built for the flight, featuring a long turtle-back fairing over the centre fuselage enclosing additional fuel tanks. It is pictured here at Brooklands during preliminary trials prior to shipment to Newfoundland.

Pictured in front of a Vimy (*not* their historic aircraft, G-EAOU) at Brooklands before the England–Australia flight are the famous Aussies, Captain Ross Smith, Lieutenant Keith Smith, Sergeant J. M. Bennett and Sergeant W. H. Shiers.

Airco D.H.4 and D.H.9

Geoffrey de Havilland always had a flair for producing aircraft that filled the bill for a specific requirement. In 1916, with World War 1 in progress, there was a need for an advanced bombing and reconnaissance aircraft, which would, in the event, make possible the RFC's entry into strategic bombing. The aircraft that more than met this need was the D.H.4.

The D.H.4 was a well-designed single-strut biplane made of spruce and ash covered with fabric, except for the front section of the fuselage which was panelled with plywood. The pilot sat beneath the centre of the wing, with the gunner behind him; between them was the 60-gal (273-litre) fuel tank. The engine was the only part that gave any problems while this aircraft was being introduced. The original prototype of the D.H.4 had a new BHP test engine, which gave just over 200 hp (149 kW) and was also used in the later versions. The D.H.4 showed such great promise that 50 were ordered. The prototype performed so well even in its first flight that large numbers were in use within a very short space of time. The second aircraft had a 250-hp (186-kW) Rolls Royce engine. The framework and the central wing struts had been modified slightly by this time, the pilot had been placed in a different position, and the gunner now had a swivelling machine gun. Other engines used in later production aircraft were the 200-hp (149-kW) RAF 3a, the Siddeley Puma with 230-hp (172-kW; a version of the BHP), the 260-hp (194-kW)

Fiat A-12 and the 250-hp (186-kW) Rolls-Royce, later the Eagle. Eventually, the 375-hp (280-kW) Eagle VIII engine was fitted, which required a higher undercarriage and a larger propeller.

The first aircraft to become operational went to France with No. 55 Squadron, RFC, which flew from Fienvilliers on 6 April 1917 to bomb Valenciennes. The aircraft was a great advance on previous bombers, having a higher ceiling, a maximum speed in excess of 100 mph (161 km/h) at 15,000 ft (4570 m) and, by flying in formation, the ability to provide a formidable fire power to tackle German fighters struggling at heights at which they were ill equipped to fight. So, at the beginning of its career, the D.H.4 was able to operate without fighter escort deep behind the enemy lines. The only disadvantage it had was the placing of the fuel tank between the pilot and gunner, making communication between the two almost impossible and ensuring that, when the aircraft was hit by enemy fire, both crew members were incinerated, giving the aircraft the soubriquet 'The Flaming Coffin'. Re-equipment went ahead, No. 57 Squadron receiving D.H.4s in May, No. 18 Squadron in June, and No. 25 Squadron in July, while new squadrons came to France already D.H.4-equipped.

The RNAS had also ordered the aircraft and this version was built by Westland at Yeovil, having the Eagle engine,

Another patrol mission for E844, a D.H.9A operated by No. 8 Sqn as part of its long association with the Middle East. Note the close proximity of pilot and observer, thus enabling effective communication – an improvement on the early D.H.4.

This is an Airco D.H.4 operated by No. 2
Sqn RNAS immediately prior to its
redesignation as No. 202 Sqn RFC in
1918. Based at Bergues and Varssenaere
during World War 1, the aircraft was used
for bombing and reconnaissance
missions over Belgium until the
Armistice. The squadron also used the
D.H.9 during the war, returning to the UK
in March 1919.

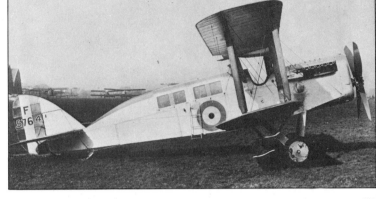

Originally one of 100 D.H.4s produced under contract by Palladium
Autocars, F5764 was converted to D.H.4A configuration to carry two
passengers in the enclosed cabin. Up to five aircraft served with the RAF,
and there were a further nine civil conversions.

two forward-firing Vickers guns in place of one, and a Scarff
ring for the observer. The naval aircraft went first to No. 2
Squadron, at the same time as No. 55 Squadron received its
D.H.4s, and then to Nos 5, 6 and 17 Squadrons. These were
all based in the north of the Western Front and were used for
a variety of tasks in addition to bombing, such as gun-
ranging with ships, reconnaissance and photographic work.
Most of their bombing targets were the naval installations at
Ostend and Zeebrugge; it was also a first for the D.H.4 when
No. 17 Squadron, by then renumbered No. 217 Squadron,
RAF, sank a U-boat off the Belgian coast on 12 August 1918.
The naval aircraft also flew with the coastal defence stations
on North Sea patrols, and with Home Defence flights in the
United Kingdom, having occasional brushes with Zeppelins;
one D.H.4, flown by Major E. Cadbury, shot down the
Zeppelin L70 on 5 August 1918, 40 miles (64 km) out over
the North Sea when operating from the base at Great
Yarmouth. To make the D.H.4 more suitable for such tasks a
floatplane version was modified and tested at Felixstowe,
but this variant was never put into production.

As well as forming part of the Independent Air Force
when it was formed as the first strategic bombing organization in the world, the D.H.4 also served in small numbers
in such overseas theatres as Italy and the Aegean.

The Americans showed much interest in the D.H.4 as they
had nothing comparable, although they had a fine new
engine, the Liberty 12, which was expected to develop
400 hp (298 kW). Accordingly, the Americans decided to
build the D.H.4 under licence in America. The American
flair for mass-production meant that by the end of 1918 some
4,587 American DH-4 aircraft (as the type was known locally)
had been built, three times more than had been produced in

An Airco D.H.4A of the Belgian airline SNETA, which began operating its
continental routes with the predecessor of this model, the Airco D.H.4.
The picture was taken in 1921. Today's commercial passengers would
hesitate before taking continental journeys in this aircraft.

the UK. In the United Kingdom the D.H.4 did not last long
after the Armistice in RAF service, being superseded first by
the D.H.9, but then overwhelmingly by the D.H.9A. Not a
few were sent to Commonwealth countries to enable them to
form their own air forces under what was known as the
'Imperial Gift Scheme'. Those which went to Canada performed a number of valuable roles, particularly in respect of
the great forests where as single-seaters they flew fire patrols,
and many were also used on early mail routes, remaining in
service until 1928. D.H.4s were also sold after the war to
Belgium, Persia and Spain from the United Kingdom. However, in the USA the DH-4 really took off after World War 1
because the government decreed that there would not be
funds for new aircraft but that they would be available for
rebuilding existing aircraft. As there were by then 4,846 DH-
4s in existence in America, the possibilities were immense
and, with the Americans' penchant for adaptation, no fewer
than 60 different versions of the DH-4 were evolved, and
even 10 years later many were still serving. The type flew
with the US Army, US Navy and US Marine Corps, and was
used as a bomber, trainer and transport. And for several
years the DH-4 was the backbone of the airmail service flown
by the US Postal Service in the United States. The type was
still on the services' inventories in 1929, by which time
many had entered civilian use.

Civilian versions of the D.H.4 appeared in the United
Kingdom as well, for the production lines were still pump-
ing out new aircraft at the time of the Armistice and an
aircraft such as the D.H.4 had a basic airframe suitable for a
variety of duties. The type entered into continental services
in 1919 with Aircraft Transport and Travel until better
aircraft were available, others went out to Australia and
figured in the first air mail services of QANTAS, and one of
their aircraft was still flying (on joy riding flights) in 1934.
The first Belgian airline, SNETA, used four D.H.4s to open
up its continental routes; but the D.H.4s did not last long in
service with the Belgians.

One D.H.4 was highly modified, with the lower wing cut
right down and the aircraft turned into a single-bay biplane

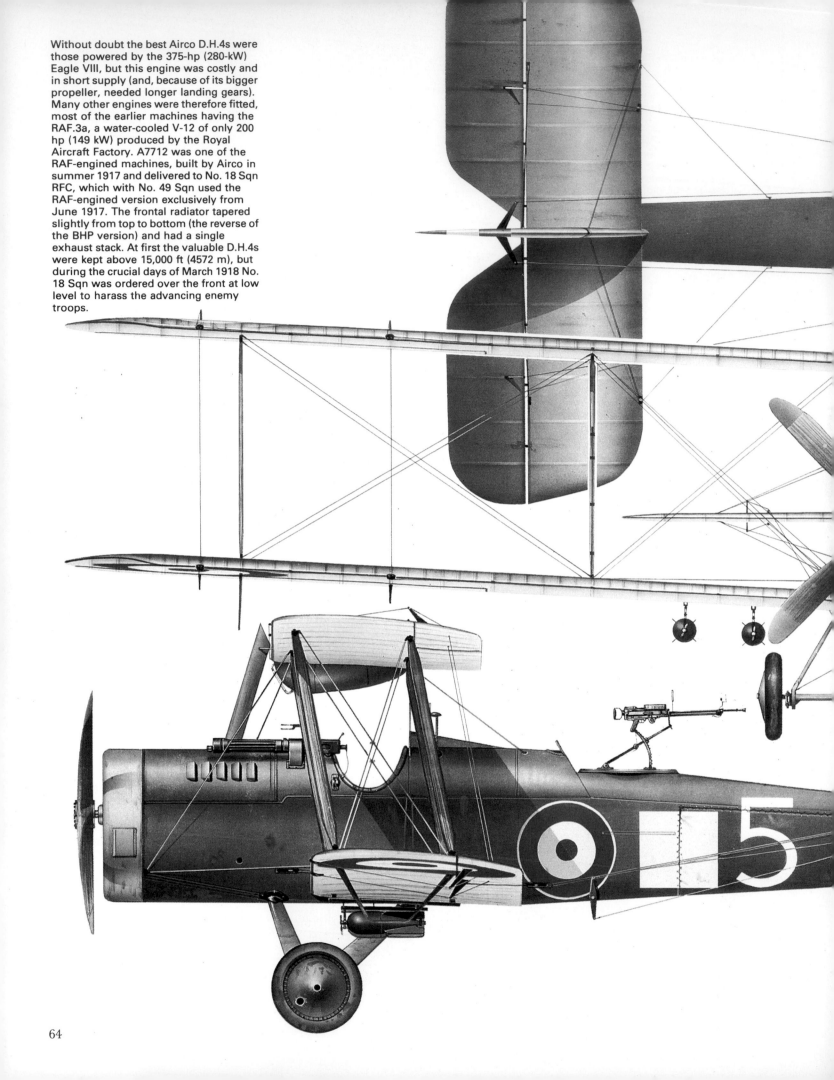

Without doubt the best Airco D.H.4s were those powered by the 375-hp (280-kW) Eagle VIII, but this engine was costly and in short supply (and, because of its bigger propeller, needed longer landing gears). Many other engines were therefore fitted, most of the earlier machines having the RAF.3a, a water-cooled V-12 of only 200 hp (149 kW) produced by the Royal Aircraft Factory. A7712 was one of the RAF-engined machines, built by Airco in summer 1917 and delivered to No. 18 Sqn RFC, which with No. 49 Sqn used the RAF-engined version exclusively from June 1917. The frontal radiator tapered slightly from top to bottom (the reverse of the BHP version) and had a single exhaust stack. At first the valuable D.H.4s were kept above 15,000 ft (4572 m), but during the crucial days of March 1918 No. 18 Sqn was ordered over the front at low level to harass the advancing enemy troops.

Airco D.H.4 and D.H.9

Specification

Airco D.H.4 (Eagle VIII)

Type: two-seat bomber

Powerplant: one 375-hp (280-kW) Rolls-Royce Eagle VIII water-cooled V-12 piston engine

Performance: maximum speed 143 mph (230 km/h) at sea level; cruising speed about 108 mph (174 km/h); time to reach 15,000 ft (4572 m) 16.5 minutes; service ceiling 22,000 ft (6700 m); endurance (maximum) 6 hours 45 minutes

Weights: empty 2,387 lb (1083 kg); loaded (clean) 3,472 lb (1575 kg) (two 230 lb [104.3 kg] bombs) 3,932 lb (1784 kg)

Dimensions: span 42 ft 4.625 in (12.92 m); length (Eagle) 30 ft 8 in (9.347 m); height (Eagle VIII) 11 ft 0 in (3.353 m); wing area 434 sq ft (40.32 m²)

Armament: one 0.303-in (7.7-mm) Vickers machine-gun firing ahead; single or twin Lewis of same calibre mounted on observer's Scarff ring; racks under lower wing for two bombs of 230 lb (104.3 kg), four of 112 lb (50.8 kg), depth charges or other stores

Airco D.H.4 and D.H.9

The lack of suitable American aircraft for use in World War 1 led to the United States producing the D.H.4 as the 'Liberty Plane', with 4,846 being built by three companies. This DH-4B served with the 168th Aero Squadron as part of the American Expeditionary Force in France, one of 13 squadrons equipped with the type. But there were severe problems with the aircraft, most notably the landing characteristics and the lethal positioning of the fuel tank between pilot and observer.

with outboard bracing struts to become the D.H.4R racer with a new Napier Lion engine, with which it set up a British closed-circuit speed record of 129.3 mph (208.08 km/h) in the Aerial Derby on 21 June 1919. It subsequently flew at 150 mph (241 km/h). This and other civil D.H.4s were one-off conversions by their new owners, mainly differing in the rearrangements made to the rear (observer's) position by the fitting of different seating arrangements. However, there was in existence in 1919 an official civil conversion of the D.H.4, known as the D.H.4A. It arose from the fact that D.H.4s were being used by No. 86 (Communications) Wing of the RAF on its cross-Channel passenger services around the time of the Armistice, providing transport for civil servants, military attachés, MPs and ministers flitting to and fro. One of the cabinet ministers, Bonar Law, requested that a modified version should be built to accommodate its passengers in a cabin. In the event this became a major variant because, by the time the windowed cabin had been built of plywood, the centre of gravity had moved considerably aft and therefore the upper mainplane had to be rerigged aft so that the biplane became unstaggered. The resulting aeroplane became known as the D.H.4A and at least eight aircraft were modified to this configuration. They went into service with No. 2 (Communications) Squadron of the wing flying the route between Kenley and Buc, and continued regular services until September 1919, when the wing was disbanded for lack of the traffic to sustain it.

The remaining aircraft were sold to Handley Page Ltd, which immediately prepared them for use on its impending routes. At the same time four brand new D.H.4s were converted to D.H.4A standard and sold to Aircraft Transport and Travel, and one such made its niche in British aviation history by flying the first British commercial cross-Channel service with one passenger and freight consisting of news-

papers, grouse, Devonshire cream and leather! AT&T carried on with services until the end of 1920, when the company went into liquidation. In the meantime, Handley Page Air Transport had started regular services using D.H.4s and D.H.4As from Cricklewood to Paris and Schiphol (Amsterdam), and two more D.H.4As were used by SNETA. A further D.H.4A served with Instone Air Line out of Croydon on the Paris route, transferring to the Central Aircraft Company in 1922 and winning the King's Cup in that year, the first in which the race was run. A further D.H.4A went to Argentina.

The D.H.4 had become one of the greats of World War 1, pioneering true strategic bombing, and also being the mainstay of budding aviation in the USA. But aircraft development does not stand still, and even as the D.H.4 was beginning to win its spurs over the Western Front a successor was starting flight trials at Hendon. As mentioned above, the original D.H.4 prototype had used a prototype BHP engine which showed much promise. As time went by this engine was developed into the Galloway Adriatic, which powered the prototype of a new aircraft with basically the same wings and tail of the D.H.4 but a new fuselage, placing the pilot and observer back to back. In the meantime, the Siddeley-Deasey Car Company had modified the BHP engine for mass production, improving it for service use and calling it the Puma. Forecasts estimated that this new engine would produce 300 hp (224 kW), but it had extended teething troubles and was derated to 230 hp (172 kW). In the meantime the new aircraft had been ordered in quantity. Aircraft came pouring off the production lines, but the commander of the RFC in France, hearing about the D.H.9 (for this was the designation of the new aircraft) and its poor performance, tried to stop its entry into squadron service as it was clearly inferior to the D.H.4 it was intended to replace. Alternative engines were tried, and

Having served in World War 1, this D.H.9 was transferred to the South African Air Force and fitted with a 200-hp (149-kW) Wolseley Viper, a change which for some inexplicable reason led to the aircraft being named the Mantis.

Prior to development of the three-passenger D.H.9C, the D.H.9B offered places for two people, one fore and one aft of the pilot. Twenty were built for civil use in the UK, this machine having passed later to the Dutch civil register for use with KLM.

some production aircraft entered service with the Fiat A-12, but with production wheels so squarely set in motion, there was no turning back and the D.H.9 entered service with the RFC and RNAS. The first units to fly them in France were Nos 6 and 11 Squadrons, RNAS, and again the type was used mainly for attacks on naval installations on the Belgian coast. The first RFC units were Nos 98 and 99 Squadrons, followed by Nos 103, 104, 107 and 108, No. 98 moving to France on 3 April 1918, two days after the Royal Air Force had been formed.

Not only was the performance of the D.H.9 poorer than that of the D.H.4, the main disadvantage being its low ceiling of 13,000 ft (3960 m), but the Puma engine was chronically unreliable. Early raids by the squadrons resulted in between one third and one half of the aircraft taking part being lost on each raid, a totally unacceptable figure. It is significant that the Netherlands army was able to operate a squadron of nine D.H.9s, all aircraft of the RAF that had force landed in the Netherlands and been interned!

What the boffins in the UK could not do, the mechanics on the squadrons in France attempted to do, namely make 'home brewed' modifications to improve the reliability of the D.H.9, and it says much for their brilliant improvisation that their squadrons stayed in business and managed to achieve some successes; for, in its favour, the aircraft was a pilot's aeroplane (like most of de Havilland's) and could manoeuvre well in a dogfight and, with the revised seating arrangements, the pilot and observer were well placed to cope with enemy fire. In fact, one observer of No. 49 Squadron managed to shoot down four enemy fighters in one sortie.

The D.H.9 was also used in overseas theatres, chiefly the Mediterranean, and here it made some outstanding long-range reconnaissance flights; whether the hot, dry climate made the Puma more reliable is not recorded.

The D.H.9 squadrons fought on through 1918, and the type was even used in the UK for anti-Zeppelin and coastal defence work, and after the Armistice was used initially on the cross-Channel mail services. This was short-lived, for by July 1919 the RAF had thankfully rid itself of the D.H.9 for its replacement. The aircraft was not finished yet, however, and various airframes continued on the research and development scene, chiefly as engine test-beds for a variety of new and alternative powerplants. A few were used for deck landing trials when the new HMS *Eagle* appeared in 1921, and the most significant piece of development that any of the D.H.9s accomplished was by H9140. This aircraft was bought by Handley Page, which used it as a test-bed for the company's new aerodynamic theory of leading-edge slats. The theory ran that these slats, being auxiliary aerofoils fitted on the front of each upper wing, would provide a smooth airflow over the upper surface even when the wing would normally stall, and thus enable the aircraft to fly under full control at a slower speed. Handley Page designated the aircraft the H.P.17 and flew it in demonstrations against a standard D.H.9, demonstrating the tremendous advantages of a slatted wing.

Captain Gerald Gattergood won the 'Aerial Derby' at Hendon in the Airco D.H.4R, registration K141, with a 450 hp (336 kw) Napier Lion engine. His average speed was 128 mph (206.88 km/h), racing over a private course.

Surplus stock operators

Although the RAF disposed of D.H.9s as quickly as possible, this was not the case elsewhere. Many emergent air forces were forming after the 'war to end all wars', and there were literally hundreds of D.H.9s in the hands of the Aircraft Disposal Company. Thus impecunious small nations could construct a sizable bomber/reconnaissance force at a price

Airco D.H.4 and D.H.9 variants

D.H.4: two prototypes and 1,449 production aircraft, the latter built by the Aircraft Manufacturing Company (Airco). F.W. Berwick & Co. Ltd, Glendower Aircraft Co. Ltd, Palladium Autocars Ltd, Vulcan Motor & Engineering Co., Waring & Gillow Ltd and Westland Aircraft Works; an additional 15 aircraft to this pattern were built for the Belgian army air arm by SABCA in Belgium; of this total 21 found their way onto the civil register after World War 1 (three in the UK, four in Belgium, two in Australia and 12 in Canada); engines used in the D.H.4 were the 200-hp (149-kW) RAF 3A, the 230-hp (172-kW) BHP, the 230-hp (172-kW) Siddeley Puma, the 250-hp (186-kW) Rolls-Royce Mk III, the 250-hp (186-kW) Rolls-Royce Mk IV, the 260-hp (194-kW) Fiat and the 275-hp (205-kW) Rolls-Royce Eagle VI; there were also 15 experimental installations
D.H.4A: designation of Liberty-engined aircraft modified to carry two passengers in a small enclosed cabin aft of the open pilot's cockpit; it is believed that five such machines were operated by the RAF, while civil conversions amounted to two Belgian and seven British aircraft
D.H.4R: designation of one special racing aircraft with the 450-hp (336-kW) Napier Lion engine and clipped lower wings
DH-4: designation applied to US-built aircraft; orders amounted to 12,348 aircraft, but of these only 4,846 were built (less than 200 being delivered to units in France before the Armistice); this baseline American model was powered by the 420-hp (313-kW) Liberty engine, though other versions of the Liberty engine were used in the various developed models listed below; manufacturers were the Dayton-Wright Airplane Co. (3,106 aircraft), the Fisher Body Corporation (1,600 aircraft) and the Standard Aircraft Corporation (140 aircraft)
DH-4Amb-1: ambulance model with the ability to carry one litter
DH-4Amb-2: ambulance model with the ability to carry two litters
DH-4Ard: dual-control cross-country model with additional fuel capacity
DH-4B: much-modified development with the pilot and main fuel tank exchanged and with the fuselage covered in ply
DH-4B-1: improved version of the DH-4B with additional tankage
DH-4B-2: revised model with 'crashworthy' fuel system
DH-4B-3: version with considerably increased fuel capacity
DH-4B-4: airways version with standard fuel tankage
DH-4B-5: US equivalent to the D.H.4A three-seater with small cabin
DH-4BD: DH-4B equipped for crop-dusting
DH-4BG: DH-4B equipped for the laying of chemical smoke screens
DH-4BK: night-flying version of the DH-4B
DH-4BM: messenger version with rear-fuselage compartment
DH-4BM-1: dual-control transport version of the DH-4BM with additional fuel capacity
DH-4BM-2: increased-tankage version of the DH-4BM-1
XDH-4BP: experimental photographic aircraft with cameras in front cockpit
DH-4BP-1: photographic aircraft
XDH-4BP-2: experimental photographic aircraft with additional tankage and the wings of the USD-9
DH-4BP-3: improved version of the DH-4BP-1
XDH-4BS: experimental version of the DH-4B with a supercharged engine
DH-4BT: dual-control trainer version of the DH-4B
DH-4BW: test-bed aircraft for the 300-hp (224-kW) Wright-Hispano 'H' engine
DH-4C: test-bed aircraft for the 350-hp (261-kW) Packard 1A-1237 engine
XDH-4L: aerodynamically improved cross-country racer with large fuel capacity
DH-4M: much improved development with steel-tube fuselage; 59 built by Boeing
DH-4M-1: improved version of the DH-4M; 97 built by Boeing, as well as another 30 used by the US Marine Corps with the designation **O2B-1**
DH-4M-1K: DH-4M-1 equipped as a target tug
DH-4M-1T: dual-control trainer version of the DH-4M-1, of which 22 were produced by conversion from standard airframes
DH-4M-2: version of the DH-4M-1 with increased fuel capacity; 135 built by the Atlantic Aircraft Corporation
DH-4M-2A: airways version of the DH-4M-2
DH-4M-2K: target tug version of the DH-4M-2
DH-4M-2P: photographic version of the DH-4M-2
DH-4M-2S: supercharged version of the DH-4M-2 with reduced fuel capacity
DH-4M-2T: dual-control trainer version of the DH-4M-2
Twin DH-4: designation of a twin-engine version developed by LWF (Lowe, Willard and Fowler) in 1919 as an airmail aircraft; span was increased to 52 ft 6 in (16.00 m) and maximum take-off weight to 5,490 lb (2490 kg), power being provided by two 200-hp (149-kW) Hall-Scott L-6 inlines for a maximum speed of 105 mph (169 km/h); twin vertical tails were added, and production amounted to 20 Post Office and 10 US Army aircraft
XCO-7: single Boeing-built corps observation development with the wings developed for the Loening COA-1 amphibian
XCO-7A: single Boeing-built development of the XCO-7 with DH-4M-1 fuselage and Loening tapered wings, larger tailplane and split oleopneumatic landing gear
XCO-7B: single Boeing-built development of the XCO-7 with an inverted Liberty engine
XCO-8: single conversion of a DH-4M-2 with Loening wings
D.H.9: recast version of the D.H.4 with the pilot and observer/gunner located closer together for enhanced tactical capability; production amounted to one prototype (converted from a D.H.4) and 3,204 production aircraft, the latter being built by the Aircraft Manufacturing Co., Alliance Aeroplane Co. Ltd, F. W. Berwick & Co. Ltd, Crossley Motors Ltd, Cubitt Ltd, Mann, Egerton & Co. Ltd, NAF 1, NAF 2, Short Bros, Vulcan Motor & Engineering Co., Waring & Gillow Ltd, G. & J. Weir Ltd, Westland Aircraft Works and Whitehead Aircraft Co. Ltd; other examples were built in Belgium by SABCA (30 aircraft) and in Spain by Hispano-Suiza (perhaps 500 aircraft); de Havilland also exported aircraft to the Netherlands, and among the many handed on to other air forces were machines redesignated **Mantis, M'pala I** and **M'pala II** by the South African Air Force when re-engined with the 200-hp (149-kW) Wolseley Viper, 450-hp (336-kW) Bristol Jupiter VI and 480-hp (358-kW) Bristol Jupiter VIII respectively; seven trial engine installations were made in British D.H.9s, but the standard powerplants were the 230-hp (172-kW) Siddeley Puma, the 250-hp (186-kW) Fiat A-12, the 430-hp (321-kW) Napier Lion and the 435-hp (324-kW) Liberty 12A; many D.H.9s later passed on to the civil registers of several countries, 34 in the UK, nine in Australia, five in New Zealand, six in Belgium, four in India and four in Denmark
D.H.9A: much-improved version of the D.H.9 designed round the Liberty engine, though the first two of three prototypes had the 375-hp (280-kW) Rolls-Royce Eagle VIII; production amounted to 2,300 aircraft built by the Aircraft Manufacturing Co., Mann, Egerton & Co. Ltd, Whitehead Aircraft Co. Ltd, Vulcan Motor & Engineering Co., Westland Aircraft Works, F. W. Berwick & Co. Ltd, Handley Page Ltd, Gloucester Aircraft, Parnall Aircraft Co. and de Havilland Aircraft Co. Ltd; civil conversions amounted to 13 British and 11 Canadian aircraft
D.H.9AJ: single prototype with 465-hp (347-kW) Bristol Jupiter VI radial and divided landing gear
D.H.9B: designation of 20 aircraft converted for the British civil register as three seaters with two passenger seats (one forward and one aft of the pilot)
D.H.9C: designation of aircraft modified to carry three passengers (one forward and two aft of the pilot); these civil conversions appeared in the UK (13 aircraft), Australia (three aircraft) and Spain (three aircraft)
D.H.9J: designation of modernized aircraft produced by conversion in the late 1920s with 385-hp (287-kW) Armstrong Siddeley Jaguar III radials, Handley Page leading-edge slats and a number of control and structural improvements; the designation was also used for the South African M'pala development; 14 such civil conversions were carried out in the UK
D.H.9R: single racing aircraft with sesquiplane wing and 465-hp (347-kW) M Napier Lion II engine
USD-9A: US version of the D.H.9, of which only 13 (nine by the engineering Division at McCook Field and four by Dayton-Wright) of a planned 4,000 were completed

Airco D.H.4 and D.H.9

Service in the Middle East saw the use of aluminium dope on the main airframe, this No. 45 Sqn D.H.9A also sporting the red rim of 'A' Flight and the winged camel badge signifying the squadron's long association with the Middle East. This aircraft was based at Heliopolis in 1928 for patrol duties in Egypt and Palestine. Note the auxiliary radiator under the nose for desert use.

they could afford. If the aircraft were not the best for fighting, they were certainly good value for training budding airmen in the arts of aerial warfare, so business was brisk. Belgium took 18 to form its day bomber force, and Poland had a squadron's worth, 12 aircraft. Afghanistan, Greece, Eire, Latvia and the Netherlands all took aircraft, and the Netherlands, having returned those interned, then purchased 46 for service at home and in the East Indies and began assembling its own. An amazing fact about the Dutch aircraft is that they were re-engined in 1934 with Wright Whirlwinds and some were still in service in 1937, a tribute to the correctness of the basic airframe. Peru, Romania, Spain and Switzerland all took D.H.9s into their complements, and the aircraft figured in the Imperial Gift to Commonwealth nations. Biggest recipient of the D.H.9 was South Africa, which acquired 48 that served in the Union for a long time, many being re-engined with Bristol Jupiters and named M'palas. They were in action in 1922 during the Boudelzvartz rebellion, and one aircraft made the first Pretoria to Cape Town flight, taking 9 hours 25 minutes in March 1924. So the D.H.9 was greater in its latter days than it had ever been in RAF service. But its fame paled when compared with that of its replacement.

Both the D.H.4 and the D.H.9 had been hampered in production because of the lack of sufficient suitable engines. To remedy this overall shortage, and when convinced that a winner could be found across the Atlantic, large orders were placed for the American Liberty 12 which produced 400 hp (298 kW). This engine was lined up for a D.H.9 replacement as quickly as possible. Unfortunately, the de Havilland design team was up to its ears in producing the organization's first production twin-engine bomber, the D.H.10, so the responsibility for developing this new single-engine day bomber was given to Yeovil-based Westland Aircraft, which had produced D.H.4s and D.H.9s for the RFC and RNAS. This was an opportunity to take the good qualities of both

earlier types, marry them to the excellent Liberty engine and produce what by any standards would be an outstanding aeroplane. And this Westland achieved by strengthening the fuselage for the heavier engine and by increasing the span and chord of the mainplanes.

The first two prototypes, in order to speed things along, were fitted with scarce Rolls-Royce Eagle VIII engines in order to work out the type aerodynamically, then the production aircraft had the Packard Liberty. The aircraft could carry up to 660 lb (299 kg) of bombs on external racks, and the observer's cockpit had provision for twin Lewis guns, otherwise the configuration was as before. By June 1918, enough production aircraft had been delivered to form one squadron. This was No. 110, which began receiving its aircraft at Kenley in that month; all its aircraft had been subscribed by the Nizam of Hyderabad and were suitably decorated, the squadron henceforth being known as the Hyderabad Squadron. It went to France on the last day of August 1918 and flew its first bombing raid on Boulay aerodrome two weeks later. This was followed by raids deeper into Germany, and losses mounted as a result not of any fault in the aircraft but of the fact that the crews were generally 'green'. The squadron fought on until the Armistice, having by then dropped 10½ tons of bombs. One other squadron, No. 99, received some 'Nineacks' (as the

One of de Havilland's 'own' D.H.9s was the D.H.9J, the most notable difference from previous models being the adoption of a 385-hp (287-kW) Armstrong Siddeley Jaguar III radial engine. Other modifications, made in the 1920s, included Handley Page leading-edge slats. Fourteen D.H.9Js were produced.

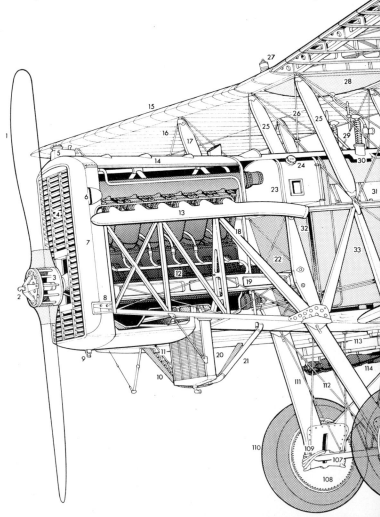

type became known in the service) in time to use them in action, and the comparison between the performance of the D.H.9A and that of the D.H.9 was very apparent as the squadron was also operating the older type at the same time.

The type also went into service with the Americans on the Western Front, principally with the Marine Corps Northern Bombing Groups which began operations in October, just before the Armistice called a halt to all bombing. By then Nos 18 and 105 Squadrons, RAF, had also received the type. As other squadrons disbanded, the D.H.9A units soldiered on with the Army of Occupation in Germany, providing a useful component to run scheduled mail services on the continent, but within a year of the Armistice this task was over and by January 1920 only No. 99 Squadron was left with the D.H.9A in service.

The aircraft, however, continued in production in the UK for it was seen to be suitable for the post-war Royal Air Force. This was soon proved to be so for already the service had become operational once more, with fighting on India's border with Afghanistan. Reinforcements were sent out to India, one such being the only D.H.9A squadron, No. 99. Flying from Mianwali, it was immediately thrown into the arid operations involved in taming the tribes up amongst the mountains. The first lesson learnt was that the Nineack's performance in the heat of India was but a fraction of its temperate abilities. Even with extra radiators, its ceiling, on a good day, was only some 13,500 ft (4115 m), so it had perforce to wind its way through the mountain passes. On 1 April 1920, No. 99 was renumbered No. 27 Squadron, sporting the flying elephant badge on its fins. Although the

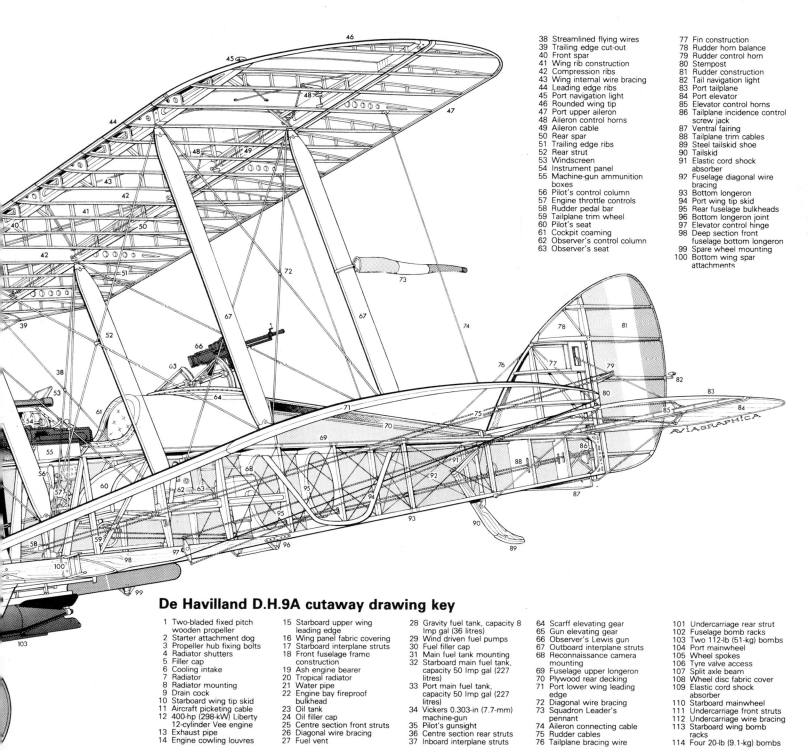

38 Streamlined flying wires	77 Fin construction
39 Trailing edge cut-out	78 Rudder horn balance
40 Front spar	79 Rudder control horn
41 Wing rib construction	80 Sternpost
42 Compression ribs	81 Rudder construction
43 Wing internal wire bracing	82 Tail navigation light
44 Leading edge ribs	83 Port tailplane
45 Port navigation light	84 Port elevator
46 Rounded wing tip	85 Elevator control horns
47 Port upper aileron	86 Tailplane incidence control
48 Aileron control horns	screw jack
49 Aileron cable	87 Ventral fairing
50 Rear spar	88 Tailplane trim cables
51 Trailing edge ribs	89 Steel tailskid shoe
52 Rear strut	90 Tailskid
53 Windscreen	91 Elastic cord shock
54 Instrument panel	absorber
55 Machine-gun ammunition	92 Fuselage diagonal wire
boxes	bracing
56 Pilot's control column	93 Bottom longeron
57 Engine throttle controls	94 Port wing tip skid
58 Rudder pedal bar	95 Rear fuselage bulkheads
59 Tailplane trim wheel	96 Bottom longeron joint
60 Pilot's seat	97 Elevator control hinge
61 Cockpit coaming	98 Deep section front
62 Observer's control column	fuselage bottom longeron
63 Observer's seat	99 Spare wheel mounting
	100 Bottom wing spar
	attachments

De Havilland D.H.9A cutaway drawing key

1 Two-bladed fixed pitch wooden propeller	15 Starboard upper wing leading edge	28 Gravity fuel tank, capacity 8 Imp gal (36 litres)	64 Scarff elevating gear	101 Undercarriage rear strut
2 Starter attachment dog	16 Wing panel fabric covering	29 Wind driven fuel pumps	65 Gun elevating gear	102 Fuselage bomb racks
3 Propeller hub fixing bolts	17 Starboard interplane struts	30 Fuel filler cap	66 Observer's Lewis gun	103 Two 112-lb (51-kg) bombs
4 Radiator shutters	18 Front fuselage frame construction	31 Main fuel tank mounting	67 Outboard interplane struts	104 Port mainwheel
5 Filler cap	19 Ash engine bearer	32 Starboard main fuel tank, capacity 50 Imp gal (227 litres)	68 Reconnaissance camera mounting	105 Wheel spokes
6 Cooling intake	20 Tropical radiator	33 Port main fuel tank, capacity 50 Imp gal (227 litres)	69 Fuselage upper longeron	106 Tyre valve access
7 Radiator	21 Water pipe		70 Plywood rear decking	107 Split axle beam
8 Radiator mounting	22 Engine bay fireproof bulkhead	34 Vickers 0.303-in (7.7-mm) machine-gun	71 Port lower wing leading edge	108 Wheel disc fabric cover
9 Drain cock	23 Oil tank	35 Pilot's gunsight	72 Diagonal wire bracing	109 Elastic cord shock absorber
10 Starboard wing tip skid	24 Oil filler cap	36 Centre section rear struts	73 Squadron Leader's pennant	110 Starboard mainwheel
11 Aircraft picketing cable	25 Centre section front struts	37 Inboard interplane struts	74 Aileron connecting cable	111 Undercarriage front struts
12 400-hp (298-kW) Liberty 12-cylinder Vee engine	26 Diagonal wire bracing		75 Rudder cables	112 Undercarriage wire bracing
13 Exhaust pipe	27 Fuel vent		76 Tailplane bracing wire	113 Starboard wing bomb racks
14 Engine cowling louvres				114 Four 20-lb (9.1-kg) bombs

Airco D.H.4 and D.H.9

While many war surplus aircraft found their way to lesser military powers, 19 D.H.9s were converted as civilian passenger aircraft carrying four people, including the pilot. Thirteen such aircraft were operated in the UK (with three going to Australia and three to Spain) with this example, operated by Northern Air Lines, being the last D.H.9C in service in 1932 at Barton.

Third Afghan War was supposed to have ended in May 1920, in fact the squadron was almost continuously in action during the 1920s, being supplemented by No. 60 on D.H.9As in 1923 when the latter shed its temperamental D.H.10s. It fell to these two squadrons to pioneer the peacetime use of the RAF in India and, apart from the intermittent operations, they flew several long-distance flights across the sub-continent. In 1925, the RAF was allowed to conduct a whole 'war' by itself, and managed to contain one such tribal war with only two casualties, largely as a result of the effectiveness of the D.H.9A squadrons. In 1928, the two squadrons were involved in the emergency flights to evacuate Kabul, escorting the Vickers Victorias of No. 70 Squadron to accomplish this feat. The Nineacks actually stayed in service in India until 1930 when Westland Wapitis, a new aircraft, but fitted with surplus D.H.9A wings, took their place.

The D.H.9A was not confined to India. It had been chosen to be the standard day bomber for the reconstituted Royal Air Force in the UK and, as and when Trenchard could form new squadrons, so the D.H.9A moved in. No. 207 Squadron re-formed at Bircham Newton on 1 February 1920 and No. 39 two months later. In the autumn of 1922 the former went to Turkey for a year because of the crisis there, returning after a fruitless year. These two squadrons maintained the light bomber force of the RAF through the 1920s, their D.H.9As being replaced by Wapitis during 1928. But they were augmented in the day bomber role during the 1920s by the formation of the Auxiliary Air Force, and six of these squadrons received D.H.9As as their initial equipment, starting with 602 (City of Glasgow) Squadron in September 1925. It was on this safe and doughty aircraft that this volunteer force cut its teeth and laid the foundations for the formidable air force it became in time for World War 2. By 1930 the Nineack had left the AAF and was virtually out of service in the UK. It had also served at Martlesham Heath where it became a ready tool of the experimental squadrons, and had spent a brief period in the early 1920s with No. 3 Squadron on coastal reconnaissance duties.

In September 1922 Captain F. L. Barnard won the first King's Cup race in this Airco D.H.4A (G-EAMU) at an average speed of 122.3 mph (196.8 km/h).

Success in the Middle East

It is probably in the Middle East, however, that the D.H.9A flew its most significant role. In 1921 it was agreed in Cairo that the Royal Air Force alone would accept responsibility for control of the area – a bold step indeed. The new Iraq Command had four squadrons, all equipped with the D.H.9A: Nos 8, 30, 55 and 84. These units had already been in action in 1919–20 when the first Arab revolt took place, although not all of them were fully equipped with the D.H.9A at the time. Now these squadrons began a system of air policing whereby, with regular flights over key areas, any inter-tribal enterprises were discouraged. If raids by tribesmen began, their villages were notified by messages dropped that bombing raids would take place at a specified time a few days later. This gave the factions the opportunity to evacuate personnel and thus preserve life while at the same time hampering the tribes by removing their possessions. It was a very effective method which had great success. Despite this, sporadic outbreaks of fighting continued during the 1920s.

The method was transferred to Palestine in the mid-1920s when trouble flared there, and a newly equipped No. 14 Squadron used its Nineacks to good effect in the fighting against Ibn Saud. Two more Middle East squadrons received the D.H.9A, No. 47 at Helwan in 1920 (remaining as a base squadron in Egypt with detachments in the Sudan) and No. 45 Squadron at Heliopolis in 1927 (converting from Vickers Vernon bomber transports).

In 1927, No. 8 Squadron transferred to Aden and started its unique control of the Protectorate, converting to Fairey IIIFs shortly after this and the Westland Wapiti began to replace the D.H.9A overseas in the late 1920s, and by 1930 the last D.H.9As were leaving the Middle East. Now there were but few of the breed left, most of them in England with training units (a two-seater trainer version had been produced and used in the flying training schools) and with experimental establishments such as Farnborough. It had been a wonderful mainstay for the decade after World War 1, had been the instrument with which the RAF's revolutionary policing methods had been worked out and honed in the Empire, and had seen the Auxiliary Air Force established at home.

The type had gone into service with Commonwealth air forces in small numbers, and a few had appeared in civil guise though to nothing like the same extent as the D.H.4. The D.H.9A racer version, the D.H.9R, had appeared in 1919 but was not as punchy as the D.H.4R. Despite this it established a closed-circuit record at 149.43 mph (240.48 km/h) in November 1919. A large number were used in research and development flying, carrying on Handley Page's slot trials, trying out a plethora of different engine types and being used to test new propellers, landing gear legs and many other ancillary devices. Even when the Nineack itself was finished, its many surplus wings flew on in the Westland Wapiti into the early years of World War 2.

All these aircraft, from the D.H.4 to the D.H.9A, were amongst the most important aircraft of World War 1 and the ten years afterwards. The specifications they fulfilled with their abilities, flexibility and adaptability were being imitated as late as the 1930s by other aircraft builders.

Fokker F.VII:
the Dutch master

After World War 1 the best-selling airliners did not come from the Allies but from defeated Germany's Junkers and 'Flying Dutchman' Anthony Fokker, whose German factory had produced the enemy's top fighters. Fokker's series of high-wing monoplane transports also supported a major industry in the USA.

Germany's military defeat in 1918 was followed by the collapse of the political system. Sailors from the navy mutinied in Wilhelmshaven, and then in Kiel. The mutiny spread to the hinterland of these cities and rebellion was in the air in many large towns. In Bavaria the Wittelsbachers had fallen and on 9 November the November Revolution, as it was called, reached its high point: Kaiser Wilhelm II was forced to abdicate. On the same day Philipp Scheidemann declared the German Republic against the will of Friedrich Ebert, and shortly afterwards Karl Liebknecht proclaimed a Free Socialist Republic. During this time of political confusion Anthony Fokker managed to escape from his aircraft factory in Schwerin, which was being guarded by revolutionaries. The guards are believed to have been shot because they failed to recognise Fokker. Fokker transferred large sums of money to his Dutch homeland, and only two years later he completed an audacious project. The Allies had strictly forbidden Germany to build large aircraft during the postwar period. But in 1920 Fokker still had large stocks of aircraft parts left over from wartime production, and using six freight trains, each with sixty wagons, he smuggled these components past the eyes of the Allies from his old factory in Schwerin to Amsterdam, where by now he had built a new factory.

However, back in early 1919 Fokker and chief designer Reinhold Platz had decided they had better start designing passenger aircraft. The first result was the F.I. There was no argument about the structure. The fuselage was to be made of steel tubes, accurately cut and, where necessary, curved, and welded together in a precision jig, with fabric covering. This was how they had made their fighters. Platz had pioneered unbraced wooden wings whose plywood covering was an early form of stressed skin. By making the wing deep it could be light yet strong enough to need no external bracing. The wing of the F.I. was almost a direct scale-up of that of the D.VIII fighter. This was to be mounted in the parasol position above the fuselage, the latter having an impressive row of open cockpits for the pilot and six passengers, the latter in three side-by-side pairs. But before this prototype (the V 44) had got very far, Fokker and Platz took a decision that probably made the difference between failure and success. They decided to redesign the fuselage to accommodate the passengers in comfort, internally.

The result was the V 45 prototype, or F.II, first flown by Fokker's trusty chief pilot and school head, Bernard de

This single-engine version of the Fokker F-VIIA was flown by Swissair in the early 1930s and has now become a museum piece.

Fokker F.VII

Specification

Fokker F.VII-3m

Type: 8/10 seat medium range passenger transport monoplane

Powerplant: three 215-hp (160-kW) Armstrong Siddeley Lynx air-cooled radial piston engines fitted with two-blade wooden fixed-pitch propellers*

Performance: maximum speed at sea level 115 mph (185 km/h); cruising speed 93 mph (149 km/h); range with standard tanks at cruising speed 477 miles (768 km); service ceiling 10,170 ft (3100 m); landing approach speed 62 mph (100 km/h)

Weights: empty weight 6,393 lb (2900 kg); maximum take-off 11,023 lb (5000 kg)

Dimensions: span 71 ft 2½ in (21.71 m); length 47 ft 7 in (14.50 m); height 12 ft 9 in (3.88 m); wing area 727.66 sq ft (67.6 m²)

Accommodation: two crew in side-by-side seating in forward enclosed cockpit and eight passengers in two rows of four seats either side of a central aisle in main cabin

* Note: Fokker F.VIIs were fitted with a variety of engines, and the performance of different aircraft varied slightly from that shown above

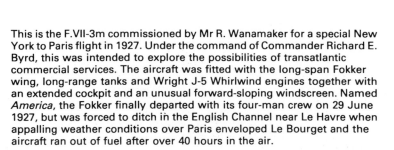

This is the F.VII-3m commissioned by Mr R. Wanamaker for a special New York to Paris flight in 1927. Under the command of Commander Richard E. Byrd, this was intended to explore the possibilities of transatlantic commercial services. The aircraft was fitted with the long-span Fokker wing, long-range tanks and Wright J-5 Whirlwind engines together with an extended cockpit and an unusual forward-sloping windscreen. Named *America*, the Fokker finally departed with its four-man crew on 29 June 1927, but was forced to ditch in the English Channel near Le Havre when appalling weather conditions over Paris enveloped Le Bourget and the aircraft ran out of fuel after over 40 hours in the air.

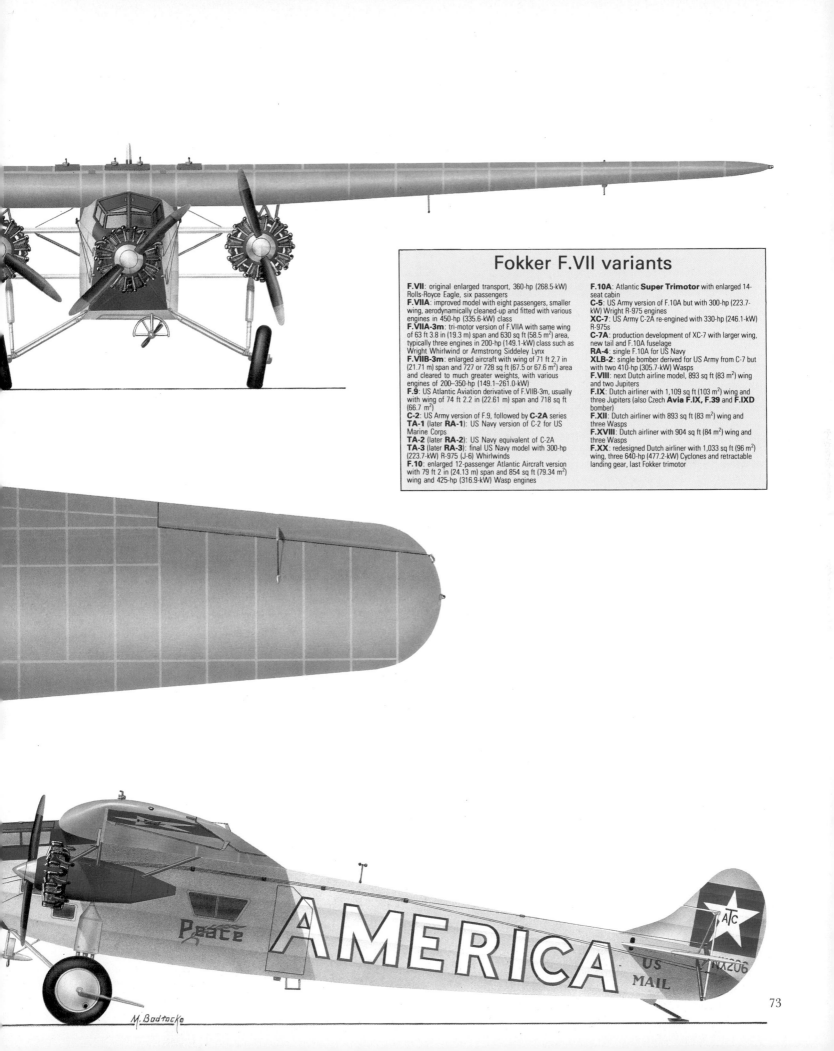

Fokker F.VII variants

F.VII: original enlarged transport, 360-hp (268.5-kW) Rolls-Royce Eagle, six passengers

F.VIIA: improved model with eight passengers, smaller wing, aerodynamically cleaned-up and fitted with various engines in 450-hp (335.6-kW) class

F.VIIA-3m: tri-motor version of F.VIIA with same wing of 63 ft 3.8 in (19.3 m) span and 630 sq ft (58.5 m²) area, typically three engines in 200-hp (149.1-kW) class such as Wright Whirlwind or Armstrong Siddeley Lynx

F.VIIB-3m: enlarged aircraft with wing of 71 ft 2.7 in (21.71 m) span and 727 or 728 sq ft (67.5 or 67.6 m²) area and cleared to much greater weights, with various engines of 200–350-hp (149.1–261.0-kW)

F.9: US Atlantic Aviation derivative of F.VIIB-3m, usually with wing of 74 ft 2.2 in (22.61 m) span and 718 sq ft (66.7 m²)

C-2: US Army version of F.9, followed by **C-2A** series

TA-1 (later **RA-1**): US Navy version of C-2 for US Marine Corps

TA-2 (later **RA-2**): US Navy equivalent of C-2A

TA-3 (later **RA-3**): final US Navy model with 300-hp (223.7-kW) R-975 (J-6) Whirlwinds

F.10: enlarged 12-passenger Atlantic Aircraft version with 79 ft 2 in (24.13 m) span and 854 sq ft (79.34 m²) wing and 425-hp (316.9-kW) Wasp engines

F.10A: Atlantic **Super Trimotor** with enlarged 14-seat cabin

C-5: US Army version of F.10A but with 300-hp (223.7-kW) Wright R-975 engines

XC-7: US Army C-2A re-engined with 330-hp (246.1-kW) R-975s

C-7A: production development of XC-7 with larger wing, new tail and F.10A fuselage

RA-4: single F.10A for US Navy

XLB-2: single bomber derived for US Army from C-7 but with two 410-hp (305.7-kW) Wasps

F.VIII: next Dutch airline model, 893 sq ft (83 m²) wing and two Jupiters

F.IX: Dutch airliner with 1,109 sq ft (103 m²) wing and three Jupiters (also Czech **Avia F.IX, F.39** and **F.IXD** bomber)

F.XII: Dutch airliner with 893 sq ft (83 m²) wing and three Wasps

F.XVIII: Dutch airliner with 904 sq ft (84 m²) wing and three Wasps

F.XX: redesigned Dutch airliner with 1,033 sq ft (96 m²) wing, three 640-hp (477.2-kW) Cyclones and retractable landing gear, last Fokker trimotor

M. Bodtocke

Fokker F.VII

Sir Charles Kingsford Smith's famous F.VII-3m – the *Southern Cross* – arrived at Brisbane's Eagle Farm Airport on 9 June 1928 following a 7,390-mile (11890-km) flight across the Pacific from Oakland, California. The American registration (1985) was changed to VH-USU.

The Italian airline Avioline-Italiane received a batch of three F.VIIa-3ms, including I-BBED (c/n 5059). This was sold by them in 1933 to Societá Aérea Mediterranea and then, in company with the other ALI aircraft, it was taken on charge by the Ala Littoria company and is believed to have been scrapped in 1939.

Waal, in October 1919. The wing, originally intended for the V 44, was simply bolted direct to the top of the enlarged fuselage. The cabin was furnished for four passengers, and a fifth could sit in the open front cockpit under the leading edge alongside the pilot. Powered by a 185-hp (138-kW) BMW IIIa 6-cylinder inline water-cooled engine, the F.II was slow but to the passenger vastly better than the crudely converted military machines produced by British and French companies. One odd feature was the absence of a fin, the weathercock stability being provided by the long flat-sided rear fuselage to which was hinged the diminutive rudder. There was nothing lacking, however, from the tailplane, elevators and ailerons, all controls being fully balanced and the ailerons projecting distinctively beyond the wingtips.

De Waal secretly flew the V 45 prototype to the Netherlands on 20 March 1920. Subsequently the type entered service with several airlines, some being built by Fokker and others

The first prototype of the single-engined Fokker F.VII is seen here making its maiden flight on 11 April 1924. The vertical tail shown in this photograph was later changed for a redesigned version with greater area and a rounded rudder profile. This aircraft was subsequently given the registration H-NACC.

Of typical Fokker design, with a plywood-covered two-spar wooden wing and fabric-covered welded steel tube fuselage, the four production F.VIIs had accommodation for eight passengers and two crew members.

under licence by Grulich, the latter having 250- or 320-hp (186.4- or 238.6-kW) BMW engines and usually some wing bracing struts and an enclosed cockpit. They firmly established Fokker as a builder of practical passenger airliners. Despite their wooden wings and fabric-covered fuselages, they proved to be robust and long-lived, and they rather

F.VIIB-3m PH-AFS was used initially by KLM, who named it *Specht* (woodpecker). It was sold in August 1936 to Crilly Airways, but did not see any further airline service because it was then passed on to the Spanish Nationalist forces, who took it on charge at Burgos and used it in the fight against the Republican army.

Sabena was a prominent F.VIIB-3m user, and flew aircraft built under licence by the Belgian manufacturing company SABCA. This particular example, OO-AGH, was delivered on 20 September 1932 and flew on European routes until May 1940, when it was taken over by the invading German forces at Haren Airport near Brussels.

The first three-engined Fokker F.VII (c/n 4900) was flown in the 1925 Ford Reliability Tour and was subsequently sold to Edsel Ford. Carrying the name *Josephine Ford*, it made an historic flight from Spitzbergen to the North Pole on 9 May 1926 under the command of Lieutenant-Commander Richard E. Byrd and piloted by Floyd Bennett.

led to an outcry among US manufacturers. Fokker overcame this by setting up a US subsidiary, Atlantic Aircraft Corporation, at Teterborough, New Jersey. Subsequently, Atlantic Fokkers tended to depart from the parent product in design details and engines, until from 1925 Atlantic's manager, R. B. C. Noorduyn (later a famed builder of his own well-liked and efficient Norseman), developed Fokker transports quite independently.

In early 1923 Fokker and Ing. Walther Rethel (later famed at Arado) began designing the F.VII, a straightforward machine with a 360-hp (268.5-kW) Rolls-Royce Eagle and six passenger seats. It had a wing of 772-sq ft (71.72-m²) area, compared with 421 sq ft (39.11 m²) for the F.III and 958 sq ft (89.00 m²) for the F.IV. It worked well enough, but the way to improve it was obvious. With a newer and more powerful engine and smaller wing it would be possible to carry more yet fly faster, and thus reduce the operating costs. Only five F.VIIs were built, but the improved F.VIIA was another smash hit.

First flown in early 1925, the Fokker was given a wing reduced in area to only 630 sq ft (58.53 m²), with the ailerons at last accommodated within the outline of the wing. The usual engine was a 450-hp (335.6-kW) Bristol or Gnome-Rhône Jupiter, but one early example had the 400-hp (298.3-kW) Packard A-1500 (improved Liberty). Carrying eight passengers and two crew, the F.VIIA was what a modern observer might call 'a real airliner'. Minor improvements were the fitting of a larger rudder with a fixed fin, and a neater landing gear with vertical shock struts (sprung by multiple elastic cords inside a fairing) pinned under the front wing spar.

surprisingly remained in scheduled service with several operators (including even Deutsche Lufthansa) well into the 1930s, one still flying in 1940.

Naturally Fokker developed the F.II, moving via the bigger F.III to the F.IV of 1921. The former, powered by a BMW, Eagle, Puma or Jupiter, was a best-seller and by far the most important airliner in northern Europe, including the Soviet Union, in 1922–5. The F.IV was much bigger but was still only single-engined, with a 420-hp (313.2-kW) Liberty. Two were sold to the US Army, which called them T-2s. One gained immediate fame on 2–3 May 1922 by flying nonstop across the USA, from New York to San Diego. This triggered off major sales to the US Army and US Navy, which in turn

The F.VIIB-3m c/n 5028 was delivered for use on the 1928 Antarctic expedition planned by Lieutenant-Commander Richard E. Byrd. In the event, a Ford Trimotor was used instead and the Fokker, named *Friendship*, was fitted with twin floats and, with the great Amelia Earhart as passenger and Wilmer Stultz piloting, made a record transatlantic flight from Trepassey Bay to Burry Port.

The US Army received eight C-2A aircraft, which differed from the normal F.VIIB-3m in having a larger, 10-seat fuselage, a modified cockpit and three 220-hp (164-kW) Wright J-5 engines. This example, named *Question Mark* and a US Army crew of Spaatz, Eaker, Quesada and Halvorsen, was used to establish an inflight-refuelling endurance record of 150 hours during January 1929.

Famous Fokker flights

2–3 May 1923: Lieutenants Macready and Kelly fly nonstop from New York to San Diego in a Fokker T-2 of the US Air Service, the flight time being 26 hours 50 minutes

24 November 1924: Van der Hoop starts the first airline flight from Amsterdam to Batavia in the Netherlands East Indies in a Fokker F.VII of KLM

27 July 1925: M. Grase sets an endurance record of 3 hours 30 minutes 30 seconds with a payload of 3,307 lb (1500 kg) in a Fokker F.VIIA

September 1925: Anthony Fokker wins the Ford Reliability Trial in the Fokker F.VII-3m

9 May 1926: Floyd Bennett flies the Byrd expedition's Fokker F.VII-3m from Spitzbergen over the North Pole

28–29 June 1927: Lieutenants Hegenberger and Maitland of the US Army fly the Fokker C-2 *Bird of Paradise* from Oakland, Cal., to Wheeler Field, Hawaii, in 25 hours 15 min

29 June–1 July 1927: The F.VIIB-3m prototype is flown by Bernt Balchen and Byrd from Roosevelt Field, USA, to Ver-sur-Mer, France, in 43 hours 21 minutes in fog

15–23 July 1927: An F.VIIA of KLM flown by Geysendorffer and Scholte makes the first revenue flight from Amsterdam to Batavia

31 May 1928: Charles Kingsford Smith and his crew in an F.VIIB-3m make the first aerial crossing of the Pacific Ocean from Oakland, California, to Sydney in Australia (via Honolulu, Suva and Brisbane) in 88 hours for the 7,800-mile (12555-km) trip

10 June 1928: Flown by Barnard and Alliott, an F.VIIA sets off for a round trip from the UK to India; the outward leg was delayed by the need for an engine change, but the return leg was accomplished in 4½ days

17–18 June 1928: Amelia Earhart piloted by Wilmer Stultz becomes the first woman to cross the Atlantic Ocean by air, flying from Trepassey Bay to Burry Port in the F.VII-3m *Friendship*

10–11 September 1928: Kingsford Smith makes the first aerial crossing of the Tasman Sea from Australia to New Zealand in an F.VIIB-3m; he makes the return flight in the same year

January 1929: The Fokker C-2A *Question Mark* is flown by a US Army crew (Spaatz, Eaker, Quesada and Halvorsen) for an inflight-refuelled record flight of 150 hours 40 min 15 sec

10 July 1929: Kingsford Smith and his crew arrive at Croydon from Australia in their F.VIIB-3m in 12 days 18 hours

24–26 June 1930: Kingsford Smith and his crew fly from Portmarnock to Harbour Grace and New York in their F.VIIB-3m

KLM specification

In the summer of 1924 the Dutch airline KLM, by then almost entirely Fokker-equipped, issued a specification for an airliner to carry 10 passengers and be able to fly with one engine stopped. It suggested the use of three Siddeley Puma engines. However, Fokker was intensely interested in the tri-motor Junkers G.23 when this flew in November 1924. Most significant of all, in his autobiography he wrote 'When Byrd sought to buy the first tri-motored Fokker he was unknown to me. That plane had been constructed on the basis of my cabled instructions to put three Wright motors on an F.VII'. It is therefore odd that Fokker later claimed that he built the F.VIIA-3m tri-motor purely in order to compete in the Ford Reliability Trial in the USA, which began in September 1925. Be that as it may, Fokker had his eye initially on the US market, and in any case was always intensely interested in publicity. So the first F.VIIA-3m was given American engines, 200-hp (149.1-kW) Wright J-4 Whirlwinds, and fitted for the American trial. Fokker wanted the outboard engines on the leading edges, but for reasons of balance and thrust-line axis designer Platz put them in separate nacelles on the vertical main legs, braced to fuselage and wings. This machine was completed with rather crude exhaust stacks wrapped round right in front of the air-cooled cylinders and discharging under the nose and above the wings. In typical

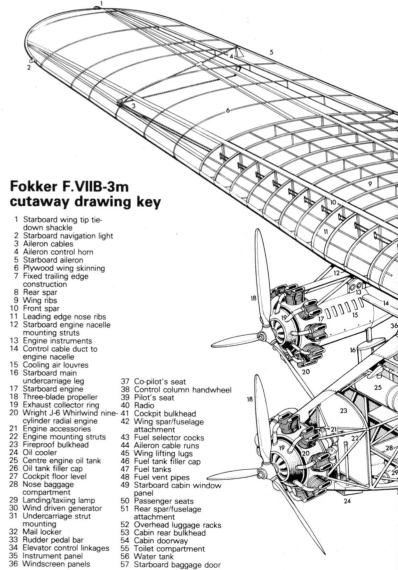

Fokker F.VIIB-3m cutaway drawing key

 1 Starboard wing tip tie-down shackle
 2 Starboard navigation light
 3 Aileron cables
 4 Aileron control horn
 5 Starboard aileron
 6 Plywood wing skinning
 7 Fixed trailing edge construction
 8 Rear spar
 9 Wing ribs
10 Front spar
11 Leading edge nose ribs
12 Starboard engine nacelle mounting struts
13 Engine instruments
14 Control cable duct to engine nacelle
15 Cooling air louvres
16 Starboard main undercarriage leg
17 Starboard engine
18 Three-blade propeller
19 Exhaust collector ring
20 Wright J-6 Whirlwind nine-cylinder radial engine
21 Engine accessories
22 Engine mounting struts
23 Fireproof bulkhead
24 Oil cooler
25 Centre engine oil tank
26 Oil tank filler cap
27 Cockpit floor level
28 Nose baggage compartment
29 Landing/taxiing lamp
30 Wind driven generator
31 Undercarriage strut mounting
32 Mail locker
33 Rudder pedal bar
34 Elevator control linkages
35 Instrument panel
36 Windscreen panels
37 Co-pilot's seat
38 Control column handwheel
39 Pilot's seat
40 Radio
41 Cockpit bulkhead
42 Wing spar/fuselage attachment
43 Fuel selector cocks
44 Aileron cable runs
45 Wing lifting lugs
46 Fuel tank filler cap
47 Fuel tanks
48 Fuel vent pipes
49 Starboard cabin window panel
50 Passenger seats
51 Rear spar/fuselage attachment
52 Overhead luggage racks
53 Cabin rear bulkhead
54 Cabin doorway
55 Toilet compartment
56 Water tank
57 Starboard baggage door

Fokker F.VIIs were pressed into service with both sides in the Spanish Civil War. This example was one of three F.VIIB-3ms originally delivered to Lineas Aereas Postales Espanolas (LAPE) in November 1933 and used by the Republicans. Makeshift external bomb racks were fitted on spars secured to the window frames.

The Avro Ten G-AASP was delivered as *Achilles* to Imperial Airways at its Cairo station during April 1931, and flew pipeline patrols on contract to the Iraq Petroleum Transport Co. It later returned to the UK, where Imperial Airlines found charter work for it. It was eventually withdrawn from use and scrapped in 1939.

Fokker fashion the aircraft was painted with the name in gigantic capitals along the wings and fuselage. It first flew on 4 September 1925, required little alteration, and was dismantled and shipped to the USA.

The machine's appearance was sensational, and it performed almost faultlessly throughout the trial. It proved it could (just) fly with one outer engine stopped, and Henry and Edsel Ford took a keen personal interest. The Fokker won the trial easily, and Edsel Ford bought the aircraft for Commander Richard E. Byrd's scientific expedition over the North Pole. Named *Josephine Ford*, and now with refined rear exhaust collector rings and fitted with skis, it was flown by Byrd and Floyd Bennett over the Pole on 9 May 1926. The same aircraft is now in the Ford Museum in Dearborn. Ford later produced his own tri-motor, with Junkers-type all-metal structure with corrugated skin.

From the start, demand for the F.VIIA-3m was almost more than Fokker's Dutch and US plants could handle. Later he did a deal with industrialists in Wheeling, West Virginia, who thought aircraft might replace part of their declining steel industry; soon Wheeling was building a 10-seat tri-motor every five days. Licences were purchased by Belgium, Italy, Poland and the UK, the British licensee being A. V. Roe, which produced several derived designs which included a nice-looking twin, the Avro 642. This was a much

more graceful design than Fokker's own derived twin, the F.VIII. The latter was a hefty 15-passenger machine, of which two were made by Manfred Weiss in Hungary.

Until 1934 Fokker's mainstream airliner developments were tri-motors. In 1926 two Dutch-built F.VIIs were ordered for Sir Hubert Wilkins' Arctic expedition. One was a Liberty-F.VIIA, but the other was a tri-motor of a new and enlarged type which gradually became the standard model, the F.VIIB-3m. This had a bigger wing of 727 or 729 sq ft (67.54 or 67.72 m²), but not as big as that on the original F.VII, which was designed at Fokker's Dutch factory for the American Fokker F.9 (see variants list). Thus the second machine was a unique in-between, for it retained the 200-hp

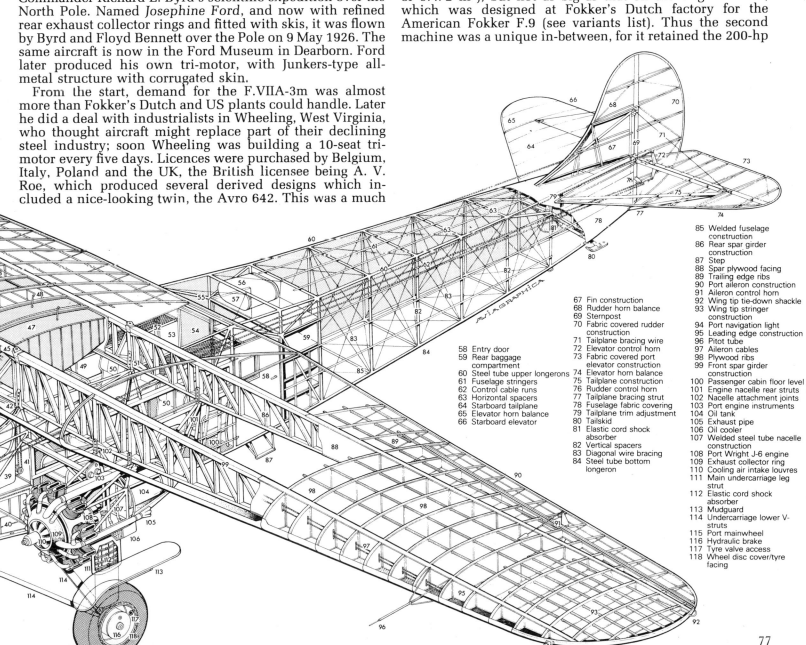

58 Entry door
59 Rear baggage compartment
60 Steel tube upper longerons
61 Fuselage stringers
62 Control cable runs
63 Horizontal spacers
64 Starboard tailplane
65 Elevator horn balance
66 Starboard elevator
67 Fin construction
68 Rudder horn balance
69 Sternpost
70 Fabric covered rudder construction
71 Tailplane bracing wire
72 Elevator control horn
73 Fabric covered port elevator construction
74 Elevator horn balance
75 Tailplane construction
76 Rudder control horn
77 Tailplane bracing strut
78 Fuselage fabric covering
79 Tailplane trim adjustment
80 Tailskid
81 Elastic cord shock absorber
82 Vertical spacers
83 Diagonal wire bracing
84 Steel tube bottom longeron
85 Welded fuselage construction
86 Rear spar girder construction
87 Step
88 Spar plywood facing
89 Trailing edge ribs
90 Port aileron construction
91 Aileron control horn
92 Wing tip tie-down shackle
93 Wing tip stringer construction
94 Port navigation light
95 Leading edge construction
96 Pitot tube
97 Aileron cables
98 Plywood ribs
99 Front spar girder construction
100 Passenger cabin floor level
101 Engine nacelle rear struts
102 Nacelle attachment joints
103 Port engine instruments
104 Oil tank
105 Exhaust pipe
106 Oil cooler
107 Welded steel tube nacelle construction
108 Port Wright J-6 engine
109 Exhaust collector ring
110 Cooling air intake louvres
111 Main undercarriage leg strut
112 Elastic cord shock absorber
113 Mudguard
114 Undercarriage lower V-struts
115 Port mainwheel
116 Hydraulic brake
117 Tyre valve access
118 Wheel disc cover/tyre facing

The Polish government ordered a bomber version of the F.VIIB-3m, which was built by the Plage & Laskiewicz factory at Lublin. This aircraft served with No. 2 Sqn of the Dywizjon Bombowy (bomber group) and was equipped with an open mid-upper turret and bomb racks under the fuselage. The engines were J-5 Whirlwinds.

(149.1-kW) Whirlwind and fuselage of the F.VIIA. After expedition flying in Alaska this special long-range Fokker was overhauled by Boeing and sold to an Australian, Squadron Leader Charles Kingsford Smith. Re-engined with 237-hp (176.7-kW) J-5 Whirlwinds and boldly painted with the name *Southern Cross*, the Fokker took off from Oakland, California, on 31 May 1928. This was the start of a career that was to make the Fokker the most famous aircraft between the world wars, surpassing even Lindbergh's Ryan. Some of its flights figure in a separate listing of famous Fokker flights. Today it is on display at Eagle Farm, Brisbane.

The 'big-wing' tri-motor had great potential, especially with greater power, and the F.VIIB-3m was formally marketed from 1928, usually with the J-6 series Whirlwind of 300–330 hp (223.7–246.1-kW). The first production example was another 'special' built in late 1927 as the *America* for the Byrd transatlantic flight. Later renamed *Friendship* (a prophetic name for Fokker) it participated in many further epic flights. Several of the enlarged tri-motors were F.VIIA rebuilds, one of the most famed starting life as H-NADP, powered by a Jupiter. This carried a wealthy American on the first KLM passenger flight to the Dutch East Indies (see list of flights). In 1928 it was rebuilt as an F.VIIB-3m with Gnome-Rhône (Bristol) Titans, and was again hired by Black for a trip to Cape Town. It was later fitted with Whirlwinds and almost commuted between Croydon, Cape Town and the Far East, amazing for 1929–30.

Licence-building

The F.VIIB-3m was the world's premier airliner of the 1927–33 period. Fokker and Atlantic built 147, and basically similar machines (with many makes of engine) were built under licence in Belgium, Czechoslovakia, France, Italy, Poland and the UK. Nine of the licensed sub-types were military, four being bombers. Probably the most important tri-motor Fokker bombers, however, were the Avia F.IXs. The Czech Avia company had built 21 F.VIIB-3m aircraft, one a bomber, and it followed with 12 F.IX bombers based on the Fokker F.IX, a much more powerful machine with 500-hp (372.9-kW) Walter-built Jupiters and able to take off at a weight of 19,842 lb (9000 kg). An ex-KLM F.IX later found its way to the Spanish Republicans where it too became a bomber.

Fokker's American team ended in a blaze of glory with 10 giant F.32s, the designation indicating the number of seats. Powered by four push/pull 575-hp (428.8-kW) Pratt & Whitney Hornets, they were generally judged too big for the market. But back in Amsterdam the traditional Fokker tri-motors just kept on being improved. In 1930 the important F.XII made its appearance, with an 893-sq ft (82.96-m²) wing and 425-hp (316.9-kW) Pratt & Whitney C-series Wasp engines. Normally seating 16 passengers, the F.IX was the KLM main liner and also served with Sweden's ABA and Denmark's DDL, two actually being built in Denmark. This model in turn led to the further-enlarged F.XVIII of 1932. These proved to be the ultimate production Fokker tri-motors. KLM's incredibly experienced crews did marvels with what were becoming outdated machines. F.XVIII PH-AIP *Pelikaan* took 1933 Christmas mail to Batavia in 73 hours 34 minutes flight time, and PH-AIS *Snip* took 1934 Christmas mail to Curaçao in under 56 hours.

In 1932 Fokker gradually realised the advantages of an all-metal fuselage. But he obstinately stuck to traditional methods. The result was the F.XX of 1933, which kept in step with technical progress with 640-hp (477-kW) Cyclone engines and retractable undercarriage. For the first time a conscious effort was being made to reduce resistance, and the new twelve-seater could reach a speed of 190 mph (305 km/h). but now it had to prove itself against the Boeing 247 and the Douglas DC-1. KLM reluctantly decided in 1933 to negotiate with Douglas. But Fokker did not give up that easily. His last two transport planes were the great F.XXXVI, which flew in June 1934, and a year later the somewhat smaller F.XXII. This time the numbering of the type was based on the American method used for the F.32, where the number represented the maximum number of passengers. Both machines were traditional high-wing aircraft made of steel tubing, fabric and wood. But they had four wing-mounted engines. The '36' had a 750-hp (559-kW) Cyclone engine, and the '22' Wasp one of 500 hp (373 kW). Four machines were fitted with these, but only two were left by the beginning of World War 2. These were kept by the RAF, which used them in Scotland together with the only F.XXXVI ever to be built.

Hugh Wells piloted this Fokker F-VII in Pan American's first official flight from Miami to Havana.

Breguet 19

Almost certainly produced in larger numbers than any other military aircraft between the world wars, the inelegant Breguet 19 established numerous world records and served with great distinction for almost a quarter of a century.

The design for the Breguet 19, which was intended to capitalise on the success of the Breguet 14, the well-known World War 1 bomber, was taken charge of by M. Vuillerme in the design offices in Vélizy-Villacoublay. The prototype Bre.19 A.2 No. 01 was displayed in the VIIe Salon d'Aéronautique from 12 to 27 November 1921 in the Grand Palais in Paris. The structure of this large two-seater was made entirely of duralumin. The front half of the fuselage had a duralumin skin, while the rear half was tensioned using lacquered fabric. The huge upper wing was also tensioned with fabric and consisted of two pre-fabricated spars and ribs made of duralumin. It sat on two tandem wing struts above the fuselage and was joined to the much smaller bottom wing above a single Y-shaped wing strut. The prototype had a single Breguet-Bugatti 16-cylinder V-engine giving 450-hp (336-kW) and driving a four-bladed propeller. In fact, two Bugatti eight-cylinder engines were used in series. As the first ground test revealed vibration and cooling problems, the 16-cylinder engine which Robert Thiery used for the maiden flight in March 1922 in Villacoublay was replaced by a Renault 12Kb 12-cylinder V-engine with direct drive.

Already assembly of 11 pre-production aircraft had started

The 'Fuel Can', as it was nicknamed, flew around the world as the *'Nungesser-Coli'* in 1927–8. This journey of 35,420 miles (57000 km) also involved the first-ever crossing of the South Atlantic.

at Vélizy-Villacoublay, it being intended to offer the Bre.19 in two versions, the A.2 (Armée-biplace) two-seat reconnaissance aircraft and the B.2 (Bombardement-biplace) two-seat bomber, with a number of alternative engines; these preliminary aircraft featured the Renault 12Kb, 480-hp (358-kW) Renault 12Kd, 370-hp (276-kW) Lorraine-Dietrich 12D, 450 hp (336-kW) Lorraine-Dietrich 12Eb, and a Hispano-Suiza 12. The pre-production aircraft also differed from the prototype in having a 2-ft (0.6-m) longer fuselage.

Following trials with the Service Technique de l'Aéronautique in August 1922, which fully justified the manufacturers' earlier confidence, plans were authorized for an initial batch of 112 aircraft.

Production and proliferation

Roughly half the first production batch was powered by the Renault 12Kd, these aircraft being delivered for service with France's Aviation Militaire; however, well aware that a huge market was opening up internationally as nation after nation sought to establish or re-establish military air services and the post-war pacifism evaporated, Breguet offered the type with the many other powerplant options. First to inspect the Bre.19 was General Uzelac, commanding Yugoslavia's army aviation (already using the Bre.14), and in 1923 a pre-production Bre.19 was delivered for evaluation in that country. Meanwhile Thiery had flown Bre.19 No. 01 at an

Unquestionably the most illustrious Breguet 19 was the record-breaking Super-Bidon, the *Point d'Interrogation*, whose manufacture was sponsored by François Coty, the perfume magnate. After Dieudonné Costes and Maurice Bellonte had failed to fly the Atlantic in July 1929, a direct-drive Hispano-Suiza 12Lb engine was fitted and in this form the aircraft established a new world record of 4,912 miles (7905 km) when the same crew flew from Le Bourget to Tsitsihkar in Manchuria on 27–29 September 1929. It was again re-engined, this time with a 650-hp (485-kW) Hispano-Suiza 12Nb engine, and made the first direct aeroplane flight from Paris to New York. Thereafter it embarked on a 'Voyage of Friendship' in the USA, its landing points being recorded on the rear fuselage chevron as shown in this illustration. Other remarkable achievements are also recorded between the chevrons.

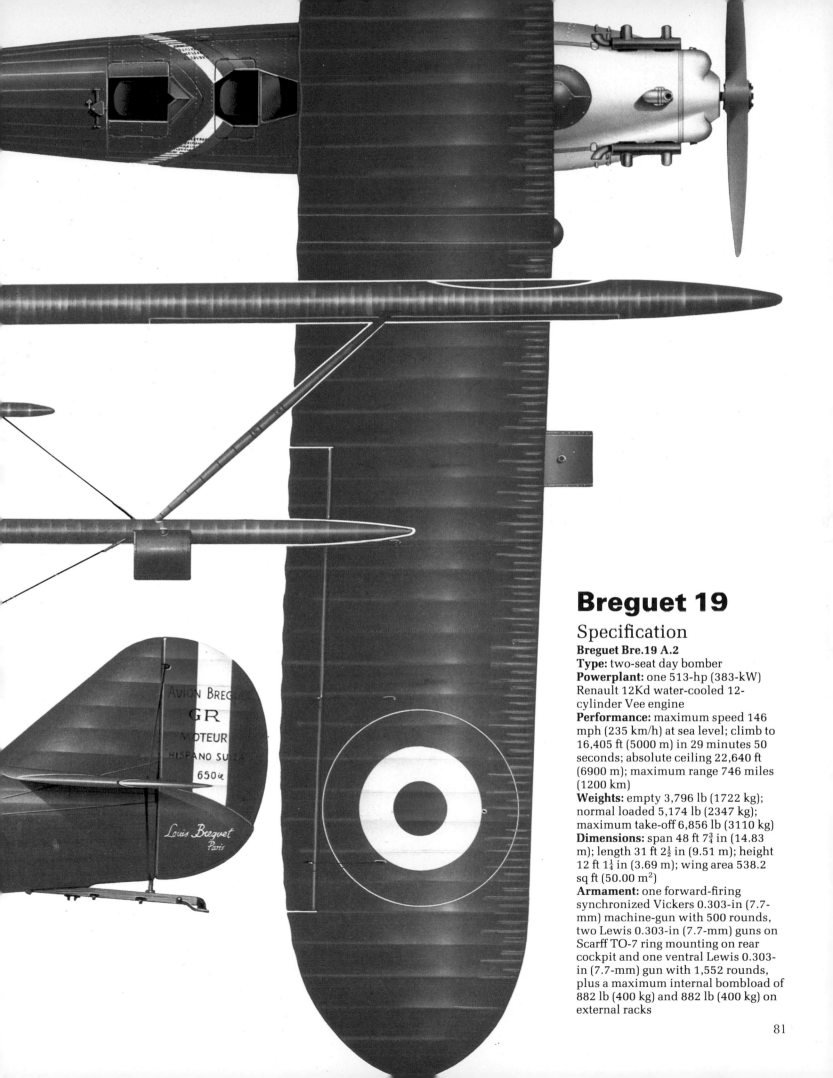

Breguet 19

Specification

Breguet Bre.19 A.2
Type: two-seat day bomber
Powerplant: one 513-hp (383-kW)
Renault 12Kd water-cooled 12-
cylinder Vee engine
Performance: maximum speed 146
mph (235 km/h) at sea level; climb to
16,405 ft (5000 m) in 29 minutes 50
seconds; absolute ceiling 22,640 ft
(6900 m); maximum range 746 miles
(1200 km)
Weights: empty 3,796 lb (1722 kg);
normal loaded 5,174 lb (2347 kg);
maximum take-off 6,856 lb (3110 kg)
Dimensions: span 48 ft 7¾ in (14.83
m); length 31 ft 2½ in (9.51 m); height
12 ft 1¼ in (3.69 m); wing area 538.2
sq ft (50.00 m²)
Armament: one forward-firing
synchronized Vickers 0.303-in (7.7-
mm) machine-gun with 500 rounds,
two Lewis 0.303-in (7.7-mm) guns on
Scarff TO-7 ring mounting on rear
cockpit and one ventral Lewis 0.303-
in (7.7-mm) gun with 1,552 rounds,
plus a maximum internal bombload of
882 lb (400 kg) and 882 lb (400 kg) on
external racks

Versatility was a characteristic of the Bre.19 design, with two main versions being produced in France: the A.2 (Armée-biplace) reconnaissance aircraft, and the B.2 (bombardement-biplace) bomber, coupled with a great range of equipment provisions, and powerplants ranging from 350 hp (261 kW) to 650 hp (485 kW). Illustrated is a French Aviation Militaire Bre.19 A.2.

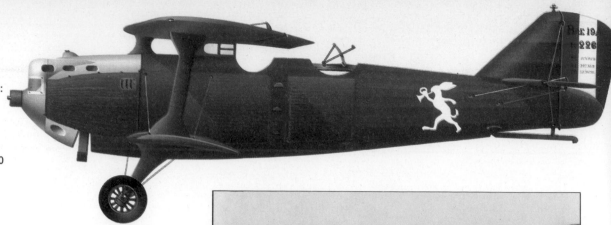

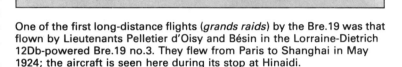

international military aircraft contest in Spain in February 1923, eclipsing all other contenders; subsequently Spain negotiated licence rights to manufacture the Bre.19.

Distributed among the first 112 production series were aircraft powered by the Lorraine-Dietrich 12Db and 12Eb, 500-hp (373-kW) Salmson 183Ma and 420-hp (313-kW) Gnome-Rhône 9Ac engines. By the time production deliveries started from Villacoublay in 1924 foreign interest in the aircraft was such that Breguet negotiated sub-contracted production with Avions Henri et Maurice Farman at Billancourt, and the Société d'Emboutissage et de Constructions Mécaniques at Colombes (SECM-Amiot). By mid-1928 no fewer than 1,936 Bre.19s had been built in France, of which more than 1,100 were exported.

Deliveries of the Bre.19 A.2 for the Aviation Militaire started in October 1924 to the 32e, 33e, 34e and 35e Regiments d'Aviation, and in June 1926 the 11e Regiment d'Aviation de Bombardement de Jour (RABJ, or day bomber regiment) took delivery of its first Bre.19 B.2s, followed by the 11e RABJ. In all, by mid-1927 46 Escadrilles de Reconnaissance, d'Observation and de Bombardement were flying the Bre.19 A.2 and B.2.

Meanwhile Breguet was hard pressed to keep pace with demand abroad. Yugoslavia had ordered 100 Bre.19 A.2s and B.2s, the former powered by the Lorraine-Dietrich 12Db and the latter by 12Eb engines; one of these aircraft, flown by Captain Radović and Lieutenant Rubčić, established a speed record between Paris and Belgrade in 8 hours 25 minutes on its delivery flight. The Yugoslav army's 2nd Regiment at Rajlovac near Sarajevo was the first to introduce the Bre.19.

In 1926 Romania ordered 50 Bre.19 A.2s and B.2s with which to start modernizing her air force, the first of a total of 108 Bre.19s (supplemented by about 12 Bre.19.7s, of which more later). In the Far East, following the purchase of four Bre.19s in 1924 by the Central Chinese government in Peking, 70 Lorraine-Dietrich 12Db-powered Bre.19s were bought for the Manchurian air arm under Marshal Chang Tso-lin, and some of these fought against the Japanese in the Manchurian campaign of 1931–2.

A measure of the high esteem in which the Breguet 19 was held at this time may be gained by the decision by Poland to create a powerful air force largely composed of Bre.19s. Following a visit by a purchasing mission from Poland,

One of the first long-distance flights (*grands raids*) by the Bre.19 was that flown by Lieutenants Pelletier d'Oisy and Bésin in the Lorraine-Dietrich 12Db-powered Bre.19 no.3. They flew from Paris to Shanghai in May 1924; the aircraft is seen here during its stop at Hinaidi.

General Wlodzimierz Zagórski authorized the first of a number of orders for Bre.19 A.2s and B.2s at the end of June 1925, and less than a month later Zagórski led a mixed formation of Bre.19s and Potez 25s from France to Poland – the first of 250 Bre.19s delivered to the Polish Lotnictwo Wojskowe between then and 1930 (including 20 examples of a special long-range version). It was a Polish Bre.19 A.2, flown by Colonel Ludomil Rayski and Sergeant Leonard Kubiak, which flew 4,660 miles (7500 km) round the entire Mediterranean between 16 and 22 September 1925. A Bre.19 was flown from Warsaw to Tokyo, a distance of 14,290 miles (23000 km) by Captain Boleslav Orlinski; on the return flight the aircraft ran into a severe storm and lost a large area of fabric from its port lower wing but, after the crew had landed in a field and torn away an equivalent area of fabric from the wing on the other side, continued safely on its way.

Polish Bre.19s served with the 2nd, 3rd, 5th and 6th Regiments of the Lotnictwo Wojskowe, but by the end of 1936 they had been relegated to training duties; 20 were sold to the Nationalists early in the Spanish Civil War. Just before the fateful events of September 1939 a small number of Polish Bre.19s took part in exercises to test the control of Warsaw's anti-aircraft defences, but were grounded immediately afterwards and took no part in the operations to fight Germany's invasion.

Greece and Turkey also purchased Bre.19s in the mid-

Yugoslav Kraljevo-built Bre.19 A.2 no. 1330 with 420-hp (313-kW) Gnome-Rhône 9AB radial of the fourth production batch, shown in the markings of the Yugoslav air force in about 1935. The engine, the French version of the Bristol Jupiter, was licence-built at a factory at Rakovica.

Operated by the 51ᵉ Escadre (2ᵉ Escadrille) of France's Aviation Militaire, this Bre.19 A.2 (Armée-biplace) was powered by a Lorraine-Dietrich 12Db 12-cylinder Vee-type engine.

Britain was among the foreign nations to acquire single examples of the Bre.19 for evaluation, this B.2 with a Renault 12Kd engine being registered J7507 and flown by pilots of the Royal Aircraft Establishment during 1925.

1920s. The former took delivery of 30 Bre.19 A.2s and B.2s (bought by popular subscription), powered by 500-hp (363-kW) Hispano-Suiza 12Hb engines, for the 1st Air Regiment newly formed at Tatoi and the 3rd Air Regiment at Salonika-Mikra; and the latter received 20 Lorraine-Dietrich 12Eb-powered Bre.19 B.2s for the 1st Air Regiment.

A number of orders were placed for Bre.19s by South American countries, a sequence initiated by Argentina with an order for 25 Lorraine-Dietrich 12Eb-powered Bre.19 A.2s and B.2s, the first of which were delivered in 1926. In 1930 a dozen of these aircraft, flying from El Palomar, played an active part in the revolution which erupted that year. In 1928 12 Bre.19 A.2s and B.2s constituted the initial combat element of Venezuela's newly-formed Military Aviation Service, and at the same time Brazil bought five Renault 12Kb-powered Bre.19s. Fifteen Bre.19 B.2s purchased by Bolivia in 1928 took part in the war with Paraguay in the following year.

Breguets under licence

As mentioned above, Robert Thiery's demonstration of the Bre.19's superiority at the Cuatro Vientos military aircraft contest in February 1923 led to Spain's decision to acquire licence manufacturing rights, but these could not be implemented until completion of the Construcciones Aeronáuticas SA (CASA) factory south of Madrid in 1924. Three pattern aircraft were delivered, together with components for 26 other aircraft for assembly by CASA; except for one, which was powered by a 500-hp (373-kW) Hispano-Suiza 12b, all were fitted with Lorraine-Dietrich 12Ebs. Simultaneously the latter engine entered licence production in Spain by Elizalde SA as the A-4. Before licence-built Bre.19s could be completed, the campaign in Spanish Morocco forced the Spanish government to import 16 Breguet-built aircraft, and these took part in military operations with the Aeronáutica Militar Espanola in July 1925. In due course the first licence-built order for 77 Bre.19s (50 with imported HS 12Hb and 27 with indigenous A-4 engines) was completed, and was followed by a contract for 80 aircraft in 1929 and one for 20

in 1931, all these aircraft having Hispano-Suiza 12b A-4.

Production of the Bre.19 in Spain ended in 1935, but in the following year the Spanish Civil War broke out, by which time about 135 Bre.19s were serving with the Aviación Militar. Owing to the disposition of the air force (a number of Bre.19s were, for example, serving in North Africa), Bre.19s fought with both Republican and Nationalist forces, but with the arrival of modern aircraft on the scene all were withdrawn from combat status by May 1937. Losses from all causes were said to have been 10 by the Nationalists and 28 by the Republicans. As already mentioned, 20 Bre.19s were also acquired by the Nationalists from Poland.

At about the time that Spain first decided on licence production of the Bre.19, Belgium ordered six Bre.19 B.2s in 1924 as pattern and evaluation aircraft. Evaluation of various alternative engines led to the choice of the Hispano-Suiza 12Ha but in the event, when production was undertaken by Société Anonyme Belge de Constructions Aéronautiques (SABCA) at Haren, aircraft were produced with both this engine and the Lorraine-Dietrich 12Eb. Belgian-built Bre.19s joined the Aéronautique Militaire in 1927, eventually equipping the 1ère Régiment d'Aeronautique and the 2ème Groupe de Bombardement until replaced by the Fairey Fox in the 1930s. Belgian production amounted to 146 Bre.19s.

A number of nations contemplated licence production, and purchased pattern and evaluation aircraft. Japan, where production by Nakajima was suggested, acquired two Bre.19 A.2s for assembly in that country, one being completed as a landplane, the other as a floatplane; licence production was not undertaken, however. Italy purchased one Bre.19 A.2 and one Bre.19 B.2 in 1924, and Persia took two Bre.19 A.2s. The UK obtained an early Bre.19 B.2 in 1925 (with Renault engine), and this was evaluated by the RAE at Farnborough as J7507.

Yugoslavia proved to be the largest foreign customer for the Breguet 19 and, following delivery of the 100 Bre.19 A.2s and Bre.19 B.2s in 1925–6 (already mentioned), a contract was signed on 14 October 1927 for the import and licence construction of a minimum of 425 aircraft. The first order covered 50 completed aircraft delivered by rail from France;

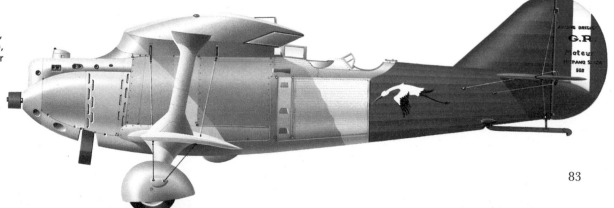

The second Bidon-type Bre.19 GR, powered by a Hispano-Suiza 12Lb, was flown by Commandants Girier and Weiss on 25 May 1929 to establish a world speed record of 116.88 mph (188.1 km/h) over a distance of 3,107 miles (5000 km).

Breguet 19

CASA-built Bre.19s served on both sides during the Spanish Civil War. This Elizalde A-4-powered aircraft was flown by a Nationalist observers' school in about 1938 after the type had been relegated to second-line duties.

an order, signed in December 1928, stipulated 35 completed aircraft delivered by rail, 25 aircraft in parts to be assembled at Kraljevo and 15 to include some Yugoslav-made components; the next order for 75 aircraft and the fourth for 100 aircraft were to be completed by Yugoslav manufacture, the last aircraft being delivered in 1932. The aircraft in the second and third batches were powered by Hispano-Suiza 12Hb or 12Lb engines, but those in the last order had Yugoslav-built Gnome-Rhône Jupiter 9Abs. The fifth batch of Yugoslav Bre.19s comprised 125 Bre.19.7s, a new version whose development is now described.

Some of the spectacular long-distance flights undertaken by modified Bre.19s have already been mentioned, and France's own Aviation Militaire had already flown a number of *grand raids* (long-distance flights), including one by Lieutenants Pelletier d'Oisy and Bésin from Paris to Shanghai in May 1924; on 3–4 February 1925 Capitaines Lemaitre and Arrachart established a new world distance record with a flight of 1,967 miles (3166 km) from Etampes to Villa Cisneros in the Spanish Sahara.

After the famous *'Point d'Interrogation'* only one other Super-Bidon was produced; this was the CASA-built Bre.19 *'Cuatro Vientos'*, which was flown by Barberián and Collar the 4,722 miles (7600 km) from Seville to Camaguey, Cuba, on 10–11 June 1933, but which disappeared on a subsequent flight to Mexico.

Breguet 'fuel cans'

As a result of international interest in these long distance flights, three standard Bre.19s were taken from the production line in 1926 and extensively modified to accommodate 641 Imp gal (2915 litres) of fuel, compared with 97 Imp gal (440 litres) in the standard Bre.19 B.2, and to feature an enlarged upper wing. These three aircraft embarked on a series of extraordinary flights, the first, flown by Capitaine Girier and Lieutenant Dordilly from Villacoublay to Omsk on 14–15 July 1926, raised the record to 2,930 miles (4715.9 km); another, flown by Breguet's chief test pilot Dieudonné Costes together with Capitaine Rignot, increased the record to 3,353 miles (5396 km) on a flight from Le Bourget to Djask on 28–29 October 1926. These achievements were crowned

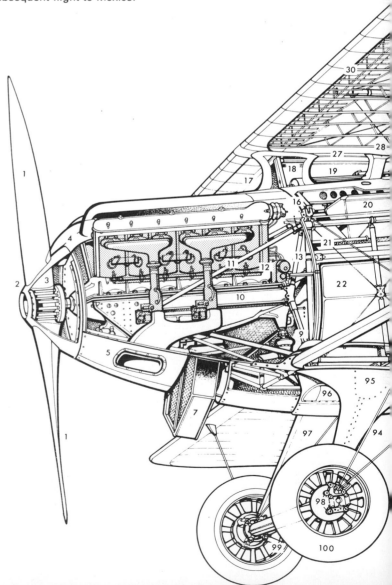

Breguet Bre.19 variants

Bre.19 A.2.01: prototype, originally with Breguet-Bugatti 16-cylinder engine but changed to Renault 12Kb for first flight in March 1922

Bre.19 A.2 and B.2.02 to 012: pre-production, nos 03, 04 and 05 with Renault 12Kb, no. 02 with Lorraine-Dietrich 12D, nos 06, 07, 08, 010 and 012 with Renault 12Kd, no. 09 with Hispano-Suiza 12, and no. 011 with LD 12EB

Bre.19 A.2 and B.2: production by Breguet, Farman and SECM; powered by LD 12Db, LD 12Eb, LD 12Ed, Renault 12Kb, Kd, Ke and Kf, Salmson 18CMa, Gnome-Rhône 9Ac and Farman 12We; 100 to Yugoslavia, 108 to Romania, 4 to China (Central government), 70 to Manchuria, 30 to Greece, 45 to Spain, 20 to Turkey, 250 to Poland, 25 to Argentina, 12 to Venezuela, 15 to Bolivia, five to Brazil, two to Japan (one completed as floatplane), two to Italy, two to Persia and two to UK; remainder (excluding experimental conversions, see below) to Service Aviation

Bre.19 A.2 and B.2: foreign licence production; assembly and production of 300 aircraft at State factory, Kraljevo, Yugoslavia, with Lorraine 12Eb, HS 12Hb or 12Lb engines; 177 by CASA, Spain, with LD 12Eb (and licence A-4) engines; 146 by SABCA of Belgium

Bre.19 Grand Raid: increased fuel capacity in French Bre.19 A.2 (converted)

Bre.19 Bidon type: Bre.19 nos 1685, 1686 and 1687

rebuilt with 641-Imp gal (2915-litre) fuel capacity; no. 1685 (later became *Nungesser-Coli*) powered in turn by HS 12Ha and HS 12Lb; nos 1686 and 1687 powered by Renault 12Kb; also one Belgian aircraft similar to no. 1685, one Greek aircraft with HS 12Hb (named *Hellas*), and two built by CASA in Spain, nos 71 and 72 (the latter named *Jesús del Gran Poder*)

Bre.19 Super Bidon: fuel capacity 1,137 Imp gal (5170 litres); one aircraft built in France (*Point d'Interrogation*) and one by CASA in Spain (*Cuatro Vientos*)

Bre.19.1132: twin-float conversion of Bre.19 no. 1132 in 1926

Bre.19ter: prototype; long-range service derivative of Bidon type; became F-AIXP; HS 12Lb engine

BRE.19.7: 10 rebuilt aircraft similar to Bre.19ter, five to Yugoslavia and five to Romania; 125 newly built in Yugoslavia; HS 12Nb engines

Bre.19.8: prototype; Yugoslav-built aircraft fitted by Breguet with GR 14Kbrs Mistral Major radial, re-engined with GR 14Kdrs; various propellers and cowlings

Bre.19.8: production; 48 Yugoslav-built Bre.19.7s completed with Wright Cyclone GR-1820-F56 radials

Bre.19.9: single Yugoslav prototype (converted Bre.19.7) with 860-hp (642-kW) Hispano-Suiza 12Ybrs

Bre.19.10: single Yugoslav prototype (converted Bre.19.7) with 720-hp (537-kW) Lorraine 12Hfrs Petrel

Breguet Bre.19 B.2 Type 1926 cutaway drawing key

1 Two-bladed fixed-pitch wooden propeller
2 Spinner
3 Propeller boss
4 Exhaust manifold (to starboard)
5 Carburettor intake
6 Port carburettors
7 Radiator
8 Engine support lower bearer
9 Water pump
10 Engine main support member
11 Upper engine bearer
12 Port magneto
13 Forward fuselage frame
14 Renault 12Kd 12-cylinder 60° Vee water-cooled engine

19 Synchronized 7.7-mm Vickers machine gun (offset to starboard)
20 Oil tank (11 Imp gal/50 litre capacity)
21 Forward fuel tank (70 Imp gal/320 litre capacity) to starboard (obscured by port tank/bomb magazine)
22 Optional 88 Imp gal (400 litre) long-range tank (replacing Type D magazine for 32 22-lb (10-kg) or eight 110-lb (50-kg) vertically-disposed bombs)
23 Diagonal bracing wires
24 Lower mainplane bracing wire

30 Leading-edge stiffeners
31 Diagonal bracing wires
32 Aileron control conduit
33 Wing ribs
34 Mainplane forward spar
35 Interplane strut upper attachments
36 Mainplane rear spar
37 Wing fabric
38 Aileron outer hinge
39 Aileron control hinge
40 Port aileron
41 Aileron inner hinge

51 Control linkage
52 Pilot's seat
53 Seat support frame
54 STIAé bomb sight (external starboard)
55 Handhold
56 F120 vertical camera installation
57 Underwing bomb release switches (starboard side)
58 Fuselage Type D (forward) and Type F (rear) bomb release switches (portside)

73 Fin navigational light
74 Rudder upper hinge
75 Rudder frame
76 Port tailplane upper bracing
77 Port elevator
78 Elevator torque tube
79 Port tailplane lower bracing
80 Rudder post and hinge
81 Tailskid
82 Tailskid attachment
83 Fuselage fabric
84 Aft-firing 7.7-mm Lewis machine gun

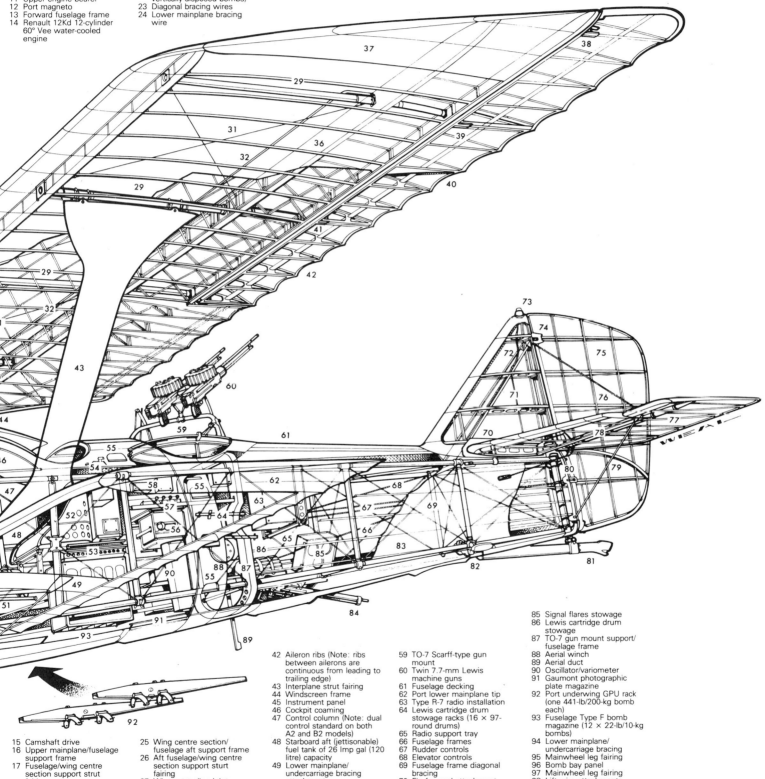

15 Camshaft drive
16 Upper mainplane/fuselage support frame
17 Fuselage/wing centre section support strut
18 Centre section forward support strut

25 Wing centre section/fuselage aft support frame
26 Aft fuselage/wing centre section support sturt fairing
27 Wing centreline joint
28 Aileron control linkage
29 Interspar bracing tubes

42 Aileron ribs (Note: ribs between ailerons are continuous from leading to trailing edge)
43 Interplane strut fairing
44 Windscreen frame
45 Instrument panel
46 Cockpit coaming
47 Control column (Note: dual control standard on both A2 and B2 models)
48 Starboard aft (jettisonable) fuel tank of 26 Imp gal (120 litre) capacity
49 Lower mainplane/undercarriage bracing attachment
50 Underwing bomb rack attachments

59 TO-7 Scarff-type gun mount
60 Twin 7.7-mm Lewis machine guns
61 Fuselage decking
62 Port lower mainplane tip
63 Type R-7 radio installation
64 Lewis cartridge drum stowage racks (16 × 97-round drums)
65 Radio support tray
66 Fuselage frames
67 Rudder controls
68 Elevator controls
69 Fuselage frame diagonal bracing
70 Fin forward attachment
71 Fin structure
72 Electrical lead

85 Signal flares stowage
86 Lewis cartridge drum stowage
87 TO-7 gun mount support/fuselage frame
88 Aerial winch
89 Aerial duct
90 Oscillator/variometer
91 Gaumont photographic plate magazine
92 Port underwing GPU rack (one 441-lb/200-kg bomb each)
93 Fuselage Type F bomb magazine (12 × 22-lb/10-kg bombs)
94 Lower mainplane/undercarriage bracing
95 Mainwheel leg fairing
96 Bomb bay panel
97 Mainwheel leg fairing
98 Lift wire attachments
99 Cross-axle fairing
100 Port mainwheel

Breguet 19

Not surprisingly the Axis powers were glad to throw any available aircraft into the fight against the numerous partisans who were active in Yugoslavia during the war. This Wright Cyclone-powered Kraljevo-built Bre.19.8 served with the Croatian air force in about 1943.

when Dieudonné Costes and Lieutenant de Vaisseau le Brix made their famous 35,420-mile (57000-km) round-the-world flight in 350 flying hours in *Nungesser-Coli* (inevitably dubbed the Bidon, or Fuel Can) between 10 October 1927 and 14 April 1928; the flight also included the first flight across the South Atlantic.

Further Bidons [and Super-Bidons with 1,137 Imp gal (5170 litres of fuel)] appeared; the most famous was *Point d'Interrogation* (Question Mark), sponsored by the perfume company Coty; flown by Dieudonné Costes and Maurice Bellonte and powered by an Hispano-Suiza 12Lb, this aircraft was flown from Le Bourget to Tsitsihkar in Manchuria between 27 and 29 September 1929, a new world distance record of 4,912 miles (7905 km). The aircraft had a theoretical range of 5,405 miles (8700 km) and the margin was to allow for unforecast headwinds.

Bre.19.7 was the name given to an aerodynamically improved version with an Hispano-Suiza 12Nb engine. These engines were produced in Kraljevo, Yugoslavia. The aircraft illustrated here was used in Turkey.

Night fighters

Bidon-type Bre.19s (termed Bre.19.7s) were acquired by Belgium (where the nickname originated), Turkey, Romania and Greece (as well as Yugoslavia, already mentioned) while in France the standard Bre.19 was being introduced as a night-fighter, equipping the 21e, 22e, 23e and 24e Escadrilles de Chasse de Nuit between 1931 and 1935. Peak inventory of Bre.19s reached 702 in July 1931, including 34 deployed in North Africa. Thereafter the total declined, until the last examples (the night-fighter models) were phased out of

This Kraljevo-built Bre.19.7, F-ALPN, was modified at Vélizy-Villacoublay by installation of a Gnome-Rhône Mistral Major but, although it established a number of records, neither it nor the engine found favour with the Yugoslavs.

operational front-line service during the spring of 1935.

Production by the parent company ended in 1932, but Breguet re-engined a Yugoslav-built Bre.19.7 with a 690-hp (515-kW) Gnome-Rhône 14Kbrs Mistral Major, this aircraft being redesignated the Bre.19.8; it was evaluated but discarded by the Yugoslav *opitna grupa* (test squadron) and attention switched to the Wright Cyclone GR-820-F56, of which an installation was undertaken at Kraljevo, retaining the Bre.19.8 designation. (An experimental version, the Bre.19.10 with 720-hp/537-kW Lorraine 12Hfrs Petrel, was also produced in prototype form.) In all, 55 Cyclone-powered Bre.19.8s were built at Kraljevo between December 1936 and November 1937. As late as 1936 Bre.19s equipped all six of Yugoslavia's air regiments.

Breuguets fly for Croatia

In the period from 1938 to 1940 most of the Yugoslavian Bre.19 bombers were used only for training purposes, 103 reconnaissance aircraft with Jupiter engines being taken out of service in 1939. But when Germany attacked Yugoslavia on 6 April 1941, more than a hundred Bre.19s were still in use in 14 Army Co-operation Squadrons. Apart from an attack on a bridge over the river Vardar, however, most of these machines stayed on the ground and were destroyed where they lay. Thirty of them fell into the hands of the German forces, and six were taken over by the Italians to equip the new Croatian Air Force. This unit was stationed in Mostar, Sarajevo and Zagreb to be used in attacks on partisans. One Br.19 pilot defected to the partisans with his aircraft, and another was used by Major Arkadije Popov in October 1943 to cross the Adriatic and join the Allies, who were fighting in Italy. The Yugoslavian liberation army discovered the last two Bre.19s in April 1945 at Sarajevo Airfield, but even these two were scrapped a year later.

Dornier Flying-boats

In April 1983 Dornier flew the Do 24TT, a big turboprop amphibian derived from the pre-war Do 24. No company is better fitted to test the market for marine aircraft than this famous German firm, with a heritage of all-metal flying-boats no other company can match.

Professor Dr Claude Dornier was probably the best builder of flying boats anywhere in the world in the years before 1930, as well as being one of the great exponents of the modern all-metal aircraft. His very first design, the RS I in 1915, was not only made almost entirely of steel and aluminium alloys, but was also the largest aircraft in existence, with a wingspan of 142 ft 8 in (43.5 m). This was the first in the RS series (RS stood for *Riesenflugzeug See*, or Extra Large Seaplane) which was used after the war ended in 1918.

As well as the RS series Dornier's company, Zeppelin-Werke Lindau GmbH, had almost completed the prototype of a smaller but still very capable flying-boat, the Gs I. Powered by two 270-hp (201-kW) Maybach Mb.IV water-cooled engines arranged in tandem at the centre of a rectangular monoplane wing, the Gs I had a slim and very efficient hull, stabilizing sponsons of the kind favoured by Dornier, and a twin-finned biplane tail. The four-seat enclosed cockpit in the bows gave an appearance like the head of a serpent, but as a tough transport flying-boat it had no equal when it flew on 31 July 1919. It was later flown from Lindau to the Netherlands, but the fact remained that the machine contravened the rules imposed by the Allies and the Allied Control Commission had it sunk off Kiel on 25 April 1920.

Dornier went ahead with small aircraft, such as the Delfin, Libelle and Komet, but he never gave up his work on big and powerful flying-boats. His wartime design for the Gs II, rather larger than the Gs I with 1,033.4 sq ft (96 m²) of wing instead of 861.1 sq ft (80 m²), and a laden weight raised from 9,513 lb (4315 kg) to 12,566 lb (5700 kg) appeared to be just what the infant airlines and air forces needed. Under the noses of the hated Control Commission, Dornier set up an Italian subsidiary, Societá di Costruzioni Meccaniche di Pisa, at Marina di Pisa. He carried on designing at Lindau, the works there being renamed Dornier Metallbauen GmbH in 1922, and licensed the big Gs II machines to the Italian subsidiary, even buying two 300-hp (224-kW) Hispano-Suiza engines from Paris for the prototype of the improved Gs II. Dornier redesignated it as the Type J, and named it Wal (whale). The prototype flew on 6 November 1922.

Dornier was correct in his assessment of the market. The Wal was ideally suited to both commercial and military operations for the next 15 years, having very satisfactory performance and payload, a robust all-metal structure and

This Wal was one of the later examples of the 17,637-lb (8000-kg) gross weight civil family, in this case with BMW VI engines. These later variants had the same 1,033-sq ft (96-m²) wing area, but rounded tips and span increased from 74 ft (22.5 m) to 76 ft (23.2 m). D-2069 *Monsun* (monsoon) served with Deutsche Lufthansa. Note the giant D/F loop aerial.

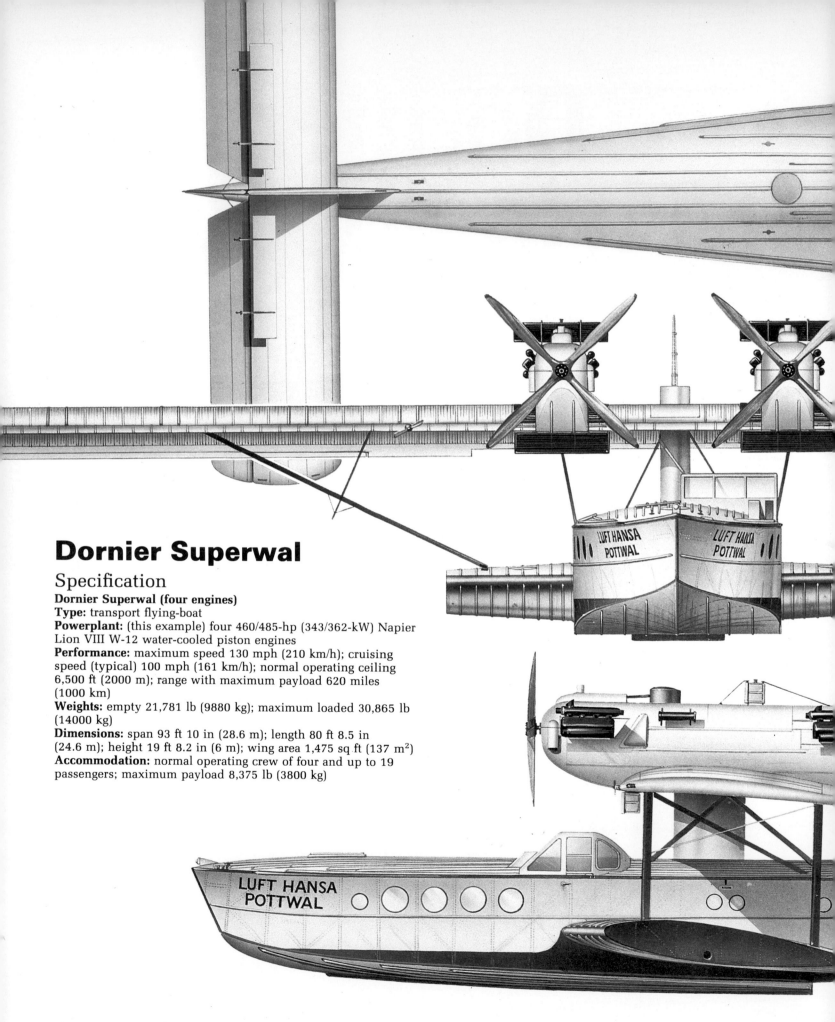

Dornier Superwal

Specification

Dornier Superwal (four engines)
Type: transport flying-boat
Powerplant: (this example) four 460/485-hp (343/362-kW) Napier Lion VIII W-12 water-cooled piston engines
Performance: maximum speed 130 mph (210 km/h); cruising speed (typical) 100 mph (161 km/h); normal operating ceiling 6,500 ft (2000 m); range with maximum payload 620 miles (1000 km)
Weights: empty 21,781 lb (9880 kg); maximum loaded 30,865 lb (14000 kg)
Dimensions: span 93 ft 10 in (28.6 m); length 80 ft 8.5 in (24.6 m); height 19 ft 8.2 in (6 m); wing area 1,475 sq ft (137 m²)
Accommodation: normal operating crew of four and up to 19 passengers; maximum payload 8,375 lb (3800 kg)

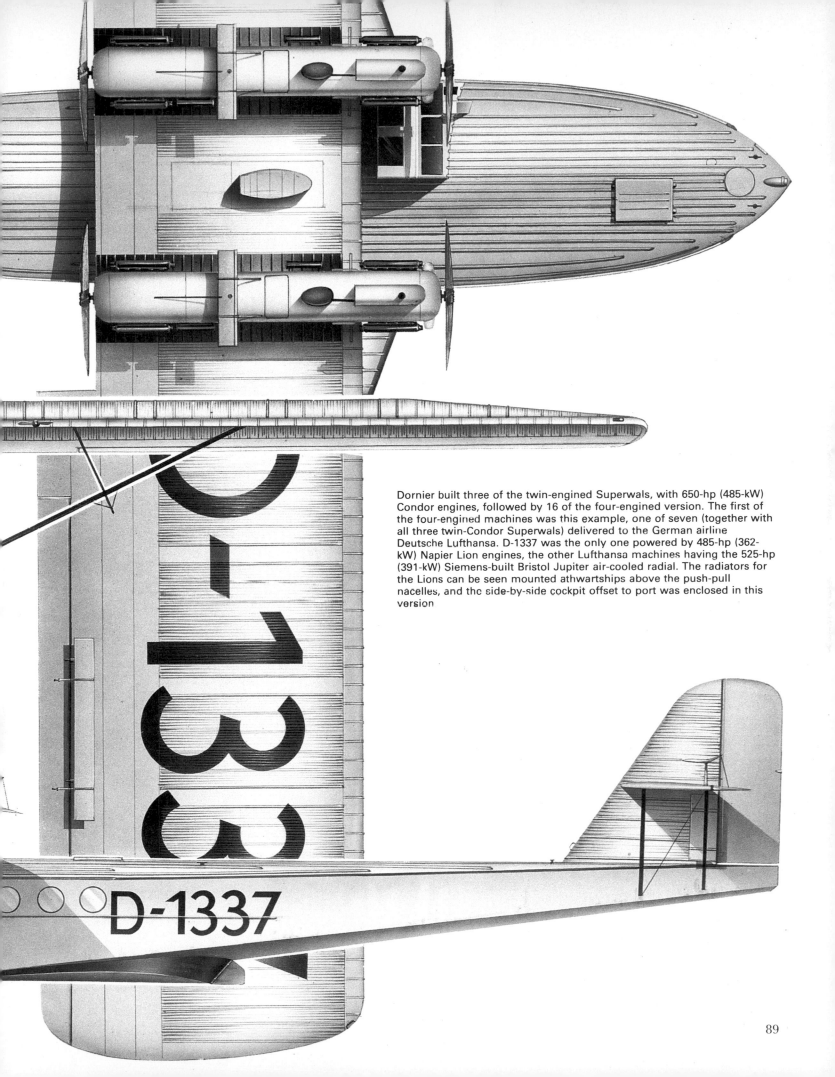

Dornier built three of the twin-engined Superwals, with 650-hp (485-kW) Condor engines, followed by 16 of the four-engined version. The first of the four-engined machines was this example, one of seven (together with all three twin-Condor Superwals) delivered to the German airline Deutsche Lufthansa. D-1337 was the only one powered by 485-hp (362-kW) Napier Lion engines, the other Lufthansa machines having the 525-hp (391-kW) Siemens-built Bristol Jupiter air-cooled radial. The radiators for the Lions can be seen mounted athwartships above the push-pull nacelles, and the side-by-side cockpit offset to port was enclosed in this version

Dornier Flying-boats

This regular Military Wal was one of a substantial number operated by the Spanish navy. Many earlier Spanish Wals had been built by CMASA, but the example shown was a Dornier-built Do J IId, with BMW VI engines. It is shown during the Civil War while serving with I-G 70 Grupo at Puerto de Pollensa, in Majorca.

The Luftwaffe Do 18D reached the peak of its brief career in 1939–40, when the type equipped four *Staffeln* (squadrons) of the *Küstenfliegergruppen* (coastal groups). This example served at Kamp, on the Pomeranian coast, with 2/KüFlGr 906. By 1941 the Do 18Ds were being converted as Do 18H crew trainers, the more powerful Do 18Gs then becoming Do 18Ns.

The 22,046-lb (10000-kg) gross weight Wal was the last and largest version, dating from 1933. Span was increased to 89 ft 2.9 in (27.2 m) and wing area to 1,206 sq ft (112 m²). This example was one of those that made 328 scheduled crossings of the South Atlantic, operating from the ships *Westfalen* and *Schwabenland*. Note the length of the hydraulic catapult.

of the hull from which bombs and other stores could be hung, and there were various schemes for defensive guns.

Of course, with the benefit of hindsight the Wal can be criticized. Tandem engines are inefficient, can lead to cooling problems and can cause severe stresses in the rear propeller. The Wal's very broad wingtips were aerodynamically poor, and the high induced drag inevitably reduced the attainable range. The large 'park bench' balancing surfaces attached to the ailerons were a scheme outmoded by 1930, and the open cockpit of most Wals would have been disliked by the softer pilots of later times. But in overall terms no other marine aircraft came near it. Altogether at least 300 and possibly more than 320 Wals were built, including between 157 and 177 in Italy (156 by SCMP and its successor CMASA of 1929, a Fiat subsidiary), at least 56 by Dornier at Friedrichshafen from 1932, 40 by CASA in Spain, about 40 by Aviolanda in the Netherlands and three by

excellent reliability. Airline Wals set new standards in interior appointments, and with glass portholes resembled staterooms in luxury yachts. The many military versions were fitted with four small stub wings along the upper part

One of the three Wals built under licence by Kawasaki. Dornier Wals were also built under licence in Italy, Spain and Holland with the result that the variations of this model were in many ways very different from one another.

Kawasaki in Japan. It is doubtful if any aircraft has left the original factory in so many different variations. There were four major and nine minor variations in span, six quite different designs of nose and cockpit, eight different designs of tail, at least 17 different basic types of engine, and a host of gross weights from 8,818 lb (4000 kg) to more than 22,046 lb (10000 kg).

Though some early customers continued to specify the Hispano, many of the pre-1925 Wals were powered by the 360-hp (268-kW) Rolls-Royce Eagle IX, and this rather outdated V-12 was fitted to a Wal that set 20 world records for speed/height/range with payloads up to 4,409 lb (2000 kg) on 4, 9, 10 and 11 February 1925. Other Wals, with three different types of engine, made crossings of the North and South Atlantic, flew from Europe to near the North Pole and to various places in the Far East, and also flew round the world. Airline Wals often had an enclosed cockpit (always from 1931) and began as six- to nine-seaters, with space for loose cargo. In 1931 Dornier began production of the '8-tonne Wal' first flown the previous year with 690-hp (515-kW) BMW VI engines and a 1,033.4-sq ft (96-m²) wing. This became the standard model, though again with many variations, and it led to the 8.5-tonner in 1933, and the corresponding Militär-Wal 33 which was produced for the Luftwaffe as the Do 15. In the same year appeared the biggest version, the 10-tonne Wal, with 1,205.6 sq ft (112 m²) of wing, which was operated by Deutsche Lufthansa from the

The original Do X 12-engined monster is seen here after its refit with Curtiss Conqueror water-cooled engines. It is shown after its long trip to the Americas in brief service with Lufthansa. It then went to the DVL research organization before becoming the biggest exhibit in the Berlin air museum, where it was destroyed by bombs.

depot ships *Westfalen* and *Schwabenland* and made 328 crossings of the South Atlantic in regular mail service. Among export customers were Argentina, Chile, Colombia, Italy, Japan, the Netherlands, Portugal, the Soviet Union, Spain, the UK and Yugoslavia.

Different enough to have a different name, Superwal, the Type R enlarged version first flew on 30 September 1926. This was constructed at another Dornier factory, at Manzell on the Swiss shore of the Bodensee (Lake Constance). The prototype of this much bigger boat had two Rolls-Royce Condors of 650 hp (485 kW) each, and another had two 800-hp (597-kW) Packard A-2500s, but most other Superwals had two push/pull pairs, the most common engines being the Siemens-built Bristol Jupiter, Pratt & Whitney Hornet, and, for the CASA-built military Superwals, the 500-hp (373-kW) Hispano-Suiza.

Model X monster

Just as the RS I had been the biggest aeroplane of its day, so did Dornier's liking for size manifest itself in an extreme

D-AEAV was one of a small batch of Fokker-built Do 24T-1 flying-boats completed as unarmed civil aeromedical transports operated by the *Reichsluftdienst* (air service). They operated mainly within and around Germany in 1941–4, carrying seven stretchers or a larger number of sitting patients or war casualties.

This Do 24T-2 was one of the later (1943) production series from the Dutch assembly line, the main external difference being the tall HDL 151 dorsal turret fitted with a Mauser MG 151/20 cannon instead of the French HS 404 cannon of the Do 24T-1. This boat served with 7 *Seenotstaffel* SBK XI in the Aegean Sea, chiefly on rescue duties.

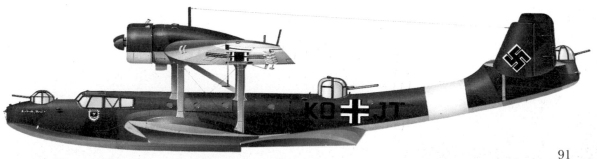

form in 1926 when work began at Manzell on the Model X. This monster flyingboat was the ultimate scaled-up Wal, with no fewer than six push/pull pairs of engines, still the largest number ever used to propel a single aircraft. The Do X first flew in the hands of Richard Wagner on 12 (often reported as 25) July 1929, powered by Siemens Jupiters. Planned as a long-range passenger machine with 66 to 72 seats, it took off on 31 October 1929 with 10 crew, 150 passengers and nine stowaways, a total not exceeded for 20 years. On 4 August 1930 the Do X emerged after a rebuild with water-cooled Curtiss Conqueror engines with plain struts instead of auxiliary wings between the nacelles, the US engines giving extra power (640 instead of 525 hp/477 instead of 391 kW) and avoiding customs problems on a visit to the USA in 1930–1. The Italian air force used two of these monsters with 580-hp (433-kW) Fiat A 22R engines.

On 26 September 1939 a Blackburn Skua flown by Lieutenant B. S. McEwan scrambled from HMS *Ark Royal* and shot down a shadowing Do 18D, the first aircraft shot down by British forces in World War 2. The Do 18 was the natural successor to the Wal, designed in early 1934 to meet both a requirement for an updated Militär-Wal and a more modern South Atlantic boat for Lufthansa. The prototype Do 18a flew on 15 March 1935, powered by tandem 540-hp (403-kW) Junkers Jumo 5 diesel engines giving great range and endurance. Similar to the 8-tonne Wal in size and weight, the Do 18 was naturally much improved aerodynamically, with a tapered wing with rounded tips and 'double wing' flaps and ailerons, a central wing pylon incorporating the cooling radiators, and a well-streamlined hull of graceful form. Small numbers of several versions were produced for civil applications, and in summer 1936 deliveries began from the Weser company of the military Do 18D series, most of which had 600-hp (447-kW) Jumo 205C diesels and were used for armed reconnaissance with coastal units. Delay in development of the Blohm und Voss Bv 138 led to continued

D-ABYM *Aeolus* was the Do 18 V3 (third prototype). Powered by tandem 600-hp (447-kW) Jumo 205C diesel engines, all three were later designated as Do 18E transports and used from 1936 on Lufthansa's routes on the North, and later South, Atlantic. Just before joining the airline, on 10–11 July 1936, *Aeolus* made a 30-hour 21-minute test flight over the Baltic.

Dornier Do 24T cutaway drawing key

1 Bow navigation light
2 Towing/mooring ring
3 Fore hull structure
4 Retractable mast
5 Ammunition magazine racks
6 Spent cartridge chute
7 Bow compartment (see equipment stowage)
8 Turret mechanism
9 Bow 7.92-mm MG 15 machine-gun
10 Bow turret
11 Removable turret dome
12 Nose decking
13 Nose mooring lug
14 Mooring rope stowage
15 Bulkhead
16 Crawlway
17 Rudder pedal assembly
18 Bulkhead door frame
19 Instrument panel shroud
20 Co-pilot's control column
21 Compass
22 Windscreen panels
23 Cockpit roof glazing
24 Sliding entry panels
25 Hatch runners
26 Flight deck windows
27 Navigator's station
28 Co-pilot seat
29 Pilot's seat
30 Seat adjustment lever
31 Side-mounted control column
32 Floors support frame
33 Radio-operator's position
34 'Vee' bottom hull structure
35 Fuselage/sponson fairing
36 Access panels
37 Sponson nose ribs
38 Sponson main fuel cells (four, approx 77 Imp gal/ 350 litre capacity each)
39 Sponson abbreviated fuel cell (36.6 Imp gal/180 litre capacity)
40 Port sponson mooring lug
41 Rib reinforcement
42 Sponson main spar/ fuselage frame
43 Sponson/forward wing strut lower attachment
44 Fuel collector tank (46 Imp gal/210 litres)
45 Access panels
46 Fuselage hull step
47 Sponson rear spar/ fuselage frame
48 Sponson/aft wing strut lower attachment
49 Mooring lug
50 Non-slip sponson walkway
51 Forward midships bay (two-stretcher accommodation; 28 oxygen bottles stowed along centre-line walkway)
52 Forward bay hinged entry hatch
53 Sponson/forward wing strut
54 Fuselage main frame bulkhead

Dornier Wal variants

Gs I: wartime flying-boat design, first flown in 1919 and sunk by Allied authorities

Wal: initial military version of 1922 built by Marina di Pisa and licensees; Rolls-Royce Eagle, Hispano, Lorraine, Napier, Bristol, Packard, Liberty, Wright, BMW, Junkers, Piaggio and other makes of engine; 1,033.4-sq ft (96-m²) wing, gross weight 5.7 tonnes

Wal Type J: initial commercial model from early 1923, generally as for military, a few with enclosed cockpit

8.0-to Wal: strengthened and more powerful 1931 model, usually with 690-hp (515-kW) BMW VI engines, still 1,033.4 sq ft (96 m²) but span increased from 73 ft 9.8 in to 76 ft 1.4 in (22.5 to 23.2 m); passenger seating increased from nine to 14

8.5-to Wal: further uprated version generally as 8.0-to but cleared to 18,739 lb (8500 kg) in 1933

10-to Wal: further enlarged 1933 model with span of 89 ft 2.9 in (27.2 m), 1,205.6-sq ft (112-m²) wing area, usually 690-hp (515-kW) BMW VI engines

Do-15: Luftwaffe designation for uprated military version of 1933; 18,739-lb (8500-kg) weight, 1,033.4-sq ft (96-m²) wing, usually BMW VI engines in German service

Superwal/2m: various twin-engine Type R Superwals usually with two 650-hp (485-kW) Condor or 800-hp (597-kW) Packard engines, 93 ft 10 in (28.6 m) span, 1,539.3-sq ft (143-m²) wing, 19 passenger seats, gross weight 10.5 tonnes

Superwal/4m: four-engine Superwal series, with 480-hp (358-kW) Jupiter VI, 525-hp (391-kW) Siemens Jupiter, 550-hp (410-kW) Hornet or 460-hp (343-kW) Napier Lion; same span but wing reduced to 1,474.7 sq ft (137 m²) area and gross weight increased to 14 tonnes

A49-4 was the fourth of five of the oldest Do 24K-1s flown from the Dutch East Indies to Australia on 19 February 1942. Many later escapees reached Broome, Northern Territory, a fortnight later, only to be destroyed there by Japanese fighters. A49-4 served with RAAF No. 41 Sqn on transport duties to the New Guinea theatre.

production of the Do 18 into World War 2 the total of all versions being in the region of 160 including 75 Do 18Ds. The main wartime version was the Do 18G and the unarmed Do 18H crew trainer, both powered by the 880-hp (656-kW) Jumo 205D. By 1941 most surviving Do 18s of all types were converted as Do 18N air/sea rescue aircraft.

The last aircraft that can be said to have descended from the Wal was the Do 24, a considerably larger boat that at last abandoned tandem engines, though it adhered to the use of sponsons for stability on the water. It had its origins in the requirement of the MLD, the Dutch naval air force, for a successor to its mainstay, the trusty Wal. In 1934 the MLD

55 Medical attendant: station
56 Fuselage/wing strut attachment fairing
57 Port engine nacelle intake
58 Fuselage porthole
59 Starboard crew entry door
60 Bulkhead
61 Radio equipment installation
62 Roof external strakes
63 Three-blade VDM metal propellers
64 Spinners
65 Starboard sponson
66 Roof (starboard) entry hatch
67 Centre engine nacelle intake
68 Engine exhausts
69 Engine upper air intakes
70 1,000-hp (746-kW) Bramo 323R-2 radial engine
71 Cowling ring
72 Hinged engine inspection/ maintenance panels

73 Cooling louvre
74 Oil tank cover
75 Servicing handgrip
76 Engine bearers
77 Firewall/bulkhead
78 Centre engine oil tank
79 Centre nacelle frames
80 Centre nacelle pick-up/ hoist bar
81 Starboard wing fuel tank
82 Starboard engine nacelle fairing
83 Starboard aerial mast
84 Wing front spar
85 Aerial
86 Wing ribs
87 Wing metal skinning
88 Starboard navigation light
89 Starboard formation/ identification light
90 Starboard aileron

91 Aileron hinge fairings
92 Wing rear spar
93 Aileron control runs
94 Aileron trim tab
95 Wing centre/outer-section join
96 Aileron inboard profile
97 Centre-section underwing flap
98 Flap actuating hinges
99 Antenna
100 D/F loop
101 Rear spar structure
102 Wing rib/flap cut-out
103 Flap control runs
104 Port engine nacelle fairing
105 Port wing fuel tank
106 Port aerial mast

113 Sponson/forward wing strut upper attachment
114 Twin landing lights
115 Sponson/wing strut diagonal bracing
116 Fuselage/wing aft inverted 'Vee' struts (housing fuel lines from sponsons)

133 Wing rear spar
134 Port navigation light
135 Port formation/ identification light
136 Port aileron
137 Hull aft step

160 Tailplane rear spar/tailfin attachment
161 Starboard tailfin structure
162 Aerial attachment
163 Rudder balance
164 Rudder frame
165 Rudder upper trim tab
166 Starboard rudder post
167 Rudder lower trim tab
168 Trim tab actuating linkage
169 Starboard elevator tab
170 Port rudder balance
171 Starboard elevator structure
172 Elevator control linkage

107 Oil tank cover
108 Front spar
109 Hinged leading-edge (inspection/servicing access)
110 Fuselage/wing centre-line diagonal brace strut
111 Fuselage/wing forward inverted 'Vee' struts (housing control runs)
112 Wing centre/outer section front spar join

117 Wing centre/outer section join rib
118 Sponson/aft wing strut upper attachment
119 Midships dorsal decking
120 Sponson/aft wing strut
121 Fuselage air ventilation plant
122 Fuselage main frame bulkhead
123 Centre-line walkway
124 Aft bay hinged entry hatch
125 Aft midships bay (four × stretcher accommodation)
126 Hull 'Vee' bottom structure
127 Galley/hot plate (port)
128 Blanket/survival clothing cupboard (starboard)
129 Fuselage midships mooring lug
130 Aileron hinge fairings
131 Bulkhead door
132 Aileron underwing mass balances

138 'Vee' bottom sternpost frame
139 Reinforced fuselage frame
140 Turret support
141 Compressed air bottles
142 Turret ring
143 Dorsal turret
144 20-mm MG 151 cannon
145 Toilet
146 Peat bag (toilet sanitary refill)
147 Porthole
148 Master compass
149 Aft fuselage centre-line catwalk
150 Tail surface control rod linkage
151 Fuselage aft frames
152 Fuselage skinning
153 Ventral stringers
154 Control rods
155 Fuselage/tailplane fairing
156 Tailplane front spar
157 Elevator control rod
158 Elevator hinges
159 Tailplane ribs

173 Rudder linkage
174 Port aerial attachment
175 Tailplane inboard end rib structure
176 Tailplane front spar/ fuselage frame attachment
177 Fuselage aft main frame
178 Control linkage
179 Stern mooring rope stowage
180 Tailplane brace struts
181 Port tailfin
182 Tailplane/fin attachment
183 Port elevator hinge
184 Rear turret ammunition stowage
185 Port rudder post
186 Rear turret
187 Turret ring
188 Tail gunner's armour plating
189 Port rudder
190 Rudder lower trim tab hinge fairing
191 Port rudder lower trim tab
192 Tail navigation light
193 Tail mooring ring
194 7.92-mm MG 15 stern machine-gun

Dornier Flying-boats

The last military flying-boats in service in Europe, the Spanish Ejercito del Aire's Do 24T-2s survived on coastal patrol and rescue duties from Puerto de Pollensa until 1970, serving with the 58th Escuadrilla de Salvamento. Their superb rough-water seaworthiness has never been equalled by any other aircraft of any size.

refined its ideas and opened talks with Dornier, soon deciding that the Do 18 was not quite big enough. The MLD wanted not only long range and more than two engines but also the ability to operate safely at great distances from land and, if necessary, alight on quite rough seas. During 1935 Dornier went ahead with the design of the three-engine Do 24 purely for the MLD, charging the Dutch government a fee for the design process as well as selling a licence to Aviolanda, which had finished building Wals in 1931. Four prototypes were put in hand, the Do 24 V3 being the first to fly and being powered, like the Do 24 V4, with the engine specified by the customer for commonality with its Martin 139WH-1 bombers, the Wright Cyclone F52. Dornier fitted the first two prototypes with the heavier and less powerful Jumo 205 diesel for possible use by the Luftwaffe, but not much was done with them before the war.

Successful trials

A wholly modern stressed-skin boat, the Do 24 hung its shapely hull under the rectangular centre section on two pairs of inverted-V struts, with a fifth diagonal strut to react to the pull of the engines (in contrast to the big streamlined pylon of the Do 18). The tail had twin fins on the ends of the wide-span tailplane, and there was provision for a gun turret in the bow, amidships and at the extreme tail. The MLD also specified wing bomb racks for up to 12 stores of 220 lb (100 kg) each, and a heavy load of mission equipment. Flight trials, including operations from very heavy seas, showed that the Do 24 possessed exceptional strength and good performance. In autumn 1937 the MLD signed for 60, to be licence-built in the Netherlands, but in the event Dornier built 12 (including the Do 24 V3 and V4 prototypes), with the designation Do 24K-1, using the 875-hp (652-kW) F52 engine, while Aviolanda, De Schelde and other Dutch companies undertook to build the other 48, designated Do 24K-2, powered by the 1,000-hp (746-kW) Cyclone G102.

Continuing the story of the Do 24 into the 1980s, this ex-Do 24T-2 has acquired a new wing and triple turboprop powerplants while retaining the original hull and tail units. Currently undergoing flight testing and research into composite materials and corrosion problems, a commercial future for the Do 24TT remains to be realized.

This Do 24MS minesweeper was one of a small number (possibly only two) converted for the task from regular Luftwaffe Do 24T-1 rescue/reconnaissance machines. An auxiliary motor/generator set in the hull fed the heavy current pulses through the duralumin ring conductor; the magnetic field exploded mines below the aircraft.

All the Do 24K-1s had been delivered by the outbreak of war, but when Germany invaded the Netherlands on 10 May 1940 only 25 of the Do 24K-2s had been despatched. Three were captured intact, and when these were tested at Travemünde the Luftwaffe discovered they were superb boats, and Dutch production was quickly restarted. Under the control of the Weser company the Do 24K-2s were modified without bomb gear but with MG15 nose and tail guns and captured Hispano 20-mm cannon in the amidships turret, as well as large hatches and comprehensive internal furnishings for the air/sea rescue mission. Designated Do 24N-1, the production boats entered Luftwaffe service from August 1941, 11 being delivered by November when the stock of engines was exhausted. Production then continued with the Do 24T-1 with the 1,000-hp (746-kW) BMW Bramo Fafnir 323, a total of 170 in all being supplied. Such was the demand for this fine boat that a second source was organized at the former Potez-CAMS factory at Sartrouville, France, where 48 additional Do 24s were built.

From early 1943 most were of the Do 24T-2 sub-type with extra radio and sometimes radar, as well as an MG 151 replacing the Hispano cannon amidships. Very similar boats designated Do 24T-3 were prepared for Spain, 12 being flown to the Spanish seaplane base at Puerto Pollensa, Majorca, in 1944.

Every Do 24 was heavily involved in the events of the war. The MLD boats in the Dutch East Indies had almost all been destroyed by the end of March 1942. Towards the end of the war, the Luftwaffe's losses of flying boats were very high, but the Spanish Do 24T-3s were still in use long after the war. As late as 1972, holidaymakers in Majorca were able to see a number of Do 24T-3s. The last of these was flown to the Dornier factory in Friedrichshafen to be preserved for posterity. A number of squadrons of the French Aéronavale were using about 40 Do 24T-2s between them, and one machine which a Luftwaffe flight engineer flew to Sweden in 1945 was used by the Flygvapen as a Tp 24 for a total of seven years.

Curtiss Hawk Biplanes

Dependence upon licence production of British aircraft at the end of World War 1 deprived the USA of design experience with which to maintain a flow of indigenous designs during the post-war period. Instead, a host of small companies scrambled for attention; the best-known results were the Curtiss Hawk fighters, manufactured by a company run by a famous American. Glenn Curtiss, a noted flier in his own right, produced the Curtiss Hawk over a period of 10 years, though fewer than 250 were built.

One of the USA's most famous pioneers of flight, Glenn Curtiss, was also one of the country's first aircraft manufacturers. He mass-produced planes based on wholly American designs, although later on the Curtiss JN ('Jenny') trainer was built mainly from designs by B. Douglas Thomas, who was working for Sopwith in England at the time. Towards the end of World War 1, trainers were the only planes designed in America and mass-produced for the US Army.

However, one of the best-known foreign combat aircraft, selected by the Bolling Commission for US production, was the Royal Aircraft Factory S.E.5a, and although the planned mass production of this excellent fighter by Curtiss never materialized the company gained important experience in the field when ordered to modify and assemble 57 British-manufactured examples. In the meantime the company also embarked on a series of racing aircraft in which military pilots were to compete in the prestigious Pulitzer contest of 1922, and the two Curtiss R-6s (68563 and 68564) were flown into first and second place by Lieutenants Russell Maughan and Lester J. Maitland; shortly after the race Brigadier General Billy Mitchell raised the world speed record over 0.62 mile (1 km) to 222.97 mph (358.84 km/h) while flying one of the racers.

The success of the R-6 encouraged the Curtiss company to enter the field of interceptor fighters (known in those days as pursuit aircraft), and before the end of 1922 a prototype was under construction at private expense. However, whereas the R-6 biplanes had employed single-bay wings (and demonstrated inadequate strength when one aircraft shed its wings at the start of the 1924 Pulitzer race), the new fighter reverted to two-bay configuration, being officially adopted by the Air Service as the XPW-8 (experimental, pursuit, water-cooled-8). In due course Curtiss won a contract for 25 PW-8 production aircraft, and these served with the 17th Pursuit Squadron between 1924 and 1926. When one of the three XPW-8s was modified (at the request of what had become the US Army Air Corps on 4 June 1920) to feature completely redesigned wings of tapered planform and Clark Y aerofoil section (similar to that on the contemporary Boeing PW-9), the resulting aircraft, the XPW-8B, became in effect the prototype of a new design family, the P-1 Hawk (under a simplified designation system omitting reference to

A few of the nine P-6As with the Prestone cooling system were fitted with three-blade propellers, this aircraft carrying the markings of an Air Base Squadron, probably in about 1930. Top speed of this version was 179 mph (288 km/h) at sea level.

The XP-6 was in fact a P-2, 25-423, experimentally powered by a 600-hp (447-kW) V-1570 Conqueror engine; the famous 'Snowy Owl' insignia suggests previous service with the 17th Pursuit Squadron, 1st Pursuit Group.

Curtiss P-6 Hawk

Specification

Curtiss P-6E Hawk
Type: single-seat pursuit aircraft
Powerplant: one 600-hp (448-kW) Curtiss
V-1570-23 12-cylinder
Vee liquid-cooled piston engine
Performance: maximum speed 197 mph
(317 km/h) at sea level;
initial climb rate 2,400 ft (732 m) per
minute; service ceiling
24,700 ft (7530 m); range 570 miles (917
km)
Weights: empty 2,699 lb (1224 kg);
maximum take-off 3,392 lb
(1539 kg)
Dimensions: span 31 ft 6 in (9.60 m); length
23 ft 2 in (7.06 m);
height 8 ft 10 in (2.69 m); wing area 252.0
sq ft (23.41 m^2)
Armament: two 0.3-in (7.62-mm) machine-
guns with 600 rounds
per gun on sides of nose

Curtiss Hawk variants

XPW-8B: serialled 23-1203, this was the third of three prototypes with single-bay wings; became P-1 Hawk prototype; Curtiss D-12 engine
P-1 Hawk: 10 aircraft (25–410 to 25–419); Curtiss V-1150-1 engines
P-1A Hawk: 25 aircraft (26-276 to 26-300); Curtiss V-1150-1 engines; fuselage lengthened by 3 in (7.62 cm); one aircraft (26-296) became **XAT-4** and one more (26-295) became **XP-6A** racer
P-1B Hawk: 25 aircraft (27-063) to 27-087); Curtiss V-1150-3 engines with modified radiators
P-1C Hawk: 33 aircraft (29-227 to 29-259); Curtiss V-1150-5 engines; wheelbrakes fitted
XP-1C: one P-1C (29-238) with Heinrich radiator and Prestone cooling
AT-4: 35 aircraft (27-088 to 27-097, and 27-213 to 27-237); trainers with Wright V-720 engines; re-engined with Curtiss V-1150-3s and designated **P-1D Hawk**
AT-5: five aircraft (27-238 to 27-242); trainers with Wright R-790-1 radial engines; re-engined with Curtiss V-1150-3s and designated **P-1E Hawk**
AT-5A: 31 aircraft (28-042 to 28-072); trainers with Wright R-790-1 radials; re-engined with Curtiss V-1150-3s and designated **P-1F Hawk**
P-2 Hawk: five aircraft (25-420 to 25-424); first aircraft (25-420) with experimental turbocharger; fourth (25-423) became **XP-6** with V-1570-1 engine; remaining three became standard **P-1A** fighter
XP-3A: conversion of last P-1A (26-300) with Pratt & Whitney R-1340-9 radial
P-3A Hawk: five aircraft (28-189 to 28-193); Pratt & Whitney R-1340-3 radials; one aircraft (28-189) became a second XP-3A
P-5 Hawk: five aircraft (27-327 to 27-331); turbocharged V-1150-3 engines; the first aircraft (27-327) was termed **XP-5**
XP-6: conversion of P-2 (25-423) with V-1570 engine for racing
XP-6A: conversion of P-1A (26-295) with high compression V-1570 for racing
P-6 (YP-6) Hawk: 18 aircraft (29-260 to 29-273, and 29-363 to 29-366); test batch with V-1570 engines; first

nine aircraft with water cooling and remainder with Prestone cooling; nine aircraft later converted to P-6D
P-6A: eight P-6s (29-260 to 29-267) converted to V-1570-23 with Prestone cooling
XP-6A: (2nd aircraft); conversion of one production P-6A (29-263) for trials
XP-6B 'Hoyt Special': long-range conversion of the last P-1C (29-259) with V-1570 engine
XP-6D: conversion of first P-6A (29-260) with turbocharged V-1570C
P-6D Hawk: conversion of nine P-6s and three P-6As with turbocharged V-1570 engines
XP-6E: conversion of third P-11 (29-374) with single-leg landing gear
P-6E Hawk: 46 aircraft (32-233 to 32-277); Curtiss V-1570-23 engines, final aircraft (32-277) became XP-23
XP-6F: conversion of XP-6E (29-374) with V-1570F engine and enclosed cockpit
XP-6G: conversion of one P-6E (32-254) with unsupercharged V-1570F engine; reverted to P-6E
XP-6H: conversion of first P-6E (32-233) to mount six machine-guns
P-11: three aircraft intended for Curtiss H-1640 engine, but two completed as P-6 (29-367 and 29-268), and one as YP-20 (29-374) with Wright Cyclone engine
XP-17: conversion of first P-1 (25-410) with V-1470 engine
YP-20: conversion of third P-11 (29-374) with Wright Cyclone engine
XP-21: conversion of XP-3A (26-300) and first P-3A (28-189) with R-985 Wasp Junior engine; 26-300 became **XP-21A**, and 28-189 became a P-1F
XP-22: conversion of third P-6A (29-262) with modified nose, tail surfaces and three-blade propeller
Y1P-22: original designation of 46 production aircraft that became P-6E
XP-23: conversion of the last P-6E (32-277) with monocoque fuselage; became **YP-23**
Export Hawk: eight aircraft for Netherlands East Indies air force, and eight for Cuba (with Pratt & Whitney R-1340 radials); one aircraft purchased by Mitsubishi, Japan

One of the two classic Army biplane pursuit aircraft designs of the 1920s and 1930s, the long-lived Hawk series was epitomized by the last of the production versions, the P-6E. Its basic shape had evolved through a long line of Hawk biplanes, originating with Army and Navy racers that Curtiss built between 1921 and 1925. The developed P-6E form was elegant, with tapered wings and a fuselage that faired into the 600-hp (448-kW) Curtiss Conqueror liquid-cooled engine. The initial order was for 46 of the E models, and most were delivered to the 17th and 94th Pursuit Squadrons during 1932. The single-leg landing gear and the belly radiator position were the major differences between the P-6E and earlier Hawks, with their more conventional landing gear and nose radiators. This particular aircraft is painted in the characteristic black and white markings and Army Air Corps insignia of the 17th Pursuit Squadron of the 1st Pursuit Group, while based at Selfridge Field, Michigan. This scheme, named after the Arctic snow owl painted on the fuselage band, was a short-lived one; but it is the best-remembered one, as well as the most elaborate, of all Hawk markings.

engine type and manufacturer) but only ten were assembled.

Adoption of the smaller, tapered wing on the XPW-8B, combined with growing familiarity with the causes and effects of wing flutter, allowed reversion to the single-bay layout, and the 10 production Curtiss P-1s, ordered on 7 March 1925, differed from the prototype only in inclusion of an extra strut in the centre-section bracing and a slightly modified rudder shape. These aircraft served with the 27th and 94th Pursuit Squadrons, 1st Pursuit Group, at Selfridge Field, Michigan, commanded by Major Thomas G. Lanphier. Power was provided by the 435-hp (325-kW) Curtiss D-12 12-cylinder water-cooled Vee engine which, under a new designation system denoting cubic capacity, became the V-1150-1. The first P-1 underwent tests at McCook Field starting on 17 August 1925.

The P-1 contract covered production of five additional

Service P-6Ds differed from the prototype XP-6D in having three-blade propellers. Fitted with turbo-superchargers, nine P-6Ds and some P-6As were converted to P-6D standard, the aircraft shown being flown by the 8th Pursuit Group in 1932.

aircraft designated P-2 and powered by the 505-hp (377-kW) Curtiss V-1400, also water-cooled. The first of these P-2s was flown in December 1925, and was later fitted with an experimental turbocharger which increased the service ceiling from 22,980 ft (7005 m) of the standard P-1 to 32,790 ft (9995 m)

Meanwhile the P-1 itself had undergone minor improvement that resulted in a contract for 25 P-1As being placed in September 1925; this version featured a fuselage lengthened by 3 in (7.62 cm), changed cowling lines and a D-12C engine, and had improved bomb release gear (all pursuit fighters were still required to feature a light bomb-carrying ability). Only 23 P-1As were completed as such, one aircraft emerging as the XAT-4 trainer with Wright-Hispano E engine, and

the other became the XP-6A racer (with XPW-8A wings).

The next production version, the P-1B with V-1150-3 engine and improved radiator, was ordered in August 1926, 23 examples serving alongside earlier Hawks and starting delivery only two months later. With larger landing wheels and some equipment changes, the normal loaded weight increased to 2,932 lb (1330 kg), and the maximum speed was reduced from the 163 mph (262 km/h) of the P-1 to 159.6 mph (257 km/h).

Largest order for the Curtiss pursuit fighters to date was for 33 P-1Cs, their delivery being completed in April 1929. The V-1150-3 was retained and once more, on account of increased weight (wheel brakes were fitted), the speed dropped, this time to 154 mph (248 km/h). One aircraft, modified with an experimental Heinrich radiator and Prestone cooling system, was termed the XP-1C. No further P-1s were produced but, following successful trials with the XAT-4 in October 1926, 35 production AT-4s with Wright V-720 engines and five AT-5s with Wright R-790 engines were ordered; the former were later re-engined with the standard Curtiss V-1150-3 and reverted to the pursuit category as P-1Ds; when similarly re-engined the five AT-5s became P1Es. These aircraft served with the 43rd School Squadron at Kelly Field; this unit became the 43rd Pursuit Squadron in 1935.

Trainers into fighters

A further conversion involved 31 Curtiss AT-5A trainers which had been ordered by the US Army on 30 July 1927 with R-790 engines; their poor performance (maximum speed only 122 mph/196 km/h) caused them to be re-engined with D-12s in 1929, their designation changing to P-1F; one other P-1F was created by reconverting an XP-21 (see below).

The designation P-2, as mentioned above, covered the last five aircraft ordered on the first P-1 contract, powered by Curtiss V-1400 engines. In the event this engine proved disappointing and three aircraft were converted to P-1As; only one aircraft (25-240) remained XP-2, and the last P-2 became the XP-6.

The P-3 was the first radial-engine Hawk pursuit fighter. The XP-3A designation was applied to the last P-1A, which was completed with a 410-hp (306-kW) Pratt & Whitney R-1340-9, this radial engine being flown both uncowled and with a variety of deep-chord NACA cowls. Later, when re-engined with the 300-hp (224-kW) Pratt & Whitney R-985-1 Wasp Junior, the aircraft was redesignated the XP-21. Five production P-3As with R-1340-3 radials were ordered in 1928 and four of these were delivered the following year to the 94th Pursuit Squadron, then commanded by the famous US Army Air Corps pilot, Major (later Major General) Ralph Royce. The other P-3A (28-189) was retained for further engine cowling trials and became the second XP-3A. Later it also became an XP-21 with R-985-1 Wasp Junior before being converted to a P-1F. Maximum speed of the standard P-3A

One of 23 P-1Bs ordered by the US Army Air Corps in August 1926, this aircraft served with the 27th Pursuit Squadron, 1st Pursuit Group, commanded by the famous Major Ralph Royce at Selfridge Field (now Air National Guard Base), Michigan, in 1929–30.

with narrow-chord cowling was 153 mph (246 km/h) at sea level; however in June 1930 one of the P-3As was flown with an SR-1340-C cowling, spinner and side fairings, refinements which resulted in a top speed of 193 mph (311 km/h).

Strangely, the US Army Air Corps decided to discontinue the radial engine 'Hawk' (despite favouring the radial-powered Boeing P-12), and the next Curtiss variant was the P-5, of which only five were ordered and delivered to the 94th Pursuit Squadron in 1928. Produced to allow service evaluation of the turbocharged Curtiss D-12F engine, this Hawk possessed a sea-level maximum speed of only 144 mph (232 km/h), but at 25,000 ft (7620 m), well above the ceiling of unsupercharged P-1s, the top speed was 166 mph (267 km/h). By the time the P-5s were delivered, however, the new Curtiss V-1570 Conqueror was ready for production. No further development was undertaken on the D-12.

Enter the P-6 Hawk

After almost four years of development the definitive Curtiss P-6 Hawk was considered ready for production. Once again aircraft prepared for racing played an important part in the development. For the 1927 National Air Races to be held at Spokane, Washington, the US Army ordered two Curtiss racers, the fourth P-2 (25-423) with the new 600-hp V-1570 Conqueror as the XP-6, and a P-1A (26-295) with a high-compression V-1570 in a different cowling as the XP-6A (this also employed wing radiators). The XP-6A won the unlimited race at a speed of 201 mph (324 km/h), and second place went to the XP-6 at a speed of 189 mph (304 km/h). The XP-6A was destroyed shortly before the 1928 air races, however.

The use of the Conqueror engine in the two racers served

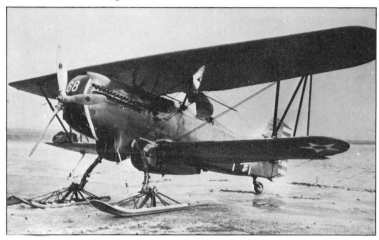

Best known of all P-6 squadrons was probably the 17th Pursuit Squadron, 1st Pursuit Group, one of whose aircraft is seen here with ski undercarriage. The rear fuselage band was black with white borders and a 'Snowy Owl' superimposed on it.

Third of the three P-11s, 29-374, was completed with a Wright R-1820 Cyclone radial engine as the XP-20; it was then given the engine and landing gear of the XP-22 and became the prototype XP-6E, later being re-designated the XP-6F.

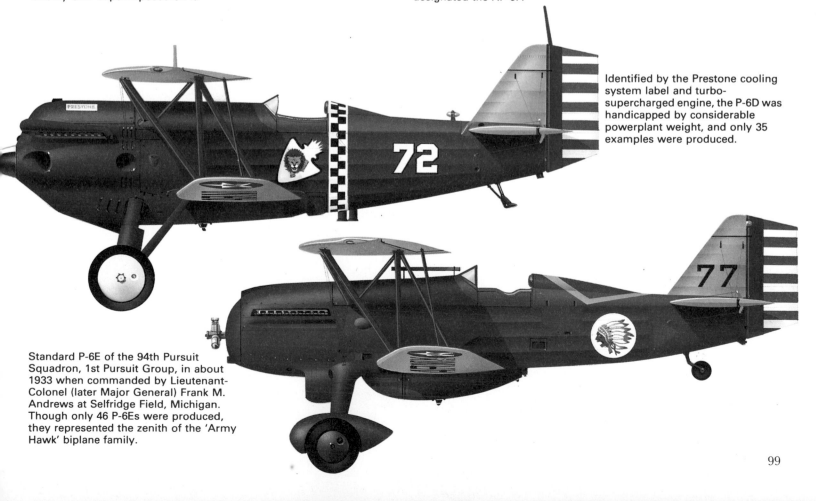

Identified by the Prestone cooling system label and turbo-supercharged engine, the P-6D was handicapped by considerable powerplant weight, and only 35 examples were produced.

Standard P-6E of the 94th Pursuit Squadron, 1st Pursuit Group, in about 1933 when commanded by Lieutenant-Colonel (later Major General) Frank M. Andrews at Selfridge Field, Michigan. Though only 46 P-6Es were produced, they represented the zenith of the 'Army Hawk' biplane family.

A P-6E retained by the 33rd Pursuit Squadron in 1938, long after re-equipment with P-12s and P-35s; the stylized badge on the blue fuselage suggests that the aircraft was regarded at worst as a 'hack', at best a museum piece.

not only to demonstrate its suitability in the Hawk but also its reliability, and on 3 October 1928 18 P-6s (sometimes referred to as YP-6s) were ordered for service evaluation; they were delivered to the 27th Pursuit Squadron in 1929. To speed delivery, the first nine aircraft were completed with V-1570-17 engines with water cooling, the remainder having the intended V-1570-23s with Prestone (ethylene glycol) cooling which permitted smaller radiators. Two additional P-6s were produced by completing two of the three P-11s (see below) on order with water-cooled V-1570-17s.

Eight of the water-cooled P-6s were subsequently re-engined with Prestone-cooled V-1570-23s their designation being changed to P-6A; some of these flew with three-blade variable-pitch propellers. One of the aircraft (29-263) was assigned to radiator trials under the designation XP-6A no. 2, and the designation XP-6B covered a special conversion of the last P-1C (29-259) with Conqueror engine, and popularly known as the Hawk Hoyt Special; intended for a long-distance flight from New York to Alaska by Captain (later Brigadier General) Ross G. Hoyt, the Hawk crashed short of its destination and, after repairs, was assigned to experimental work.

The designation P-6D referred to turbocharged aircraft. The XP-6D covered the first P-6A (29-260) fitted experimentally with a supercharged V-1570C, performance figures including a sea-level maximum speed of 172 mph (277 km/h) and a speed of 197 mph (317 km/h) at 15,000 ft (4570 m). No new production followed, but nine P-6s and three P-6As were fitted with turbochargers and redesignated P-6D; they were issued to the US Army Air Corps in April 1932.

Best known of all Hawks was the P-6E variant. The prototype XP-6E had begun life as the third XP-11 (29-374), was completed as the YP-20 (see below) and then fitted with

Last of the P-6Es, 32-278, was held at the factory and completed with aluminium monocoque fuselage, turbo-supercharged and geared G1V-1570-C engine, and designated the XP-23; after removal of the supercharger and fitting a two-blade propeller, as shown here, the aircraft was re-designated YP-23.

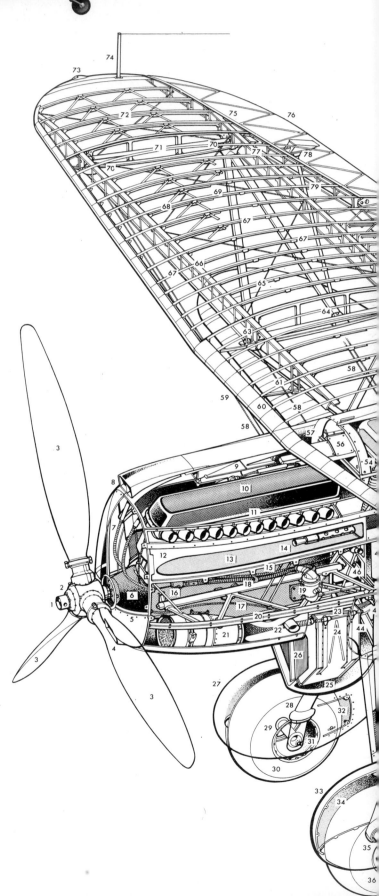

Curtiss P-6E Hawk cutaway drawing key

1 Starter dog
2 Propeller hub
3 Three-blade Hamilton Standard metal propeller
4 Oil cooler chin intake
5 Nose cowling front panel line
6 Gear housing
7 Front curved panel
8 Carburettor air intake
9 Intake trunk
10 Curtiss V-1570-C Conqueror engine
11 Exhaust stubs (2 per cylinder)
12 Stainless steel trough surround
13 Gun trough
14 Machine-gun muzzle
15 Cowling access panel line
16 Diagonal brace
17 Struts
18 Main engine support bearer
19 Filter
20 Lower panel lines
21 Oil cooler assembly
22 Telescopic access/servicing step
23 Radiator attachment mounts
24 Prestone radiator
25 Radiator fairing
26 Intake
27 Starboard mainwheel spat

28 Starboard undercarriage strut
29 Axle
30 Starboard low-pressure mainwheel tyre
31 Anchor point
32 Inboard access panel (brake servicing)
33 Port mainwheel spat
34 Flathead screw panel line
35 Port axle assembly
36 Port low-pressure mainwheel tyre
37 Hub assembly forging
38 Angled undercarriage strut
39 Removable spat half-section
40 Undercarriage leg fairing
41 Strut/fairing attachment
42 Strut support forged frame member
43 Strut pivot
44 Hinged cover plate
45 Front wires fuselage attachment
46 Engine accessories
47 Fuselage forward frame
48 Port ammunition magazine (600 rounds per gun)
49 Deflector panel
50 Cartridge chute
51 Gun support strut
52 Ammunition feed fairing
53 Oleo shock strut/rebound spring
54 Upper pivot point
55 Cabane forward attachment
56 Oil access point
57 Bulkhead panel
58 Starboard wires
59 Aluminium leading-edge panels

60 Upper wing centre-section
61 Cabane struts
62 Cabane wires
63 Cabane upper wing attachment points
64 Reinforced strut
65 Starboard lower wing plan
66 Front spar
67 Interplane 'N'-struts
68 Upper wing ribs
69 Internal bracing wires
70 Interplane strut upper attachment points
71 Reinforced rib
72 Outer rib assemblies
73 Starboard navigation light
74 Aerial mast
75 Aileron/rear spar join
76 Welded steel aileron (fabric-covered)
77 Aileron hinge link
78 Metal plate
79 Aileron interplane actuating link
80 Aileron profile
81 Rear spar
82 Trailing-edge rib assembly
83 Centre-section cut-out
84 Handhold
85 Telescopic gunsight
86 Gunsight supports
87 Hinged fuel access panel
88 Filler neck
89 Fuselage main fuel tank (50 US gals/189 litres)
90 Engine controls
91 Port 0.30-in (7.62-mm) Browning machine-gun
92 Lower longeron
93 Fuel tank bearer
94 Lower wing front spar attachment
95 Wingroot walkway

96 Diagonal strut frame
97 Lower wing rear spar attachment
98 Aileron control linkage
99 Hanging rudder pedal assembly
100 Control column
101 Fuselage frame
102 Cabane rear attachment
103 Instrument centre panel
104 Main instrument panel
105 Windscreen
106 Control grip
107 Side switch panel
108 Engine control quadrant
109 Throttle lever
110 Upper wing trailing-edge
111 Padded forward coaming
112 Cockpit cut-out
113 Headrest/turnover frame
114 Bad-weather cover (snap-on rubber tarpaulin)
115 Oxygen access panel (starboard)
116 Pilot's seat
117 Seat support frame
118 Inspection 'Vee' panel
119 Cockpit floor
120 Fuselage diagonal side frames

153 Tailfin rear beam attachment
154 Elevator control cable
155 Rudder control horns
156 Port elevator frame
157 Brace wire attachment
158 Port (adjustable) tailplane
159 Tailplane front beam
160 Tail dolly lug

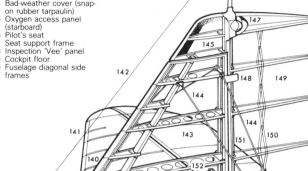

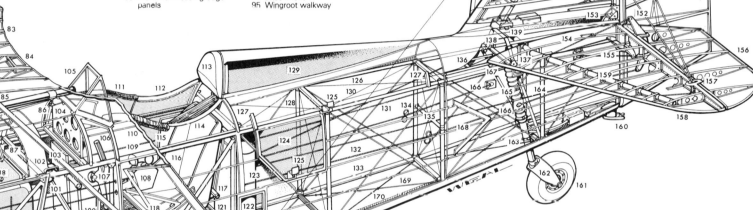

121 Oxygen cylinder (starboard)
122 Metal door flap
123 Parachute flare stowage (port)
124 Baggage compartment hinged side door
125 Hasp and lock
126 Baggage compartment hinged upper panel
127 Snap fasteners
128 Fuselage top frames
129 All-metal dorsal decking
130 Diagonal brace wires
131 Elevator control cables
132 Rudder control cables
133 Fuselage structure
134 Pulleys
135 Cross-member
136 Dorsal cross-section transition (round/point)
137 Tailplane front beam attachment
138 Bearer frame
139 Tailfin front beam attachment
140 Tailfin leading-edge
141 Starboard tailplane
142 Aerials
143 Tailfin structure
144 Tailplane brace wires
145 Rudder balance
146 Aerial post
147 Tail navigation light recess
148 Rudder upper hinge
149 Rudder frame
150 Spacers
151 Rudder post
152 Elevator control horns

161 Swivel/steerable tailwheel
162 Axle fork
163 Metal grommet collar
164 Fuselage strut
165 Tailwheel shock-strut leg
166 Leather grommets (elevator control cables)
167 Tailwheel leg upper attachment
168 Access 'Vee' panel
169 Diagonal brace wires
170 Lower longeron
171 Ventral skinning
172 Port aileron
173 Aerial mast
174 Lower wingroot cut-out
175 Ventral tank aft fairing
176 Rear spar
177 Interplane 'N'-struts
178 Upper wing leading-edge
179 Drop tank filler cap
180 Drop tank (41.6 Imp gal/189 litres)
181 Vent
182 Lower wing aluminium leading-edge panels
183 Nose ribs
184 Wire turnbuckle clamp
185 'N'-strut lower attachments
186 Port navigation light
187 Reinforced rib
188 Aileron actuating linkage
189 Lower wing trailing-edge
190 Rear spar
191 Outer rib assemblies
192 Front spar
193 Wingtip structure
194 Handling point

the engine and landing gear of the XP-22 and designated XP-6E. It later became the XP-6F.

Forty-six production aircraft (32-233 to 32-278) were ordered under the initial designation Y1P-22, subsequently changed to P-6E to simplify administration. Their most prominent distinguishing feature was the single-strut cantilever landing gear with wheel 'pants' (streamlined fairings which covered the upper halves of the wheels). The radiator was moved back from the 'chin' location to a position just forward of the main landing gear units, while the balance area of the rudder was decreased by the top rib of the fin. The two-gun nose armament was revised by moving the guns from the top of the nose cowling to the sides of the fuselage. Other airframe refinements (including a tailwheel in place of a skid) raised the sea-level speed to 197 mph (317 km/h).

P-6Es served with the 1st Pursuit Group (17th, 27th and 94th Squadrons) at Selfridge Field, California, under Lieutenant Colonel Frank M. Andrews, and with the 8th Pursuit Group (33rd, 35th and 36th Squadrons) at Langley Field, Virginia, under Major Byron Q. Jones.

A formation of P-6E Hawks, the most important version of the Hawk series, here shown in the distinctive markings of the 17th Pursuit Squadron, 1st Pursuit Group, at Selfridge Field.

Experimental developments

Several other experimental variations of the P-6E were produced, including the XP-6F – the fastest of all Hawks. This was the XP-6E with turbocharged V-1570-55 Conqueror and an enclosed cockpit; gross weight increased to 3,842 lb (1743 kg) and this limited the sea-level speed to 194 mph (312 km/h), but at 18,000 ft (5510 m) the maximum speed increased to 225 mph (362 km/h). However, the impossibility of controlling the engine cooling at greater altitudes with the possibility of disastrous failure caused tests on this aircraft to be ended on 1 August 1933.

The designation XP-6G covered a P-6E (32-254) with the supercharger removed; the 'X' was dropped when the aircraft was delivered to the 8th Pursuit Group, but it later reverted to a standard P-6E. The XP-6H had also started out as a P-6E (32-233) but was returned to the manufacturers to have four additional machine-guns fitted (two in the upper and two in the lower wings, all free-firing outside the propeller arc). Carrying a total of 3,300 rounds of 0.3-in (7.62-mm) ammunition, the six-gun XP-6H was not considered a feasible combat aeroplane by the US Army Air Corps and the project was dropped.

Export Hawks included eight P-6s for the Netherlands East

Indies and a small number for Cuba with Pratt & Whitney R-1340 radials, produced around 1930. One Hawk was purchased by Mitsubishi in Japan where the technical inspector was one Jiro Horikoshi, later the chief designer of the famous Zero-Sen naval fighter.

Unsatisfactory Chieftain

Finally, there was a host of designations tentatively applied to new projects, and many of these reverted to standard after completion of trials. Three P-11s were ordered to a standard comparable with the P-6 but powered by the new Curtiss H-1640 Chieftain engine; this powerplant proved unsatisfactory and the first two P-11s were completed as P-6s, while the third became the YP-20, which was powered by a Wright Cyclone engine.

The XP versions appear

The designation XP-17 was applied to the first P-1 (25-410) when experimentally fitted with the Curtiss V-1470, a 480-hp (358-kW) 12-cylinder inverted-Vee engine. The YP-20 was so designated when the third P-11 was fitted with a 575-hp (429-kW) Wright R-1820 Cyclone radial; after being modified with the cantilever landing gear of the XP-22, the aircraft became the XP-6E, and later still the XP-6F. The XP-22 itself was the third P-6A (29-262), with all the modifications (including the revised single-strut landing gear) subsequently adopted on the P-6E. It later reverted to a standard P-6A. As already mentioned, the Y1P-22s became P-6Es.

YP-23 was the designation given to the final P-6E (32-378), which was retained by the manufacturer and featured an entirely new monocoque aluminium fuselage, new tail surfaces and a supercharged and geared Curtiss G1V-1570-C engine; top speed of this version was 220 mph (354 km/h) at 15,000 ft (4570 m).

The delivery of the Curtiss P-6E and Boeing P-12 during 1932 and 1933 marked the end of the procurement of biplanes for pursuit fighter purposes by the US Army Air Corps.

It was becoming very evident to US and other military aircraft designers that the era of the pursuit biplane was rapidly coming to an end. Already brilliant minds overseas were dreaming of monoplane fighters capable of high speeds. Sydney Camm, for one, had the embryo Hurricane on his drawingboard.

A view under the engine cowl of an XP-6A Hawk. With its V-1570 Conqueror engine this machine won the 1927 National Air Races at a speed of 201.3 mph (324 km/h).

de Havilland Moths

A product of the 1920s, the classic Moths represented a successful venture to enable the public to enjoy the sport of flying, and sowed the seeds of private aircraft ownership that were to blossom throughout the inter-war years.

The de Havilland Moth was much more than simply a series of light aircraft. With this plane, de Havilland proved their theory that the British middle classes loved recreational flying and represented a previously untapped market. For the same reasons, in 1923 the Daily Mail sponsored a competition for light aircraft – we would call them ultra-lights today – at Lympne. There was a demand for the production of an aircraft that a small flying club or even the man in the street could afford and would be correspondingly easy to fly. A number of interesting small aircraft were entered for the competition, but de Havilland realised that a machine with a capacity of less than 1.1 litre was too under-powered for an inexperienced pilot and would be dangerous.

Accordingly the works at Stag Lane set about producing a scaled-down version of the D.H.51 three-seater, the new aircraft being a two-seat single-bay biplane, tough enough to withstand the rigours of instructional work and not so cramped as to be uncomfortable during cross-country flying. Powered by a four-cylinder 60-hp (45-kW) engine specially designed by Major F.B. Halford and named the A.D.C. Cirrus I, the new D.H.60 was a model of robust simplicity, its fuselage being in effect a plywood box built round spruce longerons and stiffened by vertical and horizontal members screwed to the plywood.

Named Moth in recognition of Geoffrey de Havilland's renown as a lepidopterist, the first D.H.60 (G-EBKT) was flown at Stag Lane by 'DH' himself on 22 February 1925. On that day was set a pattern for private flying that was to be emulated the world over until World War 2. Efforts to canvass support from government sources were successful when Sir Sefton Brancker, Director of Civil Aviation, announced the founding of five Air Ministry-subsidized Moth-equipped flying clubs, the Lancashire Aero Club, the London Aeroplane Club, the Newcastle Aero Club, the Midland Aero Club and the Yorkshire Aeroplane Club. By the end of 1925 20 Cirrus Moths had been completed, of which 16 had been delivered to the clubs and two to private owners. 1926 brought forth 35 more Moths, of which 14 were exported, nine of them to Australia; Major Halford produced an 85-hp (63-kW) Cirrus II engine which was fitted in a Moth to be piloted by Geoffrey de Havilland in the King's Cup Race, but a broken oil pipe let through Hubert Broad into first place in a Cirrus I Moth. Another famous British sporting pilot, Neville Stack, flew the second Moth proto-type (G-EBKU), powered by the first production Cirrus II, from Croydon to India where it attracted much interest as it embarked on six months joyriding in the sub-continent.

G-ATBL was a D.H.60G Gipsy Moth which was exported to Switzerland. It returned to England where it continued to fly, and is seen here at the Shuttleworth Trust at Old Warden, a perfect setting for the aircraft that established light aeroplane flying as a purely enjoyable pastime.

de Havilland D.H.82A Tiger Moth

Specification

D.H.82A Tiger Moth Mk II
Type: two-seat ab initio trainer biplane
Powerplant: one 130-hp (97-kW) de Havilland Gipsy Major 1 four-cylinder air-cooled inverted inline piston engine
Performance: maximum speed 104 mph (167 km/h) at sea level; initial climb rate 635 ft (194 m) per minute; service ceiling 13,600 ft (4145 m); range 300 miles (483 km)
Weights: empty 1,115 lb (506 kg); maximum take-off 1,825 lb (828 kg)
Dimensions: span 29 ft 4 in (8.94 m); length 23 ft 11 in (7.29 m); height 8 ft 9½ in (2.68 m); wing area 239 sq ft (22.20 m²)
Armament: none

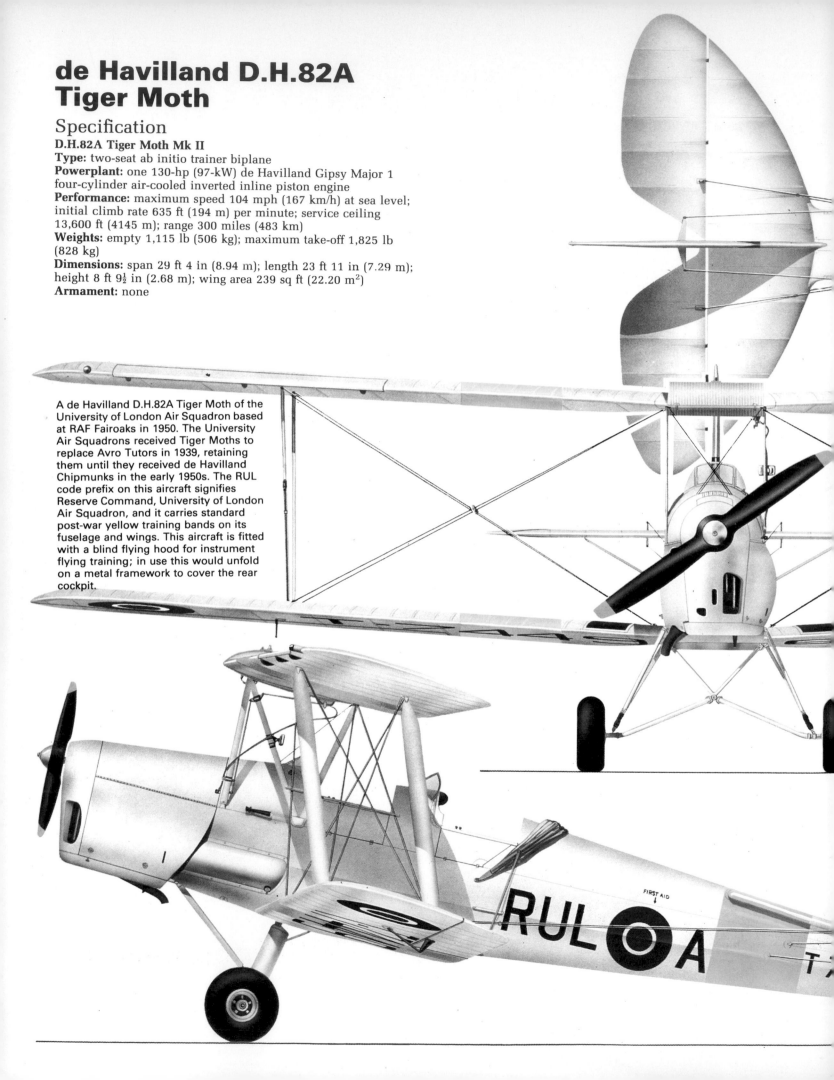

A de Havilland D.H.82A Tiger Moth of the University of London Air Squadron based at RAF Fairoaks in 1950. The University Air Squadrons received Tiger Moths to replace Avro Tutors in 1939, retaining them until they received de Havilland Chipmunks in the early 1950s. The RUL code prefix on this aircraft signifies Reserve Command, University of London Air Squadron, and it carries standard post-war yellow training bands on its fuselage and wings. This aircraft is fitted with a blind flying hood for instrument flying training; in use this would unfold on a metal framework to cover the rear cockpit.

Moth variants

D.H.60 Moth (Cirrus I): 1925–26 model; two prototypes (G-EBKT and G-EBKU); eight pre-production; 31 production aircraft
D.H.60 Moth (Cirrus II): 1926–27 model; 32 built
D.H.60 Genet Moth: six aircraft (J8816–J8821) for Air Ministry; Genet engines
D.H.60X Moth (Cirrus III): 1928 model; 338 built by de Havilland at Stag Lane
D.H.60G Gipsy Moth: introduced 1928; 595 built by de Havilland at Stag Lane; 40 aircraft built by Morane-Saulnier in France; 18 built by Moth Aircraft Corp, in USA; 32 built by Larkin Aircraft Supply, Melbourne, for Australian government
D.H.60M Moth (Metal Moth): introduced 1928; four pre-production aircraft; 536 built by de Havilland at Stag Lane; 40 built by DH Canada; 161 built by Moth Aircraft Corp, in USA; 10 built by Norwegian Army Aircraft Factory in 1931
D.H.60GIII Moth: Gipsy III in wooden Moth; introduced in 1932; 47 built by de Havilland at Stag Lane
D.H.60GIII Moth Major: Gipsy Major III or IIIA, introduced in 1934; one prototype (G-ACNP) and 96 production aircraft
D.H.60T Moth Trainer: Gipsy II; military trainer; introduced 1931; two prototypes (G-ABKS and G-ABKU) and initial production of 47 aircraft
D.H.61 Giant Moth: six/eight-passenger cabin biplane; Jupiter VI or XI, Jaguar VIC or Pratt & Whitney Hornet engines; introduced in 1928
D.H.71 Tiger Moth: two experimental monoplanes G-EBQU (Gipsy) and G-EBRV (Cirrus II) produced in 1927
D.H.75 Hawk Moth: first high-wing Moth; one D.H.75 prototype (de Havilland Ghost engine), five **D.H.75A** (Lynx, Whirlwind or Cheetah engine), and one **D.H.75B** (Whirlwind)
D.H.80A Puss Moth: high-wing cabin monoplane; Gipsy III, Gipsy Major or Gipsy (high compression) engines; introduced 1930; one **D.H.80** prototype (G-AAHZ) and 259 production aircraft built at Stag Lane; 25 built by DH Canada
D.H.81 Swallow Moth: two-seat low-wing monoplane, only one built
D.H.82T Tiger Moth: eight similar to D.H.60T but with Gipsy III; service trials led to D.H.82 and D.H.82A
D.H.82 Tiger Moth: 114 initial military training biplanes built by de Havilland at Stag Lane
D.H.82A Tiger Moth: in RAF, **Tiger Moth MkII**; basic ab initio trainer; total of about 7,290 produced between 1934 and 1945; 795 built by de Havilland at Hatfield, 3,216 by Morris at Cowley, remainder by DH Canada, DH Australia, DH New Zealand, and in Portugal (91), Norway (37) and Sweden (23); Gipsy III and Gipsy Major (various versions); total includes 786 **D.H.82C** with Menasco Pirate D4 engine built by DH Canada (200 sold to USA as **PT-24** in 1942); at least 17 converted to **Thruxton Jackaroo** (four-seat cabin conversion), 1957–9
D.H.82B Queen Bee: radio-controlled gunnery target; RAF 380, Royal Navy 420
D.H.83 Fox Moth: four-passenger cabin biplane; introduced in 1932; Gipsy Major or Gipsy Major IC
D.H.85A Leopard Moth: three seat high-wing cabin monoplane; introduced in 1933; Gipsy Major (**D.H.85**) and Gipsy Six R (D.H.85A); one prototype (G-ACHD) and 131 production aircraft
D.H.87 Hornet Moth: two-seat cabin biplane; introduced in 1934; Gipsy Major I; prototype D.H.87 (G-ACTA), **D.H.87A** with elliptical wings and tips **D.H.87B** with squared wings and tips; 163 made
D.H.94 Moth Minor: two-seat low-wing monoplane; introduced in 1937

The prototype D.H.60 Moth G-EBKT, which was first flown by Captain Geoffrey de Havilland on Sunday 22 February 1925 at Stag Lane. It differed from subsequent production aircraft in having an unbalanced rudder and exhaust pipe on the starboard side. Moving the pipe to the port side allowed access to an aft baggage locker.

The so-called 1927-model Moths, of which 150 were produced, were all powered by the Cirrus II, and one of these (G-EBPP) was shipped to Australia where Major Hereward de Havilland set up an agency in Melbourne to assemble imported Moths. Numerous outstanding lightplane flights were made by enthusiastic private owners, typical being Lady Bailey's altitude record for light aircraft of 17,283 ft (5268 m) on 5 July of that year, and Lieutenant R. R. Bentley's two extraordinary return flights between the UK and Cape Town totalling 51,652 miles (83125 km) in G-EBSO. Six aircraft, powered by 75-hp (56-kW) Armstrong Siddeley Genet radials, were bought by the Air Ministry for use at the Central Flying School.

1928 introduced the 90-hp (67-kW) Cirrus III engine and a split-axle landing gear which, on account of the new cross-braces between the landing gear, resulted in this model being termed the D.H.60X Moth. By the end of the year 403 Moths of all types had been produced and production was running at 16 per week; moreover, licences to build Moths had been negotiated with the Finnish Government Aircraft Factory and Veljekset Karhumäki O/Y (also of Finland) and the General Aircraft Co. of Sydney, Australia.

Meanwhile stocks of war-surplus Renault engine components, employed in the Cirrus engines, had been exhausted and in 1926 'DH' asked Major Halford to design a new replacement engine; the first example of this, the legendary Gipsy, was completed in July 1927 and within 16 weeks a production shop at Stag Lane was built. After trials in an early Moth (G-EBOH), the new engine gained its certificate and appeared in the production D.H.60G Gipsy Moth. One of

these, flown by W. L. Hope, won the 1928 King's Cup Race at 105 mph (169 km/h). Records tumbled, and many memorable flights followed; 'DH' himself in his own Gipsy Moth (G-AAAA) established a new lightplane height record at 19,980 ft (6090 m) on 25 July 1928, and Hubert Broad remained aloft for 24 hours (using extra fuel tanks in the fuselage); DH's son Geoffrey flew a Gipsy Moth for 600 hours in nine months during 1929; covering 51,000 miles (82075 km) with only routine inspections; when tested afterwards

de Havilland D.H.82A Tiger Moth cutaway drawing key

1 Starboard navigation light
2 Automatic leading edge slat, open
3 Slat hinges
4 Starboard upper and wing panel
5 Wing fabric covering
6 Starboard interplane struts
7 Pitot static tubes
8 Starboard lower wing panel
9 Diagonal wire bracing
10 Leading-edge stiffening ribs
11 Lattice rib construction
12 Fuel tank, capacity 22.8 Imp gal (104 litres)
13 Fuel contents gauge
14 Filler cap
15 Main spar attachment joint
16 Centre section 'N' struts
17 Cowling step
18 Detachable engine cowlings
19 de Havilland Gipsy Major four-cylinder inline engine
20 Fixed nose cowling
21 de Havilland two-bladed fixed-pitch wooden propeller
22 Spinner
23 Splined propeller shaft
24 Cooling air intake
25 Internal air duct
26 Engine mounting points
27 Engine bearer struts
28 Accessory equipment
29 Sloping engine bay bulkhead
30 Oil filler cap
31 Forward rudder pedals
32 Oil tank, capacity 2.5 Imp gal (11.4 litres)
33 Control column
34 Instrument venturi
35 Front pilot's (instructor's) seat
36 Tailplane trim control lever
37 Rear rudder pedals
38 Seat safety harness
39 Engine throttle lever
40 Instructor's instrument panel
41 Slat locking lever
42 Rear view mirror
43 Fuel tank sump and gravity feed pipe
44 Centre section root rib
45 Rear spar attachment joint
46 Cockpit side hatches
47 Cockpit bulkhead
48 Windscreen panel
49 Ignition switches
50 Student pilot's instrument panel
51 Throttle lever
52 Fire extinguisher bottle
53 Rear pilot's (student or solo flight) seat
54 Gosport speaking tube
55 Padded facia panel
56 Outline of blind flying hood closed position
57 Seat harness attachment
58 Blind flying hood, folded down
59 Starboard side locker door
60 Stowage locker
61 First aid kit
62 Plywood covered turtle decking
63 Anti-spin strakes
64 Control cable runs
65 Starboard tailplane
66 Starboard fabric covered elevator
67 Tailfin construction
68 Rudder horn balance

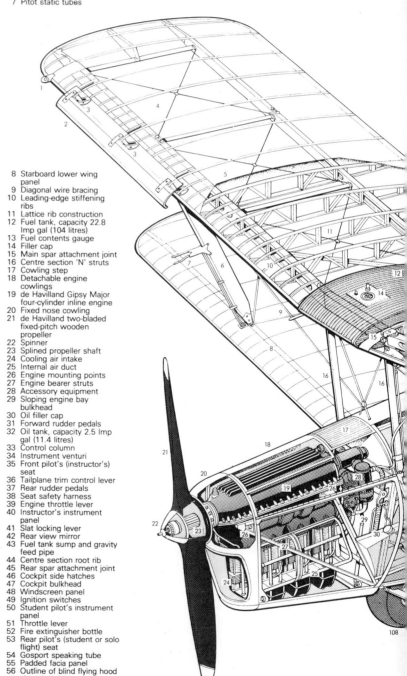

108

The Thruxton Jackaroo was a post-war four-seat cabin conversion of the Tiger Moth undertaken by Jackaroo Aircraft Ltd, starting in 1957, G-AOIR (shown here), being the fourth produced that year. Most were powered by the 145-hp (108-kW) Gipsy Major 1C in place of the more usual 130-hp (97-kW) Gipsy Major I of the Tiger.

the cost of replacement parts was only just over £7! (The cost of a Gipsy Moth, ex-works, was a mere £475.)

The introduction of the inverted Gipsy III in 1931 led to the D.H.60GIII Moth, whose prototype (G-ABUI) first flew in March 1932. This was followed by orders from all over the world. The third production aircraft was fitted with a special high-compression Gipsy IIIA which developed 133 hp (99 kW); flown by Hubert Broad, it finished fifth in the 1932 King's Cup Race at 131.34 mph (211.5 km/h). One long-distance flight by a D.H.60GIII is worthy of mention, that by the Portuguese pilot Carlos Bleck, who flew from Lisbon to Goa (Portuguese India), averaging 105 mph (169 km/h) over the 6,000 miles (9655 km) in February 1934. From the 58th airframe onwards the designation was changed to Moth Major to mark a change to the standard 130-hp (97-kW) Gipsy Major, although externally the aircraft was indistinguishable from the earlier type (the cooling fins of the Major's cylinders tapered inwards towards the crankcase, while those of the Gipsy III did not). Among British sporting owners of Moth Majors was the Duchess of Bedford; at the age of 72 the old lady took off for a solo flight in the G-ACUR over the North Sea on 23 March 1937, but was never seen again.

Last of the classic D.H.60s, and a link between them and the famous Tiger Moth ab initio trainer, was the D.H.60T Moth Trainer of which 63, including two prototypes, were produced, prompted by an order for 10 aircraft for the

Swedish air force in 1931. Light training armament (such as camera gun, light reconnaissance camera and practice bombs, etc) were specified, and subsequent batches were supplied to the Egyptian air force, the Brazilian air arms, and Iraq.

Also in 1927 were produced in great secrecy two small monoplanes, designated D.H.71 and intended for high-speed lightplane research. Given the name Tiger Moth (in no way to be confused with the later D.H.82), G-EBQU and G-EBRV were each powered initially by 85-hp (63-kW) A.D.C. Cirrus II engines, but the former was soon re-engined with Major Halford's new 135-hp (101-kW) Gipsy engine. Both were entered for the 1927 King's Cup Race, but one was scratched and the other withdrew from the race having averaged 166 mph (267 km/h). Shortly afterwards, with wings reduced in span from 22 ft 6 in (6.86 m) to 19 ft 0 in (5.79 m), the first aircraft was flown by Broad to establish a world Light-plane Class III speed record over a 62.1-mile (100 km)

69 Fabric covered rudder construction
70 Tail navigation light
71 Rudder operating lever
72 Sternpost
73 Elevator operating lever
74 Elevator construction
75 Tailplane rib construction, fabric covered
76 Sprung tailskid, linked to rudder
77 Tailplane bracing strut
78 Fuselage lower longeron
79 Elevator cables
80 Fuselage fabric covering
81 Primary fuselage structure, square-section tube
82 Rudder cables
83 Port upper wing panel rear spar
84 Inter-spar bracing strut
85 Front spar
86 Wing internal wire bracing
87 Fixed trailing-edge construction
88 Wing tip construction
89 Port navigation light

90 Port automatic leading-edge slat, closed
91 Interplane struts
92 Early type air pressure airspeed indicator
93 Diagonal wire bracing
94 Aileron pulley and operating lever
95 Port aileron construction
96 Rear spar
97 Wing tip construction
98 Main spar
99 Interplane strut attachment joint
100 Leading-edge stiffening ribs
101 Inter-spar bracing strut
102 Lattice rib construction
103 Wing walkway
104 Main undercarriage shock
105 Port mainwheel
106 Pivoted axle strut
107 Drag strut
108 Starboard mainwheel

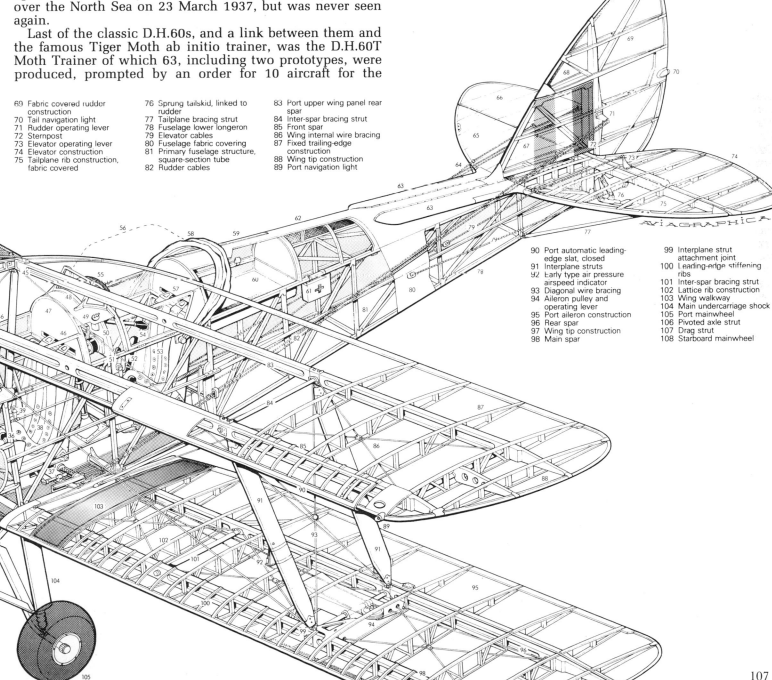

The light aeroplane that made the greatest impact on sporting aviation throughout the world in the 1920s was the D.H.60 Gipsy Moth, and it was flown in almost every country that supported flying facilities. Shown here with Australian registration, the Gipsy Moth was used by flying clubs at Adelaide, Brisbane, Longreach, Melbourne, Perth and Sydney.

The classic Tiger Moth was licence-built in Canada, New Zealand, Australia, Portugal, Norway and Sweden. The example depicted here was one of 20 D.H.82As produced by AB Svenska Järnvagsverkstaderna, Lindingö, as the Sk 11A for the Flygvapen.

closed circuit at 186.47 mph (300 km/h) on 24 August 1927.

Much closer to the true Moth tradition was the D.H.75 Hawk Moth, a four-seat cabin high-wing monoplane for which a new engine had been developed by Major Halford by inclining two Cirrus Is to mate on a common crankshaft as a V-8. The new engine, the Ghost, provided power of only 198-hp (148 kW), and after the prototype Hawk Moth had flown on 7 December 1928 the first two D.H.75A production aircraft were powered by 240-hp (179-kW) Armstrong Siddeley Lynx geared radials. Only five other aircraft were believed to have been built, of which one, designated D.H.75B, was fitted with a 300-hp (224-kW) Wright Whirlwind R-975 radial.

The next Moth, the D.H.80 Puss Moth, was also a high-wing cabin monoplane, this time a 'club three-seater' with the pilot seated forward of a two-place bench seat. This attractive little aeroplane remained in production for three years from mid-1930 until a total of 350 had been built, of which roughly half were exported. A spate of early accidents (in one of which the famous sporting pilot Bert Hinkler was killed on 7 January 1933) was diagnosed as the result of wing failure following control flutter, cured by mass-balanced ailerons and strengthened wing struts. Jim and Amy Mollison (the latter was Amy Johnson before her marriage) were the outstanding Puss Moth pilots; the former in G-ABXY *The Heart's Content* made the first solo east–west crossing of the North Atlantic on 18–19 August 1932; he also became the first to fly from England to South America, the first to make a solo east–west crossing of the South Atlantic and the first to make crossings of both North and South Atlantic.

Next in line, however, the D.H.82, was to eclipse even the magnificent D.H.60. The D.H.60T Moth Trainer had been in use by the RAF for some years when Air Ministry Specification 15/31 was issued calling for an improved version. Eight pre-production aircraft, using D.H.60 fuselages, were produced, but with the top wing centre-section moved forward and the outer sections swept back 19 in (48.26 cm) at the tips, thereby avoiding large changes in the centre of gravity position; this change in effect created the basis of the famous D.H.82 Tiger Moth. The first 35 production aircraft to Specification T.23/31 for the RAF were designated Tiger Moth Mk Is and entered service with the CFS and FTS, followed by two float-equipped aircraft to Specification T.6/33, but large-scale production started at Stag Lane early in 1934 with the issue of T.26/33, only to be switched to de

Havilland's new factory at Hatfield later in that year. Known in the RAF as the Tiger Moth Mk II, the new version departed from the Moth's traditional use of fabric and stringers behind the cockpits in favour of plywood decking, as well as provision for a blind-flying hood over the rear cockpit. Further contracts as well as Specification T.7/35 were received in 1935, so that pre-war production amounted to 1,150 at Hatfield, 227 by the de Havilland factory at Toronto, one by de Havilland at Wellington, New Zealand, and three by the DH Technical School. The vast majority had entered RAF service, but many had also gone to foreign owners and air forces as well as British flying clubs. On the outbreak of war most of the civil aircraft in the UK were impressed, the civilian schools providing the aircraft for the service's Elementary Flying Training Schools. In 1941 production of the de Havilland Mosquito at Hatfield forced the company to move Tiger Moth production to Morris Motors at Cowley, Oxford, where a total of 3,216 examples was produced before manufacture ended on 15 August 1945. Many of these Tiger Moths were shipped overseas where they provided the ab initio flying equipment of the schools that constituted the great Empire and Commonwealth Air Training Plan. Indeed, there were precious few wartime RAF pilots whose first experience of flight was not in the cockpit of a 'Tiger'.

After the war surplus Tiger Moths flooded into the civil market, while others continued to serve in the RAF for a number of years until replaced by the Percival Prentice and de Havilland Chipmunk.

Exuding nostalgia for RAF pilots of a former generation, this photo shows a de Havilland-built Tiger Moth being flown solo in 1941. So sensitive was the little trainer that it was possible to induce yaw simply by putting one's hand out into the slipstream as if to signal one's intention to turn!

Ford Tri-Motor

Popularly called the Tin Goose (and also, like the same company's Model T car, the Tin Lizzie), the Ford Tri-Motors combined the capable high-wing trimotor configuration of Fokker with the tough, all-metal construction of Junkers. This alone was enough for success in the tough airline world of the 1920s, but who could predict that these machines would make snap rolls and loops, fight fires, and still fly in the 1980s?

At the beginning of 1925 the Automobile King, Henry Ford, announced a reliability trial for transport planes. The race would begin at his company's headquarters in Dearborn, Michigan, and pass through most of the United States. Henry Ford had decided to extend his manufacturing to that of civil aircraft, and he sponsored this competition to find out who made the best transport planes. The Dutchman, Anthony Fokker, rapidly converted his remaining F.VII to run on three Wright engines and flew the first F.VII/3m to the USA in July 1925. He proved to be virtually unrivalled, and won the Ford Tour without any real problems. Henry's son, Edsel Ford, bought the Fokker for Byrd's North Pole expedition. He also persuaded his father that the three-engine high-wing aircraft was the best plane for his requirements. But Fokker was not interested in signing a licence contract with Ford to produce this model.

The Fokker was made of steel tube, wood and fabric, and after taking a lot of advice Henry Ford became convinced the future lay with what were at the time called 'all-metal ships'. Instead of just copying the Fokker, which is what Fokker himself insisted, incorrectly, was what happened, Ford decided to build an all-metal tri-motor high-wing transport of his own. In August 1925 he bought the Stout Metal

Airplane Company, whose founder, William Bushnell 'Bill' Stout, had pioneered the internally braced metal monoplane in the USA. From 1922 Stout had built reliable and aerodynamically clean transports, with Liberty, Wright and other engines, with an outer skin entirely of Alclad (described later).

Ford purchased several of these single-engine transports, and like many other companies jumped on the mail bandwagon made possible by the Kelly Act of 1925, which enabled private companies to bid for air mail routes. On 15 February 1926 Ford's Stout Air Services began flying the Detroit–Cleveland and Detroit–Chicago routes. But Ford could see that the future called for a bigger multi-engine aircraft, and he told Stout to build him a tri-motor.

Stout had the ball at his feet, but he rushed through his Model 3-AT as if timing mattered more than the result. It will probably never be known precisely what happened, but

Tri-motors nos 69, 74 and 75 were all of the Model 5-AT-CS type with twin floats for water-based operation. It is shown as built, with two engines fitted with ring cowls and registered as a US civil aircraft (NC414H). Later it is believed to have served, with at least one other Model 5-AT-CS, with the Chilean air force.

109

Ford Tri-Motor

Specification

Ford Model 5-AT-B
Type: passenger transport
Powerplant: three 420-hp (313-kW) Pratt & Whitney Wasp
C-series nine-cylinder radial piston engines
Performance: maximum speed 161 mph (259 km/h); cruising
speed 123 mph (198 km/h); normal range 440 miles (708 km)
Weights: empty (typical, as built) 7,600 lb (3447 kg); maximum
12,650 lb (5738 kg)
Dimensions: span 77 ft 10 in (23.72 m); length 50 ft 3 in (15.3 m);
height (tail down) 12 ft 0 in (3.66 m); wing area 835 sq ft (77.57 m²).
Accommodation: flight crew of two side-by-side plus normal
seating for up to 15 passengers, or (later) 13 plus steward, or
3,350 lb (1520 kg) cargo

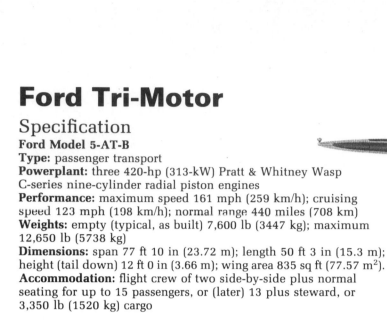

Ford Model 5-AT-39 has had a long and very active life, passing through
many minor changes and different paint schemes. She is depicted as she
was when four years old in 1933, flying for American. After leaving
American she toiled for operators in many Latin American countries as
well as Alaska and Mexico before being completely refurbished in 1962 by
Aircraft Hydro-Forming (a US company which made a prolonged attempt
in the past 20 years to re-establish production of an improved Tri-Motor,
the Stout Bushmaster 2000). A year later she was bought by American
(long since Airlines instead of Airways) and repainted with her old
number for publicity flying.

Ford Tri-Motor

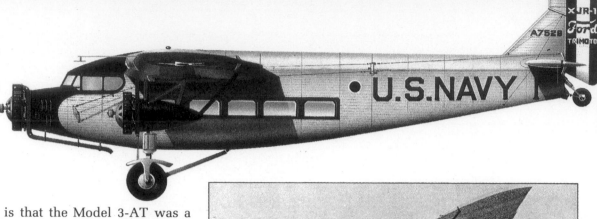

The fourth Tri-Motor built was the lone XJR-1 ordered by the US Navy in March 1927. A Model 4-AT, it was tested at Anacostia in 1928 and put into service as a cargo and personnel transport before being damaged beyond repair in April 1930. It was the precursor of eight additional Tri-Motors in navy/marines service.

what seems beyond dispute is that the Model 3-AT was a crude and unimpressive lash-up. It may have flown only once before it was destroyed in a fire on the ground, which also destroyed the factory at Ford Airport, on 17 January 1926. Ford and Stout had a violent argument which ended in Stout being fired.

In February 1926 Ford decided to proceed with an improved aircraft, the Model 4-AT, whose design was based on that of the Model 3-AT but differed in almost all details and especially in the engine installations, cockpit, landing gear and fuselage. The small engineering team was headed by Harold Hicks and Tom Towle, but it is difficult today to determine whether they or Stout should receive the main credit for this classic and long-lived aircraft.

The first of the successful Ford tri-motors was flown for the first time on 11 June 1926. Most surviving pictures, and all surviving Fords, are of the larger Model 5-AT variety, but the Model 4-AT was as important as its successor and will now be described.

Though some of the high-wing transports of the day, including the Fokkers, had their wing mounted above the fuselage, the Ford wing was recessed so that the three spars significantly reduced headroom in the cabin. Each spar was

The Model 4-At-3, the third Tri-Motor to be built, typified the early production machines with enclosed cockpit, revised cabin windows and many other changes, but still with wire wheels with mudguards. It operated on the Ford Freight Line from late 1926 with 200-hp (149-kW) Whirlwind J4 engines. Gross weight was 9,200 lb (4173 kg).

After the false start with the Model 3-AT the Stout Metal Airplane division built the first true ancestor of the Tri-Motors in the Model 4-AT-1, flown on 11 June 1926. The assistant chief engineer was a young man of Scottish ancestry named James S. McDonnell, a recent graduate from MIT, whose later aircraft went faster.

a Warren-braced truss assembled mainly by riveting, and the ribs were likewise built up from rolled strip and sections. The wing was a generation earlier in form than the superb multi-spar stressed-skin wings of John R. Northrop, one of which was the basis of the Douglas DC series in the early 1930s. The Northrop (Douglas) wings proved to have hardly any fatigue problem, but Fords have suffered a certain amount of cracking after flying over 5,000 hours, a figure seldom even approached in commercial service between the world wars.

Rugged structure

Like that of Douglas, the Ford wing was made in three parts, the rectangular centre section being integral with the fuselage. The latter was a capacious box, though unlike that of the Fokkers it had a rounded top which may have reduced drag. The three engines, which in the Model 4-AT were 200-hp (149-kW) Wright J-4 Whirlwinds driving two-blade metal propellers, were uncowled and in most Fords not even provided with cooling airflow baffles or fairings. In the Model 3-AT the nose engine had been mounted low to balance the thrust lines of the two wing-mounted engines, but in the Model 4-AT the centre engine was mounted exactly on the nose and the other pair brought down so that all thrust lines were at the same level, the wing engines now

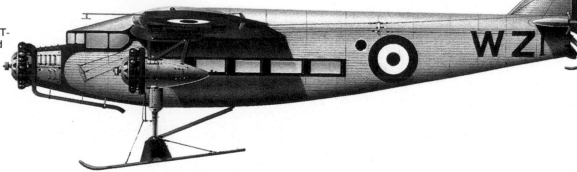

This unique Ford was Model 6-AT-1, basically a Model 5-AT-C fitted with low-powered Wright Whirlwind J6 engines, sold as a sea/ski-plane to the Royal Canadian Air Force in 1929. It is pictured with only the last two letters of its civil registration G-CYWZ. Its main duty was forest patrol and dusting, followed by radio research.

US Army Air Corps aircraft 31-401 was the first of three Tri-Motor Model 5-AT-Ds with the Army designation C-4A. It was the 91st Tri-Motor, delivered in 1931. Like most army Fords it had Townend rings round its R 1340 Wasps and spats over the mainwheels. The Army bought 13 Fords, seven being less-powerful C-3As.

being carried on the front of separate strut-mounted nacelles well below the wing. The wing engines had short stub exhausts or, from 1927, an exhaust manifold leading to a short pipe on the outboard side of the nacelle. The nose engine, however, sent its gas through a pipe running (in most versions) half way back to the tail, surrounded by a muff open at the front so that, in cold weather, heated fresh air could be admitted to the cabin.

Unlike those of many later metal stressed-skin aircraft, the movable control surfaces, as well as the fixed tail, were metal-skinned. The extreme nose and the top and bottom of the fuselage were often skinned with smooth metal sheet, but almost all other surfaces were of Junkers-style corrugated sheet. Such sheet could be made in thin gauges yet resist local impacts or buckling loads, and it was retained in Junkers aircraft up to the last Ju 52/3m in mid-1944. In fact, it was only after World War 2 that careful measurements revealed that the drag penalty of corrugated skin was con-

siderable, the air hardly ever flowing in the direction of the corrugations! The one good thing about the skin of the Fords was that, from the first Model 4-AT, the material used was Alclad, duralumin coated with non-corrosive pure aluminium. For good measure the assembled structure was then given a sprayed coating of varnish. This explains the outstanding longevity of these aircraft.

All the Fords had an oval entrance door on the right side, used for passengers, cargo and also by the two pilots. In the Model 4-AT the latter had the usual open cockpit, a feature of which was a sharply angled Vee windshield which had glass panes that were not vertical but sloped outwards from bottom to top, to give a better view for landing. Panels in the windshield could be slid open in really bad weather. The Model 4-AT had four passenger seats on each side of a central aisle, and was available with a lavatory at the rear. Light personal baggage could be placed in a typical suspended mesh rack along each side of the cabin above the windows, level with the bottoms of the wing spars. In a few Model 4-ATs further baggage and mail was stowed in drop-down lockers between the spars at the inner end of each outer wing panel, though this was really a feature of later models. Other features by no means common in 1926 were wheel brakes, which enabled a tailwheel to be used instead of a skid, and an electrical system with the battery charged by a generator in the nose engine. This system served navigation lights and, in most aircraft, leading-edge landing lamps and two-way radio. On the other hand, the Fords adhered to the old

This Ford 5-AT passenger/mail plane of National Airlines had specially built mail compartments in its wings; here they have been opened for loading.

practice of running the tail control cables along the outside of the fuselage from large rocker arms on the sides of the nose.

One of the first customers was Stout himself, who had formed Stout Air Services to fly schedules from Detroit to Chicago and other cities in the Great Lakes region. But the first and largest customer was a Los Angeles car dealer, Jack Maddux. He first had to be satisfied with the Ford's ability to operate over the mountains of California and neighbouring states, and of its reliability; then he eventually bought 16 of different versions for Maddux Air Lines.

Subsequent Fords had an enclosed cockpit with sliding side windows, and various other refinements, and almost all were more powerful. As listed in the separate Variants section, there were almost as many sub-types as there were aircraft built, partly because there were numerous rebuilds and conversions. The initial Model 4-AT-A eight-seater entered service with Ford's own air service on 2 August 1926. Ford Airport at Dearborn had by this time become the first in the world with paved runways and full electric lighting, and later Ford not only made many other improvements to the buildings but also set up one of the world's first training schools for commercial flight crews.

Most famous of all Tri-Motors, the Model 4-AT-15 was donated by Henry and Edsel Ford for the Antarctic expedition of Commander Richard E. Byrd. Pilot Bernt Balchen found it needed more range, so the span was increased to 74 ft (22.55 m), tankage was augmented and a powerful Cyclone was put on the nose. It overflew the South Pole.

One of the almost priceless survivors, Ford Model 5-AT-39 served with American Airlines in 1933–5. Then followed many years of trucking all over the Americas from Chile to Alaska. In 1962 the still highly airworthy ship was bought by American, completely refurbished and used for publicity and promotional purposes.

Though the Model 4-AT had been the biggest all-metal aircraft then built in the USA, and possibly in the world, it was rightly judged too small and the Model 4-AT-B of 1927 had a span increased from 68 ft 10 in (20.97 m) to 73 ft 11 in (22.53 m), matching the greater power of 220-hp (164-kW) J-6 Whirlwind engines. Though the fuselage was almost the

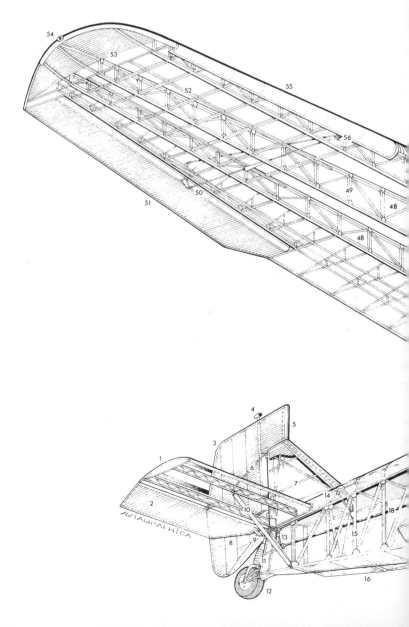

Ford Tri-Motor variants

Model 3-AT: original Stout tri-motor prototype, destroyed 17 January 1926
Model 4-AT: first Ford tri-motor; three J-4 Whirlwind radials and eight passengers
Model 4-AT-A: initial production model, similar to Model 4-AT; 14 built
Model 4-AT-B: increased span and J-5 Whirlwind radials; accommodation for two pilots and 12 passengers; 35 built
Model 4-AT-C: similar to the Model 4-AT-B but with 400-hp (298-kW) Wasp radial; 1 built
Model 4-AT-D: used wing similar to that of the Model 5-AT; total production was three, one having J-4 Whirlwind radial, another with two J-5 Whirlwind radials and one 300-hp (298-kW) J-6-9 Whirlwind radials; and the last with three J-6-9 Whirlwind radials
Model 4-AT-E: detail changes and three 300-hp (298-kW) J-6 Whirlwind radials; 24 built
Model 4-AT-F: one aircraft similar to the Model 4-AT-E and built in 1931
Model 5-AT-A: enlarged variant with three 420-hp (313-kW) Wasp radials; 3 built
Model 5-AT-B: new 15-seater of 1929 with three 420-hp (313-kW) Wasp C-1 or Wasp SC-1 radials; 42 built
Model 5-AT-C: improved 17-seat version; 48 built
Model 5-AT-D: increased-weight version with three 450-hp (336-kW) Wasp SC radials; 24 built
Model 6-AT-A: similar to the Model 5-AT-C but with J-6 Whirlwind radials; 3 built
Model 7-AT-A: rebuild of Model 6-AT-A with a nose-mounted 420-hp (313-kW) Wasp radial
Model 8-AT: single Model 5-AT-C converted as a freighter without wing-mounted engines
Model 9-AT: conversion of Model 4-AT-B with 300-hp (224-kW) Wasp Junior radials; 1 converted

Model 11-AT: one Model 4-AT-E rebuilt with 225-hp (168-kW) Packard DR-980 diesels
Model 13-A: conversion of one Model 5-AT-D with two J-6 Whirlwind radials and one 575-hp (429-kW) Cyclone radial
Model 14-A: one much larger aircraft of 1932 with two 715-hp (533-kW) and one 1,100-hp (820-kW) Hispano-Suiza engines; this 40-seater was completed but not flown
C-3: US Army no. 28-348; based on Model 4-AT-B
C-3A: US Army nos 29-220/226, seven aircraft with 235-hp (175-kW) R-790-3 Whirlwind radials
C-4: US Army no. 29-219; basically a Model 4-AT-B for military service
C-4A: US Army nos 31-401/404, four aircraft based on the Model 5-AT-D with 450-hp (336-kW) R-1340-11 radials
C-9: redesignation of all seven C-3As after the installation of 300-hp (224-kW) R-975-1 radials
XJR-1: US Navy no. A7526, based on Model 4-AT
JR-2: US Navy nos A8273/8274, two aircraft based on the Model 4-AT-E for the US Marine Corps
JR-3: US Navy nos A8457 and A8598/8599, three aircraft based on the Model 5-AT-C
RR-2: redesignation of JR-2
RR-3: redesignation of JR-3
RR-4: additional Model 5-AT-C with US Navy no. A8840
RR-5: US Navy nos 9205/9206, two aircraft based on the Model 5-AT-D, one of them delivered to the US Marine Corps
XB-906-1: single prototype (NX9652) for a bomber version with internal racks and two gunner's positions; crashed on 19 September 1931 killing Ford's chief test pilot, Leroy Manning

Possibly Model 5-AT-11, this Tri-Motor in the 5-AT series was one of four supplied in 1930 to Cia Mexicana de Aviacion, an affiliate of Pan American. All had uncowled Wasp engines, but after World War 2 various powerplants appeared on Ford Tri-Motors throughout Latin America, including cowled Wasp Juniors from BT-13s.

same as before, the seating limit went up to 12. There followed various sub-types of Model 4-AT, differing chiefly in engine arrangement. Almost all the Fords were originally built with spatted main wheels, and their modern image did much to promote sales.

When the Ford was a new and very modern aircraft, most had Wright engines in the 200/220-hp (149/164-kW) bracket, but production of this Model 4-AT family came to an end (except for the single Model 4-AT-F) in 1929. By this time the much more powerful, and further enlarged, Model 5-AT family was selling even better than its predecessors, and output of Model 5-ATs reached a remarkable four per week in 1929, before the Wall Street crash.

A8840 was the US Navy RR-4, basically a Model 5-AT-C with the enlarged wing and three 450-hp (335-kW) Wasp engines with Townend ring cowls. The Tri-Motor in the US Naval Aviation Museum at NAS Pensacola is painted and presented as this aircraft, but its true identity is not certain.

Ford Tri-motor 5-AT-D cutaway drawing key

1 Starboard tailplane
2 Starboard elevator
3 Rudder
4 Tail navigation light
5 Rudder horn balance
6 Tailplane bracing wire
7 Tailfin
8 Corrugated tailplane skins
9 Elevator hinge strut
10 Tailplane bracing strut
11 Tailwheel shock absorber
12 Tailwheel
13 Tailplane incidence screw jack
14 Fin attachment
15 Rear fuselage construction
16 Port elevator
17 Port tailplane
18 Incidence control shaft
19 Fuselage top decking
20 Corrugated fuselage skins
21 Tail control cable pulleys
22 Flare dispenser
23 Wash basin
24 Step
25 Cabin door
26 Toilet compartment
27 Fire extinguisher
28 Rear cabin seating
29 Cabin roof luggage racks
30 Cabin windows
31 Fuselage strut bracing construction
32 Bottom longeron
33 Starboard mainwheel
34 Shock absorber leg strut
35 Starboard Pratt & Whitney Wasp radial engine
36 Two bladed propeller
37 NACA cowling ring
38 Engine cooling air shutters
39 Engine mounting framework
40 Oil tank
41 Exhaust pipe
42 Engine cowling fairing
43 Engine pylon struts
44 Centre wing panel
45 Wing corrugated skins
46 Spar attachment joints
47 Drop-down mail and baggage lockers
48 Outer wing panel spars
49 Wing spar strut bracing
50 Aileron hinge control
51 Starboard aileron
52 Wing rib bracing
53 Wing tip construction
54 Starboard navigation light
55 Reinforced leading edge
56 Aileron cable pulley
57 Landing and taxi lamp
58 Corrugated leading edge skin
59 Outer wing panel attachment rib
60 Fuel tanks
61 Cabin roof fairing
62 Fuselage main frame
63 Passenger seats
64 Starboard undercarriage swing axle
65 Cabin floor
66 Cabin heater duct fairing
67 Centre engine exhaust pipe
68 Air vents
69 Battery
70 External control cables
71 Co-pilot's seat
72 Cockpit side windows
73 Instrument panel
74 Control column hand-wheel
75 Cockpit roof windows
76 Sliding windscreen panel
77 Windscreen frame
78 Centre engine fairing air louvres
79 Oil tank
80 Centre engine mounting framework
81 Rudder pedals
82 Exhaust collector ring
83 Centre Pratt & Whitney Wasp engine
84 NACA cowling ring
85 Two-bladed propeller
86 Port Pratt & Whitney Wasp engine
87 NACA cowling ring
88 Engine pylon fairing
89 Port landing and taxi lamp
90 Reinforced leading edge
91 Instrument pitot head
92 Port wing tip
93 Port navigation light
94 Outer wing panel construction
95 Aileron hinge control
96 Port aileron
97 Port mainwheel
98 Mudguard fairing
99 Shock absorber leg fairing
100 Swing axle struts

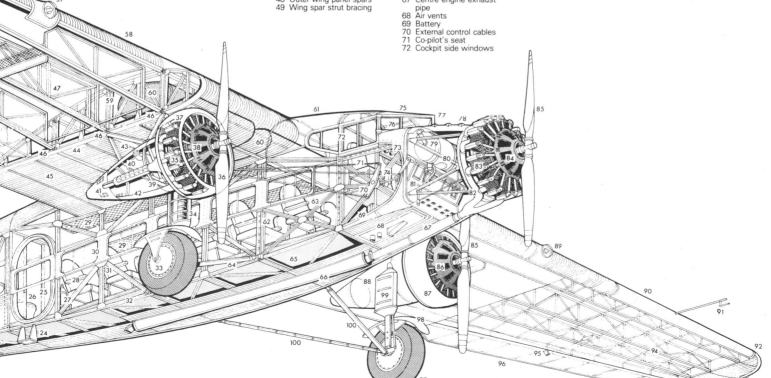

Ford Tri-Motor

On 9 May 1926 Lieutenant Commander Richard E. Byrd, USN, noted polar explorer, had reached and flown over the North Pole in a prototype tri-motor Fokker F.VIIA/3m piloted by Floyd Bennett. However, the trip was not without its problems for the Fokker, called *Josephine Ford*, developed oil-leaks in the engines, so it was Byrd's intention to use another aircraft to overfly the South Pole, his next ambition. The plane he chose was a Ford Tri-Motor Model 4-AT-15, called *Floyd Bennett*, Byrd's pilot having died of pneumonia.

But this venture proved more hazardous than the Arctic flight, for the South Pole had no occupied base within a radius of 1,000 miles (1600km) and the Tri-Motor was not up to the job, being unable to carry four men, all the necessary equipment and fuel for the return leg. A base, some 440 miles (708km) south of Little America, was established in the Bay of Whales and it was intended to use it for the return trip. A Scandinavian, Bernt Balchin, was named pilot.

The Tri-Motor rose into the air on 28 November 1929 and the plane became the first to fly over the Pole, but not without its moments. Sufficient height became a problem at one stage and food had to be jettisoned but at last Byrd became the first man to fly over both Poles.

More engines, more sales

Thanks to the use of the Pratt & Whitney Wasp engine, the Model 5-AT was a much more capable aircraft. First flown in mid-1928, the Model 5-AT had a further enlarged wing, the fuselage deepened to give more headroom under the wing, Townend-ring cowled wing engines (often a cowled nose engine also), and a structure strengthened for operation at greater weights. No fewer than 117 were built in 1929–31, many of them having float or ski landing gear. Many were built with the wing baggage/mail lockers, and others were thus equipped as a modification. The cabin could be equipped to seat up to 17, with eight seats on the right and nine on the left even with a rear lavatory.

Some of the versions of this aircraft were built for military purposes. The first companies to buy the 198 civil aircraft built were American, British Columbia, CLASSA (Spain), Colonial, Colonial Western, CMA (Mexico), Curtiss Flying Service, Eastern, Ford, Jefferson, Maddux, Mamer, Mohawk, NAT (National), Northwest, NYRBA (New York, Rio and

US Army Air Corps X (NX) 9652 was the one-off XB-906-1 bomber, built at the firm's expense and using what was mainly a Model 5-AT-D airframe (but with a redesigned vertical tail). There were guns above and below at the rear and a bombardier's station under the cockpit. This aircraft disintegrated fatally in a dive in 1931.

Buenos Aires), Pacific, Pan American, Pan American Grace, Pennsylvania, Pitcairn, Queen City (Ohio), Rapid, Robertson, SCADTA (Colombia), SAFE (Southwest Air Fast Express), Spokane, Stout, TAT (Transcontinental Air Transport) and Universal Flyers. After 1930 many Fords appeared on the secondhand market and were soon snapped up. Standard Oil was the first industrial company to buy Ford aircraft (the first one they bought was new), and Royal Typewriters wrote on the fuselage of the plane they bought: 'Capacity 210 portable typewriters'. Several aircraft were exported to England, where the airport at Ford in Sussex bought them for their name and became a maintenance base for the many triple-engined machines which people were optimistically hoping to sell in Europe.

In 1934 W.S. Shackleton, of Piccadilly, London, sent four aircraft from Piccadilly to New Guinea, where they and various Junkers were used to service mining operations. One machine belonging to the Guinness family was given a set of roundels and became no. X5000 of No. 271 Squadron of the RAF. Many flew with the US Forces, the RAAF, the RCAF, the Colombian Air Force and the Republicans in the Spanish Civil War. The many Fords sold to Latin American countries remained in service longest. The Honduran company TACA had a particularly large number: at one point it owned thirty. The plane with the most unusual history was the Model 5-AT-11 (the eleventh Model 5-AT), whose first owners were Pan American and TACA. The latter sold it in August 1945 for $4,500 to the Mexican company TATSA, which flew the aircraft between Mazatlan and a tiny airstrip at the bottom of a canyon to service a mine at Tayoltita. As this was the only aircraft TATSA used for this purpose, it transported over 65,000 passengers and 6,700 tonnes of freight without a hitch and clocked up 5,376 hours of flight. In 1966 Island Airlines in Port Clinton, Ohio, bought the aircraft, by which time it had flown 23,000 hours. By the mid-1980s the old Ford Tri-Motor was still being used.

Built as NX8499, the lone Ford Model 8-AT was a single-engined machine completed as a freighter but used from 1929 until 1933 to test the Wright Cyclone (seen here), Pratt & Whitney Hornet, Hispano-Suiza 12 and Bliss-built Bristol Jupiter. From 1933 it had a fully cowled Cyclone and served as shown with Pacific Alaska Airways.

N414H may have been the last Tri-Motor on the US active register. Owned by Scenic Airways Inc., of Las Vegas, Nevada, it is still in existence and has been used for local pleasure flying (for example, as far as the Grand Canyon). One Scenic 5-AT caught out its pilot – unused to taildragger landing gears – and ground-looped.

Bristol Bulldog

If tenacity is an attribute of the bulldog, it was certainly evident in the manner by which the outmoded Bulldog clung to service with the Royal Air Force. By no stretch of the imagination an outstanding design of fighter aircraft, even in its day it nevertheless constituted the RAF's fighter backbone during the early 1930s.

In 1924 the British Air Staff issued specifications for an interceptor; the main criterion was good climbing performance rather than the range that would be needed for longer patrol flights. If possible the machine was to have a Rolls-Royce Falcon X engine, which later became famous as the Kestrel, even though this engine was too heavy, because it was still common to cast the cylinders individually. Frank Barnwell and Roy Fedden advocated the use of a radial engine. Specification F.17/24 was then replaced by specification F.9/26, which involved either a V-engine or a radial engine. Barnwell recommended the Bristol type 102A to fulfil this specification, and for the requirements of a fighter wanted by the Navy, N.21/26, a type 102B for float planes. As none of the Rolls-Royce V-12 engines being developed in 1926 was suitable for use in an interceptor, specification F.9/26 was partially replaced by F.20/27, for which Fedden recommended a Bristol Mercury III radial engine with gears.

In due course Bristol started work on a Mercury-powered prototype, the Type 107 Bullpup (J9051), which was scheduled for competitive evaluation with designs from Hawker, Gloster, Vickers and Westland. However, as a result of the limited availability of the geared Mercury engine, Barnwell produced a private-venture design, the Type 105 Bulldog

with a Bristol Jupiter VII radial, and, as this presented no installation problems, the Bulldog prototype was first flown by Cyril Uwins on 17 May 1927 while the Bullpup still awaited its Mercury.

The Bulldog's structure employed high-tensile steel strip using flat gusset plates in place of bolted joints, the wings and fuselage being fabric-covered. The lower wing was of much reduced span and chord, and of Clark YH section, while the big upper wing, of Bristol IA section, carried the fuel in two centre-section gravity tanks. Characteristically, armament remained the time-honoured pair of forward-firing Vickers guns on the sides of the nose, firing between the engine cylinders and synchronized to avoid the propeller.

Although regarded as an outsider in the F.9/26 evaluation at Martlesham Heath, the Bulldog quickly disposed of all opposition but the Hawker Hawfinch, with which it entered the final stage. A second Bulldog (designated a Mk II and serialled J9480) was ordered in November 1927 for extended

Prototype Bulldog, referred to as the Mk I, at Filton in May 1927, with Cyril Uwins in the cockpit. Seen here in its original form with small rudder, this aircraft was subsequently fitted with enlarged rudder and wings for high altitude trials at Farnborough.

Bristol Bulldog

Specification

Bulldog Mk IIA

Type: single-seat interceptor

Powerplant: one 440-hp (328-kW) Bristol Jupiter VIIF air-cooled radial piston engine

Performance: maximum speed 178 mph (286 km/h) at 10,000 ft (3050 m); climb to 20,000 ft (6095 m) in 14 minutes 30 seconds; service ceiling 27,000 ft (8230 m); normal range 310 miles (499 km)

Weights: empty 2,222 lb (1008 kg); maximum take-off 3,660 lb (1660 kg)

Dimensions: span 33 ft 11 in (10.34 m); length 25 ft 2 in (7.67 m); height 9 ft 10 in (3.00 m); wing area 306.5 sq ft (28.47 m²)

Armament: two forward-firing synchronized 0.303-in (7.7-mm) Vickers machine-guns on the sides of the nose, plus occasional provision for four 20-lb (9-kg) bombs

A Bristol Bulldog Mk IIA of No. 32 (Fighter) Sqn, RAF. These aircraft first arrived on the squadron in September 1930 when it was based at Kenley, commanded by Squadron Leader B. E. (later Air Marshal Sir Brian, CB, DSO, MC, AFC) Baker. Two years later it moved to Biggin Hill, retaining its Bulldogs until replaced by Gloster Gauntlets in July 1936. The blue squadron flash was crossed by white diagonals, although the number of such diagonals does not appear to have been consistent throughout the squadron.

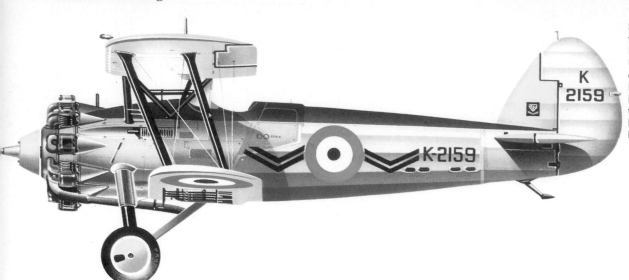

Standard-issue Bulldog Mk IIA of the flight commander, 'C' Flight, No. 17 (Fighter) Sqn, RAF, based at Upavon in 1933. The squadron was one of the first to receive Bulldog Mk IIs which replaced Woodcocks in 1928, the Mk IIA starting to arrive two years later. Note the extended Hucks starter dog on the propeller boss.

competition with the Hawfinch in 1928, and was finally judged the winner, largely on account of its steel construction.

Meanwhile the Bulldog Mk I prototype underwent extensive modification (for an attempt on the world climb and altitude records) by the installation of a high aspect ratio wing and supercharged Jupiter VII radial.

The prototype Bulldog Mk II was flown by Uwins on 21 January 1928 and after achieving success in competition against the Hawfinch was purchased by the Air Ministry for £4,800. A production batch of 26 aircraft was laid down, comprising 25 (J9567–J9591) for the RAF and one company demonstrator (G-AAHH). The first RAF Bulldog Mk IIs were allocated to Nos 3 and 17 (Fighter) Squadrons at Upavon, replacing Hawker Woodcocks. One of the first batch was diverted to the company agents in Japan, but this aircraft was replaced by an additional aircraft as J9591, and this became a test-bed for the geared Mercury IV.

The next batch of 23 RAF aircraft (K1079–K1101), delivered in 1930, completed the establishment of No. 17 Squadron as well as equipping No. 54 (Fighter) Squadron at Hornchurch.

Already the Bulldog was proving popular among RAF pilots, its manoeuvrability setting it well ahead of its predecessors, the Gloster Grebe and Gloster Gamecock, and it was this partisan esteem (not to mention the relatively low cost of the long-established Jupiter engine) that prompted considerable follow-up orders. It was thus during the depressed years of 1930–3, when defence appropriations were

strictly limited, that the unimaginative Bulldog gained preference on account of its low cost. However the competitive Kestrel V-12 engine had emerged from Rolls-Royce, first in the Hawker Hart bomber and then in the Hawker Fury fighter, both aircraft possessing a superior performance to that of the Bulldog.

The first improved Bulldog for the RAF was the Bulldog Mk IIA with Jupiter VIIF engine, revised wing spars and local strengthening to allow increased all-up weight, and was the subject of an RAF order for 92 aircraft placed in May 1930, yet the new variant's speed performance remained unaltered at 178 mph (286 km/h) at 10,000 ft (3050 m). In 1931 an additional 100 Bulldog Mk IIAs were ordered, and by the end of that year 10 of the 13 home-based RAF fighter squadrons were equipped with Bulldogs (Nos 3, 17, 19, 23, 29, 32, 41, 54, 56 and 111); the others were equipped or equipping with the Hawker Fury Mk I, while one flight of No. 23 Squadron was flying the Hart Fighter, or Demon.

As early as 1933 Bulldogs started phasing out of service, No. 23 Squadron completing a changeover to Demons in April. In 1935 Nos 19 and 29 followed with Gloster Gauntlets and Demons, and in June 1937 (only six months before the Hawker Hurricane appeared in service) No. 3 Squadron at Kenley became the last to discard its Bulldogs; No. 3 had been the only RAF fighter unit to fly Bulldogs in the Middle East, taking its aircraft to Khartoum in October during the crisis in Abyssinia. Of the 441 Bulldogs produced at Filton,

Although No. 17 Sqn, RAF, received its first new Bulldog Mk IIs in October 1928, its full complement of aircraft was achieved by taking over some of No. 3 Sqn's aircraft, also based at Upavon. In this photograph the nearest aircraft retains No. 3 Sqn's green flash and others have yet to be fully painted in No. 17's famous zig-zag flashes.

Later to be distinguished as the first squadron to fly Gauntlets, and later Spitfires, No. 19 (Fighter) Sqn received Bulldog Mk IIAs in September 1931; this ex-No 17 Sqn aircraft carried the familiar blue and white checks on the tail and wing surfaces denoting the aircraft flown by Squadron Leader (later Air Vice-Marshal) J. R. Cassidy.

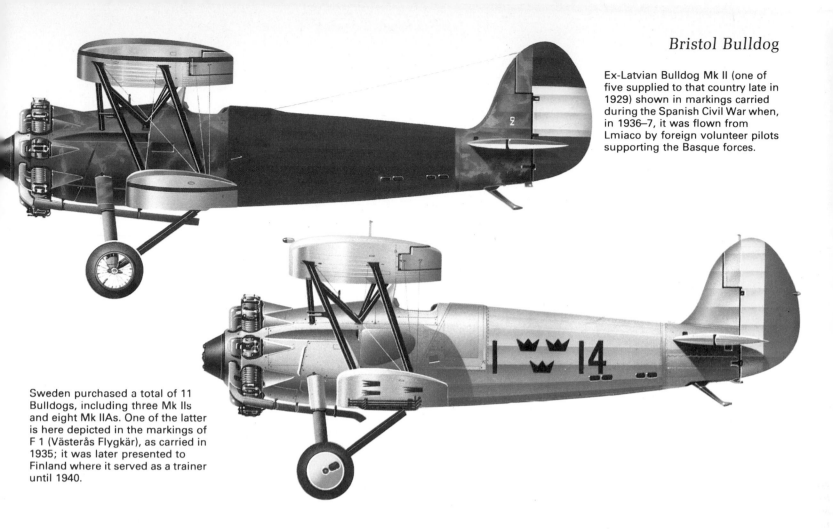

Ex-Latvian Bulldog Mk II (one of five supplied to that country late in 1929) shown in markings carried during the Spanish Civil War when, in 1936–7, it was flown from Lmiaco by foreign volunteer pilots supporting the Basque forces.

Sweden purchased a total of 11 Bulldogs, including three Mk IIs and eight Mk IIAs. One of the latter is here depicted in the markings of F 1 (Västerås Flygkär), as carried in 1935; it was later presented to Finland where it served as a trainer until 1940.

Bristol, a single example survived in flying condition in the UK until the 1960s, but this was destroyed in an accident during a display at Farnborough following what appears to have been pilot error during low-level aerobatics.

The Bulldog two-seater

At the end of 1931 one of the production batch of 100 Bulldog Mk IIAs for the RAF was retained by the manufacturer for conversion to a two-seater, and this dual-control trainer, K2188 (known as the Bulldog TM, or training machine) was evaluated by the Central Flying School during 1932. A production order for 17 aircraft followed, these

aircraft being distributed between the CFS and Coastal Area at Leuchars, as well as to six of the RAF's fighter squadrons; later aircraft served at the Royal Air Force College, Cranwell.

A total of 59 Bulldog TMs was eventually built, some of these remaining in service with flying training schools until 1939; they were also the only Bulldogs to serve on a permanent basis with the RAF in the Middle East, some examples equipping No. 4 FTS at Abu Sueir in Egypt.

As already mentioned, the final Bulldog Mk II of the first production batch was retained for test-bed work by Bristol with a geared Mercury IV engine. Thereafter numerous installations were undertaken, including an aircraft marked R-1 which flew with a Mercury III driving a four-blade

The demonstration Bulldog G-ABBB (R-II) with Bristol Aquila I sleeve-valve radial in 1935. This was the aircraft that, restored post-war with a Jupiter VIIFP engine, was made airworthy with the spurious registration K2227 and presented to the Shuttleworth Trust before being destroyed in a flying accident at Farnborough.

Characterized by the mounting of Madsen guns lower on the fuselage sides, the four Type 105D Danish Bulldogs equipped No. 1 Sqn, Danish Army Aviation Troops in 1931; three, the Type Mk IIa, were still in service as fighter trainers at the time of the German invasion of Denmark in April 1940.

propeller, followed by installation of a Gnome-Rhône Jupiter VI; in the latter guise, while practising for a foreign demonstration tour, the aircraft crashed when T. W. Campbell baled out rather than risk landing after damaging the rudder bar in a flick roll. A replacement demonstrator was produced with a Gnome-Rhône 9Asb, and after a number of demonstrations this Jupiter was replaced by a Bristol Aquila sleeve-valve radial; it was this aircraft, with a re-built Jupiter, that became the sole British survivor after World War 2.

In an early attempt to improve the Bulldog, Bristol produced the private-venture Bulldog Mk IIIA in 1931 with a Mercury IVA (later Mercury IVS2), and this was flown in competition with the Gloster SS.19B to decide a Bulldog replacement in the RAF. Pursuing much the same course as Gloster in the progressive development of a single prototype, Bristol did considerable work on the Bulldog Mk IIIA, but in the end the SS.19B emerged the winner and entered service as the Gauntlet. Bristol then produced the Bulldog Mk IVA with four guns in 1934 for competition under Specification F.7/30 requirements, with a Mercury VIS2 radial, but once again the Bulldog's 224 mph (360 km/h) speed was no match for the SS.37's 250 mph (402 km/h), and the latter entered service with the RAF as the Gladiator.

Bulldog two-seaters were also employed as engine test-beds for the Armstrong Sideley Cheetah and Alvis Leonides radials, and the Napier Rapier air-cooled inline.

Foreign Bulldogs

From the earliest days of the Bulldog's RAF service the aircraft attracted considerable interest overseas, nurtured by a constant programme of demonstrations by company pilots throughout Europe, the Bulldog's relatively low cost once more proving a considerable attraction. Apart from the aircraft diverted to Japan from the first production batch and mentioned above, the first true overseas order was for five Gnome-Rhône Jupiter VI-powered aircraft with twin Oerlikon machine-guns which followed that first batch in 1929 and were shipped to Latvia.

The next Bulldog on the production line was delivered to the United States where it underwent tests at Anacostia as a dive-bomber; this aircraft was destroyed after an aileron failed in a dive and the pilot, Lieutenant Cuddihy, was killed. With local strengthening incorporated, a replacement Bulldog Mk II was delivered in 1930 for US Navy tests.

Third of the second batch of Bulldogs, a Mk IIA, sold to Sweden and delivered in May 1931, shown at Filton shortly before delivery to Malmslätt. All the Swedish aircraft were from time to time flown with ski undercarriages.

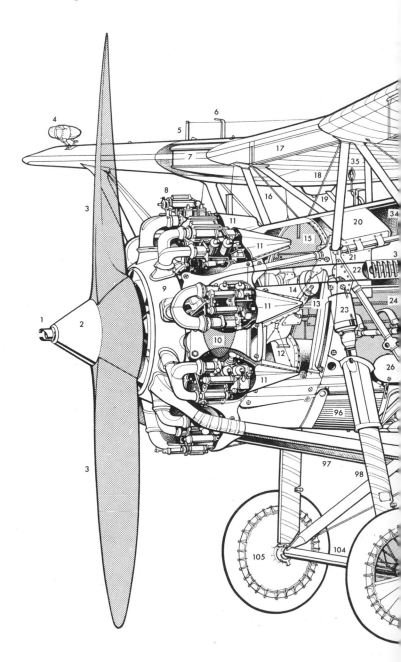

Bristol Bulldog variants

Bristol Type 105 (F.9/26): prototypes as private venture; Bristol Jupiter VII radial; no serial
Bulldog Mk I: company display aircraft; completed but not flown; no serial
Bulldog HA: conversion of private-venture prototype for high-altitude record attempt; supercharged Jupiter VII and high aspect ratio wings
F.9/26 Bulldog Mk II: prototype for RAF evaluation; J9480
Bulldog Mk II: production for RAF in 1928–29; 49 aircraft (J9567–J9591) and K1079–K1101; Jupiter VII
Bulldog Mk II: one aircraft shipped to Japan for evaluation; Nakajima Jupiter as test-bed with Mercury IVA in various cowlings
Bulldog Mk II: three aircraft (1202–1203) for evaluation in Sweden
Bulldog Mk II: European display aircraft; shipped to Chile for evaluation but returned to UK
Bulldog Mk II: European display aircraft, G-ABBB, with Gnome-Rhône 9Asb, later Bristol Aquila; restored post-war, but crashed and destroyed
Bulldog Mk II: 12 aircraft for Estonia in 1930; Gnome-Rhône Jupiter VI engines
Bulldog Mk IIA: production for RAF in 1930–1; 254 aircraft (K1603–K1694, K2135–K2234, K2476–K2495, K2859–K2872, K2946–K2963 and K3504–K3513); Jupiter VIIF; strengthened for increased all-up weight
Bulldog Mk IIA: four aircraft for Denmark in 1931; Jupiter VIFH engines and Madsen guns
Bulldog Mk IIA: eight aircraft (5211–5218) for Sweden in 1931; Jupiter VIIF; three aircraft (5214–5216) presented to Finland in 1939
Bulldog Mk IIA: one aircraft (K4189) to Spec. 11/31 with stainless-steel structure
Bristol Type 124 Bulldog TM: two-seat trainer prototype; conversion of one standard RAF

Bulldog Mk II: 12 aircraft for Latvia, 10 with Gnome-Rhône Jupiter VI and two with Gnome-Rhône 9Asb; Oerlikon guns; delivered in 1929–30
Bulldog Mk II: two aircraft for evaluation by US Navy; delivered 1929–30
Bulldog Mk II: two aircraft to Royal Siamese air force, January 1930; Jupiter VII
Bulldog Mk II: eight aircraft (A12-1 to A12-8) for Royal Australian Air Force, January 1930; Jupiter VIF
Bulldog Mk II: one test-bed, marked R-1, for Mercury III radial; later Gnome-Rhône Jupiter VI; became G-ABAC
Bulldog Mk II: conversion of J9591 (as G-AATR) Bulldog Mk IIA (K2188)
Bulldog Mk IIIA: two prototypes, marked R-5 and G-ABZW; former with Mercury IVA and Mercury IVS2; later converted to Bulldog Mk V
Bulldog Mk IV: prototype converted from Mk III with four guns; evaluation as K4292
Bulldog Mk IVA: prototype (new aircraft), G-ACJN; flown with Mercury IVS2, Perseus IA and Mercury VIS2 with Hamilton three-blade propeller
Bulldog Mk IVA: 17 aircraft for Finland; Mercury VIS2; often flown with ski landing gear
Bulldog TM: to Specification T.12/32; production two-seat trainers for RAF; 59 aircraft (K3170–K3186, K3923–K3953 and K4566–K4576); Jupiter VIF; delivered 1932–4
Bulldog test-beds: conversions of aircraft included above; Alvis Leonides and Napier Rapier in Bulldog TM (K3183), and Armstrong Siddeley Cheetah IX in Bulldog TM prototype (K2188)
JSSF: Japanese-built Bulldog derivatives; two aircraft; Nakajima Jupiter VII
Bullpup: one prototype (J9051) to F.20/27; flown in turn with Mercury IIA, Short-stroke Mercury, Jupiter VIIF and Aquila I

Bristol Bulldog Mk IIA cutaway drawing key

1 Starter dog
2 Spinner
3 Two-blade wooden propeller
4 Starboard navigation light
5 Starboard aerial mast
6 Forward-facing fuel vent pipe
7 Starboard fuel tank capacity 35 Imp gal (159 litres)
8 Bristol Jupiter VIIF or VIIF-P engine
9 Cowling ring
10 Engine mounting plate
11 Cylinder head fairings
12 Cross-bracing
13 Gun synchronizing generator (port and starboard)
14 Supercharger
15 Firewall
16 Centre-section support struts
17 Wing centre-section
18 Bracing wire
19 Starboard fuel pipe
20 Oil tank, capacity 7.5 Imp gal (34.1 litres)
21 Forward fuselage framework

22 Gun trough
23 Oleo leg attachment
24 Rudder pedals
25 Accumulator (lighting system)
26 Air bottle (high-pressure cylinder)
27 Elevator link tube
28 Aileron rockshaft
29 Ammunition box, capacity 600 rounds (one each gun)
30 Control column
31 Empty case chute
32 Port Vickers 0.303-in (7.7-mm) Mk II or Mk IIIN gun
33 Gun cooling louvres
34 Instrument panel
35 Ring sight (combined with Aldis tube front mounting)

36 Bead sight
37 Windscreen
38 Padded coaming
39 Cockpit
40 Fibre acorns
41 Pilot's adjustable seat
42 Tailplane adjusting wheel
43 Chain and sprocket
44 Handhold step
45 Elevator cable arm
46 ASI cable on strut leading edge
47 Fuselage lacing
48 Wireless compartment and crate
49 ASI horn
50 Aerial mast
51 Interplane bracing
52 Port fuel pipe

53 Fuel lead fairing
54 Port fuel tank, capacity 35 Imp gal (159 litres)
55 Front interplane strut
56 Upper mainplane leading edge ribbing
57 Front spar
58 Port navigation light
59 Wing rib
60 Spar strip steel sections
61 Upper mainplane tip
62 Aileron balance
63 Aileron construction
64 Rear spar
65 Aileron cable
66 Rear interplane strut
67 Interplane bracing
68 Aerials

69 Strut cross-bracing
70 Fuselage tubular framework
71 Rudder/tailplane controls
72 Elevator controls
73 Handholds with lifting-bars behind
74 Tailskid spring
75 Rear fuselage lacing
76 Fuselage decking
77 Fin solid section
78 Fin frame structure
79 Upper rudder hinge
80 Aerial anchor point
81 Rudder frame
82 Rear navigation light
83 Rudder post
84 Centre rudder hinge

85 Port tailplane
86 Lower rudder hinge
87 Support pad with trolley-fitting track rail
88 Stern frame construction
89 Tailskid
90 Lower mainplane tip
91 Port lower mainplane
92 Tie-down lug
93 Light bomb racks
94 Air-driven generator mounting cradle
95 Centre-section lower frames
96 Oil cooler
97 Exhaust pipes
98 V-strut undercarriage
99 Cross-bracing wires
100 Fixed-length radius rod
101 700 × 100 Palmer Cord Aero Tyre
102 Tyre valve
103 Wheel spokes
104 Axle strut
105 Wheel cover

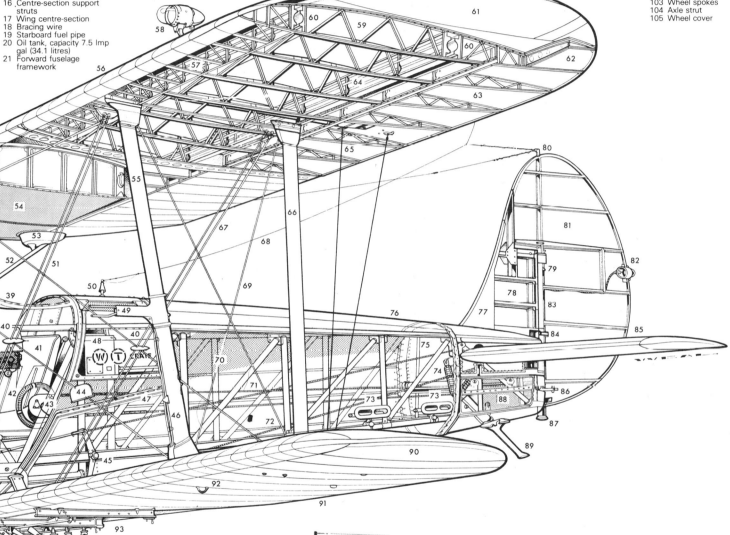

In addition to the three Bulldog Mk IIAs presented to her by Sweden in 1939, Finland had purchased from Britain 17 Mk IVA aircraft early in 1935. Powered by Mercury radials, and some operating on skis, the Bulldogs were flown in combat in the Winter War, gaining several victories. The aircraft shown served with TLeLv 35 early in 1942.

The same Bulldog seen on page 121 (bottom left) and showing the incorrect registration K-2227 and the Jupiter VIIFP motor. Here it is part of the famed Shuttleworth Collection before crashing to destruction at Farnborough in the 1960s.

In January 1930 two Bulldog Mk IIs were delivered to the Royal Siamese air force, and in the same month eight similar aircraft, with Jupiter VIF engines, were shipped out for service with the Royal Australian Air Force. Later in that year, following a demonstration in Sweden by the Bulldog G-AAHH, three Bulldog Mk IIs were shipped to that country in August for competitive evaluation with the indigenous Jaktfalk, the trials confirming the Bristol aircraft's superiority in the air. Simultaneously seven further Bulldogs (five with Gnome-Rhône Jupiter VI and two with Gnome-Rhône 9Asb engines) were shipped to Latvia. Also in August 1930 a dozen Gnome-Rhône Jupiter VI-powered Bulldogs were sold to Estonia.

Germany captures the Bulldog

The appearance of the RAF's first strengthened Bulldog Mk IIAs was accompanied by an order in 1931 for four similar aircraft (but with unsupercharged high-compression Jupiter VIFH engines, Viet gas starters and Madsen machine-guns) for the Royal Danish flying corps; these were flown by the Danish No. 1 Squadron, and three were still being used as trainers when Germany invaded the country in April 1940. At one time negotiations were in hand to build the Bulldog under licence at the Danish Naval Dockyard following evaluation of one of the Bristol-built machines by the Danish naval air service, but these plans did not come to fruition.

The four Danish Bulldogs were shipped from Filton in March 1931, and two months later eight further Bulldog Mk IIAs were flown out from the Bristol factory by Swedish service pilots to Malmslätt, where they gave long service, often operating with ski landing gear. The last three survivors of this romantic but sadly dated aeroplane were presented to Finland in December 1939 for service against the invading Soviet forces during the Winter War then raging.

Indeed it was Finland, fifth of the Baltic nations to equip with the Bulldog, that flew the old biplane into combat. The Bulldog Mk IVA attracted the Finns' attention in 1933, and in December of that year the manufacturers received an order for 17 Mercury-powered fighters. The situation was complicated by the fact that Finland lay within the Gnome-Rhône engine franchise area agreed with Bristol, and French production of the British engine was regarded by the parent company as disappointing. In due course the Bristol directors waived the licence franchise and went ahead with delivery of the aircraft with Bristol-built Mercury VIS2 radials in January 1935. Most of the 17 aircraft were still serving with the Finnish fighter squadron LLv 26 at the beginning of the Winter War of 1939–40, about five Russian aircraft being said to have been shot down by their pilots before the Bulldogs (including those presented by Sweden) were replaced by the Gladiator at the end of January 1940. A single aircraft survived both the Winter War and Continuation War, and survives to this day in superbly restored condition in Finland.

The Finnish Bulldogs were the last to be built at Filton. However, following evaluation of the original aircraft sent out to Japan in 1929, powered by a licence-built Nakajima Jupiter, the Japanese government sponsored an indigenous adaptation of the Bulldog under Bristol design supervision in Japan. Although differing in several respects (namely the fuel tank installation, landing gear and tail unit) two Nakajima Jupiter-powered prototypes (the first with cylinder helmets and the second with narrow-chord Townend ring and wheel spats) were flown. No Bulldog production was undertaken, although several subsequent Japanese aircraft incorporated Bulldog features without attribution.

It is true that in the early 1930s the RAF was very dependent on the Bulldog, but bombers were very important during this period and people were trying to spend less money on interceptors. It did not seem to matter very much that most of the fighters being used differed very little from those of World War 1.

Hawker Fury and Nimrod

Graced with superbly clean and simple lines, Sydney Camm's beautiful Hawker Fury biplane was the first RAF fighter to enter service with a top speed of over 200 mph (320 km/h). In the early 1930s the select body of Fury pilots came to be regarded as the fortunate élite in 'the best flying club in the world'.

The successful debut of the Rolls-Royce F.XI V-12 engine (which differed from the earlier Falcon in its cylinder blocks cast from a single piece of metal, giving a much better performance/weight ratio), meant that Hawker's chief designer, Sydney Camm, was able to break with the old tradition of using a radial engine for interceptors. Camm was striving for ever-improving speeds from his fighters, and had a particularly good working relationship with Rolls-Royce. As a result, he was able to take two fundamental paths in the building of the new F.XI engine: one led to the light Hart bombers, and the other to the Hornet, Fury and Nimrod fighters.

The basis of this fighter design lay in the experimental Hoopoe naval single-seater, produced as a private venture in 1927 and conforming to the general requirements of naval Specification N.21/26. Originally powered by a Bristol Mercury radial and with two-bay wings, the Hoopoe progressed to single-bay wings and finished up with a 560-hp (418 kW) Armstrong Siddeley Panther III which gave a fairly creditable top speed of 196 mph (315 km/h).

Early in 1928 the Hoopoe's design was tailored to accommodate a Rolls-Royce F.XI, it being found possible to enclose the engine totally in an exceptionally finely contoured nose with the associated radiator bath located between the landing gear legs. This design exceeded by a handsome margin the requirements of Air Ministry Specification F.20/27, and a prototype, named the Hornet, went on display at the 1929 Olympia Show where its appearance caused a sensation, the more so when, re-engined with a supercharged F.XIS, it returned a top speed of 205 mph (330 km/h) during flight trials by Flight Lieutenant P. W. S. Bulman a few weeks later.

Owing to 'shortsighted, superfluous and stultifying' demands expressed in F.20/27, the specification was officially withdrawn and a new set of requirements was drawn up around the Hornet, Camm himself frequently being consulted.

K8249 was a Fury Mk II built by General Aircraft. It differed from the Hawker-built aircraft by having a tailwheel and no spats. Eighty-nine were built in this batch and this example flew with No. 1 Sqn based at Tangmere, sporting the squadron's two red bars and winged '1' on the fin.

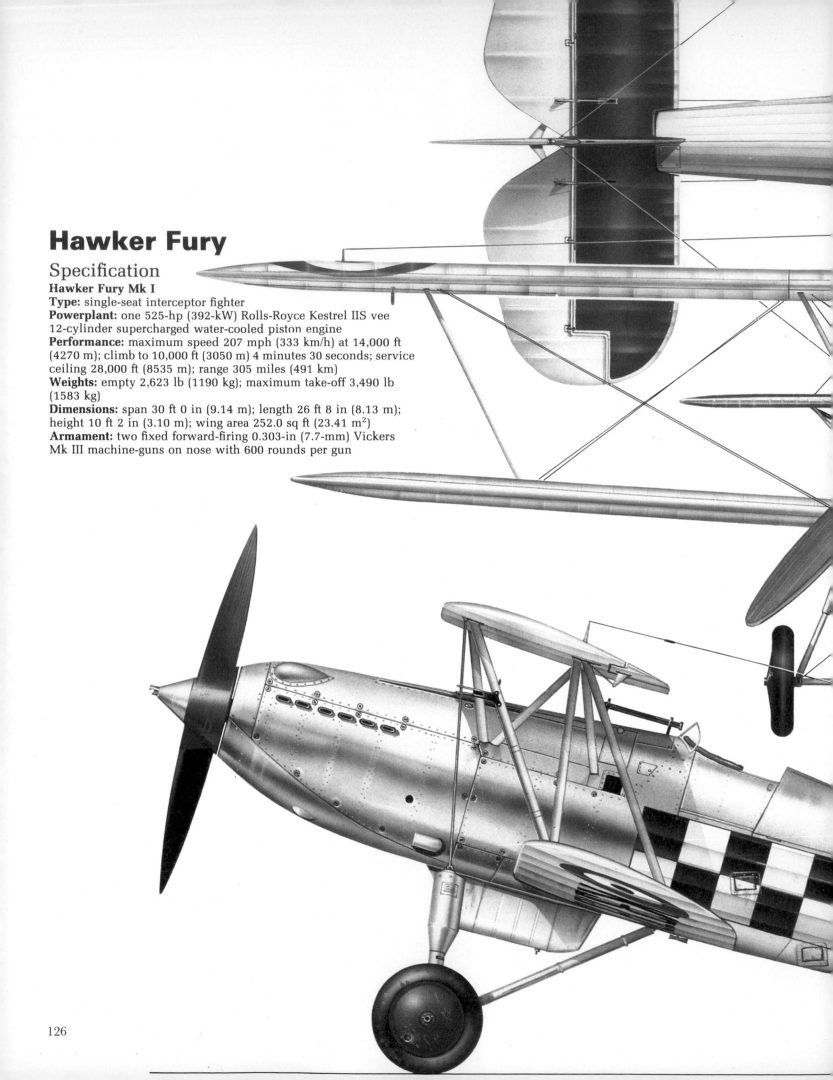

Hawker Fury

Specification

Hawker Fury Mk I
Type: single-seat interceptor fighter
Powerplant: one 525-hp (392-kW) Rolls-Royce Kestrel IIS vee 12-cylinder supercharged water-cooled piston engine
Performance: maximum speed 207 mph (333 km/h) at 14,000 ft (4270 m); climb to 10,000 ft (3050 m) 4 minutes 30 seconds; service ceiling 28,000 ft (8535 m); range 305 miles (491 km)
Weights: empty 2,623 lb (1190 kg); maximum take-off 3,490 lb (1583 kg)
Dimensions: span 30 ft 0 in (9.14 m); length 26 ft 8 in (8.13 m); height 10 ft 2 in (3.10 m); wing area 252.0 sq ft (23.41 m²)
Armament: two fixed forward-firing 0.303-in (7.7-mm) Vickers Mk III machine-guns on nose with 600 rounds per gun

During the mid-1930s, the Fury was a front-line fighter for the RAF. One squadron, No. 25(F), was based at Hawkinge, and two, Nos 1(F) and 43(F) at Tangmere. The latter is represented here in the shape of K3731, the aircraft of the red flight leader, denoted by the red coloured fin. Known as the 'Fighting Cocks', No. 43 flew Furies from May 1931 to November 1938, and often participated in the annual Hendon Air Pageant.

127

Three Hawker Furies were supplied to the Portuguese Arma de Aéronautica in 1935. Several European countries would have bought more Furies, but its cost and the slow delivery of the Kestrel engine halted several exports, while aircraft such as the Bristol Bulldog flourished.

Specification 13/30 was issued, the Hornet itself was purchased by the Air Ministry with the serial J9682, and a preliminary order for three development aircraft placed with the H.G. Hawker Engineering Company. Already the Rolls-Royce F.XI had been named the Kestrel and, despite some disappointment by the manufacturers as well as within the Air Ministry itself, the name Hornet was changed to Fury.

It was always Camm's intention that the Fury and Hart families should come to be regarded as the Bentleys and Rolls-Royces of the RAF, representing the peak of engineering expertise, yet in themselves they did little to advance technology save in an extraordinary attention to design detail. The Fury perpetuated Fred Sigrist's dumbbell-section wing spars, the wings themselves being of unswept parallel-chord configuration; the fuselage was a steel and aluminium structure with aluminium panels enclosing the nose as far aft as the cockpit, and with fabric covering on rear fuselage, wings and tail. The gun armament (twin synchronized Vickers guns) remained the same as had been introduced in RFC scouts more than a dozen years earlier. Ailerons were fitted to the top wing only, yet these were adequate to bestow extremely sensitive control and a brisk rate of roll.

As the Hornet prototype was taken abroad on a demonstration tour by Bulman, the Air Staff decided to equip a single RAF squadron with Furies (a decision possibly difficult to justify having regard to the prevailing economic depression, the fact that the Bristol Bulldog was only then just entering service as the RAF's standard interceptor and that the Fury was undeniably expensive at a unit price of £4,800, itself reflecting the new Kestrel's unamortized costs). As jigging and tooling for the new fighter got under way at Kingston-upon-Thames, an order for six Furies was received from Yugoslavia, one of them to be powered by the Hispano-Suiza 12Nb engine and the others by standard Kestrel IIS engines.

First deliveries

The three development Furies and 18 production aircraft were all flown early in 1931, 16 of them being delivered to No. 43 (Fighter) Squadron, commanded by Squadron Leader L. H. (later Air Marshal Sir Leonard) Slatter at Tangmere. The Yugoslav Furies followed on immediately after, the Hispano-powered aircraft being found to be unsatisfactory and therefore modified to standard form.

Such was the enthusiasm with which the Fury was received by Slatter's pilots that an immediate follow-on order for 48 RAF aircraft was placed, and these joined No. 25 (Fighter) Squadron, commanded by Squadron Leader Walter Bryant at Hawkinge during the winter of 1931–2, and No. 1 (Fighter) Squadron, commanded by Squadron Leader Charles Spackman at Tangmere. At once intense rivalry sprang up among these three premier fighter squadrons, particularly to win the RAF's coveted air gunnery challenge trophy (eventually won outright by No. 25 Squadron with its Furies).

Despite the type's speed superiority over the Bulldog, efforts to argue support for standardization of the Fury nevertheless failed, largely on account of the faster amortization of Bulldog costs and limited availability of Kestrel engines (already slated for the large orders being placed for the growing family of Hawker Hart variants). Thus only 48 further Fury Mk Is were ordered for the RAF, spread over the

Developed from the Mercury-powered Hoopoe and the Hornet, there were three prototype Furies. The first flew initially on 25 March 1931. Production aircraft were little different from K1926 pictured here and were soon in service with No. 43 Sqn, which was receiving aircraft, armed with Vickers Mk III machine guns, as early as May 1931.

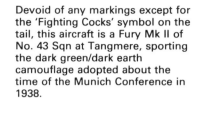

Devoid of any markings except for the 'Fighting Cocks' symbol on the tail, this aircraft is a Fury Mk II of No. 43 Sqn at Tangmere, sporting the dark green/dark earth camouflage adopted about the time of the Munich Conference in 1938.

Three Furies were delivered to Spain powered by 700-hp (522-kW) Hispano-Suiza 12Xbrs engines, and featuring a single strut undercarriage in common with contemporary types such as the Gloster Gladiator. These aircraft originally flew in aluminium colour schemes with red panels on the fuselage.

period 1932–5, the majority of these being replacements issued to the three squadrons already mentioned. That is not to suggest that the accident rate on the Fury was inordinately high, a total of 12 flying accidents being recorded on the three units in five years; however, there were other losses: on 7 August 1933 a No. 504 Squadron Horsley crashed at Hawkinge, falling on the hangar housing the Furies of No. 25 Squadron and destroying six in the fire that followed.

While the RAF Fury squadrons provided superb displays, including the memorable tied-together formation aerobatics at Hendon and elsewhere, foreign air forces were taking a lively interest in the fighter, although once more its high cost and the limited delivery rate of the Kestrel kept individual orders small. Norway ordered a single evaluation example with a Panther radial, and this was flown on a ski landing gear for a short time; the 14-cylinder engine proved too heavy, however, and this version was not considered a success. Largest overseas customer was Persia, for whose air force 16 aircraft were produced with Pratt & Whitney Hornet radials. Most of these were delivered in 1933, and were followed the next year by an order for six further aircraft with Bristol Mercury VISP radials, the Hornet engine having given persistent trouble; some of the earlier aircraft were returned to Kingston to have the British engine substituted, a small number of Mercury Furies surviving in 1941 when they were encountered by the RAF during the Raschid Ali revolt.

Further exports

Other foreign customers included Portugal (with three aircraft delivered in 1935), and Spain, which also received three aircraft; the latter were powered by 700-hp (522-kW) Hispano-Suiza 12Xbrs engines and featured Gloster Gladiator-type single-leg cantilever landing gear legs, and were flown in action during the Spanish Civil War. Yugoslavia returned one of its original Furies to Kingston to have a 720-hp (537-kW) Lorraine Petrel Hfrs engine fitted; although this example returned a top speed of 229 mph (369 km/h) on test, the Yugoslavs opted to order 10 Kestrel XVI-powered aircraft (so as to share a common powerplant with that nation's Hawker Hinds) which featured the single-leg landing gear, low-drag radiator and four-gun armament. With a top speed of 242 mph (389 km/h) these Yugoslav aircraft were the fastest of all export Furies.

Hawker was undoubtedly fortunate to gain the relatively small Fury Mk I orders it did, bearing in mind that it had been pre-empted by the Bulldog and that the 1930 depression and the pervading mood for disarmament could be held as adequate excuse to ignore the aircraft altogether. Issue of Specification F.7/30, however, showed that the Air Staff at least was looking beyond the scope of the 'Ten-Year Rule', which claimed that 10-year warning of a European conflict would be available, and which was abandoned within a year in any case. It was this covert attitude, shared among those with a favoured ear in Whitehall, that spurred Camm and the Hawker management to persist with privately-funded development of the Fury, with a descendant in mind for possible tender to the F.7/30 specification itself.

This is an exact replica of the aicraft flown by Squadron Leader L. H. Slatter of No. 43 Squadron, itself one of the first examples of the Hawker Fury delivered in 1931.

Several aircraft for export had radial engines which necessitated an enlarged fin. This example was one of the six Mercury-engined Furies supplied to Persia. Earlier, 16 Pratt & Whitney Hornet-engined aircraft had been delivered. These saw much service and were used as late at 1941.

First step was to produce an almost standard, company-owned trial installation aircraft, known as the Intermediate Fury and registered G-ABSE. On this aircraft, first flown by P. E. G. Sayer on 13 April 1932, were tested such innovations as wheel spats, Goshawk supercharger (and eventually the Goshawk engine itself) and steam-condenser evaporative cooling. The next logical step was to produce a company-funded aircraft on which high performance flight trials could be conducted without the complication of service equipment. This was the High-Speed Fury, first flown on 3 May 1933 and variously used for the exploration of low-drag tapered wings, low-drag V-type interplane struts, evaporating cooling and Goshawk engine (by then mandatory in the F.7/30 specification). When eventually it underwent service-style evaluation with the 730-hp (545-kW) Goshawk B 43 engine with semi-retractable radiator and two guns fitted, the High-Speed Fury (sometimes known in this form as the Fury Mk II) returned a top speed of 277 mph (446 km/h) at 12,500 ft (3810 m), possibly the highest speed recorded by a fully-armed British biplane. It is also worth mentioning that, although not strictly a member of the Fury family, Camm's P.V.3 contender for the F.7/30 contest was a direct development of the High-Speed Fury; compromised by the unsuitable steam-cooled Goshawk, and weighed down by the ungainly condensers, mandatory four-gun armament, night-flying equipment, wheel spats and full fuel load, the P.V.3. could manage no more than 224 mph (360 km/h), at 14,000 ft (4265 m). It is hardly surprising, therefore, that the Gloster Gladiator, which was faster by some 25 mph (40 km/h) earned the winner's verdict. Incidentally the High-Speed Fury was also flown by Rolls-Royce in 1935 with the 1,000-hp (746-kW) P.V.12 Merlin prototype engine although, as a result of considerable ballasting to restore the centre of gravity position, there were no measured top speed trials.

Fury Mk II and Nimrod

That was not, however, the end of the Fury saga. Half-way through the High-Speed Fury development the aircraft (K3586) was evaluated at Martlesham Heath with a Kestrel VI and wheel spats, returning a top speed of 228 mph (367 km/h). When formally tendered to the existing Specification F.14/32, this version was accepted as the basis of an interim RAF fighter needed to serve during the Hawker Hurricane's development period. With an additional fuel tank to compensate for higher consumption this version, the Fury Mk II, entered service with No. 25 Squadron in November 1936, followed within a year by Nos 41, 73 and 87 Squadrons.

With a speed of only 223 mph (359 km/h), and already outclassed by the Gladiator (not to mention the Hurricane and Spitfire) the Fury was virtually at the end of its front-line service by the time of the Munich Crisis of September 1938. Nevertheless, production of the Fury Mk II totalled 98.

It has often been suggested that in much the same manner that the Hart underwent 'navalization' to become the Osprey, so the Fury joined the Fleet Air Arm as the Nimrod. This is entirely incorrect, and the two fighters were no more than distant cousins rather than brothers, albeit generically descended from the Hoopoe, which was, as already explained, itself a naval fighter.

Encouraged by the initial success of the Hornet as well as continuing enquiries from Denmark, Sweden and Norway

Hawker Fury Mk I cutaway drawing key

1 Starter dog
2 Spinner
3 Watts two-bladed wooden propeller
4 Propellor attachment bolts
5 Spinner backplate
6 Propeller reduction gear
7 Engine cowling
8 Cowling fairing
9 525 hp Rolls-Royce Kestrel II.S engine
10 Cowling attachments
11 Exhaust stubs
12 Front engine mounting
13 Rear engine mounting
14 Engine support framework
15 Supercharger
16 Water system header tank
17 Water system filler cap
18 Coolant pipe
19 Supercharger air intake
20 Engine compartment bulkhead
21 Centre section 'N' struts
22 Wing centre section structure
23 Handgrips
24 Outer wing spar attachment
25 Plywood-covered leading edges
26 Pitot/static tubes
27 Tubular steel front spar
28 Tubular steel rear spar
29 Spar bracing strut
30 Diagonal bracing wires
31 Port aileron
32 Aileron crank
33 Aileron cable
34 Gravity fuel tank, 27 Imp gal (123 litres)
35 Filler cap
36 Main fuel tank, 23 Imp gal (105 litres)
37 Tank mountings
38 Filler cap
39 Oil tank
40 Fuselage tubular framework
41 Upper longeron
42 Lower longeron
43 Riveted framework joints
44 Vickers 0.303-in (7.7-mm) machine guns
45 Gun muzzle trough in fuel tank
46 Cartridge case and link ejector chute
47 Ammunition tank, 600 rounds each gun
48 Gunsight
49 Pilot's windscreen

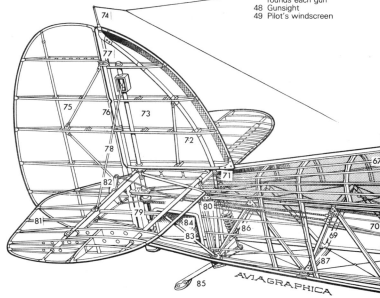

Hawker Nimrod variants

Hawker Norn: one private-venture naval prototype, later purchased by Air Ministry and renamed Nimrod; Rolls-Royce F.XIMS
Hawker Nimrod: two prototypes (S1577 and S1578) to Specification 16/30; Kestrel IIs
Hawker Nimrod Mk I: 10 production aircraft (S1579–S1588) to Specification 16/30; Kestrel IIS; interchangeable wheel/float landing gear
Hawker Nimrod Mk I: production of 43 aircraft (S1614–S1637) and K2823–K2841) in 1932–3 to amended Specification 16/30 with minor modifications
Hawker Nimrod Mk II: production of 27 aircraft (K2909–K2914), K2925, K2926, K3654–K3662 and K4620–

K4629) in 1933–5 to Specification 11/33 with strengthened rear fuselage; Kestrel V used in some aircraft; sweptback top wing K2909–K2911 of stainless-steel construction
Hawker Danish Nimrod: two pattern aircraft with Kestrel IIIS engines; supplied in 1934, followed by licence production in Denmark
Hawker Japanese Nimrod: one aircraft with Kestrel IIIS engine, supplied in 1934
Hawker Portuguese Nimrod: one aircraft supplied in 1934, first with Kestrel IIS but later changed to Kestrel V

The Fury Mk II went into service with No. 25 Sqn in November 1936 with the more powerful Kestrel VI. The first (Hawker) production batch were distinguished from their predecessors by having spats. This aircraft served with No. 25 Sqn flying from Hawkinge.

Hawker Fury variants

Hawker Hornet: one private-venture prototype (J9682) to amended Specification F.20/27; F.XIA engine (later F.XIS); first flight in March 1929
Hawker Fury Mk I: three development aircraft (K1926–K1928) with Kestrel IIS engine
Hawker Fury Mk I: production in 1931 to Specification 13/30; 18 aircraft (K1929–K1946) with Kestrel IIS; one aircraft (K1935) became Fury Mk II prototype; Vickers Mk I guns
Hawker Fury Mk I: production in 1932–3 to amended specification 13/30 with minor modifications; 63 aircraft (K2035–K2082, K2874–K2883 and K2889–K2903) with Kestrel IIS; Vickers Mk III guns
Hawker Yugoslav Fury (1st Series): six aircraft delivered in 1932; Kestrel IIS (one aircraft temporarily with Hispano-Suiza 12Nb engine)
Hawker Norwegian Fury: one aircraft delivered in November 1932; Armstrong Siddeley Panther IIIA radial; also flown with ski landing gear
Hawker Persian Fury (1st Series): 16 aircraft delivered in latter half of 1933 with Pratt & Whitney Hornet S2B1G radials and three-blade Hamilton Hydromatic propellers
Hawker Persian Fury (2nd Series): six aircraft delivered in 1935 with Bristol Mercury VIS2 radials (plus some converted from 1st Series)
Hawker Portuguese Fury: three aircraft (50–52) delivered June 1934 with Kestrel IIS
Hawker Yugoslav Fury (2nd Series): 10 aircraft delivered 1936-7 with Kestrel XVI, low-drag radiator, cantilever landing gear and four-gun armament
Hawker Spanish Fury: three aircraft (4-1 to 4-3) delivered June 1936 with Hispano-Suiza 12Xbrs, cantilever landing gear and two-gun armament
Hawker Intermediate Fury: one company-sponsored trials aircraft (G-ABSE) flown with Kestrel IIS, IVS (with Goshawk supercharger), VI and VI Special, and Goshawk III engines; also on occasion with wheel spats, cantilever landing gear and electro-magnetic bomb gear
Hawker High-Speed Fury Mk I and Mk II: one company-sponsored trials aircraft (K3586) flown with Kestrel IIS, IIIS, IVS, Kestrel (Special), Goshawk III, B41 and B43, and Rolls-Royce P.V.12 (Merlin prototype) engines; various wing configurations also flown
Hawker Fury Mk II: production in 1936 to Specification 6/35 by Hawker; 23 aircraft with Kestrel VI
Hawker Fury Mk II: production in 1936-7 to Specification 19/35 by General Aircraft Ltd; 75 aircraft (K8232–K8306); four aircraft to Habbaniyah in 1938, some others to South Africa in about 1939

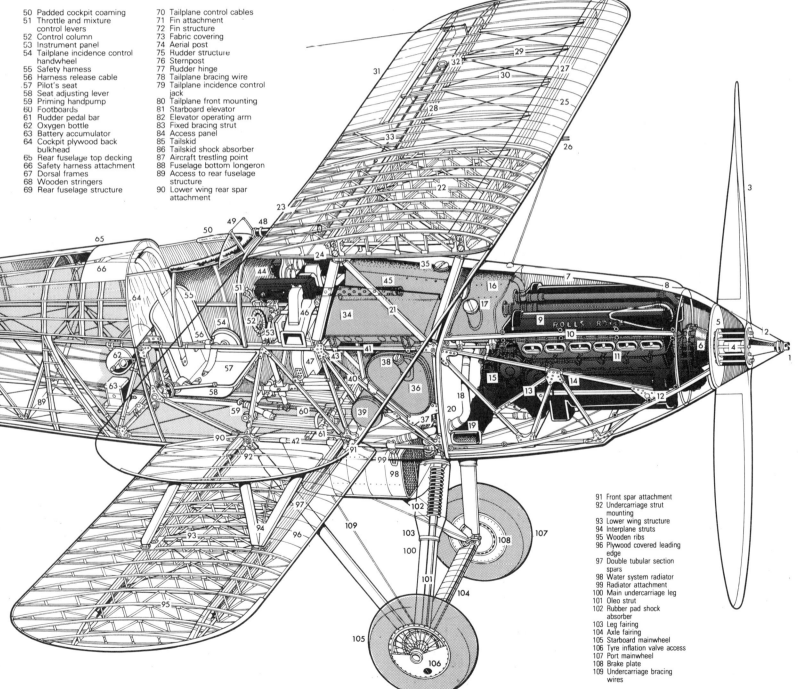

50 Padded cockpit coaming
51 Throttle and mixture control levers
52 Control column
53 Instrument panel
54 Tailplane incidence control handwheel
55 Safety harness
56 Harness release cable
57 Pilot's seat
58 Seat adjusting lever
59 Priming handpump
60 Footboards
61 Rudder pedal bar
62 Oxygen bottle
63 Battery accumulator
64 Cockpit plywood back bulkhead
65 Rear fuselage top decking
66 Safety harness attachment
67 Dorsal frames
68 Wooden stringers
69 Rear fuselage structure
70 Tailplane control cables
71 Fin attachment
72 Fin structure
73 Fabric covering
74 Aerial post
75 Rudder structure
76 Sternpost
77 Rudder hinge
78 Tailplane bracing wire
79 Tailplane incidence control jack
80 Tailplane front mounting
81 Starboard elevator
82 Elevator operating arm
83 Fixed bracing strut
84 Access panel
85 Tailskid
86 Tailskid shock absorber
87 Aircraft trestling point
88 Fuselage bottom longeron
89 Access to rear fuselage structure
90 Lower wing rear spar attachment

91 Front spar attachment
92 Undercarriage strut mounting
93 Lower wing structure
94 Interplane struts
95 Wooden ribs
96 Plywood covered leading edge
97 Double tubular section spars
98 Water system radiator
99 Radiator attachment
100 Main undercarriage leg
101 Oleo strut
102 Rubber pad shock absorber
103 Leg fairing
104 Axle fairing
105 Starboard mainwheel
106 Tyre inflation valve access
107 Port mainwheel
108 Brake plate
109 Undercarriage bracing wires

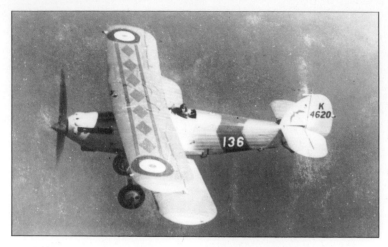

Although not the same basic aeroplane, the Nimrod was the naval equivalent of the Fury. Nearly 100 Nimrods were produced by Hawker under licence, and several were still serving with the Danes when the Germans invaded in 1940. This example was a Nimrod Mk II.

farther forward to give improved field of vision over the lower-wing leading edge.

After initial evaluation at Martlesham, the first Nimrod (S1577) was embarked early in 1931 in HMS *Eagle* to attend the British Empire Trade Exhibition at Buenos Aires, being flown in the El Palomar air display by Flying Officer C. P. Barker. On return, it completed its evaluation successfully and was joined by a second aircraft (S1578) for floatplane trials at Felixstowe. A production order for 34 aircraft was placed, and these aircraft first entered service in June 1932 with No. 408 Flight, commanded by Lieutenant Commander (later Vice-Admiral Sir Edward) E. M. C. Abel-Smith RN, aboard HMS *Glorious*, and soon after with Nos 402 and 409 Flights, in each case replacing Flycatchers. A final batch of 19 Nimrod Mk 1s included the addition of arrester hook and catapult spools, and of a headrest fairing found necessary during catapulting. Some of these modifications were retrospectively introduced to the earlier aircraft.

Production of the Nimrod continued slowly until well into 1935 with the Nimrod Mk II version, of which 27 were completed; originally intended to be a Kestrel V-powered version with swept-back top wing, strengthened rear fuselage and increased use of stainless steel in its structure, most aircraft were in fact completed with no more than the strengthening to distinguish them from Nimrod Mk Is, the Kestrel V being substituted later; only three aircraft are known to have widely employed stainless steel.

In 1933 Fleet Air Arm units underwent a change of designation, the old flights being renumbered in the 800s; Nimrods served with two flights on each of Nos 800 and 801 Squadrons (HMS *Courageous*) and No. 802 Squadron (HMS *Furious*), the third flight being equipped with Hawker Ospreys. Almost all had disappeared from service (replaced by Gloster Sea Gladiators and Blackburn Skuas) by the outbreak of World War 2. A total of four Nimrods was exported, two to Denmark as pattern aircraft for proposed licence production, one to Japan and one to Portugal.

Once it had been fitted out for ship-supported use, the Nimrod with its wheeled undercarriage and a Kestrel IIS engine was able to reach a maximum speed of only 196.4 mph (316 km/h) at a height of 11,800 ft (3600 m). But from all reports the plane handled quite well.

about a possible naval development, Camm set about adapting the Kestrel-Hoopoe concept to the requirements of naval fighter Specification N.21/26, issued to bring about a replacement for the ageing Fairey Flycatcher. By the time this had been updated in Specification 16/30 Hawker had almost completed two prototypes at company expense. At first known unofficially as the Norn (a Scandinavian Fate), these aircraft were purchased by the Air Ministry, one for flight evaluation and the other for flotation trials. Renamed Nimrod, the new naval fighters certainly resembled the Fury but differed in a number of important respects. High energy-absorption, long-travel landing gear oleos, slightly enlarged fin, and metal fuselage panels extending slightly farther aft were the main external distinguishing features; internally there were such features as flotation boxes in the top wing and rear fuselage, some use of stainless steel components in wing attachments and engine bearers, and provision for interchangeable float or wheel landing gear. Much less perceptible was the relocation of the cockpit 3 in (7.6 cm)

After having been rebuilt by Hispano-Suiza, this Fury, originally supplied to the Spanish air force, was captured by the Nationalist forces and flown by them. It features the Hispano-Suiza engine (note paired middle exhaust ports in the cowling) and single strut undercarriage.

Several ex-RAF Furies were handed over to the South African Air Force after their front-line days were over. This aircraft flew with No. 3 Sqn, SAAF, in 1942.

de Havilland Dragon and Rapide

Producing more than twice as many transport aircraft as any other British manufacturer, the de Havilland Aircraft Company carved its niche in aviation history. The Dragon family of biplane transports formed a high proportion of the company's output; with their reliable pedigree and overall performance attracting both civil and military customers, the three major designs logged over 30 years of operations, with some aircraft still flying today.

In the late 20s and early 30s, de Havilland was establishing itself a superb reputation with its series of light aircraft based on the D.H.60 Moth. The company had built the eight-passenger D.H.61 Giant Moth and the D.H.66 Hercules for

Aer Lingus flew its first passengers from Dublin to Bristol in a D.H.84 Dragon. To mark the company's 50th anniversary in 1986, a beautifully restored Dragon retraced this journey. At the speed it flew, and the height, a road map would have been enough for navigation.

Owned and operated by the Prince of Wales in the 1930s, this immaculate D.H.84 Dragon 1 wore a red, blue and silver colour scheme. Powered by two 130-hp (97-kW) Gipsy Major engines with a 30-Imp gal (136-litre) fuel tank in each nacelle, this two-bay strut and wire-braced biplane had seating for between six and 10 passengers.

use by Imperial Airways and elsewhere in the British Empire, while the needs of smaller users were covered by the D.H.83 Fox Moth.

One of the main Fox Moth operators was Hillman's Airways. It had been founded by Edward Hillman, who moved into aviation as a natural extension of his motor coach business. This colourful character was responsible for pressing de Havilland to design a larger 10-seat twin-engine aircraft to meet the expanding demand for his airline's services. Hillman's Airways was accordingly the first operator of de Havilland's new light airliner, the D.H.84 Dragon. The Dragon was actually rather smaller than Hillman's initial specification and provided accommodation for a pilot and six passengers in a slab-sided fuselage built of spruce and plywood. The biplane wings were built with outer panels which folded backwards just outboard of the engines and the shape of the wings themselves was somewhat complex. Two 130-hp (97-kW) de Havilland Gipsy Major 1 engines were mounted on the lower wings with the main landing gear legs directly mounted to the engine firewall bulkheads and, in some cases, the wheels were enclosed with streamlined spats to give some drag improvement. A swept-back fin and rudder assembly was used, perpetuating the de Havilland 'trademark' which had become familiar on the sport bi-planes, and the pilot was housed in an extensively glazed cockpit in the extreme nose of the aircraft.

The prototype Dragon (E-9, c/n 6000) made its first flight at Stag Lane on 24 November 1932. The period of flight testing was incredibly short compared with present-day experience and the prototype was soon resprayed with the registration G-ACAN and delivered to Mr Hillman during December 1932. Four production Dragons followed in quick succession and were an immediate success. Hillman's Airways offered very low fares (by the device of keeping overheads down and paying the pilots and the bus drivers the same wage rates) and this soon resulted in two further Dragons being ordered and the existing machines being converted to eight-passenger configuration by eliminating the rear baggage compartment.

Many other small airlines started to order the Dragon for passenger services and carrying mail and for ambulance operations in Scotland and other isolated areas. Another bus company, the Scottish Motor Traction Co. Ltd, had established an integrated system of coach and air services and used the Dragon for this purpose and the type entered service with Highland Airways and Aberdeen Airways,

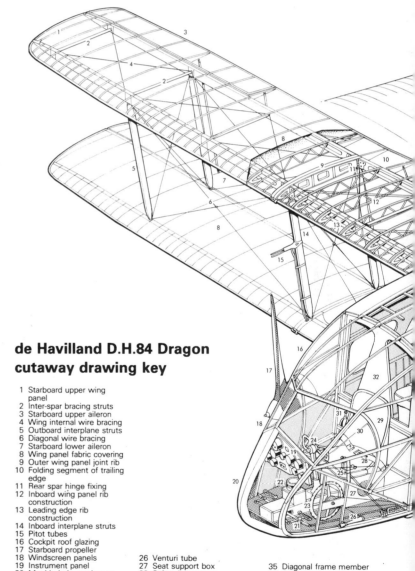

de Havilland D.H.84 Dragon cutaway drawing key

1 Starboard upper wing panel
2 Inter-spar bracing struts
3 Starboard upper aileron
4 Wing internal wire bracing
5 Outboard interplane struts
6 Diagonal wire bracing
7 Starboard lower aileron
8 Wing panel fabric covering
9 Outer wing panel joint rib
10 Folding segment of trailing edge
11 Rear spar hinge fixing
12 Inboard wing panel rib construction
13 Leading edge rib construction
14 Inboard interplane struts
15 Pitot tubes
16 Cockpit roof glazing
17 Starboard propeller
18 Windscreen panels
19 Instrument panel
20 Moulded plywood nose section
21 Rudder pedals
22 Compass
23 Tailplane rim control handwheel
24 Control column
25 Engine throttle and mixture control levers

26 Venturi tube
27 Seat support box
28 Safety harness
29 Pilot's seat
30 Direct vision opening side window panel
31 Fire extinguisher
32 Cockpit bulkhead
33 Main cabin flooring
34 Fuselage side panel framework

35 Diagonal frame member
36 Cabin window panels
37 Passenger seats (six)
38 Cabin roof framing
39 Ventilating air duct
40 Cabin wall trim panels
41 Leading-edge ventilating air scoop
42 Wing spar centre-section carry-through

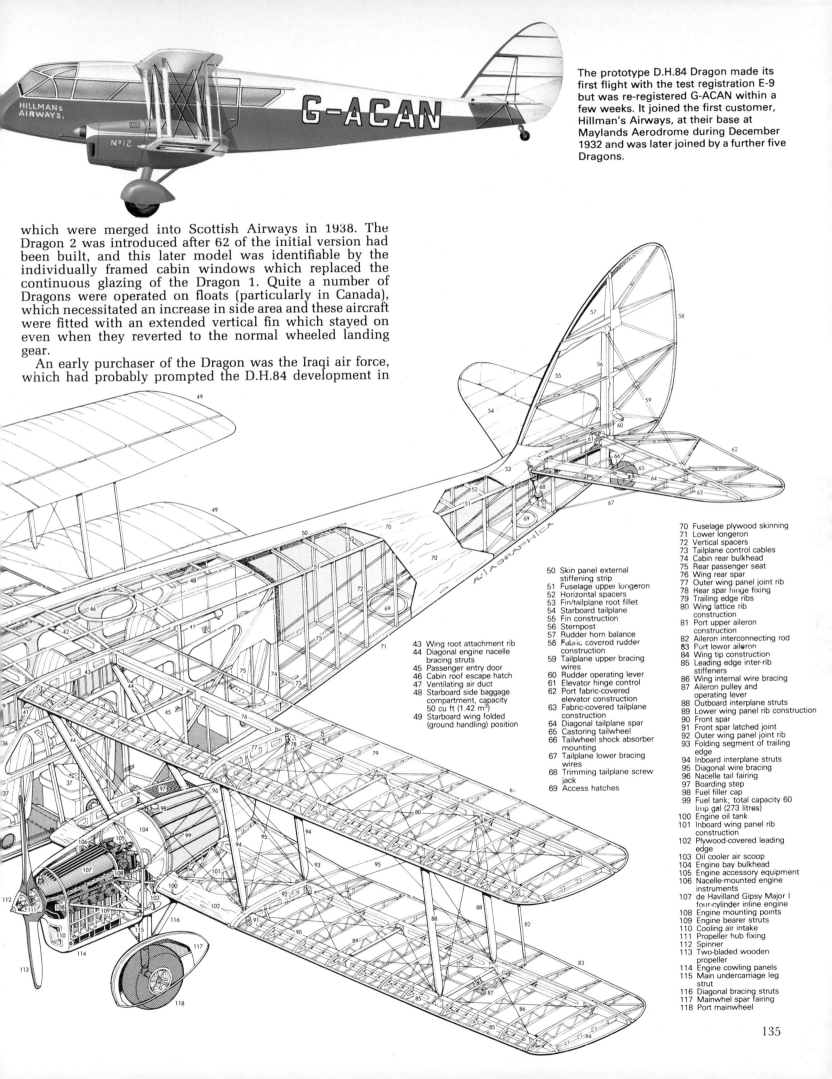

The prototype D.H.84 Dragon made its first flight with the test registration E-9 but was re-registered G-ACAN within a few weeks. It joined the first customer, Hillman's Airways, at their base at Maylands Aerodrome during December 1932 and was later joined by a further five Dragons.

which were merged into Scottish Airways in 1938. The Dragon 2 was introduced after 62 of the initial version had been built, and this later model was identifiable by the individually framed cabin windows which replaced the continuous glazing of the Dragon 1. Quite a number of Dragons were operated on floats (particularly in Canada), which necessitated an increase in side area and these aircraft were fitted with an extended vertical fin which stayed on even when they reverted to the normal wheeled landing gear.

An early purchaser of the Dragon was the Iraqi air force, which had probably prompted the D.H.84 development in

43 Wing root attachment rib
44 Diagonal engine nacelle bracing struts
45 Passenger entry door
46 Cabin roof escape hatch
47 Ventilating air duct
48 Starboard side baggage compartment, capacity 50 cu ft (1.42 m³)
49 Starboard wing folded (ground handling) position
50 Skin panel external stiffening strip
51 Fuselage upper longeron
52 Horizontal spacers
53 Fin/tailplane root fillet
54 Starboard tailplane
55 Fin construction
56 Sternpost
57 Rudder horn balance
58 Fabric covered rudder construction
59 Tailplane upper bracing wires
60 Rudder operating lever
61 Elevator hinge control
62 Port fabric-covered elevator construction
63 Fabric-covered tailplane construction
64 Diagonal tailplane spar
65 Castoring tailwheel
66 Tailwheel shock absorber mounting
67 Tailplane lower bracing wires
68 Trimming tailplane screw jack
69 Access hatches
70 Fuselage plywood skinning
71 Lower longeron
72 Vertical spacers
73 Tailplane control cables
74 Cabin rear bulkhead
75 Rear passenger seat
76 Wing rear spar
77 Outer wing panel joint rib
78 Rear spar hinge fixing
79 Trailing edge ribs
80 Wing lattice rib construction
81 Port upper aileron construction
82 Aileron interconnecting rod
83 Port lower aileron
84 Wing tip construction
85 Leading edge inter-rib stiffeners
86 Wing internal wire bracing
87 Aileron pulley and operating lever
88 Outboard interplane struts
89 Lower wing panel rib construction
90 Front spar
91 Front spar latched joint
92 Outer wing panel joint rib
93 Folding segment of trailing edge
94 Inboard interplane struts
95 Diagonal wire bracing
96 Nacelle tail fairing
97 Boarding step
98 Fuel filler cap
99 Fuel tank; total capacity 60 Imp gal (273 litres)
100 Engine oil tank
101 Inboard wing panel rib construction
102 Plywood-covered leading edge
103 Oil cooler air scoop
104 Engine bay bulkhead
105 Engine accessory equipment
106 Nacelle-mounted engine instruments
107 de Havilland Gipsy Major I four-cylinder inline engine
108 Engine mounting points
109 Engine bearer struts
110 Cooling air intake
111 Propeller hub fixing
112 Spinner
113 Two-bladed wooden propeller
114 Engine cowling panels
115 Main undercarriage leg strut
116 Diagonal bracing struts
117 Mainwhel spar fairing
118 Port mainwheel

135

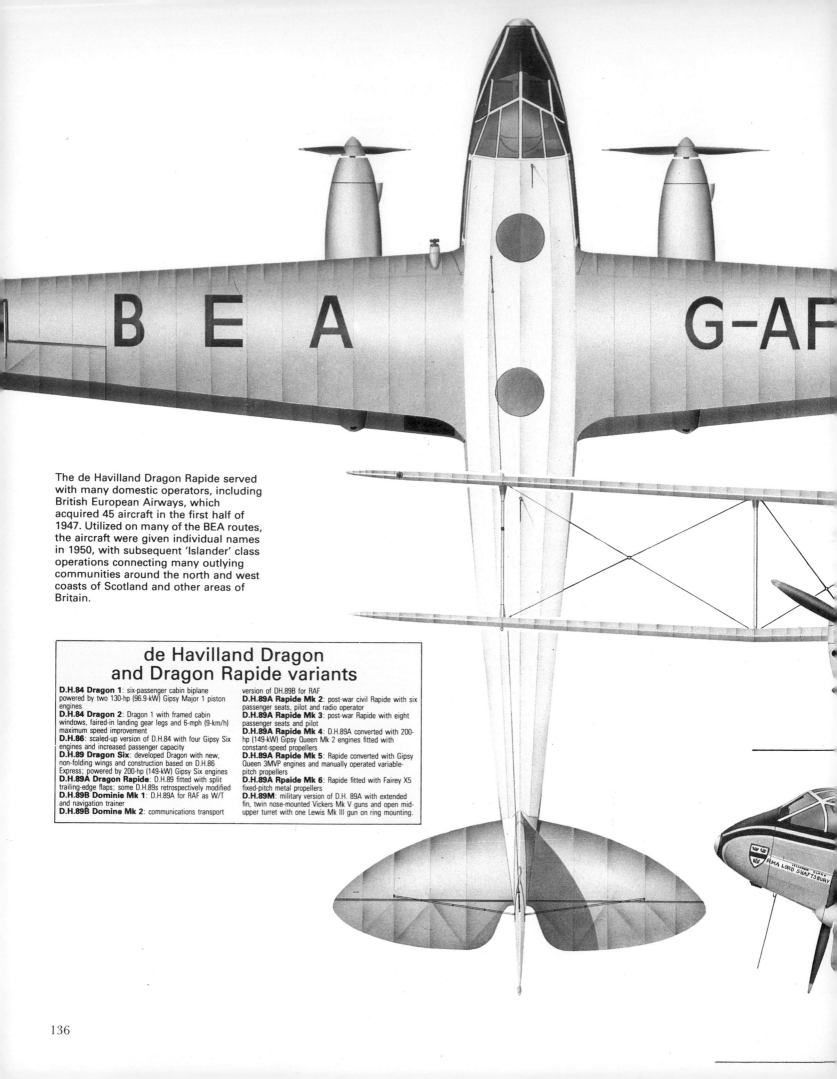

The de Havilland Dragon Rapide served with many domestic operators, including British European Airways, which acquired 45 aircraft in the first half of 1947. Utilized on many of the BEA routes, the aircraft were given individual names in 1950, with subsequent 'Islander' class operations connecting many outlying communities around the north and west coasts of Scotland and other areas of Britain.

de Havilland Dragon and Dragon Rapide variants

D.H.84 Dragon 1: six-passenger cabin biplane powered by two 130-hp (96.9-kW) Gipsy Major 1 piston engines

D.H.84 Dragon 2: Dragon 1 with framed cabin windows, faired-in landing gear legs and 6-mph (9-km/h) maximum speed improvement

D.H.86: scaled-up version of D.H.84 with four Gipsy Six engines and increased passenger capacity

D.H.89 Dragon Six: developed Dragon with new, non-folding wings and construction based on D.H.86 Express; powered by 200-hp (149-kW) Gipsy Six engines

D.H.89A Dragon Rapide: D.H.89 fitted with split trailing-edge flaps; some D.H.89s retrospectively modified

D.H.89B Dominie Mk 1: D.H.89A for RAF as W/T and navigation trainer

D.H.89B Domine Mk 2: communications transport version of DH.89B for RAF

D.H.89A Rapide Mk 2: post-war civil Rapide with six passenger seats, pilot and radio operator

D.H.89A Rapide Mk 3: post-war Rapide with eight passenger seats and pilot

D.H.89A Rapide Mk 4: D.H.89A converted with 200-hp (149-kW) Gipsy Queen Mk 2 engines fitted with constant-speed propellers

D.H.89A Rapide Mk 5: Rapide converted with Gipsy Queen 3MVP engines and manually operated variable-pitch propellers

D.H.89A Rpaide Mk 6: Rapide fitted with Fairey X5 fixed-pitch metal propellers

D.H.89M: military version of D.H. 89A with extended fin, twin nose-mounted Vickers Mk V guns and open mid-upper turret with one Lewis Mk III gun on ring mounting.

de Havilland D.H.89

Specification

de Havilland D.H.89A
Type: light piston-engine transport biplane
Powerplant: two 200-hp (149-kW) de Havilland Gipsy Queen 3 inline piston engines
Performance: maximum speed 157 mph (253 km/h); cruising speed 132 mph (212 km/h); initial rate of climb 867 ft (264 m) per minute; service ceiling 19,500 ft (5944 m); maximum range with standard fuel tanks 578 miles (930 km); take-off run 870 ft (265 m); landing run 510 ft (155 m)
Weights: empty 3,276 lb (1486 kg); maximum take-off 5,500 lb (2495 kg)
Dimensions: 48 ft 0 in (14.63 m); length 34 ft 6 in (10.52 m); height 10 ft 3 in (3.12 m); wing area 336 sq ft (31.21 m²)

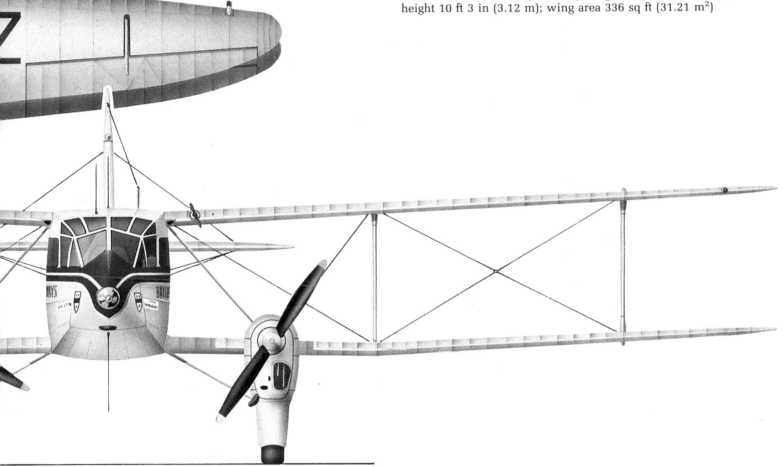

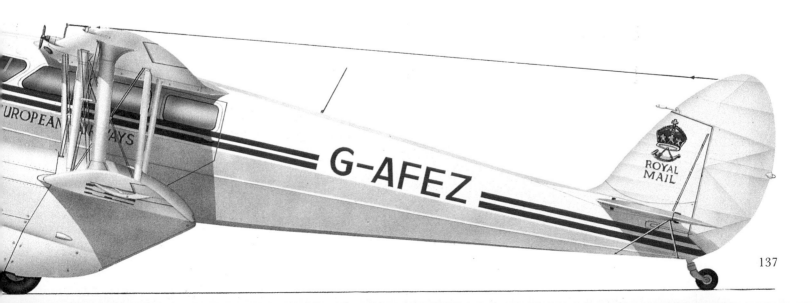

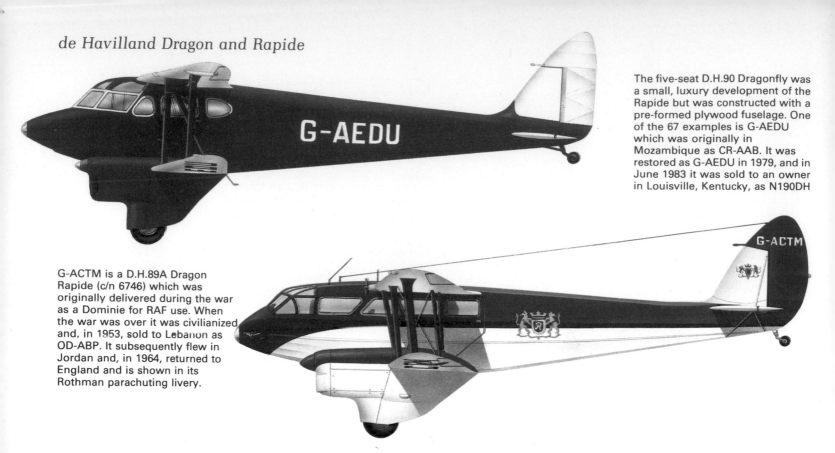

The five-seat D.H.90 Dragonfly was a small, luxury development of the Rapide but was constructed with a pre-formed plywood fuselage. One of the 67 examples is G-AEDU which was originally in Mozambique as CR-AAB. It was restored as G-AEDU in 1979, and in June 1983 it was sold to an owner in Louisville, Kentucky, as N190DH

G-ACTM is a D.H.89A Dragon Rapide (c/n 6746) which was originally delivered during the war as a Dominie for RAF use. When the war was over it was civilianized and, in 1953, sold to Lebanon as OD-ABP. It subsequently flew in Jordan and, in 1964, returned to England and is shown in its Rothman parachuting livery.

the first place. It ordered eight of the D.H.84M version, and these were delivered to Baghdad during 1933 to be used for patrolling the rather turbulent tribally-controlled areas of the country. A gunner's open position was provided on top of the fuselage just aft of the wings and the pilot was able to take aggressive action using two machine-guns fitted one on each side of the nose of the Dragon. The D.H.84M was also fitted with a seaplane-style extended fin. Other air forces which ordered the type were the Danish army air force (two aircraft), the Portuguese air force (three aircraft) and the Turkish and Irish military forces which purchased standard civil Dragons as general duties transports.

Long-distance record attempt

The most famous of all Dragons was G-ACCV (c/n 6014) named *Seafarer* and owned by Jim and Amy Mollison. As Amy Johnson, Mrs Mollison had become famous through her epic flight to Australia in 1930 and subsequent flights from England to South Africa. Together, the Mollisons planned to use *Seafarer* in an attempt on the world long-distance record, which would start with a flight to New York. The Dragon made its first attempt to leave Croydon on 8 June

G-AGSH, a Dragon Rapide Mk 6, is seen here in the markings of the Royal Air Force Sport Parachute Association. The predominantly red colour scheme reflected its use by the 'Red Devils' parachute team as the jump-ship at many air displays.

1933 but was so heavily loaded that it failed to evade a ditch and the aicraft nosed over. The aircraft was repaired and flown to Wales where it successfully took off from Pendine Sands and, after 39 hours in the air, arrived over Bridgeport, Connecticut. Attempting to land downwind *Seafarer* over-shot and was damaged beyond repair, the Mollisons ending up in hospital. The remains of G-ACCV were later canni-balized to be used in the Dragon 2 *Seafarer II* which was used by Ayling and Reid to fly the Atlantic from Canada to England in August of the following year.

In 1934, de Havilland had rushed through development of a new four-engine airliner designated D.H.86. Aimed at the requirement for a fast 10-seater which could operate the Singapore to Australia section of the proposed Croydon to Brisbane passenger service, the D.H.86 (Express Air Liner, as it was known) used much of the design layout of the Dragon but was scaled up, had a completely new wing cellule and was powered by four of the new 200-hp (149-kW) de Havilland Gipsy Six inline engines. There was also a degree of pressure from existing Dragon operators for a more com-fortable and faster replacement for the D.H.84, and this led to the company scaling down the D.H.86 and fitting it with two Gipsy Six engines to produce the D.H.89 Dragon Six. Out-wardly, the Dragon Six was not a great deal different from

Rejected by the RAF in favour of the Avro Anson for general reconnaissance, the D.H.89B Dragon Rapide was ordered for communications and training duties as the Dominie Mk I and II. This example served with No. 2 Radio School and has the direction finding loop on the upper fuselage to facilitate the training of wireless operators.

the Dragon, but it used the completely new tapered wings without the folding mechanism of the previous model and the maximum speed of 128 mph (206 km/h) which had been achieved by the Dragon 1 rose to 157 mph (253 km/h) because of improved streamlining and the higher engine power. The D.H.89 prototype (E-4, c/n 6250) was first flown from Hatfield on 17 April 1934. It had a fully faired landing gear, which was a major contributor to drag reduction, and the nose cone was tapered upwards to give a new profile to the cockpit area.

Once again, Mr Hillman was a keen purchaser of the new model, which was now named the Dragon Rapide, and the first three production examples were delivered to Hillman's Airways between July and September 1934. A further four Dragon Rapides were delivered to this operator, and these were finally transferred to British Airways when Edward Hillman sold his business in December 1935. Another Rapide operator was Railway Air Services Ltd, which had been formed by the principal railway companies in 1934 and had begun flying on routes from Croydon to the Isle of Wight, Plymouth, Birmingham and Liverpool. The expansion of mail services to Glasgow and Belfast prompted the company to buy the D.H.86 and also a total of eight D.H.89s. Other British operators of the Dragon Rapide included Olley Air Service Ltd, Northern & Scottish Airways Ltd, Jersey Airways Ltd and British Continental Airways Ltd. All of these small air carriers used the Dragon Rapide intensively, and in all weather conditions, right up to the outbreak of World War 2 in 1939.

The D.H.89 built up a good export reputation, 41 of the first 100 aircraft being sold to overseas customers. Several of the Middle East petroleum companies bought Rapides for communications with the desert oil extraction sites, and Canadian companies including Quebec Airways and Canadian Airways Ltd had fleets of them, often fitted with the extended fin and twin floats. Once the Rapide production line had built up to a fair volume, de Havilland introduced the D.H.89A version

which featured split trailing edge flaps fitted just outboard of the engine nacelles on the lower wings, and optional metal propellers. Many of the earlier D.H.89s were retrospectively modified with the flap system, and production of the D.H.89A started at G-AERN (c/n 6345) which was sold to West Coast Air Services and delivered in March 1937. At about this time, also, the Rapide was given an effective cabin heating system, the rear cabin windows were enlarged and optional provision was made for a toilet in the rear of the cabin.

Several Rapides had been sold abroad for military purposes during 1936 and 1937. The Imperial Iranian war ministry bought three, the National Government of China had five (delivered in December 1937) and the Spanish government ordered three for police work in its North African territories. These were, in fact, never used in North Africa and they joined the Republican forces when the Spanish Civil War broke out. Three ex-civil D.H.84s and approximately 10 D.H.89s also reached one side or the other. These were all aircraft which were sold by dealers who had purchased them in England and were able to break the blockade which both the British and French governments established in the summer of 1936. Both the Nationalists and the Republicans were desperate to obtain aircraft, and a number of Airspeed Envoys, Monospars, Fokker transports and Rapides were despatched, although a fair number never reached their destinations. The Rapides were fitted in Spain with open gun turrets and there is no evidence that any of these machines survived the war.

Coastal patrol version

In 1935, the British Air Ministry carried out evaluations to see if the Rapide would be suitable for the coastal patrol role

The D.H.90 Dragonfly first appeared in 1936 as a smaller version of the Dragon Rapide, intended as a luxury airliner. Most of the 66 machines built went to buyers abroad.

set out in Specification G.18/35. One example (K4772, c/n 6271) was built as a D.H.89M with the extended fin and a dorsal upper turret which housed a Lewis Mk III machine-gun, and it was tested at Martlesham Heath and Gosport but the patrol contract was awarded to the Avro 652 (which became the Anson). Despite this setback two Rapides were ordered as communications aircraft and several were ordered as navigation trainers by Airwork Services Ltd, which had gained substantial contracts from the Air Ministry during the build-up to the outbreak of war. As 1938 gave way to the fateful 1939 the Rapides in use at the School of Navigation at Shoreham received a coat of camouflage paint, and the Rapide went into battle.

Up to the start of the war on 3 September 1939, de Havilland's civil Rapide output had numbered about 180 aircraft and this gave way to military production at Hatfield

as the company started to receive direct Air Ministry orders for D.H.89s equipped as W/T and navigation trainers. These were designated D.H.89B Dominie Mk I and were externally identical to the civil model with the exception of the large loop antenna on the roof just behind the cockpit and, of course, the camouflage paint scheme. Dominies entered service with the air navigation schools, particularly No. 6 Air Observers' Navigation School (AONS) at RAF Staverton and No. 7 AONS at RAF Perth (Scone). They were also delivered as the D.H.89B Dominie Mk II for general communications duties and employed as the mainstays of station flights both with the RAF and the Royal Navy. The Air Transport Auxiliary (ATA) took over responsibility for the ferrying of military aircraft from airfield to airfield in May 1940 and used Dominies for positioning crews all over the United Kingdom and Europe. It also set up a Medical Section which used Dominies with up to two stretchers fitted into the modified D.H.89 cabin to ferry medical cases from isolated locations to its central hospital at White Waltham.

The arrival of the war had brought complete suspension of all civil air services. Once the military priorities had been sorted out some of the aircraft used by the airlines were put back in service with civil markings to run priority routes under the control of the Associated Airways Joint Committee (AAJC). Typical of the Rapides so employed were G-ACPP and G-ACPR of Great Western and Southern Air Lines, which were put to work flying three return flights each day between Land's End (St Just) and the Scilly Isles. Most of the Dragons and Rapides on the civil register, however, were impressed into military service with standard service markings and serials. Many of them suffered accidents during their war service with the result that few were still airworthy when peace came in 1945.

The overall total of Dragon Rapides built by de Havilland was 728 and the production line was closed in 1945 to make way for new types. The last 346 aircraft were built by the Brush Coachworks at Loughborough and, in common with many other aircraft, the D.H.89 was subject to some cancellation of Air Ministry contracts when peace arrived. In fact, the last batch of approximately 100 Rapides was built for post-war civil sale. These were known as the Rapide Mk 2, which was fitted with six passenger seats, and the Rapide Mk 3 which had eight passenger seats in addition to the pilot. The Rapide Mk 4 was a conversion of the standard Dominie with the Gipsy Queen 3 engines replaced by Gipsy Queen 2s with constant-speed propellers, and the single example of the Rapide Mk 5 had manually-operated variable-pitch propellers and a special version of the Gipsy Queen 3 engines. The final post-war variant was the Rapide Mk 6 which, again, was a modification of earlier aircraft with fixed-pitch Fairey X5 propellers which provided performance equivalent to that of the Rapide Mk 4 but with less mechanical sophistication.

The majority of post-war Rapides were Dominies, which had survived to be declared surplus and sold at bargain prices to various overhaul companies such as W.A. Rollason, Field Aircraft Services and Lancashire Aircraft Corporation. These Dominies initially supplemented the fleets of the AAJC operators to Shetland, Guernsey and Scilly Isles.

The Rapides found their way to small air taxi companies like Air Kruise. They were used by Skegness Air Taxi and Airwork Services, both of which did circular trips for only £1 a person.

The glassed-in, very narrow cockpit of the D.H.84 gave the pilot an excellent all-round view. This type, of which 115 were built, flew successfully with a large number of civil airlines.

Boeing P-26

One of the first successful breaks with the established biplane tradition, Boeing's classic little P-26 was America's first all-metal fighter to achieve production status, and the last to feature open cockpit and fixed landing gear.

The Boeing Airplane Company in Seattle, Washington, became a leading manufacturer of fighters for the US Army Air Corps between 1921 and 1935. This was after it had built the Thomas-Morse MB-3 followed in the mid-1920s by the Boeing PW-9. The classic P-12, the parallel to the US Navy's F4B, was still being built by the company well into the 1930s. but in 1931 Boeing proposed a small monoplane to the US Army, the Boeing Model 248. This fighter would use the successful air-cooled Pratt & Whitney R-1340 nine-cylinder radial engine.

While the US Army showed enthusiasm for these proposals, evidence of caution was provided by the stipulation in the Bailment Contract of 5 December 1931 that while the US Army would supply engines and instruments, Boeing would bear the cost of building three prototypes (XP-936) and their initial testing. The airframes remained with the company.

Construction of the first prototype started in January 1932, and in no more than nine weeks the aircraft was complete, its first flight being made on 20 March before being delivered for service trials at Wright Field; the second aircraft underwent static tests at Wright and the third went to Selfridge Field, Michigan, prior to evaluation by active USAAC squadrons. All three prototypes were successful in their various trials and were then purchased outright by the USAAC and accorded the successive designations XP-26, Y1P-26 and finally P-26.

Despite Boeing's experience in cantilever wing design and previous work on retractable landing gear, the P-26 embodied an externally-braced monoplane wing and fixed, spatted landing gear. Despite use of an engine of only 525 hp (392 kW), the prototype XP-936 returned a maximum speed of 227 mph (365 km/h) at 10,000 ft (3050 m) compared, for example, with the biplane P-12E's 189 mph (304 km/h) with

a 500-hp (373-kW) engine. All-metal semi-monocoque construction was employed, comprising aluminium bulkheads, top-hat section longerons, stiffeners and skins. The thin-section, low aspect ratio, low-set wing was supported by landing wires attached to the fuselage and by flying wires attached to the landing gear, and the pilot's cockpit was located above the wing's mid-chord. An armament of twin 0.3-in (7.62-mm) forward firing machine-guns was provided, as well as provision to carry up to 112 lb (51 kg) of bombs externally. Compared with the P-12's wing span of 30 ft 0 in (9.14 m), the XP-936 spanned only 27 ft 5 in (8.36 m).

Signed up for the Army

Trials with the XP-936 at Wright Field occupied most of 1932, and on 7 November a new specification was drawn up incorporating the experience of these trials. Thus on 11 January 1933 the US Army Air Corps and Boeing signed a contract for 111 examples of this improved design (the Model 266) to be designated the P-26A. In due course this order was increased to 136 in the largest single production order for a US military aeroplane since that for the 200 MB-3As in 1921.

Production versions of the P-26A differed externally from the prototypes only in that the streamlined wheel spats did not extend aft of the landing gear strut fairings, and span was increased. However, another alteration was included after an early aircraft overturned during landing on soft ground; the pilot was killed although the aircraft itself was scarcely damaged. Accordingly the streamlined headrest fairing was strengthened and deepened to provide better protection, and production was delayed while this modification was incorporated.

The third prototype Boeing XP-936. Trials with the Pratt & Whitney R-1340-21 engined prototypes occupied many months before a production standard was agreed, the principal differences lying in the increased depth of the pilot's headrest and the shortening of the streamlined mainwheel fairings.

Resplendent in olive drab fuselage and orange-yellow wings, wheel spats, engine cowling, tail surfaces and fuselage bands, this Boeing P-26C belonged to the 19th Pursuit Squadron, 18th Pursuit Group, based at Wheeler Field, Hawaii, in 1939. Not many were built, some ending their days in Guatemala.

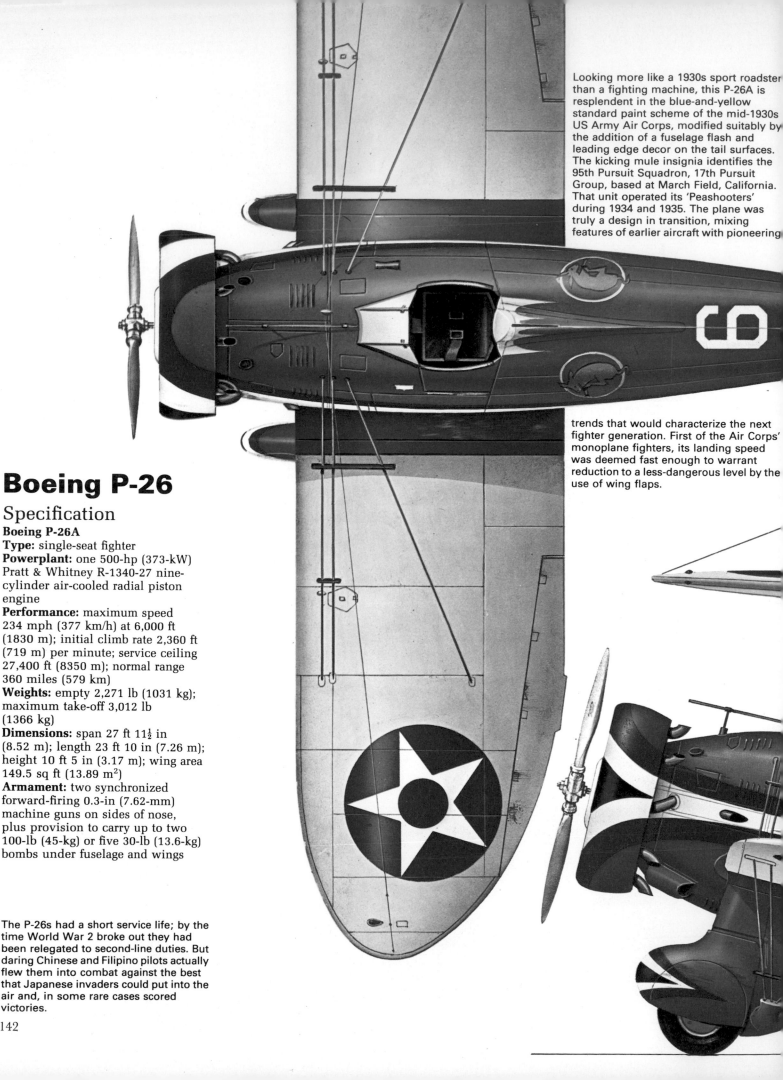

Looking more like a 1930s sport roadster than a fighting machine, this P-26A is resplendent in the blue-and-yellow standard paint scheme of the mid-1930s US Army Air Corps, modified suitably by the addition of a fuselage flash and leading edge decor on the tail surfaces. The kicking mule insignia identifies the 95th Pursuit Squadron, 17th Pursuit Group, based at March Field, California. That unit operated its 'Peashooters' during 1934 and 1935. The plane was truly a design in transition, mixing features of earlier aircraft with pioneering trends that would characterize the next fighter generation. First of the Air Corps' monoplane fighters, its landing speed was deemed fast enough to warrant reduction to a less-dangerous level by the use of wing flaps.

Boeing P-26

Specification

Boeing P-26A
Type: single-seat fighter
Powerplant: one 500-hp (373-kW) Pratt & Whitney R-1340-27 nine-cylinder air-cooled radial piston engine
Performance: maximum speed 234 mph (377 km/h) at 6,000 ft (1830 m); initial climb rate 2,360 ft (719 m) per minute; service ceiling 27,400 ft (8350 m); normal range 360 miles (579 km)
Weights: empty 2,271 lb (1031 kg); maximum take-off 3,012 lb (1366 kg)
Dimensions: span 27 ft 11½ in (8.52 m); length 23 ft 10 in (7.26 m); height 10 ft 5 in (3.17 m); wing area 149.5 sq ft (13.89 m²)
Armament: two synchronized forward-firing 0.3-in (7.62-mm) machine guns on sides of nose, plus provision to carry up to two 100-lb (45-kg) or five 30-lb (13.6-kg) bombs under fuselage and wings

The P-26s had a short service life; by the time World War 2 broke out they had been relegated to second-line duties. But daring Chinese and Filipino pilots actually flew them into combat against the best that Japanese invaders could put into the air and, in some rare cases scored victories.

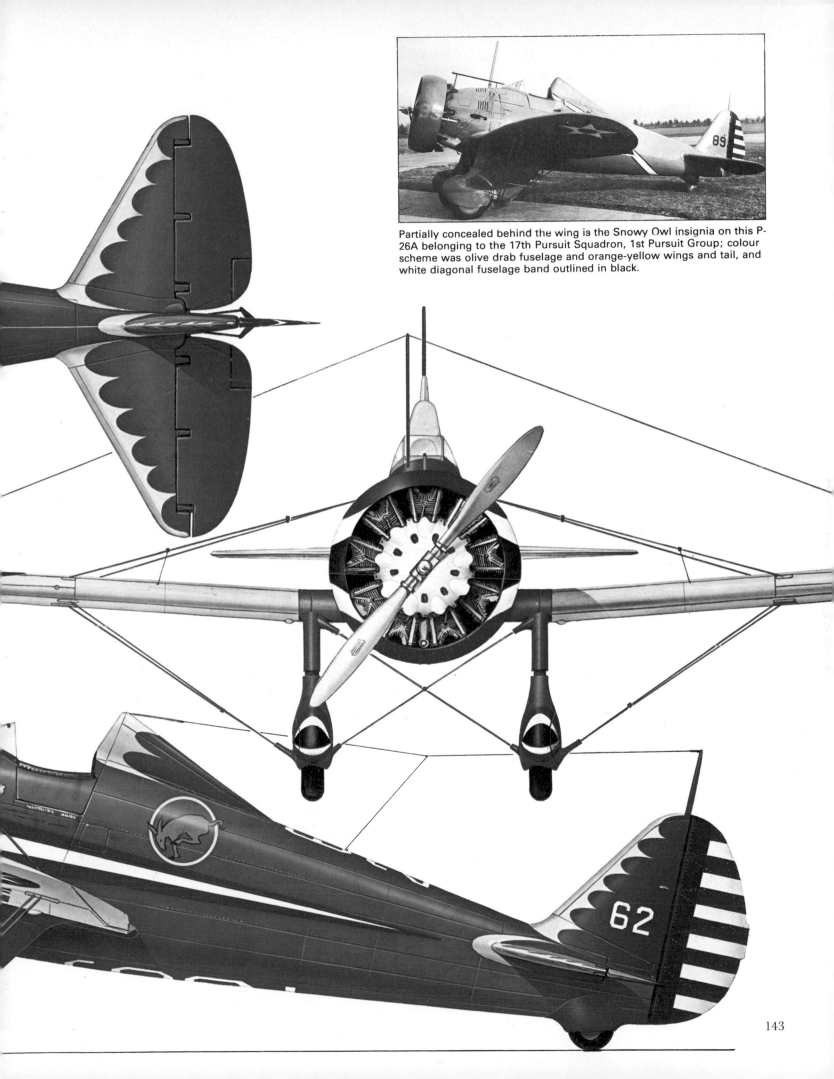

Partially concealed behind the wing is the Snowy Owl insignia on this P-26A belonging to the 17th Pursuit Squadron, 1st Pursuit Group; colour scheme was olive drab fuselage and orange-yellow wings and tail, and white diagonal fuselage band outlined in black.

Boeing P-26A of the 95th Pursuit ('Kicking Mule') Squadron, 17th Pursuit Group; the olive drab finish preceded the adoption of an all-over blue scheme, and for a short time the aircraft carried the squadron number in large characters under the fuselage. The kicking mule emblem originated during World War 1 when the unit was the 95th Aero Squadron.

Boeing P-26 variants

Model 248: three prototypes (XP-936, subsequently XP-26, Y1P-26 and P-26), with Pratt & Whitney R-1340-21 engines; serial nos 32-412, -413 and -414
Model 266 (P-26A): 111 aircraft built, with R-1340-27 engines; 33-028 to -138; some subsequently to Guatemala
Model 266A (P-26B): two aircraft built, with R 1340-

33 engines with fuel injection; 33-179 and 33-185
Model 266 (P-26C): 23 aircraft built, initially with R-1340-33 engines without fuel injection, but later modified to P-26B standard; 33-186 to -203; some subsequently to Guatemala
Model 281: 12 aircraft built, with R-1340-33 engines; one to Spain and 11 to China

Internally, however, the P-26A had undergone much improvement with the inclusion of US Army radio and the addition of flotation gear in the wing roots. Tare weight remained much the same although the 525-hp (392-kW) Pratt & Whitney R-1340-21 engine was replaced by a 500-hp (373-kW) R-1340-27 engine, though top speed was increased to 234 mph (377 km/h). The armament installation was altered to allow one of the 0.3-in (7.62-mm) guns to be replaced by a 0.5-in (12.7-mm) weapon, and the bomb rack attachment points changed to permit carriage of either two 100-lb (45-kg) or five 30-lb (13.6-kg) bombs under the wings and fuselage.

Deliveries of the first production P-26As started on 16 December 1933 and the last of the original order for 111 aircraft was completed on 30 June 1934. Unit cost per aircraft, less government-furnished equipment (GFE), came out at $9,999.00 (marginally less than the cost of a Boeing P-12E biplane).

When the P-26A entered service early in 1934 it gained the nick-name 'Peashooter' and quickly became a firm favourite among US Army pursuit pilots, being light and sensitive on the controls, and remaining the fastest US Army Air Corps fighter until joined four years later by the Seversky P-35 and Curtiss P-36A in 1938. Many of the pilots who were to achieve fame in World War 2 served their flying apprenticeships on the aircraft, and a remarkable proportion of the pre-war P-26 group and squadron commanders rose to high rank in the USAAF and USAF in later years.

Squadron service

First deliveries were made to the 1st Pursuit Group, commanded by Lieutenant Colonel Ralph Royce (who later, as a major general, commanded the III Fighter Command in 1942 and the US 1st Air Force in 1943), based at Selfridge Field, Michigan. The group included the 17th, 27th and 94th Pursuit Squadrons – the last famous as the 'Hat in the Ring' squadron. The 27th and 94th gave up their Peashooters in 1938, but the 17th continued flying them until 1941 when they were finally replaced by Curtiss P-40s.

Also equipped with P-26As in 1934 was the 17th Pursuit Group (commanded by Major Frank O'D. Hunter, who succeeded Major General Royce at the head of the 1st Air Force from 1943 until 1945). Based at March Field, California, the 34th and 95th Squadrons retained their P-26As for only one year before the group was assigned to the attack role.

Third and last of the initial P-26A pursuit groups in 1934 was the 20th at Barksdale, Louisiana, commanded by Lieutenant Colonel Armin F. Herold: the group's 55th and 77th Squadrons took delivery in 1934 and the 79th Squadron

Boeing P-26A cutaway drawing key

1 Starter dog
2 Propeller hub sleeve
3 Sleeve attachment
4 Two-blade propeller
5 Engine face plate
6 Cooling inlets
7 Engine cowling ring
8 Pratt & Whitney R-1340-27 Wasp engine
9 Cylinder heads
10 Gun barrel blast tube
11 Exhaust pipes
12 Engine bearer ring
13 Louvred exhaust stacks
14 Carburettor cold air intake
15 Engine bearer upper support struts
16 Starter primer access
17 Cowling panel fasteners
18 Hot air intake
19 Cockpit heater
20 Exhaust stub
21 Gun blast tube
22 Oil cooler
23 Lower panel access
24 Wingroot stub
25 Port gun barrel
26 Bulk head/lower longeron attachment
27 Fuselage forward frame
28 Air intake/starter controls
29 Support strut attachment
30 Cooling louvres
31 Oil tank, capacity 8 US gal (30 litres)
32 Upper louvres
33 Oil filter access
34 Gunsight tube supports
35 Tubular gunsight
36 Starboard wing fuel tank
37 Starboard landing wires support strut and brace
38 Fuel filter cap
39 Landing wires outboard attachment
40 Front spar
41 Pitot tube
42 Wing panelling
43 Aerial spring brace attachment
44 Starboard navigation lights (upper and lower surfaces)
45 Aerial lead-in
46 Electrical leads
47 Wing main rib stations

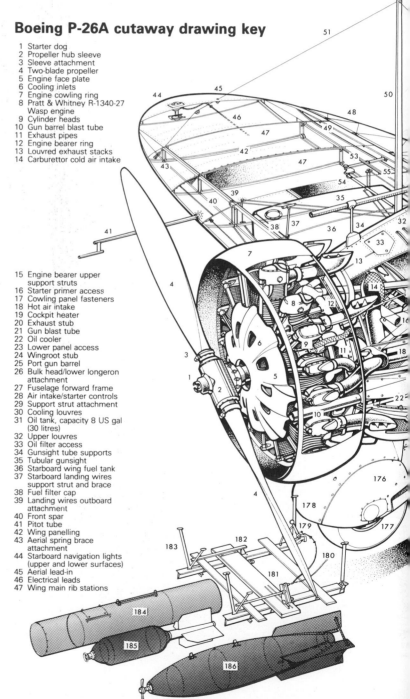

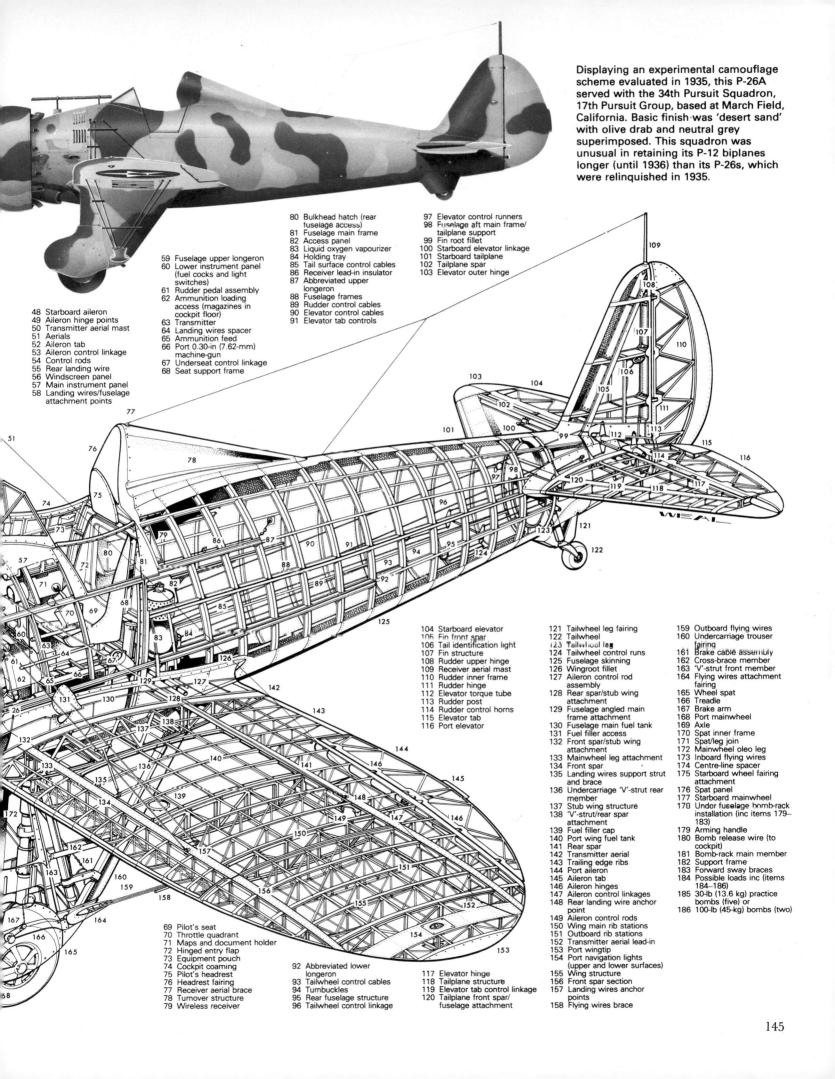

Displaying an experimental camouflage scheme evaluated in 1935, this P-26A served with the 34th Pursuit Squadron, 17th Pursuit Group, based at March Field, California. Basic finish was 'desert sand' with olive drab and neutral grey superimposed. This squadron was unusual in retaining its P-12 biplanes longer (until 1936) than its P-26s, which were relinquished in 1935.

48 Starboard aileron
49 Aileron hinge points
50 Transmitter aerial mast
51 Aerials
52 Aileron tab
53 Aileron control linkage
54 Control rods
55 Rear landing wire
56 Windscreen panel
57 Main instrument panel
58 Landing wires/fuselage attachment points
59 Fuselage upper longeron
60 Lower instrument panel (fuel cocks and light switches)
61 Rudder pedal assembly
62 Ammunition loading access (magazines in cockpit floor)
63 Transmitter
64 Landing wires spacer
65 Ammunition feed
66 Port 0.30-in (7.62-mm) machine-gun
67 Underseat control linkage
68 Seat support frame

80 Bulkhead hatch (rear fuselage access)
81 Fuselage main frame
82 Access panel
83 Liquid oxygen vapouriser
84 Holding tray
85 Tail surface control cables
86 Receiver lead-in insulator
87 Abbreviated upper longeron
88 Fuselage frames
89 Rudder control cables
90 Elevator control cables
91 Elevator tab controls

97 Elevator control runners
98 Fuselage aft main frame/ tailplane support
99 Fin root fillet
100 Starboard elevator linkage
101 Starboard tailplane
102 Tailplane spar
103 Elevator outer hinge

104 Starboard elevator
105 Fin front spar
106 Tail identification light
107 Fin structure
108 Rudder upper hinge
109 Receiver aerial mast
110 Rudder inner frame
111 Rudder hinge
112 Elevator torque tube
113 Rudder post
114 Rudder control horns
115 Elevator tab
116 Port elevator

121 Tailwheel leg fairing
122 Tailwheel
123 Tailwheel leg
124 Tailwheel control runs
125 Fuselage skinning
126 Wingroot fillet
127 Aileron control rod assembly
128 Rear spar/stub wing attachment
129 Fuselage angled main frame attachment
130 Fuselage main fuel tank
131 Fuel filler access
132 Front spar/stub wing attachment
133 Mainwheel leg attachment
134 Front spar
135 Landing wires support strut and brace
136 Undercarriage 'V'-strut rear member
137 Stub wing structure
138 'V'-strut/rear spar attachment
139 Fuel filler cap
140 Port wing fuel tank
141 Rear spar
142 Transmitter aerial
143 Trailing edge ribs
144 Port aileron
145 Aileron tab
146 Aileron hinges
147 Aileron control linkages
148 Rear landing wire anchor point
149 Aileron control rods
150 Wing main rib stations
151 Outboard rib stations
152 Transmitter aerial lead-in
153 Port wingtip
154 Port navigation lights (upper and lower surfaces)
155 Wing structure
156 Front spar section
157 Landing wires anchor points
158 Flying wires brace

159 Outboard flying wires
160 Undercarriage trouser fairing
161 Brake cable assembly
162 Cross-brace member
163 'V'-strut front member
164 Flying wires attachment fairing
165 Wheel spat
166 Treadle
167 Brake arm
168 Port mainwheel
169 Axle
170 Spat inner frame
171 Spat/leg join
172 Mainwheel oleo leg
173 Inboard flying wires
174 Centre-line spacer
175 Starboard wheel fairing attachment
176 Spat panel
177 Starboard mainwheel
178 Under fuselage bomb-rack installation (inc items 179–183)
179 Arming handle
180 Bomb release wire (to cockpit)
181 Bomb-rack main member
182 Support frame
183 Forward sway braces
184 Possible loads inc (items 184–186)
185 30-lb (13.6 kg) practice bombs (five) or
186 100-lb (45-kg) bombs (two)

69 Pilot's seat
70 Throttle quadrant
71 Maps and document holder
72 Hinged entry flap
73 Equipment pouch
74 Cockpit coaming
75 Pilot's headrest
76 Headrest fairing
77 Receiver aerial brace
78 Turnover structure
79 Wireless receiver

92 Abbreviated lower longeron
93 Tailwheel control cables
94 Turnbuckles
95 Rear fuselage structure
96 Tailwheel control linkage

117 Elevator hinge
118 Tailplane structure
119 Elevator tab control linkage
120 Tailplane front spar/ fuselage attachment

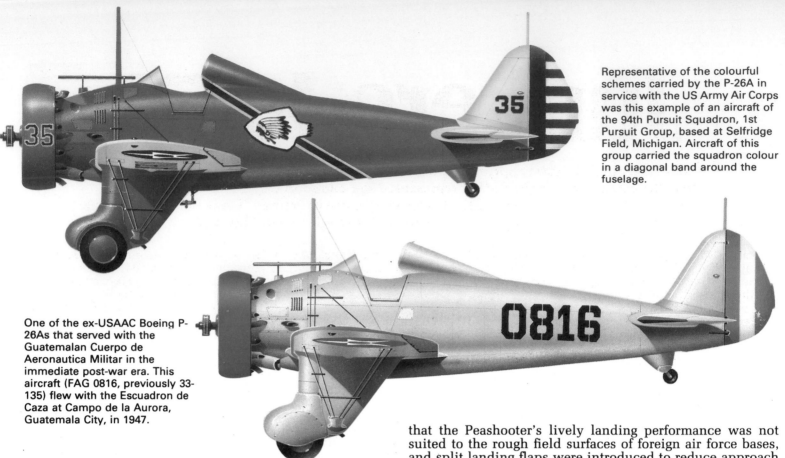

Representative of the colourful schemes carried by the P-26A in service with the US Army Air Corps was this example of an aircraft of the 94th Pursuit Squadron, 1st Pursuit Group, based at Selfridge Field, Michigan. Aircraft of this group carried the squadron colour in a diagonal band around the fuselage.

One of the ex-USAAC Boeing P-26As that served with the Guatemalan Cuerpo de Aeronautica Militar in the immediate post-war era. This aircraft (FAG 0816, previously 33-135) flew with the Escuadron de Caza at Campo de la Aurora, Guatemala City, in 1947.

in 1935. All were re-equipped with P-36s in 1938.

As the P-35s and P-36s entered service with home-based front-line squadrons in 1938 the P-26 was moved farther afield, initially to the Panama Canal Zone, and soon after to Wheeler Field. The 16th Pursuit Group, commanded by Lieutenant Colonel Willis H. Hale (later commander of the 6th Air Force in 1947–9, and of the 1st Air Force, 1950–1), included the 24th and the 29th Squadrons based at Albrook Field, Canal Zone, in 1938–9, and the 78th Squadron at Wheeler Field, Territory of Hawaii, in 1940. The 37th Pursuit Group received P-26s in 1940, its 28th and 30th Squadrons retaining them for only one year, but the 31st Squadron was still flying them in 1942 (after the US entered World War 2) and was the last first-line squadron to fly the Peashooter. This group and the 32nd Group were both based at Albrook Field: the latter, commanded by Captain Roger J. Browne (yet another commander of the 1st Air Force, in 1954–5) was equipped with P-26s for one year in 1941.

One other group, the 18th (with the 6th and 19th Pursuit Squadrons) flew P-26s from Wheeler Field between 1938 and 1941, but they had been discarded in favour of P-40s by the time of the Japanese attack on Pearl Harbor.

Returning to the development of the P-26 itself, the addition of 25 aircraft to the original order brought changes to the powerplant; the first two aircraft, designated P-26Bs and first flown on 10 January 1935, were powered by R-1340-33 engines with fuel injection, and were followed by 23 P-26Cs, also with R-1340-33 engines but initially without fuel injection. Delivery of the P-26C started in February 1936, and all were eventually modified to the P-26B standard. Both versions had a top speed of 235 mph (378 km/h) at 6,000 ft (1830 m).

Perhaps somewhat surprisingly, the P-26 was not widely exported in the late 1930s to the world's smaller air forces, for its cost and performance compared favourably with many other aircraft being offered on the international market.

Nevertheless Boeing underwrote the development of an export version, the Model 281, subsequently producing a total of 12 examples. Originally these were little different from the standard USAAC P-26A, but it soon became clear that the Peashooter's lively landing performance was not suited to the rough field surfaces of foreign air force bases, and split landing flaps were introduced to reduce approach speeds. Such flaps were also fitted to all Peashooters of the USAAC, either on the production line or as a retrofit.

One of the Boeing 281s was sold to Spain and the remainder were purchased by the Chinese for operation against the Japanese. The first arrived in China on 15 September 1934 but was destroyed in a crash during a demonstration by an American pilot; the other 10 reached Canton during the next 15 months, equipping one fighter squadron and being flown in constant action against the vastly superior numbers of Japanese aircraft. They succeeded in gaining occasional air victories, however, before the survivors were eventually forced out of service by lack of spares.

After the P-26 was declared obsolete in 1941 and given up by the USAAC, a few of the remaining machines which had been used in the Panama Canal Zone were transferred to the Cuerpo de Aeronautica Militar in Guatemala, to form that country's first fighter unit stationed in La Aurora near Guatemala City. Six of these aircraft were still in use immediately after the end of World War 2.

Led by Major (later Lieutenant Colonel) Armin F. Herold (whose aircraft featured blue, yellow and red bands round the engine cowling), this formation of 20th Pursuit Group Boeing P-26As included aircraft of the 55th, 77th and 79th Pursuit Squadrons flying from Barksdale Field, Louisiana just after 1934.

Junkers Ju 52

For all its seemingly archaic appearance, with fixed landing gear, angular lines and corrugated skin, the classic Junkers Ju 52/3m represented the common denominator of every land operation by Germany's Wehrmacht, whether in advance or retreat. 'Tante Ju' was indeed the German counterpart of America's Douglas C-46 Skytrain.

Towards the end of the 1920s, the German Lufthansa was widely regarded as the most efficient airline in the world, while other aviation companies were having problems keeping their heads above water in the major economic crisis that was occurring at the time. The company offered convenient flights throughout Europe with its large fleet of aircraft, mostly consisting of developments of the all-metal monoplane built by Professor Hugo Junkers in 1915, the J 1.

The great majority of these early aircraft (the J 10, F 13, A 20, F 24, W 33, W 34, Ju 46 and Ju 52) were single-engined low-wing monoplanes, but in 1924 there appeared a three-engine airliner, the G 23, powered by a 195-hp (145-kW) Junkers L 2 and two 100-hp (75-kW) Mercedes engines. It is thought that, as a result of Versailles Treaty restrictions imposed on German aircraft manufacture, this prototype was produced at Junkers' Fili factory near Moscow; production of about nine aircraft (as well as that of the much more numerous G 24) was subsequently undertaken in Sweden. The G 24, usually powered by three 280/310-hp (209/231-kW) Junkers L 5 inline engines, served in numerous con-

This Ju52, designated C-352-L, was built by CASA in Spain with BMW 132 radial engines produced under licence.

figurations and with a number of airlines, including Lufthansa which retained them in service until 1933–4.

The year 1926 was busy for the Junkers concern, two new designs (the G 31 tri-motor transport and the W 33/34) being the most important to fly. The former was a beefier version of the successful G 24, and the latter an excellent single-engine transport which was built in large numbers. Almost at once the Junkers designers embarked on a new, but considerably enlarged single-engine transport, the Ju 52, which embodied the cumulative experience of earlier designs and was primarily intended for freight carrying. Like its predecessors it was of standard Junkers all-metal construction with corrugated, load-sustaining duralumin skinning, and featured the patented Junkers full-span double wing. Five aircraft were built, of which four underwent development with various powerplants in Germany and one (CF-ARM) went to Canada. The first aircraft flew on 13 October 1930.

Despite its single engine (usually of around 780-825 hp/ 582–615 kW) the Ju 52 was able to carry 15–17 passengers when required. However the following year the Junkers design team, under Dipl. Ing. Ernst Zindel, undertook work to adapt the Ju 52 to feature three 525-hp (392-kW) Pratt & Whitney Hornet nine-cylinder radials, and the prototype of

The 18-seat Ju 52/3mg7e, shown here, was a major production variant and featured automatic pilot and wide cabin doors. Subsequent versions had the wheel fairings removed, as sand and mud tended to clog the wheels.

Three Junkers Ju 52/3mg6e mine clearance aircraft of the Minensuchgruppe, probably over the Mediterranean; the rudder markings are said to have denoted the number of minesweeping sorties flown – a somewhat hazardous task.

this version, the Ju 52/3m (*Dreimotoren*, or three-motor), made its maiden flight in April 1932. Subsequent deliveries were made to Finland, Sweden and Brazil, as well as to Deutsche Lufthansa. Ultimately Ju 52/3ms flew with airlines in Argentina, Austria, Australia, Belgium, Bolivia, China, Colombia, Czechoslovakia, Denmark, Ecuador, Estonia, France, Great Britain, Greece, Hungary, Italy, Lebanon, Mozambique, Norway, Peru, Poland, Portugal, Romania, South Africa, Spain, Switzerland, Turkey and Uruguay. Powerplants included Hispano-Suiza, BMW, Junkers Jumo, Bristol Pegasus, Pratt & Whitney Hornet and Wasp engines. Commercial Ju 52/3ms delivered to Bolivia were employed as military transports towards the end of the Gran Chaco war of 1932–5.

Starting late in 1932, Ju 52/3ms were delivered to Lufthansa, with D-2201 *Boelcke* and D-2202 *Richthofen* inaugurating the airline's Berlin–London and Berlin–Rome services before the end of that year. In due course no fewer than 230 Ju 52/3ms were registered with Deutsche Lufthansa, continuing to fly commercial services to Spain, Portugal, Sweden, Switzerland and Turkey almost to the end of World War 2.

Despite the stringencies of treaty restrictions imposed on Germany since 1919, clandestine adventures had continued by which potential military personnel had undergone training in foreign lands, particularly the USSR. Thus when, following her walk-out from the disarmament talks in 1932, Germany set about the covert establishment of a military air force, it fell to such aircraft as the Ju 52/3m to provide the basis of its flying equipment, and in 1934 the first military version, the Ju 52/3mg3e, appeared.

The Ju 52/3mg3e was an attempt to produce a bomber version quickly and without unduly interrupting the highly profitable commercial production line. Powered by three 525-hp (392-kW) BMW 132A-3 radials, this version normally carried a bomb load of 600 kg (1,321 lb), comprising six 100-kg (220-lb) bombs, and featured a dorsal gun position and a ventral 'dustbin', each mounting a single 7.92-mm (0.31-in) MG 15 machine-gun. Deliveries of the Ju 52/3mg3e to the new Luftwaffe totalled 450 in 1934–5, the first unit thus equipped being Kampfgeschwader 152 'Hindenburg'. In 1937 this Geschwader's IV Gruppe was re-designated KGrzbV1; this designation (*Kampfgruppe zur besonderen Verwendung*, or bomber group for special operations) was roughly comparable to the RAF's 'bomber transport' category, and was intended to reflect a dual role, bombing and military transport duties. It thereby perpetuated the originally intended function of the Ju 52/3m. In the event Ju 52/3m-equipped KGrzbV seldom if ever during World War 2 engaged in bombing operations.

When, on 18 July 1936, the Spanish Civil War broke out and Germany quickly aligned herself with the right-wing Nationalists, 20 Ju 52/3ms and six Heinkel He 51s were sent to Spain, being assembled into the Legion Cóndor under General Hugo Sperrle during the following November. And it was as transports that the Junkers were initially employed, bringing 10,000 Moorish troops to Spain from Morocco. Thereafter they were developed in three bomber *Staffeln* of Kampfgruppe 88, and were flown in raids on the Republican-held Mediterranean ports and in support of the land battle for Madrid. By mid-1937 they were deemed to be poor bombers and were largely replaced by such aircraft as the Dornier Do 17 and Heinkel He 111. Nevertheless the Ju 52/3m3ge continued to serve both as a bomber and a tran-

Junkers Ju 52/3mge cutaway drawing key

1 Starboard navigation light
2 Drooping aileron section of Junkers 'double wing'
3 Aileron hinge fairings
4 Control linkage
5 Underwing inspection panels
6 Corrugated wing skin
7 Aerial mast
8 Wing strut diagonal bracing
9 Starboard oil filler cap
10 House-flag mast
11 Starboard engine cowling (NACA cowling)
12 Junkers metal two-blade propeller
13 Centre BMW 132A radial engine (in Townend ring)
14 Exhaust
15 Filter intakes
16 Engine bearers
17 Bulkhead
18 Centre oil tank
19 Oil filler cap
20 Flat windscreen panels
21 Co-pilot's seat
22 Radio-operator's jump-seat
23 Pilot's seat
24 Control column
25 Rudder pedals
26 Raised cockpit floor level

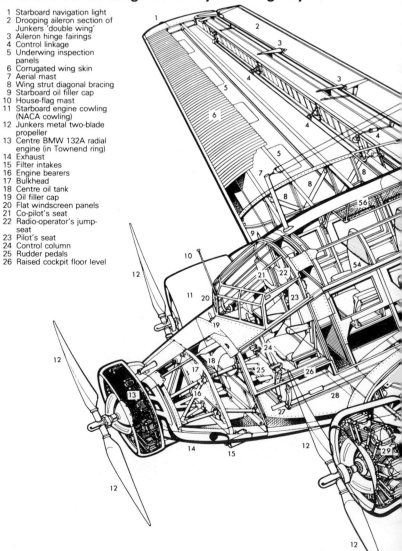

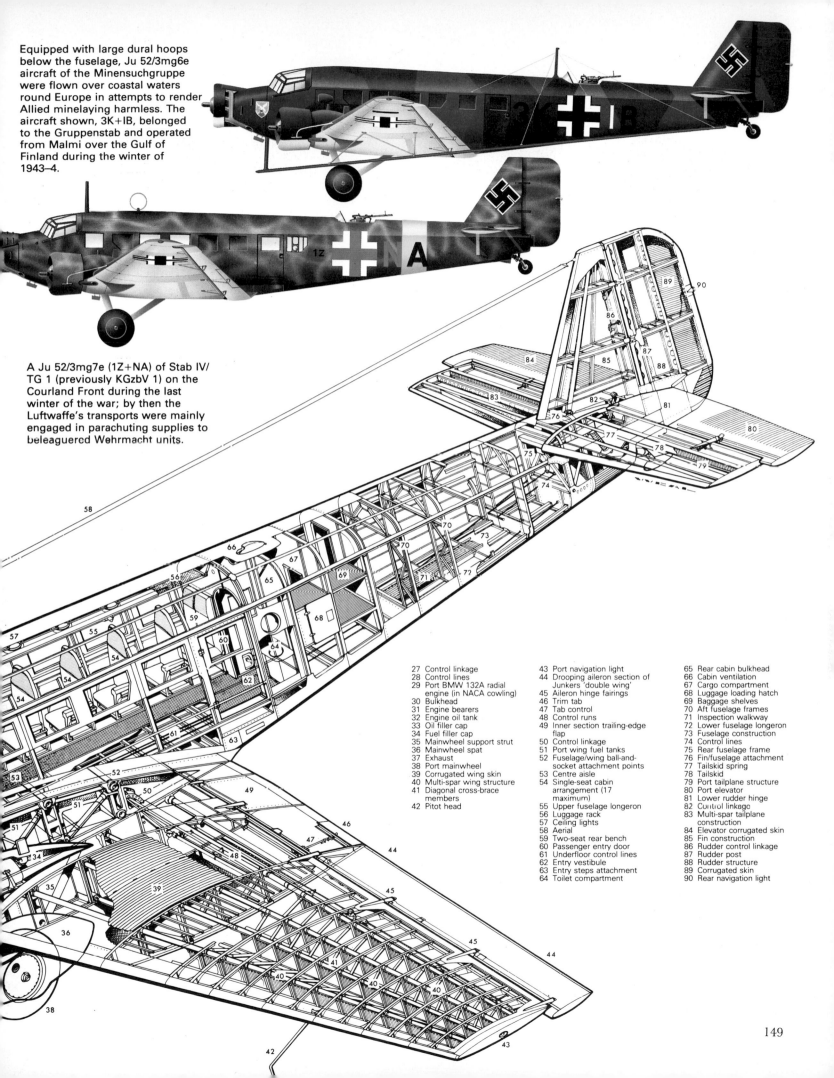

Equipped with large dural hoops below the fuselage, Ju 52/3mg6e aircraft of the Minensuchgruppe were flown over coastal waters round Europe in attempts to render Allied minelaying harmless. The aircraft shown, 3K+IB, belonged to the Gruppenstab and operated from Malmi over the Gulf of Finland during the winter of 1943–4.

A Ju 52/3mg7e (1Z+NA) of Stab IV/TG 1 (previously KGzbV 1) on the Courland Front during the last winter of the war; by then the Luftwaffe's transports were mainly engaged in parachuting supplies to beleaguered Wehrmacht units.

27 Control linkage
28 Control lines
29 Port BMW 132A radial engine (in NACA cowling)
30 Bulkhead
31 Engine bearers
32 Engine oil tank
33 Oil filler cap
34 Fuel filler cap
35 Mainwheel support strut
36 Mainwheel spat
37 Exhaust
38 Port mainwheel
39 Corrugated wing skin
40 Multi-spar wing structure
41 Diagonal cross-brace members
42 Pitot head

43 Port navigation light
44 Drooping aileron section of Junkers 'double wing'
45 Aileron hinge fairings
46 Trim tab
47 Tab control
48 Control runs
49 Inner section trailing-edge flap
50 Control linkage
51 Port wing fuel tanks
52 Fuselage/wing ball-and-socket attachment points
53 Centre aisle
54 Single-seat cabin arrangement (17 maximum)
55 Upper fuselage longeron
56 Luggage rack
57 Ceiling lights
58 Aerial
59 Two-seat rear bench
60 Passenger entry door
61 Underfloor control lines
62 Entry vestibule
63 Entry steps attachment
64 Toilet compartment

65 Rear cabin bulkhead
66 Cabin ventilation
67 Cargo compartment
68 Luggage loading hatch
69 Baggage shelves
70 Aft fuselage frames
71 Inspection walkway
72 Lower fuselage longeron
73 Fuselage construction
74 Control lines
75 Rear fuselage frame
76 Fin/fuselage attachment
77 Tailskid spring
78 Tailskid
79 Port tailplane structure
80 Port elevator
81 Lower rudder hinge
82 Control linkage
83 Multi-spar tailplane construction
84 Elevator corrugated skin
85 Fin construction
86 Rudder control linkage
87 Rudder post
88 Rudder structure
89 Corrugated skin
90 Rear navigation light

Junkers Ju 52

Specification

Junkers Ju 52/3mg7e
Type: 18-seat military transport
Powerplant: three 830-hp (619-kW) BMW
132T-2 nine-cylinder air-cooled radial
engines
Performance: 183 mph (295 km/h) at sea
level; initial climb rate 680 ft (208 m) per
minute; service ceiling 18,045 ft (5500 m);
range 802 miles (1290 km)
Weights: empty 14,462 lb (6560 kg);
maximum take-off 23,180 lb (10515 kg)
Dimensions: span 95 ft 11½ in (29.25 m);
length 62 ft 0 in (18.90 m); height 14 ft 9 in
(4.50 m); wing area 1,189.45 sq ft (110.50 m²)
Armament: (typical) one 7.92-mm (0.31-in)
MG 15 machine-gun in dorsal position
and two 7.92-mm (0.31-in) machine-guns
mounted to fire abeam through side windows

A Junkers Ju 52/3mg7e of 2.Staffel, KGzbV 1, based at Milos, Greece, in May 1941 prior to the invasion of Crete. Under the command of Generalmajor Gerhard a fleet of 493 Ju 52/3ms was assembled for the landings, known as Operation 'Mercury', but owing to confusion over the island during the initial assault subsequent waves of transports were delayed and the element of concentration was lost; of every four paratroopers dropped, one was killed or wounded. By the end of the operation more than 170 Ju 52/3ms had been lost or seriously damaged.

One of the first tasks of the German air force contingent in Spain was to lift 10,000 Moroccan troops from North Africa to the war zone. The aircraft shown, a Ju 52/3mg3e, is depicted in the markings of the Legion Cóndor's Kampfgruppe 88 late in 1936.

sport with German and Spanish Nationalist forces until the end of the Civil War.

To war in earnest

Operations from Germany's poorly surfaced military airfields had resulted in 1935 in the introduction of the Ju 52/3mg4e with tailwheel in place of tailskid, and by 1938 this version was being standardized among the KGrzbV. In March that year, at the time of the Austrian *Anschluss*, German troops were carried forward by KGrzbV 1 and 2 in a massive show of strength, the former based at Fürstenwalde with 54 aircraft, and the latter at Brandenburg-Briest.

By the time Germany was ready to crush Poland the Luftwaffe's *Transportverband* possessed an inventory of 552 aircraft, of which 547 were Ju 52/3mg3e and Ju 52/3mg4e aircraft (the balance being two obsolete He 111 transports, a Junkers G 38, a Ju 90 and a Focke-Wolf Fw 200). Losses in the month-long campaign of September amounted to 59 Junkers Ju 52/3ms, all but two to ground fire or flying accidents. In the course of 2,460 flights the aircraft carried 19,700 troops and 1,600 tons of supplies.

In the relatively swift and clinically organized invasion of Norway in the following year, the number of Ju 52/3ms available had risen to 573, equipping all four *Gruppen* of KGzbV 1, and KGrzbV 101, 102, 103, 104, 105, 106 and 107, an average of 52 aircraft in each *Gruppe*. A small number of twin float-equipped Ju 52/3m Wasser aircraft was also employed in the Norwegian campaign, alighting in the fjords to disembark troops, engineers and supplies. A new version, the Ju 52mg5e, with provision for alternative wheel, float or ski landing gear had been introduced, powered by three 830-hp (619-kW) BMW 132T-2 engines.

Among the important operations undertaken by the Junkers in Norway were the capture by airborne forces of Stavanger-Sola airport and of the Vordingborg bridge. A total of 29,000

First Junkers Ju 52/3mge to serve with Deutsche Lufthansa was this aircraft, D–2201 (c/n 4013), in May 1932, named *Boelcke* after the World War 1 fighter pilot. Early aircraft flew the Berlin–London and Berlin–Rome services.

men, 259,300 Imp gal (1,180,000 litres) of aviation fuel and 2,376 tons of supplies were airlifted during the campaign, for the significant loss of 150 aircraft.

However, before the conclusion of the Norwegian campaign, the majority of Ju 52/3ms were being withdrawn back to Germany in preparation for Operation 'Yellow', the great assault in the West. As a result of losses in Norway the number of Junkers available was only 475, to which was now added 45 DFS 230 assault gliders, the whole transport force being commanded by General Putzier. Because of the need to conserve the Ju 52/3ms for a likely air assault on the UK, the Luftwaffe's transports were largely confined to airborne attacks in the initial stage, and it was against the Netherlands and Belgium that most of these were launched, in particular on the Moerdijk bridges and on Rotterdam's Waalhaven airport. Large numbers of Ju 52/3ms were employed in each attack and losses, mainly from anti-aircraft gunfire, were extremely heavy; in the five days that it took the Wehrmacht to crush the Netherlands, no fewer than 167 Junkers were totally destroyed, and a similar number badly damaged.

By the end of 1940 a total of 1,275 Ju 52/3ms had been delivered to the Luftwaffe, of which some 700 aircraft had already been struck off charge for one reason or another. After the collapse of France no further major operations involving the use of Ju 52/3ms were launched until the advance by German forces through the Balkans in April 1941. By then a number of new versions had appeared, namely the Ju 52/3mg6e, which was similar to the Ju 52/3mg5e but equipped with improved radio and the Ju 52/3mg7e with automatic pilot, accommodation for up to 18 troops and wider cabin doors; it also featured provision for two 7.92-mm (0.31-in) machine-guns to fire through the cabin windows. Operations in the Balkans and Aegean also saw the first operations by the *Minensuchgruppe* (minesweeping group), equipped with the Ju 52/3mg6e fitted with large dural hoops energized by an auxiliary motor to explode Allied mines sown in abandoned harbours.

Despite its ultimate capture, Crete proved a disaster for the *Transportverband*. Assigned to the task of an airborne invasion of the island, the 493 Ju 52/3ms and about 80 DFS 230 gliders were intended to attack in three waves. However, as a result of confusion on the ground caused by dense clouds of

South African Airways flew a total of 15 Ju 52/3ms, of which the first, ZS-AFA *Jan Van Riebeeck* is seen here. Nine aircraft were handed on to the South African Air Force, these being employed on a transport shuttle between South Africa, Egypt and Italy.

Since April 1986, this Junkers Ju-52 has been flying for Lufthansa again, exactly 50 years after it was first brought into service by the same airline with the registration D-AQUI. Later it was used in Norway and the USA before returning to Germany to be restored. (Photo: Lufthansa, with the consent of Senat. Bremen, No. MBB 86-0402/32)

Junkers Ju 52

As well as serving with the German Legion Cóndor, Ju 52/3ms were supplied to the Spanish Nationalist forces, this 3mg4e bearing the markings of the Grupo de Bombardeo Nocturno 1-G-22 early in 1938. In Spanish service the Ju 52/3m was nicknamed *Pava* (turkey), its last bombing sortie being against Belmez on 26 March 1939.

dust, there were numerous collisions and delays, so that what had been planned as an attack concentrated in time and area degenerated into widespread confusion and dissipated effort. German causualties were more than 7,000 men (of whom about 2,000 were paratroops) and 174 Ju 52/3ms, representing more than a third of the Luftwaffe's available transport force.

It has often been averred that the Balkan campaign was a lost cause for the Allies, yet the heavy losses inflicted on this vital enemy assault arm proved of immense importance when Germany launched Operation 'Barbarossa' less than two months later, and henceforth (apart from isolated instances of commando-type operations) the use of air transport was confined within the Luftwaffe to logistic supply and evacuation. Indeed, on the opening day of 'Barbarossa' the Luftwaffe could field no more than 238 serviceable Ju 52/3ms, a far cry from the numbers available in 1939 and 1940.

The nature of warfare on the Eastern Front quickly determined the role to be played by the Ju 52/3m, with scorched earth tactics employed by the retreating Russians demanding considerable dependence by the Wehrmacht on air supplies. Production of the Ju 52/3m increased to 502 in 1941, 503 in 1942 and 887 in 1943. New versions continued to appear; the Ju 52/3mg8e dispensed with the wheel spats (found to be a hindrance in the quagmire conditions on the Eastern Front), but included a 0.51-in (13-mm) MG 131 gun in the dorsal position, while some aircraft had 850-hp (634-kW) BMW 132Z engines; the Ju 52/3mg9e, which appeared in 1942, featured strengthened landing gear to permit a take-off weight of 25,353 lb (11500 kg) and was equipped to tow the Gotha Go 242 glider; the Ju 52/3mg10e was a naval version with provision for floats, and the Ju 52/3mg12e had 800-hp (597-kW) BMW 132L engines. Only one other version reached the Luftwaffe (late in 1943), namely the Ju 52/3mg14e with an MG 15 machine-gun mounted in a streamlined position over the pilot's cabin.

It may be said of the Ju 52/3m that its star shone brightest in adversity from 1942 onwards. When in February that year six German divisions were trapped at Demyansk, the Luftwaffe performed the prodigious task of sustaining 100,000 troops, and in three months delivered 24,300 tons of material, airlifted 15,446 men into the pocket and evacuated 20,093 casualties: the cost of this effort was a loss of 385 flying personnel (including Major Walter Hammer, commanding KGrzbV 172) and 262 aircraft. Far greater disasters befell the German armies at Stalingrad and in North Africa, and in a single raid on Sverevo in the dreadful winter of 1942–3 52 Junkers were destroyed by Russian bombers. In the final attempts to succour (and eventually to evacuate) the Axis armies in Tunisia in April 1943 the Luftwaffe lost 432 transport aircraft, almost all of them JU 52/3ms, in less than three weeks.

The story of 'Tante Ju' did not end on VE-Day, when fewer than 50 such aircraft remained airworthy of the 4,835 said to have been built in Germany. The principal post-war operator of the aircraft was France where Ateliers Aéronautiques de Colombes produced more than 400 examples of a version known as the AAC1 Toucan; apart from 85 which flew post-war services for Air France, others were operated by Aéro-

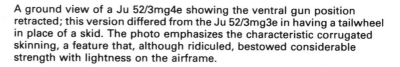

A ground view of a Ju 52/3mg4e showing the ventral gun position retracted; this version differed from the Ju 52/3mg3e in having a tailwheel in place of a skid. The photo emphasizes the characteristic corrugated skinning, a feature that, although ridiculed, bestowed considerable strength with lightness on the airframe.

Cargo, Air Atlas, Aigle Azur, Air Nolis, Air Ocean, TAI and many other airlines. The Toucan served with the Armée de l'Air and Aéronavale, and was used in fairly large numbers in the Algerian and Indo-China wars. In Spain CASA produced 170 aircraft, known as the C-352-L, with licence-built BMW 132 radials. Ten aircraft were reconditioned by Short Bros and Harland at Belfast, and entered service with British European Airways as G-AHOC to G-AHOL on 18 November 1946 on the Croydon–Liverpool–Belfast service. In Switzerland three Ju 52/3mg4e transports which were originally delivered to the Swiss Fliegertruppe on 4 October 1939 were still flying in the early 1980s.

In common with most of Germany's successful wartime aircraft, the Ju 52/3m underwent extensive development, resulting in the appearance of the Ju 252 and Ju 352. The former, whose prototype first flew in October 1941, was a larger aircraft than the Ju 52/3m, powered by three 1,340-hp (1000-kW) Junkers Jumo 211F liquid-cooled engines in annular cowlings, and had accommodation for 21 passengers in a pressurized cabin; the corrugated skinning was dispensed with. Originally it was intended to produce 25 aircraft for Lufthansa, but in view of the deteriorating war situation the order was reduced to 15, and all were delivered to the Luftwaffe. Some Ju 252As served with Lufttransportstaffel 290 (later redesignated Transportstaffel 5).

A quartet of early Ju 52/3mg3es bearing pre-war Luftwaffe markings; note the extended and awesomely situated ventral 'dustbin' gun positions and tailskids. The ventral gunner was protected from the slipstream by a fairing in which very exposed steps were incorporated to allow entry to the fuselage while the aircraft was airborne.

Grumman Single-seat Biplane Fighters

Grumman has been associated with US Navy fighters for so long that the names Tomcat, Cougar, Panther, Bearcat, Tigercat, Hellcat and Wildcat awake vivid memories of the last 45 years of carrier-based flying. To the older generation who remember the days before American naval aircraft had official names, the Grumman image evoked is that of the brightly coloured single-seaters with the F2F/F3F designations.

These sturdy-looking aircraft were almost the last biplanes when most other aircraft manufacturers had gone over to monoplanes. The Boeing P-12F acquired by the US Army in May 1932 was their last-ever single-seater biplane, more than a year before the first Grumman single-seater was produced for the Navy. Leroy Grumman's first aircraft was the two-seater FF-1, flown for the first time on 21st December 1931; this was also the first fighter in the US Navy to have a retractable undercarriage and closed cockpit. The plane was much faster than others of the same format, and this led to the conviction that a smaller, single-seat version would give much better performance than the Boeing F4B-4 and Curtiss F11C-2 fighters which the US Navy had ordered.

On 2 November 1932 the US Navy ordered an XF2F-1

The predecessor of the Grumman F2F and F3F fighters, the two-seater FF-1, was fitted with the 4½ ft (1.37 m) Wright R-1820 nine-cylinder radial engine.

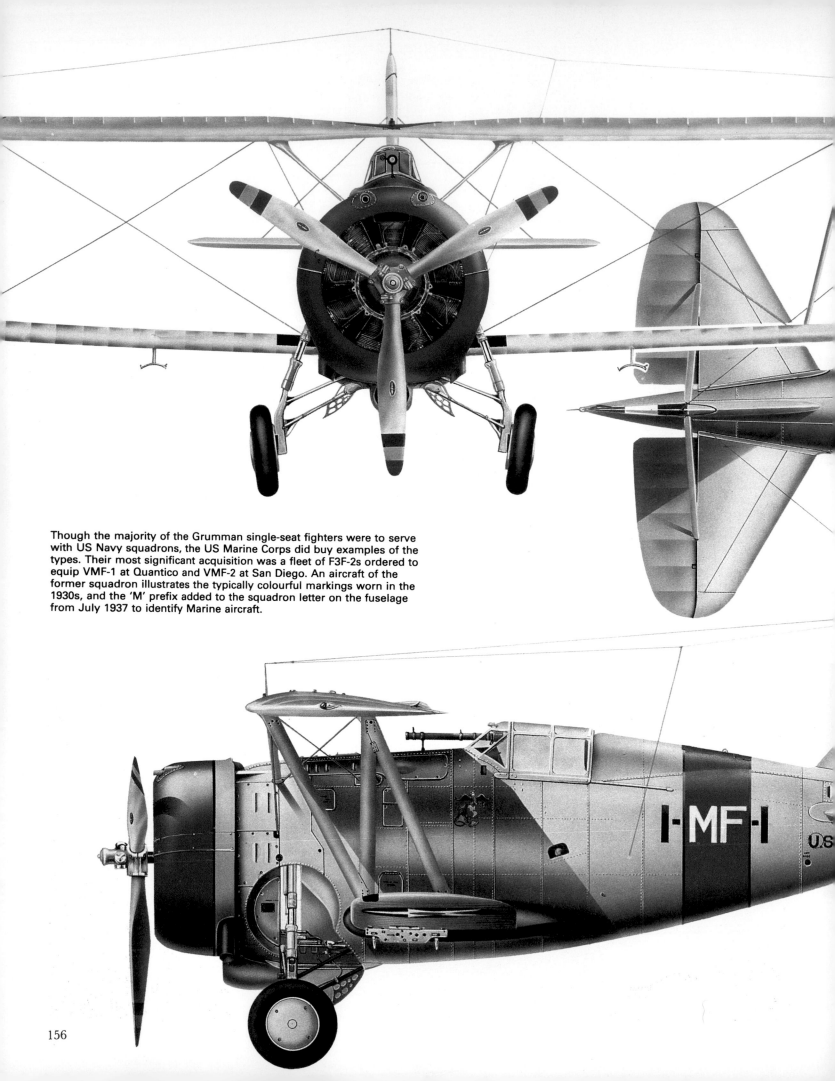

Though the majority of the Grumman single-seat fighters were to serve with US Navy squadrons, the US Marine Corps did buy examples of the types. Their most significant acquisition was a fleet of F3F-2s ordered to equip VMF-1 at Quantico and VMF-2 at San Diego. An aircraft of the former squadron illustrates the typically colourful markings worn in the 1930s, and the 'M' prefix added to the squadron letter on the fuselage from July 1937 to identify Marine aircraft.

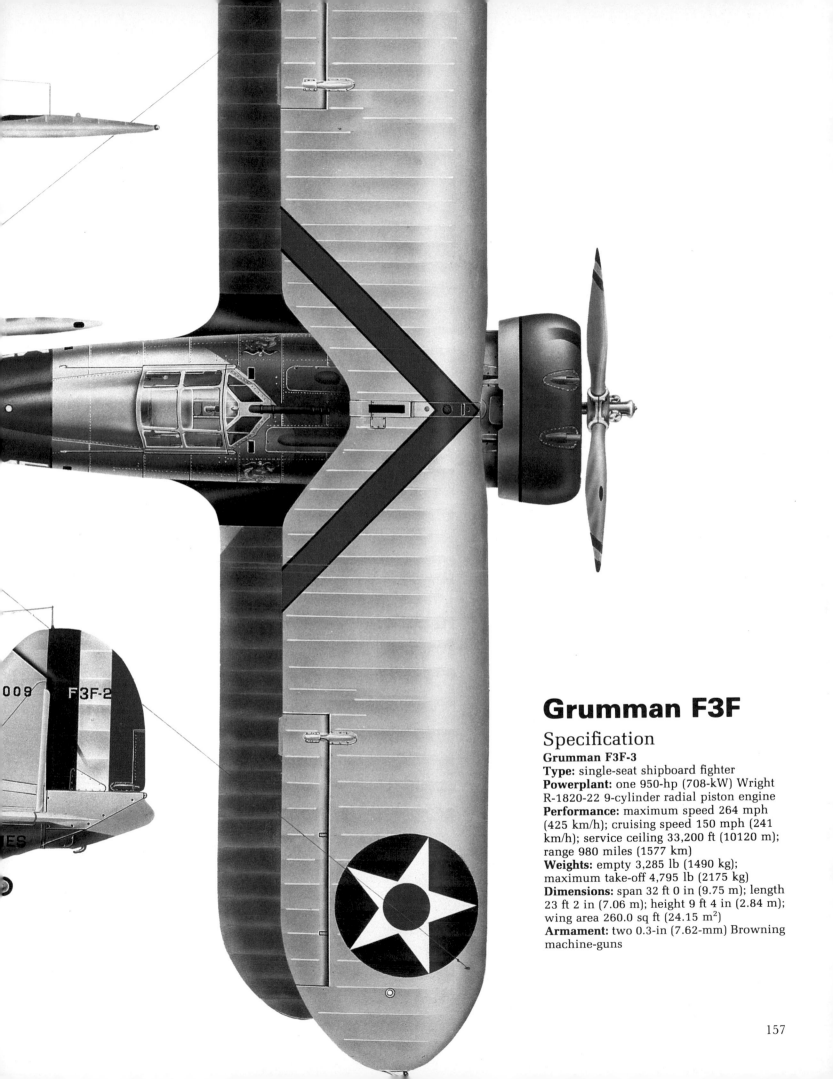

Grumman F3F

Specification

Grumman F3F-3
Type: single-seat shipboard fighter
Powerplant: one 950-hp (708-kW) Wright R-1820-22 9-cylinder radial piston engine
Performance: maximum speed 264 mph (425 km/h); cruising speed 150 mph (241 km/h); service ceiling 33,200 ft (10120 m); range 980 miles (1577 km)
Weights: empty 3,285 lb (1490 kg); maximum take-off 4,795 lb (2175 kg)
Dimensions: span 32 ft 0 in (9.75 m); length 23 ft 2 in (7.06 m); height 9 ft 4 in (2.84 m); wing area 260.0 sq ft (24.15 m²)
Armament: two 0.3-in (7.62-mm) Browning machine-guns

Grumman Biplanes

single-seat prototype, and on 19 December the small Grumman company also received its first production contract for 27 FF-1 two-seaters. A factory was rented in Farmingdale, Long Island, and construction began. The US Navy had decided on air-cooled radial engines for all of its fighters back in 1927. Instead of the 54 in (1.37 m) wide Wright R-1820 Cyclone of the FF-1, with its nine cylinders circled in a single row, a new 44 in (1.12 m) diameter twin-row 14-cylinder Pratt & Whitney XR-1535-44 Twin Wasp Junior was selected better to fit into the shape of the XF2F-1's short, deep all-metal fuselage.

The main wheels retracted into the fuselage behind the engine, wound up by about 32 turns of a hand crank, and the tail wheel also disappeared, along with the arresting hook in the tail. The small size (span of 28 ft 6 in/8.69 m and length of 23 ft 1 in/8.56 m) promised to occupy less space on aircraft-carrier decks. Another advantage was that the water-tight compartments in the fuselage below the cockpit floor provided flotation in an emergency water landing, eliminating the complicated rubber bags in the wings of older types. Like previous US Navy fighters, the XF2F-1 was armed with two synchronized 0.3-in (7.62-mm) machine-guns, under the cowl ahead of the enclosed cockpit.

On 18 October 1933 the XF2F-1 (serial number 9342) was first flown from Farmingdale and soon displayed its superior performance. With the XR-1534-44 giving 625 hp (466.1 kW) at 8,400 ft (2560 m), top speed was 229 mph (369 km/h) at that critical altitude compared with 207 mph (333 km/h) for

the production FF-1s delivered in the same year. Weighing only 3,536 lb (1604 kg) compared with 4,677 lb (2121 kg) for the two-seater, the XF2F-1 showed so much better manoeuvrability than its predecessor that the US Navy gave up the two-seat fighter configuration until after World War 2.

Grumman still faced competition from five other single-seat fighter designs built for the US Navy within a year of the XF2F-1's appearance. Curtiss was able to get its XF11C-3 into the air first, on 11 March 1933, because the airframe was essentially that of the 1925 Curtiss Hawk with fabric-covered fuselage and open cockpit. Like the Grumman aircraft, it had the wheels retracting into the fuselage, just behind a 700-hp (522.0-kW) R-1820 Cyclone.

Boeing offered the most modern-looking design, a low-wing monoplane flown on 14 September 1933 that made 239 mph (385 km/h) on only 550 hp (410.1 kW). Unfortunately it was judged unsuitable for carrier work because it required too long a take-off run and landed too fast. Northrop's low-wing XFT-1 and the high-wing Curtiss XF13C-1 monoplane appeared in January 1934 with most of the Boeing's speed and much of the same problems, while the Berliner-Joyce XF3J-1 biplane delivered in March 1934 had a conservative

Success with the two-seat Grumman FF-1 fighter provided the fledgling design team with a sound basis for a single-seat development with better performance. As the Grumman F2F-1, it began replacing the Boeing F4B-2s of VF-2B in 1935. This example carries the red tailplane and fuselage codes of VF-5B 'Red Rippers'.

Looking rather sombre in its black trim when compared with the bright colours of other US Navy squadrons, this F3F-1 served with VF-7 (later designated VF-72), the last squadron to operate the F3F-1, with final withdrawal taking place on 10 February 1941. This model continued to serve in the pilot training role at NAS Norfolk and Miami.

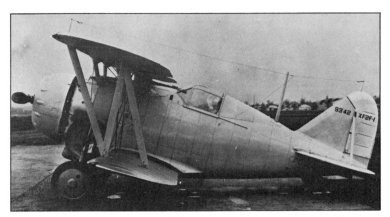

In this view of the Grumman XF2F-1 fighter prototype, the barrel-like lines of the fuselage are well illustrated. Various modifications were introduced, including a smaller-diameter engine cowl with rocker arm blisters, a Mk III Mod 2 telescopic gunsight, and various radio aerials.

design that was much too slow and too late to be competitive.

The US Navy ordered 27 Curtiss biplanes on 26 February 1934 and 54 Grumman F2F-1s on 17 May. When the first Curtiss was delivered on 8 October 1934, it carried a BF2C-1 (for Bomber Fighter) designation, as it could carry a 474-lb (215-kg) bomb or a drop tank; neither was provided on the Grummans. A severe vibration problem caused the retirement of the BF2C-1 by March 1936, and Curtiss won no more US Navy fighter production contracts.

Far more success was enjoyed by the F2F-1, first delivered on 19 January 1935, which remained in squadron service more than five years. Powered by a production Twin Wasp Jr, the R-1535-72 of 700 hp (522.0 kW) at take-off and 650 hp (484.7 kW) at 7,500 ft (2286 m), the F2F-1's top speed went from 203 mph (327 km/h) at sea level to 231 mph (372 km/h) at 7,500 ft (2286m). Landing at a reasonable 66 mph (106 km/ h), the fighter climbed to 5,000 ft (1524 m) in 2.1 minutes and reached a 27,100-ft (8260-m) service ceiling. The 110-US gal (416-litre) fuel capacity allowed an 985-mile (1585-km) maximum range. It might be mentioned that the Royal Navy's standard carrier fighter at that time, the Hawker Nimrod, had a maximum speed of 195 mph (314 km/h).

As was the custom of the time, the first production F2F-1 (9623) went to the US Navy's test station at Anacostia, in Washington DC, during January 1935. The next 22 were painted in the markings of VF-2B, the fighter squadron of the USS Lexington, and flown across the country from Farmingdale to San Diego, California, by US Navy pilots.

During this movement, the US Navy lost a Grumman when the aircraft painted 2-F-10 ran into a blinding dust storm over Mississippi on 16 March 1935. Lieutenant-Commander Arthur W. Radford bailed out at 3,000 ft (914 m), landed safely, and went on to become the top admiral in the US establishment in 1953, as the chairman of the Joint Chiefs of

Staff. A replacement aircraft (9997) was ordered on 29 June 1935, at a price of $12,000.

Twenty F2F-1s went to the USS Ranger for VF-3B from April to June 1935 while production continued until the last two of 55 aircraft were delivered on 2 August 1935, the last group going to the Battle Force Storage Pool in San Diego. Nine of these were issued to replace the FF-1s of VF-5B on the Ranger in October 1935.

Improved design

Even before F2F-1 deliveries began, Grumman prepared a new design intended to improve that design's directional stability and manoeuvrability, spin tendencies, and to add a bombing capability. On 15 October 1934 the US Navy ordered the design and construction of one XF3F-1 for $75,850, but Grumman would have to build three aircraft, all with the serial 9727, to complete the contract.

The XF3F-1 had the same R-1535-72 engine, but the fuselage was lengthened, and the wing area increased from 230 to 260.6 sq ft (21.37 to 24.21 m²). Reduction of the wheel diameter from 32 to 26 in (0.81 to 0.66 m) eliminated the bulge behind the engine and allowed a more streamlined fuselage. Jimmy Collins, company test pilot and a well-known aviation writer, made the first three XF3F-1 test flights on 20 March 1935.

Two days later tests resumed with two flights by US Navy pilots in the morning and then Collins began a series of six flights to demonstrate recovery from high-speed dives. The tenth dive was begun from 18,000 ft (5486 m) with a pull-out planned at 5,000 ft (1524 m) at 9g, nine times the stress of gravity on the airframe. But this time the biplane pulled out at 8,000 ft (2438 m) so sharply that the accelerometer

Despite the loss of the first and second prototypes (the first machine crashed during a test flight) the US Navy was convinced of the XF3F-1's performance improvements over the F2F-1. The second prototype was rebuilt and successfully completed the test phase. Operating squadrons included VF-6B, one of whose aircraft is shown here.

indicated some 14 g, the overstressed airframe broke up in mid-air and crashed in a cemetery, and Collins was killed.

A second strengthened prototype was quickly built and flown on 9 May at Farmingdale and delivered to the Anacostia test station. During a 10-turn spin demonstration, the XF3F-1 failed to recover, company pilot Lee Gehlbach bailed out, and the prototype struck the ground after 42 flat turns. The wreck was shipped back to Grumman and rebuilt in three weeks and redelivered to Anacostia on 20 June 1935 by William McAvoy.

On 24 August 1935 the US Navy ordered 54 F3F-1 fighters for $1,102,885; the batch was enough for two 18-plane squadrons with 50 per cent spares. The R-1535-84 engine had the same 650-hp (484.7-kW) rating as the R-1535-72, with the addition of a dynamic damper and fittings for the hydraulic pitch control of the Hamilton Standard 96-in (2.44-m) two-bladed propeller. While gross weight increased from 3,847 lb (1745 kg) on the F2F-1 to 4,170 lb (1892 kg) on the F3F-1, top speed remained 231 mph (372 km/h) at 7,500 ft (2286 m), and landing speed remained 66 mph (106 km/h), while range could be stretched to 998 miles (1606 km). Service ceiling was elevated to 28,500 ft (8687 m) by the slightly lower wing loading.

Armament included the usual 0.3-in (7.62-mm) M2 gun under the port side of the cowl with 500 rounds, but the starboard weapon was a 0.5-in (12.7-mm) M2 with 200 rounds. A 116-lb (52.6-kg) MkIV bomb could be attached below each wing and was aimed in a dive by the same three-power telescopic sight used for the guns. Other equipment included a radio, life raft, and oxygen, as on the F2F-1.

Wing span was now 32 ft (9.75 m) and length 23 ft 3 in (7.09 m). The typical Grumman biplane wing structure with metal ribs, twin spars, and leading edges, had fabric surfaces and was joined by metal N struts. Between the wings was a 5-ft (1.52-m) gap, and the lower wing had 2° dihedral.

The first F3F-1 (0211) was delivered 29 January 1936 and went to Anacostia as was usual. Squadrons VF-5B on the *Ranger* and VF-6B on the USS *Saratoga* got new F3F-1s between March and July, while the last delivery was made on 21 September 1936. A new US Marine squadron, then VF-4M at San Diego, got six in January 1937.

Grumman proposed a version to take advantage of the power offered by the new Wright Cyclone G series with a two-stage super-charger. Work on a prototype began before the contract, which was not approved until the aircraft was completed. On 27 July 1936 the XF3F-2 (0452) was flown to Anacostia by James Taylor. Powered by a single-row XR-1820-22 of 950 hp (708.4 kW) at take-off and driving a 9-ft (2.74-m) three-bladed propeller, the SF3F-2 achieved 255

mph (410 km/h) at 12,000 ft (3658 m) and could take off from a carrier in a 25-kt wind in only 131 ft (40 m). The increased engine diameter of 54 in (1.37 m) again altered the barrel-shaped appearance.

A civilian version, the G-22, was built for the Gulf Oil company's Major Alford Williams and delivered 6 December 1936 in bright orange paint and blue trim. Costing $12,225, the *Gulfhawk II* was flown on promotional tours. Powered by a 1,000-hp (745.7-kW) Wright R-1820-G1 and looking like an F3F-2, it actually had F2F wings of 28 ft 6 in (8.69 m) span

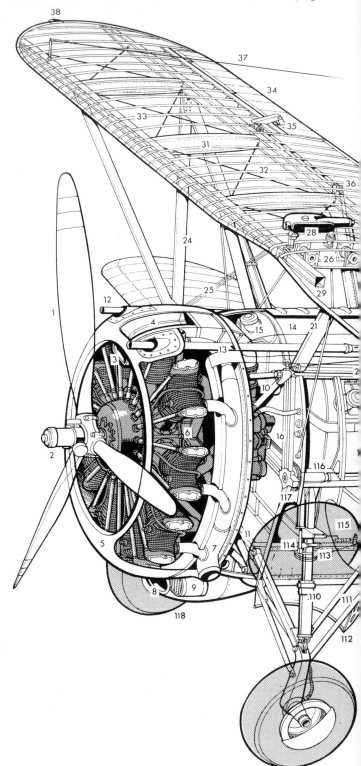

Sentiment for the biplane and a lack of belief in the attributes of monoplane fighters for the US Navy helped to buy time for the F3F. Fitted with a large-diameter Wright Cylcone powerplant, which necessitated a major revision of the nose contours, the F3F-1 became the F3F-2, and 81 were ordered for the US Navy, deliveries of which were all completed during 1936.

Grumman F3F-3 cutaway drawing key

1 Three-bladed constant-speed controllable-pitch 9-ft (2.74-m) diameter Hamilton Standard propeller
2 Propeller pitch change mechanism
3 Carburettor air intake
4 Supercharger air intake
5 NACA-type cowling
6 Wright R-1820-22 Cyclone nine-cylinder single-row radial air-cooled engine
7 Exhaust pipe
8 Oil cooler intake
9 Oil cooler (9 in/22.9 cm diameter)
10 Upper engine mounting struts
11 Lower engine mounting struts
12 Starboard gun blast tube
13 Port gun blast tube
14 Oil tank (9 US gal/34 litre capacity)
15 Oil filler cap
16 Engine bulkhead
17 Main fuel tank (83 US gal/314 litre capacity)
18 Fuel tank filler cap
19 Tank fixing
20 Fuselage main longeron
21 Centre section forward strut
22 Centre section aft strut
23 Strut attachment lug
24 Light alloy interplane N-struts
25 Flying wires
26 Upper wing centreline joint
27 Aircraft sling attachments
28 Mk VII gun camera
29 Front spar
30 Rear spar
31 Spar bracing rib
32 Diagonal wire bracing
33 Wing ribs (of truss construction)
34 Starboard aileron
35 Aileron actuating arm
36 Aileron control rod
37 Aerial cable
38 Starboard navigation light
39 Mk III Mod 4 telescope sight
40 Windscreen frame
41 Port 0.3-in (7.62-mm) Browning machine-gun
42 Starboard 0.5-in (12.7-mm) Browning machine-gun
43 Ammunition tanks (500 rounds 0.3-in/7.62-mm and 200 rounds 0.5-in/12.7-mm)
44 Ammunition feed chute
45 Cartridge case ejector chute
46 Pressure fire extinguisher
47 Auxiliary fuel tank (47 US gal/178 litre capacity)
48 Auxiliary tank filler
49 Very pistol cartridge holder
50 Rudder pedal
51 Instrument panel
52 Pilot's seat
53 Throttle and propeller controls
55 Bomb release levers
56 Tailplane trim control
57 Access step
58 Cockpit floor structure
59 Adjustable seat support structure
60 Headrest
61 Aft-sliding canopy
62 Life raft stowage
63 D/F loop
64 Junction box
65 Equipment bay access door
66 Dynamotor unit
67 Radio transmitter
68 Radio receiver
69 First aid kit
70 Emergency rations and water supply
71 Dorsal light
72 Fuselage frames (Z section)
73 Tailplane incidence control rod
74 Lift/hoist tube
75 Controls access cover
76 Rudder and elevator control cables
77 Fin structure (solid section ribs)
78 Fin/fuselage attachment
79 Rudder post
80 Rudder structure (fabric covered)
81 Rudder hinge
82 Trim tab
83 Trim actuator
84 Tailcone
85 Arrester hook fairing
86 Tail light
87 Variable-incidence tailplane
88 Tailplane structure
89 Elevator (fabric covered)
90 Arrester hook (extended)
91 Retractable tailwheel (solid rubber tyre)
92 Tailwheel shock absorber strut
93 Port upper wing structure
94 Port navigation light
95 Interplane 'N' struts
96 Lower wing front spar
97 Lower wing rear spar
98 Spar bracing rib
99 Wing ribs
100 Leading edge construction
101 Wire bracing
102 Retractable landing light
103 Mk XLI bomb rack
104 Mk IV 116-lb (52.6-kg) demolition bomb
105 Fuse unit
106 Wing spar root fitting
107 Flying wire attachment
108 Wing root fillet
109 Port mainwheel (26 in × 6 in/66 cm × 15 cm)
110 Oleo strut
111 Radius arms
112 Fairing door
113 Retraction strut
114 Lock actuator
115 Wheel well
116 Retraction strut axle mounting
117 Retraction chain drive
118 Starboard mainwheel

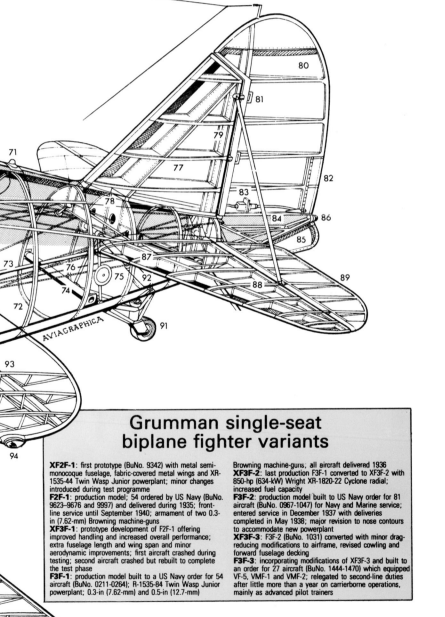

Grumman single-seat biplane fighter variants

XF2F-1: first prototype (BuNo. 9342) with metal semi-monocoque fuselage, fabric-covered metal wings and XR-1535-44 Twin Wasp Junior powerplant; minor changes introduced during test programme
F2F-1: production model; 54 ordered by US Navy (BuNo. 9623–9676 and 9997) and delivered during 1935; front-line service until September 1940; armament of two 0.3-in (7.62-mm) Browning machine-guns
XF3F-1: prototype development of F2F-1 offering improved handling and increased overall performance; extra fuselage length and wing span and minor aerodynamic improvements; first aircraft crashed during testing; second aircraft crashed but rebuilt to complete the test phase
F3F-1: production model built to a US Navy order for 54 aircraft (BuNo. 0211-0264); R-1535-84 Twin Wasp Junior powerplant; 0.3-in (7.62-mm) and 0.5-in (12.7-mm) Browning machine-guns; all aircraft delivered 1936
XF3F-2: last production F3F-1 converted to XF3F-2 with 850-hp (634-kW) Wright XR-1820-22 Cyclone radial; increased fuel capacity
F3F-2: production model built to US Navy order for 81 aircraft (BuNo. 0967-1047) for Navy and Marine service; entered service in December 1937 with deliveries completed in May 1938; major revision to nose contours to accommodate new powerplant
XF3F-3: F3F-2 (BuNo. 1031) converted with minor drag-reducing modifications to airframe, revised cowling and forward fuselage decking
F3F-3: incorporating modifications of XF3F-3 and built to an order for 27 aircraft (BuNo. 1444-1470) which equipped VF-5, VMF-1 and VMF-2; relegated to second-line duties after little more than a year on carrierborne operations, mainly as advanced pilot trainers

The urgent need to replace the obsolescent F2F-1s in service with VF-2 and VF-5, while development of the first generation of monoplane fighters continued, led to a contract for 27 'improved' F3F-2s in 1938, which were designated F3F-3. Various modifications helped to reduce drag in addition to new features such as the curved Plexiglas windscreen and revision of the engine cowling.

and was credited with 290 mph (467 km/h). In October 1948 it was donated to the Smithsonian Institution (which now operates the National Air and Space Museum) and is the only Grumman single-seat biplane surviving today. Gulf also purchased a two-seat version, the G-32 delivered on 12 May 1938.

New Model welcomed

Eighty-one production F3F-2s, ordered on a contract approved on 23 March 1937, were built in the new Grumman factory at Bethpage, New York, except for the wings and tail, which were subcontracted to Brewster. The first F3F-2 (0967) was flown to Anacostia by Lee Gehlbach on 17 July 1937. Although not officially accepted until November the new model was hailed in the test report as 'the most satisfactory single-seat fighter developed for the Navy to date, taking into account all the factors ... '.

Powered by a Wright R-1820-22 with 950 hp (708.4 kW) for take-off and 750 hp (559.3 kW) at 15,200 ft (4633 m), the F3F-2 had a wing span of 32 ft (9.75 m) and was 23 ft 2 in (7.06 m) long. According to US Navy characteristics charts it weighed 3,254 lb (1476 kg) empty and 4,498 lb (2040 kg) with normal load, the top speed went from 234 mph (377 km/h) at sea level to 260 mph (418 km/h) at 15,250 ft (4648 m). Landing speed was 69 mph (111 km/h). Rate of climb began at 2,800 ft (853 m) per minute and the service ceiling was 32,300 ft (9845 m), while 130 US gal (492 litres) of fuel allowed a range between 975 to 1,130 miles (1569 and 1819 km). Armament remained the same as on the F3F-1.

The second F3F-2 was delivered 1 December 1937 for VF-6 on the USS *Enterprise*, and by April 1938 26 had been allocated to replace that squadron's F2F-1s. US Marine Squadron VMF-1 at Quantico got some to replace, at long last, its 188-mph (303-km/h) Boeing F4B-4s in March

1938, while VMF-2 (formerly VF-4M) at San Diego also re-equipped with the F3F-2.

When the last F3F-2 was accepted in May 1938, all seven US Navy and US Marine fighter squadrons had Grumman single-seaters. These units had been renumbered in 1937, the US Navy squadrons now corresponding to their carriers: VF-2 with CV-2, etc. All of their fighters were painted chrome yellow on the upper wing surface to facilitate their location in emergencies, and a tail colour went with each carrier. Thus the F2F-1s of VF-2 on the *Lexington* wore yellow tails, the F3F-1s of VF-3 the *Saratoga*'s white and the F3F-1s of VF-4 the *Ranger*'s green, the F2F-1s of VF-5 the *Yorktown*'s red, and the F3F-2s of VF-6 the *Enterprise*'s blue. Colourful stripes on the cowls and fuselages denoted each machine's place within the squadron, and US Marine F3F-2s had vertical red, white, and blue rudder stripes.

By this time the biplane fighter seemed ready for replacement, for the US Navy ordered 54 Brewster F2A-1 monoplanes in June 1938 and Grumman's own XF4F-2 monoplane was showing great promise. Nevertheless, the US Navy decided to order 27 F3F-3 fighters on 21 June 1938 as these could be delivered before the Brewsters. These aircraft incorporated drag-reducing refinements made to F3F-2 number 1031, which became the XF3F-3. That plane had been returned to Grumman for modification of the cowling and windshield, a new 105-in (2.67-m) Hamilton propeller, and other details. At one point, it also tried an upper wing with landing flaps that had been made for a company aircraft, the G-32A two-seater version of the F3F-2, but tests in August indicated this change was unnecessary, and the standard wing was restored.

The XF3F-3 arrived at Anacostia in October, and after successful tests some of its improvements were incorporated on the production F3F-3. On 16 December 1938 the first F3F-3 (1444) came to Anacostia for Production Acceptance Trials. The first 18 were painted with the red tails of VF-5 on the *Yorktown*, whose F2F-1s they were replacing, while the others remained ashore as spares.

Using the same engine and armament as its predecessor, the F3F-3 weighed 4,543 lb (2061 kg), had a top speed of 239 mph (385 km/h) at sea level and 264 mph (425 km/h) at 15,200 ft (4633 m), and landed at 68 mph (109 km/h). Service ceiling was 33,200 ft (10119 m), and range varied from 980 to 1,150 miles (1577 to 1851 km).

When the last F3F-3 was delivered on 10 May 1939, American production of biplane fighters ended, although abroad the Gloster Sea Gladiator, Polikarpov I-153, and Fiat CR.42 would continue into World War 2. Grumman's plump single-seaters would retire from US Navy service without firing a shot in combat.

In December 1939, VF-3 received ten Brewster F2A-1 monoplanes and was able to exchange half of its F3F-1s for VF-7s. This was the squadron with black tailplanes set up for the new USS *Wasp*. From September 1940 deliveries of F2A-2s replaced VF-2's F2F-1s and the remaining machines still in use by VF-3.

The Grumman J2F 'Duck' was a special version of the F2F with a large main float. A small rudder at the end of the float made manoeuvring on water easier.

Dornier's Flying Pencils

From 1937 the Dornier 'Flying Pencil' was one of the most notorious and active fast bomber and reconnaissance aircraft in the world. Subsequently, it was tripled in weight and quadrupled in power, but without real success, and the overall production total of all models only just exceeded 3,000.

It is generally accepted that in the mid-1930s the Luftwaffe was clandestinely developing its new fast bombers in the guise of civil transport aircraft. Anyone looking closely at the Do 17 V1, the first prototype of a completely new high-speed land plane built in mid-1934 by Dornier's factory in Friedrichshafen, could be in no doubt about its purpose. This aircraft type, whose slim fuselage soon earned it the nickname of 'Flying Pencil', with its sleek lines, small, simple tail and undercarriage which retracted into the nacelles of the BMW engines, looked distinctly like a fast bomber. As a transport plane this aircraft, which squeezed two passenger seats in behind the cockpit, and a further four in a 'cabin'

Fitted with BMW-Bramo 323P Fafnir engines rated at 1,000 hp (745.7 kW) for take-off, the Dornier Do 17Z-2 appeared in 1939 capable of carrying a 2,205-lb (1000-kg) bombload. This example was one of the last in front-line service, fighting on the Eastern front in 1942 with 15.(Kroat)/KG 53.

behind the wings with a clear height of only 4 ft (1.22 m), would have been wholly unsuitable. It was obvious that the high-wing configuration allowed room for a large bomb compartment underneath the wing.

From first flight on 23 November 1934 the Do 17 handled well, but though two further prototypes were speedily completed and tested by the airline Deutsche Lufthansa, it was reluctantly agreed that the type was not suited to carrying passengers. For despite all appearances, the Do 17 really had been designed as a fast six-passenger mailplane! The prototypes languished in a hangar at the Löwenthal factory, where by chance they were spotted by Flugkapitän Robert Untucht, famed Lufthansa test pilot and RLM (air ministry) liaison officer. He instantly drew the obvious conclusion, which apparently had not occurred to anyone else, and tested one of the aircraft. His enthusiasm led to the Do 17 V4, a bomber prototype with twin fins. Further prototypes followed, the

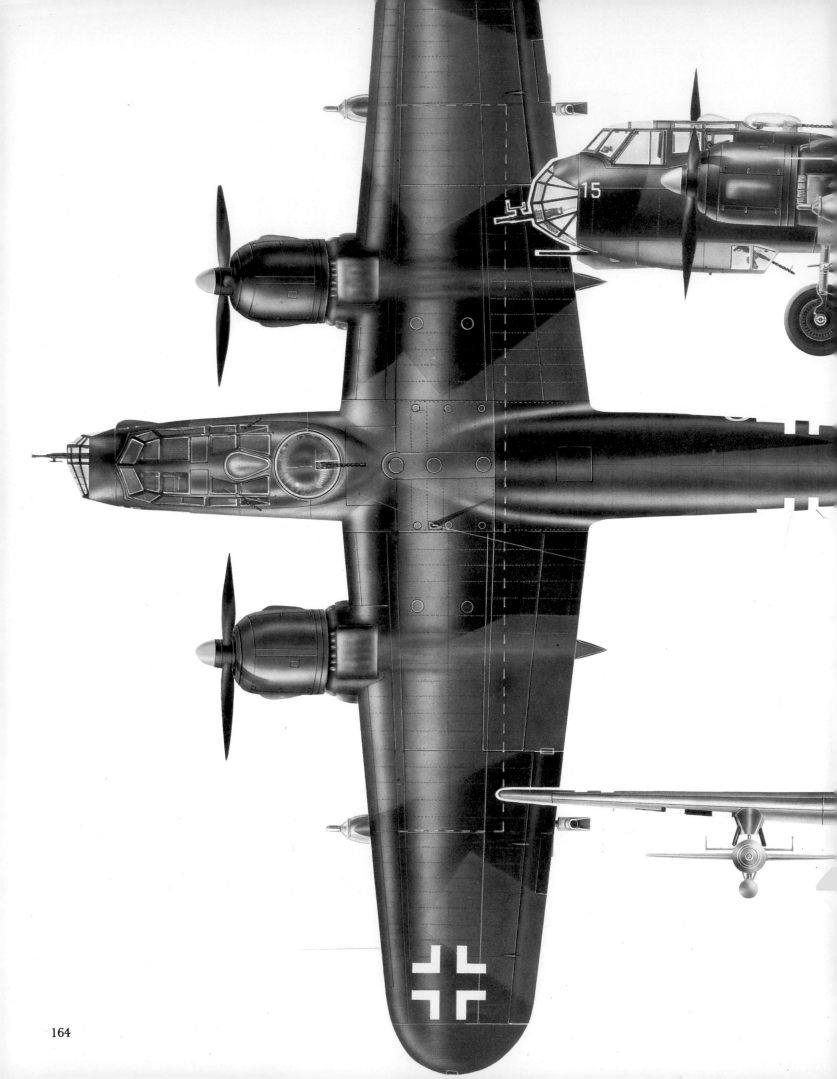

Dornier Do 217

Specification

Dornier Do 217E-2
Type: four-seat bomber
Powerplant: two 1,580-hp (1178-kW) BMW 801ML 14-cylinder radial piston engines
Performance: maximum speed 320 mph (515 km/h) at 17,060 ft (5200 m); service ceiling (with bombload) 24,600 ft (7500 m); range with normal fuel 1,430 miles (2300 km)
Weights: empty 18,522 lb (8855 kg); maximum loaded 26,299 lb (16465 kg)
Dimensions: span 62 ft 4 in (19.0 m); length 59 ft 8.5 in (18.2 m); height 16 ft 6 in (5.03 m); wing area 613.5 sq ft (57.0 m²)
Armament: (as depicted) one fixed 20-mm MG 151/20 in nose fired by the pilot, one hand-aimed 20-mm MG FF, one 13-mm MG 131 in turret and one hand-aimed MG 131 to lower rear; two Hs 293A anti-ship missiles

One of the ultimate sub-types of the basic Do 217E-series was the E-5, built from the start with wing pylons for the Hs 293A stand-off radio-guided anti-ship missile, together with the associated Kehl/Strassburg guidance system. This model entered service with II/KG 100 in April 1943 and quickly made its mark against Allied ships in the Bay of Biscay and Atlantic, the first attack being against British destroyers on 25 August 1943. This Do 217E-5, from 6/KG 100, is very unusual in retaining its fixed MG 151 cannon under the nose; normally this was removed when the 20-mm MG FF hand-aimed cannon was added in the glazed part of the nose.

Many of the Do-17s surviving into 1941 served with KG 2, and this Do 17Z-2 flew with that unit's I Gruppe based at Tatoi, Greece, in May 1941. Do 17Zs could undertake shallow diving attacks at speeds up to 370 mph (595 km/h) on account of their sturdy structure. KG 2 was soon to take its Do 17s to the USSR.

Early in 1942, Hermann Goering presented 15 ex-Luftwaffe Do 17Z-2s to the Finnish air force where they supplanted Bristol Blenheims with PLeLv 46 and enjoyed considerable success against the Russians. This example survived the war and was flown for several years after by PLeLv 43 on reconnaissance duties.

Hispano-engined Do 17 V5 reaching 243 mph (391 km/h). As this was well above the speed of any fighter in service it was hoped defensive guns would not be needed, but eventually the Do 17E-1 went into production at the company's new factories at Löwenthal, Manzell and Allmansweiler in 1936 with hand-aimed MG 15s firing above and below at the rear, and with a bomb load of up to 1,653 lb (750 kg). With a shortened, glazed nose the Do 17E-1 and corresponding Do 17F-1 reconnaissance aircraft were not quite so elongated, but when a *Staffel* of 15 F-1s went to Spain in spring 1937 its Do 17s easily outpaced Republican fighters, and aircraft of this type quickly replaced the Heinkel He 70 in reconnaissance wings. Do 17E-1s also served in Spain, with 1 and 2/K 88, along with a more powerful version, the Do 17P with 865-hp (645-kW) BMW 132N radials. Both remained standard types, serving with Grupo 27 of the Spanish EdA (air force) until 1949.

The initial production bomber version was the Do 17E-1, which began equipping the *Kampfgeschwader* in 1937. It was soon to receive its baptism of fire in Spanish skies, alongside the similar Do 17F-1 reconnaissance version. This E-model of 7./KG 255 is seen with national insignia painted over the 1938 war games.

Foreign service and operations

In July 1937 the Do 17 V8 (also known as the Do 17M V1) appeared at the prestigious International Military Aircraft Competition at Zurich. It impressed everyone with its clean lines, and when it easily won the Circuit of the Alps, pulling far ahead of every fighter at the meeting, the media had a field-day. What was not reported was that its 1,000-hp (746-kW) DB 600A engines had been earmarked for fighters, so the production Do 17M bomber had Bramo 323A-1 Fafnir radial engines of the same power. They also had the short rounded nose of the Do 17E and Do 17F, but Yugoslavia was so impressed at Zurich that its delegation bought 20 Do 17Ks plus a manufacturing licence, this model retaining the original long nose but being powered by Gnome-Rhône 14N

radials of 980 hp (731 kW). The Do 17K had a 20-mm cannon and three machine-guns, but still reached 259 mph (417 km/h). When Germany invaded Yugoslavia on 6 April 1941 70 Do 17Ks of various sub-types were on strength, 26 being destroyed on the ground but others seeing prolonged and hectic action. A few were eventually put into service by the Croatian puppet air force against Soviet partisans, while on 19 April 1941 two escaped to Heliopolis, Egypt, with cargoes of gold, afterwards serving with the RAF as AX 706/707.

Fighting over Spain against the Polikarpov I-16 had suddenly showed the Dornier's vulnerability, and in late 1937 a completely new forward fuselage was designed to provide much more room for an enlarged crew and better arcs of fire for the guns. First flown in early 1938 on the DB-engined Do 17s and Do 17U versions, the new front end went into major production with the Do 17Z series of bombers, reconnaissance aircraft and night-fighters, all powered by the Fafnir. With a maximum load of 2,205 lb (1000 kg) the Do 17Z-2 was virtually the standard 'Dornier' during the great battles of 1940. Over 500 had been built when production was stopped in mid-year, and these aircraft saw much service with KG 2, KG 3, KG 53 (Croatian) and the Finnish air force.

The Do 17Z-7 Kauz (screech-owl) was a night-fighter fitted with the nose of a Ju 88C-2 complete with one cannon and three MG 17s. This was followed by the properly planned Do 17Z-10 Kauz 11, with the world's first FLIR (forward-looking infra-red) detector, two cannon and four machine-guns. The first of several Do 17Z-10 kills was gained by Oberleutnant Becker on 18 October 1940; it was a Vickers Wellington over the Zuyder Zee. By late 1940 the Do 17Z-10 was being

The original 'flying pencil': Dornier's Do 17V1 fast mailplane caused much anxiety in Britain and France when it appeared in late 1934, as its military potential was both obvious and frightening. A year later all fears were realized when the twin-fin Do 17V4 bomber prototype was rolled out.

Laid down to a Swedish air force order, this Do 215B-1 was converted on the production line for Luftwaffe use following the arms embargo in 1939. It was configured for long-range reconnaissance and served with 3.Aufkl. St./Ob.d.L. attached to the Luftwaffe High Command at Stavanger in April 1940.

replaced by the Do 215B. The 215 designation was chosen by the RLM for export versions of Do 17Z, the only sale being to Sweden in late 1939, which selected the 1,100-hp (820-kW) DB 601A engine. The 18 Do 215B-1 aircraft involved were never exported, but were taken over by the Luftwaffe as fast reconnaissance machines. At least 20 of the last batch of Do 215B-4s were completed as Do 215B-5 night-fighters with not only the IR sensor but also the first Lichtenstein radar. Again Becker scored the first kill, on 9 August 1941, with four more by 2 October to become the first night ace.

In 1937 the RLM had called for an enlarged Do 17Z with much heavier bombload and considerably greater fuel capacity, able to accept any of a range of engines, and equally capable at level or dive bombing. First flown in August 1938, the Do 217 V1 was powered by 1,075-hp (802-kW) DB 601A engines, but despite its similar appearance to the Do 17/215 it was a totally new design. It soon showed that it was less pleasant to fly, and in fact crashed, but development continued. Prototypes flew with Junkers Jumo 211A and BMW 139 engines before the big BMW 801 was used in the Do 217 V9 prototype of January 1940. By this time handling was acceptable, the leading edges of the fins being slotted, but the unique dive brake, which opened like a giant cross at the extreme tail, caused endless difficulty. In mid-1941, after wing brakes had been tried and several aircraft lost, the RLM abandoned its stance that the heavy Do 217 had to be a dive bomber.

The heavyweight arrives

First to enter service, in late 1940, the Do 217E-1 was the first bomber model, with the massive bombload of 8,818 lb

(4000 kg), of which 5,550 lb (2517 kg) was inside the bomb bay. A handful to fly, but still a most effective bomber, the Do 217E-1 had a hand-held 20-mm MG FF in the nose, used by KG 40 against ships in the Atlantic, and seven MG 15s. The Do 217E-2 introduced the EDL 131 electric dorsal turret with the excellent MG 131 gun, a hand-aimed MG 131 being in the ventral position, a fixed MG 151/15 firing ahead and three hand-aimed MG 15s completing the defence, though R19 (the 19th in the *Rüstsatz* series of field kits) added twin or quadruple MG 81 machine-guns firing aft from the tailcone. Other *Rüstsätze* added barrage cable cutters and various weapon kits, by far the biggest of which hung two Hs 293 anti-ship missiles under the wings, with Kehl/Strassburg radio command guidance link. The first operational missile carrier was the Do 217E-5 flown by II/KG 100, which went into action with increasingly devastating effect against British ships from 25 August 1943.

With the Do 217E subtypes Dornier got the much heavier Do 217 family into service, and all subsequent models proved adequate but generally (and in the case of the Do 217K-2, severely) underpowered. Despite this, and the absence of the 2,000-hp (1491-kW) engines that were needed, Dornier proposed in early 1941 to develop a night intruder fighter version. The result was the Do 217J, with plenty of fuel and weapons for missions over the UK, but Hitler personally stopped further such flights from 12 October 1941 so the Do 217J served only over Germany and, from September 1942, over Italy with the Regia Aeronautica. Equipped with early radar, usually FuG 202 Lichtenstein BC, the Do 217J-2 retained the turret and lower rear gun of the Do 217E-2 but had a new nose with four MG FFs and four MG 17s. Eight 100-lb (50-kg) SC50 bombs could be carried in the rear bomb bay, though this provision was removed from the Do 217J-2 version.

On 31 July 1942 Dornier flew the first Do 217N, with 1,850-hp (1380-kW) DB 603A engines. A much better, but

Featuring a redesigned nose packed with guns, the Do 217J was the night fighter/intruder version of the Do 217E. This example, the Do 217J-2, differed from the J-1 by having no rear bomb bay. Do 217Js often operated in concert with Messerschmitt Bf 110s, whose manoeuvrability and speed were greater than the Do 217.

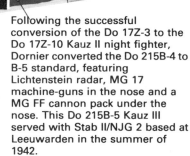

KG 2 became the only *Geschwader* to be completely equipped with the Do 217. Originally beginning replacement of the Do 17Z in 1941, KG 2 pulled back from the Russian front and relocated to the Netherlands for bombing and anti-shipping strikes over the North Sea. This is a Do 217E-2/R19 of 9./KG 2 with two MG 81 machine-guns in the tailcone.

Following the successful conversion of the Do 17Z-3 to the Do 17Z-10 Kauz II night fighter, Dornier converted the Do 215B-4 to B-5 standard, featuring Lichtenstein radar, MG 17 machine-guns in the nose and a MG FF cannon pack under the nose. This Do 215B-5 Kauz III served with Stab II/NJG 2 based at Leeuwarden in the summer of 1942.

The Do 317 was an advanced extension of the Do 17/217 line, featuring a pressurized cabin. No real increase in performance over the Do 217P was found, and apart from the Do 317V1 (illustrated), the other five prototypes were completed without pressurization and used by KG 100 as missile carriers.

of this family reached heights up to 53,000 ft (16155 m) and speeds of over 400 mph (644 km/h). (Dornier's literature states 785 km/h, or 488 mph, but this is an error.)

Total production of Do 217s amounted to 1,541 bombers and 364 night fighters, not including the five Do 217Rs. These were five of the six prototypes of the Do 317 with which Dornier wanted to ensure the order for highly developed 'B-bombers' – fast, long-range bombers with pressurised cabins which were intended to raze Britain to the ground, and remote-controlled machine guns. In 1943 test flying of the Do 317-V1 began; this aircraft resembled a Do 217M with triangular tail fins, and the Do 317B with DB 610A/B twin engines of 2,870 hp (2,140 kW) never actually flew.

still not brilliant, night-fighter, the Do 217N carried a heavier load of avionics and, for use on the Eastern Front, restored the rear bomb bay. The Do 217N-2 had wooden fairings in place of the turret and lower rear gun, but most had the new SN-2 radar and an increasing number were fitted with *schräge Musik* oblique upward-firing cannon, the usual fit being four 20-mm MG 151 of the type which by the start of Do 217N-2 production had also replaced the forward-firing MG FFs. Only 364 Do 217Js and Do 217Ns were delivered, and they had faded from the NJG (night fighter wings) front line by mid-1944. The blind spot in most bombers was directly below the centre section and the upward-firing 20-mm cannon took full advantage of this.

In come the guided bombs

In 1941 Dornier had again enlarged the crew compartment, this time eliminating the windscreen and glazing the whole nose as in many other German types of the period. The Do 217K-1 bomber entered service with KG 2, replacing the last of the Do 17Z-2s, in October 1942. Crews initially felt vulnerable surrounded by Plexiglas, but the Do 217K-1 was better arranged and also introduced a braking parachute made of Perlon, a Nylon-like material. In December 1942 the Do 217K-2 followed it into service, this having the span greatly increased to lift two of the formidable FX, or FX 1400 or Fritz X, guided bombs. Each of these weighed 3,461 lb (1570 kg) and the Kehl/Strassburg command link steered it in azimuth and pitch.

Major Bernhard Jope's III/KG 100 based at Istres had a field-day on 9 September 1943 when the Italian fleet sailed from La Spezia to join the Allies. One of the world's biggest battle-ships, the brand-new *Roma*, took two direct hits, blew up and sank in minutes; and her sister *Italia* just reached Malta with 800 tons of water on board. Later FX sent many other ships to the bottom. Most Do 217K-2 aircraft had a paired R19 *Rüstsatz* in the tail with four aft-firing MG81 guns.

Last production Do 217 was the Do 217M, essentially a Do 217K-1 with DB 603As, or alternatively a bomber version of the Do 217N. Only a few were built, the priority being on the Do 217N night-fighter, but one hit by AA fire near London on 23 February 1944 was abandoned by its crew and then flew on to make an excellent belly landing near Cambridge! Even at light weights height could not be maintained on one engine, and as with all the Do 217s the feeling was that there was too much aeroplane for the available wing area and power.

The last of the Do 217s, and by far the fastest, the Do 217P family was for high-altitude use and had the same complex *HZ-Anlage* system as the Henschel Hs 130: a DB 605T in the rear fuselage drove a giant two-stage blower which supercharged the two DB 603B propulsion engines, the underside of the fuselage and inboard wings being filled by giant radiators and intercoolers. The three engines provided 2,880 hp (2148 kW) at 45,000 ft (13715 m), and aircraft

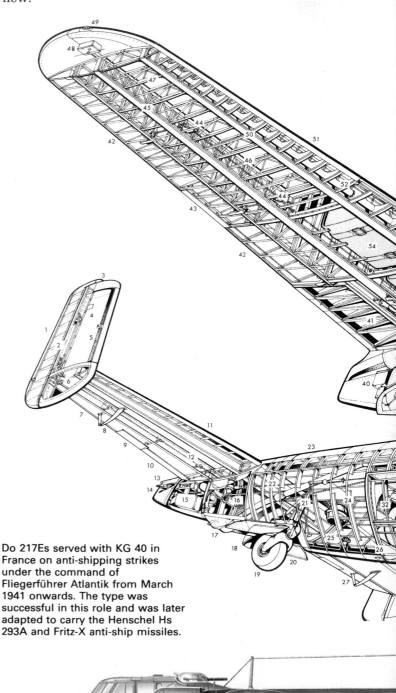

Do 217Es served with KG 40 in France on anti-shipping strikes under the command of Fliegerführer Atlantik from March 1941 onwards. The type was successful in this role and was later adapted to carry the Henschel Hs 293A and Fritz-X anti-ship missiles.

Seen wearing hastily applied RAF roundels and Air Ministry registration, this Do 217M-1 shows the Daimler-Benz DB 603A engines which distinguished it from the BMW 801D-powered Do 217K-1. Later Do 217M versions featured carriage for Fritz-X and Hs 293A missiles, but these did not attain series production.

Dornier Do 217K-1 cutaway drawing key

1 Starboard rudder tab
2 Rudder controls
3 Rudder mass balance (lead insert)
4 Starboard tailfin
5 Leading-edge slot
6 Tailplane/tailfin attachment
7 Elevator
8 Elevator mass balance
9 Fixed tab
10 Trim tab
11 Tailplane construction
12 Elevator controls
13 Rear navigation light
14 Four aft-firing 7.9-mm MG 81 machine-guns (*Rüstsatz* [field conversion set] 19)
15 Ammunition boxes
16 Tailplane trim control
17 Fuel emergency jettison
18 Mudguard
19 Tailwheel
20 Tailwheel doors
21 Tailwheel retraction mechanism

22 Tailplane carry-through
23 Fuselage skinning
24 Master compass
25 Dipole antenna
26 Anti-collision beacon
27 Elevator mass balance
28 Port tailfin
29 Leading-edge slot
30 Bomb bay division
31 Bomb bay hinge line
32 Bomb bay rear bulkhead entry/inspection hatch
33 Spherical oxygen cylinders
34 Starboard mainwheel

35 Mudguard
36 Mainwheel doors
37 Mainwheel retraction mechanism
38 Mainwheel well
39 FuG 25 (A-A recognition)
40 EuG 101 radio altimeter
41 Outer section split flaps
42 Starboard aileron
43 Aileron tab
44 Control lines
45 Rear spar
46 Braced wing ribs
47 Intermediate ribs
48 EGS 101 antenna
49 Starboard navigation light
50 Front spar
51 Leading-edge hot-air de-icing
52 Hot-air duct
53 Balloon-cable cutter in leading-edge
54 Starboard outer fuel tank (35 Imp gal/160 litre capacity)
55 Starboard oil tank (51.7 Imp gal/235 litre capacity)
56 Flame-damping exhaust pipes
57 Sliding-ring cooling air exit
58 BMW 801D 14-cylinder two-row radial engine
59 Annular oil cooler
60 VDM Three-blade metal propeller of 12.79 ft (3.90 m) diameter
61 Cooling fan
62 Cowling sliding nose-ring
63 Propellor boss

64 Starboard inner fuel tank (175 Imp gal/795 litre capacity)
65 Fuselage main fuel tank (231 Imp gal/1050 litre capacity)
66 Wing spar carry-through
67 Bomb bay top hinge line
68 Load-bearing beam
69 Bomb shackle
70 Bomb bay centre hinge line

71 Typical bomb load: two 2,250-lb (1000-kg) SC 1000 bombs
72 Forward bomb doors
73 13-mm MG 131 machine-gun in ventral position (1,000 rounds)
74 Ammunition ejection chute
75 Ventral gunner's station
76 Armoured bulkhead
77 Cartridge collector box
78 Batteries (two 24-Volt)
79 Radio equipment
80 Dorsal gunner's seat support

81 Cabin hot-air
82 Dorsal gunner's station
83 Armoured turret ring
84 Aerial mast
85 Gun safety guard
86 Starboard beam-mounted 7.9-mm MG 81 machine-gun (750 rounds)
87 13-mm MG 131 machine-gun (500 rounds)
88 Electrically operated dorsal turret
89 Revi gunsight
90 Angled side windows
91 Jettisonable decking
92 Bomb-aimer's folding seat
93 Navigator's position
94 Pilot's contoured table seat
95 Rear-view gunsight
96 Upper instrument panel
97 Nose glazing
98 Control horns
99 Engine controls
100 One 13-mm MG 131 in strengthened nose glazing (alternatively twin 7.9-mm MG 81Z)
101 Balloon-cable cutter in nose horizontal frame
102 Cartridge ejection chute
103 Ammunition feed
104 Lotfe 7D bombsight
105 Bomb aimer's flat panel
106 Control column counterweight
107 Nose armour
108 Ventral gunner's quilt
109 Ammunition box (nose MG 131)
110 Cartridge collector box
111 Entry hatch
112 Entry hatch (open)
113 Entry ladder
114 Port mainwheel doors
115 Mudguard
116 Port mainwheel
117 Mainwheel leg cross struts
118 Port engine cowling
119 Landing light (swivelling)
120 Control linkage
121 Pitot head
122 Port navigation light
123 Port aileron
124 Aileron trim tab

Dornier Do 17, 215 and 217 variants (simplified, omitting many prototypes)

Do 17 V1: original civil mailplane prototype, two 750-hp (559-kW) BMW VI engines, wing area 592 sq ft (55 m²), speed 270 mph (435 km/h)
Do 17 V4: first bomber prototype, twin fins, BMW VI
Do 17 V8: first Do 17 M-series, DB 600 engines, long glazed nose
Do 17E: initial production bomber, 750-hp (559-kW) BMW VI, short rounded nose, speed 221 mph (355 km/h)
Do 17F: initial production reconnaissance version, similar to Do 17E
Do 17M: bomber, 900-hp (671-kW) Bramo 323A engines, broadly as E
Do 17P: day/night reconnaissance, 865-hp (645-kW) BMW 132N engines
Do 17R: test-beds with 1,100-hp (820-kW) DB 601A or other engines
Do 17S: new forward fuselage with roomy crew compartment, 1,000-hp (746-kW) DB 600G engines
Do 17U: five-seat pathfinder (two radio/radar operators) with new nose and DB 600A engines (according to Dornier, Bramo 323A)
Do 17Z: four-seat bomber with new nose, basically Do 17M with modified crew compartment; later **Do 17Z-2** with 1,000-hp (746-kW) Bramo 323P engines, **Do 17Z-3** reconnaissance bomber, **Do 17Z-4** crew trainer and **Do 17Z-5** maritime reconnaissance aircraft
Do 17ZKauz: **Do 17Z-6 Kauz 1** night-fighter with nose of Ju 88C-2, followed by **Do 17Z-10 Kauz II** designed from start for role, both with Bramo 323P engines
Do 215B: most four-seat reconnaissance/bomber with 1,100-hp (820-kW) DB 601Aa; **Do 215B-5** night-fighter with first Lichtenstein radar
Do 217 V1: new enlarged bomber/dive bomber with 614-sq ft (57-m²) wing and 1,075 (802-

kW) DB 601 As
Do 217 V2/3/4: prototypes with 1,200-hp (895-kW) Jumo 211As
Do 217 V7/8: prototypes with 1,550-hp (1156-kW) BMW 139
Do 217A: long-range reconnaissance/bomber, long-span 700-sq ft (65-m²) wing, 1,350-hp (1007-kW) DB 601R/C3
Do 217C: similar to Do 217A but regular 614-sq ft (57-m²) wing, revised ventral contour, no cameras, more defensive guns
Do 217E: major family of four-seat bombers, 1,580-hp (1178-kW) BMW 801 MA or ML engines: **Do 217E-2** introduced turret, **Do 217E-4** BMW 801 C engines, **Do 217E-5** either Hs 293 or FX 1400 missiles
Do 217J: interim three-seat night-fighter, 1580-hp (1178-kW) BMW 801L, FuG 202 Lichtenstein BC radar
Do 217K-1: four-seat night bomber, 1,700-hp (1268-kW) BMW 801D engines, new glazed nose
Do 217K-2: carrier for FX 1400 missiles, long-span 721-sq ft (67-m²) wing, R19 tail guns
Do 217L: high-altitude reconnaissance aircraft, 2,000-hp (1491-kW) DB 603HC-3 engines, 753-sq ft (70-m²) wing, 360 mph (580 km/h), ceiling 42,650 ft (13000 m)
Do 217M: bomber, 1,850-hp (1380-kW) DB 603A engines
Do 217N: four-seat night-fighter and intruder, 1,850-hp (1380-kW) DB 603A engines
Do 217P: ultra-high altitude pressurized bomber with third supercharging engine to boost DB 603B main engines, Do 217-2 wing
Do 217R: Hs 293 missile carrier modified from Do 317A prototypes
Do 317A: four-seat high-altitude bomber, 1,750-hp (1305-kW) DB 603A engines

The Lockheed Twins

The introduction of the small Lockheed airliner in the mid-1930s pulled the company back from penury, and set the Burbank-based organization on the road to recovery. When war came the shortage of patrol bombers and fast transports immediately became evident, and Lockheed grasped the opportunity with both hands.

In 1932, Lockheed was on the verge of financial ruin. Its trustees valued the assets of the company at $129,961 and ordered it to sell them. While the founder of the firm, Allan Loughead, tried to raise the money to buy his old company, the stockbroker and banker Robert Ellsworth Gross snapped up the almost totally run-down aircraft company for the legendary amount of $40,000. Like many other businessmen who speculated with their money, Gross had little idea of the complex world of the flying industry, but had plenty of sound business sense and gradually came under the spell of the new generation of commercial transport planes. After he had made a careful assessment of the company, Gross declared that the company's future lay not in the production of mail planes or military aircraft, but in the development of fast and relatively small commuter and supply planes, which could eventually represent a challenge to the new machines from Boeing and Douglas which dominated the market at the time. With Gross came Hall Hibbard, a young aircraft engineer from the Massachusetts Institute of Technology, who worked with Lloyd Stearman on a number of different projects which looked promising. But it was Gross who gradually developed the idea of a small, twin-engine all-metal plane. The construction team was joined by George Prudden and James Gerschler, and later on by C. L. 'Kelly'

Johnson, who early on demonstrated his brilliant ability by solving the problems of the new Lockheed in the wind tunnel which later became known as the Lockheed Model L-10.

Roll-out for the Lockheed Model L-10 Electra took place on 23 February 1934. It was a beautiful little twin-engine aircraft resplendent in glistening polished natural aluminium. Power came from two 450-hp (336-kW) Pratt & Whitney R-985-SB radials, cabin and crew seats numbered 12, empty weight was 6,454 lb (2928 kg), and the gross weight was 10,300 lb (4672 kg). Tests gave a maximum speed of 202 mph (325 km/h), and a spanking maximum continuous cruising speed of 190 mph (306 km/h). After exhaustive tests the prototype L-10 Electra was flown by Marshall Headle to Mines Field, Los Angeles, for FAA certification which was granted a few weeks later. On the return to Burbank a heart-

Lockheed A-29 in US Army Air Force colours of early 1942 vintage. Initially all 800 A-29 and A-29A aircraft were allocated to the RAF under Lend-Lease, but with the crisis taking place in the Pacific and the Far East a large number were repossessed and pressed into service with the USAAF: some were used as crew trainers, and others as bombers and maritime patrol aircraft, one being the first USAAF aircraft to sink a U-boat in World War 2.

This Howard 500 is a conversion of a Lockheed Super Ventura. It has a newly-built fuselage and two Pratt & Whitney R-2800 engines. It now belongs to the British company, Baker Petroleum.

Lockheed PV2 Harpoon

Specification

Type: four/five-seat patrol bomber
Powerplant: two 2,000-hp (1491-kW) Pratt & Whitney R-2800-31 Double Wasp 18-cylinder radials
Performance: maximum speed (clean) 282 mph (454 km/h) at medium altitudes; service ceiling 23,900 ft (7285 m); range (with outer-wing tanks available, after curing major sealing problem) 1,790 miles (2880 km)
Weights: empty 21,028 lb (9538 kg); maximum 36,000 lb (16330 kg)
Dimensions: span 74 ft 11 in (22.84 m); length 52 ft 0½ in (15.86 m); height 11 ft 10 in (3.63 m); wing area 686 sq ft (63.77 m²)
Armament: internal bay for bombload of 4,000 lb (1814 kg), plus underwing racks for two 1,000-lb (454-kg) bombs, depth charges or other stores, or (as illustrated) eight HVAR (high-velocity aircraft rockets) in addition to drop tanks

This Lockheed PV-2 Harpoon served at the end of World War 2 with US Navy squadron VPB-142 in the Marianas Islands. It was one of the original and most common variant with a forward-firing armament of five guns, two high in the nose and three below; later the number was increased to eight. In fact hardly any of the PV-2 was identical with the corresponding parts of any PV-1, the unchanged portions being confined to small portions of the fuselage, inboard wing ribs and the cowlings (but not the nacelles). Another item common to some PV-1s was the type of Martin dorsal turret, but the lower rear guns were changed to the same 0.5-in (12.7-mm) calibre as used elsewhere.

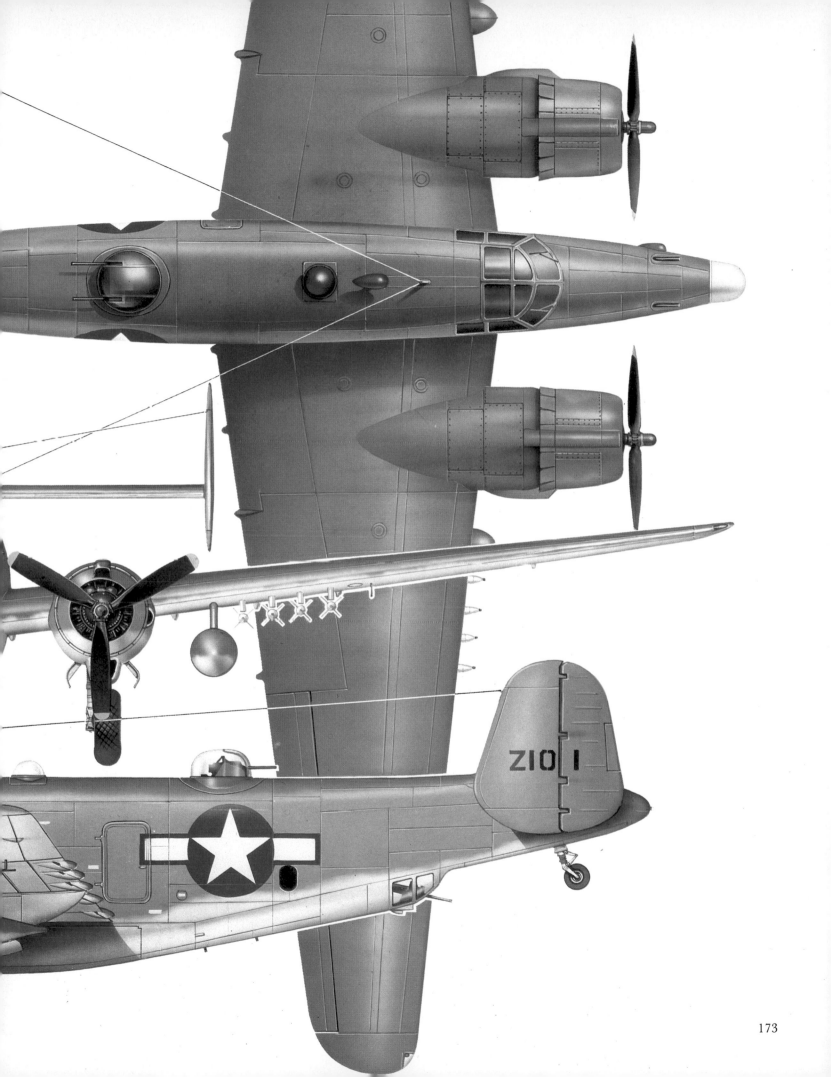

Lockheed PV-1 of the US Navy's VB-135 operational over the Pacific area in 1944. Powered by twin 2000-hp (1491-kW) Pratt & Whitney R-2800-31 radials, the first PV-1s entered service with Navy Squadron VP-82 to replace the PBO-1 (Hudsons) in December 1942. Approximately 1,600 PV-1s were procured by the US Navy. The much cleaner Martin turret helped boost the PV-1 maximum speed to 312 mph (502 km/h) at 13,800 ft (4200 m).

The Lockheed XC-35 was built to a US Army Air Corps contract of 1936, to investigate high-altitude flight. Modified from a Model 12, its circular-section fuselage was stressed up to 10 lb/sq in (0.69 bars) pressure differential. It was the first aircraft to feature a pressure cabin and engine-driven turbo-superchargers, and flew for the first time on 7 May 1937.

stopping incident took place. Up to the time of the L-10's first flight Lockheed had gone into debt for $139,404 for its development, and as its priceless prototype, newly certificated, made its approach all attempts by the crew to lower one of the main wheels ended in stubborn failure: only a skilfully handled one-wheel landing at nearby Union Air Terminal by pilot Headle, with minimal damage to the Electra, prevented a major lay-off of the work force and the renewal of financial straits. There the matter rested: sales of the Model L-10 Electra rocketted skywards with examples going to Mid-Continent Airlines, Northwest Airlines, Northeast Airlines, Cia Nacional Cubana, Pan American Airways, Panair do Brasil, Braniff Airways, National Airlines, British Airways, Delta Air Lines, Eastern Air Lines, Chicago and Southern, LAV (Venezuela), LOT (Poland), LARES

(Romania), AEROPUT (Yugoslavia), LAN-Chile, and to a host of private buyers including Amelia Earhart.

An L-10 Electra was the seventh Lockheed successfully to fly the Atlantic Ocean when Dick Merill and John Lambie flew NR16055 on a round-trip to London to collect photos of King George VI's coronation in 1937. Also that year, somewhere in the Pacific Ocean wastes between Lae, New Guinea, and Howland Island, aviatrix Amelia Earhart and her navigator disappeared for ever during a record attempt in their L-10 Electra. A total of 149 L-10s was built and delivered between 29 June 1934 and 18 July 1941, and many saw military service in the RCAF and Argentine navy, and with the US Army, US Navy and US Coast Guard as redesignated C-36, C-37, R20 and R30 sub-types.

Bigger and better

The interim Model L-12 Electra Junior was taken into the air for the first time by Marshall Headle at 12.12 on 27 June 1936, exactly on the scheduled time. By now business was booming, with Lockheed getting $2 million worth of orders in the previous year. Price-tagged at $40,000 the Model L-12, with six-seat capacity, was aimed squarely at the business and commuter markets, and in fact was a scaled-down version of its predecessor with two Pratt & Whitney R-985-SB radials. Grossing 8,650 lb (3924 kg), the Electra Junior's top speed was 225 mph (362 km/h) and service ceiling 22,300 ft (6800 m). Its performance and handling qualities exceed those of the majority of contemporary fighters, and it became another good seller. Several records fell to the Model L-12, including a new route average of 210 mph (338 km/h) by test pilot E. C. McLead, despite four fuel stops, from Amsterdam to India on a delivery flight of a L-12 for the Maharaja of Jodhpur. A total of 130 Model L-12s was built before work stopped in mid-1942.

Incorporating many of the latest aviation developments, the larger and more powerful Lockheed Model L-14 Super Electra took to the air for the first time on 29 June 1937. New features on this 14-seat aircraft included use of 24SRT

The Lockheed Model 14 Super Electra of South African Airways is very similar in design to the models succeeding the Hudson which was destined to have a memorable career in World War 2 in a number of very useful roles. The Model 14 was all-metal, with Fowler flaps, two 820 hp (611 kW) Wright Cyclones GR-1820-G3B radial engines and flew for the first time on 29 July 1937.

One of the 625 Lockheed Model L-18 Lodestars, with its higher-mounted tail designed to avoid pitch and Pratt & Whitney engines. The Model 18 was flown for the first time on 2 February 1940 by Marshall Headle and was used by several airlines. Only a few were sold in Europe. There were also US Army and RAF versions.

After World War 2 many Venturas remained in service around the world. This former GR.Mk V of the Royal Canadian Air Force was replaced by a Lancaster MR.Mk 10, but went on into the 1950s as a target tug at Sea Island, Vancouver. The orange/black livery was called 'Oxydol special' after a popular brand of soap powder.

By far the most important of the post-war users of the Ventura was the South African Air Force, which gathered its own survivors (including this GR.Mk V) and many former B-34s and PV-1s to serve as ocean patrol and medium bomber aircraft until Shackletons arrived in 1958. No 6472 served with No. 17 Sqn.

duralumin, high-speed aerofoil (NACA 23018 and 23009 at root and tip respectively), single main spar, and high wing loading, massive Lockheed-Fowler flaps, and two of the latest Wright Cyclone engines, the GR-1820-G3B. With an empty weight of 10,700 lb (4854 kg) and a gross of 17,500 lb (7938 kg), the new L-14 had a top speed of 257 mph (414 km/h): its cruising speed was some 30 mph (48 km/h) faster than that of any other commercial transport in the United States and, at a cruise speed of 237 mph (381 km/h) the Super Electra cut the West Coast—New York flight time of the Douglas DC-3 by four hours. Such was the reputation of the company that even before roll-out over 30 L-14s were on the order book, and the aircraft itself was soon to justify all expectations. Millionaire Howard Hughes purchased a Model L-14, and increased tankage from the normal 644 to 1,844 US gal (3438 to 6980 litres) for a round-the-world record attempt. Departing from New York on 10 July 1938, Hughes and his crew flew via Paris, Moscow, Yakutsk, Fairbanks and Minneapolis to land at Floyd Bennett Field after a 14,709-mile (23670-km) flight achieved within the time of three days 17 hours 14 minutes and 10 seconds. But the 112 Model L-14s are remembered today as the progenitors of what was to be one of Lockheed's most successful warplanes. Licence production of the L-14 in Japan amounted to 64 by Tachikawa and 55 by Kawasaki.

Enter the Hudson

To the United States in April 1938 came the British Purchasing Commission in search of good-quality American aircraft to bolster the strength of the Royal Air Force in its preparations for an inevitable war: the mission had $25 million with which to acquire its finds. At that time Lockheed engaged only 2,000 workers, and had eschewed the design of military types in favour of the commercial market. But in 10 days of frantic labour the concern had cobbled together something that might whet the appetites of the commission: this was nothing other than a mockup of a Model L-14 provided with bomb-bay, bomb-aimer's panel and nose-glazing, and provision for various armaments. The British, with a need for a medium-range maritime patrol bomber for North Sea operations with RAF Coastal Command, were impressed. At the invitation of Sir Henry Self, the contracts director at the Air Ministry in London, Courtlandt Gross (brother of Robert Gross) travelled to the UK with Carl Squier, C. L. Johnson, Robert Proctor and R. A. van Hake for consultations. The

initial order for 175 Model B14s, now known as the Hudson, was signed on 23 June 1938, with provision of up to a maximum of 250 by December 1939: it was the largest military order gained by a US company to date. The first Hudson Mk I bomber took to the air on 10 December 1938, with the company, now numbering a work force of 7,000, hard at work to fill the orders which rose in value with additional orders for P-38s and B-34s to an impressive $65 million.

Arriving by sea, the first Hudson Mk Is reached the UK on 15 February 1939. The type was powered by two 1,100-hp (820-kW) Wright GR-1820-G102A Cyclones with two-speed Hamilton propellers. For reconnaissance duties the Hudson Mk I carried an F.24 camera, assorted flares and a bombload of up to 1,100 lb (499 kg) comprising either four 250-lb (114-kg) GP, SAP or AS, or 10 110-lb (50-kg) anti-submarine bombs; an overload of 12 112-lb (51-kg) Mk VIIc AS bombs could be carried, but in this event the bomb doors could not be fully closed. Modified with extra items at the Lockheed-Vega subsidiary at Speke (Liverpool), the first Hudson Mk Is and Mk IIs (the latter differing in the installation of Hamilton Standard Type 611A-12/3E50-253 constant-speed propellers) were delivered to Wing Commander E. A. Hodgson's No. 224 Squadron at Leuchars, Scotland, in

Venturas of the Royal New Zealand Air Force featured prominently in the campaigns in the south-west Pacific, in the Solomons and against the Japanese bastions at Rabaul and Kavieng. These PV-1s, three of 388 procured under Lend-Lease, flew as the Ventura GR.Mk V with the RNZAF in the Solomons during 1943-4. The nearest aircraft is NZ4534, coded ZX-D. They are demonstrating single-engine flight.

The Lockheed Twins

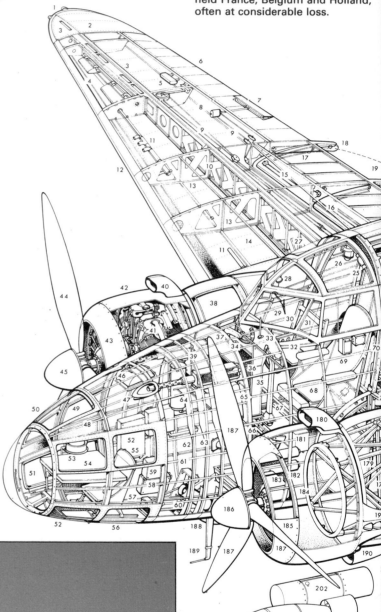

Ventura Mk II of No. 21 Sqn, RAF, operating from Methwold airfield, Norfolk, under No. 2 (Bomber) Group. RAF Venturas entered service in November 1942, and one of their first large missions was that against the Philips concern at Eindhoven on 6 December 1942. The spring and summer of 1943 saw Nos 21, 464 and 487 Sqns operating the Ventura over enemy-held France, Belgium and Holland, often at considerable loss.

August 1939. Although less manoeuvrable than the lighter Avro Anson, the Hudson was considered by the squadron to be eminently suitable for its patrols over the North Sea as far as Norway, the Skaggerak and the German Bight. Cruising at 2,000 ft (610 m) at 190 mph (306 km/h), a fuel consumption of 71 Imp gal (323 litres) per hour gave the Hudson an endurance of over six hours with 20 per cent reserves and a 570-mile (917-km) radius of action. Armament was light initially, and the twin 0.303-in (7.7-mm) nose guns, beam guns and the Boulton Paul Type 'C' Mk II turret were retrofitted during the autumn of 1939 and the spring of 1940.

With the outbreak of war the Hudsons of RAF Coastal Command were among the first RAF aircraft to go into action, and the first combat with a German aircraft was recorded on 4 September 1939, when No. 224 Squadron's T-Tommy (N7214), captained by Flying Officer H. D. Green, engaged a Dornier Do 18 over the Dogger Bank. In addition to No. 224 Squadron, Nos 206, 269, 233, 320 and 220 Squadrons were equipped with Hudsons during 1939–40, and much action was seen off Norway during the *Altmark* incident and the subsequent German invasion of Scandinavia, and over the Channel during the Dunkirk evacuations in addition to patrol work over the Western Approaches and the North Sea. During 1941 RAF and RCAF Hudsons, operating from the UK, Iceland, and Newfoundland, conducted a difficult war against the U-Boat menace: on 27 August 1941 a Hudson of No. 269 Squadron from Kaldadarnes forced the crew of the *U-570* to surrender after repeated attacks. Use of the Hudson was not limited to the RAF and RCAF, and in early 1942 US Army A-28s and A-29s, and US Navy PBO-1s did much work along the eastern seaboard of the United States, while in the Far East those of Nos 1 and 8 Squadrons RAAF fought well against great odds during the Japanese invasions of Malaya, Java and Burma. Six primary marks of Hudson, in maritime and transport work, came from Lockheed's 2,941 made up to June 1943 when production ceased, seeing service on all Anglo-American war fronts.

The Lockheed PV-2 was the last version of the twin-engined Lockheed craft, with a wingspan almost 10 ft (3 m) longer than that of the PV-1.

Lockheed Hudson Mk 1 cutaway drawing key

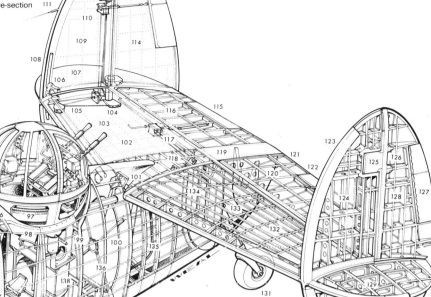

1 Starboard navigation/identification lights
2 Starboard wingtip
3 De-icing slots
4 Internal vanes
5 Aileron internal mass balance
6 Starboard aileron
7 Aileron tab
8 Tab mechanism
9 Control cables
10 Wing main spar structure
11 De-icing tubes
12 Leading-edge de-icing boot
13 Main wing rib stations
14 Wing skinning
15 Flap control cables
16 Flap tracks
17 Flap cables/pulleys
18 Track fairings
19 Port flap (extended)
20 Aerial mast

35 Central instrument console
36 Starboard nose compartment entry tunnel
37 Bulkhead
38 Starboard engine oil tank
39 Fixed forward-firing 0.303-in (7.7-mm) Browning machine-guns (two)
40 Carburettor intake
41 Wright R-1820-G102A radial engine
42 Starboard nacelle
43 Cowling nose ring
44 Three-blade propeller
45 Spinner

69 Pilot's radio control boxes
70 Forward (canted) fuselage frame
71 Frame wing pick-up
72 Hydraulics reservoir
73 Wireless-operator's table
74 Wireless-operator's seat
75 Transmitter
76 Receiver
77 Main spar centre-section carry-through

46 Nose compartment cold air
47 Machine-gun muzzles
48 Nose structure
49 Roof glazing
50 Window frames
51 Nose cone
52 Navigator's side windows
53 Compass
54 Navigator's table
55 Navigator's (sliding) seat
56 Bomb-aimer's flat panels
57 Bomb-aimer's prone position
58 Bomb selector switch panel
59 Navigator's instrument panel
60 Forward flare chute
61 Bombsight support
62 Nose frames
63 Nose compartment warm air
64 Windscreen de-icing tank
65 Machine gun ammunition magazine
66 Rudder pedal assembly
67 Pilot's control column
68 Pilot's seat

78 Spar/frame attachment
79 Wireless bay racks
80 Cabin cold air
81 Astrograph table/supply locker
82 Wing flaps actuating cylinder
83 Smoke-float stowage rack
84 Port cabin windows
85 Beam machine-gun positions (field modification)
86 Gun support frame
87 Starboard cabin windows
88 Astrodome (Mk III and retrofit)
89 Fuselage frames
90 Stringers
91 Flare stowage racks
92 Aft fuselage bulkhead
93 Aft fuselage bulkhead
94 Aerials
95 Boulton Paul dorsal turret
96 Turret support canted frame

97 Turret ring
98 Dorsal cut-out former
99 Bulkhead
100 Rear bulkhead/tailplane support
101 Tail surface control linkage
102 Starboard tailplane
103 Twin 0.303-in (7.7-mm) machine-guns
104 Rudder control quadrant
105 Cable linkage
106 De-icing tube
107 Starboard end plane
108 Tailfin de-icing boot
109 Tailfin skinning
110 Rudder tab actuator
111 Aerial attachment
112 Rudder upper balance
113 Rudder tab
114 Starboard rudder
115 Elevator tab
116 Starboard elevator
117 Tab actuating linkage
118 Elevator control mechanism

119 Fixed centre-section
120 Tail navigation light
121 Port elevator
122 Elevator tab
123 Port tailfin de-icing boot
124 Tailfin structure
125 Rudder upper balance
126 Rudder upper hinge
127 Rudder tab
128 Port rudder structure
129 Port end plane
130 Rudder lower balance
131 Fixed tailwheel
132 Port tailplane structure
133 Tailwheel shock-absorber leg
134 Tailplane support bulkhead
135 Warm air conduit
136 Bulkhead cover plate
137 Control pulley quadrant
138 Turret mechanism support
139 Aft flare tube
140 Toilet location
141 Step
142 Entry door (jettisonable dinghy housing)
143 Ammunition feed magazine
144 Dinghy release cylinder/hand lever
145 Tunnel (ventral) gun station (optional)
146 Cabin entry walkway (port)
147 Ventral camera port
148 Ventral gun well
149 Bomb-doors operating quadrant
150 Bomb-bay rear well
151 Port flap section
152 Flap track fairings
153 Aileron tab
154 Port aileron
155 Aileron internal mass balance
156 Port wing tip structure
157 Port navigation identification lights
158 Internal vanes
159 Wing slots
160 Wing structure

161 Main spar
162 Nose ribs
163 Port wing leading-edge de-icing boot
164 Rib assembly
165 Mainwheel recess
166 Port nacelle fairing
167 Rear spar wing join
168 Main spar wing join
169 Port wing aft fuel tank
170 Fuselage bomb-bay actuating cylinder
171 Port wing foward fuel tank
172 Control servos
173 Undercarriage retractor cylinder
174 Undercarriage support attachment strut
175 Port engine oil tank bay
176 Engine support frame
177 Carburettor anti-icing tank
178 Engine bearer assembly
179 Bomb-bay forward wall
180 Carburettor intake
181 Battery
182 Smoke floats
183 Propeller anti-icing tank (fuselage)
184 Engine bearer ring
185 Cowling nose ring
186 Spinner
187 Three-blade propeller
188 Starboard mainwheel
189 Pitot head
190 Oil cooler intake
191 Exhaust louvres
192 Landing gear fulcrum
193 Drag strut
194 Exhaust stub
195 Side strut
196 Mainwheel oleo leg
197 Torque links
198 Port mainwheel
199 Axle hub
200 Towing lug
201 Undercarriage door
202 Float marker
203 250-lb (113.5-kg) A S bomb

21 D F loop fairing
22 Supported structure
23 Aerial lead-in
24 Cockpit cold air
25 Flight deck sun-blind frames
26 Windscreen wiper motor
27 Jettisonable canopy hatch
28 Console light
29 Windscreen wipers
30 Second-pilot's jump seat
31 Adjustable quarterlight
32 Windscreen frame support member
33 External gunsight
34 Second-pilot's (back-up) control column (cantilevered)

The Model 18 Progeny

A direct development of the L-14 series, the Lockheed L-18 Lodestar first flew on 21 September 1939: the fuselage had been stretched by 5 ft 6 in (1.68 m), and to minimize tail flutter the elevator was raised slightly. By the end of 1940 some 54 of the 17-seat Model 18s had been sold to such varied customers as Mid Continent (first to buy the $90,000 aircraft), Regie Air Afrique and the Netherlands East Indies, BOAC and South African Airways. During World War 2 the Model 18 series was adopted by the US Army and the US Navy as a transport: US Army versions included the C-56 (in models up to C-56E), C-57 and C-57B, C-59, C-60 and C-60A, C-66 and C-111, all of which featured differences either in engines, seating or ancillary equipment. Naval versions included the R50 (in models up to R50-6), while the RAF used Lodestar Mks I, IA and II models.

In response to a request from the British, Vega Aircraft Corporation developed a military version of the Model L-18 series which was employed by the RAF as the Ventura, by the US Army Air Force as the B-34 and B-37, and by the US Navy as the PV-1 patrol bomber. All were powered by two 2,000-hp (1492-kW) Pratt & Whitney R-2800-31 radials, with the exception of the RAF's Ventura Mk I which had Pratt & Whitney R-2800-S1A4G engines, and the few B-37s which featured Wright R-2600-13s. The first Ventura Mk I flew on 31 July 1941 and, together with the up-rated Mk II and Mk IIA versions, entered service with No. 2 (Bomber) Group in November 1942. On daylight missions over France and the Low Countries the Ventura fared badly against the dangerous Focke-Wulf Fw 190As of the Luftwaffe, and losses to flak and enemy fighters were consistently high. During the summer of 1943 the type was withdrawn from No. 2 Group, its place being taken by North American Mitchells and Douglas Boston Mk IIIA bombers. The B-34s of the USAAF saw little action, while the B-37 (Ventura Mk III) saw none at all. However, in the Solomons and South Pacific

A Lockheed Hudson Mk IVA in the colours of the Royal Australian Air Force. In the 1970s this machine belonged to the Stathallan Collection in Scotland, and has since been moved to the RAF Museum, Hendon.

area Ventura Mk IVs and GR.MK Vs of the RNZAF saw considerable action against the Japanese bastions at Kavieng and Rabaul, and proved their worth. The last-mentioned marks were known in the US Navy as PV-1s, of which 1,800 were built. Carrying a crew of four or five, the PV-1 weighed in at 20,197 lb (9161 kg) empty and 31,077 lb (14097 kg) gross, and was capable of a maximum speed of 312 mph (502 km/h) at 13,800 ft (4205 m). Armament consisted of two forward-firing 0.5-in (12.7-mm) guns, two more guns of the same calibre in a Martin CE250 dorsal turret, and two 0.3-in (7.62-mm) guns in the ventral position: up to four 1,000-lb (454-kg) bombs could be stowed internally, with another two under the wings, while an alternative was a single Model 13 Mk II torpedo. US Navy PV-1s operated from Aleutian bases during 1943–5 in all weathers on anti-shipping strikes and attacks on the Japanese bases at Paramushiro and Shimushu, and fought off frequent aggressive attacks by the Mitsubishi A6M3 Reisens of the 13th Koku Kantai (Air Fleet) which defended the area. The PV-1 more than compensated for the relatively poor showing by the Ventura in Europe, and performed useful service against the Japanese in all sectors of the Pacific.

The last version of this long and successful series of twin-engine Lockheed aircraft, begun in 1934 with the little Model L-10, was the maritime patrol bomber, the PV-2 Harpoon. In this model, the fuselage and tailplane were rebuilt and the wingspan increased from 65 ft 6 in (19.96 m) to 75 ft (22.86 m). The PV-2's maiden flight was on 3 December 1943, and the first planes were delivered to the US Navy for use on its supply bases in the Aleutians. Wing flexing caused additional problems during production, but PV-2s flew until the end of the war and remained in service for years afterwards with reserve squadrons of the US Navy.

Wartime-vintage Lockheed Venturas were converted in many instances to luxury executive-type aircraft in the years of peace. This smart twin, N5390N, is a Howard Aero Super Ventura.

Featuring a luxury custom-fitted interior, new fuselage contours and a totally new nose section, this beautifully finished ex-US Navy PV-1 illustrates one of several executive conversions of the type.

Swordfish: Taranto Tinfisher

Archaic in appearance even when it first flew, the venerable Swordfish survived as an anachronism throughout World War 2, outlived its replacement and destroyed a greater tonnage of enemy shipping than any other Allied torpedo bomber.

The beginnings of the Swordfish came with the privately-financed tender for Specification S.9/30 from the Air Ministry made by the Fairey Aviation Company. The tender went out at the beginning of the 1930s and was for a torpedo bomber. The TSR I prototype, with an air-cooled 635 hp (474 kW) Bristol Pegasus IIM nine-cylinder radial engine, flew on 21 March 1933. But it soon became apparent that its engine was underpowered and the plane's directional stability left something to be desired. Six months later it crashed after failing to recover from a spin.

A revised specification, S.15/33, was drafted and Fairey produced the TSR II with lengthened fuselage, revised tail unit and an uprated Pegasus IIIM3 developing 775 hp (578 kW). Its structure was largely of fabric-covered metal with split-axle wheel landing gear capable of replacement by twin single-step Fairey floats. With a maximum sea level speed of 146 mph (235 km/h) and first flown on 17 April 1934, this aircraft exceeded the specified performance demands and three prototype development aircraft, named Swordfish, were ordered to meet Specification S.38/34; the third aircraft was completed as a floatplane, making its first flight on 10 November 1934.

The first production order for 86 aircraft was placed in 1935 and initial deliveries were made the following

February to No. 823 Squadron, which embarked in HMS *Glorious* later that year, replacing Shark Mk IIs. The standard three-seat production aircraft had a maximum speed of 138 mph (222 km/h) and was easily capable of lifting a standard 18-in (457-mm) 1,610-lb (731-kg) torpedo from the decks of all British carriers with full load, its range in this configuration being 546 miles (879 km).

Further orders continued with Fairey until by the outbreak of war in 1939 a total of 689 Swordfish aircraft had been completed or were on order. Mk I floatplanes were serving with Nos 701, 702 and 705 Catapult Flights of the Fleet Air Arm, being embarked in most of the Royal Navy's battleships, battle-cruisers and cruisers in commission, as well as serving with wheel landing gear in 13 squadrons, of which eight were at sea in the carriers HMS *Ark Royal*, *Argus*, *Courageous*, *Eagle*, *Furious*, *Glorious* and *Hermes*.

Swordfish were in action from the earliest days of the war and it was a floatplane flown by Lieutenant Commander W. M. L. Brown from HMS *Warspite* during the Battle of Narvik on 13 April 1940 that was used to direct the fire of

A Swordfish Mk II of the main Blackburn-built production batch. Carrying a smoke float under the starboard wing, this aircraft would probably have been from a carrier-based squadron.

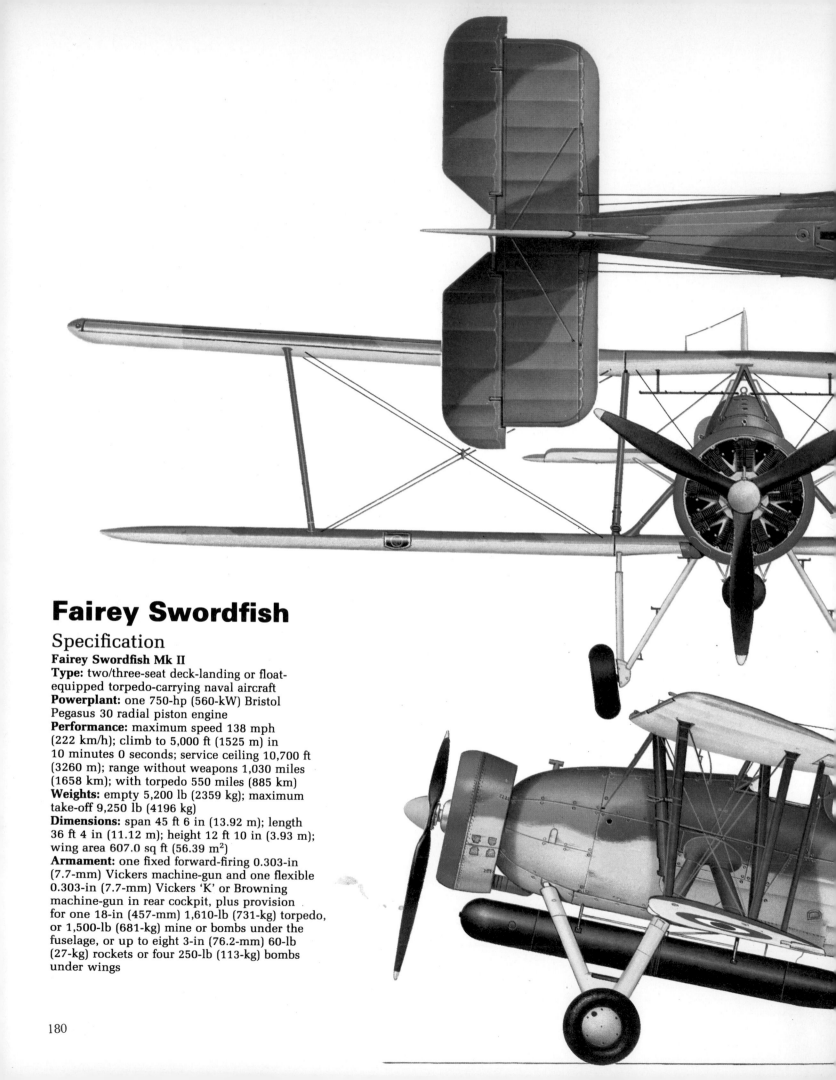

Fairey Swordfish

Specification

Fairey Swordfish Mk II
Type: two/three-seat deck-landing or float-
equipped torpedo-carrying naval aircraft
Powerplant: one 750-hp (560-kW) Bristol
Pegasus 30 radial piston engine
Performance: maximum speed 138 mph
(222 km/h); climb to 5,000 ft (1525 m) in
10 minutes 0 seconds; service ceiling 10,700 ft
(3260 m); range without weapons 1,030 miles
(1658 km); with torpedo 550 miles (885 km)
Weights: empty 5,200 lb (2359 kg); maximum
take-off 9,250 lb (4196 kg)
Dimensions: span 45 ft 6 in (13.92 m); length
36 ft 4 in (11.12 m); height 12 ft 10 in (3.93 m);
wing area 607.0 sq ft (56.39 m²)
Armament: one fixed forward-firing 0.303-in
(7.7-mm) Vickers machine-gun and one flexible
0.303-in (7.7-mm) Vickers 'K' or Browning
machine-gun in rear cockpit, plus provision
for one 18-in (457-mm) 1,610-lb (731-kg) torpedo,
or 1,500-lb (681-kg) mine or bombs under the
fuselage, or up to eight 3-in (76.2-mm) 60-lb
(27-kg) rockets or four 250-lb (113-kg) bombs
under wings

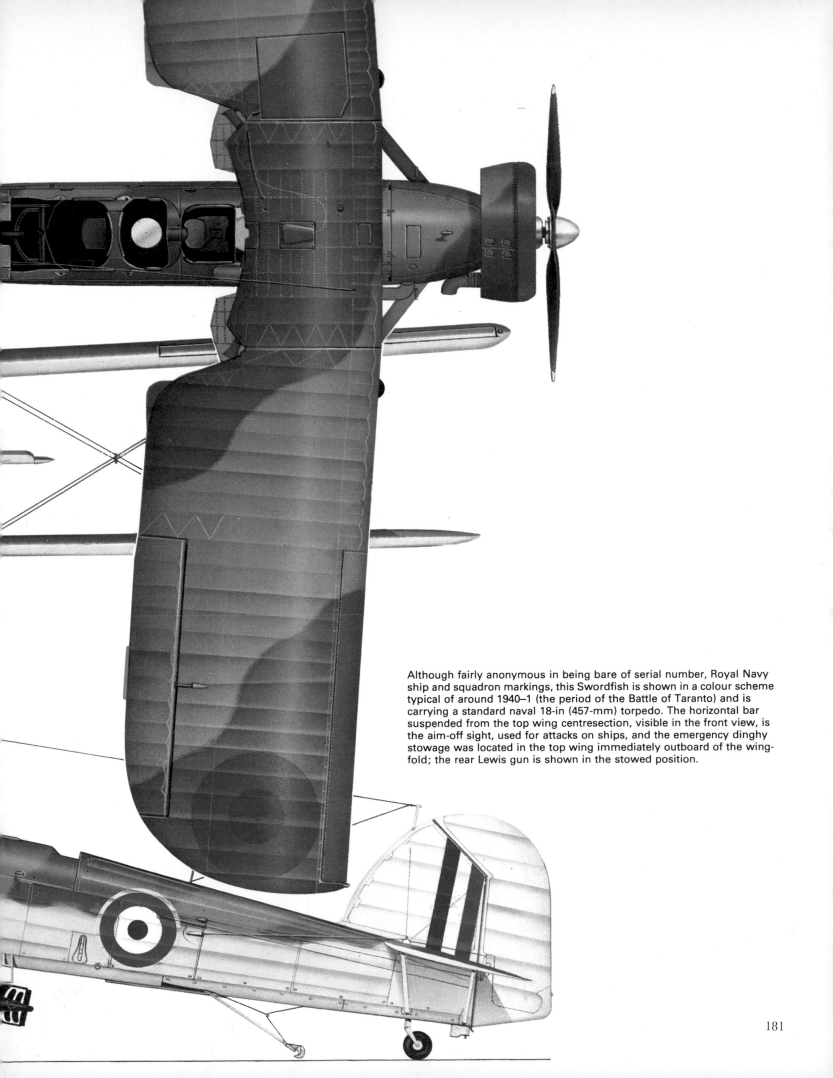

Although fairly anonymous in being bare of serial number, Royal Navy ship and squadron markings, this Swordfish is shown in a colour scheme typical of around 1940–1 (the period of the Battle of Taranto) and is carrying a standard naval 18-in (457-mm) torpedo. The horizontal bar suspended from the top wing centresection, visible in the front view, is the aim-off sight, used for attacks on ships, and the emergency dinghy stowage was located in the top wing immediately outboard of the wing-fold; the rear Lewis gun is shown in the stowed position.

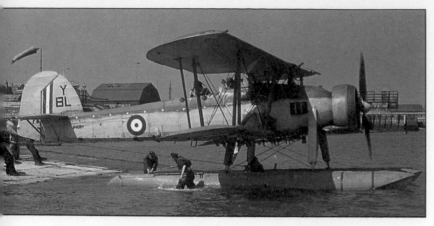

Super wartime photo of a Swordfish Mk 1 (P4084) with float undercarriage being launched from a slipway. These aircraft were widely used aboard Royal Navy ships during World War 2 for reconnaissance and gunnery spotting duties.

Fairey Swordfish II cutaway drawing key

1 Rudder structure
2 Rudder upper hinge
3 Diagonal brace
4 External bracing wires
5 Rudder hinge
6 Elevator control horn
7 Tail navigation light
8 Elevator structure
9 Fixed tab
10 Elevator balance
11 Elevator hinge
12 Starboard tailplane
13 Tailplane struts
14 Lashing down shackle
15 Trestling foot
16 Rear wedge
17 Rudder lower hinge
18 Tailplane adjustment screw
19 Elevator control cable
20 External bracing wires
21 Elevator fixed tab
22 Tailfin structure
23 Bracing wire attachment
24 Aerial stub
25 Bracing wires
26 Port elevator
27 Port tailplane
28 Tailplane support struts
29 Dinghy external release cord
30 Tailwheel oleo shock absorber
31 Non-retractable Dunlop tailwheel
32 Fuselage framework
33 Arrester hook housing
34 Control cable fairleads
35 Dorsal decking
36 Rod aerial
37 Lewis gun stowage trough
38 Aerial
39 Flexible 0.303-in (7.7-mm) Lewis machine gun
40 Fairey high-speed flexible gun mounting
41 Type O-3 compass mounting points
42 Aft cockpit coaming
43 Aft cockpit
44 Lewis drum magazine stowage

45 Radio installation
46 Ballast weights
47 Arrester hook pivot
48 Fuselage lower longeron
49 Arrester hook (part extended)
50 Aileron hinge
51 Fixed tab
52 Starboard upper aileron
53 Rear spar
54 Wing ribs
55 Starboard formation light
56 Starboard navigation light
57 Aileron connect strut
58 Interplane struts
59 Bracing wires
60 Starboard lower aileron
61 Aileron hinge
62 Aileron balance
63 Rear spar
64 Wing ribs
65 Aileron outer hinge
66 Deck-handling/lashing grips
67 Front spar
68 Interplane strut attachments
69 Wing internal diagonal bracing wires
70 Flying wires
71 Wing skinning
72 Additional support wire (fitted when underwing stores carried)
73 Wing fold hinge
74 Inboard interplane struts
75 Stub plane end rib
76 Wing locking handle
77 Stub plane structure
78 Intake slot
79 Side window
80 Catapult spool
81 Drag struts
82 Cockpit sloping floor
83 Fixed 0.0303-in (7.7-mm) Vickers gun (deleted from some aircraft)
84 Case ejection chute
85 Access panel
86 Camera mounting bracket
87 Sliding bomb-aiming hatch
88 Zip inspection flap
89 Fuselage upper longeron
90 Centre fairing
91 Inter-cockpit fairing
92 Upper wing aerial mast

93 Pilot's headrest
94 Pilot's seat and harness
95 Bulkhead
96 Vickers gun fairing
97 Fuel gravity tank (12.5 Imp gal/57 litre capacity)
98 Windscreen
99 Handholds
100 Flap control handwheel and rocking head assembly
101 Wing centre section
102 Dinghy release cord handle
103 Identification light
104 Centre section pyramid strut attachment
105 Diagonal strengtheners
106 Dinghy inflation cylinder
107 Type C dinghy stowage well
108 Aileron control linkage
109 Trailing edge rib sections
110 Rear spar
111 Wing rib stations
112 Aileron connect strut
113 Port upper aileron
114 Fixed tab
115 Aileron hinge
116 Port formation light
117 Wing skinning
118 Port navigation light
119 Leading-edge slot
120 Front spar
121 Nose ribs

122 Interplane struts
123 Pitot head
124 Bracing wires
125 Flying wires
126 Port lower mainplane
127 Landing lamp
128 Underwing bomb shackles
129 Underwing strengthening plate
130 Rocket-launching rails
131 Four 60-lb (27-kg) anti-shipping rocket projectiles
132 Three-blade fixed-pitch Fairey-Reed metal propeller
133 Spinner
134 Townend ring
135 Bristol Pegasus IIIM3 (or Mk 30) radial engine
136 Cowling clips
137 Engine mounting ring
138 Engine support bearers
139 Firewall bulkhead
140 Engine controls
141 Oil tank immersion heater socket
142 Filler cap
143 Oil tank (13.75 Imp gal/62.5 litre capacity)
144 Centre section pyramid struts
145 External torpedo sight bars
146 Fuel filler cap
147 Main fuel tank (155 Imp gal/705 litre capacity)

the battleship's guns, resulting in the destruction of seven German destroyers, one of which was finished off by a bomb from Brown's aircraft; he also sank with bombs the German submarine *U-64* in Herjangsfjord.

In 1940, as production of the Fairey Fulmar fleet fighter increased at Fairey's Hayes factory, responsibility for the Swordfish was taken over entirely by Blackburn Aircraft Limited at Sherburn-in-Elmet, Yorkshire, the first aircraft being completed on 29 December. After 300 Mk Is had been delivered in nine months, Blackburn production switched to the Mk II with strengthened lower wing with metal skin to permit the carriage of eight rocket projectiles. The provision for interchangeability of wheel and float landing gear was discarded after termination of the Mk I production.

Mk Is continued in service throughout 1940, and once again it was Lieutenant Commander Brown who provided excellent spotting services for HMS *Warspite*'s main armament in the action off Calabria against the Italian fleet on 9 July.

Later that year, however, the brilliantly executed attack on the Italian fleet in Taranto harbour on 11 November constituted the pinnacle on which the Swordfish's fame was forever to stand. Following a remarkable feat of low-level reconnaissance by a Maryland crew which disclosed a concentration of Italian naval vessels in the port, it was decided to launch a night strike by the Swordfish of Nos 813, 815, 819 and 824 Squadrons from HMS *Illustrious* (Rear Admiral Lumley Lyster, himself an experienced naval pilot who had served at Taranto during World War 1). Led by Lieutenant Commander Kenneth Williamson, the first wave of 12 aircraft (six with torpedoes, four with bombs and two with bombs and flares) was launched 10 minutes before a second wave of nine aircraft (five with torpedoes, two with bombs and two with bombs and flares) led by Lieutenant

Fairey Swordfish variants

Fairey TSR 1: one prototype to Specification S.9/30; Pegasus IIM of 635 hp (474 kW); crashed from spin and destroyed

Fairey TSR II: one prototype (K4190) to Specification S.15/33; Pegasus IIIM3 of 775 hp (578 kW); first flight 17 April 1934

Fairey Swordfish Mk I: to Specification S.38/34, and powered by Pegasus IIIM3 of 690 hp (515 kW) (three prototypes, K5660·K5662·K5662 being completed as floatplane)

Fairey Swordfish Mk I: Fairey production 1935–40, with Pegasus IIIM3; all convertible to floatplanes; K,L and P serials (689 built)

Fairey Swordfish Mk I: Blackburn production 1940–

1, aircraft as Fairey-built Mk Is; V serials (300 built)

Fairey Swordfish Mk II: Blackburn production 1941–4, with Pegasus 30 of 750 hp (560 kW); wheel landing gear only and metal-covered lower wings; W, DK, HS, LS, NE and NF serials (1,080 built, some later converted to Swordfish Mk IV with enclosed cockpit)

Fairey Swordfish Mk III: Blackburn production 1944, with Pegasus 30; wheel landing gear only; ASV radar (most aircraft with provision for rocket projectiles); FF, NF, NR and NS serials (327 built, many converted to Swordfish Mk IV with enclosed cockpit)

Fairey Swordfish Mk IV: conversions from Mks II and III with enclosed cockpit

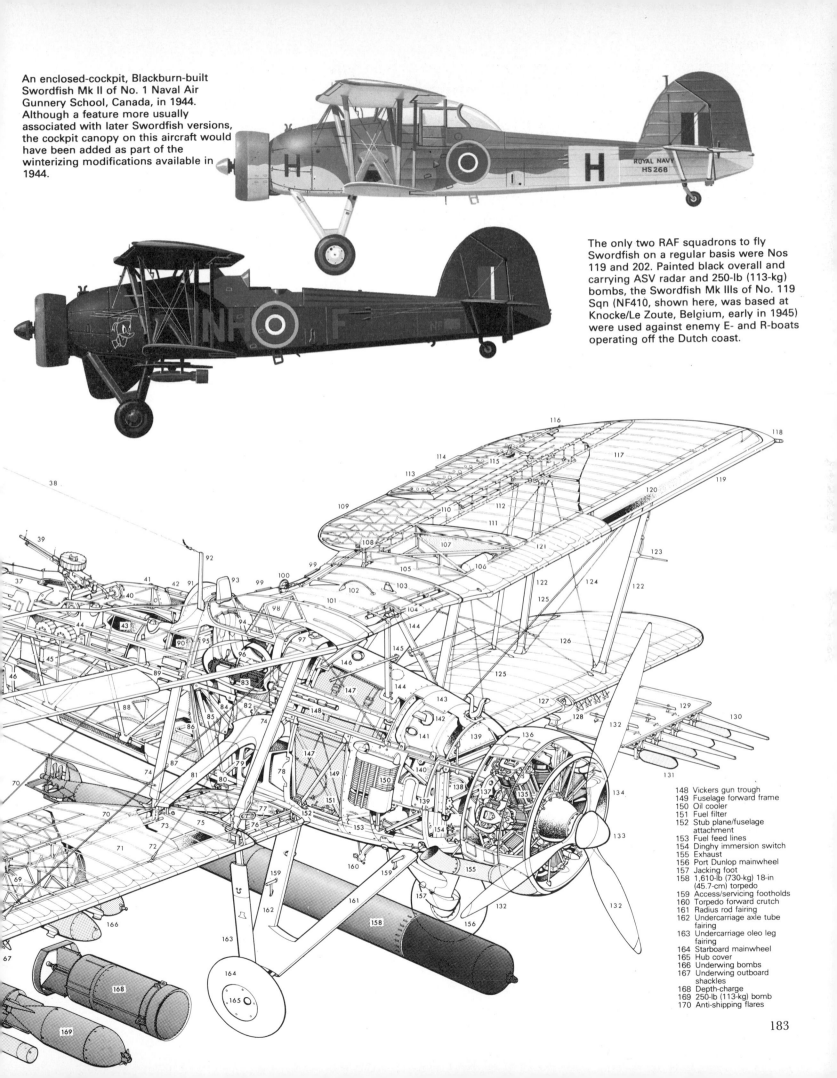

An enclosed-cockpit, Blackburn-built Swordfish Mk II of No. 1 Naval Air Gunnery School, Canada, in 1944. Although a feature more usually associated with later Swordfish versions, the cockpit canopy on this aircraft would have been added as part of the winterizing modifications available in 1944.

The only two RAF squadrons to fly Swordfish on a regular basis were Nos 119 and 202. Painted black overall and carrying ASV radar and 250-lb (113-kg) bombs, the Swordfish Mk IIIs of No. 119 Sqn (NF410, shown here, was based at Knocke/Le Zoute, Belgium, early in 1945) were used against enemy E- and R-boats operating off the Dutch coast.

148 Vickers gun trough
149 Fuselage forward frame
150 Oil cooler
151 Fuel filter
152 Stub plane/fuselage attachment
153 Fuel feed lines
154 Dinghy immersion switch
155 Exhaust
156 Port Dunlop mainwheel
157 Jacking foot
158 1,610-lb (730-kg) 18-in (45.7-cm) torpedo
159 Access/servicing footholds
160 Torpedo forward crutch
161 Radius rod fairing
162 Undercarriage axle tube fairing
163 Undercarriage oleo leg fairing
164 Starboard mainwheel
165 Hub cover
166 Underwing bombs
167 Underwing outboard shackles
168 Depth-charge
169 250-lb (113-kg) bomb
170 Anti-shipping flares

183

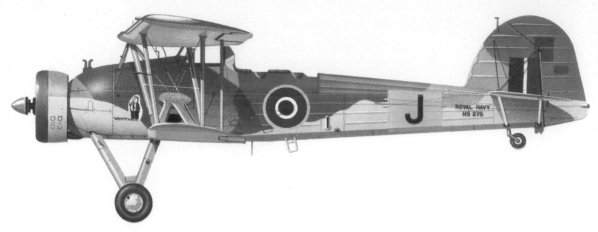

Blackburn-built Swordfish Mk II, HS275, of No. 1 Naval Air Gunnery School, Yarmouth, Nova Scotia, 1943. By this stage in the war most Swordfish had acquired a wide variety of camouflage schemes, that shown here being fairly commonplace.

Commander John Hale. Achieving almost total tactical surprise, the Swordfish crews attacked at low level, sinking the new 35,000-ton battleship *Littorio* at her moorings, and crippling the two older battleships *Conte di Cavour* and *Caio Duilio*, as well as a heavy cruiser and a destroyer. At a single stroke Italy's naval power in the Mediterranean was reduced by a half, at a cost of two Swordfish (Williamson himself being shot down and taken prisoner). A postscript to this attack lay in the fact that the Japanese naval attaché in Rome was recalled to Tokyo and became the architect of the Japanese attack on Pearl Harbour one year later.

Thereafter, and for many months to come, Fleet Air Arm Swordfish, based on Malta, became the scourge of Axis shipping in the Mediterranean, between them sinking more than a million and a half tons of German and Italian ships during 1941–3. Among their other widely varying tasks in that theatre were minelaying, fleet reconnaissance, gunnery spotting, coastal bombing attacks and even agent-dropping. One Swordfish is recorded as having flown 12 minelaying sorties in a single 24-hour period.

The attack on *Bismarck*

The most famous of all Swordfish pilots now joins the story. Lieutenant Commander Eugene Esmonde, a peacetime Imperial Airways pilot from Ireland, and who now commanded a Swordfish squadron aboard HMS *Victorious*, led a torpedo attack by nine aircraft on the German battleship *Bismarck* at large in the Atlantic on 26 May 1941 as it made its way towards Brest. The attack resulted in at least one vital hit, which crippled the vessel's steering mechanism, thereby allowing the British fleet to catch and sink her. Esmonde was awarded the DSO for his part in the operation, and now joined HMS *Ark Royal* in the Mediterranean; however, when the carrier was torpedoed he managed to fly off all his Swordfish and make for Gibraltar before the ship sank.

By the end of the year Esmonde was stationed in Kent, commanding No. 825 Squadron, deployed to counter any attempt by the German warships *Scharnhorst* and *Gneisenau* to break out of Brest and escape up the English Channel to Germany. On 12 February 1942 the worst British fears were realized when the German ships evaded all patrols and reached the eastern end of the Channel before being spotted. Esmonde's six Swordfish were thus the only aircraft readily available for an initial strike. Flying from Manston, the Swordfish crews missed their fighter rendezvous but pressed home their attack in the face of overwhelming enemy fighter and flak defences. Esmonde, in a Swordfish Mk II (W5984), was himself one of the first to be shot down by a Focke-Wulf Fw 190, followed by all five of his fellow pilots; none of their torpedoes found their mark. Of the 18 crew members only five survived to be rescued from the sea and all received the DSO or CGM. Esmonde was awarded a posthumous Victoria Cross.

Meanwhile efforts had been made to speed a replacement

A formation of early Swordfish Mk Is in November 1938 from the second and third production batches; these aircraft had provision for interchangeable wheel and float undercarriage. The aircraft shown here were clearly squadron aircraft, although probably not embarked in a carrier (note absence of fuselage chevron).

Originally referred to as the Fairey TSR 2, the prototype Swordfish, K4190, was designed and built to Specification S.15/33 and carried the Fairey works no. F2038 in small characters aft of the service serial number on the rear fuselage.

One of the last working examples of the Fairey Swordfish is now owned by the Fleet Air Arm Museum in Yeovilton, and regularly appears at air displays in the UK. (Photo: Air Portraits).

A Swordfish Mk 1, K5972, of the initial Fairey-built production batch in the markings of No. 823 Sqn, embarked in HMS *Glorious* in 1936. The fin stripes identify the Flight aircraft.

for the now-famous old 'Stringbag' biplane. The Fairey Albacore had been in production for some months but never lived up to its modest expectations (800 were produced, but manufacture stopped in 1943, while that of the Swordfish continued for a further year). The Fairey Barracuda (a Merlin-powered monoplane) for all its grotesque appearance might have had a distinguished career had it not been severely delayed after the abandoning of its original Rolls-Royce Exe engine.

Later Blackfish

As it was, Blackburn continued to produce Swordfish Mk IIs (known locally as 'Blackfish') until 1944, completing the last of 1,080 examples on 22 February that year. Production then switched to the Mk III, which was fitted with a large ASV scanner between the landing gear legs, thereby preventing carriage of the torpedo; when employed on anti-shipping torpedo strikes it was normal practice for one Mk III to assume the search role, while Mk IIs in the strike unit carried bombs and torpedoes. Swordfish were widely used aboard

the relatively small escort carriers which were hurriedly introduced for convoy duties, particularly in the North Atlantic in the mid-war years, their normal complement of six Swordfish and six Grumman Martlet fighters being permanently ranged on their steeply pitching decks at the mercy of the elements.

The final version was the Mk IV, retrospectively modified Mk IIs and Mk IIIs with a rudimentary cockpit enclosure, and this version continued in service until the end of the war in Europe. A small number of Swordfish were sent to Canada for operational and training purposes, some serving with No. 1 Naval Air Gunnery School at Yarmouth, Nova Scotia.

The last Mk III (N204) was completed on 18 August 1944 in Sherburn, and on 28 June 1945 a Swordfish was the last biplane to fly a solo mission for the Fleet Air Arm. By 1967 there were only six complete Swordfish left out of the 2,396 production aircraft built. One of these (LS326, previously registered as G-AJVH), is still in working order and often makes appearances at air displays in England.

This Swordfish, the same aircraft as that pictured on the previous page, is taxying during a display by the Fleet Air Arm Memorial Flight. The aft navigators' compartment must have seemed frighteningly exposed during World War 2 actions.

PBY Catalina: Ocean Patroller

Designed in 1935, the PBY transformed the oceanic patrolling capability of the US Navy. It was evaluated and purchased for the RAF before the war and was also built under licence in the Soviet Union; as a result, there were more Catalinas than any other flying-boat in history. And nearly 50 years after its inception, it still flies many oceans.

The Consolidated Catalina was one of the slowest fighters of World War 2. It was jokingly said of this plane that there was no point in its crew using a stop watch to rendezvous with a convoy because it took a whole month to get to its destination. It was already flying in 1935 and therefore, even when war broke out, it was not a young aircraft. What was more, the US Navy had ordered the next generation of flying boat, the Martin PBM, to replace the Catalina, even before the war. But the much-loved 'Cat' did not accept defeat that easily. In 1938 the Soviet Union had declared that it was better than anything built by their own factories, and throughout the war it was built under licence in Russia. Furthermore, the original American craft lived on in many new versions and more of these were sold during the war than the newer machines that replaced them.

The genesis of the PBY, as the aircraft was known to US forces, lay in a 1933 requirement by the US Navy for a new long-range patrol flying-boat. At that time the principal aircraft in this category was the Consolidated P2Y, designed at Buffalo by Isaac M. 'Mac' Laddon, a gifted seaplane engineer and a director of Consolidated Aircraft. To meet the new demand he cleaned up the P2Y by giving it an almost cantilever wing mounted above the shallow but broad hull on a central pylon housing the flight engineer. The wing differed from that of the P2Y in having a rectangular centre section and tapered outer panels, all of stressed-skin all-metal construction (ailerons were fabric-skinned). A unique feature was that the wing-tip floats were mounted on pivoted frames which could be retracted electrically so that in flight the floats formed the wingtips. The hull, likewise all-metal, was quite different from that of most large boats in being all on one deck, with a broad semicircular top. In the bows was a mooring compartment and transparent sighting window with a venetian blind giving seawater protection. The bow cockpit was a turret with large all-round windows in pro-

A US Navy PBY-5A pictured in 1944 over the Aleutians. In areas such as this, with consistent bad weather, the range and endurance of these reliable amphibious boats brought many crews to a safe landing either on land or water.

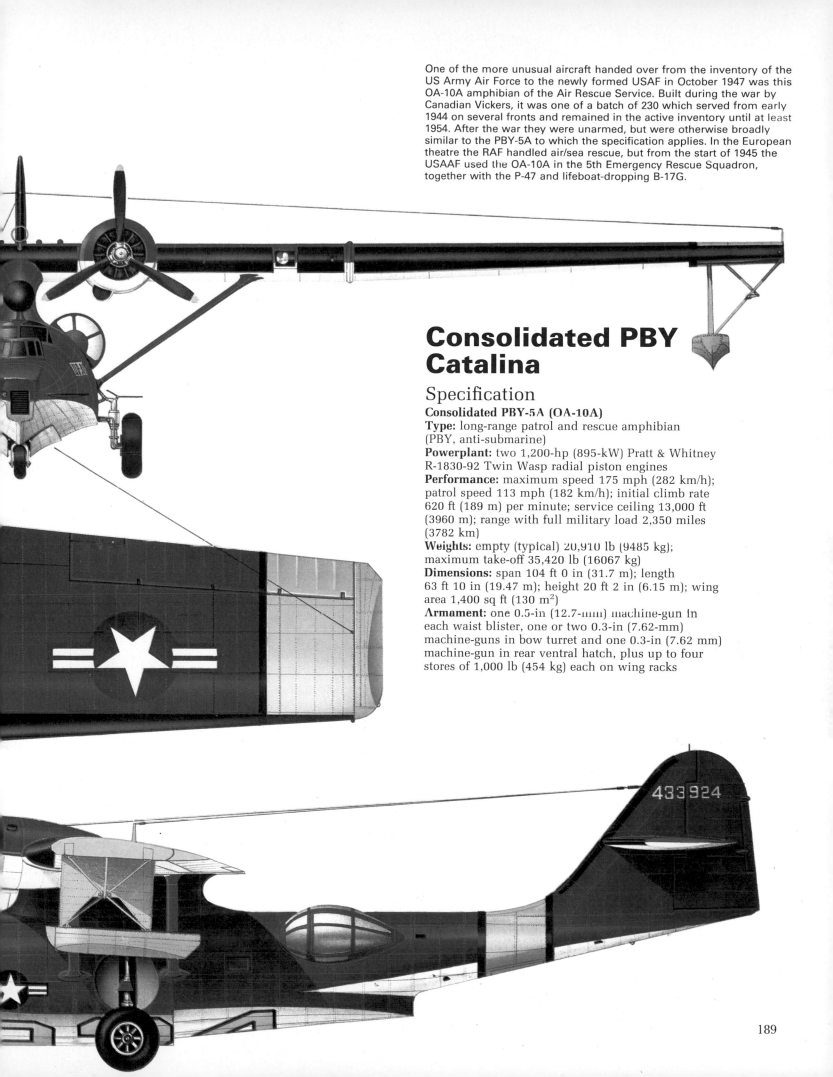

One of the more unusual aircraft handed over from the inventory of the US Army Air Force to the newly formed USAF in October 1947 was this OA-10A amphibian of the Air Rescue Service. Built during the war by Canadian Vickers, it was one of a batch of 230 which served from early 1944 on several fronts and remained in the active inventory until at least 1954. After the war they were unarmed, but were otherwise broadly similar to the PBY-5A to which the specification applies. In the European theatre the RAF handled air/sea rescue, but from the start of 1945 the USAAF used the OA-10A in the 5th Emergency Rescue Squadron, together with the P-47 and lifeboat-dropping B-17G.

Consolidated PBY Catalina

Specification

Consolidated PBY-5A (OA-10A)
Type: long-range patrol and rescue amphibian (PBY, anti-submarine)
Powerplant: two 1,200-hp (895-kW) Pratt & Whitney R-1830-92 Twin Wasp radial piston engines
Performance: maximum speed 175 mph (282 km/h); patrol speed 113 mph (182 km/h); initial climb rate 620 ft (189 m) per minute; service ceiling 13,000 ft (3960 m); range with full military load 2,350 miles (3782 km)
Weights: empty (typical) 20,910 lb (9485 kg); maximum take-off 35,420 lb (16067 kg)
Dimensions: span 104 ft 0 in (31.7 m); length 63 ft 10 in (19.47 m); height 20 ft 2 in (6.15 m); wing area 1,400 sq ft (130 m²)
Armament: one 0.5-in (12.7-mm) machine-gun in each waist blister, one or two 0.3-in (7.62-mm) machine-guns in bow turret and one 0.3-in (7.62 mm) machine-gun in rear ventral hatch, plus up to four stores of 1,000 lb (454 kg) each on wing racks

Consolidated PBY Catalina

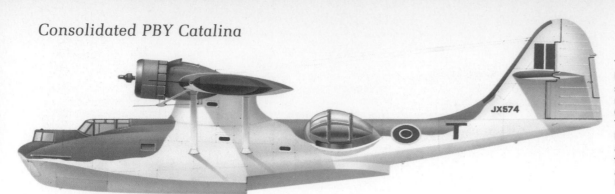

This Catalina IVA from Royal Air Force No. 210 Squadron shows the standard colour scheme for maritime patrol aircraft of Coastal Command from 1942 onwards. This particular machine has ASV Mk II radar without the dipole aerial array on the hull. One 'Cat' skipper from No. 210 won a VC and another sank the Command's last U-boat.

duction aircraft, with a machine-gun above. Two pilots sat side-by-side in the wide cockpit with large windows all round. Aft of the wing were left and right gunner's stations each with a sliding hatch. Unlike the P2Y the tail was clean and simple, with the horizontal tail mounted well up the single fin. The powerplant switched from Cyclones to the new two-row Pratt & Whitney Twin Wasp, neatly cowled on the centre section with cooling gills and driving Hamilton variable-pitch propellers.

Designated Consolidated Model 28, the new boat received the US Navy designation XP3Y-1, the prototype (BuAer number 9459) flying from Lake Erie on 28 March 1935. It proved to be an excellent aircraft, though tests at Coco Solo (Panama Canal Zone) showed the need for a larger rudder. The new Douglas XP3D-1 was also good, but the Consolidated boat was cheaper, at $90,000, and an order for 60 was placed on 29 June 1935. The designation was changed to PBY-1 because of the increase in underwing weapon load to 2,000 lb (907 kg). Defensive armament comprised four 0.5-in (7.62-mm) Browning machine-guns, one in the manual nose turret, one in each waist position and the fourth in a tunnel hatch which was located on the underside of the rear fuselage.

With the massive order for 60, Consolidated had plenty of work to support its 2,000-mile (3220-km) move to San Diego, in southern California, where weather was fine all through the year. In October 1935 the XP3Y made a non-stop flight of almost 3,500 miles (5633 km) from Coco Solo to San

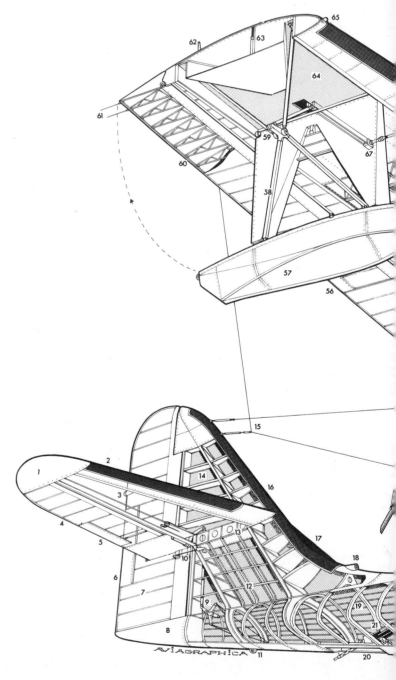

An original colour photograph taken at about the time of the start of the long Aleutians campaign in early 1942 shows a PBY-5 of the US Navy before slipping its moorings for a patrol. A pair of bombs can be seen under the wing (maximum load was four at 1,000-lb [454-kg]). Defensive guns would be two 0.3-in (7.62-mm) and two 0.5-in (12.7-mm). The photographer picked an unusually sunny, clear day.

NZ4017 was one of a batch of Boeing-built PB2B-1 Catalinas, approximately equivalent to the PBY-5, which were supplied under the Lend-Lease Act to the Royal New Zealand Air Force in 1943–4. Equipped with ASV radar transmitters on the wings, it served in the South West Pacific theatre until after VJ-Day.

Consolidated PBY-5A Catalina cutaway drawing key

1 Starboard tailplane
2 Tailplane leading edge de-icing
3 Tail navigation light
4 Starboard fabric-covered elevator
5 Elevator tab
6 Rudder trim tab
7 Fabric-covered rudder construction
8 Tailcone
9 Elevator push-pull control rod
10 Rudder control horn
11 Tail mooring point
12 Lower fin structure integral with tail fuselage
13 Tailplane centre section attachment
14 Upper fin construction

15 Aerial cables
16 Fin leading edge de-icing
17 Port tailplane
18 Cooling air intake
19 Rear fuselage frame and stringer construction
20 Ventral tunnel gun hatch
21 0.3-in (7.62-mm) machine gun
22 Fuselage skin plating
23 Target-towing reel
24 Flare launch tube
25 Rear fuselage bulkhead
26 Bulkhead door
27 0.5-in (12.7-mm) beam machine gun
28 Starboard beam gun cupola
29 Cupola opening side window
30 Flexible gun mounting
31 Port beam gun cupola
32 Gunner's folding seat
33 Semi-circular gun platform
34 Walkway
35 Hull bottom V-frames
36 Wardroom bulkhead
37 Crew rest bunks
38 Wardroom
39 Starboard mainwheel
40 Hull planing bottom step

41 Planing bottom construction
42 Fuselage skin plating
43 Mainwheel housing
44 Hydraulic retraction jack
45 Telescopic leg strut
46 Fore and aft wing support struts
47 Wing mounting centre pylon construction
48 Pylon tail fairing
49 Starboard wing integral fuel tank, capacity 875 US gal (3312 litres)
50 Fuel jettison pipe
51 1000-lb (454-kg) bomb
52 Smoke generator tank
53 Trailing edge ribs
54 Fabric covered trailing edge
55 Rear spar
56 Aileron trim tab
57 Starboard retractable wing-tip float
58 Float support struts
59 Retraction linkage
60 Fabric-covered starboard aileron
61 Static discharge wicks
62 Wing-tip aerial mast
63 Float up-lock
64 Float leg housing
65 Starboard navigation light

66 Leading edge de-icing boot
67 Float retracting gear
68 Front spar
69 Wing rib-stringer construction
70 ASV radar aerial
71 Outer wing panel attachment joint
72 Wing lattice ribs
73 Bomb carrier and release unit
74 Two 500-lb (227-kg) bombs
75 Leading-edge nose ribs
76 Position of pitot tube on port wing
77 Landing lamp
78 Landing lamp glare shield
79 Starboard engine nacelle fairing
80 Hydraulic accumulator
81 Engine oil tank
82 Fireproof bulkhead
83 Exhaust stub
84 Engine bearer struts
85 Detachable engine cowlings
86 Curtiss Electric three-bladed constant-speed propeller, 12-ft (3.66-m) diameter
87 Propeller hub pitch-change mechanism

88 Pratt & Whitney R-1830-92 Twin Wasp two-row radial engine
89 Aerial cable lead-in
90 D/F loop aerial
91 Oil cooler
92 Control runs through pylon front fairing
93 Pylon step
94 Engineer's control panel
95 Flight engineer's seat
96 Wing mounting fuselage main frame
97 Radio and radar control units
98 Cabin heater
99 Front cabin walkway
100 Port main undercarriage leg strut
101 Torque scissor links
102 Port mainwheel
103 Mk 13-2 torpedo
104 450-lb (204-kg) depth charge
105 Forward fuselage frame construction
106 Navigator's seat
107 Radio/radar operator's seat
108 Radio rack
109 Cabin side window
110 Autopilot servo controller
111 Navigator's chart table
112 Fuselage chine member
113 Cockpit bulkhead
114 Co-pilot's seat
115 Pilot's seat
116 Pilot's electrical control panel

117 Sliding side window
118 Engine cowling cooling air gills
119 Port engine nacelle
120 Cockpit roof escape hatch
121 Overhead throttle and propeller controls
122 Windscreen wipers
123 Curved windscreens
124 Instrument panel
125 Control column yoke and handwheels
126 Rudder pedals
127 Cockpit flooring
128 Nose undercarriage hatch doors
129 Nosewheel bay
130 Port aileron
131 Nosewheel
132 Port retractable wing-tip float
133 Float support struts
134 Port navigation light
135 Leading edge de-icing boot
136 Nosewheel forks
137 Nose undercarriage retraction jack
138 Front gunner/bomb aimer's station
139 Curtained bulkhead
140 Gunner's footboards
141 Spare ammunition containers
142 Front rotating gun turret
143 0.3-in (7.62-mm) machine gun
144 Bomb aimer's instrument panel
145 Drift sight
146 Bomb aiming window with protective blind
147 Anchor cable

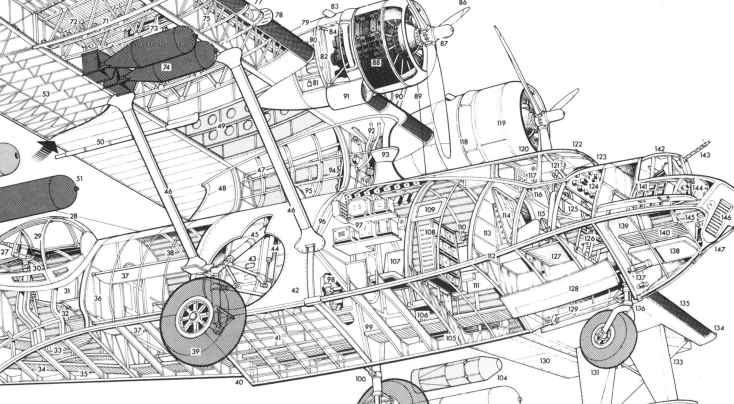

This Catalina was the third of a batch of 36 GR.IIAs produced by Canadian Vickers, ex-RCAF and the only ones of this species. They were assigned mainly to No. 209 Squadron, the original Catalina operator, after having been fitted with ASV.II radar complete with the hull-mounted dipole aerials ahead of the struts.

Shown in 1942 markings, this PBY-5 was supplied to the Royal Australian Air Force and assigned to No. 11 Squadron. It was one of a batch of 18 ordered as a commercial sale before the Lend-Lease Act became law. British ASV radar was fitted in 1942 (on this aircraft without the wing-mounted transmitter aerials).

Francisco. It then went on to participate in the dedication of the giant new San Diego plant on 20 October before returning to Buffalo to be modified to PBY standard with a broad rounded rudder, de-icer boots on all leading edges (with pull-out steps up the leading edge of the fin), full armament and combat equipment. It flew again in March 1936 and reached US Navy squadron VP-11F at the same time as the first production machines in October 1936. Unquestionably this was the best patrol flying-boat in the world at that time.

In July 1936 Consolidated received a contract for 50 PBY-2s with all four wing racks stressed to 1,000-lb (454-kg) loads and with 0.5-in (12.7-mm) guns in the waist positions. In November 1936 an order followed for 66 PBY-3s with R-1830-66 Twin Wasps uprated from 900 to 1,000 hp (671 to 746 kW), and in December 1937 a contract followed for 33 PBY-4s, all but one with large bulged transparent blisters instead of lateral sliding hatches for the beam gunners and with 1,050-hp (783-k/W) engines. Two more PBYs were sold in 1937 to explorer Dr Richard Archbold, who named them *Guba I* and *Guba II* (Motu word for a sudden storm). *Guba II* spent an arduous year in New Guinea, finally making the first flight across the Indian Ocean to survey the route known in World War 2 as the 'horseshoe route' on which hundreds of military and BOAC Catalinas were to fly. It then crossed Africa and the Atlantic, the first aircraft to circle the globe near the Equator. *Guba I* was sold to a Soviet expedition led by Sir Hubert Wilkins who flew 19,000 miles (30600 km) through the worst weather in the world fruitlessly searching for S. A. Levanevskii, who vanished near the North Pole on 13 August 1937. So outstanding was the Model 28 in this work that the Model 28-2 was put into production at Taganrog on the Azov Sea as the GST (civil transport version, MP-7), over 1,000 being used in World War 2 with 950-hp (709-kW) M-62 engines in Polikarpov I-16 type shuttered cowlings and with Soviet equipment and armament.

Another Model 28-5 (PBY-4) was bought by the British Air Ministry and tested at Felixtowe as RAF P9630, proving so outstanding that it was adopted as a standard boat for Coastal Command. Named Catalina I – a name later adopted by the US Navy – the first RAF variant was similar to the latest US Navy type, the PBY-5 with 1,200-hp (895-kW) R-1830-92 engines, an order for 200 of which had been placed on 20 December 1939. No flying-boat – in fact no large US Navy aircraft – had ever been ordered in such quantities, and the vast open-ended British orders called for massive extra capacity. British officials helped arrange for licence production by Canadian Vickers at Cartierville (Montreal) and Boeing of Canada at Vancouver. The San Diego plant also much more than doubled in size and was joined by an even larger plant a mile down the road building B-24s.

Amphibian conversion

On 22 November 1939 Consolidated flew a PBY-4 rebuilt as the XPBY-5A with retractable tricycle landing gear. This excellent amphibian conversion was a great success and had only a minor effect on performance. The final 33 PBY-5s were completed as PBY-5As, and another 134 were ordered in November 1940. At the time of Pearl Harbor (7 December 1941) the US Navy had three squadrons of PBY-3s, two of PBY-4s and no fewer than 16 flying the new PBY-5. Before sunrise on that day a PBY crew spotted the periscope of a Japanese submarine at Pearl Harbor, marked it with smoke and guided the destroyer USS *Ward*, which sank it – the first US shots of World War 2, over an hour before the air attack began.

By this time a further 586 PBY-5s had been ordered, and the export list had risen to: Australia 18, Canada 50, France 30 and the Netherlands East Indies 36. In 1942 another 627 PBY-5As were added, of which 56 were to be OA-10s for the USAAF, used for search and rescue. The first Lend-Lease batch for the RAF comprised 225 non-amphibious PBY-5Bs (Catalina IAs) followed by 97 Catalina IVAs fitted in Britain with ASV Mk II radar. RAF Catalinas usually had a Vickers K (VGO) machine-gun in the bow and twin 0.303-in (7.7-mm) Brownings in the waist blisters.

This PBY-1 of VP-12, the second squadron of the US Navy to receive these boats in 1937, shows the appearance of the pre-war version with sliding rear hatches instead of blisters. Pre-war aircraft were finished in silver or natural metal.

An unusual stern view of a US Navy PBY-5 shows the waist gunners (who appear to have non-standard installations of 0.5-in/12.7-mm guns, with saddle-type ammunition boxes). This close-up shows how the rudder, almost divided into upper and lower halves, swings across a fixed portion of tailplane.

Based on a PBY-6A, this Catalina is one of a substantial number modified in the immediate post-war era for use as civilian water-bombers to fight forest fires, mainly on the US West Coast and in Canada. They were the ancestors of today's purpose-designed Canadair CL-215, which has a similar layout but engines of twice the power.

Operational with the RAF

RAF Catalina operations began in spring 1941 with Nos 209 and 210 Squadrons, and one of the first to become operational was a machine of No. 209 from Castle Archdale which on 26 May 1941 was far out over the Atlantic, with the crew under Pilot Officer Briggs being checked out by a 'neutral' lieutenant in the US Navy. Suddenly they spotted a giant warship; it was the *Bismarck*, which had eluded all pursuers for 31½ hours. Despite heavy flak the Catalina radioed the battleship's position and kept her in view until another Catalina from No. 240 Squadron took over and guided the British fleet to the spot. Apart from this epic, almost all Coastal Command missions by over 650 Catalinas were against U-boats, many of the 15- to 20-hour trips ending at Grasnaya (Murmansk) and Arkhangelsk protecting convoys supplying the Soviet Union. The only shortcoming of the Catalina was that its slow speed often gave a U-boat time to dive after being spotted. By 1943 they stayed on the surface, bristling with guns, and two Catalina skippers won the VC, one posthumously, for pressing home their attacks on heavily armed U-boats under almost unbelievable conditions.

Black Cats

Life was equally tough in the Pacific where the Catalina was from 7 December 1941 by far the most important US patrol aircraft. In the northern campaign along the Aleutians many Catalinas had to make overloaded downwind take-offs in blizzards at night, with ice over the windscreen. The PBY was the first US aircraft (other than the obsolete Douglas B-18) to carry radar. They fulfilled diverse missions including those of torpedo-bomber, transport and glider-tug. Perhaps the most famous of all Catalinas were the Black Cat PBY-5A amphibians which, painted matt black, roamed the western

Pacific from December 1942 finding Japanese ships of all kinds by radar at night and picking up Allied survivors from ships and aircraft in boats and dinghies. In addition to radar, bombs, depth charges and fragmentation grenades, the Black Cats often carried crates of empty beer bottles whose eerie whistling descent deterred Japanese gunners and caused wasted time looking for unexploded bombs.

By late 1941 the Cartierville plant was in full production. Canadian Vickers delivered 230 amphibians ordered as PBV-1As but actually passed to the USAAF as OA-10As, as well as 149 Canso I amphibians for the RCAF. Boeing, which came on stream later, built 240 PB2B-1 flying-boats, mainly as Catalina IVBs for the RAF, RAAF and RNZAF, and 17 Catalinas and 55 Cansos for the RCAF. Yet a further plant was brought into the programme in 1941 to produce its own improved models. The NAF (Naval Aircraft Factory) at Philadelphia had been the source of all US Navy flying-boat designs, and its experience enabled it to improve on 'Mac' Laddon's design in a way that could have been done by the parent company had it not been for the frantic demand for production. The NAF Catalina, the PBN-1, had a restressed wing for 38,000-lb (17237-kg) gross weight, with increased tankage, redesigned wing-tip floats and struts, and a new hull with a longer and sharper bow, 20° step amidships, and rear step extended about 5 ft (1.52 m) aft; most obvious of the changes was the tall vertical tail, with a horn-balanced rudder, and armament was generally increased to three or more 0.5-in (12.7-mm) machine-guns (only the ventral tunnel retained the rifle-calibre gun) with a rounded bow turret and improved continuous-feed magazines. Another change was a redesigned electrical system of increased capacity, with the batteries moved from the leading edge down to the hull.

The NAF itself delivered 138 PBN-1 Nomads, and Consolidated (by this time Convair) opened yet another plant at New Orleans to build the best Catalina of all, the amphibious version of the PBN. Called PBY-6A, this usually carried a

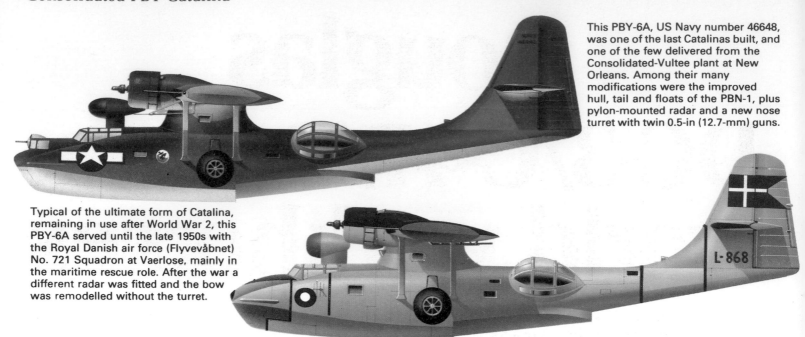

This PBY-6A, US Navy number 46648, was one of the last Catalinas built, and one of the few delivered from the Consolidated-Vultee plant at New Orleans. Among their many modifications were the improved hull, tail and floats of the PBN-1, plus pylon-mounted radar and a new nose turret with twin 0.5-in (12.7-mm) guns.

Typical of the ultimate form of Catalina, remaining in use after World War 2, this PBY-6A served until the late 1950s with the Royal Danish air force (Flyvevåbnet) No. 721 Squadron at Vaerlose, mainly in the maritime rescue role. After the war a different radar was fitted and the bow was remodelled without the turret.

centimetric radar in a neat pod above the cockpit, and the bow turret usually had twin 0.5-in (12.7-mm) guns. An order was placed for 900, but the end of the war cut this to 48 for the Soviet Union (which also received all but one of the PBNs), 75 as OA-10Bs for the USAAF and 112 for the US Navy. Fifty more were delivered by Boeing from Vancouver as PB2B-2s, designated Catalina VI by the RAF.

Total production of all versions of the Consolidated Model 28 considerably exceeded 4,000. Of these 2,398 were delivered by Consolidated Aircraft and Convair (the March 1943 name for the merged Consolidated and Vultee-Stinson companies). Some 892 were built in Canada and by the two Canadian plants, and about 1,500 built in Russia.

After the war most users of the Catalina continued to operate the type. In the Soviet Union the GST remained the chief patrol boat until replaced by the Beriev Be-6 in 1950–3, but continued in fishery protection and other offshore roles until 1959. Likewise the lower-powered (870-hp/649-kW M-62IR) MP-7 transport remained in civil use until at least 1958. The RAF withdrew Lend-Lease aircraft after VJ-Day, but the USN continued to use flying-boat and amphibious versions until after 1950. In the 1950s the Naval Reserve and Coast Guard used the PBY-6A and the JSAAF and USAF used the OA-10B in most cases in the air-sea rescue role with an airborne lifeboat under each wing. France and Israel made important use of the Catalina in the 1950s, together with Argentina, Brazil, Ecuador, Dominica, Indonesia, Nationalist China, Mexico and Peru. The last active PBY-6A was retired from NARTU (Naval Air Reserve Training Unit), Atlanta, Georgia, on 3 January 1957. Canada, Australia and New Zealand retained Catalinas of various marks after 1960, and the last in service was Latin American air forces were retired in 1965–6.

Post-war Catalinas found wide employment as civil transports and water bombers for firefighting. The amphibious variants were in special demand, at one time more than 80 being in use by Latin American civil operators (headed by Panair do Brasil which used them on a major network with 22 passenger seats). Some dozen served mainly as freighters in North America, and the water bomber was the first aircraft able to scoop up a load and dump it on a forest fire.

One disadvantage of the later, heavier versions of the Catalina, which was criticised, perhaps justly, was its inadequate engine performance, particularly when one engine stopped working. Various American companies, including Timmins and Steward-Davis, offered conversions or conversion packages to improve the performance and reliability

of the aircraft with a heavier payload. In 1966 the Bird Innovator led to a bigger change. The Bird Corporation, the largest manufacturer of respirators for medical purposes, was using a PBY-5A as a company aircraft. To improve its performance, the company mounted two 340-hp (254 kW) Lycoming piston engines on the outer wing sections, strengthened the tailplane, increased the fuel capacity, rebuilt the tail fin and with other alterations the four-engined Catalina could cruise at 200 mph (322 kmph).

Catalina variants

Consolidated 28 XP3Y-1: original prototype; two 825-hp (615-kW) Pratt & Whitney R-1830-58 Twin Wasp engines,; redesignated XPBY-1 after modification
Consolidated PNY-1: first production model, 900-hp (671-kW) R-1830-64 engines
Consolidated PBY-2: various modifications
Consolidated PBY-3: two 1,000-hp (746-kW) R-1830-66 and other changes
Consolidated PBY-4: two 1,050-hp (783-kW) R-1830-72 and other changes, e.g. waist blisters
Consolidated PBY-5: two 1,200-hp (895-kW) R-1830-92 and numerous other changes, e.g. further modified vertical tail (RAF Catalina I and II)
Consolidated PBY-5A: retractable tricycle landing

gear (RCAF: Canso; RAF: Catalina III; USAAF: OA-10 and OA-10A
NAF PBN-1: revised design by Naval Aircraft Factory
Consolidated PBY-6A: amphibian version of PBN (USAAF: OA-10B)
Consolidated PB2B-1: Boeing-built PBY-5 (RAF/RAAF/RNZAF; Catalina IVB)
Consolidated PB2B-2: Boeing-built PBY-6A (RAF/RAAF: Catalina VII)
GST: Licence-built version in Soviet Union, two 950-hp (709-kW) M-62
MP-7: civil transport version of GST; two 850-hp (634-kW) M-621R

Even today a considerable number (probably more than 100) of Catalina flying-boats and amphibians are still in operation. One of these survivors is OB-T-051 of Lorasa (Loretana de Aviación SA) of Peru. It is a PBY-5A, used for charters and for passenger and cargo services. Note the spats of a Cessna Skyhawk parked just beyond.

Douglas DC-3/C-47/Dakota: world workhorses

The Douglas C-47 and its numerous derivatives has for nearly half a century remained the most versatile workhorse aviation has known. Born in the brassy years of the American mid-1930s as the Douglas DC-3, it became the standard pre-war airliner, went to war in uniform the world over, and returned to civilian clothes afterwards.

In the middle of 1935 C. R. Smith, then President of American Airlines, ordered a larger and more luxurious version of the DC-2 from Douglas, so as to gain the upper hand over competing companies with their Boeing 247s and DC-2s.

The project leader at Douglas, Fred Stineman, had his team design a new type of aircraft known as the Douglas Sleeper Transport, with 14 sleeping berths. Soon, however, it was realised that if 21 seats were installed instead, and a pair of

The Finnish Air Force was still using four Douglas C-47s in its Transport Flight at Utti in 1983.

Douglas C-47 Skytrain

Specification

Douglas C-47 Skytrain

Type: cargo, supply or 21/28-seat troop transport, 14-litter ambulance, or glider tug

Powerplant: two 1,200-hp (895-kW) Pratt & Whitney R-1830-92 radial piston engines

Performance: maximum speed 227 mph (365 km/h) at 7,500 ft (2285 m); initial climb rate 940 ft (287 m) per minute; service ceiling 24,000 ft (7315 m); range 1,600 miles (2575 km)

Weights: empty 18,200 lb (8256 kg); maximum take-off 26,000 lb (11794 kg)

Dimensions: span 95 ft 6 in (29.11 m); length 63 ft 9 in (19.43 m); height 17 ft 0 in (5.18 m); wing area 987 sq ft (91.69 m^2)

Payload: 8,000 lb (3629 kg) to 10,000 lb (4536 kg) of military cargo (depending on aircraft variant)

General Eisenhower is on record as having stated that the C-47 was one of the four principal instruments of Allied victory in World War 2 (the others being the bazooka, Jeep and atom bomb). Typical example of the Skytrain was this C-47A-65-DL of the 81st Troop Carrier Squadron, 436th Troop Carrier Group, based at Membury in England between 3 March 1944 and February 1945 (it also took part in the airborne assault on Southern France, based at Voltone, Italy, during July and August 1944). The mission tally on 'Buzz Buggy', together with invasion stripes, suggest participation in the Normandy, South France, Nijmegen and Bastogne operations, both as a paratrooper and glider tug.

One of the 98 US Navy R4D-8s, modified to 'Super DC-3' standard with swept wings, lengthened fuselage, enlarged tail and fully enclosed undercarriage. Redesignated the C-117D, this version had a top speed of 270 mph (435 km/h).

The RCAF contributed three Article VI transport squadrons with Dakotas (Nos 435, 436 and 437) to the RAF during World War 2, the first two in the Far East and No. 437 in Europe. Shown here is an RCAF Dakota used for training pilots in airborne forces duties.

Wright Cyclone 900 hp (671 kW) engines installed, the increased payload could increase their income by 50% more than the DC-2, with fuel costs rising by only 3%. At 3 p.m. on 17 December 1935, the 32nd anniversary of the Wright Brothers' first flight, the prototype, X14988, set off on its maiden flight from Clover Field (now Santa Monica). It was piloted by Carl A. Cover and still designated DST (Douglas Sleeper Transport).

The prototype entered service as American Airlines' flagship on 11 July 1936 as orders poured in to Douglas. By the end of 1939 the DC-3 (third Douglas Commercial) had joined Braniff, Eastern, Northwest, Pennsylvania-Central, Transcontinental & Western, and United, as well as American in the United States, while overseas KLM was the first to take deliveries, followed by Panagra, Panair do Brasil, LAV, CMA, Australian National, Sweden's ABA, Czechoslovakia's CLS, Swissair, Air France, Sabena, LOT, LARES, and MALERT. Licences to build were negotiated with Nakajima in Japan (the first aircraft being completed on 30 September 1938), and with the Soviet Union, which purchased 18 DC-3s before World War 2 and went on to produce huge numbers which served with Aeroflot and the military, first as the PS-84 and later as the Lisunov Li-2.

When war broke out in Europe most of the commercial airlines reduced their operations and in due course many of the DC-3s of subjugated nations found themselves serving with Lufthansa, while others were seized by the Italians.

Douglas C-47 Dakota IV cutaway drawing key

1 Hinged nose cone access to instruments and controls
2 Rudder pedals
3 Instrument panel
4 Windscreen de-icing fluid spray nozzle
5 Starboard propeller
6 Windscreen panels
7 Co-pilot's seat
8 Engine throttles
9 Control column
10 Cockpit floor level
11 Access panels to control cable runs
12 Pitot static tubes
13 Aerial cables
14 Propeller de-icing fluid tank
15 Pilot's seat
16 Cockpit bulkhead
17 Cockpit roof escape hatch
18 Whip aerial
19 Starboard landing/taxying lamp
20 Windscreen de-icing fluid tank
21 Starboard baggage compartment
22 Electrical fuse panel
23 Crew entry door
24 ADF loop aerial housing
25 Life raft stowage
26 Port baggage compartment
27 Main cabin bulkhead
28 Radio operator's seat
29 Air scoop
30 Heating and ventilating system heat exchanges
31 Astrodome observation hatch

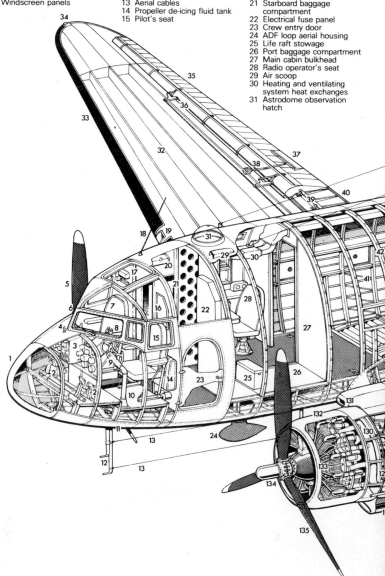

The single Douglas XC-47C (42-5671) of 1943 had Edo amphibious floats, each incorporating two retractable landing wheels and a 300-US gal (1136-litre) fuel tank.

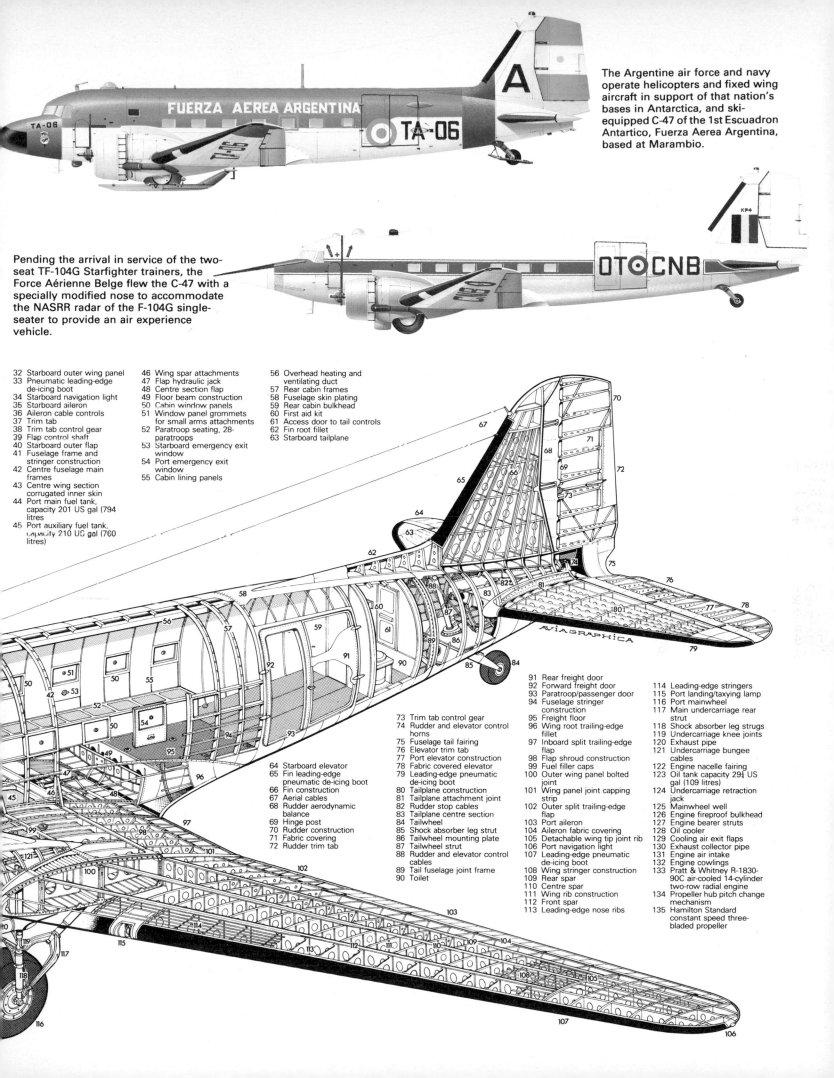

The Argentine air force and navy operate helicopters and fixed wing aircraft in support of that nation's bases in Antarctica, and ski-equipped C-47 of the 1st Escuadron Antartico, Fuerza Aerea Argentina, based at Marambio.

Pending the arrival in service of the two-seat TF-104G Starfighter trainers, the Force Aérienne Belge flew the C-47 with a specially modified nose to accommodate the NASRR radar of the F-104G single-seater to provide an air experience vehicle.

FUERZA AEREA ARGENTINA

TA-06

O T O CNB

32 Starboard outer wing panel
33 Pneumatic leading-edge de-icing boot
34 Starboard navigation light
35 Starboard aileron
36 Aileron cable controls
37 Trim tab
38 Trim tab control gear
39 Flap control shaft
40 Starboard outer flap
41 Fuselage frame and stringer construction
42 Centre fuselage main frames
43 Centre wing section corrugated inner skin
44 Port main fuel tank, capacity 201 US gal (794 litres)
45 Port auxiliary fuel tank, capacity 210 US gal (760 litres)

46 Wing spar attachments
47 Flap hydraulic jack
48 Centre section flap
49 Floor beam construction
50 Cabin window panels
51 Window panel grommets for small arms attachments
52 Paratroop seating, 28-paratroops
53 Starboard emergency exit window
54 Port emergency exit window
55 Cabin lining panels

56 Overhead heating and ventilating duct
57 Rear cabin frames
58 Fuselage skin plating
59 Rear cabin bulkhead
60 First aid kit
61 Access door to tail controls
62 Fin root fillet
63 Starboard tailplane

64 Starboard elevator
65 Fin leading-edge pneumatic de-icing boot
66 Fin construction
67 Aerial cables
68 Rudder aerodynamic balance
69 Hinge post
70 Rudder construction
71 Fabric covering
72 Rudder trim tab

73 Trim tab control gear
74 Rudder and elevator control horns
75 Fuselage tail fairing
76 Elevator trim tab
77 Port elevator construction
78 Fabric covered elevator
79 Leading-edge pneumatic de-icing boot
80 Tailplane construction
81 Tailplane attachment joint
82 Rudder stop cables
83 Tailplane centre section
84 Tailwheel
85 Shock absorber leg strut
86 Tailwheel mounting plate
87 Tailwheel strut
88 Rudder and elevator control cables
89 Tail fuselage joint frame
90 Toilet

91 Rear freight door
92 Forward freight door
93 Paratroop/passenger door
94 Fuselage stringer construction
95 Freight floor
96 Wing root trailing-edge fillet
97 Inboard split trailing-edge flap
98 Flap shroud construction
99 Fuel filler caps
100 Outer wing panel bolted joint
101 Wing panel joint capping strip
102 Outer split trailing-edge flap
103 Port aileron
104 Aileron fabric covering
105 Detachable wing tip joint rib
106 Port navigation light
107 Leading-edge pneumatic de-icing boot
108 Wing stringer construction
109 Rear spar
110 Centre spar
111 Wing rib construction
112 Front spar
113 Leading-edge nose ribs

114 Leading-edge stringers
115 Port landing/taxiing lamp
116 Port mainwheel
117 Main undercarriage rear strut
118 Shock absorber leg strugs
119 Undercarriage knee joints
120 Exhaust pipe
121 Undercarriage bungee cables
122 Engine nacelle fairing
123 Oil tank capacity 29¼ US gal (109 litres)
124 Undercarriage retraction jack
125 Mainwheel well
126 Engine fireproof bulkhead
127 Engine bearer struts
128 Oil cooler
129 Cooling air exit flaps
130 Exhaust collector pipe
131 Engine air intake
132 Engine cowlings
133 Pratt & Whitney R-1830-90C air-cooled 14-cylinder two-row radial engine
134 Propeller hub pitch change mechanism
135 Hamilton Standard constant speed three-bladed propeller

AVIAGRAPHICA

Douglas DC-3, C-47

A Douglas Dakota III of No. 24 Squadron, RAF. The squadron was strictly speaking a communications unit, based at Hendon during World War 2, and flew Dakotas on mail and VIP services to Malta from 1943 onwards.

Douglas C-47 of the small Arkia Israel Inland Airlines Ltd, shown carrying military recognition markings at the time of the Israeli-Egyptian conflict of 1956 (the Suez Crisis).

In the USA, however, Air Transport Command had, between the wars, grown into a sizeable military carrier, albeit to a great extent employing aircraft leased from commercial operators. Indeed it was not until September 1940 that transport aircraft featured significantly in the procurement programme. At this time an order was placed for 545 DC-3s, to be designated C-47 Skytrain. None of these had been delivered at the time of Pearl Harbor when the total transport inventory consisted of about 50 Douglas C-32s, Douglas C-33s and Douglas C-39s – all military versions of the DC-2. By the end of 1941 military orders had been increased by 70 C-47s and nearly 100 C-53s – the US Army's passenger version. In the meantime the USAAC had established the 50th Transport Wing (on 8 January 1941) to administer all transport duties, this being followed by the 51st, 52nd and 53rd in 1942, the 54th, 60th and 61st in 1943, and the 322nd in 1944. Together these Wings comprised a peak total of 32 Groups, in turn comprising over 190 transport squadrons during the war.

The military C-47 differed from the DC-3 principally in its stronger cabin floor and rear fuselage, large loading doors and 1,200-hp (895-kW) Pratt & Whitney R-1830-92 engines. Utility bucket seats along the cabin walls replaced the airline type, window grommets were inserted to permit the use of small-arms in combat, and the all-up weight increased from 25,000 lb (11340 kg) to 29,300 lb (13290 kg).

Production of the C-47 was undertaken at a new plant at Long Beach, California, a total of 953 being completed before production switched to the C-47A, which differed principally in having a 24-volt electrical system in place of the previous 12-volt system. Long Beach could not cope with the quickly increasing military orders, however, and in 1942 a Douglas-operated plant at Tulsa, Oklahoma, joined the programme, producing 2,099 C-47s while Long Beach completed 2,832. The third major production version was the C-47B, characterized by R-1830-90 or Dash-90B engines with superchargers and extra fuel (originally intended specifically for flight over the 'Hump' in the China-Burma-India theatre); of this variant Long Beach built 300 and Tulsa, 2,808, plus 133 TC-47B trainers with Dash-90C engines. Almost all the 600-odd US Navy R4D Skytrain and Skytrooper transports procured during the war were diverted from US Army contracts, and acquired sub-designations under the overall designation R4D.

In service the C-47 went wherever Allied troops served, being among the first to cross to the UK after the USA's entry to the war. In 1942 Troop Carrier Command was formed to provide mobility for airborne forces, and as a result the C-47

assumed the roles of paratroop transport and glider tug. In the first major Allied airborne assault, the invasion of Sicily in July 1943, C-47s (with a handful of other aircraft types) dropped 4,381 paratroops; in the massive assault on Normandy in June the following year C-47s carried more than 50,000 airborne troops in the first 50 hours.

In the RAF the C-47 and its derivatives were named Dakota (the choice of name being alliterative rather than geographically significant), the Dakota I corresponding to the C-47, the Dakota II to the C-53, the Dakota III to the C-47A and the Dakota IV to the C-47B. Some 1,895 aircraft served with 25 RAF squadrons, first joining No. 31 Squadron on the Burma front in June 1942. It remained with that service until 1950, when it was replaced by the Vickers Valetta.

As transport demands increased, so variations of the basic C-47 proliferated. A float-equipped amphibian, the XC-47C (42-5671) was produced with twin Edo floats each accommodating two retractable wheels and a 300-US gal (1136-litre) fuel tank. The impressed DC-3s were all accorded distinct US Army designations to distinguish between those equipped as 21-seat or 14-berth aircraft, variations in sub-type of Twin Wasp or Cyclone engines, entry and loading door configuration (some had doors on the starboard side of the fuselage), and all-up weight limitations. Most of these ex-airliners were retained for staff transport purposes so as to avoid maintenance and operating complications on the operational squadrons. The ex-DC-3s were designated C-48 to C-52 (with many sub-variants), while the C-53 Skytrooper included not only 193 impressed DC-3s but also many new-built aircraft to airliner standard. The two C-68s were late model DC-3s impressed in 1942, but the four C-84s were early 28-seat DC-3Bs with Wright R-1820-71 engines. The C-117 was a Tulsa-built VIP transport version with 28 seats in an airliner-style cabin; only 17 were completed of a contract for 131 (the remainder being cancelled after VJ-day), some of them having their superchargers removed and being given the designation C-117B. Eleven VC-47 staff transports were restyled C-117Cs, and as late as 1962 were serving as VC-117As and VC-117Bs. Finally there was a strange experiment involving the conversion of a C-47 (41-18496) to a glider, the XCG-17, in an attempt to produce a suitable vehicle for towing behind a C-54 Skymaster.

After the war many Skytrains and Skytroopers were declared surplus and sold to civil operators at home and abroad. The superchargers were removed from the C-47Bs, these aircraft becoming C-47Ds, service staff transports being designated VC-47As and VC-47Ds. When the Military Air Transport Service (MATS) was formed on 1 June 1948, 248

This Douglas C-47 Dakota is still in use, over 50 years after the first flight by this sturdy aircraft type, flying between Antigua and neighbouring islands for Seagreen Air Transport.

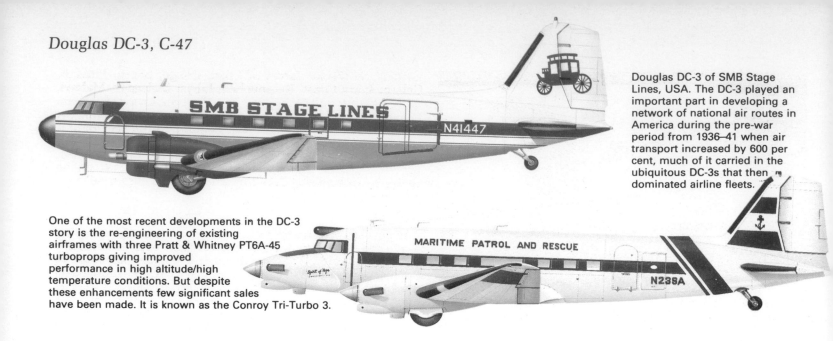

Douglas DC-3 of SMB Stage Lines, USA. The DC-3 played an important part in developing a network of national air routes in America during the pre-war period from 1936–41 when air transport increased by 600 per cent, much of it carried in the ubiquitous DC-3s that then dominated airline fleets.

One of the most recent developments in the DC-3 story is the re-engineering of existing airframes with three Pratt & Whitney PT6A-45 turboprops giving improved performance in high altitude/high temperature conditions. But despite these enhancements few significant sales have been made. It is known as the Conroy Tri-Turbo 3.

C-47s were taken on charge, including a batch of SC-47Bs and SC-47Ds equipped to carry a lifeboat for sea rescue. A total of 105 C-47s operated with MATS during the Berlin Airlift of 1948.

During the Korean War Combat Cargo Command of the USAF employed C-47s to drop and supply parachute forces, while RC-47Ds, were used for flare dropping during night bombing raids. In 1953 26 aircraft were modified as AC-47Ds for use by MATS to check air-ways navigation aids.

Service with the US Navy ...

As mentioned above, the C-47 and its derivatives served with the US Navy as the R4D. The R4D-1 with R-1830-82 engines corresponded to the early C-47; two R4D-2s (equivalent to the C-49) were staff transports, later styled R4D-2F and R4D-2Z, and were the only R4Ds with Wright R-1820 engines. The R4D-3 and R4D-4 matched the US Army's C-53 and C-53C Skytrooper, while the US Navy's principal cargo variant was the R4D-5 with Dash-92 engines and 24-volt system, corresponding to the C-47A. The R4D-6 was equivalent to the C-47B with Dash-90B engines, and the R4D-7 to the TC-47B trainer.

Immediately after Pearl Harbor the Naval Air Transport Service came into being, almost exclusively equipped with R4Ds, and Squadrons VR-1, VR-2 and VR-3 were soon flying naval and marine personnel on quasi-airline schedules throughout the Pacific theatre. US Marine Corps paratroops were flown on combat missions in R4D-3s and R4D-5s.

All manner of technical duties demanded special US Navy variations, radio and radar countermeasures being undertaken by the R4D-4Q, R4D-5Q and R4D-6Q, electronic warfare by the R4D-5E and R4D-6E, Antarctic operation by the ski-equipped R4D-5L and R4D-6L, and navigation training by the R4D-5T and R4D-6T. Other versions of this remarkable aircraft included the R4D-5S and R4D-6S air-sea warfare trainers and the R4D-5Z and R4D-6Z (and R3D-2Z already mentioned) staff transports.

The other major US Navy variant was the R4D-8 which materialized from Douglas' venture to modernize the DC-3 as the Super DC-3 after the war, with swept-back, angular wings, lengthened and strengthened fuselage, enlarged tail, uprated R-1820-80 engines and deepened engine nacelles. Some 98 conversions from earlier R4Ds were authorized, and these appeared in R4D-8L (winterized), R4D-8T (trainer) and R4D-8Z (staff transport) versions, while in Korea the US Marine Corps night fighter squadron VMF(N)-513 flew R4D-8s as flare droppers on close support missions.

... and other forces

Dakotas (to use their RAF name) served with the British Commonwealth air forces during World War 2, being flown by Nos 33, 34, 36 and 38 Squadrons of the Royal Australian Air Force in the Far East; Nos 435, 436 and 437 Squadrons of the Royal Canadian Air Force; and Nos 40 and 41 Squadrons of the Royal New Zealand Air Force. Many of their aircraft continued to serve in the post-war services, No. 38 Squadron of the RAAF flying operational sorties in Malaya, and No. 91 Wing, RAAF, in Korea. Ex-USAAF C-47s and derivatives were supplied to the air forces of Argentina, Belgium, Bolivia, Brazil, Burma, Cambodia, Chile, Nationalist China, Colombia, Cuba, Denmark, Ecuador, Egypt, Ethiopia, France, West Germany, Greece, Guatemala, Haiti, Honduras,

The cockpit of one of the oldest DC-3s still in use, built in 1937. It has 85,000 hours on the clock and belongs to Air BVI (British Virgin Islands) and still looks in good condition.

Brainchild of Captain Ronald Terry at the USAF Aeronautical Systems Division, the AC-47 gunships of the 1st Special Operations Wing carried a number of laterally-firing multi-barrel guns with which to saturate jungle targets in Vietnam as the aircraft circled slowly overhead.

India, Indonesia, Iran, Israel, Italy, South Korea, Laos, Mexico, Netherlands, Norway, Nicaragua, Paraguay, Peru, Philippines, Portugal, Rhodesia, Salvador, Saudi Arabia, South Africa, Spain, Sweden, Syria, Thailand, Turkey, Uruguay, Venezuela, Vietnam, Yemen and Yugoslavia. Russian-built Li-2s were also provided for the air forces of Bulgaria, Communist China, Czechoslovakia, Hungary, North Korea, Mongolia, Poland and Romania. To these should be added aircraft supplied during the past 30 years, either by the USA or from surplus stocks held by the above

nations, to the air forces of Chad, Congo, Benin, Finland, Gabon, Ivory Coast, Kampuchea, Libya, Malagasy, Malawi, Mali, Mauretania, Morocco, Niger, Nigeria, Oman, Pakistan, Panama, Papua/New Guinea, Rwanda, Senegal, Somalia, Sri Lanka, Togo, Uganda, Zaire and Zambia. At the last count it was estimated that more than 2,200 C-47s (etc) were still performing quasi-military duties outside the United States, not to mention the many commercial DC-3s still giving useful service among the smaller airlines of the world.

Vietnam

It is perhaps also worth mentioning that a handful of ageing C-47s are still being used by the US Air Force, particularly for shuttle flights. The aircraft made a notable comeback in 1972 after the delivery of the military AC-47, nicknamed 'Puff the Magic Dragon', for use at the air support base at Ton Son Nut. This version had three rapid-firing 7.62-mm 'miniguns' on swivel mounts on the port side of the cabin and was used by a special activity group of the US Air Force for overflying jungle targets: the on-board gunners would spray the area concerned with a veritable hail of bullets from their miniguns. This method was also used later on by newer, more heavily-armed aircraft. The EC-47 was used by tactical electronic warfare squadrons for radio monitoring purposes, and the EC-47Q was so laden down with electronic defence equipment that it could only get off the ground using more powerful Pratt & Whitney R-2000 engines. Of the total of nearly 13,000 machines built, there are now, half a century after the DC-3's first flight, nearly 700 still in use for both civil and military purposes. In short-distance transport and as a supply plane, it is still very much holding its own. It has become a legend in its own time.

An example of the vast spectrum of duties undertaken by the ubiquitous DC-3 is afforded by this aircraft operated by the Finnish company Kar-Air for geophysical survey duties featuring sensors in nose, wings and tail.

Douglas DC-3/C-47 variants

DST: prototype plus six aircraft in initial production batch, plus 18 built subsequently; majority for American Airlines; Wright Cyclone engines
DST/DC-3: mix of 14-berth, and 18- or 21-seat aircraft built 1936–7; 13 aircraft for TWA; Cyclone or twin Wasp engines
DC-3: commercial airliner to individual furnishing requirements; 417 aircraft, many subsequently commandeered for military use
C-41(DC-3-253): only one, modified from DC-2(38-502)
C-41A(DC-3-253A): only one, equivalent to luxury DC-3 for 23 passengers (40–70)
C-47: 953 aircraft for War Department built at Long Beach; 12-volt system. Twin Wasp engines (41-7722/7866; -18337/18699; -38564/38763; 42-5635/5704; -32768/32923; 43-30628/36639; 49-2612/2641 for Greece post-war; among these were 106 US Navy **R4D-1s** 3131-3143; 4692-4706; 01648-01649; 01977-01990; 05051-68687/89, -1074222, 44-83228/29)
C-49J: 34 R-1820-71 powered ex-DC-3s fitted as troopers with side seating (43-1961/94)
C-49K: 23 R-1820-71 powered ex-DC-3s fitted as troopers with side seating (43-1995/-2017)
C-50: designation applied to ex-DC-3s with minor variations in interiors and engine powers; four R-1820-85-powered aircraft (41-7697/7700)
C-50A: two aircraft similar to above but fitted as troopers (41-7710/11)
C-50B: three R-1820-81 powered ex-DC-3s with starboard door (41-7703/05)
C-50C: one R-1820-79 powered ex-DC-3 (41-7695)
C-50D: four R-1820-79 powered ex-DC-3s fitted as troopers (41-7696, -7709, 7712/13)
C-51: one R-1820-83 powered ex-DC-3 (41-7702)
C-52: one Pratt & Whitney R-1830-51 powered ex-DC-3 with 27,700-lb (12565-kg) all-up weight (41-7708)
C-52A: one R-1830-51 powered ex-DC-3 (41-7714)

C-52B: two R-1830-51 powered ex-DC-3s fitted as troopers (41-7706/07)
C-52C: one R-1830-51 powered ex-DC-3 (41-7701)
C-53: named Skytrooper, 193 impressed aircraft and 16 new-build aircraft, all powered by Pratt & Whitney R-1830-92 engines (41-20045/46, -20051, -20053, -20060, -20136, 42-6455/79, -6481/-6504, -15530/69, -15870/94, -47371/82, 43-14404/05; included 20 **R4D-3** for US Navy 05073-05084, 06992-06999)
SX-53A: one prototype with full span slotted flaps (42-6480) and 15 production **C-53A** examples (42-6455/79)
C-53B: five ex-airline long-range DC-3s (41-20047, 20052, 20057/59)
C-53C: 17 ex-DC-3s fitted as troopers with side seats (43-2018/34; included 10 **R4D-4** for US Navy, 07000-07003, 33815-33820)
C-53D: similar to C-53C; 159 aircraft (42-68693/851)
C-68: two 21-seat ex-DC3s impressed in 1942 with Wright R-1820-92 engines (42-14297/98)
C-84: four 1937-type DC-3b 28 seat airliners with R-1820-71 engines (42-57157, 42-57511/13)
C-117A: 17 Tulsa-built military airliner-style aircraft completed in 1945 with R-1830-90C supercharged engines; some converted to **C-117B** (45-2545/61); **C-117C** designation covered 11 **VC-47C** staff transport conversions which later became **VC-117A**s and **VC-117B**s
05072; 12393-12404; 30147; 37660-37685; 91104)
C-47A; 4,931 aircraft built at Long Beach and Tulsa; 24-volt system (42-23300/24419; -32924/32935; -92024/93158; -93160/93823; -100436/101035; -108794/108993; 43-15033/16132; -30640/30761; -47963/48262; among these were 248 US Navy **R4D-5s** 12405-12446; 17092-17248; 39057-39095)
C-47B: 3,241 aircraft built at Long Beach and Tulsa with supercharged R-1830-90 or -90B engines; included 133 TC-47B trainers (42-93159; 43-16133/16432; -48263/

49962; 44-76195/77294; 45-876/1139; among these were 147 **R4D-6s** for US Navy 17249-17291; 39096-39098; 39100; 50740-50752; 50753-50839, and 43 **R4D-7s** 39099, 39101-39108; 99824-99857)
YC-47F: prototype Super DC-3 (51-3817) originally termed **YC-129**; transferred to US Navy as prototype **R4D-8**
C-48: designation applied to 36 DC-3s impressed from US airlines in 1941; all with R-1830 engines and maximum all-up weight of 26,850-lb (12179 kg); one C-48 21-seater (41,7681); three **C-48A** 18-seaters (41-7682/4); 16 **C-48B** 14-berth DSTs (42-38324/26, 42-56089/91, 42-56098/102, 42-56609/12, 42-56629); 16 **C-48C** 21 seat DC-3s with R-1830-51 engines (42-38327, 42-38332/38, 42-38358/60, 42-78026/28)
C-49: designation applied to six impressed Wright R-1820-powered DC-3s (41-7685/89, 41-7694; two of these

became US Navy **R4D-2F** and **R4D-2Z** VIP transports)
C-49A: one R-1820-powered ex-DC3 (41-7690)
C-49B: three R-1820-powered ex-DC-3s with seating variation and starboard entry door (41-7691/93)
C-49C: two R-1820-powered ex-DC-3s fitted as troopers with side seats (41-7715 and 41-7721)
C-49D: 12 R-1820-71-powered ex-DC-3s fitted as troopers with side seats (41-7716/20, 42-38256,-43624, -65583/84,-68860, 44-52999)
C-49E: 23 R-1820-79-powered ex-DC-3s (42-43619/23, -56092/97,-56103/07,-56617/18,-56625/27,-56634)
C-49F: nine R-1820-71-powered 14-berth ex-DSTs (42-56613,-56616,-56620/21,-56623,-56628,-56633, -56636/37)
C-49G: eight R-1820-97-powered ex-DC-3s (42-38252, -38255,-56614/15,-56630/32,-56635)
C-49H: 19 R-1820-97-powered ex-DC-3/DSTs (42-38250/51,-38253/54,-38257,-38328/31,-57506,-65580/82)

Quetzalcoatl, the feathered snake-god of the Toltecs, creates a very unusual green and brown livery on the fuselage of this DC-3 belonging to a club in Fort Lauderdale, Florida.

Hawker Hurricane

Never displaying the glamour of Mitchell's immortal Spitfire, Sydney Camm's Hurricane nevertheless represented the vital instrument on which the RAF's newly formed Fighter Command cut its teeth during the 18 months before World War 2. It was the RAF's first eight-gun monoplane fighter and the first to exceed 300 mph.

The Hawker Hurricane came into being in 1933, as a result of specification no. F.7/30, which did not represent the most up-to-date technology. It was an attempt to bring out a new monoplane version of the Hawker Fury biplane. But the aircraft builder, Sydney Camm, was limping along a whole generation behind the monocoque construction method which Mitchell consistently used for the Spitfire. In fact it was due to precisely the simple construction of the Hurricane that it made such a good showing in the hectic months of 1939 and 1940, when RAF fighters had to fly and fight in extremely primitive conditions, for it sustained considerable damage but was easy to repair.

The first Hurricane (K5083) was flown from Brooklands on 6 November 1935 by the late Group Captain P. W. S. Bulman. Powered by a 1,025-hp (764-kW) Rolls-Royce Merlin 'C' 12-cylinder liquid-cooled inline engine, developed from the private-venture PV-12, the prototype weighed 5,420 lb (2460 kg) all-up and featured a two-blade wooden Watts propeller; its top speed was 315 mph (507 km/h) at 15,000 ft (4575 m).

As production of the first 600 Hurricanes, ordered in June 1936, built up during 1937 (albeit somewhat delayed by abandonment of the Merlin I in favour of the Merlin II, necessitating alterations to the nose contours), the wing-mounted eight-Browning gun battery was confirmed and minor alterations were made to the airframe, including an improved radiator bath, a strengthened hood canopy and the discarding of tailplane struts.

Initial service deliveries were made to No. 111 (Fighter) Squadron at Northolt before the end of 1937, and the next year Nos 3 and 56 Squadrons followed suit. Early spinning trials disclosed a need to increase keel area, provided by a ventral fairing added forward of the fixed tailwheel, and by a 3-in (7.62-cm) downward extension of the rudder.

Within the limitations imposed by the basic airframe structure and by the desperate need to accelerate production in the threatening international climate, little could be done initially to improve the Hurricane I before the outbreak of war. However, the fixed-pitch wooden propeller was replaced by a two-position, three-blade de Havilland metal propeller, and later by a Rotol constant-speed propeller – the latter bestowing much improved climb and performance at altitude. These alterations were made possible by the arrival of the 1,030-hp (768-kW) Merlin III with universal propeller shaft. Metal-covered wings also appeared in production by 1939.

By the outbreak of war a total of 497 Hurricane Is had been completed for the RAF, and 18 home-based fighter squadrons had taken deliveries. Some export orders had been authorized to friendly nations, these including Yugoslavia (12, plus licence production), South Africa (7), Romania (12), Canada (20), Persia (2), Poland (1), Belgium (20, plus licence production) and Turkey (15). Plans were

Amid the dust and sand of the Western Desert, which not only reduced visibility but caused severe wear to aircraft engines, these Hurricane IID anti-tank fighters of No. 6 Squadron taxi out for take-off at Sidi Bu Amud in January 1943 during the rout of the Afrika Korps which followed the 2nd Battle of Alamein.

This Hawker Hurricane belongs to the Battle of Britain Flight, a group of enthusiasts who re-enact scenes from the Battle of Britain at air displays. *(Photo: Air Portraits)*

Hawker Hurricane

Specification

Hawker Hurricane Mk I
Type: single-seat interceptor fighter
Powerplant: one 1,030-hp (768-kW) Rolls-Royce
Merlin III inline iston engine
Performance: maximum speed 318 mph (511 km/h)
at 18,000 feet (5500 m); initial climb rate 2,520 ft
(770 m) per minute; service ceiling 36,000 ft (10970 m);
maximum range 460 miles (740 km)
Weights: empty 4,670 lb (2118 kg); maximum take-off
6,600 lb (2994 kg)
Dimensions: span 40 ft 0 in (12.20 m); length
31 ft 4 in (9.59 m); height 12 ft 11½ in (3.96 m); wing
area 257.6 sq ft (23.93 m²)
Armament: eight 0.303-in (7.7-mm) Browning
machine-guns with 2,660 rounds of ammunition

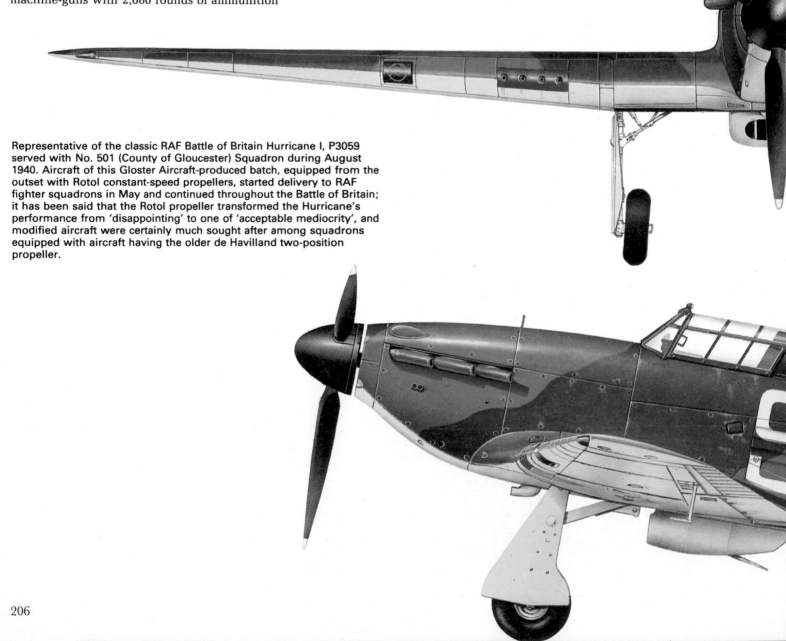

Representative of the classic RAF Battle of Britain Hurricane I, P3059
served with No. 501 (County of Gloucester) Squadron during August
1940. Aircraft of this Gloster Aircraft-produced batch, equipped from the
outset with Rotol constant-speed propellers, started delivery to RAF
fighter squadrons in May and continued throughout the Battle of Britain;
it has been said that the Rotol propeller transformed the Hurricane's
performance from 'disappointing' to one of 'acceptable mediocrity', and
modified aircraft were certainly much sought after among squadrons
equipped with aircraft having the older de Havilland two-position
propeller.

P3059

Hawker Hurricane

The Hurricane prototype (K5083) in a relatively late photograph of the aircraft being flown by P. G. Lucas in 1937 after removal of tailplane struts, installation of gunsight, modification to the radiator bath and with additional strengthening members on the cockpit canopy.

well advanced to create another production line at the Gloster Aircraft Company, and tooling up to produce Hurricanes at the Canadian Car and Foundry Company at Montreal was under way (a total of 1,451 Hurricanes was built in Canada during the war). In 1941 the Austin Motor Company, Longbridge, also produced 300 Hurricanes.

Into successful action

Four Hurricane I squadrons (Nos 1, 73, 85 and 87) accompanied the RAF to France in September 1939, and it was to Pilot Officer P. W. O. Mould of No. 1 Squadron that the first German aircraft, a Dornier Do 17, fell on 30 October. The Hurricane proved able to cope with the primitive airfield conditions in France, principally on account of its sturdy, wide-track landing gear – while the Spitfire was held at home to meet any threat to the British Isles.

By 1940 Hurricane Is were beginning to roll off the Gloster production line, as well as from the new Hawker factory at Langley, Bucks. A Hurricane squadron, No. 46, served at Narvik during the last days of the Norwegian campaign but all its aircraft were lost when the carrier HMS *Glorious* was sunk while bringing them home. Over Dunkirk, and in the closing stages of the Battle of France, Hurricanes were in constant action against the Luftwaffe, and those of the

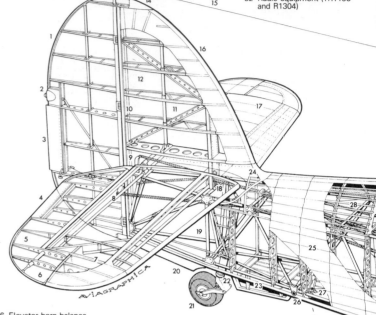

Hawker Sea Hurricane II cutaway drawing key

1 Fabric-covered rudder construction
2 Tail navigation light
3 Rudder tab
4 Elevator tab
5 Fabric-covered elevator construction
6 Elevator horn balance
7 Tailplane construction
8 Rudder control horn
9 Elevator hinge control
10 Sternpost
11 Tailfin construction
12 Fabric covering
13 Rear aerial mast
14 Rudder balance weight
15 Aerial cable
16 Tailfin aluminium leading edge
17 Port tailplane
18 Control cable pulleys
19 Port access panel to tailplane controls
20 Ventral fin
21 Tailwheel
22 Dowty shock absorber tailwheel strut
23 Fin framework
24 Fin/tailplane root fillet
25 Fuselage fabric covering
26 Lifting bar socket
27 Arresting hook latches
28 Dorsal stringers
29 Fuselage diagonal wire bracing
30 Upper longeron
31 Aluminium alloy fuselage frames
32 Bolted joint fuselage tubular construction
33 Deck arrest hook
34 Arresting hook pivot point
35 Bottom longeron
36 Arresting hook damper
37 Wooden dorsal fairing formers
38 Aerial mast
39 Upper identification light
40 Upward firing recognition flare launcher
41 Tailplane control cables
42 Fuselage access panel
43 Ventral stringers
44 Trailing edge wing root fillet
45 Downward identification light
46 Radio racks
47 Radio equipment (R3002 and R3108)
48 Parachute flare launch tube
49 Sliding canopy track
50 Canopy rear fairing construction
51 Turn-over crash pylon struts
52 Radio equipment (TR1196 and R1304)
53 Radio equipment (TR1143 and TR1133)
54 Battery
55 Oxygen bottle
56 Hydraulic system equipment
57 Dinghy stowage
58 Seat back armour plate
59 Head armour
60 Rearward sliding canopy cover
61 Canopy framework
62 Safety harness
63 Pilot's seat
64 Seat adjusting lever
65 Fuselage/wing spar attachment joint
66 Ventral oil and coolant radiator
67 Position of flap hydraulic jack (fitted on port side only)
68 Gun heater air duct
69 Inboard flap housing
70 Trailing edge ribs
71 Outer wing anel rear spar joint
72 Breech-block access covers

The Sea Hurricane IB was a conversion of the RAF's Mk I, and this Fleet Air Arm version featured catapult spools, arrester hook and naval radio. The Gloster-built aircraft shown here features exhaust glare shields forward of the windscreen. Sea Hurricanes were in constant action in the Mediterranean, particularly in 1942.

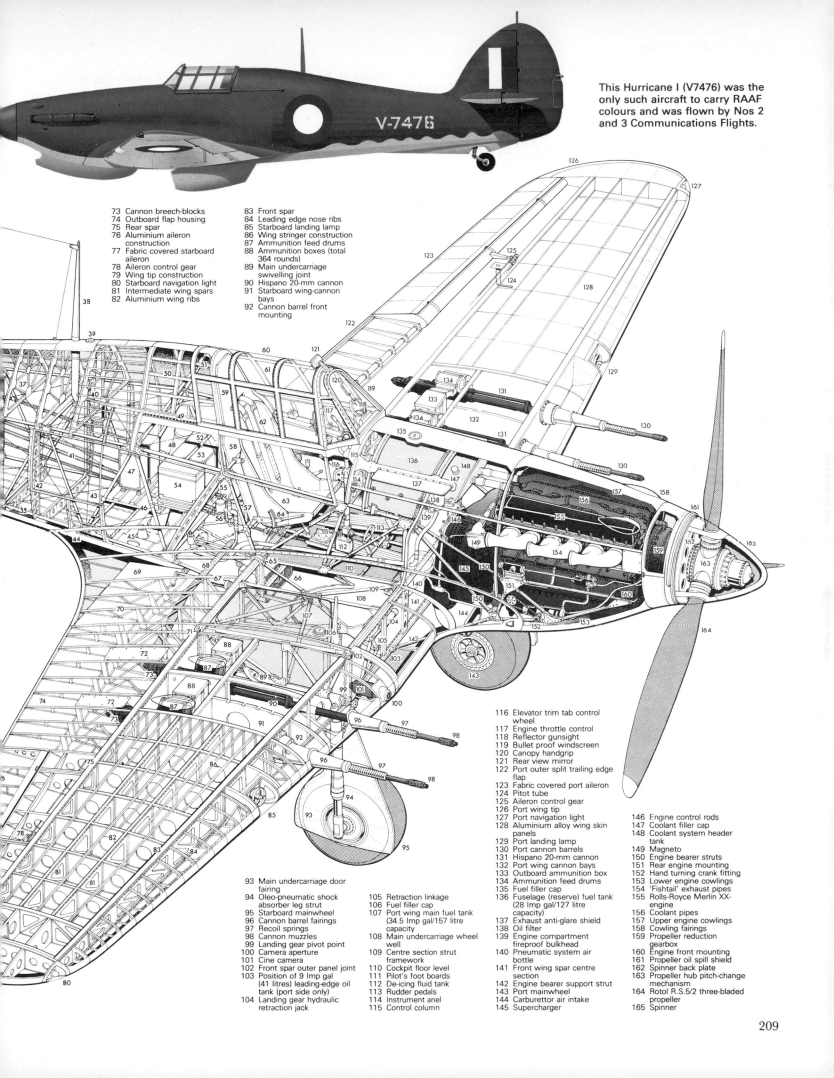

This Hurricane I (V7476) was the only such aircraft to carry RAAF colours and was flown by Nos 2 and 3 Communications Flights.

73 Cannon breech-blocks
74 Outboard flap housing
75 Rear spar
76 Aluminium aileron construction
77 Fabric covered starboard aileron
78 Aileron control gear
79 Wing tip construction
80 Starboard navigation light
81 Intermediate wing spars
82 Aluminium wing ribs

83 Front spar
84 Leading edge nose ribs
85 Starboard landing lamp
86 Wing stringer construction
87 Ammunition feed drums
88 Ammunition boxes (total 364 rounds)
89 Main undercarriage swivelling joint
90 Hispano 20-mm cannon
91 Starboard wing-cannon bays
92 Cannon barrel front mounting

93 Main undercarriage door fairing
94 Oleo-pneumatic shock absorber leg strut
95 Starboard mainwheel
96 Cannon barrel fairings
97 Recoil springs
98 Cannon muzzles
99 Landing gear pivot point
100 Camera aperture
101 Cine camera
102 Front spar outer panel joint
103 Position of 9 Imp gal (41 litres) leading-edge oil tank (port side only)
104 Landing gear hydraulic retraction jack

105 Retraction linkage
106 Fuel filler cap
107 Port wing main fuel tank (34.5 Imp gal/157 litre capacity
108 Main undercarriage wheel well
109 Centre section strut framework
110 Cockpit floor level
111 Pilot's foot boards
112 De-icing fluid tank
113 Rudder pedals
114 Instrument anel
115 Control column

116 Elevator trim tab control wheel
117 Engine throttle control
118 Reflector gunsight
119 Bullet proof windscreen
120 Canopy handgrip
121 Rear view mirror
122 Port outer split trailing edge flap
123 Fabric covered port aileron
124 Pitot tube
125 Aileron control gear
126 Port wing tip
127 Port navigation light
128 Aluminium alloy wing skin panels
129 Port landing lamp
130 Port cannon barrels
131 Hispano 20-mm cannon
132 Port wing cannon bays
133 Outboard ammunition box
134 Ammunition feed drums
135 Fuel filler cap
136 Fuselage (reserve) fuel tank (28 Imp gal/127 litre capacity)
137 Exhaust anti-glare shield
138 Oil filter
139 Engine compartment fireproof bulkhead
140 Pneumatic system air bottle
141 Front wing spar centre section
142 Engine bearer support strut
143 Port mainwheel
144 Carburettor air intake
145 Supercharger

146 Engine control rods
147 Coolant filler cap
148 Coolant system header tank
149 Magneto
150 Engine bearer struts
151 Rear engine mounting
152 Hand turning crank fitting
153 Lower engine cowlings
154 'Fishtail' exhaust pipes
155 Rolls-Royce Merlin XX-engine
156 Coolant pipes
157 Upper engine cowlings
158 Cowling fairings
159 Propeller reduction gearbox
160 Engine front mounting
161 Propeller oil spill shield
162 Spinner back plate
163 Propeller hub pitch-change mechanism
164 Rotol R.S.5/2 three-bladed propeller
165 Spinner

209

Ninth production Hurricane I
(L1555) of No. 111 (Fighter)
Squadron, Northolt, December
1937. Carrying the Co's pennant,
this aircraft was flown by
Squadron Leader John
('Downwind') Gillan. Note the
absence of ventral fin fairing that
was added in 1938 and was a
characteristic of the Hurricane in
later years.

Dramatic dusk launch of a Sea Hurricane IA from the bow-mounted
catapult of a merchant ship. Introduced to provide Allied convoys with on-
the-spot fighter defence against enemy aircraft, the catapult Sea
Hurricanes enjoyed limited success in 1941; with nowhere to go, the pilot
was forced to bale out or ditch in the hope he would be fished out of the
sea by a passing ship.

small Belgian air force suffered almost total destruction.

The Hurricane I provided Fighter Command's mainstay in
the Battle of Britain, equipping a maximum of 32 squadrons
(compared with 18½ of Spitfires) between July and October
1940, no fewer than 2,309 having been delivered by 7
August. Top speed of the Rotol-equipped Hurricane I was
328 mph (528 km/h) at 16,500 ft (5030 m), a performance
which fell far short of that of the superlative Messerschmitt
Bf 109E, and it was this shortfall that caused it to be
committed – whenever possible – against enemy bombers
rather than the German single-seaters. The Hurricane proved
to be exceptionally popular among its pilots as a highly
manoeuvrable dogfighter with rock-steady gun-aiming pro-
perties and the tightest of turning radii, which helped
to make the type particularly effective against the heavy
Messerschmitt Bf 110 fighter. It was, however, the extraordinary teamwork between the various elements of the air
defences that won the great battle.

In September 1940, when the battle was still at its height,
the first Hurricane Mk IIs were beginning to appear with the
1,185-hp (883-kW) two-stage supercharged Merlin XX with
Rotol propeller and slightly lengthened nose. Still armed
with eight Browning guns in the Mk IIA Series 1 version, this
Hurricane possessed a top speed of 342 mph (550 km/h). The
Mk IIA Series 2 introduced pick-up points for a 'universal'
wing capable of mounting 44-Imp gal (200-litre) underwing
fuel tanks; this variant was originally developed to enable
Hurricanes to be supplied by air to the Middle East, but the
fall of France ended this venture after fewer than a dozen
aircraft had attempted the flight. Hurricane IIAs were also

capable of carrying a pair of 250-lb (113-kg) bombs under
the wings and were flown on offensive sweeps across the
English Channel early in 1941.

The Hurricane IIB introduced a new 12-Browning gun
wing (as well as retaining the bomb shackles) and came to be
known as the Hurribomber, while the Mk IIC featured an
armament of four 20-mm Oerlikon/Hispano cannon – at that
time (mid-1941) still regarded as an extraordinary armament
for a single-seater (although one such Hurricane had been
fought experimentally in the Battle of Britain with limited
success). These two sub-variants equipped no fewer than 96
RAF squadrons during 1941–4 and saw continuous action in
northern Europe, North Africa and the Far East, being
employed principally in the ground attack role. They also
played a significant part in the Greek, Iraqi, Syrian
and Malayan campaigns. Last of the Merlin XX-powered
Hurricanes was the Mk IID, introduced in 1942, with a 40-
mm Vickers or Rolls-Royce anti-tank gun under each wing.
Although a small number of this variant remained home-
based, the majority was shipped to the Western Desert
(where the type played a major part in the Battle of Bir
Hakeim) and later to Burma. Following early experience in
the Western Desert, whose abrasive dust and sand wrought
havoc with aero engines, all Hurricanes supplied to the
Middle and Far Eastern theatres were fitted with Vokes air
filters over their carburettor intakes, an ungainly but
necessary modification which reduced performance by some
8 per cent.

The Hurricane II remained the principal variant in service
during the war, eventually providing the major ground-
attack element of the RAF in the Far East. A total of 2,952

Hurricane IIC night-fighter of No. 87 (Fighter) Squadron being flown by
Sqdn Ldr D. G. Smallwood, DSO, DFC; note the CO's pennant aft of the
exhaust glare shield. No. 87 Squadron, which flew Hurricane IICs from
June 1941 until March 1944, was one of the longest-serving Hurricane
night-fighter squadrons in the RAF.

Hurricanes was supplied to the Soviet Union, of which all but about 30 were Mk IIs or their Canadian-built equivalents. The majority was shipped as deck cargo on the North Cape convoys (and suffered heavy losses accordingly), though many were also supplied from Middle East stocks. Another important duty undertaken by the Mk II was night fighting, at one time participating in the almost fruitless Turbinlite venture over the UK but also serving as night intruders over France and Belgium during 1941 and 1942 until this task was taken over almost exclusively by the Bristol Beaufighter and de Havilland Mosquito.

Final variant for the RAF was the Hurricane IV (the Mk III was an unbuilt project intended to introduce the Packard-built Merlin 28 into the Hawker production line). This version, originally termed the Mark IIE, featured the 1,280-hp (954-kW) Merlin 24 or 27 and a new universal wing capable of mounting anti-tank guns, rocket projectiles or other external stores. Owing to the need for only limited airframe modifications, many Mk IIs were converted to accommodate the new wing and, with new engine, remained in service with the RAF until after the war. The final Hurricane built for the RAF, a Mark IIC (LF363), was delivered to No. 309 (Polish) Squadron in February 1944, while the last of all to be built (also a Mark IIC, PZ865), was purchased by the manufacturers and survives to this day.

When the Hawker Hurricane Mk IIC was fitted with four Oerlikon/Hispano 20 mm cannons it was somewhat unprecedented and gave the fighter an awesome punch against enemy aircraft and ground armour. Approximately 3,400 of this model were built.

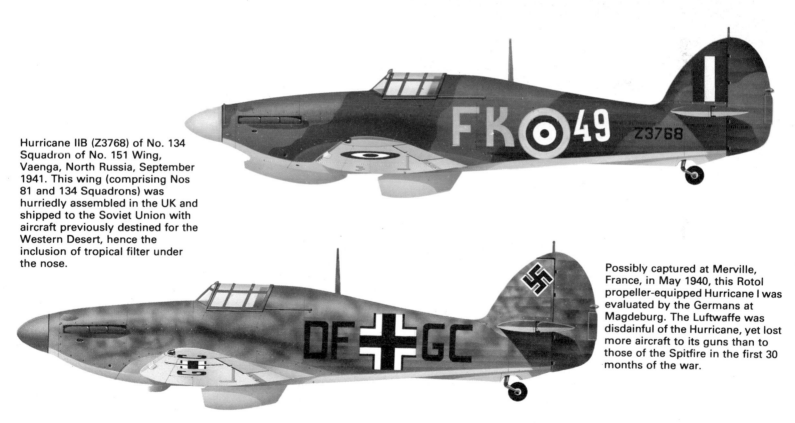

Hurricane IIB (Z3768) of No. 134 Squadron of No. 151 Wing, Vaenga, North Russia, September 1941. This wing (comprising Nos 81 and 134 Squadrons) was hurriedly assembled in the UK and shipped to the Soviet Union with aircraft previously destined for the Western Desert, hence the inclusion of tropical filter under the nose.

Possibly captured at Merville, France, in May 1940, this Rotol propeller-equipped Hurricane I was evaluated by the Germans at Magdeburg. The Luftwaffe was disdainful of the Hurricane, yet lost more aircraft to its guns than to those of the Spitfire in the first 30 months of the war.

Total production of the Hurricane amounted to 14,231, including those produced in Canada. In addition the extensive repair organization, created in 1939, returned 4,537 repaired Hurricanes to the RAF.

Sea Hurricanes

Loss of the French Atlantic seaboard in 1940 exposed the vital British convoys to increasing action by long-range German bombers such as the Heinkel He 111 and Focke-Wulf Fw 200, and it was decided to adapt the Hurricane I for catapulting from merchant ships (CAM-ships) to provide some measure of protection against this menace. The first such variant, the Sea Hurricane IA, was a simple adaptation of ex-RAF Hurricane Is to feature catapult spools. Limited success attended these operations in 1941, for it was intended that, once launched, the 'Hurricat' pilot had no alternative after action but to ditch his aircraft or make a forlorn search for land.

The next venture was to convert a number of merchantmen (MACs) to provide a small flight deck from which Sea Hurricane Mk IBs might operate, and these aircraft featured

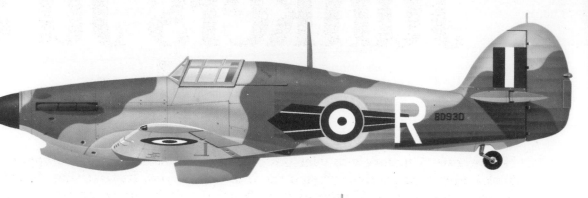

Unofficially adorned with peacetime squadron flash, this tropicalized Hurricane IIB (BD930) was flown by No. 73 Squadron in the Western Desert in 1942. Veteran of the French campaign and Battle of Britain, No. 73 Squadron was rushed to the Middle East to meet the crisis of 1940, becoming separated from its ground crews and losing many aircraft en route.

A No. 6 Squadron Hurricane IID with 40-mm anti-tank guns, based at LG89 and LG91 in the Western Desert, July 1942. First to receive this Hurricane version, No. 6 Squadron played a major part in destroying enemy vehicles in the desert during the months immediately prior to the decisive 2nd Battle of Alamein.

an arrester hook. A third version, the Sea Hurricane Mk IC, carried the four-cannon armament but was still powered by the Merlin III. It was followed by a full conversion of the Hurricane IIC, the Sea Hurricane IIC with Merlin XX, four-cannon wing, catapult spools, arrester hook, underwing store provision and naval radio. It possessed a top speed of 318 mph (512 km/h) at 17,500 ft (5340 m), a service ceiling of 30,500 ft (9300 m) and a maximum range of 1,062 miles (1710 km). It was withdrawn from service at sea in October 1943.

At one time, late in 1942, the Fleet Air Arm held on charge a total of more than 600 Sea Hurricanes, and almost every fleet and escort carrier of the Royal Navy at one time or another mustered at least a partial complement of these aircraft. One of their most memorable actions was fought over the Malta convoy of August 1942 when Sea Hurricanes from HMS *Indomitable*, *Eagle* and *Victorious* beat off attacks by 600 Axis aircraft, destroying 39 for the loss of seven of their own number.

Although RAF Hurricanes were relegated to second-line duties at home from mid-1944 onwards, particularly in the training role and on meterological and radar calibration work, Hurricane IIs and IVs remained in first line service in the Mediterranean and Far East theatres until 1945, providing outstanding support for the 14th Army's advance through Burma in the latter theatre.

Many experiments were carried out on Hurricanes between 1939 and 1945, mostly aimed at increasing the theatre-reinforcement capabilities (i.e. ferry range); these experiments included the carriage of a jettisonable auxiliary upper wing (the Hillson Bi-Mono project), pickaback trials aboard a Consolidated B-24 Liberator, and towing trials behind an Avro Lancaster. Other trials included the carriage of outsize rocket projectiles and the fitting of a semi-laminar flow wing. A floatplane version was proposed at the time of the 1940 Norwegian campaign, and skis were fitted to at least one Canadian Hurricane. Alternative engines were proposed from time to time although the only such project believed to

have reached construction was a Yugoslav Hurricane fitted with a Daimler-Benz DB 601A in 1941.

After the war, many Hurricanes were declared surplus to requirements in Britain and many of them were refitted for export. During the war, the Irish Air Corps had acquired a few Mk Is, and from 1945 to 1947 a further 13 aircraft were delivered. In the mid-1940s, Hurricanes were also flying in the Turkish, Egyptian and South African air forces. Around 50 Hurricane IIBs and IICs were sent to Portugal (although some of these were used only as sources of spare parts), and 16 were delivered to Persia to fulfil an order received before the war. A further Hurricane, a unique two-seater trainer converted from a Mk IIC, was also sold to Persia (now Iran) in 1947.

Hawker Hurricane variants

F.36/34 prototype: one aircraft (K5083) with 1,025-hp (764-kw) Merlin C; eight-gun armament fitted later; first flown 6 November 1935

Hurricane I: original production model with 1,030-hp (768-kW) Merlin II or III, eight Browning 0.303-in (7.7-mm) guns; early aircraft with fabric-covered wings, later metal-clad (total 2,719 excluding Canadian-built; about 90 exported)

Canadian Hurricane I: built by Canadian Car and Foundry Co. in Montreal, 1940; Merlin III and DH propellers; batch included Hillson Bi-Mono slip-wing Hurricane (total 40)

Hurricane IIA Series 1: introduced 1,185-hp (883-kW) Merlin XX two-stage supercharged engine in September 1940; eight-gun wing; some converted from Marks Is

Hurricane IIA Series 2: introduced provision for wing stores on Universal wing; some converted from Mark I; included some PR Mk I Conversions and PRMkIIA

Hurricane IIB: introduced 12-Browning gun wing and bomb-tank shackles for 500-lb (227-kg) bombs (total approximately 3,100 built by Hawker, Gloster and Austin, plus many converted from other versions; included the PR Mark IIB)

Hurricane IIC: introduced four 20-mm gun armament in 1941; bomb and drop tank provision; worldwide service; also tropicalized (total approximately 3,400 built by Hawker, Gloster and Austin, plus many conversions)

Hurricane IID: introduced pair of 40-mm Vickers or Rolls-Royce anti-tank guns plus two Brownings in 1942; many tropicalized (total approximately 800 built, plus many conversions)

Hurricane IV: introduced 1,280-hp (954-kW) Merlin 24 or 27 and Universal wing to carry alternative rockets, drop tanks, bombs or anti-tank guns in 1942, many tropicalized (total approximately 2,000 built plus numerous coversions)

Hurricane V: two prototypes (KZ193 and NL255, converted Mark IVs) with ground-boosted Merlin 32 and four-blade Rotol propeller

Canadian Hurricane X: Packard Merlin 28, about 100 with eight-gun wing, remainder with IIB wing; many converted to IIC wing (total 489 built in 1940–1)

Canadian Hurricane XI: 150 aircraft with 12-gun or four-cannon armament; majority shipped to Russia

Canadian Hurricane XII: 248 aircraft with Hurricane IIC modifications; one ski-equipped example

Canadian Hurricane XIIA and Sea Hurricane XIIA: Packard Merlin 29; 150 aircraft shipped principally to Soviet Union and Burma in 1943

Sea Hurricane IA: catapult fighter for CAM-ship operations (50 aircraft converted from Hurricane I, 1941)

Sea Hurricane IB: catapult spools and arrester hook for operations from CAM-ships or MACs (total approximately 340 converted from Hurricane IIA Series 2 in 1941–2)

Sea Hurricane IC: as Sea Hurricane IB but four-cannon armament included (total approximately 400 converted from Hurricane IIB and IIC in 1942–3)

Sea Hurricane IIC: full-standard conversion of Hurricane IIC with hook, spools and naval radio (total approximately 400 converted from Hurricane IIC)

Although it is possible to state the total number of Hurricanes built, no exact records exist – or were ever kept – of the number of each variant owing to ad hoc conversions both by the manufacturers and in the field

Junkers Ju 87 Stuka

No aircraft in history was ever quite so deadly effective (when unopposed) as the infamous Stuka, nor so vulnerable (when it ran into opposition). Its terrifying effect in Poland, Norway, France and the Low Countries was equalled only by its complete failure to survive against RAF Fighter Command a few weeks later.

Virtually no other aircraft struck such terror into the hearts of battle-hardened infantry as the Junkers Ju 87, known as the Stuka (for *Sturzkampfbomber*, or dive bomber). It holds the world record for sinking ships and still today comes second only to the Soviet Ilyushin Il-2 for the number of tanks it destroyed. Its most important feature in battle was its ability to place heavy bomb-loads accurately onto pinpoint targets, and only enemy fighters could put a halt to its progress. So during the first year of World War 2 it acquired legendary status, which it lost suddenly and irretrievably in the Battle of Britain. For the rest of the war it operated only at night and at low level, and only one group on the Eastern Front flew it during the daytime. The commander of this group himself flew 2,530 missions.

The technique of dive-bombing was familiar in World War 1, but no aircraft designed for the job existed until the 1920s. One of the first was the Junkers K 47, of which two were flown in 1928 with Jupiter engines and 12 with Pratt & Whitney Hornet engines sold to China. These did extensive research, and demonstrated that a 90° dive is the most accurate. In turn this demands a strong aircraft and resolute pilot, as well as an indicator of dive angle (60° feels like almost 90°). Many who later were to head Hitler's Luftwaffe became convinced that the dive-bomber had to be a central weapon in an air force dedicated to close support of ground forces. When plans could be made for new combat aircraft for the Luftwaffe, in 1933, the immediate need was ultimately met by a trim biplane, the Henschel Hs 123, while Junkers worked on the definitive Stuka.

The design staff under Hermann Pohlmann adopted the same configuration as that of the K 47; a single-engined low-wing monoplane with prominent fixed landing gear and twin fins and rudders. The Ju 87 differed in having an all-metal stressed-skin structure, without the corrugated skin previously used on Junkers all-metal aircraft, and a cranked wing of so-called inverted-gull form. Like that of the K 47, the entire trailing edge was occupied by patented double-wing flaps and ailerons, and the crew of two sat back-to-back under a large glazed canopy. The prototype flew in the spring of 1935 with a 640-hp (477-kW) Rolls-Royce Kestrel engine. Divebrakes were then added under the outer wings,

One of the surviving colour photographs from World War 2, this was taken by the 'backseater' of a Ju 87B-2 flying with StG 77 on a mission over the Balkans – believed to be after dive-bombing British ships during the invasion of Crete. Identical markings can be seen in the colour profile of Ju 87R coded S2 + MR.

Like another famed, or infamous, Nazi warplane, the Bf 109 fighter, the Ju 87 first took to the air on the power of a Rolls-Royce Kestrel engine. This photo shows the original appearance of the V1 (first prototype) at Dessau in mid-1935. The dive-brakes were not ready at this time and the radiator required changes.

All the Luftwaffe's early Stukageschwäder (dive-bomber wings) using the Ju 87 were formed on the Ju 87A, with 600-hp (448-kW) engine and trousered landing gear. This Ju 87A-2 was assigned to III/StG 165 (later renumbered StG 51) in early 1938. The camouflage and Balkankreuz insignia were revised in October 1939.

but on one of the first pull-outs the tail collapsed and the aircraft crashed.

Full-scale production

After much further development, in the course of which the engine was changed to the intended German unit, the 640-hp (477-kW) Junkers Jumo 210Ca, driving a three-blade variable-pitch propeller, a new single-fin tail was adopted, and the JU 87A-1 entered full-scale production in early 1937.

About 200 of the A-0, A-1 and A-2 series were built, all with large trouser fairings over the landing gears and the A-2 with the 680-hp (507-kW) Jumo 210Da and an improved VDM propeller. They equipped four Gruppen, of which StG 163 sent three aircraft to see action with the Legion Cóndor in Spain, where the type proved outstandingly effective. But in 1939 all A-series aircraft were transferred to training units, and the swelling ranks of Stukageschwäder (dive-bomber wings) were equipped with the much more capable Ju 87B. Visually this differed in having neater spats over the main wheels, but the chief difference was that it had double the power, in the form of the new Jumo 211A, driving a broad-blade constant-speed propeller. The full production sub-type, the B-1, had the 1,200-hp (895-kW) Jumo 211Da with a direct-injection fuel system giving immunity from icing, or engine-cuts in inverted flight, or negative-g manoeuvres (the Ju 87 could perform all normal aerobatics). Another important feature was an automatic dive-control, set by the pilot to a chosen pull-out height on a contact altimeter. Having gone through a list of 10 vital actions the pilot opened the underwing dive-brakes, which automatically set up the dive, the pilot adjusting the angle manually by lining up the visual horizon with red lines painted at various angles on the canopy. The pilot then aimed at the target manually as in a fighter, using aileron alone to achieve the correct bomb line. Often the angle was 90°, the dive being entered in a wing-over from directly above the target. Curiously, the Ju 87 was the one aircraft in which 90° did not feel like an over-the-vertical bunt; indeed, it seemed more at home in its rock-steady dive than in normal cruising flight, when its vulnerability (accentuated by the transparent canopy down to elbow-level) was all too evident. When a signal light on the contact altimeter came on, the pilot pressed a knob on top of the control column for the pull-out at 6 g to happen by itself, with usual terrain clearance of 450 m (1,476 ft). If it did not, the pilot had to haul back with all his strength, assisted by very careful use of elevator trimmer.

There was a pair of MG 81s, light but fast-firing weapons with belt feed instead of 75-round magazines. Additionally, the entire aircraft was refined to reduce drag, the most noticeable improvement being to the cowling and canopy. The landing gear was cleaned up, but from 1942 the spats and leg fairings were increasingly discarded.

The most numerous variant was the Ju 87D-3, which embodied better protection for the crew and vital parts of the aircraft, reflecting the Ju 87's increasing use as a Schlachtflugzeug (close-support aircraft). From 1942 all versions were often called upon to fly missions other than dive-bombing, such as glider-towing, anti-partisan attacks and general utility transport with a great diversity of loads. A few Ju 87D-4s were equipped as torpedo-bombers, but the next main variant was the Ju 87D-5 with extended wingtips to help counter the considerably increased weight of Ju-87D versions. Reflecting the increasing peril of day operations, the Ju 87D-7 was a night variant with the more powerful Jumo 211P engine and long exhaust pipes extending back across the wing. Together with the day-flying Ju 87D-8 it replaced the wing guns by the far more powerful 20-mm MG 151, and dive-brakes were at last omitted. The Ju 87D-8 was the last version in production, the total number built by late September 1944 – when almost all aircraft other than fighters were terminated – being generally accepted as 5,709.

Anti-armour

There were several schemes for successors, including the Ju 87F and Ju 187, but the only other Stuka variants were built by conversions of the ubiquitous D models. The most important sub-type was the Ju 87G series, of which only the Ju 87G-1 became operational. The Ju 87G was a specialized anti-armour version, fitted with two BK 3.7 (Flak 18) guns hung under the wings just outboard of the landing gears. This 37-mm gun was a formidable weapon weighing over 800 lb (363 kg) and in wide service as ground-based flak (anti-aircraft artillery) equipment. In 1942 a trial installation was tested in a converted Ju 87D-5 and found more effective than the many other Luftwaffe anti-tank aircraft such as the Henschel Hs 129 and Junkers Ju 88P. Fed by clips of six rounds, the BK 3.7 had a muzzle velocity with armour-piercing ammunition exceeding 2,790 ft (850 m) per second, and the greatest exponent of the Ju 87G-1, Hans-Ulrich Rudel, was ultimately credited with the personal destruction of 519 Russian armoured vehicles. It was he who flew 2,530 combat missions mentioned above and continued to lead Stuka formations in daylight long after the other Stukagruppen had replaced their vulnerable aircraft with the Focke-Wulf Fw 190.

Another variant produced by converting aircraft of the Ju 87D series was the Ju 87H dual-control trainer. No trainer had been considered necessary in the early days of Ju 87 service, but by 1943 the art of surviving in the type had become so specialized and important on the Eastern Front that even experienced bomber and fighter pilots had to go out with a Ju 87 instructor before taking up their places in the decimated ranks of the Stukagruppen. Almost all versions of Ju 87D were converted into H models, retaining the same suffix numbers. Outwardly the differences included removal of armament and the addition of bulged side panels in the rear cockpit to give the instructor a measure of forward vision.

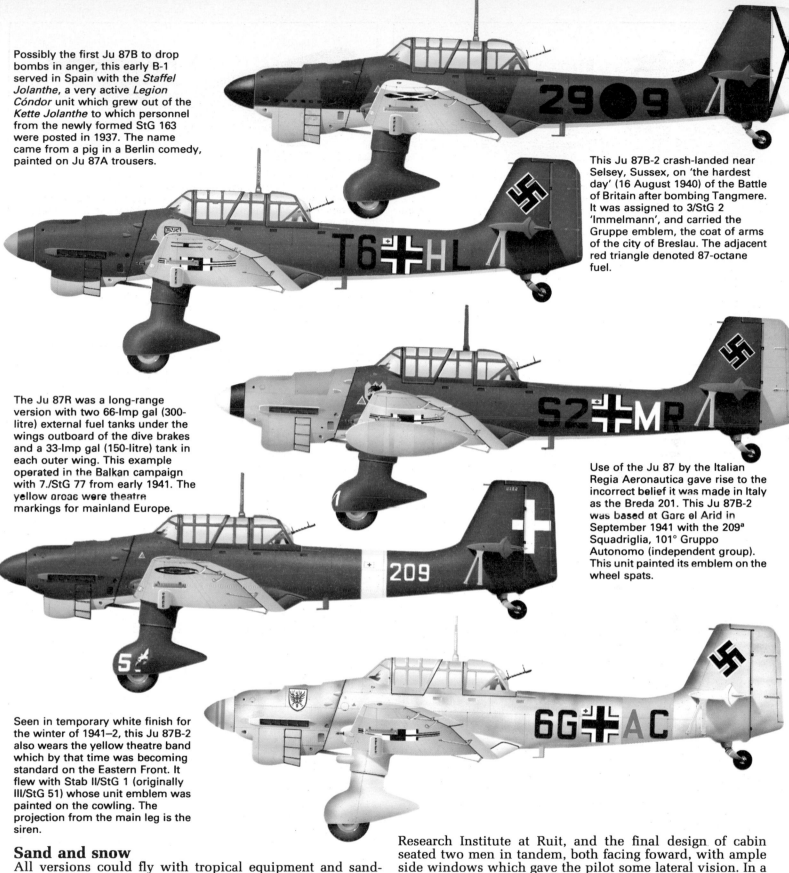

Possibly the first Ju 87B to drop bombs in anger, this early B-1 served in Spain with the *Staffel Jolanthe*, a very active *Legion Cóndor* unit which grew out of the *Kette Jolanthe* to which personnel from the newly formed StG 163 were posted in 1937. The name came from a pig in a Berlin comedy, painted on Ju 87A trousers.

This Ju 87B-2 crash-landed near Selsey, Sussex, on 'the hardest day' (16 August 1940) of the Battle of Britain after bombing Tangmere. It was assigned to 3/StG 2 'Immelmann', and carried the Gruppe emblem, the coat of arms of the city of Breslau. The adjacent red triangle denoted 87-octane fuel.

The Ju 87R was a long-range version with two 66-Imp gal (300-litre) external fuel tanks under the wings outboard of the dive brakes and a 33-Imp gal (150-litre) tank in each outer wing. This example operated in the Balkan campaign with 7./StG 77 from early 1941. The yellow areas were theatre markings for mainland Europe.

Use of the Ju 87 by the Italian Regia Aeronautica gave rise to the incorrect belief it was made in Italy as the Breda 201. This Ju 87B-2 was based at Gars el Arid in September 1941 with the 209ª Squadriglia, 101° Gruppo Autonomo (independent group). This unit painted its emblem on the wheel spats.

Seen in temporary white finish for the winter of 1941–2, this Ju 87B-2 also wears the yellow theatre band which by that time was becoming standard on the Eastern Front. It flew with Stab II/StG 1 (originally III/StG 51) whose unit emblem was painted on the cowling. The projection from the main leg is the siren.

Sand and snow

All versions could fly with tropical equipment and sand-dust filters, and many aircraft on the Eastern Front operated on skis in winter. There were several experimental variants, mainly concerned with tests of weapons intended for later aircraft. One of the most striking test programmes concerned one Ju 87D-3 fitted with large streamlined overwing passenger cabins. The idea was that the Ju 87, an aircraft well used to front-line operations, should become a vehicle for putting down agents behind enemy front lines. The trials programme got under way in early 1944 at the Graf Zeppelin Research Institute at Ruit, and the final design of cabin seated two men in tandem, both facing forward, with ample side windows which gave the pilot some lateral vision. In a shallow dive the two pods were to be pulled off the wing by streaming large parachutes, but there is no record of this actually being done, though the pods were flown with passengers.

The Ju 87 was widely used by all the Axis air forces, including those of Italy, Hungary, Slovakia, Romania and Bulgaria. When Ju 87s were discovered in Italian markings the totally fictitious belief arose among the British that the type was being made in Italy, even the invented type-

Junkers Ju 87 Stuka

Specification

Junkers Ju 87G-1
Type: anti-tank aircraft
Powerplant: one 1,400-hp (1044-kW) Junkers Jumo 211J-1 inline piston engine
Performance: maximum speed about 195 mph (314 km/h); cruising speed normally about 118 mph (190 km/h); rate of climb and service ceiling not known, but extremely poor; combat radius about 199 miles (320 km)
Weights: empty about 9,700 lb (4400 kg); maximum take-off about 14,550 lb (6600 kg)
Dimensions: span 49 ft 2½ in (15.00 m); length 37 ft 8¾ in (11.50 m); height 12 ft 9¼ in (3.90 m); wing area 362.6 sq ft (33.69 m²)
Armament: two 37-mm BK 3.7 cannon and one flexible 0.331-in (7.92-mm) MG 81 machine-gun, plus a useful bombload when the underwing cannon were not been carried

The last variant of the Ju 87 to become operational apart from the Ju 87H trainer was the Ju 87G-1 anti-tank model. This was not built as such, but rather converted from Ju 87D-5 airframes. The concept was the brainchild of the extraordinary Hans-Ulrich Rudel, who despite being shot down 30 times flew no fewer than 2,530 combat missions and destroyed 519 Russian tanks: the basic Ju 87D-5 was adapted to carry a pair of massive Flak 18 (BK 3.7) 37-mm cannon pods under its outer wing panels. The aircraft illustrated was on the strength of II/Schlachtgeschwader 3, more specifically the unit's 5. Staffel, serving on the Eastern Front in late 1944. The Ju 87G-1 could carry bombs instead of guns, but had no dive-brakes.

Junkers Ju 87 Stuka

designation of Breda 201 Picchiatelli being widely published! In fact, from 1939 every Ju 87 was made by Weser in the same Tempelhof building.

The usual load on the Ju 87B series was an SC 500 (1,102-lb) bomb on crutches which swung out from the belly to let go of the bomb well away from the propeller. Speed built up to about 324 mph (550 km/h), and it became common practice to fit sirens to the landing gears – they were called 'Trombones of Jericho' – to strike extra terror into those near the target. Over short ranges, four SC50 (110-lb) bombs could also be hung under the wings. The pilot could fire two 0.31-in (7.92-mm) MG 17 guns mounted in the wings outboard of the kink, while the radio operator had an MG 15 of the same calibre to give protection above and behind. Production was transferred from Dessau to Weser Flugzeugbau in the great oval building at Berlin-Tempelhof airport, where it built up to 60 a month by mid-1939. Three B-1s made the first combat mission of World War 2 when they took off from Elbing at 04.26 on 1 September 1939 and devastated the approaches to the Dirschau bridge over the Vistula at 04.34, some 11 minutes before the Nazis declared war on Poland. Subsequently the Ju 87B-1 played a tremendous part in the Polish campaign, destroying all but two of the Polish surface warships, heavily bombing Polish troops on many occasions within 330 ft (100 m) of advancing German forces, and on one ghastly occasion virtually wiping out an entire Polish infantry division at Piotrkow railway station.

Carrier-borne variant

Alongside the improved Ju 87B-2 variants, which as single-seaters could carry an SC100 (2,205-lb) bomb, Weser built a batch of Ju 87C-0s with folding wings, hooks and many other changes to suit them to use abroad the carrier *Graf Zeppelin*, which was never completed. Another derived model was the extended-range Ju 87R series, with extra tanks in the outer wings and provision for underwing drop tanks. They entered service in time for the Norwegian campaign – where one put a radio station off the air by ramming the aerials – and then proved useful in the Balkans, Greece and Mediterranean theatres. One Ju 87R tested a large container, hung on the main bomb crutch, intended to carry spares and other cargo.

The Ju 87B and derivatives wrought havoc throughout Europe in the first two years of World War 2, meeting only one serious setback. Over England its losses were unacceptably heavy, 41 being shot down in the period 13–18 August 1940, so that from 19 August Stukas were withdrawn from attacks against UK targets. The type had already shown that, with German air supremacy, it could knock out the vital British coastal radars; but it was the same radars that enabled the defending fighters unfailingly to intercept, and the

vulnerability of the Ju 87 was suddenly apparent. The aircraft had been designed on the basis of good fighter protection, and in such conditions it had demonstrated such devastating effectiveness that many in the UK – foot-soldiers, journalists and politicians alike – cried 'Where are our dive-bombers?' In fact, the country had dive-bombers, such as the Blackburn Skua and Hawker Henley, but they played little part in the war, and the whole concept of the dive-bomber became a subject of violent argument. The success of the Stuka in ideal conditions also warped German procurement and the large Dornier Do 217 and Heinkel He 177 were wrongly designed as dive-bombers.

Even at the outbreak of war the Ju 87 was recognized as a somewhat dated design, but this was masked by its fantastic successes. As with so many other old Luftwaffe types, lack of a replacement resulted in planned termination of production being countermanded, and like that of the Messerschmitt Bf 110 and He 111, Ju87 output increased from 1941 to 1944. The standard basic type throughout this period was the Ju 87D, designed in 1940, first flown in early 1941 and in action

Junkers Ju 87D-3 cutaway drawing key

1 Spinner
2 Pitch-change mechanism housing
3 Blade hub
4 Junkers VS 11 constant-speed airscrew
5 Anti-vibration engine mounting attachments
6 Oil filler point and marker
7 Auxiliary oil tank (5.9 Imp gal/26.8 litre capacity)
8 Junkers Jumo 211J-1 12-cylinder inverted-vee liquid cooled engine
9 Magnesium alloy forged engine mount
10 Coolant (Glysantin-water) header tank
11 Ejector exhaust stubs
12 Fuel injection unit housing
13 Induction air cooler
14 Armoured radiator
15 Inertia starter cranking point
16 Ball joint bulkhead fixing (lower)
17 Tubular steel mount support strut
18 Ventral armour (8 mm)
19 Main oil tank (9.9 Imp gal/45 litre capacity)
20 Oil filling point
21 Transverse support frame
22 Rudder pedals
23 Control column
24 Heating point
25 Auxiliary air intake
26 Ball joint bulkhead fixing (upper)
27 Bulkhead
28 Oil tank (6.8 Imp gal/31 litre capacity)
29 Oil filler point and marker (Intava 100)
30 Fuel filler cap
31 Self-sealing starboard outer fuel tank (33 Imp gal/150 litre capacity)
32 Underwing bombs with *Dienartstab* percussion rods
33 Pitot head
34 Spherical oxygen bottles
35 Wing skinning
36 Starboard navigation light
37 Aileron mass balance
38 'Double wing' aileron and flat (starboard outer)
39 Aileron hinge
40 Corrugated wing rib station
41 Reinforced armoured windscreen
42 Reflector sight

No picture could better illustrate the cranked wings of the Stuka than this shot taken through the windscreen by the pilot of an accompanying aircraft. This 1940 Ju 87B is still wearing four-letter factory codes and may be on flight test from Tempelhof. From this angle the dive-brakes are visible, but not the 'double wing'.

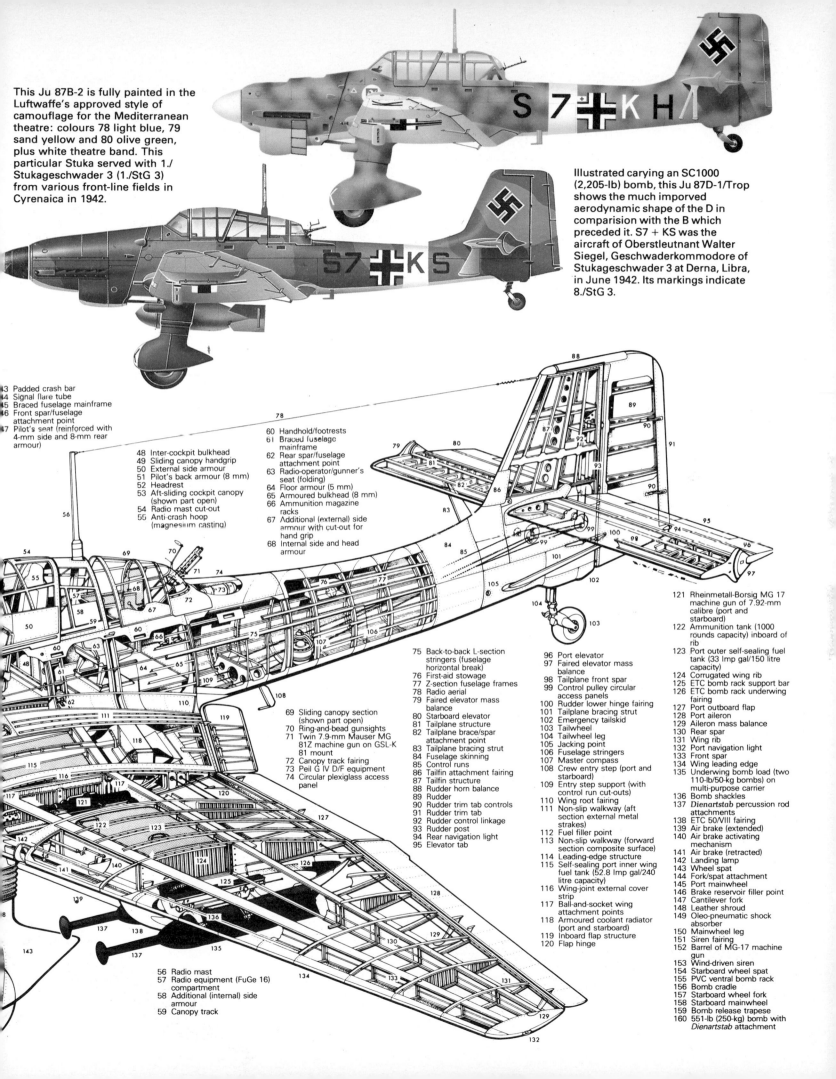

This Ju 87B-2 is fully painted in the Luftwaffe's approved style of camouflage for the Mediterranean theatre: colours 78 light blue, 79 sand yellow and 80 olive green, plus white theatre band. This particular Stuka served with 1./Stukageschwader 3 (1./StG 3) from various front-line fields in Cyrenaica in 1942.

Illustrated carying an SC1000 (2,205-lb) bomb, this Ju 87D-1/Trop shows the much imporved aerodynamic shape of the D in comparision with the B which preceded it. S7 + KS was the aircraft of Oberstleutnant Walter Siegel, Geschwaderkommodore of Stukageschwader 3 at Derna, Libra, in June 1942. Its markings indicate 8./StG 3.

43 Padded crash bar
44 Signal flare tube
45 Braced fuselage mainframe
46 Front spar/fuselage attachment point
47 Pilot's seat (reinforced with 4-mm side and 8-mm rear armour)
48 Inter-cockpit bulkhead
49 Sliding canopy handgrip
50 External side armour
51 Pilot's back armour (8 mm)
52 Headrest
53 Aft-sliding cockpit canopy (shown part open)
54 Radio mast cut-out
55 Anti-crash hoop (magnesium casting)
56 Radio mast
57 Radio equipment (FuGe 16) compartment
58 Additional (internal) side armour
59 Canopy track
60 Handhold/footrests
61 Braced fuselage mainframe
62 Rear spar/fuselage attachment point
63 Radio-operator/gunner's seat (folding)
64 Floor armour (5 mm)
65 Armoured bulkhead (8 mm)
66 Ammunition magazine racks
67 Additional (external) side armour with cut-out for hand grip
68 Internal side and head armour
69 Sliding canopy section (shown part open)
70 Ring-and-bead gunsights
71 Twin 7.9-mm Mauser MG 81Z machine gun on GSL-K 81 mount
72 Canopy track fairing
73 Peil G IV D/F equipment
74 Circular plexiglass access panel
75 Back-to-back L-section stringers (fuselage horizontal break)
76 First-aid stowage
77 Z-section fuselage frames
78 Radio aerial
79 Faired elevator mass balance
80 Starboard elevator
81 Tailplane structure
82 Tailplane brace/spar attachment point
83 Tailplane bracing strut
84 Fuselage skinning
85 Control runs
86 Tailfin attachment fairing
87 Tailfin structure
88 Rudder horn balance
89 Rudder
90 Rudder trim tab controls
91 Rudder trim tab
92 Rudder control linkage
93 Rudder post
94 Rear navigation light
95 Elevator tab
96 Port elevator
97 Faired elevator mass balance
98 Tailplane front spar
99 Control pulley circular access panels
100 Rudder lower hinge fairing
101 Tailplane bracing strut
102 Emergency tailskid
103 Tailwheel
104 Tailwheel leg
105 Jacking point
106 Fuselage stringers
107 Master compass
108 Crew entry step (port and starboard)
109 Entry step support (with control run cut-outs)
110 Wing root fairing
111 Non-slip walkway (aft section external metal strakes)
112 Fuel filler point
113 Non-slip walkway (forward section composite surface)
114 Leading-edge structure
115 Self-sealing port inner wing fuel tank (52.8 Imp gal/240 litre capacity)
116 Wing-joint external cover strip
117 Ball-and-socket wing attachment points
118 Armoured coolant radiator (port and starboard)
119 Inboard flap structure
120 Flap hinge
121 Rheinmetall-Borsig MG 17 machine gun of 7.92-mm calibre (port and starboard)
122 Ammunition tank (1000 rounds capacity) inboard of rib
123 Port outer self-sealing fuel tank (33 Imp gal/150 litre capacity)
124 Corrugated wing rib
125 ETC bomb rack support bar
126 ETC bomb rack underwing fairing
127 Port outboard flap
128 Port aileron
129 Aileron mass balance
130 Rear spar
131 Wing rib
132 Port navigation light
133 Front spar
134 Wing leading edge
135 Underwing bomb load (two 110-lb/50-kg bombs) on multi-purpose carrier
136 Bomb shackles
137 Dienartstab percussion rod attachments
138 ETC 50/VIII fairing
139 Air brake (extended)
140 Air brake activating mechanism
141 Air brake (retracted)
142 Landing lamp
143 Wheel spat
144 Fork/spat attachment
145 Port mainwheel
146 Brake reservoir filler point
147 Cantilever fork
148 Leather shroud
149 Oleo-pneumatic shock absorber
150 Mainwheel leg
151 Siren fairing
152 Barrel of MG-17 machine gun
153 Wind-driven siren
154 Starboard wheel spat
155 PVC ventral bomb rack
156 Bomb cradle
157 Starboard wheel fork
158 Starboard mainwheel
159 Bomb release trapese
160 551-lb (250-kg) bomb with Dienartstab attachment

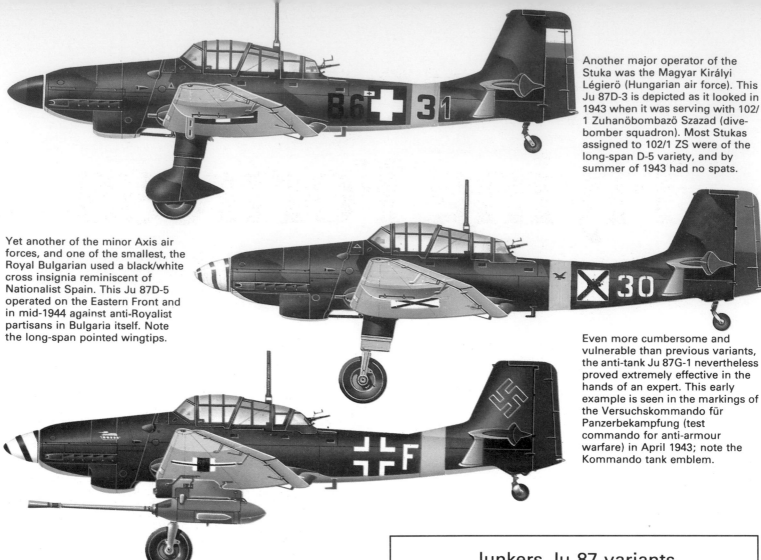

Another major operator of the Stuka was the Magyar Királyi Légierö (Hungarian air force). This Ju 87D-3 is depicted as it looked in 1943 when it was serving with 102/1 Zuhanöbombazö Szazad (dive-bomber squadron). Most Stukas assigned to 102/1 ZS were of the long-span D-5 variety, and by summer of 1943 had no spats.

Yet another of the minor Axis air forces, and one of the smallest, the Royal Bulgarian used a black/white cross insignia reminiscent of Nationalist Spain. This Ju 87D-5 operated on the Eastern Front and in mid-1944 against anti-Royalist partisans in Bulgaria itself. Note the long-span pointed wingtips.

Even more cumbersome and vulnerable than previous variants, the anti-tank Ju 87G-1 nevertheless proved extremely effective in the hands of an expert. This early example is seen in the markings of the Versuchskommando für Panzerbekampfung (test commando for anti-armour warfare) in April 1943; note the Kommando tank emblem.

on the Eastern and North African fronts by the end of 1941. This was powered by the 1,400-hp (1044-kW) Jumo 211J-1 driving a VS 11 propeller with very broad blades, making a major difference to flight performance, which was put to use in carrying much heavier loads. Maximum bomb load rose to 1800 kg (3,968 lb), the main crutch being able to take the PC1400 (3,086-lb) armour-piercing bomb and the wing racks the SC500 (1,102-lb) or a wide range of other stores including gun pods each housing either twin 20-mm cannon or six 0.31-in (7.92-mm) MG 81 machine-guns.

Junkers Ju 87 variants

Junkers Ju 87 V1: first prototype, with 640-hp (477-kW) Rolls-Royce Kestrel
Junkers Ju 87 V2: second rototype 610-hp (455-kW) Jumo 210Aa, hurriedly fitted single-fin tail unit
Junkers Ju 87 V3: third prototype properly designed tail, engine lowered to improve pilot view
Junkers Ju 87A: first production series, 640-hp (477-kW) Jumo 210Ca or (A-2) 680-hp (507-kW) Jumo 210Da about 200 built 1937–8)
Junkers Ju 87B: 1,200-hp (895-kW) Jumo 211Da, redesigned canopy and fuselage, larger vertical tail, spatted instead of trousered landing gears, bombloads up to 1000 kg (2,205 lb) (total deliveries in various sub-types about 1,300)
Junkers Ju 87C: navalized version intended for use from aircraft-carrier, folding wings, hook, catapult hooks,

jettisonable landing gear, flotation gear and extra tankage, operated from land bases
Junkers Ju 87D: major production version, 1,400-hp (1044-kW) Jumo 211J-1 or 1,500-hp (1119-kW) Jumo 211P-1, redesigned airframe with lower drag, bombload up to 3,968-lb (1800 kg), D-2 glider tug, D-3 increased armour, D-4 for torpedo-carrying, D-5 with extended wingtips, D-7 twin MG 151 cannon and night equipment, D-8 as D-7 without night equipment
Junkers Ju 87G-1: conversion of D-3 to attack armoured vehicles with two 37-mm BK 3,7 (Flak 18) guns
Junkers Ju 87H: dual-control trainers without armament, kinked rear canopy with side blisters
Junkers Ju 87R: derivative of Ju 87B-2 with augmented tankage and provision for drop tanks to increase range normally with single SC250 (551-lb) bomb

Weatherbeaten Ju 87B-2s of II/StG 1 on the Eastern Front, probably in autumn 1941. Nine more Ju 87s are in the distance at lower level. These aircraft are probably returning from a combat mission, with bomb racks empty. Spats were still in use at this time, and opposition to the Stuka still generally feeble.

The Ju 87D-5 introduced a wing of greater span to allow the heavy weapon loads to be carried with a better margin of safety. This D-5 was photographed on final landing approach, with full flap, on return from a mission with 8./StG 2 in the Kursk area in the summer of 1943. Its code was T6 + AS, T6 being that of StG 2 itself.

Boeing B-17 Flying Fortress

The B-17 Fortress flew through frost, flak, fire and fear to set a combat record which in terms of sheer courage and staying power of its crews has never been surpassed, and seldom equalled. At first the great olive-drab armadas returned smoking and riddled with holes. By late 1944 the shining silver Forts had almost defeated the Luftwaffe.

The huge fleet of the US 8th Air Force consisted mostly of Boeing B-17s. These flew the length and breadth of Germany and from 1942 to 1945, with their bombing of factories and other pinpoint targets, dominated the European theatre of war. Under their onslaught, even Goering's powerful Luftwaffe crumbled in the greatest and bloodiest air war the world had ever known. But in 1934, when American bombers were at best flying to such militarily insignificant destinations as Canada, Mexico or a few far-flung British islands, no one believed there would be conflict on such a scale. As money was short in the economic depression of the time, people thought they could bring in the Martin monoplane bomber to help them.

But when the US Army Air Corps put out a request for a new multi-engine bomber a few far-sighted engineers at the Boeing Airplane Company decided to interpret 'multi-engined' as meaning not two engines (as had generally been done before) but four. Admittedly they did this mainly in order to get more height over the target, but it had the effect of making the Boeing Model 299 significantly larger than its rivals. Design began on 18 June 1934, and the prototype made a very successful first flight in the hands of Les Tower

Prior to January 1944, when camouflage paint was generally discontinued in the USAAF, various olive drab and green paint schemes were in use. This 1942 picture of B-17Fs of the 8th Air Force's 91st Bomb Group (322nd Bomb Squadron) shows the irregular blotching of Medium Green (officially styled Shade 42) on a few B-17s.

Boeing B-17F-25-BO
Flying Fortress

Specification

Type: heavy bomber with crew 8 to 10

Powerplant: four 1,200-hp (895-kW) Wright R-1820-97 Cyclone radial piston engines

Performance: maximum speed 295 mph (475 km/h); initial climb rate 900 ft (274 m) per minute; service ceiling 36,000 ft (10975 m); combat radius with 5,000-lb (2270-kg) bombload 800 miles (1287 km)

Weights: empty (typical) 34,000 lb (15422 kg); loaded (normal) 56,000 lb (25400 kg), (war overload from 1943) 72,000 lb (32660 kg)

Dimensions: span 103 ft 9 in (31.60 m); length 74 ft 9 in (22.80 m); height 19 ft 2½ in (5.85 m); wing area 1,420 sq ft (131.92 m²)

Armament: maximum bombload 9,600 lb (4355 kg), later increased to 17,600 lb (7983 kg); defensive firepower normally 11 guns of 0.5-in (12.7-mm) calibre and one of 0.30-in (7.62-mm) calibre

Fast Woman was a B-17F serving with the 359th Bomb Squadron, 303rd Bomb Group, 8th Air Force, based at Molesworth. Its finish was olive drab (weathered a purplish hue) and medium green. Lettering at this time was in yellow, black being used after the switch on 1 January 1944 to natural metal finish. Note the pre-July 1943 national insignia.

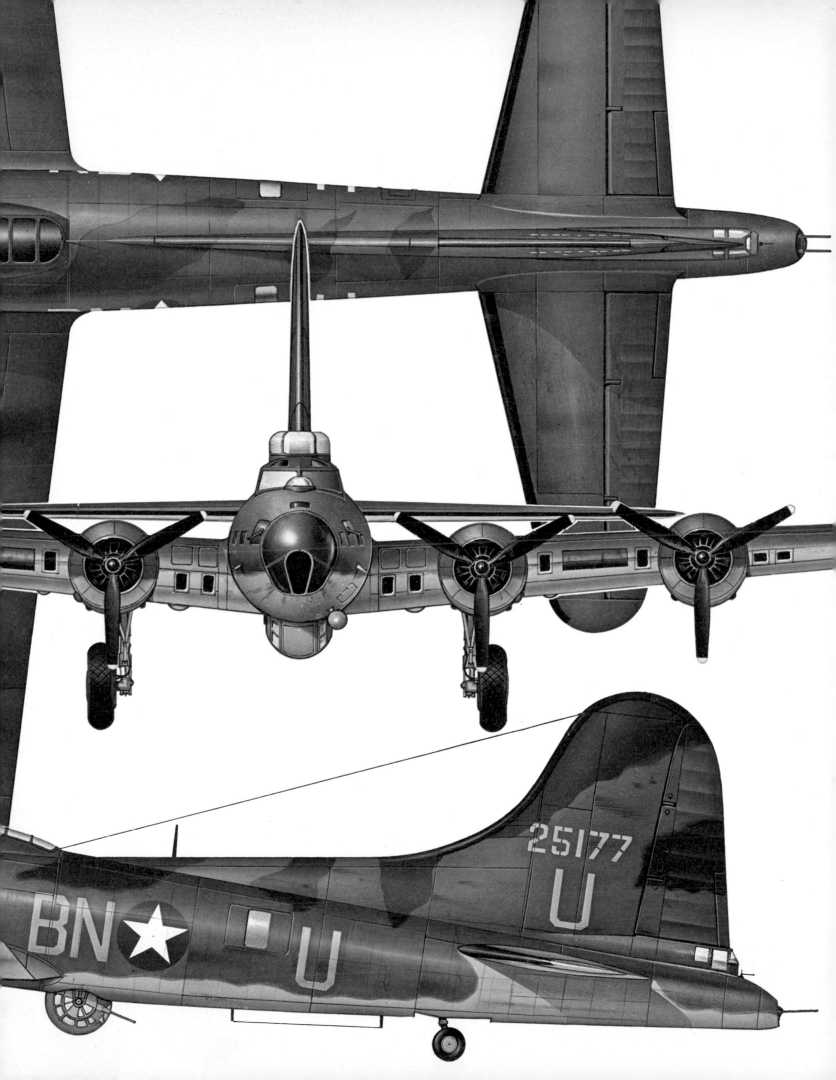

Boeing B-17

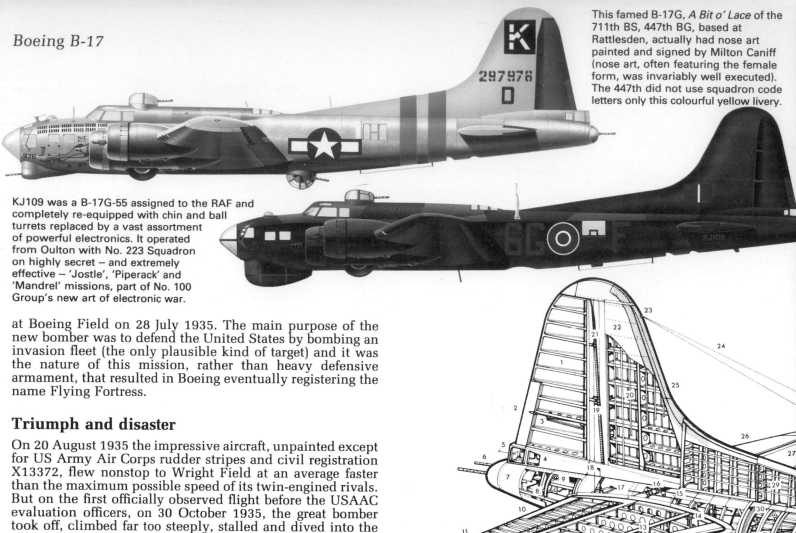

This famed B-17G, *A Bit o' Lace* of the 711th BS, 447th BG, based at Rattlesden, actually had nose art painted and signed by Milton Caniff (nose art, often featuring the female form, was invariably well executed). The 447th did not use squadron code letters only this colourful yellow livery.

KJ109 was a B-17G-55 assigned to the RAF and completely re-equipped with chin and ball turrets replaced by a vast assortment of powerful electronics. It operated from Oulton with No. 223 Squadron on highly secret — and extremely effective — 'Jostle', 'Piperack' and 'Mandrel' missions, part of No. 100 Group's new art of electronic war.

at Boeing Field on 28 July 1935. The main purpose of the new bomber was to defend the United States by bombing an invasion fleet (the only plausible kind of target) and it was the nature of this mission, rather than heavy defensive armament, that resulted in Boeing eventually registering the name Flying Fortress.

Triumph and disaster

On 20 August 1935 the impressive aircraft, unpainted except for US Army Air Corps rudder stripes and civil registration X13372, flew nonstop to Wright Field at an average faster than the maximum possible speed of its twin-engined rivals. But on the first officially observed flight before the USAAC evaluation officers, on 30 October 1935, the great bomber took off, climbed far too steeply, stalled and dived into the ground, bursting into a ball of fire. The accident was caused entirely by someone having omitted to remove the external locks on the elevators, and though the immediate winner of the official trials had to be the Douglas B-18, the much greater potential of the great Boeing bomber resulted in a service-test order for 13, designated Y1B-17, placed on 17 January 1936.

These had many changes, especially to the landing gear, armament and in having 930-hp (694-kW) Wright Cyclone engines instead of 750-hp (560-kW) Pratt & Whitney Hornets. In 1937 the machines were delivered to the 2nd Bombardment Group at Langley Field, which subsequently flew almost 10,000 hours with no serious trouble and did more than any other unit in history to solve the problems of long-distance bombing, especially at high altitude. A 14th aircraft was built as the Y1B-17A with engines fitted with General Electric turbo-superchargers, which increased the speed from 256 mph (412 km/h) to 311 mph (500 km/h) and raised the operating height to well over 30,000 ft (9145 m).

Results with the B-17 (as the Y1B was called after its test period was complete) were so good the USAAC not only

The short-lived Model 299 prototype had Hornet S1EG engines, and twin-strut main landing gears. On the fin is the Boeing Airplane emblem and model number, and the rudder carries US Army stripes and serial. Gross weight of 16 US tons (32,000 lb) was just half that of a laden B-17G. Making the Model 299 was a gigantic financial risk.

Boeing B-17F Flying Fortress cutaway drawing key

1 Rudder construction
2 Rudder tab
3 Rudder tab actuation
4 Tail gunner's station
5 Gunsight
6 Twin 0.5-in (12.7-mm) machine guns
7 Tail cone
8 Tail gunner's seat
9 Ammunition troughs
10 Elevator trim tab
11 Starboard elevator
12 Tailplane structure
13 Tailplane front spar
14 Tailplane/fuselage attachment
15 Control cables
16 Elevator control mechanism
17 Rudder control linkage
18 Rudder post
19 Rudder centre hinge
20 Fin structure
21 Rudder upper hinge
22 Fin skinning

23 Aerial attachment
24 Aerials
25 Fin leading edge de-icing boot
26 Port elevator
27 Port tailplane
28 Tailplane leading-edge de-icing boot
29 Dorsal fin structure
30 Fuselage frame
31 Tailwheel actuation
32 Toilet
33 Tailwheel (retracted) fairing
34 Fully-swivelling retractable tailwheel
35 Crew entry door
36 Control cables
37 Starboard waist hatch
38 Starboard waist 0.5-in (12.7-mm) machine gun

39 Gun support frame
40 Ammunition box
41 Ventral aerial
42 Waist gunners' positions
43 Port waist 0.5-in (12.7-mm) machine gun
44 Ceiling control cable runs
45 Dorsal aerial mast
46 Ball turret stanchion support
47 Ball turret stachion
48 Ball turret actuation mechanism
49 Support frame
50 Ball turret roof

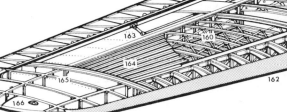

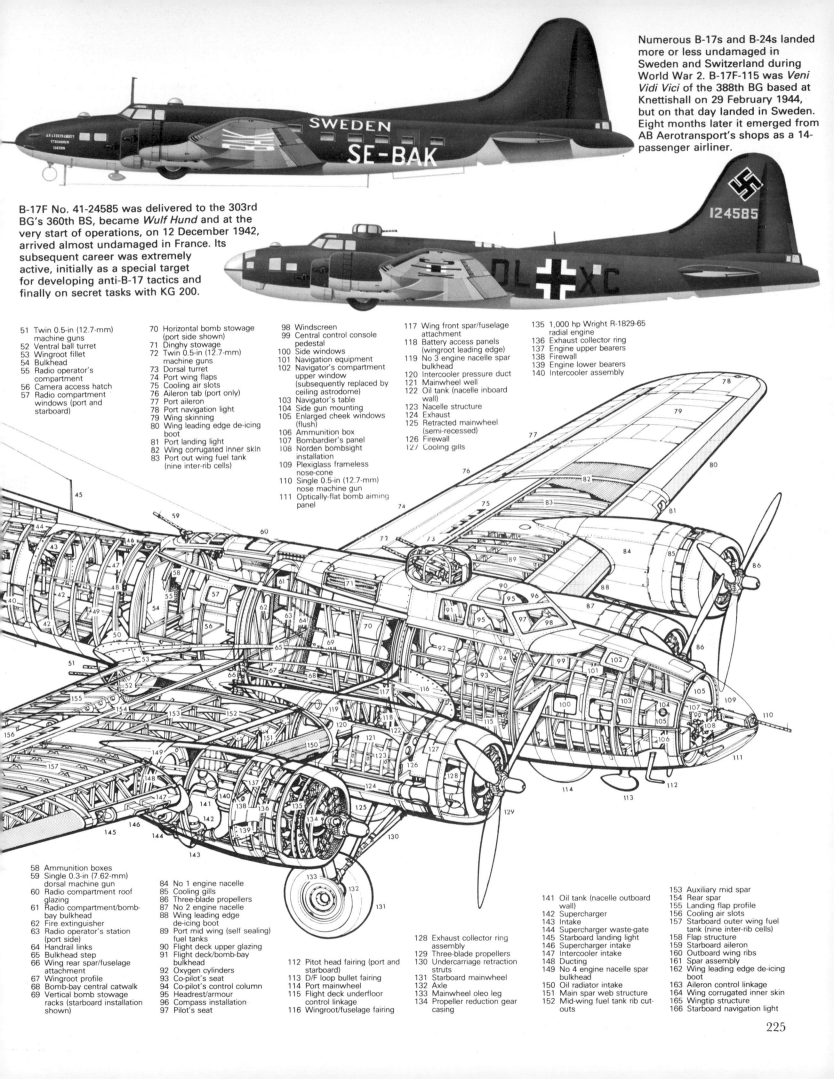

Numerous B-17s and B-24s landed more or less undamaged in Sweden and Switzerland during World War 2. B-17F-115 was *Veni Vidi Vici* of the 388th BG based at Knettishall on 29 February 1944, but on that day landed in Sweden. Eight months later it emerged from AB Aerotransport's shops as a 14-passenger airliner.

SWEDEN

SE-BAK

B-17F No. 41-24585 was delivered to the 303rd BG's 360th BS, became *Wulf Hund* and at the very start of operations, on 12 December 1942, arrived almost undamaged in France. Its subsequent career was extremely active, initially as a special target for developing anti-B-17 tactics and finally on secret tasks with KG 200.

124585

DL+XC

51 Twin 0.5-in (12.7-mm) machine guns
52 Ventral ball turret
53 Wingroot fillet
54 Bulkhead
55 Radio operator's compartment
56 Camera access hatch
57 Radio compartment windows (port and starboard)
58 Ammunition boxes
59 Single 0.3-in (7.62-mm) dorsal machine gun
60 Radio compartment roof glazing
61 Radio compartment/bomb-bay bulkhead
62 Fire extinguisher
63 Radio operator's station (port side)
64 Handrail links
65 Bulkhead step
66 Wing rear spar/fuselage attachment
67 Wingroot profile
68 Bomb-bay central catwalk
69 Vertical bomb stowage racks (starboard installation shown)

70 Horizontal bomb stowage (port side shown)
71 Dinghy stowage
72 Twin 0.5-in (12.7-mm) machine guns
73 Dorsal turret
74 Port wing flaps
75 Cooling air slots
76 Aileron tab (port only)
77 Port aileron
78 Port navigation light
79 Wing skinning
80 Wing leading edge de-icing boot
81 Port landing light
82 Wing corrugated inner skin
83 Port out wing fuel tank (nine inter-rib cells)
84 No 1 engine nacelle
85 Cooling gills
86 Three-blade propellers
87 No 2 engine nacelle
88 Wing leading edge de-icing boot
89 Port mid wing (self sealing) fuel tanks
90 Flight deck upper glazing
91 Flight deck/bomb-bay bulkhead
92 Oxygen cylinders
93 Co-pilot's seat
94 Co-pilot's control column
95 Headrest/armour
96 Compass installation
97 Pilot's seat

98 Windscreen
99 Central control console pedestal
100 Side windows
101 Navigation equipment
102 Navigator's compartment upper window (subsequently replaced by ceiling astrodome)
103 Navigator's table
104 Side gun mounting
105 Enlarged cheek windows (flush)
106 Ammunition box
107 Bombardier's panel
108 Norden bombsight installation
109 Plexiglass frameless nose-cone
110 Single 0.5-in (12.7-mm) nose machine gun
111 Optically-flat bomb aiming panel
112 Pitot head fairing (port and starboard)
113 D/F loop bullet fairing
114 Port mainwheel
115 Flight deck underfloor control linkage
116 Wingroot/fuselage fairing

117 Wing front spar/fuselage attachment
118 Battery access panels (wingroot leading edge)
119 No 3 engine nacelle spar bulkhead
120 Intercooler pressure duct
121 Mainwheel well
122 Oil tank (nacelle inboard wall)
123 Nacelle structure
124 Exhaust
125 Retracted mainwheel (semi-recessed)
126 Firewall
127 Cooling gills
128 Exhaust collector ring assembly
129 Three-blade propellers
130 Undercarriage retraction struts
131 Starboard mainwheel
132 Axle
133 Mainwheel oleo leg
134 Propeller reduction gear casing

135 1,000 hp Wright R-1829-65 radial engine
136 Exhaust collector ring
137 Engine upper bearers
138 Firewall
139 Engine lower bearers
140 Intercooler assembly
141 Oil tank (nacelle outboard wall)
142 Supercharger
143 Intake
144 Supercharger waste-gate
145 Starboard landing light
146 Supercharger intake
147 Intercooler intake
148 Ducting
149 No 4 engine nacelle spar bulkhead
150 Oil radiator intake
151 Main spar web structure
152 Mid-wing fuel tank rib cut-outs
153 Auxiliary mid spar
154 Rear spar
155 Landing flap profile
156 Cooling air slots
157 Starboard outer wing fuel tank (nine inter-rib cells)
158 Flap structure
159 Starboard aileron
160 Outboard wing ribs
161 Spar assembly
162 Wing leading edge de-icing boot
163 Aileron control linkage
164 Wing corrugated inner skin
165 Wingtip structure
166 Starboard navigation light

fought for massive production numbers, in the teeth of opposition from the US Navy, but also with Boeing collaboration even planned a next-generation bomber which became the B-29. US Navy anger was so intense that production numbers had to be scaled down, and the production batch of the first series model, the B-17B, numbered only 39. These had numerous minor changes as well as a redesigned nose and larger rudder. They were the first aircraft in the world to enter service with turbocharged engines. The B-17B entered service in 1939 and was the fastest, as well as the highest-flying, bomber in the world. The US Army Air Corps had by this time embarked on a major programme of perfecting long-range strategic bombing by day, using the massed firepower of a large formation to render interception hazardous. It was expected that, because of the B-17's speed and height, opposing fighters would be hard-pressed to keep up and would present an almost stationary (relative to the bombers) target that could be blasted by the fire from hundreds of machine-guns.

Further power and speed

Boeing and Wright Field continued to improve the B-17 and in 1939 a further 39 were ordered under the designation B-17C. These were much heavier, weighing 49,650 lb (22520 kg) compared with about 43,000 lb (19505 kg) for a B-17, because of increased armour, self-sealing tanks, heavier defensive armament (with twin 0.5-in/12.7-mm guns above and in a new ventral 'bathtub', twin 0.3-in/7.62-mm guns in the nose and new flush side gun positions) and extra equipment. Despite the greater weight, the fitting of 1,200-hp (895-kW) engines made this the fastest of all versions, with a maximum speed of 320 mph (515 km/h). In spring 1941 a batch of 20 was assigned to the RAF, following 15 months of negotiations which finally resulted in the aircraft being supplied in exchange for complete information on their combat performance (this was prior to the 1940 Lend-Lease Act). As RAF Fortress Is they had a disastrous and mismanaged career which dramatically reduced their numbers to a handful (about nine) which were transferred to Coastal Command and the Middle East.

Further extensive internal improvements, a new electrical system and engine-cowl cooling gills, led to the B-17D, of which 42 were ordered in 1940. This was the latest model in

Some idea of how deadly the German heavy radar-predicted flak could be is afforded by this picture taken during the bomb run of the 486th Bomb Group on the hated Merseburg oil plants on 2 November 1944. One of the 100-plus heavy guns scored a direct hit through solid cloud on a B-17G of the 834th Bomb Squadron.

Provision of adequate forward-firing defensive armament was always a problem with the B-17, but culminated in the B-17G series with four 0.5-in (12.7-mm) guns in two turrets (dorsal and chin, each with two guns) supplemented by a pair of manually operated cheek guns, one on each side of the nose.

service at the time of Pearl Harbor (7 December 1941) when 30 were destroyed on the ground at Hickham Field and at Clark Field, Philippines, the following day. But by this time Boeing had developed a visually different model which incorporated all the lessons learned in World War 2 in Europe. Called Boeing 299O, it entered US Army Air Force service in December 1941 as the B-17E. Its most striking change was the much larger tail, with a giant dorsal fin and long-span tailplane giving better control and stability at high altitude. Armament was completely revised, with paired 0.5-in (12.7-mm) guns in a powered turret behind the cockpit, in a ventral turret at the trailing edge, and in a new manual turret in the tail. Another pair of guns could be fired by hand from the roof of the radio compartment, and with a single hand-aimed gun at each waist position this made a total of 10 heavy machine guns, plus two 0.3-in (7.62-mm) guns aimed from the nose. Further improvements in armour and equipment all helped to increase gross weight to 54,000 lb (24494 kg), so cruising speed inevitably fell from 231 to only 210 mph (338 km/h). This was the first B-17 in large-scale production, and deliveries totalled 512 including 45 sent to the RAF as Fortress IIAs.

Massive production

On 30 May 1942 Boeing flew the first B-17F with many further changes which allowed gross weight to soar to 65,000 lb (29484 kg) with a potential bomb load for short ranges of 20,800 lb (9435 kg), though on normal combat missions the load seldom exceeded 5,000 lb (2268 kg). The only obvious external change on the F-model was the more pointed nose moulded in one piece of Plexiglas. This type went into production not only at Boeing but also in a great nationwide pool with assembly lines at Douglas (Long Beach) and Vega (a Lockheed subsidiary at Burbank). Boeing built 2,300 of this model, and Douglas and Vega added 605 and 500.

With the B-17E and B-17F the US 8th Air Force built up its early strength in England. The first combat mission was flown on 17 August 1942 by 12 B-17Es of the 97th Bomb Group against a marshalling yard near Rouen. This was the small beginning to the greatest strategic striking force ever created, which was to lead to a three-year campaign in the course of which 640,036 US tons of bombs were dropped on German targets and, at the cost of grievous losses, supremacy was eventually obtained even over the heart of Germany in daylight.

By far the most numerous model of B-17 was the last. The B-17G was the final result of bitterly won combat experience and among other changes it introduced a chin turret firing

ahead with twin accurately aimed 0.5-in (12.7-mm) guns. Previously German fighters had brought down many B-17s with head-on attacks, but the B-17G, with the chin turret plus two more 0.5-in (12.7-mm) cheek guns (and possibly the dorsal turret) firing ahead was a tougher proposition. The B-17G had enclosed waist positions, much greater ammunition capacity and, like most B-17Fs, paddle-blade propellers to handle the greater weight and prevent too much deterioration in performance. Most B-17Gs had improved turbochargers which actually increased service ceiling to 35,000 ft (10670 m), but these bombers were so heavy the cruising speed fell to 182 mph (293 km/h). This increased the time the gigantic formations were exposed to rocket and cannon attack by the German fighters; conversely, of course, it lengthened the time the B-17 guns had to destroy those fighters.

Electronic versions

Boeing built 4,035 B-17Gs. Douglas 2,395 and Vega 2,250, a total of 8,680. The total of all versions was 12,731, of which 12,677 were formally accepted by the USAAF. The B-17F was used by the RAF as the Fortress II and the B-17G as the Fortress III, the main user being Coastal Command. Some were modified with a radar in place of the chin or ball turret, and for use against surfaced U-boats a 40-mm Vickers S gun was fitted in a nose mount. The B-17G was also the chief heavy carrier of special electronics for the RAF's No. 100 Group, Nos 214 and 223 Sqns being the pioneers of spoofing, decoy, jamming and intelligence missions with 19 distinct types of electronic or related device including the superpower emitters coded 'Jostle' and 'Piperack'. The only electronic device often carried by USAAF B-17s was the early H$_2$X or Micky Mouse radar used for bombing through cloud. This set's scanner was normally housed in a retractable radome under the nose or in place of the ball turret.

Elimination of paint from the B-17 gave a measurable gain in speed or reduced fuel consumption (because cruising speed was preset at a figure all aircraft could easily maintain at full load). These B-17Gs, built by Douglas, were photographed with the 381st Bomb Group (VE code, 532nd BS; VP, the 533rd). Home base was Ridgewell.

The ball turret, a retractable installation on the B-24 Liberator, was fixed on the B-17. Originally the B-17E had been fitted with a drum-type ventral turret aimed by a gunner in the fuselage, sighting via a periscope. This was soon replaced by the aptly named spherical ball-turret made by the Sperry company. The gunner had to climb into this and squat with his knees fully bent for perhaps five or six hours. A belly landing could flatten the ball-turret and its occupant, and there were many occasions when because of combat damage the turret doors jammed and a belly landing would have killed the ball-turret gunner. Normal procedure for a belly landing was to get the gunner out and then, using special tools, disconnect the whole turret from the aircraft and let it fall free. On one occasion a B-17 returned with severe combat damage and jammed landing gears, and near its home airfield it was found that the special tools were not on board. The executive officer of the station was notified by radio; within minutes he had grabbed a set of tools and taken off. For more than two hours he circled in close formation with the stricken B-17 trying to pass the tools on the end of a cable. He succeeded.

In 1942 various special versions of B-17 were produced by Vega to serve as escort fighters. The first was the second Vega-built B-17F, which was rebuilt as an XB-40 with many armament changes including a second dorsal turret and a bomb bay full of ammunition. It was followed by 20 YB-40s

The subject of this colour profile is a B-17C, which introduced the ventral bathtub also used on the D, but had flush waist gun positions instead of blisters. The B-17D's differences were mainly internal.

Ship 41-9023 was named *Yankee Doodle*, and was one of the most famous of all US bombers. Assigned to the 414th BS, 97th BG, it carried General Ira C. Eaker, commanding general of the VII Bomber Command, on the very first mission in Europe, to Rouen railway workshops on 17 August 1942. The total force: just 12 Fortresses.

Boeing B-17

In a typical story of amazing nerve and skulduggery, the infant Israeli air force, the Heyl Ha'Avir, managed to get hold of three B-17Gs in 1948. Devoid of guns, and with turret holes gaping open or with wood/plaster sealing (for the chin hole), and devoid of navigation gear, they bombed Cairo on their way to Israel!

Boeing B-17 variants

Boeing 299: prototype with four 750 hp (560 kW) Pratt & Whitney Hornet engines often called XB 17 but in fact had no military designation (total 1)
Y1B-17: service test batch four 930 hp (694 kW) Wright R-1820-39 engines operational equipment five 0.3 in (7.62-mm) guns, 4,800 lb (2177 kg) bombload later redesignated B-17 (total 13)
Y1B-17A: single aircraft with R-1820-51 turbocharged Cyclone engines
B-17B: Boeing 299E; later styled 299M first production model (total 39)
B-17C: Boeing 299H four R-1820-65 engines improved armament and equipment (total 38)

B-17D: Boeing 299H further improvements (total 42)
B-17E: Boeing 299O complete redesign and heavier armament, first major production version (total 512)

B-17F: Boeing 299P, restressed for higher weights R-1820-97 engines, frameless plastic nose (total 3,405)

Boeing B-17F

B-17G: standard bomber from 1943 Dash 97 engines with B 2 (from late 1944 B-22) turbo, chin turret (normal defensive armament 13 .05 in (12.7 mm guns) basis for numerous conversions and post war variants (total 8,680)

Boeing B-17C

Boeing B-17E

with even heavier armament including quadruple gun mounts at nose and tail and a total of as many as 30 guns of up to 37- or 40-mm calibre! So heavy were these 'fighters' that they could not even keep formation with the B-17 bombers, and though they flew nine combat missions in 1943 they were judged unsuccessful.

In 1943 Boeing converted the ninth production B-17E to have liquid-cooled Allison engines of 1,425 hp (1063 kW) each; these naturally resulted in improved performance but it remained a one-off prototype (designated XB-38). Another unique machine was the plush XC-108 VIP transport which began life as a B-17E (41-2593) but was converted for General Douglas MacArthur, supreme commander in the Pacific, with a comfortable interior for 38 passengers. The XC-108A was a similar conversion but for cargo, with a large door on the left side. The YC-108 was a VIP conversion of a B-17F, and the XC-108B was a B-17F tanker which ferried fuel 'over the hump' from India to China.

Oddities and other developments

The F-9s were a batch of 16 B-17Fs rebuilt by United Airlines at Cheyenne as strategic reconnaissance machines with from six to ten cameras in fuselage installations. Another 45 B-17Fs were converted as F-9As or F-9Bs, while 10 B-17Gs were turned into F-9Cs, the post-war designation for survivors being FB-17 up to 1947 and RB-17 thereafter. One B-17F served with the US Navy, and late in the war 40 B-17Gs were transferred to the US Navy to pioneer the technique of AEW (airborne early warning) with the newly developed APS-120 radar in a vast chin blister; this variant was designated PB-1W.

A strange wartime rebuild was the Aphrodite cruise-missile conversion in which war-weary B-17Fs and B-17Gs were stripped of everything that could be removed and

packed with 10 tons of Torpex, a British explosive with 50 per cent greater blasting power than Amatol. Under the project names 'Perilous' and 'Castor' many tests were made, the take-off being made by two pilots in an open cockpit who then baled out to leave the Fortress (official designation BQ-17) under radio control from an accompanying aircraft such as a B-17 or PV-1. Though 11 combat launches were made on German targets the idea was judged rather too perilous after one BQ-7 had made a crater over 100 ft (30 m) in diameter in England and another had broken radio link and orbited a British city before heading out to sea.

In 1944 British experience was used in converting B-17Gs into B-17H air/sea rescue aircraft with an airborne lifeboat and search radar; post-war these were designated SB-17G. Other post-war variants included the CB-17 and VB-17 transports, TB-17 trainers, radio-guided QB-17 versions and DB-17 radio director aircraft. These soldiered on with the USAF after its formation in 1947, and also with various minor air forces. Many others became civil airliners.

No history of the B-17 would be complete, however, without reference to its exciting cloak-and-dagger operations with I/KG 200, the clandestine Gruppe of the Luftwaffe whose story has only recently come into the open. The B-17, mainly the G model, was its most important captured type, used for numerous long-range missions under the cover-designation Dornier Do 200. These machines carried out daring operations throughout Europe from Norway to Jordan and the Western Desert. They were not specifically intended to deceive the Allies, and wore German markings; they were used just because they were better for the job than any German aircraft!

It is difficult to praise any Allied aircraft more highly. It is undoubtedly due to the B-17 that the Allies gained air supremacy in Europe towards the end of the war.

From a distance this B-17G, ship number 43-37716, merely looks a trifle dirty or weatherbeaten. On closer inspection it can be seen to be the famous 5 Grand, the 5,000th B-17 built by Boeing, covered with the names of every Seattle worker who found a space.

Messerschmitt Bf 109

Longest-serving of all German interceptors, Willy Messerschmitt's classic Bf 109 was the cornerstone of the Luftwaffe's fighter arm throughout World War 2, being built in greater numbers than any other aircraft and credited with more air victories than any other fighter in the history of aerial warfare.

When aircraft designer Willy Messerschmitt began planning the Bf 109 in his Bavarian aircraft factory, he adapted some of the features of his four-seater passenger aircraft, the Bf 108 Taifun, and created a small, angular low-wing monoplane with a retractable undercarriage and an enclosed cockpit. The new Junkers Jumo 210A was to have been the engine, but this was not yet complete. Instead, the 695-hp (518-kW) Rolls Royce Kestrel VI was imported, and the new machine was completed in September 1935.

When flown in competition with the Ar 80 V1, Fw 159 V1 and He 112 V1, at the Travemünde trials, the Bf 109 V1 performed well despite minor problems and, amid general surprise, was rewarded by a contract for 10 prototype development aircraft (although it was not in fact declared the outright winner, 10 Heinkel aircraft also being ordered).

Three further prototypes (the Bf 109 V2 registered D-IUDE, Bf 109 V3 D-IHNY and Bf 109 V4 D-IOQY) were flown in 1936, powered by Jumo 210A engines and with provision for two synchronized Mg 17 machine-guns in the nose decking. However, rumours abounded that the British Hawker Hurricane and Supermarine Spitfire were to be armed with four guns, so that by the time the Bf 109 V4 prototype flew a third Mg 17 was planned to fire through the propeller hub.

The proposed two-gun Bf 109A production version did not therefore materialize, and the first pre-production Bf 109 B-0 examples were flown early in 1937, at the same time as the Bf 109 V5, Bf 109 V6 and Bf 109 V7 prototypes. Considerable operational experience was gained by three Staffeln of Jagdgruppe 88, which were equipped with production examples of the Bf 109B-1, Bf 109B-2 and Bf 109C-1 versions during the Spanish Civil War, experience that not only assisted in the development of the aircraft itself

but of air combat in general; for it was largely through men such as Werner Mölders and Adolf Galland (the former arguably the finest fighter pilot of all time, and the latter to become Germany's General of Fighters during World War 2), who fought in Spain with the Bf 109, that there came to be evolved the basic air fighting tactics which were to last until the end of the era of gun fighting air-combat.

By the beginning of World War 2 in September 1939, the Luftwaffe had standardized its fighter equipment with the Bf 109. The Bf 109D series, although produced in fairly large numbers and still in service, was giving place to the Bf 109E (widely known as the 'Emil'). Ten pre-production Bf 109E-0s appeared late in 1938 with two nose-mounted MG 17 machine-guns and two in the wings, and powered by the 1,100-hp (812-kW) DB 601A engine. Production Bf 109E-1s started leaving the Augsburg factory at the beginning of 1939 with alternative provision for two 20-mm MG FF cannon in place of the wing machine-guns. Maximum speed was 354 mph (570 km/h) at 12,305 ft (3750 m) and service ceiling 36,090 ft (11000 m), performance figures which helped the Bf 109E to eclipse all of its opponents in the first eight months of the war. A sub-variant, the Bf 109E-1/B, introduced soon after, was a fighter-bomber capable of carrying a 551-lb (250-kg) bomb under the fuselage.

Production of the Emil was shifted from Augsburg to Regensburg in 1939 (to make way for the Bf 110 twin-engine fighter) as a massive subcontract programme was undertaken by Ago, Arado, Erla and WNF, no less than 1,540 aircraft being delivered that year. On the eve of the invasion of Poland the Jagdverband comprised 12 Gruppen flying 850 Bf 109E-1s and Bf 109E-1/Bs and one with Ar 68s. Some 235 Bf 109D-1s were still serving with the Zerstörergeschwader.

One of the earliest known air-to-air photographs of a Bf 109, this November 1936 picture shows the Bf 109V4 (no. 4 prototype), with Jumo 210A engine and armament of three MG 17 machine-guns, each with 500 rounds. The similarity to later production Bf 109 versions is strikingly apparent.

To speed production by an as-yet small industry the Bf 109 was licensed in 1937 to Fieseler and in 1938 to Focke-Wulf and Erla. This photograph was taken at Bremen in August 1938 and shows the first 10 Bf 109C-2s completed by Focke-Wulf. The C-2 was the final Jumo-engined version, with five MG 17s.

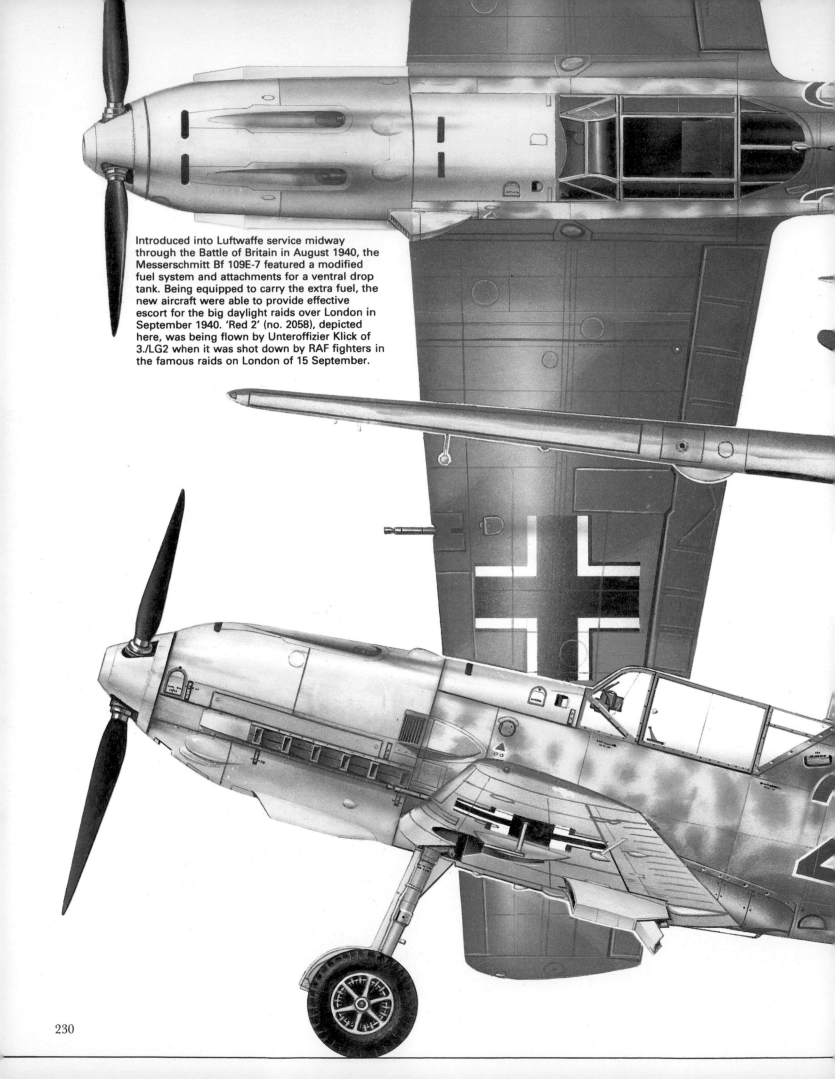

Introduced into Luftwaffe service midway through the Battle of Britain in August 1940, the Messerschmitt Bf 109E-7 featured a modified fuel system and attachments for a ventral drop tank. Being equipped to carry the extra fuel, the new aircraft were able to provide effective escort for the big daylight raids over London in September 1940. 'Red 2' (no. 2058), depicted here, was being flown by Unteroffizier Klick of 3./LG2 when it was shot down by RAF fighters in the famous raids on London of 15 September.

Messerschmitt Bf 109

Specification

Messerschmitt Bf 109E-7
Type: single-seat interceptor fighter
Powerplant: one 1,200-hp (895-kW) Daimler Benz DB 601N 12-cylinder inverted-vee liquid-cooled inline engine
Performance: maximum speed 359 mph (578 km/h) at 12,300 ft (3749 m);
Initial climb rate 3,300 ft (1006 m) per minute; service ceiling 36,500 ft (11125 m); range 680 miles (1094 km)
Weights: empty 4,440 lb (2014 kg); maximum take-off 6,100 lb (2767 kg)
Dimensions: span 32 ft 4½ in (9.86 m); length 28 ft 8 in (8.74 m); height 11 ft 2 in (3.40 m); wing area 174 sq ft (16.16 m²)
Armament: one hub-firing 20-mm (MG FF/M cannon and four 7.9-mm (0.31-in) MG 17 machine-guns in nose decking and wings

Messerschmitt Bf 109

The first occasion on which Bf 109s fought the RAF was during the daylight raid by 24 unescorted Vickers Wellingtons on Wilhelmshaven on 18 December 1939, 12 of the bombers being destroyed for the loss of two Bf 109Es of JG 77.

Deadly production

In 1940 production of the Emil increased to 1,868 aircraft, the D-series being almost entirely discarded from front-line use. Principal sub-variants produced that year were the Bf 109E-2, Bf 109E-3 (with two MG 17s in the nose and two in the wings, plus an MG FF/M firing through the propeller shaft) and the Bf 109 E (with two nose MG 17s and two wing MG FF cannon). All these versions saw widespread action during the great daylight battles over southern England in the Battle of Britain. When employed in the 'free chase' tactic they proved deadly, being generally superior to the Hurricane and well matched with the Spitfire. However, as is now well known, the capabilities of the Bf 109E were frequently squandered when the aircraft were too often tied to close escort on bomber formations, a role in which the Bf 109Es were deprived of their greatest assets, speed and manoeuvrability. Later in the Battle of Britain they were also employed as fighter-bombers (the Bf 109E-4/B). Other variants, which appeared soon after the Battle of Britain, included the Bf 109E-5 and Bf 109E-6 reconnaissance fighters, the latter with DB 601N engine, the Bf 109 E-7 with provision for belly drop-tank, and the Bf 109E-7/Z with GM-1 nitrous oxide engine boost.

Early in 1941 the Emil was beginning to appear in the Mediterranean theatre, tropicalized versions of the above sub-variant serving with JG 27 in North Africa. However, by the time Germany opened its great attack on the Soviet Union in June 1941, the Bf 109F series was beginning to go in the front-line fighter squadrons although the Emil continued to serve for a long time yet.

Powered by the 1,200-hp (895-kW) DB 601E, the Bf 109F was generally regarded as the most attractive of the entire Bf 109 family introducing extended and rounded wingtips and enlarged spinner while Frise ailerons and plain flaps replaced the Emil's slotted flaps. A fully retractable tailwheel superseded the earlier fixed type, and a cantilever tailplane was introduced. In the matter of gun armament, however, the Bf 109F was widely criticized, for it reverted to the hub cannon and two nose decking MG 17s. While this tended to satisfy the German *Experten* (aces) as benefitting the aircraft's performance, it was pointed out that the majority of Luftwaffe fighter pilots needed a heavier armament with which to achieve a 'kill'.

Pre-production Bf 109F-0s were evaluated by the Luftwaffe during the second half of 1940, and Bf 109F-1s were delivered early the following year. A number of accidents indicated that removal of the tailplane struts left the entire tail unit vulnerable to sympathetic vibration at certain oscillating frequencies of the engine, and strengthening modifications were quickly put in hand. After the Bf 109F-2 (with 15-mm

J-310 was the first Bf 109 to serve Switzerland's Fliegertruppe, delivered on 17 December 1938. Powered by a 680-hp (507-kW) Jumo 210Da engine (like the German Bf 109B) it had an armament of four MG 17 machine-guns (as fitted to the Bf 109C). The Swiss used Bf 109s until the end of 1949, some being assembled locally.

Messerschmitt Bf 109G-14/U4 cutaway drawing key

1 Starboard navigation light
2 Starboard wingtip
3 Fixed trim tab
4 Starboard Frise-type aileron
5 Flush-riveted stressed wing-skinning
6 Handley Page leading-edge automatic slot
7 Slot control linkage
8 Slot equalizer rod
9 Aileron control linkage
10 Fabric-covered flap section
11 Wheel fairing
12 Port fuselage machine-gun ammunition-feed fairing
13 Port Rheinmetall Borsig 13-mm MG 131 machine-gun
14 Engine accessories
15 Starboard machine-gun trough
16 Daimler Benz DB 605AM 12-cylinder inverted-vee liquid-cooled engine
17 Detachable cowling panel
18 Oil filter access
19 Oil tank
20 Propeller pitch-change mechanism
21 VDM electrically-operated constant-speed propeller
22 Spinner
23 Engine-mounted cannon muzzle
24 Blast tube
25 Propeller hub
26 Spinner back plate
27 Auxiliary cooling intakes
28 Cooling header tank
29 Anti-vibration rubber engine-mounting pads
30 Elektron forged engine bearer
31 Engine bearer support strut attachment
32 Plug leads
33 Exhaust manifold fairing strip
34 Ejector exhausts
35 Cowling fasteners
36 Oil cooler
37 Oil cooler intake
38 Starboard mainwheel
39 Oil cooler outlet flap
40 Wing root fillet
41 Wing/fuselage fairing
42 Firewall/bulkhead
43 Supercharger air intake
44 Supercharger assembly
45 20-mm cannon magazine drum
46 13-mm machine-gun ammunition feed
47 Engine bearer upper attachment

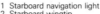
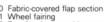

Called 'tripala' by the Spanish (the earlier models had a two-blade propeller) the Bf 109E-1 was by far the best fighter in Spain in early 1939, when this picture was taken at a Légion Kóndor base. Armament was two cannon and two MG 17 machine-guns. The Légion transferred 40 Bf 109s to Spain, which built other models post-war.

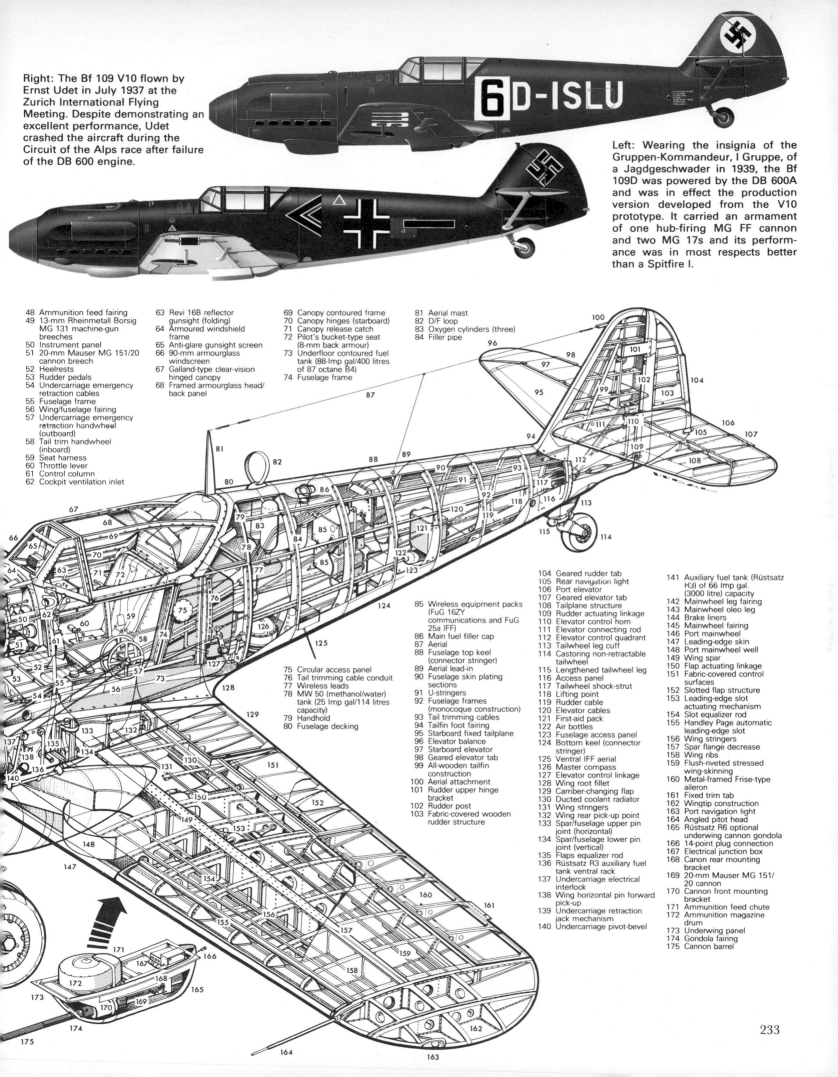

Right: The Bf 109 V10 flown by Ernst Udet in July 1937 at the Zurich International Flying Meeting. Despite demonstrating an excellent performance, Udet crashed the aircraft during the Circuit of the Alps race after failure of the DB 600 engine.

Left: Wearing the insignia of the Gruppen-Kommandeur, I Gruppe, of a Jagdgeschwader in 1939, the Bf 109D was powered by the DB 600A and was in effect the production version developed from the V10 prototype. It carried an armament of one hub-firing MG FF cannon and two MG 17s and its performance was in most respects better than a Spitfire I.

48 Ammunition feed fairing
49 13-mm Rheinmetall Borsig MG 131 machine-gun breeches
50 Instrument panel
51 20-mm Mauser MG 151/20 cannon breech
52 Heelrests
53 Rudder pedals
54 Undercarriage emergency retraction cables
55 Fuselage frame
56 Wing/fuselage fairing
57 Undercarriage emergency retraction handwheel (outboard)
58 Tail trim handwheel (inboard)
59 Seat harness
60 Throttle lever
61 Control column
62 Cockpit ventilation inlet

63 Revi 16B reflector gunsight (folding)
64 Armoured windshield frame
65 Anti-glare gunsight screen
66 90-mm armourglass windscreen
67 Galland-type clear-vision hinged canopy
68 Framed armourglass head/back panel

69 Canopy contoured frame
70 Canopy hinges (starboard)
71 Canopy release catch
72 Pilot's bucket-type seat (8-mm back armour)
73 Underfloor contoured fuel tank (88-Imp gal/400 litres of 87 octane B4)
74 Fuselage frame

81 Aerial mast
82 D/F loop
83 Oxygen cylinders (three)
84 Filler pipe

85 Wireless equipment packs (FuG 16ZY communications and FuG 25a IFF)
86 Main fuel filler cap
87 Aerial
88 Fuselage top keel (connector stringer)
89 Aerial lead-in
90 Fuselage skin plating sections
91 U-stringers
92 Fuselage frames (monocoque construction)
93 Tail trimming cables
94 Tailfin foot fairing
95 Starboard fixed tailplane
96 Elevator balance
97 Starboard elevator
98 Geared elevator tab
99 All-wooden tailfin construction
100 Aerial attachment
101 Rudder upper hinge bracket
102 Rudder post
103 Fabric-covered wooden rudder structure

104 Geared rudder tab
105 Rear navigation light
106 Port elevator
107 Geared elevator tab
108 Tailplane structure
109 Rudder actuating linkage
110 Elevator control horn
111 Elevator connecting rod
112 Elevator control quadrant
113 Tailwheel leg cuff
114 Castoring non-retractable tailwheel
115 Lengthened tailwheel leg
116 Access panel
117 Tailwheel shock-strut
118 Lifting point
119 Rudder cable
120 Elevator cables
121 First-aid pack
122 Air bottles
123 Fuselage access panel
124 Bottom keel (connector stringer)
125 Ventral IFF aerial
126 Master compass
127 Elevator control linkage
128 Wing root fillet
129 Camber-changing flap
130 Ducted coolant radiator
131 Wing stringers
132 Wing rear pick-up point
133 Spar/fuselage upper pin joint (horizontal)
134 Spar/fuselage lower pin joint (vertical)
135 Flaps equalizer rod
136 Rüstsatz R3 auxiliary fuel tank ventral rack
137 Undercarriage electrical interlock
138 Wing horizontal pin forward pick-up
139 Undercarriage retraction jack mechanism
140 Undercarriage pivot-bevel

75 Circular access panel
76 Tail trimming cable conduit
77 Wireless leads
78 MW 50 (methanol/water) tank (25 Imp gal/114 litres capacity)
79 Handhold
80 Fuselage decking

141 Auxiliary fuel tank (Rüstsatz H3) of 66 Imp gal. (3000 litre) capacity
142 Mainwheel leg fairing
143 Mainwheel oleo leg
144 Brake liners
145 Mainwheel fairing
146 Port mainwheel
147 Leading-edge skin
148 Port mainwheel well
149 Wing spar
150 Flap actuating linkage
151 Fabric-covered control surfaces
152 Slotted flap structure
153 Leading-edge slot actuating mechanism
154 Slot equalizer rod
155 Handley Page automatic leading-edge slot
156 Wing stringers
157 Spar flange decrease
158 Wing ribs
159 Flush-riveted stressed wing-skinning
160 Metal-framed Frise-type aileron
161 Fixed trim tab
162 Wingtip construction
163 Port navigation light
164 Angled pitot head
165 Rüstsatz R6 optional underwing cannon gondola
166 14-point plug connection
167 Electrical junction box
168 Canon rear mounting bracket
169 20-mm Mauser MG 151/20 cannon
170 Cannon front mounting bracket
171 Ammunition feed chute
172 Ammunition magazine drum
173 Underwing panel
174 Gondola fairing
175 Cannon barrel

Aircraft VK + AB was Bf 109 V24 (prototype no. 24), works number 5604. It was built in 1940 alongside V23 (CE + BP) as the third and fourth development aircraft for the Bf 109F, with round wingtips, a better-streamlined engine installation and other changes. The Bf 109F was the nicest of all 109s to fly.

JG 54 Grünherz ('Green Heart') moved from northern France to the Soviet Union in 1941, and this photograph was taken on an airfield near the Leningrad front in summer 1942. These Bf 109-G2s bear the badges of III/JG 54 (left) and II/JG 54 (right). The G-2 was the first 'Gustav' to enter service, in late April 1942.

MG 151 replacing the 20-mm MG FF) came the principal version, the BF 109F-3, early in 1942 with a top speed of 390 mph (628 km/h) at 21,980 ft (6700 m).

Bf 109Fs had joined the Geschwaderstab and III Gruppe of Adolf Galland's JG 26 'Schlageter' early in 1941 on the Channel coast, and during the early stages of Operation 'Barbarossa' in the East this version equipped Major Günther Lützow's JG 3 'Udet', Werner Mölders' JG 51, Major Günther von Maltzahn's JG 53 'Pik As' and Major Johannes Trautloft's JG 54. The superiority of the new fighter (even over the Spitfire Mk V in the West) quickly became apparent as the German fighter pilots' victory tallies soared.

The Bf 109F underwent progressive improvement and development: the BF 109F-4 had an MG 151 rebarrelled to 20-mm, the Bf 109F-4/R1 could be fitted with *Rüstsatz* (field conversion kit) comprising two 20-mm MG 151 guns in underwing packs for the bomber-destroyer role, the Bf 109F-4/B fighter-bomber was capable of carrying up to 1,102 lb (500 kg) of bombs, and the Bf 109F-5 and Bf 109F-6 reconnaissance fighters were introduced later in 1942. It was principally in the tropicalized Bf 109F-4 that the 22-year-old Oberleutnant Hans-Joachim Marseille became the highest-scoring Luftwaffe fighter pilot in the West with 158 air victories, although he died baling out from a BF 109G-2 on 30 September 1942 in North Africa.

The Bf 109G (dubbed the 'Gustav' by German pilots) was introduced into service in the late summer of 1942 and came to be built in larger numbers than any other version. It was powered by the 1,475-hp (1100-kW) DB 605A, although pre-production Bf 109G-0s retained the DB 601E. Basic arm-

ament remained two nose-mounted MG 17s and hub-firing 20-mm MG 151/20 cannon. The Bf 109G-1 with pressure cabin, was powered by the DB 605A-1 with GM-1 power boosting, and the tropical version, the Bf 109G-1/Trop, carried 0.51-in (13-mm) MG 131s in place of the MG 17s, necessitating larger breech blocks and giving rise to the nickname *Beule* (bump) on account of the raised fairings foward of the windscreen. The Bf 109G-2 dispensed with the pressure cabin and the Bf 109G-2/R1 was a fighter-bomber; the Bf 109G-3 was similar to the Bf 109G-1 but with FuG 16Z radio, and the Bf 109G-4 was an unpressurized version of the Bf 109G-3. The Bf 109G-5 introduced the DB 605D engine with MW-50 water-methanol power-boosting (making possible a maximum power of 1,800 hp/1343 kW) for combat bursts), while the Bf 109G-5/R2 featured a taller rudder and lengthened tailwheel leg in an effort to counter the aircraft's swing on take-off.

Improvements and add-ons

Most important of all the Gustavs was the Bf 109G-6 which, in various sub-variants, was powered by AM, AS, ASB, ASD or ASM versions of the DB 605 engine; basic armament was the hub-firing 30-mm MK 108 cannon, two nose MG 131s and two underwing 20-mm MG 151/20 guns. Numerous *Rüstsatz* kits were produced including those to produce the Bf 109G-6/R1 fighter-bomber with a bombload of

The illustration shows a Bf 109E-4N of Jagdgeschwader 27, used in North Africa in 1941. It was equipped with four 7.92-mm machine guns.

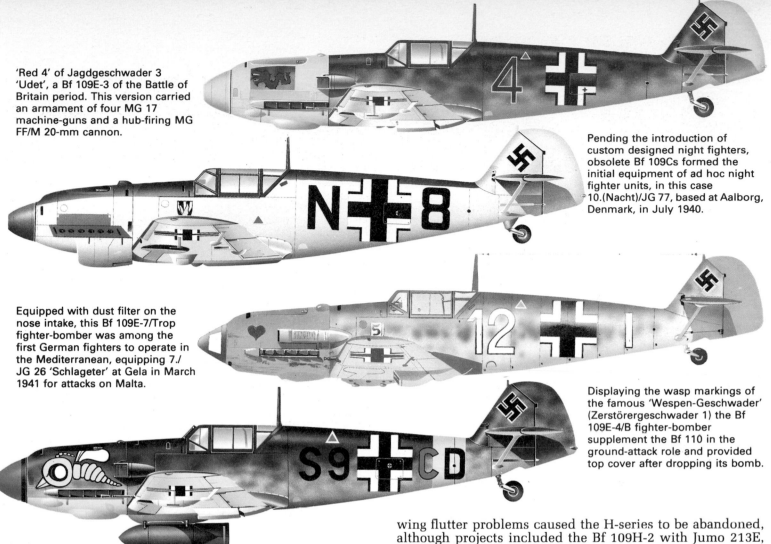

'Red 4' of Jagdgeschwader 3 'Udet', a Bf 109E-3 of the Battle of Britain period. This version carried an armament of four MG 17 machine-guns and a hub-firing MG FF/M 20-mm cannon.

Pending the introduction of custom designed night fighters, obsolete Bf 109Cs formed the initial equipment of ad hoc night fighter units, in this case 10.(Nacht)/JG 77, based at Aalborg, Denmark, in July 1940.

Equipped with dust filter on the nose intake, this Bf 109E-7/Trop fighter-bomber was among the first German fighters to operate in the Mediterranean, equipping 7./JG 26 'Schlageter' at Gela in March 1941 for attacks on Malta.

Displaying the wasp markings of the famous 'Wespen-Geschwader' (Zerstörergeschwader 1) the Bf 109E-4/B fighter-bomber supplement the Bf 110 in the ground-attack role and provided top cover after dropping its bomb.

up to 1,102 lb (500 kg), and the Bf 109G-6/R2 bomber-destroyer with two 21-cm (8.27-in) WGr 210 'Dodel' rockets replacing the underwing cannon. The Bf 109G-6.U4 (with an *Umrüst-Bausatz* or factory conversion set) was armed with two 30-mm MK 108 underwing cannon, and the Bf 109G-6U4N night-fighter carried radar. Tropicalized versions of most of these were also produced. The Bf 109G-7 was not built, but the Bf 109G-8 reconnaissance fighter formed part of the equipment of Nahaufklärungsgruppe 13 late in 1943 on the Channel coast. Fastest of all Gustavs was the Bf 109G-10 with the DB 605D with MW-50 and bulged cockpit canopy (known as the 'Galand hood'); top speed was 429 mph (690 km/h) at 24,280 ft (7400 m); the Bf 109G-10/R2 and R6 possessed the revised tail and tailwheel assembly of the Bf 109G-5/R2 and were equipped with FuG 25a IFF equipment; the Bf 109G-10/U4 had provision for a belly gun pack containing two MK 108 30-mm guns, but this could be replaced by a non-jettisonable fuel tank known as the *Irmer Behalter*. The Bf 109G-12 was a two-seat trainer, field-modified from the Bf 109G-1 to provide conversion training on the Schulejagdgeschwader, notably JG 101, 102, 104, 106, 107 and 108 in 1944. Last operational version was the 'universal' Bf 109G-14 with lightened fixed armament but with provision for external guns, WGr210 rockets or bombs. The Bf 109G-16 heavily armoured ground-attack fighter-bomber entered production before Germany's surrender but did not see operational service.

Development of the Bf 109H high-altitude fighter started in 1943, being a progression from the F-series with increased wing span and the GM-1 boosted DB 601E. Maximum speed was 466 mph (750 km/h) at 33,135 ft (10100 m). Pre-production aircraft were evaluated operationally in France and a few sorties were flown by production Bf 109H-1s, but wing flutter problems caused the H-series to be abandoned, although projects included the Bf 109H-2 with Jumo 213E, and the Bf 109H-5 with DB 605 engines.

Last main operational version of the Bf 109 was the K-series, developed directly from the Gustav; indeed the Bf 109K-0 pre-production aircraft were converted G-series airframes. The Bf 109K-2 and Bf 109K-4 (pressurized) were powered by MW-50 boosted 2,000-hp (1492-kW) DB 605 ASCM/DCM engines and armed with one 30-mm MK 103 or MK 108 cannon and two 15-mm (0.59-in) MG 151 heavy machine-guns, and the Bf 109K-6 had provision for two underwing 30-mm MK 103s. Only two Bf 109K-14s (DB 605L with MW-50 and a top speed of 450 mph/725 km/h) saw action before the end of the war, being delivered to Major Wilhelm Batz's Gruppenstab, II/JG 52, in April 1945.

Trials and experiments

With the Focke-Wulf Fw 190 reaching full operational status only after two years of war, the Bf 109 provided the backbone of the Luftwaffe's fighter arm throughout World War 2: with more than 30,000 examples produced (because of confusion caused by the bombing of factories, an accurate production total could not be arrived at, but only the Russian Ilyushin Il-2 had a higher figure, with 36,163 models built), it was natural that experiments and projects abounded.

For example, among the more bizarre trials were those conducted on Bf 109Es to carry a parachutist in an over-wing 'paracapsule'. Another (in the Starr-Schlepp programme) involving the mounting of a Bf 109E on a DFS 230 troop-carrying glider as a means of delivering airborne forces; this experiment was followed later in the war by the well-known *Beethoven-Gerät* composite weapon system involving the use of Bf 109s and Fw 109s mounted atop unmanned Junkers Ju 88s loaded with explosives. A number of radical operational tactics were pioneered by Bf 109 units, including the aerial bombing of American bomber formations with 551-lb (250-kg)

Wearing the white 'theatre band' on the rear fuselage (denoting service in the Mediterranean), this Bf 109F-4/Trop belonged to 6./JG 53 based at Comiso in May 1942 during the Luftwaffe's assault on Malta.

The Bf 109G-14 with 'Galland' hood was a fighter-bomber version of the G-6, this 'Gustav' bearing the markings of III./JG 53. The 'Spiralschnauze' has no significance in this instance. Note the bulges over the breech blocks of the nose-mounted 13-mm (0.51-in) MG 131 guns.

bombs dropped from Bf 109Gs (pioneered by JG 1 in 1943), and the use by JG 300 of day fighters for freelance night combat against night bombers, known as *wilde Sau* tactics.

A development of the Emil was the Bf 109T carrierborne fighter, intended for deployment abroad the German carrier *Graf Zeppelin*. Featuring folding wings, arrester hook and catapult spools, 10 pre-production Bf 109T-0s and 60 Bf 109T-1s were produced between 1939 and 1941, but when the carrier's construction was abandoned most of these aircraft were delivered to the Luftwaffe for land-based operation.

Perhaps the most ambitious of all projects was the Bf 109Z *Zwilling*, involving the union of two Bf 109F airframes and outer wing panels by means of new wing and tail sections; the pilot was to have been accommodated in the port fuselage and two versions were proposed, a *Zerstörer* with five 30-mm guns and a fighter-bomber with a 2,205-lb (1000-kg) bombload. A prototype was built but this was never flown.

Bf 109s were supplied to numerous foreign air forces from 1939 onwards, and considerable licence-production of the Gustav was undertaken by Avia at Prague and IAR at Brasov in Romania. The most successful of the foreign air arms with Bf 109s was the Finnish air force, its highest scoring pilot, Lentomestari Eino Juutilainen, achieving 94 victories, of which 59 were scored in Gustavs; he was the highest-scoring non-German/Austrian fighter pilot of all time and his aircraft was never once hit in combat.

Despite the absence of unit markings it is known that this Bf109 was serving in autumn 1943 with II/JG 26, one of the crack fighter units in northern France. It is a G-6/R6, the R6 modification adding the pair of 20-mm MG151 cannon and ammunition in underwing gondolas. The slats are clearly visible here.

Taken in 1944, when many Bf 109s were being used in the anti-bomber role with heavy rocket mortars, this photograph shows a pair of G-6/Rs2 with the most common of these weapons, the Wfr Gr21 which lobbed 21-cm rockets from the tubes under the wings. They were called *Pulk Zerstörer* ('formation destroyer').

Messerschmitt Bf 109 variants

Bf109a (later Bf109V1): D-IABI, first prototype; 695-hp (518-kW) Rolls-Royce Kestrel V engine; first flight in September 1935
Bf109 V2, V3 and V4: three prototypes, (D-IUDE, D-IHNY and D-IOQY); Jumo 210A engines
Bf109B: pre-production **Bf109B-0** with Jumo 210B; **Bf109B-1** with Jumo 210D; **Bf109B-2** with Jumo 210E and later, 210G engines
Bf109 V10 and V13: two prototypes, (D-ISLU and D-IPKY); Daimler-Benz DB 600 engines
Bf109C: developed from **Bf109 V8** prototype; **Bf109C-0** and **Bf109C-1** with four MG17 guns; **Bf109C-2** with five MG17s
Bf109 V13: modified with boosted DB 601 engine; world speed record of 379.38 mph (610.54 km/h) on 11 November 1937
Bf109D: developed from Bf109 V10 and V13 prototypes; **Bf109D-0** with DB 600Aa and armament of one 20-mm and two 7.92-mm (0.31-in) guns; **Bf109D-1** similar; **Bf109D-2** with two wing MG 17s; **Bf109D-3** with two MG FFs in wings
Bf109 V14: prototype (D-IRTT); fuel-injection DB 601A engine; two 20-mm and two 7.92-mm (0.31-in) guns; **Bf109 V15** (D-IPHR) similar but one 20-mm gun
Bf109E: **Bf109E-0** with four 7.92-mm (0.31-in) guns; **Bf109E-1** (and **Bf109E-1/B** bomber) similar; **Bf109E-2** with two 20-mm and two 7.92-mm (0.31-in) guns; **Bf109E-3** with one hub 20-mm and four 7.92-mm (0.31-in) guns; **Bf109E-4** (also **Bf109E-4/B** and **Bf109E-4/Trop**) similar to Bf109E-3 but no hub gun; **Bf109E-4/N** with DB610N engine; **Bf109E-5** and **Bf109E-6** reconnaissance fighters with two 7.92-mm (0.31-in) guns; **Bf109E-7** similar to Bf109E-4/N with provision for belly tank (**Bf109E-7/U2** ground attack sub-variant); **Bf109E-7/Z** with GM-1 boost; **Bf109E-8** with DB601E engine; **Bf109E-9** reconnaissance fighter
Bf109F: **Bf109F-0** from E-airframes with DB 601N engine; **Bf109F-1** wih one 20-mm and two 7.92-mm (0.31-in) guns; **Bf109F-2** with one 15-mm and two 7.92-mm (0.31-in) guns (**Bf109F-2/Z** with GM-1); **Bf109F-3** with DB601E engine; **Bf109F-4** and **Bf109F-4/B** with one 20-mm and two 7.92-mm (0.31-in) guns and DB 601E; **Bf109F-5** and **Bf109F-6** reconnaissance fighters with two 7.92-mm (0.31-in) guns; trials aircraft included one with BMW 801 radial, one with Jumo 213, one with butterfly tail and one with wing fences
Bf109G: **Bf109G-0** with DB601E engine; **Bf109G-1** with DB 605A-1 and GM-1; **Bf109G-1/Trop** with one

20-mm and two 15-mm guns (*Beule*); **Bf109G-2** was unpressurized version of Bf109G-1 (also **Bf109G-2/R1** fighter-bomber); **Bf109G-3** with FuG 16Z radio; **Bf109G-4** unpressurized version of Bf109G-3; **Bf109G-5** with enlarged rudder had DB605D with MW-50; **Bf109G-6** with variations of DB 605 (see text) and two 13-mm (0.51-in), one 30-mm and two underwing 20-mm guns (also R and U sub-variants, see text); **Bf109G-8** reconnaissance fighter; **Bf109G-10** with DB605G and MW-50; **Bf109G-12** was two-seat trainer; **Bf109G-14** with one 20-mm and two 15-mm guns plus provision for underwing guns or rockets; **Bf109G-16** ground-attack fighter
Bf109H: high-altitude fighter developed from F-series; **Bf109H-0** pre-production; **Bf109H-1** with DB601E, **Bf109H-2** and **Bf109H-3** with Jumo 213; **Bf109H-5** with DB 605L
Bf109J: proposed Spanish licence-built version, not proceeded with
Bf109K: development from Bf109G-10; **Bf109K-0** with DB 605D and GM-1; **Bf109K-2** and **Bf109K-4** (pressurized) with DB 605ASCM/DCM and MW-50, and one 30-mm and two 15-mm guns; **Bf109K-6** with three 30-mm and two 15-mm guns; **Bf109K-14** with DB605L and MW-50
Bf109L: proposed version with Jumo 213E engine; maximum estimated speed 474 mph (763 km/h); not built)
Bf109S: proposed version with blown flaps; not built
Bf109T: carrierborne version of Bf109E for carrier *Graf Zeppelin*; 10 **Bf109T-0** converted by Fieseler; 60 **Bf109T-1** with DB601N; **Bf109T-2** was conversion of T-1 with deck gear removed
Bf109TL: project based on near-standard Bf109 with two underwing Jumo 109-004B turbojets; abandoned in 1943
Bf109Z Zwilling: twin Bf109F airframes with single pilot and five 30-mm guns (**Bf109Z-1**); **Bf109Z-2** with two 30-mm guns and 2,205-lb (1000-kg) bombload; **Bf109Z-3** and **Bf109Z-4** conversion of Bf109Z-1 and Bf109Z-2 respectively with Jumo 213 engines; one prototype built but not flown; led to Me 609 project
Me 209 V1, V2, V3 and V4: D-INJR, D-IWAH, D-IVFP and D-IRND; high-speed prototypes developed for speed records
Me 309 V1, V2, V3 and V4: GE-CU, GE-CV, GE-CW and GE-CX; high-speed, high-altitude fighter prototypes intended to replace Bf109F
Me609: projected development of Bf109Z *Zwilling* twin-Bf109; abandoned

236

Heinkel He 111: big Blitz bomber

Although a 1934 design, the Heinkel He 111 not only provided the muscle of Germany's 'strategic' bombing force at the beginning of World War 2 but, with surprisingly little alteration to its basic design, came to constitute the backbone of the Luftwaffe's bomber force until Hitler's eventual defeat in 1945.

When the Luftwaffe asked for a fast commercial transport plane to be built secretly, one which could be converted quickly and cheaply into a bomber, Siegfried and Walter Günter built the He 111. This was a twin-engined, larger version of the He 70 Blitz, which had been put into service by Lufthansa in 1934. The new machine had the same elliptical wings and the same tail. The first prototype, powered by 600-hp (448-kW) BMW VI 6, OZ engines, was flown from Marienehe by Gerhard Nitschke on 25 February 1935. After less than three weeks it was followed by the second. The third prototype, a forerunner of the bomber version of the He 111A, performed much better than many fighter planes of its time.

As six commercial He 111C-0s entered service as 10-seat airliners with Lufthansa during 1936, the first of 10 military He 111A-0s were being evaluated at Rechlin but, owing to inadequate engine power when carrying warload, were summarily rejected, all 10 aircraft being sold to China.

Anticipating the problem of power shortage, Heinkel produced the He 111B, of which the pre-production He 111B-0 series were powered by 1,000-hp (746-kW) Daimler-Benz DB 600A engines. Despite a considerable weight increase this version returned a top speed of 224 mph (360 km/h). By the end of 1936 the first production He 111B-1s, with 880-hp (656-kW) DB 600C engines appeared and, following successful trials, joined 1./KG 154 (later renamed KG 157), KG 152, KG 155, KG 253, KG 257 and KG 355.

Few examples of the He 111D-0 and D-1, with 950-hp (709-kW) DB 600Ga engines, were built as a result of a

Armourers handling an SC 500 (1,102-lb/500-kg) bomb on an airfield at the Eastern Front during the summer of 1941, with a Heinkel He 111H-6 of Kampfgeschwader 55 in the background. The He 111 provided the Luftwaffe's main heavy bomber strength for much of World War 2.

Heinkel He 111

Specification

Heinkel He 111H-16

Type: five-seat medium night bomber/pathfinder and glider tug

Powerplant: two 1,350-hp (1006-kW) Junkers Jumo 211F-2 inline piston engines

Performance: maximum speed 270 mph (435 km/h) at 19,685 ft (6000 m); service ceiling 27,890 ft (8500 m); normal range 1,212 miles (1950 km)

Weights: empty 19,136 lb (8680 kg); maximum take-off 30,864 lb (14000 kg)

Dimensions: span 74 ft 1¾ in (22.60 m); length 53 ft 9½ in (16.40 m); height 13 ft 1¼ in (4.00 m); wing area 931.1 sq ft (86.50 m²)

Armament: one 20-mm MG FF cannon, one 0.51-in (13-mm) MG 131 and up to seven 0.31-in (7.92-mm) MG 15 and MG 81 machine-guns, plus one 4,409-lb (200-kg) bomb carried externally and one 1,102-lb (500-kg) bomb internally, or eight 551-lb (250-kg) bombs all internally

The aircraft depicted here, Wkr Nr 3340, 'Yellow B' of the 9th Staffel, Kampfgeschwader 53 Legion Cóndor is shown with the escort identity wing bars carried during the big Luftwaffe day-light raids on London during Sunday 15 September 1940 – the climax of the Battle of Britain. The three white panels have always been said to indicate the III Gruppe of a Geschwader, although many anomalies exist as to throw doubt on this assumption. This aircraft was in fact damaged in action on that day and force landed at Armentiers with two wounded crew members; recent computerized research suggests that it was probably attacked by Spitfires of No. 66 (Fighter) Sqn.

239

shortage of this engine, and in 1938 production switched to the Hc 111E with 1,000-hp (746-kW) Junkers Jumo 211A-1s. Some 200 of these aircraft were produced, and they proved capable of lifting a 4,409-lb (2000-kg) bombload – roughly similar to that of the RAF's much slower Armstrong Whitworth Whitley III heavy bomber.

Meanwhile efforts had been made to simplify the He 111's wing structure for ease of production, and a new planform with straight leading and trailing edges had appeared on the seventh prototype. This wing was introduced into production with the He 111F, which emerged from the shops of Heinkel's new showpiece factory at Oranienburg in 1938; powered by 1,100-hp (821-kW) Jumo 211A-3s, 24 He 111F-1s were sold to Turkey, while the Luftwaffe's version was

the F-4. The He 111G series comprised nine examples, of which five (powered variously by B.M.W.132Dc and B.M.W.132H-1 radials and DB 600G inlines) were delivered to Lufthansa and the remainder went to Turkey as He 111G-5s. Produced simultaneously with the He 111G series, the He 111J series was developed as a torpedo-carrying version, of which about 90 were produced, but in fact served as a normal bomber with the Kriegsmarine-allocated KGr 806 in 1939.

Hitherto all He 111s had featured a conventional 'stepped' windscreen profile but, following the appearance of the eighth prototype in January 1938, the He 111P adopted the smooth nose profile with extensive glazing that so characterized the aircraft thereafter. This design incorporated a nose gun mounted offset to port, and a small hinge-up windscreen to improve the pilot's view during landing. The He 111P series entered production before the end of 1938, the type joining KG 157 in the following April. Intended as an interim version pending arrival of the He 111H, it survived in Luftwaffe service long after the outbreak of war in 1939.

Devastation in Poland

By September that year the He 111H was well-established with operational units, the Luftwaffe deploying 400 such

He 111 variants

He 111a (He 111 VI): 1st prototype, two 600-hp (448-kW) B.M.W. VI6,0Z with two-blade propellers
He 111 V2: 2nd prototype (D-ALIX)
He 111 V3: 3rd prototype (D-ALES)
He 111 V4: 4th prototype (D-AHAO)
He 111C-0: six aircraft (D-ABYE, -AMES, -AQUY, -AQYF -ATYL, -AXAV); two delivered to Kommando Rowehl for clandestine reconnaissance
He 111A-1: 10 aircraft based on V3; rejected
He 111 V5: DB 600A; all-up weight 18,959 lb (8600 kg)
He 111B-0: pre-production version accepted by Luftwaffe; one aircraft with Jumo 21Ga
He 111B-1: production bombers; early aircraft with DB 600Aa, later DB 600C; all-up weight 20,536 lb (9323 kg); maximum bombload 3,307 lb (1500 kg)
He 111B-2: supercharged DB 600CG engines, all-up weight 22,046 lb (1000 kg)
He 111 V7: prototype with straight tapered wing
He 111 G-01: also termed **He 111 V12** (D-AEQU), B.M.W. VI 6.0Zu, passed to DLH
He 111 G-02: also termed **He 111 V13** (D-AYKI),
He 111G-3: two aircraft, **V14** (D-ACBS) with B.M.W. 132Dc and **V15** (D-ADCF) with B.M.W. 132H-1; both passed to DLH and re-styled **He 111L**
He 111G-4: also termed **He 111 V16** (D-ASAR); DB 600G; used by Milch as personal transport
He 111G-5: four aircraft with DB 600Ga engines, sold to Turkey
He 111 V9: modified from B-2 airframe wit DB 600Ga; became He 111D prototype with wing radiators
He 111D-0: pre-production batch with DB 600Ga and radiators moved to engine nacelles
He 111D-1: small number of production aircraft, abandoned due to shortage of DB engines
He 111V6: prototype (D-AXOH) from modified B-0 with Jumo 610Ga
He 111V10: prototype He 111E (D-ALEQ) from modified D-0 with Jumo 211A-1
He 111E-0: pre-production aircraft, 3,748-lb (1700-kg) bombload; all-up weight 22,740 lb (10315 kg)
He 111E-1: production bombers, 4,409-lb (2000-kg) bombload all-up weight 23,754 lb (10775 kg)
He 111E-3: minor internal alterations, internal bombload only
He 111E-4: half bombload carried externally
He 111E-5: as E-4 with extra internal fuel tanks
He 111 V11: prototype He 111F with straight-tapered wing; Jumo 211A-3
He 111F-0: pre-production aircraft, all-up weight 24,250 lb (11000 kg)
He 111F-1: 24 aircraft sold to Turkey in 1938
He 111F-4: 40 aircraft for Luftwaffe with E-4 bombload
He 111J-0: pre-production aircraft, DB 600CG; external bombload only
He 111J-1: 90 production aircraft intended as torpedo-bombers but served as bombers only
He 111V8: modified B-0 (D-AQUO) with stepped cockpit profile
He 111P-0: pre-production batch similar to V8, following J-1 in factory
He 111P-1: production DB 601A-1; maximum speed 247 mph (398 km/h)

He 111P-2: as P-1 but with FuG 10 radio
He 111P-3: P-1s and P-2s modified as dual-control trainers
He 111P-4: provision for additional defensive armament; extra internal fuel; external bombload
He 111P-6: introduced DB 601N engines; reverted to internal bombload; P-6R2 was later conversion to glider tug; others transferred to Hungary
He 111V19: prototype (D-AUKY); Jumo 211 engines
He 111H-0: pre-production batch similar to P-2 (FuG10) but with Jumo 211
He 111H-2: as H-1 but with Jumo 211A-3 engines
He 111H-3: introduced anti-shipping role with forward-firing 20-mm gun in gondola Jumo 211D-1 engines
He 111H-4: early aircraft had Jumo 211D-1, but later 211F-1 engines
He 111H-5: provision for 5,511-lb (2500-kg) bombload; all-up weight increased to 30,982 lb (14055 kg)
He 111H-6: included all previous modifications and provision for two 1,686-kg (765-kg) LTF5b torpedoes and increased defensive armament, Jumo 211F-1; He 111H-7 and H-9 were similar but with minor equipment changes
He 111H-8: H-3 and H-5 airframes with balloon cable-fender and cutters, H-8 R2 had fenders removed and was modified as glider tug
He 111H-10: H-6 development with 20-mm gun moved from gondola to nose. Kuto-Nase balloon cable-cutters, Jumo 211F-2
He 111H-11: fully enclosed dorsal gun position with increased armament and armour, H-11 R1 had twin MG 81 guns in beam positions, H-11 R2 was glider tug
He 111H-12: ventral gondola omitted to allow carriage of Hs 293A missiles, FuG 203b radio equipment
He 111H-14: pathfinder development of H-10, 20H-14 R2s were glider tugs
He 111H-16: 'standard' bomber H-16 R1 had electric dorsal turret, H-16 R2 was glider tug with rigid boom; H16 R3 was pathfinder with reduced bombload
He 111H-18: pathfinder similar to He 111H-16 R3 with special flame-damped exhausts
He 111H-20: built as glider tug transport, H-20 R1 was paratrooper with jump hatch, H-20 R2 was freighter tug with 30-mm gun in electric dorsal turret, H-20 R3 modified as bomber, H-20 R4 modified as bomber with external load of 20 110-lb (50-kg) bombs
He 111H-21: introduced Jumo 213, maximum speed 298 mph (480 km/h) bombload 6,614 lb (3000 kg), all-up weight increased to 35,275 lb (16000 kg). *Rüstsatz* as for He 111H-20
He 111H-23: similar to H-20 R1 with Jumo 213 engines
He 111V32: single H-6 modified with turbocharged DB 601U engines as prototype for proposed He 111R high-altitude bomber, **He 111R-1** and **R-2** were proposed but not built
He 111Z-1: two He 111 composited with fifth engine added, glider tug, all-up weight 62,831 lb (28500 kg)
He 111Z-2: long-range bomber project similar to Z-1 intended to carry four Hs 283A missiles
He 111Z-3: proposed version of Z-1 for long-range reconnaissance

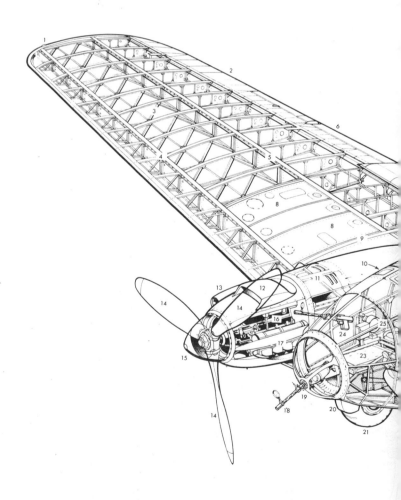

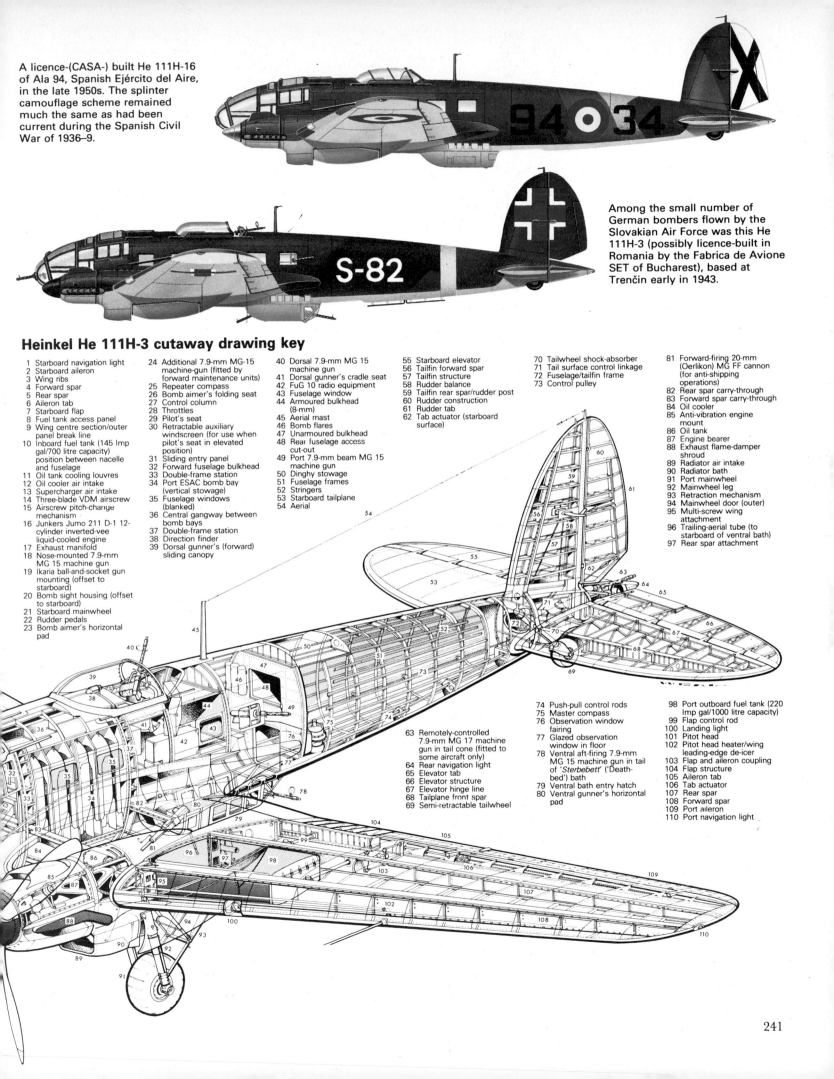

A licence-(CASA-) built He 111H-16 of Ala 94, Spanish Ejército del Aire, in the late 1950s. The splinter camouflage scheme remained much the same as had been current during the Spanish Civil War of 1936–9.

Among the small number of German bombers flown by the Slovakian Air Force was this He 111H-3 (possibly licence-built in Romania by the Fabrica de Avione SET of Bucharest), based at Trenčin early in 1943.

Heinkel He 111H-3 cutaway drawing key

1 Starboard navigation light
2 Starboard aileron
3 Wing ribs
4 Forward spar
5 Rear spar
6 Aileron tab
7 Starboard flap
8 Fuel tank access panel
9 Wing centre section/outer panel break line
10 Inboard fuel tank (145 Imp gal/700 litre capacity) position between nacelle and fuselage
11 Oil tank cooling louvres
12 Oil cooler air intake
13 Supercharger air intake
14 Three-blade VDM airscrew
15 Airscrew pitch-change mechanism
16 Junkers Jumo 211 D-1 12-cylinder inverted-vee liquid-cooled engine
17 Exhaust manifold
18 Nose-mounted 7.9-mm MG 15 machine gun
19 Ikaria ball-and-socket gun mounting (offset to starboard)
20 Bomb sight housing (offset to starboard)
21 Starboard mainwheel
22 Rudder pedals
23 Bomb aimer's horizontal pad

24 Additional 7.9-mm MG-15 machine-gun (fitted by forward maintenance units)
25 Repeater compass
26 Bomb aimer's folding seat
27 Control column
28 Throttles
29 Pilot's seat
30 Retractable auxiliary windscreen (for use when pilot's seat in elevated position)
31 Sliding entry panel
32 Forward fuselage bulkhead
33 Double-frame station
34 Port ESAC bomb bay (vertical stowage)
35 Fuselage windows (blanked)
36 Central gangway between bomb bays
37 Double-frame station
38 Direction finder
39 Dorsal gunner's (forward) sliding canopy

40 Dorsal 7.9-mm MG 15 machine gun
41 Dorsal gunner's cradle seat
42 FuG 10 radio equipment
43 Fuselage window
44 Armoured bulkhead (8-mm)
45 Aerial mast
46 Bomb flares
47 Unarmoured bulkhead
48 Rear fuselage access cut-out
49 Port 7.9-mm beam MG 15 machine gun
50 Dinghy stowage
51 Fuselage frames
52 Stringers
53 Starboard tailplane
54 Aerial

55 Starboard elevator
56 Tailfin forward spar
57 Tailfin structure
58 Rudder balance
59 Tailfin rear spar/rudder post
60 Rudder construction
61 Rudder tab
62 Tab actuator (starboard surface)

63 Remotely-controlled 7.9-mm MG 17 machine gun in tail cone (fitted to some aircraft only)
64 Rear navigation light
65 Elevator tab
66 Elevator structure
67 Elevator hinge line
68 Tailplane front spar
69 Semi-retractable tailwheel

70 Tailwheel shock-absorber
71 Tail surface control linkage
72 Fuselage/tailfin frame
73 Control pulley

74 Push-pull control rods
75 Master compass
76 Observation window fairing
77 Glazed observation window in floor
78 Ventral aft-firing 7.9-mm MG 15 machine gun in tail of 'Sterbebett' ('Death-bed') bath
79 Ventral bath entry hatch
80 Ventral gunner's horizontal pad

81 Forward-firing 20-mm (Oerlikon) MG FF cannon (for anti-shipping operations)
82 Rear spar carry-through
83 Forward spar carry-through
84 Oil cooler
85 Anti-vibration engine mount
86 Oil tank
87 Engine bearer
88 Exhaust flame-damper shroud
89 Radiator air intake
90 Radiator bath
91 Port mainwheel
92 Mainwheel leg
93 Retraction mechanism
94 Mainwheel door (outer)
95 Multi-screw wing attachment
96 Trailing-aerial tube (to starboard of ventral bath)
97 Rear spar attachment

98 Port outboard fuel tank (220 Imp gal/1000 litre capacity)
99 Flap control rod
100 Landing light
101 Pitot head
102 Pitot head heater/wing leading-edge de-icer
103 Flap and aileron coupling
104 Flap structure
105 Aileron tab
106 Tab actuator
107 Rear spar
108 Forward spar
109 Port aileron
110 Port navigation light

Though to some extent superseded by the H-series, the Heinkel He 111P continued in widespread service well into the war. This P-2 of Kampfgeschwader 55 flew from Villacoublay, France, during the autumn of 1940 on night raids over Britain and displays the Geschwaderstab marking on the nose; crudely applied mottled camouflage has obscured Geschwaderziechen and fin swastika.

By the beginning of the Battle of Britain the He 111H had almost entirely replaced the He 111P series (although most staff crews still flew the older aircraft, and it was in an He 111P that Oberst Alois Stoeckl, commanding KG 55, was shot down and killed near Middle Wallop on 14 August 1940). From the outset the He 111H, with its 270-mph (435-km/h) top speed, proved a difficult aircraft to shoot down (compared with the Dornier Do 17), and showed itself capable of weathering heavy battle damage. The 17 Gruppen flying the He 111H during the battle operated an average strength of about 500 aircraft (compared with about 100 He 111P series aircraft, of which some 40 served in the reconnaissance role with the *Aufklärungsgruppen*), losing some 246 of their number in air combat in the course of the four-month battle. Among the outstanding attacks by He 111s were those by KG 55 on the Bristol aircraft factory on 25 September, and the same unit's devastating raid on Supermarine's factory at Southampton the following day.

The majority of the He 111Hs employed during the Battle of Britain were He 111H-1s, -2s, -3s, and -4s, the latter two initially powered by 1,100-hp (821-kW) Jumo 211D engines, and perhaps the main significance of their losses lay in their five-man crews, whereas the other bombers, the Junkers Ju 88 and Do 17, were crewed by only four.

The next variant to join the Kampfgeschwäder was the He 111H-5, which incorporated additional fuel tanks in place of the wing bomb cells, and featured two external racks each capable of lifting a 2,205-lb (1000-kg) bomb; its maximum all-up weight was increased to 30,985 lb (14055 kg). He 111H-5s were widely used during the winter Blitz of 1940–1, these aircraft carrying the majority of the heavy bombs and parachute mines to fall on British cities in that campaign. The He 111H-5 could also carry a single 3,968-lb (1800-kg) bomb externally.

The He 111H-6 came to be the most widely used of all He 111s, entering production at the end of 1940. With provision to carry a pair of 1,687-lb (765-kg) LT F5b torpedoes, this version was armed with six 7.92-mm (0.31-in) MG 15 machine-guns and a forward-firing 20-mm cannon, and some aircraft featured a remotely operated grenade-launcher

First prototype of the He 111 was the He 111a (later styled the He 111V1), flown by Gerhard Nitschke at Marienehe on 24 February 1934 while powered by 660-hp (492-kW) BMW VI 6.0Z engines. Although built as a bomber, British Intelligence authorities persisted in believing it to be a high-speed commercial aircraft.

aircraft compared with 349 He 111P series, 38 He 111E series and 21 He 111J series aircraft. Of this total of 808 aircraft, 705 were serviceable on the eve of Germany's attack on Poland. In that fateful campaign the Heinkels of KG 1, KG 4, KG 26, KG 27, KG 53, KG 152 and II/LG1 were in constant action, starting with raids far beyond the front line but, as the Poles fell back towards Warsaw, launching devastating raids on the Polish capital.

Owing to the lack of suitable airfields, only three He 111-equipped units (KG 4, KG 26 and KGr 100) operated in the Norwegian campaign, the other Geschwäder deploying in readiness for the German attack in the West, which opened on 10 May 1940. Four days later the campaign was besmirched by the apparently wanton attack by 100 Heinkels of KG 54 on Rotterdam.

Serving with the Legion Cóndor's bomber element, Kampfgruppe 88, during the Spanish Civil War in 1937, this He 111B-1 carried a variety of individual markings, including the name *Holzauge* (literally 'Wooden Eye') and a black scottie-dog on fin. German aircrews gained much experience over Spain, albeit against soft targets and little opposition.

A Jumo-powered He 111E-1 whose maximum bomb load (carried internally) had been increased to 4,410 lb (2000 kg); this version eventually equipped all four bomber Staffeln of Kampfgruppe 88 of the Legion Cóndor in Spain during the extremely vicious and bloody civil war that gripped the country in 1938.

One of the last surviving operational He 111s was this He 111H-20 of I Gruppe, Kampfgeschwader 4 'General Wever', based at DresdenKlotzsche in April 1945 for supply-dropping missions to isolated Wehrmacht units.

in the extreme tail. Despite its torpedo-carrying ability, most He 111H-6s were used as ordinary bombers, the first unit to fly torpedo-equipped He 111H-6s being I/KG 26, flying these aircraft from Bardufoss and Banak in northern Norway against the North Cape convoys from June 1942 onwards and participating in the virtual annihilation of the convoy PQ 17.

Following the successful use of He 111Hs as pathfinders by KGr 100, this role featured prominently in subsequent development of the aircraft, the He 111H-14, He 111H-16/R3 and He 111H-18 being specially fitted with FuG Samos, Peil-GV, APZ5 and FuG Korfu radio equipment for the task; He 111H-14s were flown on operations by Sonderkommando Rastedter of KG 40 in 1944.

As the He 111 was joined by such later bombers as the Heinkel He 177 Greif, Dornier Do 217 and others, it underwent parallel development as a transport; the He 111H-20/R1 was fitted out to accommodate 16 paratroops and the He 111H-20/R2 was equipped as a freight-carrying glider tug. Nevertheless bomber versions continued to serve, particularly on the Eastern Front where the He 111H-20.R3 with a 4,410-lb (2000-kg) bombload and the He 111H-20/R4, carrying 20 110-lb (50-kg) fragmentation bombs, operated by night.

Perhaps the most outstanding, albeit forlorn of all operations by the He 111H bombers and transports was that in support of the Wehrmacht's attempt to relieve the German 6th Army at Stalingrad between November 1942 and February 1943. As the entire available force of Junkers Ju 52/3m transports was inadequate for the supply task, He 111 bombers of KG 27, KG 55 and I/KG 100 joined KGrzbV 5 and KGrzbV 20 (flying an assortment of He 111D, F, P and H transports) and embarked on the job of flying in food and ammunition to the beleaguered army. Although the bombers were occasionally able to attack the Russian armour as it tightened its grip on the city, bad weather severely hampered the supply operations, and by the end of the Stalingrad campaign the Luftwaffe had lost 165 He 111s, a sacrifice from which the Kampfgeschwäder never fully recovered.

The Heinkel He 111 also underwent two of what were unquestionably the most bizarre of all the Luftwaffe's wartime operational experiments. The first involved the carriage of a Fieseler Fi 103 flying-bomb (the V-1) under one wing. Following trials at Peenemünde in 1943, about 20 He 111H-6s, He 111H-16s and He 111H-21s (all re-designated He 111H-22s) were modified and delivered to III/KG 3 in July 1944. Within six weeks this unit, based in the Netherlands, had launched 300 flying-bombs against London, 90 against Southampton and 20 against Gloucester, the tactics being to approach the British shoreline at low level to escape radar detection before the aicraft climbed to about 1,475 ft (450 m) to release the weapon and then dived to escape.

Believing this campaign to have achieved worthwhile results, the Luftwaffe equipped all three Gruppen of KG 53 with about 100 He 111H-22s and, based in western Germany, these joined the assault on the UK in December, one raid being launched against far-distant Manchester on Christmas Eve. In seven months the four Gruppen launched 1,200 flying-bombs but lost 77 aircraft; no more than 20 per cent of the bombs reached their target cities.

The other experiment involving the He 111 resulted in the extraordinary five-engine He 111Z (Z denoting Zwilling, or twin), achieved by joining together two He 111s by means of a new wing centre-section carrying a fifth engine. The resulting aircraft, with a span of 115 ft 6 in (35.20 m), was intended to tow the huge Messerschmitt Me 321 Gigant glider or three Gotha Go 242 gliders at 140 mph (225 km/h) at 13,125 ft (4000 m).

One of the last important uses to which the He 111 bomber was put was the attack on the airfield at Poltava in the Soviet Union on the night of 21-22nd June 1944. On the previous day, 114 Boeing B-17s of the United States Army Air Force and the North American P-51s which had been escorting them were flown to the USSR after the bombing of Berlin. The Americans were taken by surprise by Heinkel 111s of the 4th, 27th, 53rd and 55th Kampfgruppen, and by the light of flares the bombers destroyed 43 B-17s and 15 P-51s on the ground. More than 7,300 He 111s were produced.

The Heinkel He 111H-6 was the most widely-used version of the aircraft and is pictured here carrying a pair of practice torpedoes on fuselage PVC racks. Among the operational units to employ torpedo-carrying He 111s was KG 26, based in Norway for attacks on the Allied Murmansk-bound convoys.

The Heinkel He 111H-11 with 13-mm (0.51-in) MG 131 heavy machine gun in the extreme nose and five 550-lb (250-kg) bombs on a special rack-plate under the fuselage; this version also featured considerably increased armour protection, some of which could be jettisoned in the interests of speed in an emergency.

North American Harvard/Texan

There may have been more versions of this aircraft than of any other in history. Certainly it was in its day the world's most widely used trainer, though it was used for many other purposes – as a dive-bomber, fighter, tug, racer, forward air control (FAC) aircraft, crop sprayer, and even as a three-passenger executive transport.

This series of solidly built, all-metal monoplanes is so large and varied that it is difficult to find a name for the whole range. The Swedes called it the Sk 14, the Japanese the K10W or K5Y, the Australians the Wirraway, the Spaniards the C.6 and the Luftwaffe the NAA 57. But most flyers remember it as the AT-6, the T-6, the Texan, Harvard or SNJ. And in fact it is an aircraft that for many people is unforgettable. There are still pilots today who can remember exactly how the trim tab on the rudder should be set for take-off (fully to the right) or the maximum temperature which should not be exceeded on the cylinder heads (240°C or 464°F, reduced after the war to 230°C, or 446°F), or where the

fuel indicators were located (on the upper surface of both wing tanks forming the floor of the cockpit).

Including post-war modifications, but excluding one-offs such as the racers, or the phoney conversion to simulate Zeros for Hollywood, the total number of different sub-types in this family is not fewer than 260. (The chief ones are listed separately.) Their story goes back even before North American

The Harvard Formation Team uses only machines belonging to this successful series of trainers for its flying displays: a Mk IIA, a Mk IIB and two Mk IVs.

The North American Texan/Harvard had the largest production run of any trainer aircraft ever. This Harvard Mk IIB was produced under licence by the Canadian manufacturers, Noorduyn. (Photo: *Austin J. Brown*)

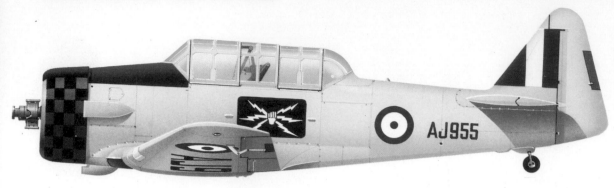

AJ955 was one of 450 NA-66s built with what was then (1940) a new designation, Harvard Mk II. No. 955 was the first of 33 in that total that went to the RCAF, and it is depicted as it looked whilst serving in 1943 with No. 2 Wireless School. Oddly, no radio aerial is visible; more than 50 radio fits were used on T-6 variants.

Aviation put its name on its aircraft but served as the parent to General Aviation at Dundalk, Maryland, where types GA-1 to GA-15 were created. In late 1934 the US Army issued a requirement for a new basic trainer, the next type encountered by pupil pilots after they had mastered the lower-powered primary trainer. The General Aviation design team, under vice-president J. Lee Atwood, quickly produced a cantilever low-wing monoplane with all-metal structure (including a wing covered with flush-riveted stressed skin, though the rest of the aircraft was mainly fabric-covered), fixed cantilever main legs, a 400-hp (298-kW) Wright R-975 Whirlwind engine and tandem open cockpits. Instead of becoming the GA-16 it was styled the NA-16, reflecting the company's change of name.

The NA-16 was flown at Dundalk in April 1935, with civil registration X-2080. The US Army pilots at Wright Field thought it the best design submitted, and the nearest approach to a tactical aircraft then achieved in a trainer, but requested several changes. This classic prototype thus became the NA-18 with enclosed cockpits (covered by tandem sliding canopies), a faired landing gear and the 600-hp (448-kW) Pratt & Whitney R-1340 Wasp engine. This aircraft was later sold to Argentina, but in late 1935 the US Army adopted the NAA trainer and placed an order for 42, with the designation BT-9. On the strength of this the company moved to sunny California, paying a $600 annual rental for a site at Inglewood on what is today Los Angeles International Airport and building a completely new factory with 150 employees (nine years later the payroll had reached 91,000).

The BT-9s were delivered in training colours of blue fuselage and chrome-yellow wings and tail, with blue/red/white-striped rudder. Most BT-9s had fixed slats on the outer wings and were used as unarmed pilot trainers, fitted with

First of the many: few photographs exist of the original General Aviation NA-16, but the same machine is pictured here after it had been modified with enclosed cockpits and faired main legs, though retaining the small-diameter Whirlwind engine. Later it was given a Pratt & Whitney 600 hp (448 km) R-1340 Wasp engine and redesignated NA-18 and exported to Argentina.

North American Harvard Mk IIB cutaway drawing key

1. Pitot tube
2. Wing tip fairing
3. Starboard navigation lights
4. Starboard outer wing panel
5. Aileron tab
6. Tab control rod
7. Starboard fabric-covered aileron
8. Aerial mast
9. Starboard split trailing edge flap
10. Flap control rod
11. Aileron hinge control
12. Aileron cables
13. Starboard landing/taxiing lamp
14. Detachable engine cowling panels
15. Hamilton Standard two-bladed variable-pitch propeller
16. Feathering bobweights
17. Propeller hub pitch change mechanism
18. Engine oil tank sump
19. Bottom cowling panels
20. Starboard mainwheel
21. Carburettor air intake duct
22. Exhaust collector
23. Pratt & Whitney R-1340-49 Wasp nine-cylinder radial engine
24. Engine mounting bulkhead
25. Cockpit heater muff
26. Engine oil tank
27. Oil filler cap
28. Battery
29. Engine hand cranking lever attachment
30. Engine bearer struts
31. Filtered air intake
32. Air intake heater duct
33. Lower engine bearers
34. Mainwheel well
35. Fuel pump
36. Intake fairing
37. Engine control rod runs
38. Fireproof bulkhead
39. Forward rudder pedals
40. Fuse box
41. Generator control unit
42. Electrical control panel
43. Front pilot's instrument panel
44. Instrument panel shroud
45. Aerial cable lead-in
46. Windscreen panels
47. Forward sliding canopy section
48. Front pilot's seat
49. Safety harness
50. Throttle mixture and propeller control levers
51. Cockpit light
52. Tailplane trim control wheels
53. Footboards
54. Wing spar/fuselage attachment joint
55. Fuel contents gauge
56. Hydraulic system emergency handpump
57. Fuel cock control
58. Dynamotor
59. Cockpit step
60. Rear rudder pedals
61. Hydraulic reservoir
62. Engine and propeller control rods
63. Radio equipment stowage
64. Sliding canopy rail
65. Rear instrument panel
66. Undercarriage warning horn
67. Roll-over protection frame
68. Canopy fixed centre-section
69. Rear sliding canopy section
70. Rear pilot's seat
71. Canopy emergency exit side panel
72. Emergency exit handle
73. Rear pilot's throttle box
74. Fire extinguisher
75. Trim handwheels
76. Flap lever
77. Rear seat mounting
78. Forward fuselage steel tube primary structure
79. Non-structural side panels
80. Rear cockpit step
81. Baggage compartment
82. Oxygen bottles
83. Oxygen filler valve
84. Rear fuselage frame and stringer construction
85. Control system access panels
86. Upper identification light
87. Fin mounting box
88. Fin root fairing
89. Starboard tailplane
90. Starboard elevator
91. Elevator tab

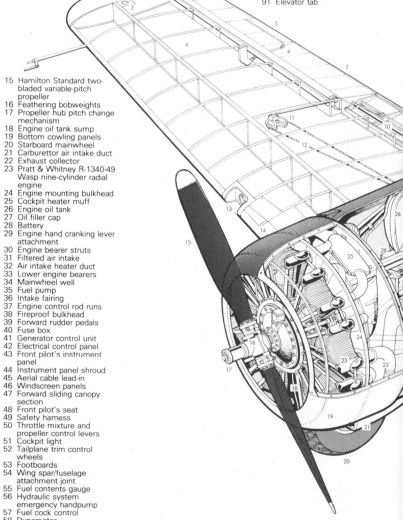

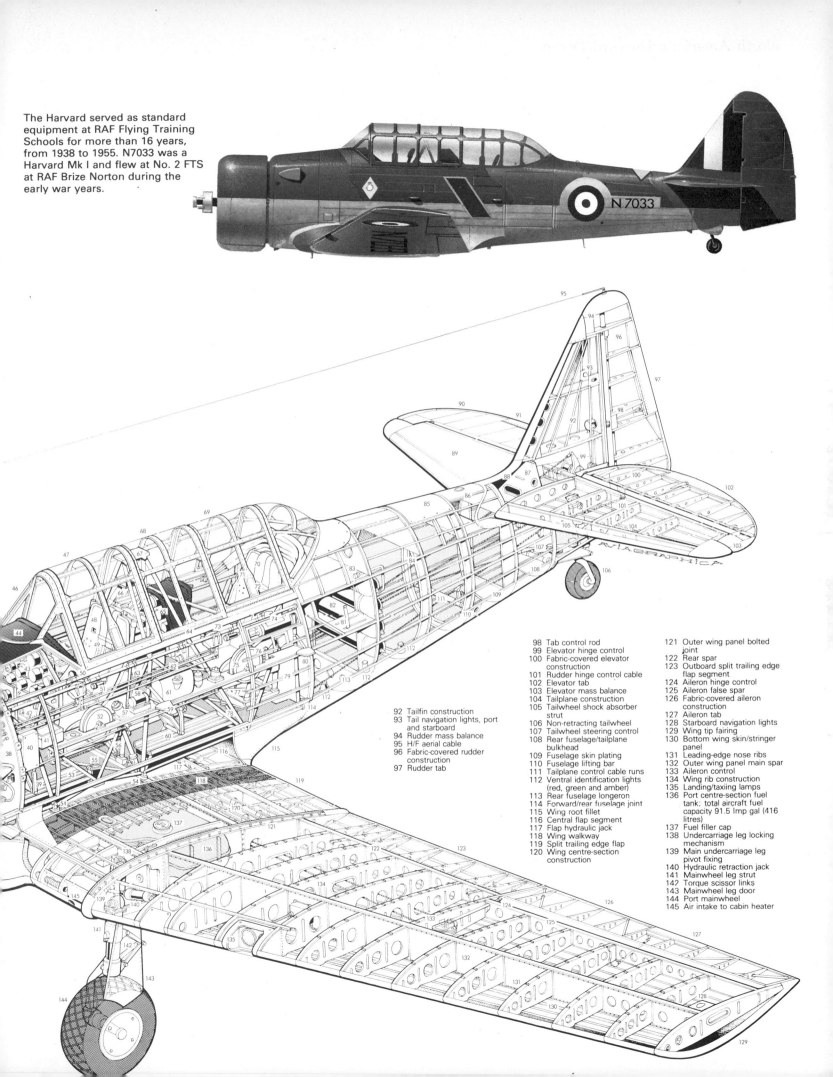

The Harvard served as standard equipment at RAF Flying Training Schools for more than 16 years, from 1938 to 1955. N7033 was a Harvard Mk I and flew at No. 2 FTS at RAF Brize Norton during the early war years.

92 Tailfin construction
93 Tail navigation lights, port and starboard
94 Rudder mass balance
95 H/F aerial cable
96 Fabric-covered rudder construction
97 Rudder tab
98 Tab control rod
99 Elevator hinge control
100 Fabric-covered elevator construction
101 Rudder hinge control cable
102 Elevator tab
103 Elevator mass balance
104 Tailplane construction
105 Tailwheel shock absorber strut
106 Non-retracting tailwheel
107 Tailwheel steering control
108 Rear fuselage/tailplane bulkhead
109 Fuselage skin plating
110 Fuselage lifting bar
111 Tailplane control cable runs
112 Ventral identification lights (red, green and amber)
113 Rear fuselage longeron
114 Forward/rear fuselage joint
115 Wing root fillet
116 Central flap segment
117 Flap hydraulic jack
118 Wing walkway
119 Split trailing edge flap
120 Wing centre-section construction

121 Outer wing panel bolted joint
122 Rear spar
123 Outboard split trailing edge flap segment
124 Aileron hinge control
125 Aileron false spar
126 Fabric-covered aileron construction
127 Aileron tab
128 Starboard navigation lights
129 Wing tip fairing
130 Bottom wing skin/stringer panel
131 Leading-edge nose ribs
132 Outer wing panel main spar
133 Aileron control
134 Wing rib construction
135 Landing/taxiing lamps
136 Port centre-section fuel tank; total aircraft fuel capacity 91.5 Imp gal (416 litres)
137 Fuel filler cap
138 Undercarriage leg locking mechanism
139 Main undercarriage leg pivot fixing
140 Hydraulic retraction jack
141 Mainwheel leg strut
142 Torque scissor links
143 Mainwheel leg door
144 Port mainwheel
145 Air intake to cabin heater

North American Harvard

Specification

Type: two-seat advanced trainer

Powerplant: one 600-hp (447-kW) Pratt & Whitney R-1340-49 Wasp radial piston engine

Performance: maximum speed 210 mph (338 km/h); initial climb rate 1,350 ft (411 m) per minute; range 740 miles (1191 km); endurance 8 hours

Weights: empty typically 4,020 lb (1823 kg); maximum take-off 5,250 lb (2381 kg)

Dimensions: span 42 ft 0¼ in (12.81 m); length 28 ft 11⅞ in (8.836 m); height 11 ft 8½ in (3.57 m); wing area 253.7 sq ft (23.57 m²)

Armament: none on this aircraft, but see text for many options

This Harvard Mk IIB typified the variants made in great numbers during the middle war years. The penultimate Harvard for the RAF produced under licence by Noorduyn of Canada, it also had the USAAF designation AT-16 (and for a time an assigned US tail number) because most of the 2,485 Mk IIBs were Lend-Lease, paid for by US funds. The pupil (in front) canopy slid back outside the fixed central portion while the instructor's canopy slid forward on the inside. On this Mk IIB the rearmost part of the canopy was fixed, but aircraft fitted for gunnery pupils had a rear section (distinguished by a straight lower edge) which rocked up and over and travelled forward with the main rear hood section.

A fine portrait of a North American BT-9 basic trainer with the R-975 Whirlwind engine and fixed slats and landing gear, of the 46th School Sqn, USAAC, in 1939. This colour scheme was replaced in 1940.

flaps pumped down by a manual hydraulic system. These were probably the first flapped basic trainers, and flaps were provided on all subsequent models. The R-975 Whirlwind fitted to most of the fixed-gear versions, except for the US Navy NJ-1 and a batch for China, was of smaller diameter than the Pratt & Whitney Wasp used on the much more numerous retractable-gear models, and resulted in a slightly better forward view.

The main landing wheels were far forward, making nosing over difficult, and on most of these variants the exhaust was collected at the front of the engine and discharged through the right side of the cowl. Many sub-types including the first two big orders for France, had the original curved wingtips and rudder; but the NA-57 for France had the new wing and tail, first flown on the NA-54, which was structurally better and easier to make. Large numbers of the former type had Et.2 (Entrainement biplace) or P.2 (Perfectionnement biplace) in black on their striped rudders, and they were put to various uses by the Vichy forces and Luftwaffe. Aircraft of the second batch were diverted to become Yales in Canada,

mostly with the exhaust stack extended back over the right wing root.

Export sales came thick and fast, no two batches being exactly alike but all having the R-975 or R-1340 engines, except for wartime licence-built Swedish Sk 14 versions which had to use an Italian Piaggio engine, and the Imperial Japanese Navy models which had a Kotobuki engine driving a wooden propeller. The Japanese variants, designated K10W and K5Y1, had many local modifications, notably to the canopy, rear fuselage and vertical tail.

Competitive attack trainer

The real mainstream began with the US Army Air Corps competition in 1937 for a BC (basic combat) trainer, able to undertake pilot instruction while at the same time simulating the handling and cockpit controls of a combat type, with the option of being able to mount fixed and movable guns and carry bombs if necessary so that one type could almost turn out a fully fledged combat pilot or gunner. The same NA-16 was taken as the starting point, but it was fitted with a big Wasp engine, driving a Hamilton variable-pitch propeller and a hydraulic pump feeding a 1,000-lb/sq in (70.3-kg/cm^2) system which worked the flaps and also the new retractable main landing gears, which folded inwards ahead of the spars with the wheels in compartments causing curved projections ahead of the wing roots. This NA-26 prototype of 1937 won the competition, and the first production model was the US Army's BC-1, some of which were the first specially designed instrument trainers, designated BC-1I.

Further changes, listed in the variants, brought in stressed-skin fuselages, integral wing tanks (soon followed by removable aluminium wing tanks), and the new angular wingtips and rudder. In 1940 the BC category was superseded by AT

SNJs lined up at NAS Pensacola during World War 2. The SNJ was almost identical to the USAAF AT-6 Texan, each major development having variants for both services. A few of the navy trainers were used for carrier training with arrester hooks.

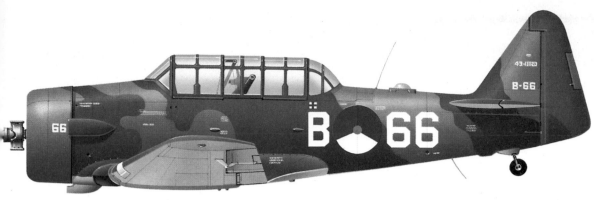

Many well-loved old-stagers were some years ago found in the Royal Netherlands air force light-aircraft units based at Deelen and Soesterberg, and operated on tactical missions mainly for the army. This ex-RAF Harvard Mk 2B (USAAF AT-16 no. 43-13120) was flying until at least 1965 with Deelen's photo flight.

EZ316 was a Harvard Mk IIA (NA-81) supplied under Lend-Lease to the Fleet Air Arm (the large batch involved is often omitted from listings of RN Harvards). It was used from 1942 onwards as an advanced pilot trainer and is shown in post-war (about 1958) markings, still with wartime insignia, serving at Stretton with No. 1832 Sqn, RNVR.

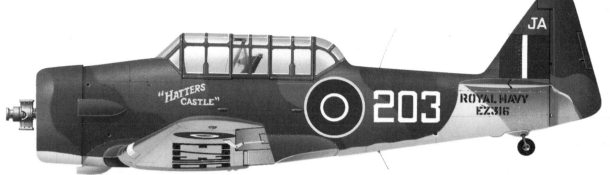

Large numbers of ex-US Navy aircraft were passed on to the French Aeronavale after World War 2. This machine is an SNJ-4, modified with the rear canopy fairing fixed and used in the pilot training role. The unit was 56S, which later became a navigator training unit equipped with C-47s.

Massive production

Almost all the gigantic wartime contracts were for the AT-6A, AT-6C, and AT-6D, plus the corresponding US Navy SNJ-3, SNJ-4 and SNJ-5, which were externally similar with the straight-edged airframe, stressed-skin fuselage and provision for a hand-aimed gun in the rear cockpit, the usual canopy having a rear fairing which rocked up and forward as the main section was slid open. On most earlier versions the rear fairing was fixed. Structurally, the big exception was launched by the NA-88 of 10 April 1941, when production was already on a massive scale even though the United States was still neutral. There was a fear that aluminium would run out, and in this model NAA redesigned the aircraft to have a basic wing structure, flaps, fin and all control surfaces of spot-welded low-alloy steel, and the forward fuselage side panels, whole rear fuselage, cockpit floor and tailplane of plywood. This saved 1,246 lb (565 kg)

(advanced trainer, a category dormant for 13 years), the NAA aircraft becoming the AT-6.

NAA was unable to meet demand, even with an Inglewood plant whose floor areas had expanded from 159,000 sq ft (14770m²) to almost 2,000,000 sq ft (185800 m²)! A new factory was therefore built at Dallas, Texas (others were built elsewhere for other NAA types), and from 1942 the AT-6 was accordingly named Texan, though since 1938 the name Harvard had taken firm hold in the British Commonwealth for the same basic type. British industry had been totally unable to meet the RAF's need for aircraft in 1938, because orders had not been placed in time, and a great outcry went up when foreign aircraft were ordered. The NAA trainer was the first, soon followed by the Lockheed Hudson and Consolidated Catalina. The Harvard Mk I was a BC-1 with British instruments and radio, and bucket seats tailored to the seat-pack parachutes. The first of 400 entered service in December 1938 at No. 3 FTS, Grantham, camouflaged on top and down to the mid-line of the fuselage, and yellow below. Subsequently the RAF received about half of the 4,768 Harvards supplied from NAA or from Noorduyn on US Lend-Lease contract, a further 1,380 Harvards being supplied direct from Noorduyn and (post-war) from Canadian Car and Foundry, as well as 285 post-war T-6Js for European air forces.

One of the post-war T-6G trainers that began life as wartime AT-6s and were then remanufactured in 1949-53. Note the spinner, rear-fuselage D/F loop acorn fairing, larger canopy side windows and flat-tread steerable tailwheel. The total thus updated was 2,068. This one went to the USAF; many went to the Air National Guard.

North American Harvard/Texan

Most Swedish aircraft of the general NA-16 family were not the locally built Sk 14 series (which were basic trainers with fixed landing gear) but ex-US aircraft supplied as war surplus in 1946-9. This Sk 16A (ex-USAAF AT-6A 41-16098) was still intensively utilized on pilot training at F9 at Sävar as late as 1967.

The Forca Aérea Brasileira (Brazilian air force) was not only one of the last T-6 operators but in fact still had two EMRAs (reconnaissance and attack squadrons) flying armed T-6s as late as 1977! Another operator was the Esquadrilha da Fumaca (Smoke Squadron), shown right, one of the established FAB aerobatic display teams, whose mounts were distinctive. The metal-covered rear canopy is a local modification.

of aluminium or light alloy per aircraft, with a surprisingly modest weight penalty and not much difference in manufacturing cost. Designations were AT-6C, SNJ-4 and Harvard Mk IIA, but after a while it was accepted that there would be no shortage of aluminium and the original structure was restored (still as the NA-88) in the AT-6D, SNJ-5 and Harvard Mk III, though these introduced 24-volt electrics.

One of the electric items much appreciated by ground crew was the starter. Of the inertia type, the flywheel was spun by the pilot depressing his heel on a treadle in the floor between the rudder pedals. A healthy rising whine ensued, and when the pitch was high enough the pilot would instead depress his toe, rocking the treadle and engaging the flywheel.

Trainer variants

NA-16: original prototype, 400-hp (298-kW) R-975 engine; modified as **NA-18** with enclosed cockpit and 600-hp (448-kW) R-1340
Na-19: USAAC BT-9 with R-975, fixed slats, 42 built
Na-19A: USAAC BT-9A with nose and dorsal 0.3-in (7.62-mm) guns and recording camera, 40 for USAAC Reserve
NA-22: ninth BT-9 temporarily evaluated as primary trainer, open cockpits, Townend-ring cowl simpler equipment
NA-23: USAAC BT-9B for 1937 production, 117 built
NA-28: US Navy model, NJ-1, 500-hp (373-kW) R-1340-6, 40 built (last flown temporarily as NJ-2 with 490-hp/366-kW XV-770-4)
NA-29: USAAC Reserve BT-9C with nose and dorsal guns, 67 built, first completed as Y1BT-10 with 600-hp (448-kW) R-1340 and another with RC-1A type wings and tail as BT-9D
NA-30: Y1BT-10 (see above)
NA-58: USAAC BT-14 with stressed-skin fuselage, 450-hp (336-kW) R-985-25 Wasp Junior, BC-1A outer wings and tail, 251 built of which 27 re-engined 1941 with 400-hp (298-kW) R-985-11 as BT-14A
NA-20: (NA-16-2H); R-1340-engined NA-18, sold to Honduras
NA-31 (NA-16-4M); as BT-9 with 450-hp (336-kW) R-975-E3, one sold to Sweden with licence to ASJA, see licence production p. 253
NA-32 (NA-16-1A); two pattern aircraft sold with licence 1937 to Commonwealth Aircraft (Australia); as NA-26 (see below) but fixed landing gear
NA-34(NA-16-4PI); for Argentine, two nose and one dorsal guns, full radio, bomb racks, 30 built
NA-37 (NA-16-4R); demonstrator for Japan, 450-hp (336-kW) R-985-9CG, three-blade propeller, via Mitsubishi to Imperial Japanese Navy as KXA1
NA-38 (NA-16-4M); one NA-31 supplied in kit form to Sweden
NA-41 (NA-16-4C); as BT-9C with R-975 for China, 35 built
NA-42 (NA-16-2A); as NA-20 plus nose/dorsal guns, two to Honduras
NA-46 (NA-16-4); as BT-9C plus two guns, bomb racks under centre section, R-975, 12 for Brazilian navy
NA-47 (NA-16-4RW); as NA-37 but R-975-E3 with two-

blade prop. supplied as kit to Imperial Japanese Navy.
NA-56: new BC-1A airframe but fixed gear, 600-hp (448-kW) R-1340, 50 for China
NA-57: as NA-23 for French Armée de l'Air (200) and Aéronavale (30); 214 on strength of Luftwaffe, Vichy French air force 1941
NA-64: as NA-57 but new BC-1A wings and tail; for Armée de l'Air (200) and Aéronavale (30), but at 111th delivery France fell and other 119 diverted to RAF and passed on as Yale Mk I to RCAF as wireless (radio) trainer
NA-26: first of retractable-gear family, 600-hp (448-kW) R-1340, combat equipment, one demonstrator evaluated by USAAC as BT-9D
NA-27 (NA-16-2H): European demonstrator as NA-26, sold to Fokker with licence as PH-APG, later air force no. 997, destroyed 11 May 1940
NA-33 (NA-16-2K): second pattern for CAC (Australia), see licence production p. 253
NA-36: USAAC BC-1, armament, 600-hp (448-kW) R-1340-7 or -47, 150 built, plus 30 BC-1 I instrument trainers; last three completed as NA-54
NA-45 (NA-16-1GV): as BC-1, three for Venezuela
NA-48 (NA-16-3C): as BC-1, 15 for China
NA-49 (NA-16-1E): as BC-1 but British equipment, usually unarmed, 400 for RAF as Harvard Mk I (first US aircraft bought for RAF)
NA-52: SNJ-1 for USN, as BC-1 but stressed-skin fuselage and integral tanks, 16 built
NA-54: last three BC-1 completed with redesigned outer wings and rudder to speed production, also R-1340-45 with three-blade propeller, stressed-skin fuselage, integral tanks
NA-55: USAAC BC-1A, as BC-1 but new wings and tail and stressed-skin fuselage, 29 for National Guard and 54 for USAAC Reserve, plus nine more completed as AT-6
NA-59: continuation of BC-1A under new designation AT-6, total 94 including nine ordered as NA-55
NA-61 (NA-16-1E): as NA-49 but for RCAF, 30 built
NA-65: USN, as NA-52 but R-1340-56 and controllable-pitch propeller, 36 built as SNJ-2
NA-66: NA-59 with British equipment as Harvard Mk II with R-1340-49; 600 built, 20 RAF, 67 RNZAF, 511 assigned RCAF but 486 delivered
NA-71 (NA-16-3); as NA-59, three for Venezuela

NA-75: as NA-66, Harvard Mk II, 100 for RCAF
NA-76: as NA-66, order for 450 for Armée de l'Air placed June 1940 two weeks before capitulation, all taken over by RAF as Harvard Mk II of which 259 to RCAF
NA-77 as NA-59 with removable fuel tanks and R-1340-9,517 for US Army as AT-6A plus 120 for US Navy as ANJ-3
NA-78: as NA-77 but built at new Dallas plant, 1,130 AT-6A plus 150 SNJ-3
NA-79: further (1940) contract for 25 SNJ-2
NA-81: Harvard Mk II as NA-66, 24 for RAF, 101 for RCAF
NA-84: as NA-77 but R-1340-AN-1 and one 0.3-in (7.62-mm) dorsal gun (in other AT-6s merely provision for this); AT-6B gunnery trainer, 400 from Dallas
NA-88: as NA-84 but extensive substitutes for aluminium in AT-6C and SNJ-4; during run, decision to revert to original structure but switch to 24-volt electrics, still as NA-88 but with US Army/US Navy designations AT-6D/SNJ-5; totals, all from Dallas, 9,331 comprising 2,970 AT-6Cs (of which 726 to RAF as Harvard Mk IIA), 2,400 SNJ-4s, 2,604 AT-6Ds (351 to RAF as Harvard Mk III), and 1,357 SNJ-5s
NA-119: standard AT-6Ds supplied to Brazil 1944 as 10 assembled airframes, 10 sets of major airframe sections and 61 in kit form for completion by Construcciones Aeronauticas SA
NA-121: final batch of 800 AT-6Ds plus 956 AT-6Fs with redesigned outer wings and rear fuselage for sustained 6g manoeuvres and clear-view rear canopy; 411 (not, as often reported, 931) AT-6Fs transferred to USN as SNJ-6s
NA-168: first major post-war contract for remanufacture of NA-88 to T-6G standard with updated cockpit, new avionics, steerable tailwheel, modified main gears, extended fuel capacity, square-tip propeller (with spinner, often removed in service) and AN-1 series engine; this batch, 691 for USAF (serials 49-2897/3536 and 50-1317/1326), plus 59 LT-6Gs equipped for FAC duties in Korea (49-3537/3596)
NA-182: further batches of remanufactured T-6Gs, total 824 (51-14314/15137)

NA-188: further remanufactured T-6Gs, total 107 (51-15138/15237 and -16071/16077)
NA-195: more T-6Gs, total 11 (51-17354/17364)
NA-197: June 1952, last T-6G remanufacture contract, total 110 (52-8197/8246, 53-4555/4614) Many T-6G blocks were assigned to friendly air forces under MDAP, and numerous other wartime aircraft were modified without NA type numbers, examples being the AT-6D re-engined with 500-hp (373-kW) Ranger V-770-9 as XAT-6E, the USN SNJ-3Cs, -4Cs and -5Cs with hooks for carrier training, the AT-6Fs rebuilt by the USAF as T-6Fs for front-line observation in Korea, and the large numbers of USN aircraft (mainly SNJ-4s) remanufactured at NAS Pensacola in 1951-53 to approximately T-6G standard with designation SNJ-7 and (armed) SNJ-7B. NAA's contract for 240 NA-198 (Navy SNJ-8) new aircraft to similar standard was cancelled

NAA Attack variants

NA-44: prototype attack model with 785-hp (586-kW) Wright R-1820-F52 Cyclone, stressed-skin throughout, two wing guns, two cowl guns, one (optional 0.5-in/12.7-mm) in rear cockpit and 400-lb (181-kg) bombload; prototype became no. 3344 of RCAF, served to 1947

NA-69: batch of 10 for Siam, requisitioned by USAAC and put into combat duty in Philippines as A-27s (41-18890/18899)

NA-72: batch of 30 delivered to Brazil

NA-74: batch of 12 for Chile

Licence production

Sweden: after studying NA-31 and NA-38, ASJA built 35 similar with R-975-E3 with air force designation Sk 14 in 1938-9, while Saab (which took over ASJA) followed in 1940-41 with 18 more; lack of US engines led to Piaggio P.VIIRC 35 (500 hp/373 kW) in next wartime batch of 23 Sk14A, followed by 60 built in 1943-4; these fixed-gear aircraft were unrelated to large Sk16 family of ex-US T-6/SNJ purchases post-war

Australia: CAC began to tool for NA-33 in 1937 with name Wirraway as multi-role aircraft with two 0.303-in (7.7-mm) forward guns and up to 500 lb (227 kg) of bombs; total 755 in 10 variants; post-war rebuilds included CA-28 Ceres crop-sprayers

Canada: to meet urgent need, which NAA could not fulfil, Canadian government nominated Noorduyn in 1940 as additional source for Empire Air Training Scheme. Type basically AT-6A, with US instruments and radio (unlike RAF Harvards), but designated Harvard Mk IIB; first batch 100 (1-40), followed by 110 (7-40); then USAAF took over contracts for remainder under Lease-Lend programme, with US designation AT-16, but delivered with RAF serials as Harvard Mk IIB; total 1,800 (500 + 233 + 67 + 339 + 361 + 300); Noorduyn built a further 900 Harvard Mk IIBs for RAF; in 1946 CCF (Canadian Car & Foundry) took over Noorduyn and in 1951 received order for 270 new aircraft for RCAF designated Harvard Mk IV, basically similar to T-6G; the USAF also bought 285 more for MCAP recipients with designation T-6J

Japan: Imperial Japanese Navy evaluated NA-37 and NA-47 and ordered K10W1 version from Watanabe in 1941 with 600-hp (448-kw) Kotobuki (Bristol Jupiter derived) engine and one/two guns; after 26 delivered, programme transferred to Nippon Hikoki as K5Y1, as which 150 more delivered 1943-4

Other familiar items included Ki-Gass manual engine priming, a wobble pump for building up fuel pressure before starting, a manual selector for building up hydraulic pressure, and massive diecast trim wheels and levers for the landing gear and flaps. Every example was pleasant to fly, and of course fully aerobatic, but if harshly handled would flick dangerously through 270°, and landing with excessively vigorous stick pressure would likewise result in violent wing-drop which, at the very least, would break the spars and often caused a write-off. Thus, the NAA trainers fulfilled the requirement in not being so easy that pilots did not have to fly correctly.

New designations and equipment

As far as possible the variants list includes all the models produced by NAA or its licensees, or modified post-war by the USAF or USN. In June 1948 the AT category was superseded by T (trainer), and the standard post-war model was defined as the T-6G, with over 250 engineering changes including a redesigned cockpit with better instruments, controls and pilot view, repositioned aerial masts usually with a D/F loop acorn over the rear fuselage), different propeller, increased fuel capacity with extra tanks at the inner end of the outer-panels, and such new avionics as a VHF command set, range receiver and marker-beacon receiver, new interphone, radio compass and ILS, as well as up-to-date instruments training equipment as in the next generation T-28. Most of the remanufactured T-6Gs came from NAA's Downey (Los Angeles) plant, but some were converted at Columbus, where they were at first called T-6H, later reverting to T-6G-NT.

Harvard's vast war experience

Though primarily trainers, the NA-16 family have played a notable part in many wars. Harvard Mk Is carried bombs in July 1940. Much later the USAF 6147th Tactical Air Control Squadron pioneered what were called 'Mosquito' observation tactics over the front line in Korea, and purpose-built T-6F and LT-6G Texans pioneered the FAC (forward air control) mission. In Kenya RAF No. 1340 Flight did similar work, flying round the clock against the Mau Mau. In infant Israel the Heyl Ha'Avir bought all the T-6s it could get, using them from November 1948 as front-line dive-bombers with eight 110-lb (50-kg) bombs and often carrying three guns, at least one being of 0.5-in (12.7-mm) calibre. By 1953 no fewer than 90 were in use, though by this time their main role was that of armed trainer. Even these numbers are small compared with the 450-odd used by the Armée de l'Air and Aéronavale in the bitter Algerian war in 1956–60. As late as 1969 Harvards of all species had been gathered in Biafra to form a mercenary squadron used effectively against Nigeria's jet air force on its home airfields.

For many long years the North American Harvard/Texan wore large numbers of different liveries for many countries and has been the advanced flying training platform for hundreds of pilots, many of whom went on to master the thoroughbreds of the time, the Spitfires and Hurricanes of World War 2. The Harvard bridged the considerable gap between the low powered elementary trainers such as the D.H. Tiger Moth and those fierce, high-powered front line fighters.

Excluding the later aircraft built under licence, 21,342 aircraft of the NA-16 series were built. In addition, NAA built 53 fighters with higher engine performance, and these are shown in the list of variations.

This Harvard Mk 2A was one of several hundred serving with the South African Air Force in 1943–75, many of them passed on from wartime schools in 'The Union' or in Southern Rhodesia to the north. No. 7698 was one of the many used by the ACF (Active Citizen Force) No. 40 Sqn, in both refresher training and COIN roles.

Spitfire: fighter supreme

Comment on the Supermarine Spitfire is almost superfluous: this magnificent thoroughbred fighting machine is perhaps the best-known British aircraft of all time. It remained in production right through World War 2, remaining a fully competitive interceptor while also being developed into a number of other roles such as PR aircraft, tactical fighter-bomber and shipboard fighter.

The Spitfire is perhaps the most famous British aircraft of all time. Though it played a minor role in the Battle of Britain compared with the less glamorous Hawker Hurricane, it was probably the most important single type of aircraft on the Allied side in World War 2. It was built in larger numbers than any Allied type outside the Soviet Union, remained in production throughout the entire war and was developed to a greater extent than any other aircraft in history. Britain was fortunate that, as a purely private venture by the chief designer with the support of his board, the nation possessed a prototype in 1936 of a fighter which was capable of being developed to much more than twice the engine power and much more than twice the laden weight in order to stay in the very forefront of the air-combat battle.

Had Britain relied upon official specifications the only 1936 fighter would have been the Supermarine 224, a clumsy machine with an airframe structurally resembling the Schneider Trophy seaplanes, with a 660-hp (492-kW)

No exponents of the Spitfire deserved a greater reputation than the Free Poles, many of whom had relatives living under the Nazi yoke. This Spitfire IX was the mount of the CO of No. 303 (Polish) Sqn, RAF.

Goshawk engine and armed with four machine-guns, two in the fuselage and two in the fixed 'trousered' landing gears. The designer, Reginald Mitchell, was unimpressed with his creation, went back to his drawing board and created the Type 300. This was much smaller and better streamlined, had retractable landing gear, was of all stressed-skin construction, and was intended to be powered by the new Rolls-Royce PV.12 engine of some 900 hp (671 kW). All the guns were in the wings, firing outside the disc of the propeller; and, thanks to young Squadron Leader Ralph Sorley, the Air Ministry had decided that future fighters might need eight machine-guns. Moreover, the absence of a modern British gun was being made up by a licence to make the American Browning (itself a World War 1 gun), and by late 1935 this

254

gun in British 0.303-in (7.7-mm) calibre was being planned for production at the BSA company. Mitchell schemed the wing of the Type 300 with a distinctive elliptical shape to accommodate all eight guns well outboard, with belt magazines quickly replenished through hatches in the skin.

It so happened that this wing, so characteristic of the Spitfire, was one of the best ever designed for a fighter of this era. The elliptical shape played no part in this, and merely made it difficult to make. But aerodynamically the profile was good for speed over 90 per cent that of sound (over Mach 0.9), and during World War 2 Spitfires were dived to Mach 0.92, much faster than any of the German jets. By this time Supermarine had developed a new wing, and when it was later fitted to the first Supermarine jet fighter many pilots, including the chief test pilot, wished the old Spitfire wing had been used instead!

Flight test and production
Like its lifelong enemy the Messerschmitt Bf 109, the new Supermarine fighter had a narrow landing gear pivoted near the fuselage and retracting out and up into the wings. Again like the Bf 109, the Spitfire used a water/glycol engine cooling liquid which was piped to radiators under the rear

around it and assigned the serial number K5054 (curiously, an earlier number than that of the prototype Hurricane, K5083, which was built six months earlier). The trim new prototype was flown unpainted by chief test pilot 'Mutt' Summers at Eastleigh airfield (now Southampton airport) on 5 March 1936. The aircraft handled like a dream, but such was the difficulty of training workers to make modern stressed-skin aircraft that the planned mass production was slow to get under way. The first Spitfire I reached No. 19 Squadron at Duxford in July 1938, and only five had been delivered at the time of the Munich crisis in September that year. By 1939 the Mk I was being made more effective as the clouds of war gathered. The Merlin engine, into which the PV.12 (used in the prototype) had been developed, was being improved in more powerful versions. The first de Havilland and Rotol constant-speed three-blade propellers were at last becoming available. The cockpit was given a bulged hood providing more room and a better view, and a thick slab of Perspex and glass was added at the front to make the windscreen bulletproof. The seat and engine bulkhead were given armour, and the two rather small fuel tanks (total 85 Imp gal/386 litres) ahead of the cockpit were made self-sealing against bullet holes. Previously the engine

A fine study of a Spitfire VB (EP622) belonging to No. 40 Sqn, South African Air Force, operating in the Taranto area of Italy during late 1943. The clipped wings bestowed greater speed and roll-rate at low altitudes, but the outline is marred by the bulging filter on the carburettor air intake.

part of the inner wing, though in the British aircraft an odd asymmetric arrangement was chosen, with the coolant radiator under the right wing and a slim oil-cooler radiator under the left. Other features included split flaps (worked, like the landing gear, by a hydraulic system with a hand pump in the cockpit), a comfortable cockpit with a Perspex (ICI transparent acrylic plastic) hood that the pilot could slide to the rear on runners, six plain stub exhausts on each side, a fixed tailskid and a hefty but crude two-blade wooden propeller (because none of the new variable-pitch propellers was available in the UK).

Altogether the new fighter was the most beautiful of its era. The Air Ministry had written specification F.37/34

had been fitted with ejector exhaust stacks and a pump to work the hydraulic system, and after the outbreak of war improved radio was fitted together with IFF (identification friend or foe), an automatic radio interrogator which gave positive identification of other aircraft in the vicinity (though this did not stop many tragic mistakes).

In 1938 Joe Smith, who on Mitchell's untimely death had become chief designer, had begun a planned process of development of later marks of Spitfire. One major scheme involved a 'B' series wing with the two inboard guns on each side replaced by a large 20-mm Hispano cannon, with drum feed. In early 1940 a batch of 30 Mk IBs was delivered, but the cannon were not then reliable. The corresponding 'C' type wing removed all the machine-guns and provided the formidable armament of four cannon in close pairs. This remained relatively rare.

By 1941 there had been many experimental or special variants, including the intended speed-record Speed Spit-

Supermarine Spitfire VA

Specification

Type: single-seat interceptor fighter
Powerplant: one 1,478-hp (1103-kW) Rolls-Royce Merlin
45 Vee piston engine
Performance: maximum speed 369 mph (594 km/h) at
19,500 ft (5945 m); initial climb rate 4,740 ft (1445 m)
per minute; service ceiling 36,500 ft (11125 m);
maximum range 1,135 miles (1827 km)
Weights: empty 4,998 lb (2267 kg); maximum take-off
6,417 lb (2911 kg)
Dimensions: span 36 ft 10 in (11.23 m); length 29 ft 11 in
(9.12 m); height 9 ft 11 in (3.02 m); wing area
242 sq ft (22.48 m²)
Armament: eight 0.303-in (7.7-mm) Browning machine-
guns with 350 rounds per gun

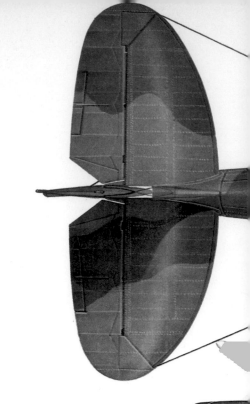

A formation of Spitfires with one aircraft missing in honour of Sir Douglas
Bader, over Greenham in July 1983.

The personal aircraft of Wing Commander Douglas Bader when he
commanded the Tangmere Wing in early 1941, this Mk VA was one of the
last Spitfires built without cannon armament, which was distrusted by
Bader. The aircraft was one of a batch of 450 Mk Is ordered from Vickers-
Armstrongs (Supermarine) on 22 March 1940. The order was
subsequently amended to cover Mk V aircraft: most were Spitfire VBs, but
a small batch of Spitfire VAs was also built. Bader was flying this aircraft,
which unlike others had no provision for bomb armament, when he
collided with a Messerschmitt Bf 109 over France and baled out to
captivity on 7 August 1941.

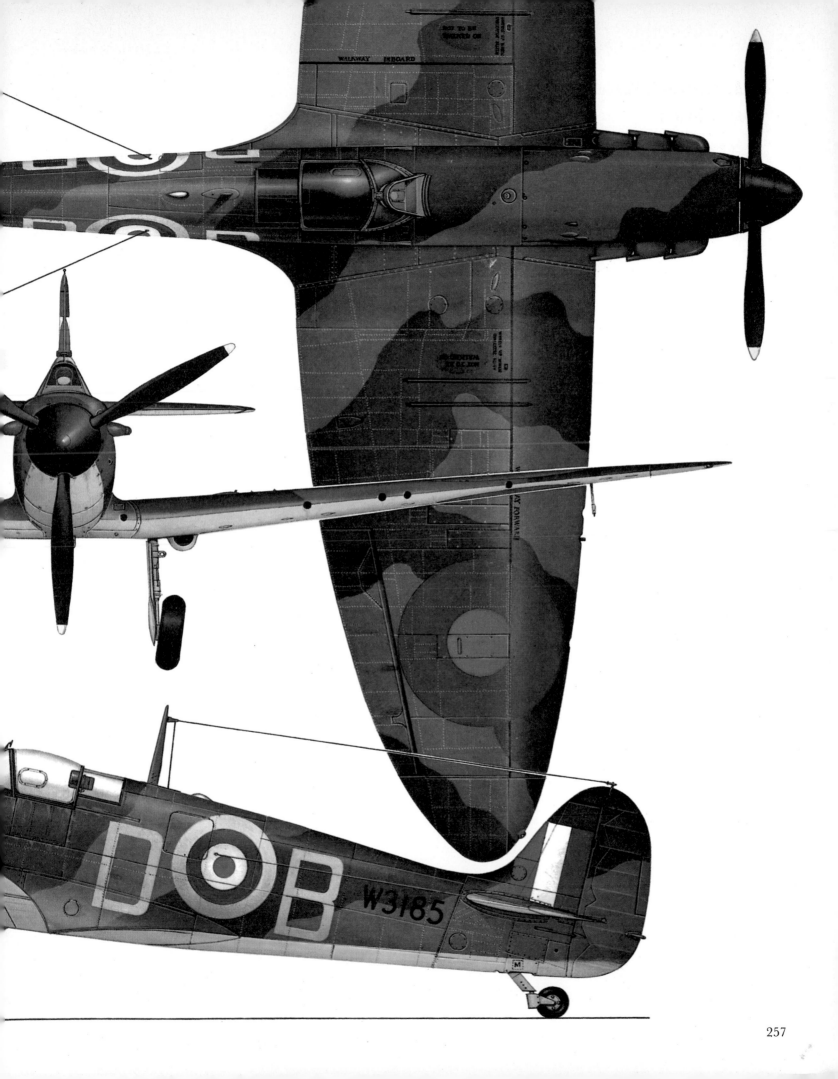

fire, two seaplanes, a part-plastic example to conserve scarce materials, a strengthened Mk III and two Mk IVs which introduced the larger Griffon engine and a four-blade propeller. Production, however, had been confined to the Mk I and the almost identical Mk II which was built at a vast shadow factory at Castle Bromwich near Birmingham. And the next major production model, the Mk V, was not greatly different. It had a strengthened fuselage like the Mk III, a more powerful Merlin with wider blades on its three-blade propeller, provision for 'A', 'B' or 'C' wings, attachments under the belly for a 30-Imp gal (136-litre) drop tank (on occasion a much larger tank could be attached here) or a bomb of up to 500 lb (227 kg). The most common model was the Mk VB with two cannon and four machine-guns, but at the end of Mk V production the four-cannon 'C' armament became more common. Aircraft destined for the Mediterranean theatre had a dust and sand filter under the nose which spoilt both the appearance and performance. Aircraft expected to operate mainly at low level had the tips of the wings removed, which was effected by the undoing of two bolts. These so-called 'clipped-wing Spits' needed a slightly longer take-off and landing run and were poorer at high altitude, but at low level they were faster and even more agile. Manoeuvrability in the Mk V was in any case improved by the use of aluminium instead of fabric to skin the ailerons. No fewer than 6,479 Spitfire Vs were built, more than any other mark.

Large numbers of Spitfires were given to the Soviet Union in World War 2, 1,188 of them being Mk IXs. This particular example was the subject of an interesting local modification: its armament was removed and a second cockpit for an instructor added behind the first.

Supermarine Spitfire IX cutaway drawing key:

1 Starboard wingtip
2 Navigation light
3 Starboard aileron
4 Browning 0.303-in (7.7-mm) machine-guns
5 Machine-gun ports (patched)
6 Ammunition boxes (350 rounds per gun)
7 Aileron control rod
8 Bellcrank hinge control
9 Starboard split trailing-edge flap
10 Aileron control cables
11 Cannon ammunition box (120 rounds)
12 Starboard 20-mm Hispano cannon
13 Ammunition feed drum
14 Cannon barrel
15 Rotol four-bladed constant speed propeller
16 Cannon barrel fairing
17 Spinner

18 Propeller hub pitch control mechanism
19 Armoured spinner backplate
20 Coolant system header tank
21 Coolant filler cap
22 Rolls-Royce Merlin 61 liquid-cooled 12-cylinder Vee piston engine
23 Exhaust stubs
24 Forward engine mounting
25 Engine bottom cowling
26 Cowling integral oil tank (5.6-Imp gal/25.5-litre capacity)
27 Extended carburettor air intake duct
28 Engine bearer struts
29 Main engine mounting member
30 Oil filter
31 Two-stage supercharger
32 Engine bearer attachment

33 Suppressor
34 Engine accessories
35 Intercooler
36 Compressor air intake scoop
37 Hydraulic reservoir
38 Hydraulic system filter
39 Armoured firewall/fuel tank bulkhead
40 Fuel filler cap
41 Top main fuel tank (48-Imp gal/218-litre capacity)
42 Back of instrument panel
43 Compass mounting
44 Fuel tank/longeron attachment fitting
45 Bottom main fuel tank (37-Imp gal/168-litre capacity)
46 Rudder pedal bar
47 Sloping fuel tank bulkhead
48 Fuel cock control
49 Chart case
50 Trim control handwheel

51 Engine throttle and propeller controls
52 Control column handgrip
53 Radio controller
54 Bullet-proof windscreen
55 Reflector gunsight
56 Pilot's rear view mirror
57 Canopy framing
58 Windscreen side panels
59 Sliding cockpit canopy cover
60 Headrest

61 Pilot's head armour
62 Safety harness
63 Pilot's seat
64 Side entry hatch
65 Back armour
66 Seat support frame
67 Pneumatic system air bottles
68 Fuselage main longeron
69 Optional long-range auxiliary fuel tank (29-Imp gal/132-litre capacity)

70 Sliding canopy rail
71 Voltage regulator
72 Cockpit aft glazing
73 IFF radio equipment
74 HF aerial mast
75 Aerial cable lead-in
76 Radio transmitter/receiver
77 Radio compartment access hatch
78 Upper identification light
79 Rear fuselage frame construction
80 Fuselage skin plating
81 Oxygen bottle
82 Signal cartridge launcher

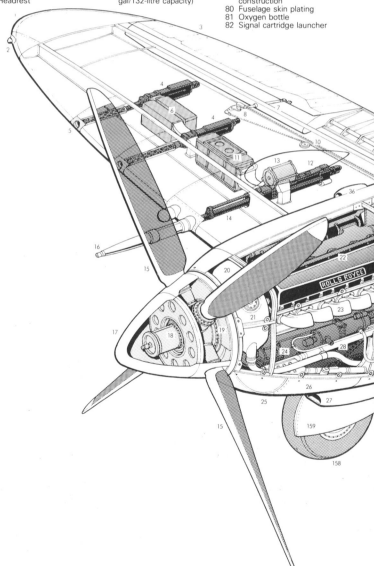

Test pilot 'Mutt' Summers taxis the prototype Supermarine Spitfire (K5054) in its immaculate pale blue finish. Note the massive two-blade propeller and flush exhaust stubs, one for each of the six cylinders on the engine's right-hand bank. However, the narrow-track landing gear was always a tactical problem.

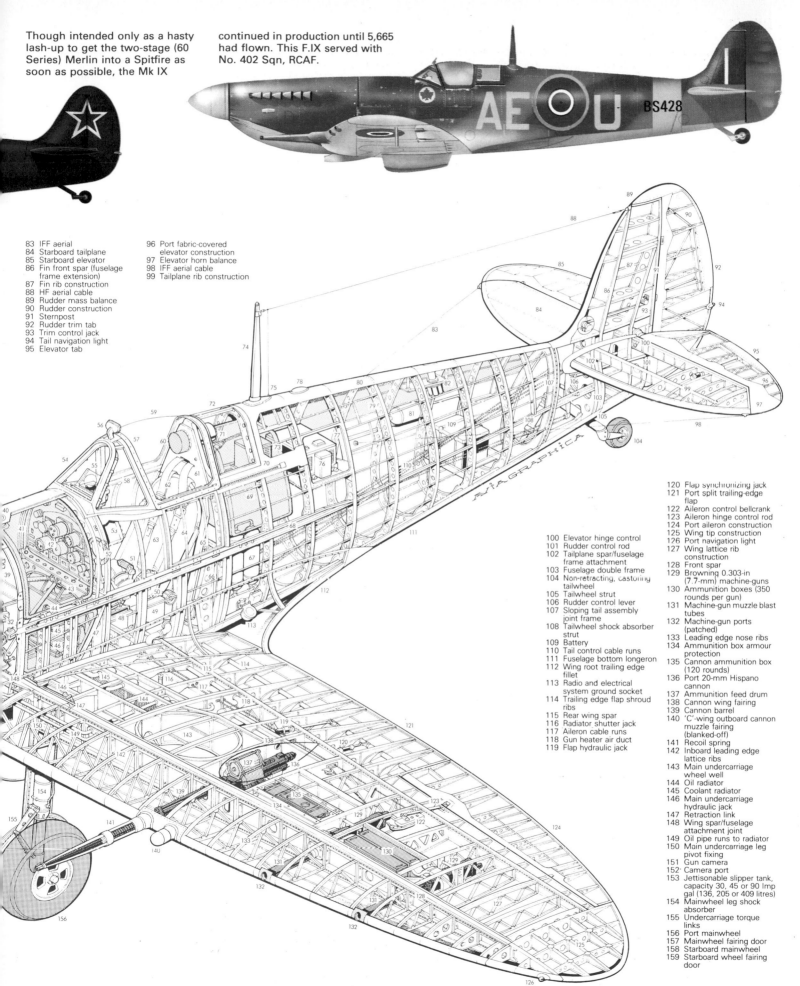

Though intended only as a hasty lash-up to get the two-stage (60 Series) Merlin into a Spitfire as soon as possible, the Mk IX continued in production until 5,665 had flown. This F.IX served with No. 402 Sqn, RCAF.

BS428

83 IFF aerial
84 Starboard tailplane
85 Starboard elevator
86 Fin front spar (fuselage frame extension)
87 Fin rib construction
88 HF aerial cable
89 Rudder mass balance
90 Rudder construction
91 Sternpost
92 Rudder trim tab
93 Trim control jack
94 Tail navigation light
95 Elevator tab

96 Port fabric-covered elevator construction
97 Elevator horn balance
98 IFF aerial cable
99 Tailplane rib construction

100 Elevator hinge control
101 Rudder control rod
102 Tailplane spar/fuselage frame attachment
103 Fuselage double frame
104 Non-retracting, castoring tailwheel
105 Tailwheel strut
106 Rudder control lever
107 Sloping tail assembly joint frame
108 Tailwheel shock absorber strut
109 Battery
110 Tail control cable runs
111 Fuselage bottom longeron
112 Wing root trailing edge fillet
113 Radio and electrical system ground socket
114 Trailing edge flap shroud ribs
115 Rear wing spar
116 Radiator shutter jack
117 Aileron cable runs
118 Gun heater air duct
119 Flap hydraulic jack

120 Flap synchronizing jack
121 Port split trailing-edge flap
122 Aileron control bellcrank
123 Aileron hinge control rod
124 Port aileron construction
125 Wing tip construction
126 Port navigation light
127 Wing lattice rib construction
128 Front spar
129 Browning 0.303-in (7.7-mm) machine-guns
130 Ammunition boxes (350 rounds per gun)
131 Machine-gun muzzle blast tubes
132 Machine-gun ports (patched)
133 Leading edge nose ribs
134 Ammunition box armour protection
135 Cannon ammunition box (120 rounds)
136 Port 20-mm Hispano cannon
137 Ammunition feed drum
138 Cannon wing fairing
139 Cannon barrel
140 'C'-wing outboard cannon muzzle fairing (blanked-off)
141 Recoil spring
142 Inboard leading edge lattice ribs
143 Main undercarriage wheel well
144 Oil radiator
145 Coolant radiator
146 Main undercarriage hydraulic jack
147 Retraction link
148 Wing spar/fuselage attachment joint
149 Oil pipe runs to radiator
150 Main undercarriage leg pivot fixing
151 Gun camera
152 Camera port
153 Jettisonable slipper tank, capacity 30, 45 or 90 Imp gal (136, 205 or 409 litres)
154 Mainwheel leg shock absorber
155 Undercarriage torque links
156 Port mainwheel
157 Mainwheel fairing door
158 Starboard mainwheel
159 Starboard wheel fairing door

259

Photo-reconnaissance

A small proportion of the Mk Vs (229) were completed as photo-reconnaissance aircraft, and though this was confusing they were then designated PR.IV (there had already been the quite different Griffon-engined Mk IV). PR versions had the guns replaced by 66½ Imp gal (302 litres) of extra fuel in the leading edge of the wing. Two cameras were fitted in the rear fuselage, in a heated bay, taking photographs on either side of the track with a small overlap in the centre. The pilot had extra oxygen and the engine a larger oil supply.

The Mk VI was the first high-altitude interceptor version, with a pressurized cockpit and pointed wingtips that increased span to 40 ft 2 in (12.24 m). Such aircraft were needed in 1941 to catch ultra-high-flying Junkers Ju 86P and 86R raiders, a problem which posed severe problems with extreme cold that iced up the windscreen and stopped guns working. An even more important advance in the high-altitude regime was being provided by Rolls-Royce with the 60-series of Merlin engines. These had two superchargers in series, with an intercooler to reduce the temperature of the air and thus increase its density still further. At altitudes of about 30,000 ft (9145 m) these engines gave twice the power of earlier Merlins, and when fitted to a Spitfire they were instantly distinguishable by a slightly longer nose, six instead of three exhaust stubs on each side, a four-blade propeller and symmetrical radiators, the oil cooler being joined by an extra cooling radiator on the left side. In combat none of these differences was obvious, so in 1942 the much more formidable Mk IX Spitfire was an unpleasant surprise that removed the previous advantage enjoyed by the Focke-Wulf Fw 190.

The definitive Spitfire VIII

The Mk IX was simply a Mk V with the new engine – in fact a hasty lash-up to get the Merlin 61 (later the 63, 66 or 70) into action quickly. The definitive model was the Mk VIII, a much better aircraft; yet the Mk IX was kept in production to the amazing total of 5,665 and was still being built in 1945! It came with a profusion of variations, including LF (32 ft 7 in/9.88 m), F (the regular 36 ft 10 in/11.23 m) and HF (40 ft 2 in/12.24 m) wings, the three previous armament schemes plus an 'E' wing with two cannon and two 0.5-in (12.7-mm) guns, and bomb loads up to 1,000 lb (454 kg). Even more remarkably, when Spitfires were built with the American-made Packard V-1650 (Merlin 266) they were not the Mk VIII type but the lash-up Mk IX airframes, the result being designated Mk XVI. Large numbers of LF.XVIE with 'E' armament and clipped wings were used by the 2nd TAF in 1945.

One of the rarest and most interesting Spitfires was this early Mk I, from the second production batch at the Supermarine works ordered in 1937 and delivered just after the outbreak of war. It was converted as a PR Type C, one of the first photo-reconnaissance aircraft assigned to Benson in 1941.

This Spitfire VB was one of more than 600 Spitfires handed to the USAAF as reverse Lend-Lease. In the markings of the 78th Fighter Group as a trainer, it was actually operated in 1942 by the 4th FG, the group formed from the four RAF Eagle Squadrons, based at Debden, Essex.

Operators of the Spitfire throughout World War 2, and the only unit to see action with the Mk 21, RAF No. 91 Sqn used the Mk VC with a tropical filter in the Mediterranean theatre in 1943. This Mk VC was made at Castle Bromwich; with the extra drag of the filter it was on the slow side.

The prototype Spitfire XII shows off its purposeful lines. All Mk XIIs had the clipped wings shown, suiting the type to the low-level interception role, and also introduced into production Spitfires the larger Rolls-Royce Griffon engine, housed in a lengthened nose with 'bumps' over the tops of the cylinder banks.

Only relatively small numbers were produced of the beautiful Mk VIII – in the opinion of most pilots, the nicest of all Spitfires to fly – and the Mk VII. The latter was a marriage of the two-stage Merlin engine with the pressurized cockpit of the Mk VI, with double-layer sealed canopy and a modified 'C' type wing with reduced-span ailerons. Some Mk VII aircraft had a broader rudder with pointed top, later made standard on Merlin 60-series aircraft, and another refinement was a retractable tailwheel. These were also features of the Mk VIII which in addition introduced a neat tropical filter, most of this type going to overseas theatres including the Pacific. The last of the Merlin Spitfires, the Mk XI, or PR.XI, was the most important Allied reconnaissance aircraft in the European theatre, being used by the RAF and USAAF on lone unarmed sorties from England to target areas as distant as Berlin. Most had the pointed rudder, and all a

The Forca Aérea Portuguesa, the air force of the UK's oldest ally, was handed 110 Spitfires in 1943, 92 of them Mk VBs and the other 18 early Mk Is. This Mk I was assigned to Esquadrilha XZ and served with a Grupo de Caca (fighter wing) until 1948. (The Mk VBs served till 1952.)

P7666 was a Spitfire IIA made at the Castle Bromwich shadow factory. It was paid for by members of the Observer Corps (soon to be the Royal Observer Corps) and was the personal aircraft of Squadron Leader Don Finlay, a pre-war Olympic hurdler who was CO of No. 41 Sqn at Hornchurch in 1940.

retractable tailwheel, but the one distinctive feature of this unarmed mark was the deep underside of the engine cowl, as a result of the oversize oil tank necessary on such long missions.

Apart from the original Mk IV, the first Spitfire with a Griffon engine was the Mk XII. The bigger engine resulted in a longer nose with bumps on top to accommodate the fronts of the cylinder blocks. The Mk XII was a hastily contrived low-level interceptor to catch Fw 190 hit-and-run raiders, and it reached almost 350 mph (563 km/h) at sea level, compared with 312 mph (502 km/h) for a Mk IX. A batch of 100, in two versions, was supplied to two RAF home-defence squadrons in 1942. They were totally unlike earlier Spitfires, notably in that on take-off they swung violently to the right instead of gently to the left, because the propeller rotated in the opposite direction. All had clipped wings, and some had retractable tailwheels.

One of the few operational units to use the pointed-wing high-altitude. F.VII, No. 131 Sqn RAF had previously used the Mks I, II, V and IX. The pressurized F.VII was painted in the high-altitude scheme of Medium Sea Grey and PRU (Photo Reconnaissance Unit) Blue, and is seen here with 'invasion stripes'.

Undoubtedly the nicest of all 'Spits' to fly or fight with, the Mk VIII got into the war late because of the prolonged output of the 'interim' Mk IX. This Mk VIII belonged to Wing Commander Glenn Cooper, CO of No. 457 Sqn, RAAF, based at Darwin and, from December 1944, Morotai in the Moluccas.

More powerful engines

Predictably, Rolls-Royce fitted two-stage supercharging to the big Griffon and the result, the 65-series engine, was much more than twice as powerful as the original Merlin at all heights. It also made the Spitfire 3 ft (0.91 m) longer and gave it two deep radiators. This great engine was first used in the Mk XIV, which though to some extent a quick lash-up of 1943, was an outstanding aircraft in all respects. On the ground it could be distinguished, apart from the massive nose, by its five-blade propeller. This affected directional stability, so a larger vertical tail was fitted. Directional stability again became marginal in later F (fighter) and FR (fighter-reconnaissance, with rear-fuselage camera) versions which had a cut-down top to the rear fuselage and a beautiful teardrop, or 'bubble', canopy giving uninterrupted view to the rear.

The Mk XIV was the most important Spitfire in the final year of World War 2. It was joined by a few of the definitive Mk XVIII version, but the Mk VIII/IX saga was repeated and only a few XVIIIs were built. Last of the Spitfires with the original basic wing was the PR.XIX, the two-stage Griffon successor to the PR.XI and the type used on the RAF's last Spitfire sortie in Malaya in 1954. Post-war arabic numerals were used for the surviving aircraft such as the LF.16, FR.18 and PR.19.

After World War 2 three generally similar models of Spitfire entered service with a new airframe which took full advantage of the power of the two-stage Griffon and was markedly heavier. The wing, no longer of simple curving (so-called elliptical) shape, was even stronger than before and carried four cannon, extra fuel and stronger landing gear covered by wing doors when retracted. The large tail had metal-skinned rudder and elevators and the systems were totally re-engineered.

The first model of this new Spitfire family was the F.21, in production from September 1944; some had the Griffon 85 with a six-blade contra-rotating propeller. The F.22 introduced a teardrop canopy and (like the last F.21s) 24-volt electrics; late F.22s had a long-span tailplane and the new vertical tail of the Spiteful, and a rear-fuselage fuel tank whose use was prohibited on grounds of directional instability. The last mark of all, the F.24, had a usable rear tank, and minor changes such as rocket launchers and electrical gun-firing. The last of 20,334 Spitfires, an F.24, was delivered in February 1948.

To meet an urgent Fleet Air Arm need for a modern carrier-based fighter in 1941, Air Service Training produced a navalized Spitfire VB called the Seafire IB. At this time the FAA also had many earlier Seafires, produced by converting Spitfires already built. The chief wartime Seafire, the Mk III, was a navalized Mk VC with a Merlin 32 or 55 giving high power at low level via a four-blade propeller, and with manually folded wings which gave some loss of performance and torsional rigidity; Westland (which made many Spitfires) and Cunliffe-Owen shared production. The single-stage Griffon powered the Seafire XV, a much more deadly machine, and the trim Mk XVII with teardrop canopy. After the war the powerful Mks 45, 46 and 47 brought the Spitfire/Seafire family to a close with aircraft weighing up to 12,750 lb (5783 kg) yet capable of impressive all-round performance fully demonstrated in the Korean war. Seafire production amounted to 2,556 excluding conversions.

Deck handlers 'spot' Seafire IIC fighters at the stern of the flight deck of a Royal Navy fleet carrier in 1943. Right at the stern is a Fairey Albacore with wings folded. The Seafire IIC, the first mark built as such rather than converted from a Seafire, did not have folding wings but was a hooked Spitfire VC.

The prototype of the Spitfire 21 in flight. This last variant entered Royal Air Force service very late in World War 2. The airframe had been totally redesigned and was powered by a Griffon 61 or 64 driving a Rotol five-blade propeller (though some examples had the Griffon 85 driving a six-blade contra-rotating propeller) and had a standard gun armament of four 20-mm Hispano cannon. Records show that 122 mark 21 Spitfires were produced.

Standard unarmed photo-reconnaissance version of the Spitfire for the second half of the war, the Mk XI (No. 541 Sqn, Benson, 1944) could be distinguished by its deeper nose (housing an enlarged oil tank for missions as far as Berlin and back) and windscreen without bullet-proof panel.

Spitfire variants

Spitfire I: original production model with 1,030-hp (768-kW) Merlin II, eight Browning 0.303-in (7.7-mm) guns (at first four not fitted because of short supply) or (Mk IB) two 20-mm and four 0.303-in (7.7-mm) guns (total 1,566)

Supermarine Spitfire I (early)

A Spitfire FXIV at the Greenham Airshow.

Spitfire II: Castle Bromwich aircraft with small changes and 1,175-hp (877-kW) Merlin XII (total 750 IIA and 170 IIB)

Supermarine Spitfire IIA

Spitfire III: experimental prototype (1 only) with 1,280-hp (955-kW) Merlin XX

Supermarine Spitfire III

Spitfire IV: Griffon prototype; same mark number used for 229 PR versions of Mk V

Spitfire V: strengthened fuselage for 1,440-hp (1074-kW) Merlin 45 or 1,470-hp (1097-kW) Merlin 50; drop tank and bomb provisions; F or LF span; 'A', 'B' or 'C' armament (total 94 Mk VA, 3,923 Mk VB and 2,447 Mk VC)

Supermarine Spitfire VB

Spitfire VI: high-altitude interceptor with 1,415-hp (1056-kW) Merlin 47, pressurized cockpit and HF 40 ft 2 in (12.24 m) pointed wings (total 100)

Supermarine Spitfire HF.VI

Spitfire VII: high-altitude interceptor with two-stage Merlin 61, 64 or 71, pressurized cockpit, retractable tailwheel, often broad pointed rudder (total 140)

Supermarine Spitfire HF.VII

Spitfire VIII: definitive fighter with two-stage Merlin 61, 63, 66 or 70; unpressurized; LF, F or HF wings (total 1,658)

Supermarine Spitfire VIII

Spitfire IX: temporary stop-gap marriage of two-stage Merlin 61, 63, 66 or 70 with Mk V airframe; LF, F or HF wings; 'B', 'C' or 'E' armament (total 5,665)

Supermarine Spitfire IXC

Spitfire X: pressurized version of PR.XI; Merlin 77; one example with HF wing (total 16)

Spitfire XI: unarmed reconnaissance aircraft; Merlin 61, 63 or 70 (total 471)

Spitfire XII: low-level interceptor; single-stage Griffon II or IV of 1,735-hp (1294-kW); LF wing; 'B' guns (total 100)

Supermarine Spitfire XII

Spitfire XIII: low-level PR aircraft based on Mk V but with Merlin 32 (three-blade propeller, of DH type unlike other late Spitfires); four 0.303-in (7.7-mm) guns only (total 18)

Spitfire XIV: two-stage Griffon 65 or 66 of 2,050-hp (1529-kW) driving five-blade propeller and redesigned and strengthened airframe with symmetric deep radiators, broad tail and often teardrop canopy; F or LF span; 'C' or 'E' guns (total 957)

Supermarine Spitfire XIVE

Spitfire XVI: Mk IX with Packard Merlin 266; F or LF span; usually 'C' or 'E' guns; many with teardrop canopy (total 1,054)

Supermarine Spitfire LF.XVI

Spitfire XVIII: definitive fighter with two-stage Griffon; F span; 'E' guns; teardrop canopy and extra wing fuel; FR.XVIII (postwar FR.18) with rear-fuselage reconnaissance camera (total 300)

Spitfire XIX: unarmed PR version; two-stage Griffon; most pressurized (total 225)

Spitfire XX: single prototype rebuilt from Mk IV and prototype MK XII

Spitfire 21: redesigned airframe; mainly Griffon 61 or 64 driving five-blade propeller; four 20-mm guns (total 122)

Supermarine Spitfire 21

Spitfire 22: minor changes; some with 2,375-hp (1772-kW) Griffon 85 and contraprop (total 278)

Supermarine Spitfire 22

Spitfire 24: minor changes; Spiteful tail; short-barrel Mk V cannon (total 54)

Seafire IB: navalized Spitfire VB (total 166)

Seafire IIC: catapult hooks and strengthened landing gear; Merlin 32 and four-blade propeller (total 372)

Seafire III: double-folding wing; 1,585-hp (1182-kW) Merlin 55M (total 1,220)

Seafire XV: single-stage 1,850-hp (1380-kW) Griffon VI and asymmetric radiators as Spitfire XII; most with sting hook; late production teardrop canopy (total 390)

Seafire XVII or 17: as Seafire XV with teardrop canopy; often strengthened landing gear; some (FR.17) with camera in place of rear tank (total 232)

Seafire 45: same new airframe as Spitfire 21; non-folding wing; Griffon 61 (five-blade) or 85 (contraprop) (total 50)

Seafire 46: as Seafire 45; teardrop canopy; FR.46 with rear fuselage camera; late production Spiteful tail (total 24)

Seafire 47: folding wing (most hydraulic); 2,375-hp (1772-kW) Griffon 87 or 88 with contraprop and carburettor air inlet just below spinner; increased fuel; late production all FR type with camera (total 140)

TZ114 was one of the last wartime Spitfires, built as an FR.XIV at the Supermarine works with teardrop hood and cut-down rear fuselage. After the war it was assigned to the Indian Air Force where it served with No. 6 Sqn. The reconnaissance camera (see FR.XVIII) was no longer fitted.

First of the new-generation aircraft with the two-stage Griffon and five-blade propeller, the impressive Mk XIV was one of the few types able to catch 'V-1' flying bombs. This F.XIV was used in 'anti-Diver' duties by S/L R. A. Newbury, CO of No. 610 Sqn at Lympne, Kent.

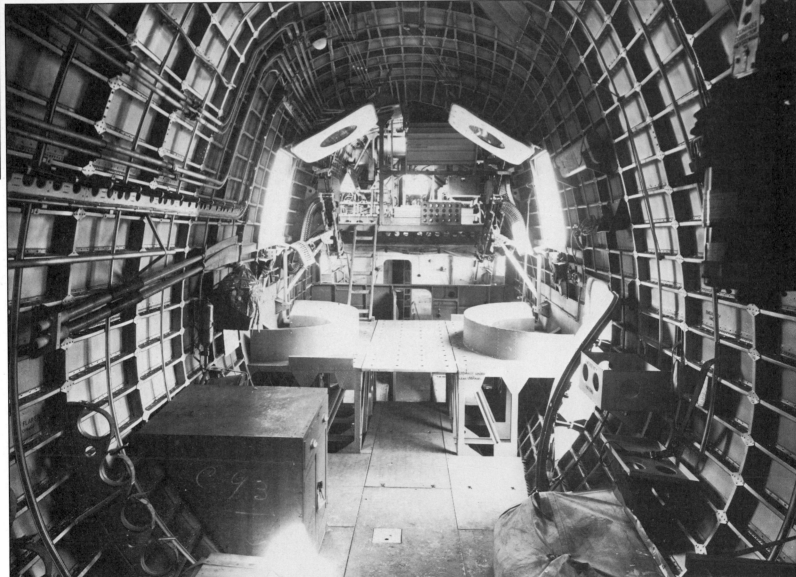

Top: A standard wartime Sunderland Mk III on the slipway. Note the forward ASV radar aerial above the cockpit and the dorsal search radar array aft.

Above: Looking forward, with the engine instruments just visible. The pairs of twin Browning 303 in MGs are stowed upright. Dinghy paddles are on the left.

Sunderland: sealane sentinel

Derived from the civil Empire Flying Boat, the Sunderland gained a legendary reputation in World War 2 as the chief patrol flying-boat of the Commonwealth forces. It was tough, reliable and could turn its hand to almost any maritime task including U-boat sinking, air-sea rescue and evacuation. The Germans found it a very prickly customer and nicknamed it 'The Flying Porcupine'.

Just as the Short S.23 C-class 'Empire' flying-boat marked a startling advance on all previous civil transport aircraft in Imperial Airways, so did its military derivative, the Sunderland, mark an equally great advance on marine aircraft in the RAF. Sometimes called 'The Pig' (not unkindly) by its crews, it was dubbed 'The Flying Porcupine' by Luftwaffe pilots who tried to attack it. When the last of these well-loved boats was retired from the RAF on 20 May 1959 it had set a record of 21 years' continuous service in the same oceanic duty. On the side, it had performed many other missions, including remarkable feats as a transport.

The Sunderland had its origins in a 1933 Air Ministry specification, R.2/33, calling for a new maritime reconnais-

This photograph was probably taken in the last year of the war, in Lough Erne, Northern Ireland. It shows a Z-Zebra, Mk V (renamed Mk 5 after the war) of 201 Squadron, which had previously used the code letters ZM.

sance flying-boat to replace the Short Singapore III biplane then just coming off the production line at the Rochester works of Short Brothers. The same company's chief designer Arthur (later Sir Arthur) Gouge immediately began to prepare a tender to the new requirement. He was already well advanced with planning a new civil transport flying-boat. Almost alone among British designers, Gouge realized that the all-metal stressed-skin monoplanes being built in the USA and Germany were a better species of flying machine,

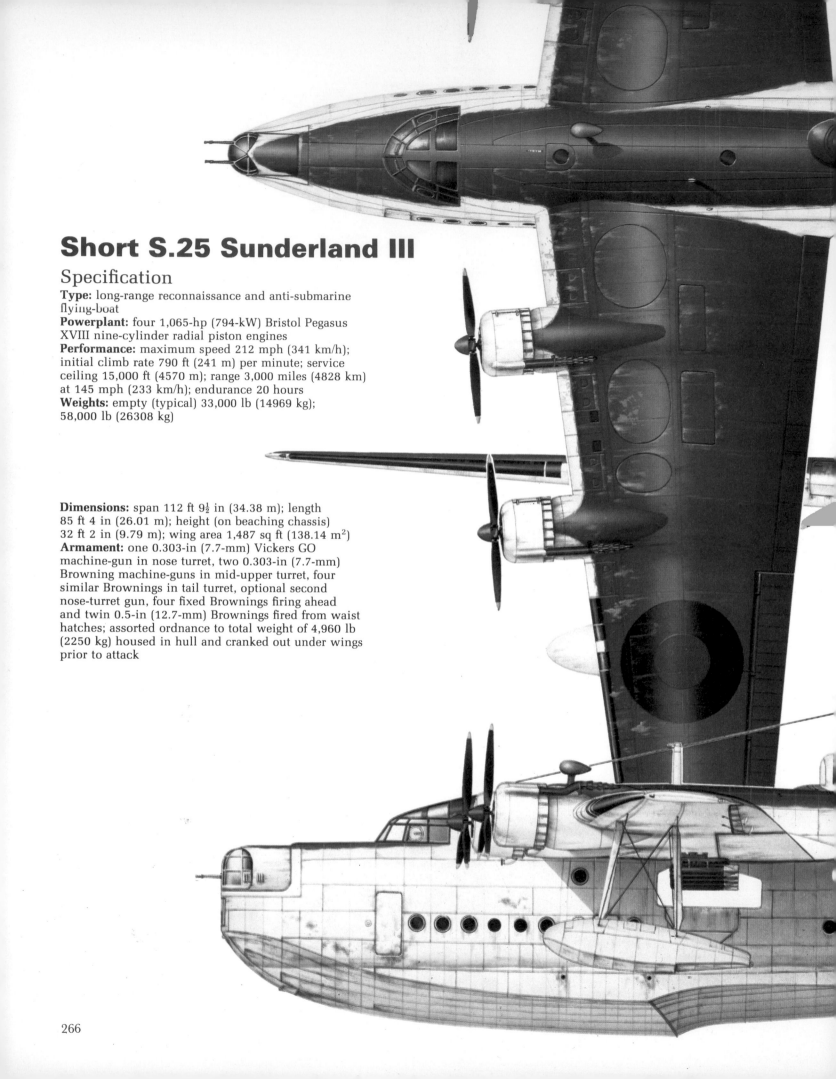

Short S.25 Sunderland III

Specification

Type: long-range reconnaissance and anti-submarine flying-boat

Powerplant: four 1,065-hp (794-kW) Bristol Pegasus XVIII nine-cylinder radial piston engines

Performance: maximum speed 212 mph (341 km/h); initial climb rate 790 ft (241 m) per minute; service ceiling 15,000 ft (4570 m); range 3,000 miles (4828 km) at 145 mph (233 km/h); endurance 20 hours

Weights: empty (typical) 33,000 lb (14969 kg); 58,000 lb (26308 kg)

Dimensions: span 112 ft 9½ in (34.38 m); length 85 ft 4 in (26.01 m); height (on beaching chassis) 32 ft 2 in (9.79 m); wing area 1,487 sq ft (138.14 m²)

Armament: one 0.303-in (7.7-mm) Vickers GO machine-gun in nose turret, two 0.303-in (7.7-mm) Browning machine-guns in mid-upper turret, four similar Brownings in tail turret, optional second nose-turret gun, four fixed Brownings firing ahead and twin 0.5-in (12.7-mm) Brownings fired from waist hatches; assorted ordnance to total weight of 4,960 lb (2250 kg) housed in hull and cranked out under wings prior to attack

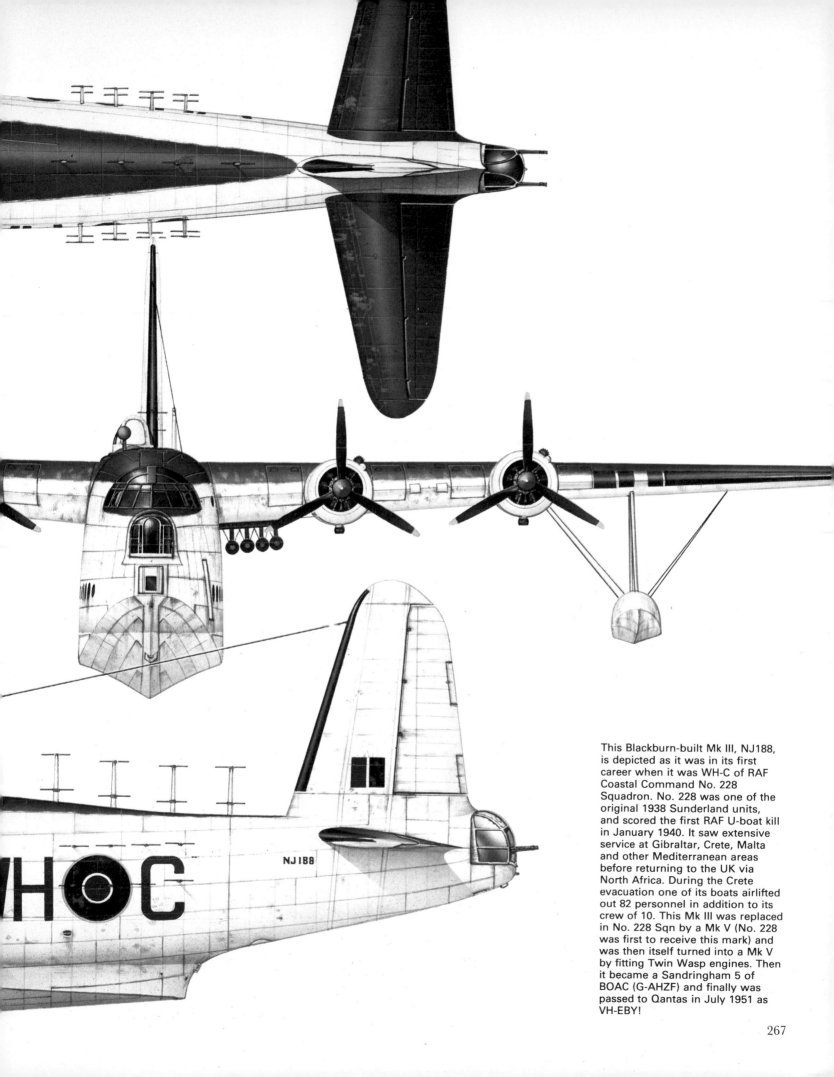

This Blackburn-built Mk III, NJ188, is depicted as it was in its first career when it was WH-C of RAF Coastal Command No. 228 Squadron. No. 228 was one of the original 1938 Sunderland units, and scored the first RAF U-boat kill in January 1940. It saw extensive service at Gibraltar, Crete, Malta and other Mediterranean areas before returning to the UK via North Africa. During the Crete evacuation one of its boats airlifted out 82 personnel in addition to its crew of 10. This Mk III was replaced in No. 228 Sqn by a Mk V (No. 228 was first to receive this mark) and was then itself turned into a Mk V by fitting Twin Wasp engines. Then it became a Sandringham 5 of BOAC (G-AHZF) and finally was passed to Qantas in July 1951 as VH-EBY!

Short Sunderland

Another early-war Sunderland was this Mk II of No. 201 Squadron, one of the first to have both ASV radar and the dorsal turret (which was offset to starboard). By this time the mid-upper and tail guns were belt-fed Brownings, though the nose guns were usually Vickers. Propellers had spinners, and the engines flame-damped exhausts.

and he designed the S.23 as a stressed-skin cantilever monoplane with a smooth skin and the greatest attention to the reduction of drag. It was an ideal basis for the new RAF machine, the S.25.

Military changes

Gouge made his submission in 1934, the specified armament being a 37-mm Coventry Ordnance Works gun in a bow cockpit or turret and a single Lewis machine-gun in the extreme tail. Compared with the civil S.23, the military boat had a completely new hull of much deeper cross-section, and with a long nose projecting ahead of a flight deck quite near the wing. When construction was well advanced it was decided to alter the armament to a nose turret with one machine-gun and a tail turret with four, a complete reversal of original thoughts on firepower. The shift in centre of gravity could only be countered by moving back the wing or altering the planform so that taper was mainly on the leading edge. The first prototype, K4774, now named Sunderland, was completed with the original wing, basically similar to that of the C-class transport, and flown without armament by J. Lankester Parker from the River Medway on 16 October 1937. After preliminary trials it went back into the factory to have the 'swept-back' wing fitted, flying again on 7 March 1938.

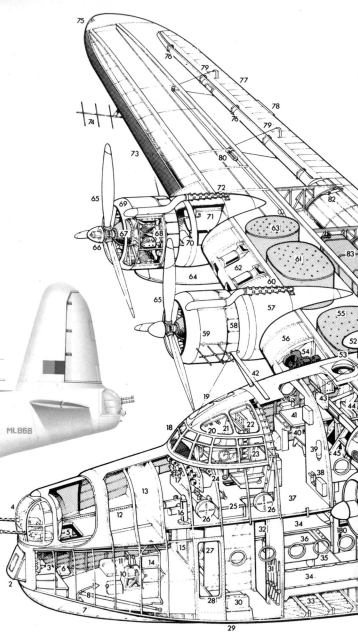

No. 230 Sqn was one of the original recipients of the Mk I in 1938, when it was based at Seletar (Singapore). In 1944 it returned to the Far East and operated in the Burma campaign, with Mk IIIs equipped with ASV II radar and painted in these Pacific theatre markings. After the war this squadron took part in the British North Greenland expedition.

Powered by 1,010-hp (753-kW) Bristol Pegasus XXII engines, more powerful than those of the civil machine, the Sunderland was far more capable than any previous RAF aircraft. Fuel was housed in six vertical drum tanks between the spars with a capacity of 2,025 Imp gal (9206 litres), later increased to 2,552 Imp gal (11602 litres) by four further cells aft of the rear spar. In the original Sunderland I the normal crew was seven, accommodated basically on two decks and with comprehensive provision for prolonged habitation, with six bunks, galley with cooking stove, workshops and stowage for a considerable quantity of equipment including

Short Sunderland III cutaway drawing key

1 Twin Vickers 0.303-in (7.7-mm) machine guns
2 Bomb aiming window, retractable
3 Bomb aimer's station
4 Retractable nose turret
5 Front entry/mooring hatch
6 Mooring cable stowage
7 Hull planing bottom
8 Anchor
9 Parachute stowage
10 Anchor winch
11 Dinghy
12 Front turret rails
13 Cockpit bulkhead
14 Mooring ladder
15 Toilet compartment door, starboard side
16 Nose gun turret hydraulic reservoir
17 Instrument panel
18 Windscreens
19 Cockpit roof glazing
20 Overhead control panels
21 Co-pilot's seat
22 Signal cartridge rack
23 Pilot's seat
24 Control column
25 Raised cockpit floor level
26 Autopilot controllers
27 Stairway between upper and lower decks
28 Front entry door
29 Fuselage chine member
30 Crew luggage locker
31 Rifle rack
32 Wardroom door
33 Planing bottom hull construction
34 Wardroom bunks
35 Window panels
36 Folding table
37 Upper deck floor level
38 Parachute stowage
39 Fire extinguisher

40 Navigator's seat
41 Chart table
42 Forward ASV radar aerial mast
43 Navigator's instrument panel
44 Flight engineer's aft-facing seat
45 Radio operator's station
46 Air intake duct
47 Wing/fuselage attachment main frames
48 Wing root rib cut-outs
49 Air conditioning plant
50 Engineer's control panels
51 Carburettor de-icing fluid tank
52 D/F loop aerial
53 Astrodome observation hatch
54 Auxiliary power unit
55 Forward inner fuel tank, 529-Imp gal (2405-litre) capacity
56 Fold-down, leading-edge maintenance platform
57 Starboard inner engine nacelle
58 Cowling air flaps
59 Detachable engine cowlings
60 Flame suppressor exhaust pipe

61 Forward inner fuel tank 325-Imp gal (1477-litre) capacity
62 Oil coolers
63 Forward outer fuel tank, 132-Imp gal (600-litre) capacity
64 Starboard wing tip float
65 De Havilland three-bladed, constant speed propeller, 12 ft 9 in (3.89 m) diameter
66 Propeller hub pitch change mechanism
67 Engine reduction gearbox
68 Bristol Pegasus XVIII, nine cylinder radial engine, 1065 hp
69 Exhaust collector ring
70 Oil filter
71 Oil tank, 32-Imp gal (145-litre) capacity
72 Flame suppressor exhaust pipe
73 Leading edge de-icing
74 Starboard ASV aerial array

75 Starboard navigation light
76 Aileron hinges
77 Starboard aileron
78 Fixed tab
79 Aileron control horns
80 Control cable runs
81 Starboard 'Gouge-type' trailing-edge flap
82 Flap guide rail
83 Rear outer fuel tank 147-Imp gal (668-litre) capacity
84 Flap jack
85 Rear inner fuel tank 111-Imp gal (505-litre) capacity
86 Pitot tubes
87 Aerial mast
88 Observation window
89 Propeller de-icing fluid tank
90 Windscreen de-icing fluid tank
91 Bomb carriage traversing drive motor
92 Smoke floats and flame floats
93 Tailplane control cable runs

94 Reconnaissance flares
95 Turret fairing
96 Mid-upper gun turret, offset to starboard
97 Twin Browning 0.303-in (7.7-mm) machine guns
98 Fuselage skin plating
99 Spare propeller blade stowage
100 Fire extinguisher
101 Rear entry door
102 Maintenance platform stowage
103 Observation window
104 Fuselage frame and stringer construction
105 ASV Mk II search radar aerial array
106 Leading edge de-icing
107 Starboard tailplane
108 Starboard elevator
109 Fin root attachments

110 Fin construction
111 Leading edge de-icing
112 Fin tip construction
113 Fabric covered rudder construction
114 Rudder tabs
115 Tail gun turret
116 Four Browning 0.303-in (7.7-mm) machine guns
117 Elevator tab
118 Fabric-covered elevator construction
119 Port tailplane construction
120 Leading edge de-icing
121 Tailplane spar fixing fuselage double frames
122 Tail fuselage fabric draught screen
123 Smoke and flame floats

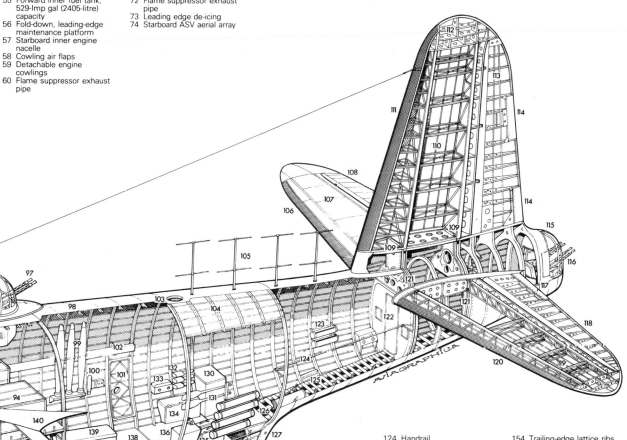

124 Handrail
125 Tail fuselage walkway
126 Reconnaissance flare chute, stowed
127 Mooring shackle
128 Tow bar
129 Rear beaching trolley
130 Camera stowage
131 Dinghy paddles
132 Distress flares
133 Emergency ration container
134 Dinghy stowage
135 Crew luggage locker
136 Tool locker
137 Bilge keel construction
138 Rear fuselage deck level
139 Crew rest bunks
140 Trailing-edge wing root fillet
141 Reconnaissance camera mounting
142 Ditching flare chutes
143 Ladder to upper deck level
144 Rear wardroom
145 Twin bunks
146 Fuselage bomb door, open
147 Retractable bomb carriage
148 Four 100-lb (45.4-kg) bombs
149 Bomb store and loading room: maximum bomb load, 2,000 lb (907 kg)
150 Port flap shroud
151 Port 'Gouge-type' trailing-edge flap
152 Fabric-covered aileron construction
153 Aileron tab, fixed

154 Trailing-edge lattice ribs
155 Wing tip construction
156 Port navigation light
157 Rear spar
158 Wing rib construction
159 Front spar
160 Leading edge de-icing
161 Port ASV radar aerial
162 Wing-tip float construction
163 Float support struts
164 Diagonal wire bracing
165 Wing spar girder construction
166 Landing lamps
167 Leading-edge rib construction
168 Diagonal wire-braced wing ribs
169 Fold-down, leading-edge maintenance platform
170 Engine nacelle construction
171 Engine mounting ring
172 Port outer engine nacelle
173 Oil cooler intakes
174 Oil coolers
175 Exhaust shroud heat exchangers
176 Port inner engine nacelle
177 Emergency escape hatch
178 Ice chest
179 Drogue container
180 Galley compartments, port and starboard
181 Watertight trailing aerial socket
182 Main beaching gear leg strut
183 Twin beaching wheels

When the Sunderland was young four Pegasus XXII engines of 1,050 hp (783 kW) each were ample, but later the portly boats were burdened by tons of extra gear and festooned with radar dipole arrays. This early example of the popular flying-boat was the third production Sunderland, L2160, photographed about June 1938.

than for the much smaller biplane Singapore III. Wing loading was, of course, in the order of twice that common on RAF aircraft of the mid-1930s, but Gouge's patented flaps (which had broad chord and rotated aft about a part-cylindrical upper surface) provided increased area and added 30 per cent to lift coefficient for landing. Hydro-dynamically, a new feature was the bringing of the planing bottom to a vertical knife-edge at the rear (second) step, thereafter sweeping the bottom line smoothly up and back to the tail. Flight-control surfaces were fabric-covered and driven manually, with no servo-tab assistance, but the Sunderland responded admirably to powerful control demands. A twin-wheel beaching chassis could be attached under the main spar and at the rear of the planing bottom.

Into RAF service

RAF service began in June 1938 when the second production Mk I (L2159) was ferried out to No. 230 Sqn at Seletar, Singapore. About 40 were in service at the outbreak of war, and by late 1941 the total output of the Mk I had risen to 90, of which 15 were built by a second-source supplier, a works set up at the Denny shipyard at Dumbarton and run by Blackburn. From late 1939 until 1942 Sunderlands were camouflaged, though in their harsh environments paint flaked off rapidly. Early home-based units, such as Nos 204, 210 and 228 Sqns, plus No. 10 Sqn of the RAAF which arrived to collect its aircraft and stayed in the UK for the next $6\frac{1}{2}$ years, were intensively in action from the first day of the war. Successes against U-boats were at first non-existent, but rescues of torpedoed crews made the headlines, starting on 18 September 1939 when two of No. 228 Sqn's aircraft took the whole crew of 34 from the *Kensington Court* and got them to hospital in Plymouth an hour after their ship sank off the Scillies.

By 1940 Sunderlands were being improved in various ways, notably by the addition of two VGO guns aimed from hatches at the rear of the upper deck on each side, with the front part of each hatch opening into the slipstream to give the gunner a calmer area for aiming. Other changes included the progressive addition of a second gun to the nose turret,

four rifles and three spare propeller blades. At the upper level it was possible to walk aft from the two-pilot flight deck past the cubicles of the radio operator (left) and navigator (right) and through the deep front spar into the domain of the flight engineer with extensive instrument panels inside the wing centre section. One could crawl through the rear spar to an aft upper deck filled with reconnaissance flares, smoke and flame floats, marine markers and other pyrotechnics. The main offensive load, comprising up to 2,000 lb (907 kg) of bombs, depth charges, mines or other stores, was hung beneath the centre section on carriers running on lateral tracks. In combat large side hatches were opened beneath the wing and the weapons run out under the wings by a drive motor which cut out when the bomb carriages had reached full travel on each side. Defensive armament was concentrated in a Nash and Thompson FN.13 hydraulic tail turret with four of the new Browning 0.303-in (7.7-mm) guns. In the bows was an FN.11 turret with a single VGO (Vickers gas-operated) machine-gun, with a winching system for retracting the turret aft so that the big anchor could be passed out through a bow hatch.

Despite its great bulk the hull was well shaped, and drag at the nominal 100 ft (30.5 m) per second was actually lower

The final production Sunderland was the Mk V, with American Twin Wasp engines giving more power than the old nine-cylinder Pegasus. The Mk V was accepted by 228 Sqn in February 1945. This example was serving at the end of the war with No. 4 OTU (Operational Training Unit); its serial number was SZ568. The Mk V was fitted as standard with ASV Mk VIc radar with scanners faired into underwing blisters.

After the start of World War 2 the patrol flying-boats of RAF Coastal Command were at first painted in this style of marine camouflage, switching to grey/white in 1942. This Sunderland I served with No. 230 Sqn, which in late 1938 had been the first full RAF Sunderland squadron. In 1940 it moved to the Mediterranean, N9029 operating from Crete.

replacement of the bracket-type (Hamilton-licence) de Havilland propellers by 12 ft 6 in (3.81-m) constant-speed propellers with spinners, addition of pulsating rubber-boot de-icers to the wings and tail and, from October 1941, ASV Mk II radar which covered the upper rear of the hull with matched dipole Yagi aerials in groups of four and added long dipole-equipped horizontal poles under the outer wings to give azimuth (homing) guidance. At the 150-mph (241-km/h) speeds which were hardly ever exceeded by Coastal Command Sunderlands on patrol these prominent arrays had little effect on performance.

In any case, though the defensive armament was actually quite light, and contained no gun greater than rifle calibre, the Sunderland soon gained great respect from the enemy. On 3 April 1940 a Sunderland off Norway was attacked by six Ju 88s, shot one down, forced another to land immediately, and drove the rest off. Later another was attacked by eight Ju 88s over the Bay of Biscay and shot down three (confirmed by the grateful skippers of the convoy it was escorting in that notorious area).

Further development

In late 1941 production switched to the Mk II, with Pegasus XVIIIs with two-speed superchargers and, in the last few of this mark, improved armament in a twin-Browning nose turret, two more Brownings in an FN.7 dorsal turret on the right side of the hull at the trailing edge, and four Brownings in an FN.4A tail turret with ammunition doubled to 1,000 rounds per gun. Only 43 of this mark were produced, 15 of them at a third source, the Short & Harland company at Queen's Island, Belfast (later the home of the parent company). This limited production resulted from the fact that in June 1941 a Mk I had begun testing an improved planing bottom, with the Vee-type main step smoothly faired to reduce drag in the air. This hull resulted in the designation Mk III, and it succeeded the Mk II from December 1941. No fewer than 461 were delivered, 35 coming from a fourth

The cockpit of a Sunderland Mk 5, which flew with the RAF until 15 May 1959. Sunderlands landed on the Wannsee during the Berlin Blockade.

assembly shop on Lake Windermere. The Mk III was effectively the standard wartime boat, and its exploits were legion in all theatres.

In the Mediterranean, Sunderlands were called upon to undertake many dangerous missions, none worse than the prolonged evacuation from Crete when many trips were made with as many as 82 armed passengers in addition to the crew, which by this time had grown to 10. A Sunderland made the necessary visual reconnaissance of Taranto before the Fleet Air Arm attack of 11 November 1940. Over the Atlantic the Sunderland shared with the Consolidated Catalina the main effort against U-boats, but when the latter received Metox passive receivers tuned to ASV Mk II they received ample warning of the presence of British aircraft and kills dropped sharply. The RAF response was the new ASV Mk III, operating in the band well below 50 cm and with the aerials neatly faired into blisters under the outer wings. When thus fitted the Sunderland became a Mark IIIA.

The U-boat sensors could not pick up this radar, and once again, in early 1943, kills became frequent. The response of the U-boats was to fit batteries of deadly Flak, typically one or two 37-mm and two quadruple 20-mm, and fight it out on the surface. Now the odds were heavily against the flying-boat, which needed forward-firing fire-power. Curiously, though the bow was ideally arranged for it, really heavy forward-firing armament was never fitted to the Sunderland, nor was the Leigh light, though many aircraft received four fixed 0.303-in (7.7-mm) Brownings, firing straight ahead,

Sunderlands were flown by France's Aéronavale up until 1960. Flotilla 7E received a number of them after World War 2 and in 1951 added another 19 of the RAF's redundant Mk 5s. The RNZAF operated this flying-boat, still looking spic and span after years of service in and on an inhospitable sea, right up to 1967.

No. 35 Sqn of the South African Air Force had a total of 15 of these Sunderland GR.5s in service, using them to transport troops home from the various war fronts. Later they were used to form a long-distance patrol unit, stationed in Congella, Durban. The turrets on the back of the fuselage were removed, but the ASV Mk VIc radar was retained (the radome is under the wing).

together with a pilot gunsight. The one thing these guns did sometimes succeed in doing was to knock out the U-boat gunners as they ran from the conning-tower hatch the few metres to their guns. In addition, heavier lateral armament became common, to combat the more numerous and more heavily armed Luftwaffe long-range fighters. Though the latter's cannon always gave a considerable edge at stand-off range, Sunderlands did at least fit locally contrived installations of single VGOs or Brownings from the escape hatches in the galley compartments (last but one in the main row of portholes). This became a standard fit in late 1943, at which time Short also added an installation of one or two of the much more effective 0.5-in (12.7-mm) Brownings from upper rear hatches behind the trailing edge. Thus the number of guns rose in a year from five to 18, believed the greatest number of guns carried by any regular British service aircraft.

In late 1942 severe shortage of equipment by BOAC, the national civil airline, resulted in six Sunderland IIIs being stripped of all armament (turrets were replaced by bulbous fairings) and put into joint BOAC-RAF service between Poole and Lagos (West Africa) and Calcutta (India). BOAC investigated the engine installation and cruising angle of

This Mk I, stationed in Mount Batten (Plymouth) with No. 10 Squadron of the Royal Australian Air Force, was photographed in 1941 when it was equipped with ASV radar. The censor retouched this top-secret equipment before the photograph was published. The gunning position was at the back of the fuselage.

A Sunderland Mk V moored opposite the Tower of London and Traitors' Gate. The flying-boat was taxied through the open Tower Bridge in London in October 1982.

attack to such effect that mean cruising speed – which had seldom bothered the RAF – was improved by more than 40 per cent. Spartan bench seats for seven passengers, the main payload being mail, gradually gave way in the BOAC Hythe class to an excellent airline interior for 24 passengers (16 with sleeping accommodation), plus 6,500 lb (2948 kg) of mail, and the engines were modified to Pegasus 38 (later 48) standard. By 1944 the number of civil Sunderland IIIs had grown to 24, and after the war the Hythes, eventually totalling 29, were supplemented by a complete civil rebuild, the S.26 Sandringham, which went into production as a basic post-war transport for BOAC (as the Plymouth class) and other airlines.

Meanwhile the increasing demands made on the military Sunderland, especially after the start of warfare in the Pacific, led in 1942 to specification R.8/42 for a more powerful long-range flying-boat, to which Short Brothers responded with the Hercules-engined Sunderland IV. Eventually this grew so different from the Sunderland, with an improved hull, new tail and completely revised armament, that it was renamed the Seaford I. Surprisingly, this saw only brief post-war service, but formed the basis for the civil Solent. The need for more power remained, however, and in early 1944 the decision was taken simply to re-engine

building 47, 48 and 60. This version entered service with No. 228 Sqn in February 1945. A further 33 were produced by conversion from Mk IIIAs. In August 1945 large contracts were cancelled, the last Sunderland coming from Belfast in June 1946, where, as at Dumbarton, some dozens of new boats were packed with new military equipment and deliberately sunk shortly after the end of the war.

Subsequently the Sunderland V was redesignated Sunderland MR.5, as which it remained the standard RAF ocean flying-boat until retirement (appropriately, from Seletar) on 15 May 1959. In post-war years Sunderlands played a very large role in the Berlin Airlift; they were also the only RAF aircraft to be in action throughout the Korean War, flying 13,380 hours in 1,647 sorties. Aircraft of Nos 201 and 230 Sqns provided the entire heavy transport support for the 1951–4 British North Greenland Expedition. Others served as close-support bombers in Malaya, and one flew a doctor to HMS *Amethyst* in the Yangtse river while under fire from Chinese shore artillery. Sunderlands also formed an important part of the post-war strength of the RAAF, RNZAF, SAAF and France's Aéronavale. The last was stood down by the RNZAF in March 1967, but the surviving boat in the RAF Museum came from the Aéronavale in the Pacific.

This was one of more than 100 Sunderlands from which armament was removed to facilitate operations in the transport role. NZ4103, with individual name *Mataatua*, served in the south-west Pacific theatre with the RNZAF Flying Boat Transport Unit in 1944–6. These Mk IIIs were later replaced by the GR.5 which equipped Nos 5 and 6 Sqns post-war.

a Mk III with Pratt & Whitney R-1830-90B Twin Wasps, almost the same engine as used in the Catalina and Dakota and many other types and already in widespread RAF service. The 14-cylinder engine conferred a substantial improvement in climb, ceiling and engine-out performance, yet had hardly any effect on range, though cruising speed tended to be slightly higher. Operationally the US-engined machine had a big advantage in being able to cruise with two engines out on one side whereas the Sunderland III in this state lost height steadily. (In fairness to Bristol, the Twin Wasp was a larger engine than the 9-cylinder Pegasus, and nothing like as powerful as the 1,800-hp/1343-kW Hercules used in the Seaford.)

After trials in March 1944 the Twin Wasp Sunderland was accepted for production as the Mk V, with de Havilland Hydromatic propellers without spinners. ASV Mk III was fitted as standard, and in the course of 1944 Rochester, Belfast and Dumbarton all switched to the Mk V, respectively

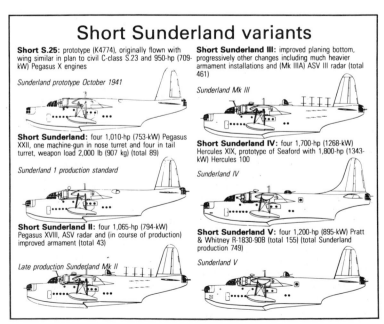

Short Sunderland variants

Short S.25: prototype (K4774), originally flown with wing similar in plan to civil C-class S.23 and 950-hp (709-kW) Pegasus X engines

Sunderland prototype October 1941

Short Sunderland: four 1,010-hp (753-kW) Pegasus XXII, one machine-gun in nose turret and four in tail turret, weapon load 2,000 lb (907 kg) (total 89)

Sunderland 1 production standard

Short Sunderland II: four 1,065-hp (794-kW) Pegasus XVIII, ASV radar and (in course of production) improved armament (total 43)

Late production Sunderland Mk II

Short Sunderland III: improved planing bottom, progressively other changes including much heavier armament installations and (Mk IIIA) ASV III radar (total 461)

Sunderland Mk III

Short Sunderland IV: four 1,700-hp (1268-kW) Hercules XIX, prototype of Seaford with 1,800-hp (1343-kW) Hercules 100

Sunderland IV

Short Sunderland V: four 1,200-hp (895-kW) Pratt & Whitney R-1830-90B (total 155) (total Sunderland production 749)

Sunderland V

Focke-Wulf Fw 190

When the Focke-Wulf Fw 190 appeared in the skies over France in September 1941 RAF Intelligence simply could not credit that this squat, angular fighter really had the measure of the sleek, slender Spitfire V. Yet Kurt Tank's 'Butcher Bird' not only came to dominate those skies for eight months but remained one of the finest fighters in Europe until the end of Hitler's war.

Conceived in 1937 as a contemporary of the Hawker Typhoon and for the same reason, to replace the first generation of monoplane interceptors (the Hawker Hurricane and the Messerschmitt Bf 109), the design of the Focke-Wulf Fw 190 was tendered with two alternative engines, the Daimler-Benz DB601 inline and the B.M.W. 139 radial, the latter being selected to power the prototype on account of its assumed higher power development potential. Detail design commenced under the leadership of Oberingenieur Blaser and the first prototype was flown by test pilot Hans Sander at Bremen on 1 June 1939.

The first two aircraft featured large, low-drag ducted spinners but these were soon discarded as they were thought to cause engine overheating, and after the B.M.W. 139 had been abandoned the Fw 190A entered production with the B.M.W. 801 14-cylinder radial with fan-assisted cooling. The first nine pre-production Fw 190A-0s featured small wings of 161.46 sq ft (15.00 m²) area, but the definitive version had larger wings of 196.99 sq ft (18.30 m²) area.

Service trials at Rechlin went ahead in 1940 without undue problems, although Luftwaffe pilots suggested that the proposed armament of the Fw 190A-1 (four synchronized 7.92-mm/0.31-in MG 17 machine-guns) would meet with spirited criticism in combat service. Production of the 100 Fw 190A-1s at Hamburg and Bremen was completed by the end of May 1941, and these were powered by 1,600-hp (1194-kW) B.M.W. 801C engines which bestowed a top speed of 388 mph (624 km/h). The aircraft were flown by Erprobungsstelle at Rechlin and 6./JG 26, the latter based at Le Bourget in August. The following month the first combats were reported with RAF Supermarine Spitfire Vs, showing the German fighters to be markedly superior, albeit lacking in weapon punch.

New armament

Already, however, the early gun criticisms had led to the Fw 190A-2 version with two wing root-mounted synchronized 20-mm MG FF cannon and two MG 17 guns; with a speed of 382 mph (614 km/h), this up-gunned version still had the edge over the Spitfire V. By the end of March 1942 JG 26, commanded by Adolf Galland, was fully equipped with Fw 190A-2s. Thirty Fw 190As had accompanied the escort forces during the famous Channel break-out by the battle-cruisers *Scharnhorst* and *Gneisenau* in February, Fw 190A-2s of III/JG 26 being involved in the one-sided action against Lieutenant Commander Eugene Esmonde's Fairey Swordfish torpedo strike.

As the RAF desperately sought to introduce an answer to the Fw 190, production of the German fighter was stepped up as Focke-Wulf factories at Cottbus, Marienburg, Neubrandenburg, Schwerin, Sorau and Tutow joined the programme, as well as the Ago and Fieseler plants. The Fw 190A-3, with 1,700-hp (1268-kW) B.M.W. 801Dg, four 20-

Fw 190Gs of II Gruppe, Schlachtgeschwader 2 'Immelmann', probably in mid-1943. The unit, commanded by Major Heinz Frank, had been the first to equip with this ground-attack version in North Africa but moved to the Eastern Front (note the yellow theatre panels).

Focke-Wulf Fw 190

Specification

Focke-Wulf Fw 190A-8
Type: single-seat fighter and fighter-bomber
Powerplant: one 2,100-hp (1567-kW) B.M.W. 801D-2
Performance: maximum speed (clean) 408 mph
(654 km/h); initial climb 2,363 ft (720 m)/min; normal
range 500 miles (805 km); service ceiling 37,400 ft
(11400 m)
Weight: empty 7,000 lb (3170 kg); maximum loaded
10,800 lb (4900 kg)
Dimensions: span 34 ft 5½ in (10.5 m); length
29 ft 0 in (8.84 m); height 13 ft 0 in (3.96 m); wing area
196.98 sq ft (18.3 m²)
Armament: (A-8/R2) two 7.9-mm MG17 machine-
guns, four 20-mm MG151/20 cannon, one 1,100-lb
(500-kg) and two 550-lb (250-kg) bombs, or one
66-Imp gal. (300-litre) drop tank

Major production version of the Focke-Wulf Fw 190 was the A-8
'Panzerbock', shown here in its basic configuration with the ETC 501
centreline store rank moved forward 7.9 in (20 cm) and carrying a 66-Imp
gal (300-litre) drop tank. Armed with four long-barrelled MG 151/20 20-
mm cannon in the wings and two MG 17 machine-guns in the nose, 'Red
19' was flown by Unteroffizier Ernst Schröder of 5.Staffel,
Jagdgeschwader 300, in 'Defence of the Reich' operations during October
and November 1944. II (Sturm) Gruppe of JG 300 had been formed with
Fw 190A-8s in July 1944 under Major Kurd Peters (awarded the Knight's
Cross in October that year), and was one of the fighter units opposing the
Western Allies during the invasion of Europe, adopting Wilde Sau night-
fighting tactics during the autumn. Staffelkapitän of 5.Staffel was
Oberleutnant Klaus Bretschneider, also a Knight's Cross holder, of whose
31 combat victories 14 were gained during Wilde Sau sorties, and who
was shot down and killed in combat with P-51s on 24 December 1944.

mm and two 7.92 mm (0.31-in) guns, joined II/JG 26 in
March 1942 and shortly afterwards the only other Luftwaffe
fighter Geschwader in the West, JG.2

Thus by the time the RAF was ready to introduce its new
Spitfire IX and Typhoon fighters to combat over the Dieppe
landings in August 1942, the Luftwaffe could field some 200
Fw 190As in opposition. Unfortunately not only had the
RAF underestimated the number of these fighters available
but were unaware that a new version, the Fw 190A-4, had
appeared with a water-injected 2,100-hp (1567-kW) B.M.W.
801D-2 engine and a top speed of 416 mph (670 km/h), and
that a bomb-carrying variant, the Fw 190A-3/U1, was in
service. (The suffix U indicated Unrüst-Bausatz, or factory
conversion set.) The result was a stinging defeat for the RAF,
which lost a total of 106 aircraft including 97 to Fw 190s. As
a result largely of mismanagement, neither the Spitfire IX
nor the Typhoon had been able to redress the balance.

It would have been of little comfort had the RAF known
that the Germans had for many months devoted all their Fw
190 resources to the Channel front, such was the esteem held
for the Spitfire V. Indeed, despite the ferocious tempo of
battle on the Eastern Front, which had opened in June 1941,
no Fw 190A fighters fought on that front until well into 1942
when I/JG 51 received Fw 190A-4s. Fw 190A-3s and A-4s
were also issued to IV/JG 5 and to JG 1 for home defence and
protection of German fleet units in Norway. A reconnaissance
version of the Fw 190A-3 was first flown by 9.(H)/LG 2 in
March 1942 on the Russian Front. The Fw 190A-4/U4 reconnaissance fighter joined NAufklGr 13 in France, and Fw
190A-4/Trop ground-attack fighter-bombers appeared in
North Africa with I/SG 2 during 1942. Before the end of that
year Fw 190A-3/U1s and A-4/U8s of SKG 10, each able to
carry a 1,100-lb (500-kg) bomb, had embarked on a series of
day-light low-level 'tip and run' attacks against cities and

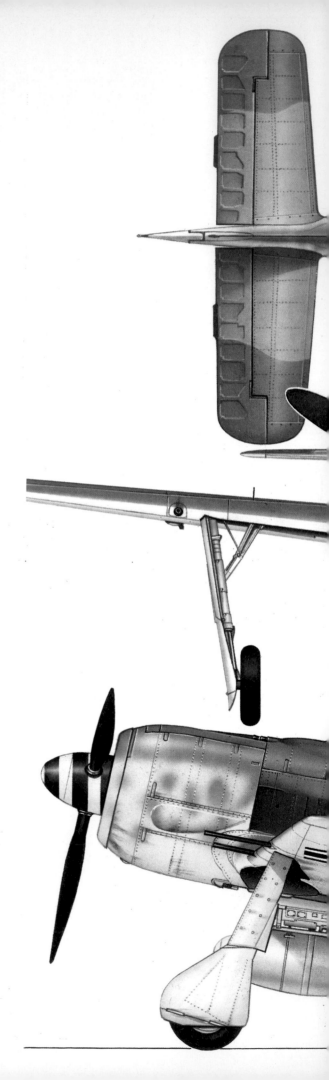

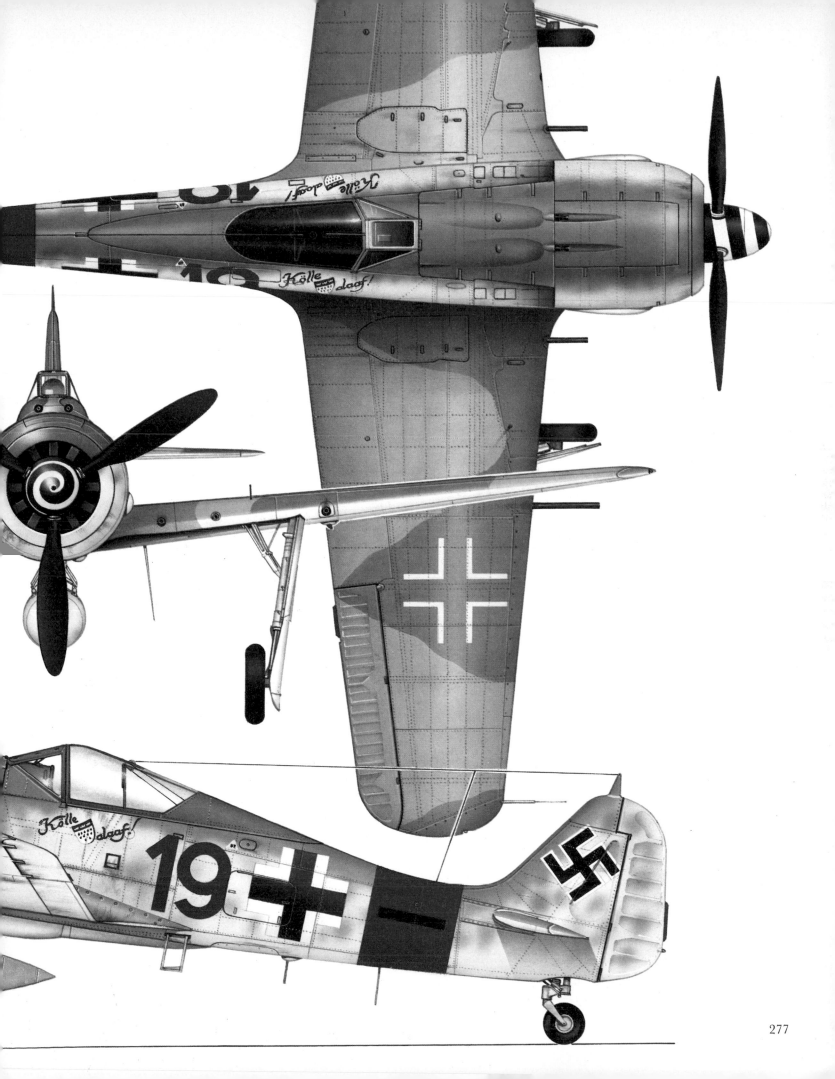

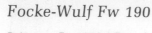

Focke-Wulf Fw 190

Pale grey Fw 190A-6/R11 of 1./NJG 10 flown by Oberleutnant Hans Krause from Werneuchen in August 1944. The pilot's insignia consisted of his nickname 'Illo' beneath the *Wilde Sau* emblem. Note *Neptun* radar arrays and two-shade grey on upper wing surface. Krause was later awarded the Knight's Cross.

'Defence of the Reich' Fw 190A-8 (note red fuselage band) of I Gruppe, Jagdgeschwader 1, based at Twenthe in the Netherlands in December 1944. An aircraft with white 'double chevrons' was being flown by Major Hans Ehlers, the Gruppenkommandeur, when he was shot down and killed on 27 December 1944.

ports in southern England, forcing Fighter Command to deploy disproportionately heavy fighter defences to counter the threat. Some measure of the dependence now placed on the Fw 190 may be judged from the fact that more than 1,900 Fw 190A-3s and A-4s had reached the Luftwaffe in 1942 (compared with 500 RAF Typhoons and Spitfire IXs).

Rocket launchers

Early in 1943 there appeared the Fw 190A-5 with slightly lengthened engine mountings, and with it a much increased range of *Rüstsätze* (field conversion kits), including the R6 that enabled the Fw 190A-5 (in modified form Fw 190A-5/R6) to carry two under-wing WG21 8.27-in (21-cm) rocket-launchers for use against the growing Boeing B-17 and Consolidated B-24 bomber fleets operated by the USAAF. The Fw 190A-5/U2 night bomber could carry a 1,102-lb (500-kg) bomb and two 66-Imp gal (300-litre) drop tanks, the Fw 190A-5/U3 carried up to 2,205 lb (1000 kg) of bombs, the Fw 190A-5/U12 was a heavily armed fighter with six 20-mm MG 151/20 cannon and two MG 17s, while the Fw 190A-5/U15, of which three examples were built in November 1943, was equipped to carry a 2,094-lb (950-kg) LT950 torpedo (a torpedo-carrying Fw 190A-5/U14, a lighter version of the U15 torpedo-fighter, is said to have been flown in action by Hauptmann Helmut Viedebannt of SKG 10).

The Fw 190A-6, in its standard form with reduced wing structure weight, was armed with four fast-firing 20-mm

First of the 190 series to be powered by the 1,660-hp (1238-kW) B.M.W. 801C-0 engine were the Fw 190 V5k and V5g, the former with small wing (161.46 sq ft/15.0 m² area), illustrated here, and the latter with enlarged wing (196.98 sq ft/18.3 m² area). The latter was chosen for production on account of superior manoeuvrability.

Focke-Wulf Fw 190A-3 cutaway drawing key

1 Rudder fixed tab
2 Tail navigation light
3 Leads
4 Rudder hinge/attachment
5 Tailwheel extension spring
6 Tailwheel shock-absorber leg retraction guide
7 Tailfin spar
8 Rudder post assembly
9 Rudder frame
10 Rudder upper hinge
11 Aerial attachment
12 Tailfin structure
13 Canted rib progression
14 Port elevator fixed tab
15 Port elevator
16 Mass balance
17 Port tailplane
18 Tailplane incidence motor unit
19 Tailwheel retraction pulley cables
20 Tailplane attachment
21 Starboard tailplane structure
22 Elevator fixed tab
23 Starboard elevator frame
24 Mass balance
25 Tailplane front spar
26 Semi-retractng tailwheel
27 Drag yoke
28 Tailwheel recess
29 Tailwheel locking linkage
30 Access panel
31 Actuating link
32 Push-pull rod
33 Rudder cables
34 Rudder control differential linkage
35 Fuselage/tail unit join
36 Elevator control differential
37 Fuselage lift tube
38 Elevator control cables
39 Bulkhead (No. 12) fabric panel (rear fuselage equipment dust protection)
40 Leather grommets
41 Rudder push-pull rods
42 Fuselage frame
43 Master compass

44 Flat-bottomed (equipment bay floor support) frame
45 First-aid kit
46 Optional camera (2 × Rb 12) installation (A-3/U4)
47 Control runs
48 Access hatch (port side)
49 Electrical leads
50 Distribution panel
51 Canopy channel slide cut-outs
52 Canopy solid aft fairing
53 Aerial
54 Head armour support bracket
55 Aerial attachment/take-up pulley
56 Equipment/effects stowage
57 FuG 7a/FuG 25a radio equipment bay
58 Battery
59 Cockpit aft bulkhead
60 Control runs
61 Cockpit floor/centre-section main structure
62 Wingroot fillet
63 Underfloor aft fuel tank (64 Imp gals/291 litres)
64 Underfloor forward fuel tank (51 Imp gal/232 litres)
65 Cockpit sidewall control runs
66 Seat support brackets
67 Armoured bulkhead
68 Pilot's seat
69 Canopy operating handwheel
70 14-mm armoured backplate
71 Pilot's headrest
72 Canopy
73 Windscreen frame assembly
74 Armoured-glass windscreen
75 Revi gunsight
76 Instrument panel shroud
77 Throttle
78 Port control console

79 Control column
80 Seat pan
81 Starboard control console (circuit breakers)
82 Underfloor linkage
83 Electrical junction box
84 Rudder pedal assembly
85 Instrument panel sections
86 Screen support frame
87 Two 7.9 mm MG 17 machine-guns
88 Ammunition feed chute
89 Panel release catches
90 Fuselage armament ammunition boxes
91 Forward bulkhead
92 Inboard wing cannon ammunition boxes
93 Engine mounting lower attachment point
94 Cooling air exit louvres
95 Engine mounting upper attachment point
96 Oil pump assembly
97 Engine mounting ring
98 Fuselage MG 17 ammunition cooling pipes
99 Machine gun front mounting brackets

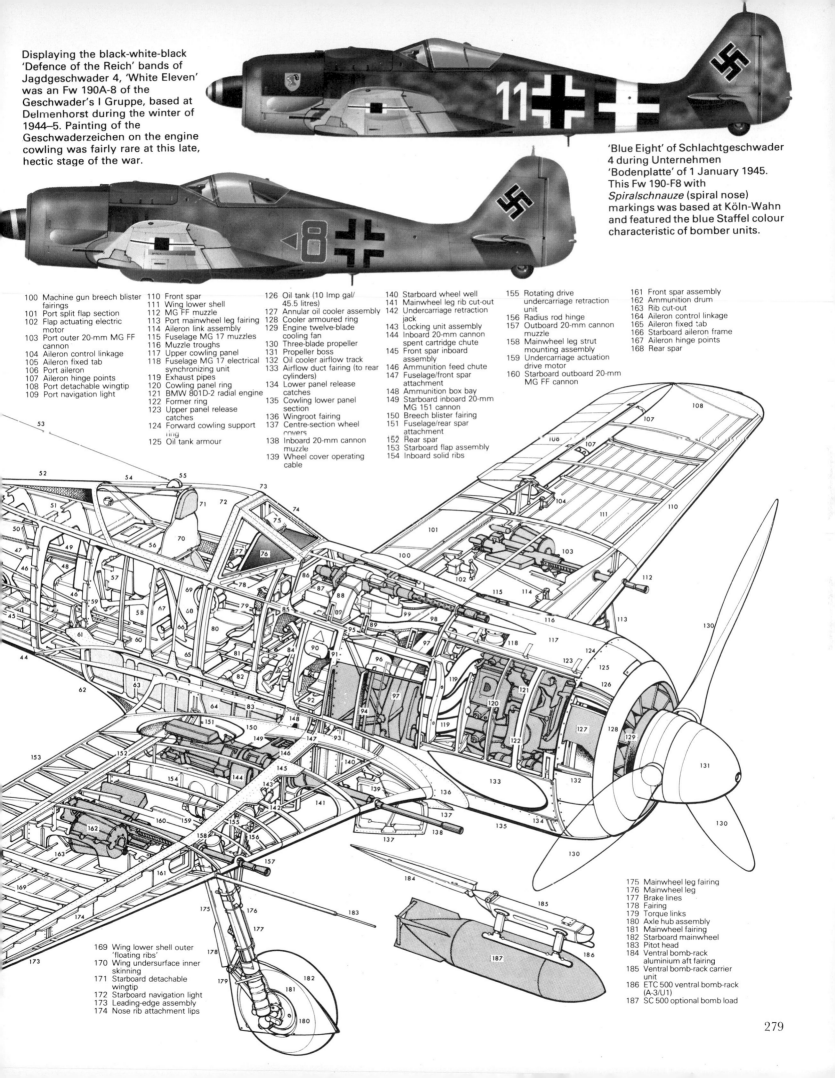

Displaying the black-white-black 'Defence of the Reich' bands of Jagdgeschwader 4, 'White Eleven' was an Fw 190A-8 of the Geschwader's I Gruppe, based at Delmenhorst during the winter of 1944–5. Painting of the Geschwaderzeichen on the engine cowling was fairly rare at this late, hectic stage of the war.

'Blue Eight' of Schlachtgeschwader 4 during Unternehmen 'Bodenplatte' of 1 January 1945. This Fw 190-F8 with *Spiralschnauze* (spiral nose) markings was based at Köln-Wahn and featured the blue Staffel colour characteristic of bomber units.

100 Machine gun breech blister fairings
101 Port split flap section
102 Flap actuating electric motor
103 Port outer 20-mm MG FF cannon
104 Aileron control linkage
105 Aileron fixed tab
106 Port aileron
107 Aileron hinge points
108 Port detachable wingtip
109 Port navigation light
110 Front spar
111 Wing lower shell
112 MG FF muzzle
113 Port mainwheel leg fairing
114 Aileron link assembly
115 Fuselage MG 17 muzzles
116 Muzzle troughs
117 Upper cowling panel
118 Fuselage MG 17 electrical synchronizing unit
119 Exhaust pipes
120 Cowling panel ring
121 BMW 801D-2 radial engine
122 Former ring
123 Upper panel release catches
124 Forward cowling support ring
125 Oil tank armour
126 Oil tank (10 Imp gal/45.5 litres)
127 Annular oil cooler assembly
128 Cooler armoured ring
129 Engine twelve-blade cooling fan
130 Three-blade propeller
131 Propeller boss
132 Oil cooler airflow track
133 Airflow duct fairing (to rear cylinders)
134 Lower panel release catches
135 Cowling lower panel section
136 Wingroot fairing
137 Centre-section wheel covers
138 Inboard 20-mm cannon muzzle
139 Wheel cover operating cable
140 Starboard wheel well
141 Mainwheel leg rib cut-out
142 Undercarriage retraction jack
143 Locking unit assembly
144 Inboard 20-mm cannon spent cartridge chute
145 Front spar inboard assembly
146 Ammunition feed chute
147 Fuselage/front spar attachment
148 Ammunition box bay
149 Starboard inboard 20-mm MG 151 cannon
150 Breech blister fairing
151 Fuselage/rear spar attachment
152 Rear spar
153 Starboard flap assembly
154 Inboard solid ribs
155 Rotating drive undercarriage retraction unit
156 Radius rod hinge
157 Outboard 20-mm cannon muzzle
158 Mainwheel leg strut mounting assembly
159 Undercarriage actuation drive motor
160 Starboard outboard 20-mm MG FF cannon
161 Front spar assembly
162 Ammunition drum
163 Rib cut-out
164 Aileron control linkage
165 Aileron fixed tab
166 Starboard aileron frame
167 Aileron hinge points
168 Rear spar

169 Wing lower shell outer 'floating ribs'
170 Wing undersurface inner skinning
171 Starboard detachable wingtip
172 Starboard navigation light
173 Leading-edge assembly
174 Nose rib attachment lips
175 Mainwheel leg fairing
176 Mainwheel leg
177 Brake lines
178 Fairing
179 Torque links
180 Axle hub assembly
181 Mainwheel fairing
182 Starboard mainwheel
183 Pitot head
184 Ventral bomb-rack aluminium aft fairing
185 Ventral bomb-rack carrier unit
186 ETC 500 ventral bomb-rack (A-3/U1)
187 SC 500 optional bomb load

Participating in the great tank battle of Kursk in July 1943, this Fw 190A-4/U3 of the Gefechtsverband Druschel (II/SG 1) features yellow theatre panels, fighter arm staff marks (forward black bar), Gruppe marks (aft black bar) and 4.Staffel (red) individual letter. Oberst Alfred Druschel, one of the most experienced assault pilots in the Luftwaffe, was killed on 1 January 1945.

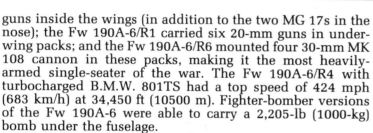

Temporarily painted matt black, an Fw 190 A-5/U8 of I Gruppe, Schnellkampfgeschwader (SKG) 10, with centreline bomb rack and wing drop tanks, during the Jabo attacks on southern England during summer 1943. Based at Poix in France, this unit virtually obliterated all national insignia in the interests of camouflage.

'Yellow Nine' of II Gruppe (denoted by the yellow horizontal bar), Jagdgeschwader 54 'Grünherz' was an Fw 190A-5 flown by Leutnant Helmut Sturm at Petseri in Estonia during June 1944. The yellow panels indicate the theatre.

guns inside the wings (in addition to the two MG 17s in the nose); the Fw 190A-6/R1 carried six 20-mm guns in under-wing packs; and the Fw 190A-6/R6 mounted four 30-mm MK 108 cannon in these packs, making it the most heavily-armed single-seater of the war. The Fw 190A-6/R4 with turbocharged B.M.W. 801TS had a top speed of 424 mph (683 km/h) at 34,450 ft (10500 m). Fighter-bomber versions of the Fw 190A-6 were able to carry a 2,205-lb (1000-kg) bomb under the fuselage.

The greatest single victory by Fw 190A-6s of JG1, JG5, JG 26, JG51 and JG 54 was gained on 14 October 1943, when they decimated the US 8th Air Force's daylight bombers attacking Regensburg and Schweinfurt, destroying 79 and damaging 121 out of the force of 228. Had it not been for the introduction of superlative American close-escort fighters, particularly the North American P-51 Mustang, the Fw 190-equipped Jagdflieger must have decisively suppressed American daylight bombing attempts early in 1944.

Notwithstanding these successes, the changing fortunes of war forced the Luftwaffe to adopt a wholly defensive stance, of an increasingly desperate nature. As the RAF night bomber offensive increased in weight the Luftwaffe employed Fw 190As (in particular Fw 190A-5/U2s) in the night-fighting role on moonlit nights, and the 'Wild Boar' tactics of Hajo Hermann's 30 Jagddivision, with three Geschwäder, are reckoned to have accounted for some 200 RAF heavy bombers during the latter half of 1943.

While Fw 190A fighter-bombers were in action in the Mediterranean theatre, there appeared the Fw 190A-7 with a pair of 20-mm cannon in the nose decking (in addition to the various wing gun combinations), and the Fw 190A-8 with GM-1 nitrous-oxide power-boosting and all the adaptability afforded by earlier *Rüstsatz* additions. The Fw 190A-8/U1 was a two-seat version, of which three examples were produced to assist the conversion training of Junkers Ju 87 pilots to the Fw 190 for the ground-attack squadrons on the Eastern Front. The Fw 190A-8/U3 was the upper component of the *Mistel* (Mistletoe) composite weapon, riding the back of explosive-packed, unmanned Junkers Ju 88 aircraft. The Fw 190A-8/U11 anti-shipping strike aircraft, with a BT700

The unarmed Focke-Wulf Fw 190 V1 (first Prototype, D-OPZE) with fan-cooled B.M.W. 139 and ducted spinner, at the time of its first flight on 1 June 1939. Numerous other differences from subsequent production versions are evident, including small tail-wheel, absence of fuselage wheel doors, and the hinged door covers on the wheel leg.

Early Focke-Wulf Fw 190A-1s undergoing final assembly at Bremen in 1941. Particularly evident in this picture is the exceptionally wide-track main landing gear and the large number of hinged panels providing access to the compact B.M.W. 801 radial engine. Just visible are the pair of nose-mounted MG 17 machine-guns.

'Black Twelve', an Fw 190D-9 (with early-style cockpit canopy) of 10.Staffel, Jagdgeschwader 54 'Grünherz'. Participating in Unternehmen 'Bodenplatte' on January 1, 1945, the aircraft crashed at Wemmel, Belgium. The yellow panels possibly indicate an aircraft withdrawn from the Eastern Front for the occasion.

Displaying pale blue-grey finish with dark grey dappling, this Fw 190D-9 of III/JG 2 'Richthofen' was based at Altenstadt in December 1944. Note the absence of white on fuselage and fin markings.

1,543-lb (700-kg) torpedo-bomb, was flown in attacks against the Russian Black Sea Fleet in February 1944. The Fw 190A-9, with armoured wing leading edge, was powered by a 2,000-hp (1490-kW) B.M.W. 801F (although the Fw 190A-9/R11 had a turbocharged B.M.W. 801TS). The Fw 190A-10, of which only prototypes were completed, featured provision for an increased range of bombs. Among the purely experimental versions of the Fw 190A were the Fw 190V74 with a seven-barrelled 30-mm SG117 Rohrblock cannon aimed by a Revi 242 gunsight, and the extraordinary Fw 190V75 with seven 17.72-in (45-cm) downward-firing mortars intended for low-level anti-tank use from a height of about 30 ft (10 m). Another interesting experiment was the use of large *Doppelreiter* overwing fuel tanks on the Fw 190A-8, evaluated by Erprobungskommando 25 under Major Georg Christl in July 1944.

New power
The arrival of the Spitfire IX in Fighter Command and its threat to combat domination by the Fw 190A led to the development of the Fw 190B series with GM-1 power-boosted B.M.W. 801D-2 engine and pressure cabin, but trouble with the latter led to the abandonment of this version after only a few prototypes had been produced. The Fw 190C series, of which five prototypes were completed with DB603 inline engines, annular radiators, Hirth 9-2281 superchargers and four-blade propellers, was also abandoned early in 1944.

The Fw 190D, with 1,770-hp (1320-kW) Junkers Jumo 213A-1 engine and annular radiator in a much-lengthened nose (necessitating increased fin and rudder area), proved very successful after it had first flown at Langenhagen in May 1944. The first production Fw 190D-9s (so termed as they followed the Fw 190A-8s at the factories, and widely known as Dora-Nines in the Luftwaffe) joined III/JG 54 in September 1944 to defend the jet base of Kommando Nowotny. Among the sub-variants of the Fw 190D series was the Fw 190D-10 with a single 30-mm MK 108 cannon located between the engine cylinder banks and firing through the propeller hub. The Fw 190D-12/R21, a ground-attack version of the hub-gunned Fw 190D-10 and power-boosted with MW50 water-methanol injection, was almost certainly the fastest of all Fw 190s with a top speed of 453 mph (750 km/h) at 36,090 ft (11000 m). Dora-Nines equipped most of the Luftwaffe's fighter units during the last fateful months of the Third Reich, but in combat with the P-51s and Spitfire XIVs were frequently overwhelmed. The problems centred on fuel shortage which allowed only small formations with battle-hardened veteran pilots. For instance, when JG 6 (commanded by Major Gerhard Barkhorn, who had a record of 301 air victories) in April 1945 took delivery of 150 new Dora-Nines, it could only fly patrols of four against massed Allied fighters.

The Fw 190F and Fw 190G series were essentially ground-attack versions, the Fw 190F ('Panzer-Blitz') armoured assault aircraft appearing in the spring of 1944. Externally similar to the Fw 190A series, but with a bulged hood, this version featured gun armament reduced to two MG 17s and two 20-mm cannon, but had the ability to carry the 2,205-lb (1000-kg) bomb plus two 110-lb (50-kg) fragmentation bombs. Most important sub-variant was the Fw 190F-8, which could carry 14 8.27-in (21-cm) rocket bombs, six 11.02-in (28-cm) rocket-launchers or 24 R4M unguided rockets; Fw 190F-8s first joined III(Pz)/KG 200 in the autumn of 1944.

First of several torpedo-carrying versions of the Fw 190 was the A-5/U14 (c/n 871), shown here carrying an LT F5b torpedo. It probably saw action with SKG 10. The rack fairing of this version was deeper than that on the U15 which carried an LT 950 2094-lb (950-kg) weapon. Note the considerably lengthened tailwheel assembly.

Second unarmed prototype for the proposed high-altitude Fw 190C-series was the V18, shown here in its U1 guise with DB 603A-engine (which replaced the earlier DB 603G), four-blade propeller and Hirth 9-2281 turbocharger. Inclusion of a pressure cabin is evidenced by strengthening members on the canopy.

Captured at Marienburg, East Prussia, by the advancing Russians, this Fw 190D-9 flew with an IAP of the Red Banner Baltic Fleet Air Force in the spring of 1945. The addition of a ventral mast presumably indicates the inclusion of Soviet radio equipment.

The Fw 190G series actually entered operational service long before the Fw 190F, the first aircraft being sent to North Africa, joining SG 2 at Zarzoun, Tunisia, following the 'Torch' landings in November 1942. The majority, however, went to the Eastern Front where they played an active part at the great tank battle of Kursk in early July 1943. The Fw 190G-1 version, with greatly strengthened undercarriage, could lift a 3,968-lb (1800-kg) bomb.

Long-nose derivative

Mention must also be made of a development of the Fw 190, the Ta 152 (its designation finally reflecting Kurt Tank's overall design responsibility). This 'long-nose' derivative of the Fw 190D series retained the hub-firing 30-mm gun but introduced increased electrical systems. Various prototypes of the Ta 152A, B and C variants were produced, but it was the Ta 152H-1 version with one 30-mm and two 20-mm guns and a maximum speed of 472 mph (760 km/h) at 41,010 ft (12500 m) that was selected for operational service; only about a dozen aircraft of this type had been completed and delivered to JG 301 when the war ended. A total of 26 Ta 152

prototypes and 67 pre-production and production aircraft was completed.

Having regard to the nature of the Luftwaffe's defensive operations during the last 30 months of the war, it is scarcely surprising that production assumed impressive proportions, no fewer than 20,087 Fw 190s (including 86 prototypes) being produced during the 1939–45 period, the peak daily production rate of 22 aircraft per day being reached early in 1944.

By the same token many Luftwaffe pilots achieved remarkable combat feats at the controls of Fw 190s (not forgetting that of Josef Würmheller who shot down seven Spitfire Vs in one day over the Dieppe beaches – despite concussion and a broken leg suffered in a recent accident). Pride of place must go to Oberleutnant Otto Kittel, the Luftwaffe's fourth highest scoring pilot, of whose 267 air victories some 220 were gained in Fw 190A-4s and -5s. Other very high scorers in Fw 190s included Walter Nowotny, Heinz Bär, Hermann Graf and Kurt Bühligen, all of whose scores included more than 100 victories gained with the guns of the aptly named Butcher Bird.

Focke-Wulf Fw 190 and Ta 152 variants

Fw 190V1 to V80 (plus six others): prototypes and progressive development aircraft, 1939–44; served as prototypes for Fw 190A to G series and some Ta 152s
Fw 190A-0: nine aircraft with small wings, remaining 11 with large wings; B.M.W. 801C-1; four 7.92-mm (0.31-in) guns
Fw 190A-1: four 7.92-mm (0.31-in) guns
Fw 190A-2: two 20-mm and two 7.92-mm (0.31-in) guns; B.M.W. 801C-2

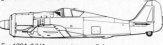
Fw 190A-3/U4 reconnaissance fighter

Fw 190A-3: four 20-mm and two 7.92-mm (0.31-in) guns; B.M.W. 801D-2; also U1 fighter-bomber, U3 ground-attack fighter, U4 reconnaissance fighter and U7 fighter-bomber; 'Trop' sub-variants

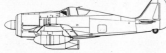
Fw 190A-4/U8 with SC500 bomb and underwing tanks

Fw 190A-4: FuG16Z radio; B.M.W. 801D-2 with MW50 injection; U1 and U8 fighter-bombers, U4 ground-attack fighter, R6 bomber-destroyer; 'Trop' sub-variants; introduced first *Rüstsatz*

Fw 190A-5/U14 with LT F5b torpedo

Fw 190A-5/U17 with SC500 and four SC50 bombs

Fw 190A-5: slightly lengthened mounting for B.M.W. 801D-2; U2 night ground-attack aircraft, U3 similar with increased bombload, U4 reconnaissance aircraft, U6 and U8 fighter-bombers, U11 bomber-destroyer, U13 ground-attack fighter, U14 and U15 torpedo-fighters, U16 bomber-destroyer, U17 was prototype for Fw 190F-3; 'Trop' sub-variants

Fw 190A-6/R1 with four underwing 20-mm cannon

Fw 190A-6: FuG16Ze and FuG25 radio; lighter wing structure; R1 to R4 bomber-destroyers, R4 with B.M.W. 801TS; R6 bomber-destroyer with underwing rockets; 'Trop' sub-variants
Fw 190A-7: two 20-mm and two 13-mm (0.51-in) guns; *Rüstsatz* conversions as for Fw 190A-6

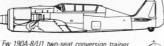
Fw 190A-8/U1 two-seat conversion trainer

Fw 190A-8 with SG 116 Zellendusche vertical-firing 30-mm weapons

Fw 190A-8: FuG16ZY radio; GM-1 power boosting; *Rüstsatz* conversions R1 to R6 as for Fw 190A-6; R7 had armoured cockpit; R11 all-weather fighter had PKS12 and FuG125 radio; R12 similar but with two 30-mm guns; U1 two-seat trainer; U3 upper component of Mistel weapon; U11 fighter/torpedo-bomber
Fw 190A-9: B.M.W. 801F; *Rüstsatz* conversions similar to Fw 190A-6, but R11 had B.M.W. 801TS, and R12 similar but two 30-mm guns
Fw 190A-10: numerous prototypes only; B.M.W. 801TS/TH; three bomb or drop tank stations; four 20-mm and two 13-mm (0.51-in) guns
Fw 190B-0: three prototypes modified from Fw 190A-1s; various wing planforms; failure of pressure cabin caused discontinuation; one Fw 190B-1 not completed

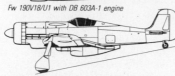
Fw 190V18/U1 with DB 603A-1 engine

Focke-Wulf Fw 190C high altitude fighter project

Fw 190C-0: six prototypes, including one modified Fw 190A-0; various engines with Hirth supercharger; development abandoned
Fw 190D-0: 10 aircraft converted from Fw 190A-7s; Junkers Jumo 213A engines with annular radiators; first 'long-nose' Fw 190s
Fw 190D-9: Jumo 213A; two 20-mm and two 13-mm (0.51-in) guns; most aircraft had bulged hoods; R11 all-weather fighter with FuG125 radio
Fw 190D-10: two prototypes converted from Fw 190D-0s; single 30-mm hub-gun replaced guns in nose decking
Fw 190D-11: seven prototypes only; two 20-mm and two 30-mm guns; R20 with PKS12 radio; R21 with FuG125 radio
Fw 190D-12: one 30-mm and two 20-mm guns; armoured Jumo 213F, R5 ground-attack fighter; R11 all-weather fighter; R21 with MW50 injection; R25 with Jumbo 213EB
Fw 190D-13: Jumo 213EB; three 20-mm guns; R5, R11, R21 and R25 as for Fw 190D-12
Fw 190D-14: DB603A; two prototypes converted from Fw 190D-9 and Fw 190D-12
Fw 190E: reconnaissance fighter project; not built
Fw 190F-1: armoured fighter-bomber; one ETC501 and two ETC50 bomb racks; bulged canopy

Fw 190F-2 with centreline ETC501 and ER-4 racks

Fw 190F-2: similar to Fw 190F-1 but additional ER4 adaptor bomb rack
Fw 190F-3: provision for underwing drop tanks; R3 with two underwing 30-mm guns

Fw 190F-8/U14 carrying LT 950 torpedo

Fw 190F-8 with Sg 113A Förstersonde 45-mm Sabot-firing weapons

Fw 190F-8: provision for variety of rockets and anti-personnel weapons; U1 was proposed two-seat trainer; U2 and U3 had provision to carry various torpedo-bombs and U14 was torpedo-fighter; R1, R2, R3, R5, R8, R11, R14, R15 and R16 all provided for various armament combinations

Fw 190F-8/U2 with Bt 700 torpedo bomb

Fw 190F-9: armoured version of Fw 190A-9 and produced in parallel; B.M.W. 801TS
Fw 190F-10 to F-14: unbuilt projects
Fw 190F-15: one prototype; Fw 190A-8 wing; B.M.W. 801TS/TH
Fw 190F-16: one prototype; increased armour
Fw 190G-0: two 20-mm guns; maximum bombload 2,205 lb (1000 kg)
Fw 190G-1: strengthened undercarriage; one 3,968-lb (1800-kg) bomb; Junkers bombrack
Fw 190G-2: as above but Messerschmitt bombrack
Fw 190G-3: as above but Focke-Wulf bombrack; R5 could carry four fragmentation bombs under the wings
Fw 190G-4: three ETC503 bombracks
Fw 190G-7: was intended to carry single 198-Imp gal (900-litre) drop tank
Fw 190G-8: B.M.W. 801D-2, otherwise similar to Fw 190A-8, R4 had GM1 power boost
Fw 190H-1: proposed high-altitude fighter with DB603G, but not built
Ta 152A-1: unbuilt project similar to Fw 190D-9 with FuG24 radio
Ta 152A-2: unbuilt project as above but with four 20-mm guns
Ta 152B-1, Ta 152B-2: unbuilt projects
Ta 152B-3: armoured ground-attack fighter project
Ta 152B-4: heavy fighter project; R1 with two 13-mm and two 20-mm guns; R2 with three 30-mm and two 20-mm guns
Ta 152B-5: one prototype built (Fw 190V53); three 20-mm guns; R11, three prototypes built (Ta 152V19, V20 and V21)
Ta 152C: three prototypes built; DB603L
Ta 152C-0 and C-1: three prototypes completed; DB603L; many gun combinations proposed
Ta 152E-1: photo-reconnaissance aircraft; two prototypes completed
Ta 152E-2: high-altitude version of Ta 152E-1; one prototype (Ta 152V26) completed
Ta 152H: high-altitude fighter; Jumo 213E; three modified Fw 190 prototypes (Fw 190V29, V30 and V32)
Ta 152H-0: 20 pre-production aircraft built at Cottbus in 1944; Jumo 213Eb; R11, R21 and R31 variants with engine boost and radio variations
Ta 152H-1: one prototype (Ta 152V26) modified from Ta 152E-2 and about a dozen production examples
Ta 153: one prototype (Fw 190V32) modified from Ta 152H prototype to include very high aspect ratio wing

Ilyushin Il Shturmovik

Outside the USSR the Ilyushin Il-2 and Il-10 remain, almost unbelievably, a lesser-known type, even to young enthusiasts. But more were built than of any other aircraft in history. And Stalin said: 'They are needed by the Red Army like it needs air or bread'.

For every Hurricane built there were three Il-2s, and for every Lancaster or Mosquito there were five. No flying machine of man's creation has ever poured off assembly lines at such a sustained high rate as the Il-2, despite its immense manufacturing problems. And the most serious of these problems centred on the fact that the Il-2 was almost a flying tank, with better armour protection than any previous production aircraft. Remarkably, apart from this crucial factor of armour, the Il-2's specification was almost identical to that of the UK's disastrous Fairey Battle, which was shot down in droves. The big difference was that the Battle was conceived as a level day bomber, whereas the Il-2 was a specialized armoured ground-attack aircraft.

Until recently the USSR has generally regarded air power as an adjunct to ground forces, and in the 1930s it paid much more attention than any other country to creating survivable close-support and attack aircraft. In addition to numerous technically fascinating prototypes, its large air armament organization, NII-AV, managed the development of the world's best air weapons, including excellent large-calibre guns, heavy recoilless cannon, hollow-charge armour-piercing bombs and similar warheads fitted to air-launched rockets. From 1929 a succession of heavily armed attack aircraft appeared, and in 1935 the Kremlin issued a requirement for a BSh (*Bronirovanyi Shturmovik*, or armoured attacker) aircraft specifically for knocking out armoured vehicles and ground strong-points. Polikarpov's team built a potentially outstanding twin-engined attacker, the VIT-1, with great speed and four 37-mm cannon, but this pro-

Il-2s depart from a forward base on a combat mission, probably in 1942. These are quite early single-seaters, though the nearest aircraft has VYa cannon whose barrels were longer than those of the ShVAK. Note the twin-oleo main landing gears with low-pressure tyres.

Ilyushin Il-2/Il-10

Specification

Ilyushin Il-10

Type: two-seat attack and anti-armour aircraft

Powerplant: one 2,000-hp (1492-kW) Mikulin AM-42 inline piston engine

Performance: maximum speed at sea level 319 mph (513 km/h); initial climb rate 1,970 ft (600 m) per minute; range 621 miles (1000 km)

Weight: empty 9,921 lb (4500 kg); maximum take-off 14,409 lb (6536 kg)

Dimensions: span 43 ft 11 in (13.4 m); length 36 ft 8¾ in (11.2 m); height 11 ft 5¾ in (3.50 m); wing area 323.0 sq ft (30.0 m²)

Armament: in this example, four 23-mm NS-23 and one 20-mm cannon, plus four wing bomb cells for total of 2,205 lb (1000 kg) or external carriage of bombs up to 1,323-lb (600-kg) size, plus eight RS-82 rockets on underwing launch rails

Il-2/Il-10 variants

TsKB-55: original two prototypes, both two-seaters with AM-35 engine

TsKB-57: third prototype, single-seater with AM-38 engine and better protection and armament; basis for initial production aircraft

BSh-2: designation of original production aircraft, with numerous detail refinements, deliveries from April to May 1941

Il-2: designation of BSh-2 under revised 1941 policy of designating according to design team rather than by function.

Il-2M: first modified version with revised structure to save aluminium

Il-2M2: second modified version with VYa-23 guns and AM-38F engine

Il-2M3: third modified version with rear gunner and other changes including improved protection; remained in production with successive refinements to reduce drag and increase flight performance

Il-2U: tandem dual-control trainer with glasshouse canopy over two pilots both facing ahead

Il-2T: torpedo-carrier with reduced armour and firepower but 21-in (533-mm) torpedo

Il-8: revised design with improved airframe and 2,000-hp (1492-kw) AM-42 engine

Il-10: succeeded Il-2 in production in 1944; completely new airframe, AM-42 engine and improved armament and systems; also **Il-10U** trainer

Il-16: prototype with AM-43 engine

Subject of the three-view illustration, the Il-10 was greatly cleaned up compared with the Il-2, and also differed greatly in airframe shape, structure and systems. The fuselage was deeper and better streamlined, the armoured cockpits closer together and the gunner had a 20-mm gun in a better mounting with a glazed cupola fairing. Though heavier, the Il-10 had simpler main landing gears, with single legs and wheels that rotated to lie flat inside the wing. The Il-10, operated by the Soviet tactical air force in Germany in 1945, had four 23-mm wing guns, a choice often associated with a single or twin UB at the rear.

gramme ground to a halt, partly because the VIT and derived designs could not safely fly from short front-line airstrips. By 1938 the need was even more urgent, and the OKBs (design bureaux) of Sergei V. Ilyushin and Pavel O. Sukhoi were set in head-on competition. Sukhoi was overloaded, but Ilyushin put a strong team on the project at once, though he personally was handicapped by being injured in a crash.

Both designers adopted a conventional low-wing single-engined configuration, but in the spring of 1939 Ilyushin's was ready much quicker. Designated TsKB-55, with the service designation BSh-2, it was powered by a large 1,350-hp (1007-kW) AM-35 liquid-cooled engine, and seated the pilot and radio operator/rear gunner/observer in tandem.

Colour schemes of Soviet aircraft in World War 2 were often irregular or non-standard. One of these Il-2s appears to be in white winter garb, while the nearer machine is probably green and fawn. Both are single-seaters of the pre-1943 type, with ShVAK cannon and eight rocket rails under the broad metal-skinned wings.

Each main landing gear had twin shock struts and retracted backwards into an underwing container. The wing, hydraulic flaps and tail were of light alloy, but the fuselage comprised a challenging forward section with a light alloy and steel-tube structure above, and a lower part made up of 1,543 lb (700 kg) of armour which covered the underside of the engine, coolant pipes, radiator, fuselage tanks and cockpits, other parts being attached directly to it (thus the armour was a structural part of the aircraft). The rear fuselage was wood. Four 7.62-mm (0.3-in) guns were mounted in the wings outboard of the main landing gear legs, with a fifth in the rear cockpit, and four compartments in the centre sections housed up to 1,323 lb (600 kg) of bombs.

Crash programme

Ilyushin was dissatisfied with the poor armament, and on test in the hands of Vladimir K. Kokkinaki the TsKB-55 showed, as predicted, poor stability. An improved second prototype, with the centre of gravity shifted forward and a larger tailplane, flew on 30 December 1939, but NII (State) testing in the summer of 1940 considered the good features outweighed by poor stability, range and general performance. Ilyushin therefore launched a 'crash programme' which in four months produced the TsKB-57. This was fitted with the 1,600-hp (1194-kW) AM-38, had an extra fuel tank instead of a rear cockpit, thicker and better distributed armour, two of the wing guns replaced by 20-mm ShVAK cannon and new underwing rails for eight RS-82 rockets. This was a much better machine, which reached 292 mph (470 km/h) and had good agility. All that now had to be done was improve the engine and oil cooling, raise the seat, redesign the canopy and cut-down rear fuselage, and refine the engine installation for better airflow, better access and flame-damping ejector exhausts. Very large scale production was then put in hand at three factories, in Moscow, at Fili to the north and at Voronezh to the south.

The Il-2M3 is also seen in one of the accompanying photographs. It was by no means uncommon to remove the rear cockpit canopy to give the gunner a free field of fire. It was also common for the gunner to have twin UB guns, though with reduced ammunition. The slogan *mstitel* painted on the side means 'Avenger'.

The Russian national insignia assumed many forms, including stars with circles in the centre, or with dark/light shades in each of the five arms, or with a yellow (less often, white) border when on a dark background. This unidentified Il-2M3 on the Stalingrad front in early 1943 had stars without borders.

Taken in the latter part of 1944, this photograph shows Il-2M3 two-seaters on the Eastern Front, which by this time had almost everywhere been pushed beyond the frontiers of the Soviet Union and into Poland, Romania and other countries.

This Il-10 was captured from the People's Republic of North Korea during the Korean War in 1951, and was photographed at Wright Field after its armament had been removed. It was found to handle extremely well, but of course was generally thought to be obsolescent. The use of the Skyraider in Vietnam questions this assessment.

This photograph shows the Czech-built dual-control pilot trainer version of the Il-10, with Czech designation of BS-33. The cockpits were spaced farther apart, the rear seat (occupied by the instructor) in this case of course facing ahead. Most BS-33s retained most of the armour, but this example appears to be unarmed.

When the Germans invaded on 22 June 1941, 249 had been delivered and a few were in service; but this was far below target. The director of the Kirov works at Leningrad, whence came the vital steel armour, tried to exonerate himself by showing Stalin a large drawing that had been used at a design conference and covered with doodles by Ilyushin, saying: 'How can I work from such shoddy drawings?' Stalin was naive enough to be taken in by this crude trick, and struck fear into Ilyushin with a telephone call telling him he would be 'brought to account'. Eventually Stalin was told the true state of affairs; the Kirov director was replaced, and Ilyushin's 2nd-class Stalin Prize was upped to 1st-class. In October the Moscow and Fili plants had to be closed and their tooling and workers evacuated far to the east, the chief new production centre being at Kuybyshyev. But output was slow to build up, and Stalin (by this time left in no doubt of the crucial value of the Il-2) sent a telegram to the factory directors telling them their performance was 'an insult'. He went on: 'The Red Army needs the Il-2 as it needs air or bread. I demand more. This is my last warning!'

This really put a spurt into the output, but, as well as the evacuation and the onset of winter, the aircraft itself still needed changes. Major parts of the outer wings and tail were redesigned in wood, to save aluminium, and in early 1942 the ShVAK guns were replaced by the much harder-hitting 23-mm VYa. Later in 1942 the designation changed to Il-2M2 with the introduction of the 1,750-hp (1306-kW) AM-38F engine, which improved all-round performance even with an increase in armour to 2,094 lb (950 kg). But losses to fighters were severe, and it was not practical to provide adequate armour against fire from above and behind. Many front-line regiments had taken the matter into their own

hands and fitted a rear cockpit for a gunner, who was usually one of their own ground crew. Despite Stalin's reluctance to sanction any further modifications, Ilyushin was authorized to produce prototypes with a rear gunner, and these flew in March 1942. The gunner had a 0.5-in (12.7-mm) UB with 150 rounds and, differently from original TsKB-55, was separated from the pilot by the amidships fuel tank. Production was eventually sanctioned in October 1942 as the Il-2M3; this new two-seater was in action with the Central Front by the end of October, and with the Stalingrad Front by November.

Streamlining modifications

Losses were immediately sharply curtailed, while casualties among Luftwaffe fighters increased. Production by this time was running at close to 1,000 per month, despite the introduction of a succession of minor changes which in the main were aimed at improving flight performance, which had fallen to a maximum speed of 251 mph (404 km/h). No detailed record was kept of these changes, but 18 have been identified in photographs in the West, and there were probably others. Almost every part that could be better streamlined was modified if it could be done without disrupting production, and among the more obvious were the windshield, cowling panels, radiators and ducts, wing roots, main-gear pods, tailwheel, and control-surface gaps and hinges. By mid-1943 maximum speed had improved to 273 mph (439 km/h) despite continuing growth in weight.

Part of the weight growth was due to increased armament, which benefitted from the superb products of the air weapon design staff. Most important was the new family of 37-mm guns, unrelated to earlier weapons of this calibre and firing high-velocity ammunition fully capable of penetrating Pzkpfw V (Panther) and Pzkpfw VI (Tiger) tanks, except in a head-on attack (these big guns are still in widespread use, notably on Su-7 series attack aircraft). Additional types of bombs could be carried in the wing cells, while underwing loads were expanded to include the large (132-mm/5.2-in calibre) RS-132 rocket and boxes of 200 small PTAB anti-armour bombs.

In 1942 Engineer-Colonel Alexei Sidorov, who had managed two-seat conversions of several fighters including the Hawker Hurricane Mk II, led a small team (curiously, at naval aviation workshops) which produced the first dual-control Il-2. Several were produced by field conversion, and by 1943 small numbers were factory-built as the Il-2U, most

This Il-2M3 was serving at the end of World War 2 with the 3rd Attack Regiment (*Szturmowego Pulk*) of the Polish 1st Mixed Air Corps, one of the first non-Soviet units to be equipped with these aircraft. This aircraft was replaced by the Il-10 in about 1947 or possibly early 1948, the Poles again being some of the first foreign recipients.

Ilyushin Il-2

with reduced armament. Another field modification resulted in the Il-2T torpedo-carrier, which with the greatest ease carried a 21-in (533-mm) torpedo. The VMF (today the separate AV-MF, or naval air force) used this version operationally, though it is not known if they were factory-built. There were countless local modifications, notably various kinds of tug and several semi-standard reconnaissance conversions with either one or two cameras in the rear fuselage. It also became common practice to use the Il-2 as a front-line passenger transport with one passenger or casualty lying in the rear fuselage, loaded through the rear cockpit, and two in the main-gear pods, the pilot having to remember to leave the wheels extended throughout the flight!

Altogether at least 36,163 Il-2s had been built when production switched to the Il-10 in August 1944. By that time monthly acceptances were running at the record level of 2,300, almost 16,000 being delivered in the eight months of 1944, the figure for the whole year of 1943 being 11,200. Where before it had been difficult to gather Il-2s to form a trained regiment, by 1944 they were operating in corps strength, as many as 500 being committed at a time on a single localized area and generally leaving no vehicle able to move. The usual method of attack was a follow-my-leader orbit which gave a long firing run from the rear of heavy armour, while individual aircraft dropped cluster bombs, 100-kg (220-lb) HE bombs or anti-armour PTABs from above on armour or Flak (anti-aircraft) vehicles. To the Soviet forces the Il-2 was commonly the *Ilyusha*, but to the invaders it was soon the *schwarz Tod* (Black Death).

In 1943 the first foreign unit, the 3rd Regiment of the 1st Polish Mixed Aviation Division, received Il-2 equipment. Subsequently an estimated 3,000 were supplied to Polish, Czech, Yugoslav and even turncoat Bulgarian regiments, while large numbers were supplied to China and North

Ilyushin Il-2M3 cutaway drawing key

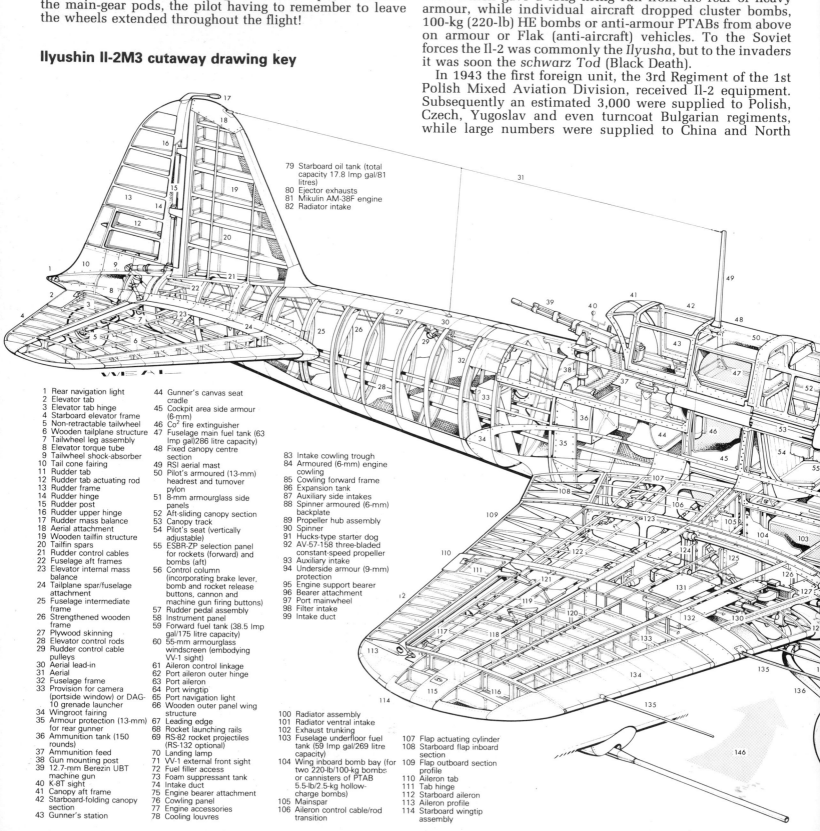

79 Starboard oil tank (total capacity 17.8 Imp gal/81 litres)
80 Ejector exhausts
81 Mikulin AM-38F engine
82 Radiator intake

1 Rear navigation light
2 Elevator tab
3 Elevator tab hinge
4 Starboard elevator frame
5 Non-retractable tailwheel
6 Wooden tailplane structure
7 Tailwheel leg assembly
8 Elevator torque tube
9 Tailwheel shock-absorber
10 Tail cone fairing
11 Rudder tab
12 Rudder tab actuating rod
13 Rudder frame
14 Rudder hinge
15 Rudder post
16 Rudder upper hinge
17 Rudder mass balance
18 Aerial attachment
19 Wooden tailfin structure
20 Tailfin spars
21 Rudder control cables
22 Fuselage aft frames
23 Elevator internal mass balance
24 Tailplane spar/fuselage attachment
25 Fuselage intermediate frame
26 Strengthened wooden frame
27 Plywood skinning
28 Elevator control rods
29 Rudder control cable pulleys
30 Aerial lead-in
31 Aerial
32 Fuselage frame
33 Provision for camera (portside window) or DAG-10 grenade launcher
34 Wingroot fairing
35 Armour protection (13-mm) for rear gunner
36 Ammunition tank (150 rounds)
37 Ammunition feed
38 Gun mounting post
39 12.7-mm Berezin UBT machine gun
40 K-8T sight
41 Canopy aft frame
42 Starboard-folding canopy section
43 Gunner's station

44 Gunner's canvas seat cradle
45 Cockpit area side armour (6-mm)
46 CO_2 fire extinguisher
47 Fuselage main fuel tank (63 Imp gal)/286 litre capacity)
48 Fixed canopy centre section
49 RSI aerial mast
50 Pilot's armoured (13-mm) headrest and turnover pylon
51 8-mm armourglass side panels
52 Aft-sliding canopy section
53 Canopy track
54 Pilot's seat (vertically adjustable)
55 ESBR-ZP selection panel for rockets (forward) and bombs (aft)
56 Control column (incorporating brake lever, bomb and rocket release buttons, cannon and machine gun firing buttons)
57 Rudder pedal assembly
58 Instrument panel
59 Forward fuel tank (38.5 Imp gal/175 litre capacity)
60 55-mm armourglass windscreen (embodying VV-1 sight)
61 Aileron control linkage
62 Port aileron outer hinge
63 Port aileron
64 Port wingtip
65 Port navigation light
66 Wooden outer panel wing structure
67 Leading edge
68 Rocket launching rails
69 RS-82 rocket projectiles (RS-132 optional)
70 Landing lamp
71 VV-1 external front sight
72 Fuel filler access
73 Foam suppressant tank
74 Intake duct
75 Engine bearer attachment
76 Cowling panel
77 Engine accessories
78 Cooling louvres

83 Intake cowling trough
84 Armoured (6-mm) engine cowling
85 Cowling forward frame
86 Expansion tank
87 Auxiliary side intakes
88 Spinner armoured (6-mm) backplate
89 Propeller hub assembly
90 Spinner
91 Hucks-type starter dog
92 AV-57-158 three-bladed constant-speed propeller
93 Auxiliary intake
94 Underside armour (9-mm) protection
95 Engine support bearer
96 Bearer attachment
97 Port mainwheel
98 Filter intake
99 Intake duct

100 Radiator assembly
101 Radiator ventral intake
102 Exhaust trunking
103 Fuselage underfloor fuel tank (59 Imp gal/269 litre capacity)
104 Wing inboard bomb bay (for two 220-lb/100-kg bombs or cannisters of PTAB 5.5-lb/2.5-kg hollow-charge bombs)
105 Mainspar
106 Aileron control cable/rod transition

107 Flap actuating cylinder
108 Starboard flap inboard section
109 Flap outboard section profile
110 Aileron tab
111 Tab hinge
112 Starboard aileron
113 Aileron profile
114 Starboard wingtip assembly

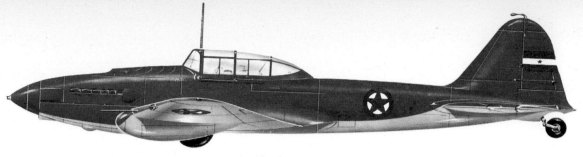

After World War 2 many Soviet aircraft supplied to Yugoslavia were subjected to local modifications. One example was the Il-2M3, which (as in this case) was sometimes rebuilt as a dual-control trainer with both seats facing ahead and with a streamlined canopy. Note the repositioned radio aerial mast.

Korea in the post-war era. Several countries, including Poland and Czechoslovakia, applied their own local designations, while many Il-2s were modified in various ways with different equipment, weapons or (in Yugoslavia) a rear fuselage of fabric-covered welded steel tubes. At least six are preserved, four being on public view in Moscow (2), Warsaw and Prague.

Fundamental improvements

Like so many aircraft, the Il-2 was the best that could be done at the time, and it is only with hindsight that one can say: 'Why was it not designed like the Il-10?' The Il-10 was the aircraft that replaced it on the production line in August 1944, and it was a total redesign, though superficially similar. It was the end result of a large Moscow conference held in early 1942 attended not only by engineers, staff officers and Ilyushin and his team, but also by front-line *Shturmovik* pilots who were encouraged to think of possible improvements. Most of the improvements were not possible without more power, and that is a good answer to the question posed above, because more powerful engines simply were not

available (though many were running on testbeds). One Il-2 was flown with the 1,700-hp (1268-kW) ASh-82 radial; it was good, but not really worth disrupting the production line. The ideal engine was Mikulin's AM-42, but this did not become available until December 1943.

Around this fine engine, driving a four-blade propeller to absorb its 2,000 hp (1492 kW), Ilyushin designed the Il-8 with an all-metal stressed-skin airframe, considerably greater fuel capacity, neater main gears with single legs folding flat under the wings with the large soft-tyred wheels turning 90° to lie in wing compartments, and greatly cleaned-up cowling with radiators in the wing roots. Armament was increased to 2,205 lb (1000 kg) of bombs or up to eight RS-132s, and guns comprised two VYa-23s and two ShVAK-20s, plus a UB at the rear. In parallel the bureau designed the Il-10 in which the same engine installation (with three-blade propeller) and landing gear were fitted to a completely redesigned airframe with a wing of different profile and planform, an improved tail, and a new cockpit for the pilot and a gunner immediately behind him in a turret. Both prototypes were on test in the spring of 1944, and though both were markedly better than the Il-2, the Il-10 was in a class of its own. While the Il-8 handled like an Il-2 (rather sedate, and hard work) the Il-10 could almost tangle with a Yak or La-5 if competently handled!

If only the 36,000 Il-2s could have been Il-10s, victory in the East could have come a little sooner and at much less cost. An absolute winner, the Il-10 was ordered into immediate production, and the first regiments were equipping in October 1944. Standard armament comprised two NS-23s and two small ShKAS machine-guns for sighting, plus a 20-mm cannon at the rear. Some had N-37 guns instead of the 23-mm NS-23s, and a few had four NS-23s with only a UB in the rear cockpit. Curiously, though it weighed the same as its predecessors and had a much smaller wing, the Il-10 had about the same top speed as the Il-8 and the same landing speed as both the Il-8 and Il-2. Its great advantages lay in agility, efficiency and much faster and simpler rearming and servicing. About 3,500 were built in the six months from November 1944 and, despite the emergence of the more powerful AM-43-powered Il-16 in 1945, production of the Il-10 continued at a low rate for about eight further years to a total of 4,966, plus another 1,200 built as B-33s by Avia in Czechoslovakia. The trainer version was the Il-10U, the Czech designation for this being BS-33. Small numbers were built of the Il-10M with redesigned square-tipped wings and other changes, one of the Il-10Ms having a booster rocket engine in the tail.

Ilyushin persisted with more powerful *Shturmoviki*, the next major type being the lumpy Il-20 powered by a 2,700-hp (2014-kW) AM-47F piston engine, followed by the Il-40 in which the same well-proven armoured two-place cockpit was fitted into a twin-jet air-frame. What killed off the *Shturmoviki* was the decision that the general ground-attack role could be fulfilled more efficiently and at less cost by the versatile MiG fighter-bombers. This policy has been followed for over 25 years, but now is again giving way to specialist *Shturmovik* aircraft (perhaps triggered by the USAF A-10A), the first of which, said to be a design from the OKB named for the late P. O. Sukhoi, was serving in numbers in Afghanistan.

115 Starboard navigation light
116 Wing outer rib
117 Aileron outer hinge
118 Wooden wing structure
119 Flap control linkage
120 Wing ribs
121 Aileron tab control
122 Flap rods
123 Wing centre/outer section joint/capping strake
124 Wing attachment points
125 Undercarriage retraction cylinder
126 Forward extremity of weapons bay
127 ShKAS 7.62-mm machine gun
128 Machine-gun barrel support
129 Cannon barrel fairing
130 Volkov-Yartsev VYa-23 23-mm cannon
131 Ammunition access panel
132 Magazine for starboard VYa-23 cannon (150 rounds)
133 Forward spar
134 Leading edge panels
135 Alternative pitot head positions

136 Undercarriage retraction linkage
137 Mainwheel leg cross-brace
138 Undercarriage fairing doors
139 Starboard mainwheel
140 Axle
141 Undercarriage oleo legs
142 Barrel of VYa-23 cannon
143 Undercarriage pivot point
144 Fairing nose section
145 Starboard bomb load comprising three (two internal and one external) 220-lb (100-kg) bombs which could be released singly or in salvo
146 Alternative main armament (II02 Type 3M) of 37-mm Nudelman-Suranov NS-11-P-37 (NSK-OKB-16) cannon

This Mitsubishi A6M5 was restored in 1980 by the Fame Museum in Chino, California, and is one of the very few examples still flying. It was used by the 261st Kokutai of the Japanese Naval Air Force in Saipan during the war.

Mitsubishi A6M 'Zero'

Built in far greater numbers than any other Japanese aircraft, the A6M was a sudden terrible shock to the Allies from Pearl Harbor onwards. But once the Allies had armed themselves properly, the once-feared 'Zero' was on the defensive.

When the Japanese Navy struck at Pearl Harbor on Sunday, 7 December 1941, the Americans already possessed files on the A6M in the form of detailed combat reports from Colonel Claire Chennault in far-off Chungking, China. Nobody had bothered to disseminate the information, and for a second time this agile and well-armed fighter caused a great shock and made mincemeat of the motley collection of aircraft that opposed it. In six months the Sentais (fighter groups) equipped with A6M had so dominated the sky that the Imperial forces had conquered over 12 million square miles (37.3m km²), a far greater area than had ever previously been overrun by one nation. The A6M kept appearing in places where Japanese fighters had been judged 'impossible', sometimes almost 1,000 miles (1609 km) from the nearest advanced Japanese airbase or carrier. In combat it could outmanoeuvre practically every Allied fighter, and its firepower was also superior.

The A6M came to symbolize the previously unappreciated fact that Japanese weapons were not made of bamboo and rice-paper, nor were they inferior copies of Occidental ones. In its own homeland it was the focal point of a part-religious belief in Nipponese invincibility. The name of Jiro Horikoshi was better-known in Japan even than that of Reginald Mitchell in the UK, because he was the genius who had created the miraculous fighter that decimated its enemies.

Of course the A6M was not really miraculous. Back in 1937 the British Gloster company had flown a prototype fighter that almost precisely paralleled the A6M in size, shape, weight, power and performance – and it was not even accepted for the RAF. At that time Horikoshi was making the first drawings of his new fighter to try to meet a newly issued Imperial Navy specification that called for a shipboard

This frame from a Japanese ciné film shows an A6M2 (foreground) and B5N2 torpedo bombers ranged on the deck of a 1st Koku Kantai carrier early on Sunday 7 December 1941: destination, Pearl Harbor. The US Navy caption gives the carrier as the *Hiryu* but the insignia are not those of the 2nd Sentai.

Mitsubishi A6M Reisen

Specification

Mitsubishi A6M5c Reisen
Type: carrier-based fighter-bomber
Powerplant: one 1,130-hp (843-kW) Nakajima NK1F
Sakae 21 radial piston engine
Performance: maximum speed 351 mph (565 km/h);
cruising speed 230 mph (370 km/h); climb to 19,685 ft
(6000 m) in 7 minutes; service ceiling 38,520 ft
(11740 m); maximum range 1,194 miles (1922 km)
Weights: empty 4,136 lb (1876 kg); maximum take-off
6,025 lb (2733 kg)
Dimensions: span 36 ft 1 in (11.00 m); length
29 ft 11¼ in (9.12 m); height 11 ft 6 in (3.50 m); wing
area 229.27 sq ft (21.3 m²)
Armament: one 0.52-in (13.2-mm) Type 3 heavy
machine-gun in the fuselage decking (breech in the
cockpit), two 20-mm Type 99 cannon in the wings and
two 0.52-in (13.2-mm) Type 3 guns in the wings
outboard of the cannon, plus two 132-lb (60-kg)
bombs under the wings (suicide mission, one 551-lb/
250-kg bomb)

The subject of this illustration was
one of the rare late-war stop-gap
variants which tried to stem the
tide of Allied air power until the
A7M Reppu could be cleared for
production. An A6M5c of the 210th
Kokutai, it combined the non-
folding rounded wingtips and thick
wing skins, separate exhaust
stacks and other improvements of
the basic A6M5 (Model 52) with
heavier firepower from two 0.52-in
(13.2-mm) guns added in the wings
outboard of the cannon. Most had
better protection, with rear armour
and self-sealing wing tanks, but the
crucial fault of inadequate power
was not rectified and only 93 of this
model were built. Note the absence
of a white border to the Hinomaru
insignia.

210-118
B

Mitsubishi A6M

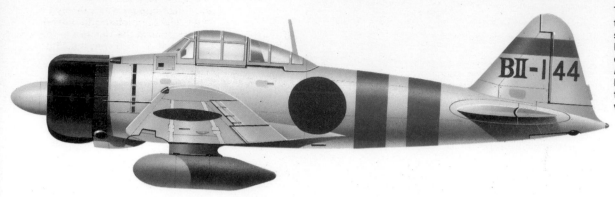

Typical of the early A6M2 Reisens that administered a paralysing shock to the Allied aircraft in the Pacific in the first half of 1942, this example served aboard the carrier *Hiryu* with the 2nd Sentai (two blue bands) of the 1st Koku Kantai (air fleet). Ruling colour was sky grey, with matt black engine cowling.

A mainstream production Reisen, this A6M2 was based at Rabaul, New Britain, with the 6th Kokutai in late 1942. By this time the grey had been sprayed with blotches of dark green, requiring a white outer ring around the Hinomaru (the red disc representing the rising sun). Over 500 Reisens were lost in this region.

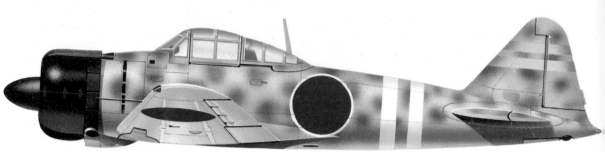

fighter with the manoeuvrability of his earlier A5M (one of the most agile aircraft ever built) despite the burden of two 20-mm cannon as well as the two machine-guns carried by the A5M, two 132-lb (60-kg) bombs, full radio, an engine to give a speed of 311 mph (500 km/h) and an endurance of eight hours with a drop tank. (It should be noted that the Imperial Navy measured speeds in knots, so that required of the new fighter was 270 knots.)

The result was wholly conventional, with stressed-skin structure, split flaps, wide-track inwards-retracting landing gear and a radial engine driving a variable-pitch propeller. After some argument a sliding canopy was added over the cockpit, and the newly demanded cannon (Type 99 Model 1, derived from the Oerlikon) were fitted in the wings, outboard of the propeller disc. Its designation was naturally A6M, A for carrier-based fighter and 6M for the sixth such type by Mitsubishi. Its popular name was Reisen (Rei-sen, zero fighter), from the Japanese year 2600 (1940 A.D.). The first A6M1, with a 780-hp (582-kW) Mitsubishi Zuisei 13 engine, flew at Kagamigahara on 1 April 1939, and showed outstanding qualities except in its speed of 304 mph

(489 km/h), which just missed the target. A constant-speed propeller gave an increase in all-round performance, but more power was needed and on 28 December 1939 the third prototype, designated A6M2, flew with the 925-hp (690-kW) Nakajima Sakae 12. This prototype exceeded all expectations, and by July 1940 the A6M2 had been cleared for production. It was decided to send 15 to China to test them in action with the 12th Rengo Kokutai. They got their first victim on 13 September 1940, and though two A6M2s were shot down by ground fire their air combat record was a remarkable 99 victories for no losses before they were redeployed for the war in the Pacific.

Countdown to 'Zero'

From the 22nd A6M2 the rear spar was strengthened, and from the 65th the outermost 20 in (50.8 cm) of the wings was hinged to fold upwards manually. In June 1941 the A6M3 had these tips omitted, and with the 1,130-hp (843-kW) Sakae 21 engine offered higher speed and more rapid roll, though turn radius was slightly worsened. At Pearl Harbor the Imperial Navy had 328 A6Ms embarked aboard carriers, and from the start they achieved complete mastery over the Curtiss P-40, Curtiss-Wright CW-21A, Brewster Buffalo, Hawker Hurricane I and other opponents. For example the hapless Buffaloes of the RAF, RAAF, RNZAF and Dutch East Indies were so outflown their 0.5-in (12.7-mm) guns were replaced by 0.303-in (7.62-mm) weapons, ammunition was cut by half and fuel by more than one-third, and still they could not bring their guns to bear over the more agile and much harder-hitting A6M.

Not knowing what the fighter was called, the Allies named it 'Ben' then 'Ray' and finally 'Zeke'. The clipped-wing model was called 'Hap', until someone recalled that that was the nickname of the USAAF Chief of Staff, General H. H. Arnold, when it became 'Hamp'. When the type was recognized as merely another version of the 'Zeke' it was called 'Zeke 32'. But desperate attempts to gather even pieces of the almost supernatural fighter proved elusive, until suddenly US troops found a perfect A6M2 in the Aleutians. Petty Officer Koga had taken off from the carrier *Ryujo* on 3 June to attack Dutch Harbor, but two bullets had

Few air-to-air photographs survive from Japanese air operations in World War 2. This picture was taken a year before Pearl Harbor as pre-series A6M2 fighters were blooded in combat over China with the 12th Rengo Kokutai. Nobody today knows what happened to the reports of the new fighter that were sent to Washington from Colonel Claire Chennault, who saw them in combat in Chungking.

Mitsubishi A6M

One of the very first Reisens to reach the Imperial Navy, this pre-series A6M2 operated with brilliant success against the Chinese in the second half of 1940 with the 12th Rengo Kokutai (combined naval air corps) in the Hankow region. These aircraft lacked folding wingtips and numerous other small refinements.

severed the fuel supply pipe and he had glided in to the uninhabited island of Akutan. Landing on marshy ground, the A6M had somersaulted and Koga had broken his neck. The valuable prize was soon on test at NAS North Island, San Diego, where the myths were blown away and the A6M's numerous shortcomings revealed.

For one thing, it is possible to do only so much on 1,130 hp (843 kW). The A6M airframe was lightly built, and the vital parts were by Western standards deficient in armour. Tactics were worked out to gain superiority in combat, but at least as important was the first flight, on the other side of the United States, of the first Grumman F6F Hellcat in June 1942. Larger and heavier than the A6M, this US Navy fighter had a 2,000-hp (1492-kW) engine: this enabled it to be stronger, tougher and better protected and yet outfight the A6M in a dogfight. Another US Navy and Marines fighter, the bent-wing Vought F4U Corsair, was even more formidable, and the US Army's P-38 was not only much faster but could stay with an A6M at all heights above 10,000 ft (3050 m) despite being much larger. And all these Allied fighters had firepower that could actually cause an A6M to break up into pieces.

Off Okinawa in April 1945 hundreds of aircraft of the Imperial Navy were lost trying to stem the Allied advance. About half were suicide (so-called Kamikaze) attacks by various fighter and attack aircraft carrying bombs. Here an A6M5 just fails to reach the deck of the USS *Missouri* on 28 April 1945, glancing off the side.

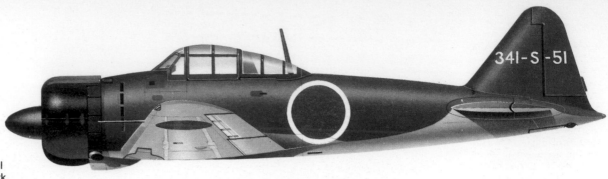

Later in the war many Imperial Navy aircraft were painted dark green over the entire upper surface and sides, often with a black forward upper decking or engine cowling. This A6M2 was based with the 402nd Chutai (squadron) of the 341st Kokutai (the basic naval air unit of some 150 aircraft) at Clark Field, Manila.

Seaplane variant

In autumn 1940 an Imperial Navy specification called for a fighter seaplane to operate over isolated beachheads and beyond the range even of the A6M, and, while the powerful Kawanishi N1K1 (which in turn was eventually to lead to a formidable land-based fighter) was developed, the Nakajima company was instructed to build a seaplane A6M. The resulting A6M2-N flew on the day of Pearl Harbor and was soon in action. Though as neat a conversion as could be imagined, it was inevitably inferior to Allied fighters and though 327 were delivered, the last in September 1943, they did not achieve very much. Another off-mainstream variant was the tandem dual-control A6M2-K advanced trainer, which was the responsibility of the 21st Naval Air Arsenal, at Sasebo. No even started until 1943, the first two-seater flew in November that year, and eventually 515 were built in two versions, with cannon and landing-gear doors removed to save weight. At Mitsubishi, Horikoshi had from 1940 pressed for a successor to the A6M, with his company's 2,200-hp (1641-kW) MK9 engine, but this was repeatedly delayed, and the old A6M had to be kept in production, both at the parent firm and (in even greater numbers) by Nakajima.

A 1943 attempt to improve performance at medium and high altitudes came to nothing: the 1st Air Technical Arsenal

Mitsubishi A6M2 'Zero' cutaway drawing key

1 Tail navigation light
2 Tail cone
3 Tailfin fixed section
4 Rudder lower brace
5 Rudder tab (ground adjustable)
6 Fabric-covered rudder
7 Rudder hinge
8 Rudder post
9 Rudder upper hinge
10 Rudder control horn (welded to torque tube)
11 Aerial attachment
12 Tailfin leading-edge
13 Forward spar
14 Tailfin structure
15 Tailfin nose ribs
16 Port elevator
17 Port tailplane
18 Piano-hinge join
19 Fuselage dorsal skinning
20 Control turnbuckles
21 Arrester hook release/retract steel cable runs
22 Fuselage frame/tailplane centre-brace
23 Tailplane attachments
24 Elevator cables
25 Elevator control horns/torque tube

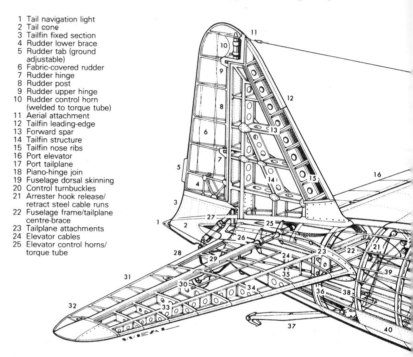

26 Rudder control horns
27 Tailwheel combined retraction/shock strut
28 Elevator trim tab
29 Tailwheel leg fairing
30 Castored tailwheel
31 Elevator frame (fabric-covered)
32 Elevator outer hinge
33 Tailplane structure
34 Forward spar
35 Elevator trim tab control rod (chain-driven)
36 Fuselage flotation bag rear wall
37 Arrester hook (extended)
38 Arrester hook pivot mounting
39 Elevator trim tab cable guide
40 Fuselage skinning
41 Fuselage frame stations
42 Arrester hook position indicator cable (duralumin tube)
43 Elevator cables
44 Rudder cables
45 Trim tab cable runs
46 Arrester hook pulley guide
47 Fuselage stringers
48 Fuselage flotation bag front wall
49 Fuselage construction join
50 Wingroot fillet formers
51 Compressed air cylinder (wing gun charging)
52 Transformer
53 'Ku'-type radio receiver
54 Oxygen cylinder (starboard), CO$_2$ fire-extinguisher cylinder (port)
55 Battery
56 Radio tray support
57 Radio transmitter
58 Canopy/fuselage fairing
59 Aerial mast support/lead-in

60 Aerial
61 Aerial mast (forward raked)
62 Canopy aft fixed section
63 Aluminium and plywood canopy frame
64 Crash bulkhead/headrest support
65 'Ku'-type D/F frame antenna mounting (late models)
66 Canopy track
67 Turnover truss
68 Pilot's seat support frame
69 Starboard elevator control bell-crank
70 Aileron control push-pull rod
71 Wing rear spar/fuselage attachment
72 Fuselage aft main double frame

73 Aileron linkage
74 Landing-gear selector level
75 Flap selector level
76 Seat adjustment lever
77 Pilot's seat
78 Cockpit canopy rail
79 Seat support rail
80 Elevator tab trim handwheel
81 Fuel gauge controls
82 Throttle quadrant
83 Reflector gunsight mounting (offset to starboard)
84 Sliding canopy

Mitsubishi A6M Reisen variants

Mitsubishi A6M1: first two prototypes, powered by the 780-hp (582-kW) Zuisei 13 engine.
Mitsubishi A6M2: initial production version, powered by the 940-hp (701-kW) Sakae 12 engine, with an armament of two 20-mm and two 0.303-in (7.7 mm) guns, span 39 ft 4½ in (12.00 m) and normal take-off weight 5,313 lb (2410 kg); initial aircraft of the batch, up to c/n 21, had an unreinforced rear spar, aircraft from c/n 22 onwards had the reinforced rear spar (both sub-types being designated **Model 11**), and from c/n 65 the wingtips were capable of manual folding.
Mitsubishi A6M3 Model 32: improved production model powered by the 1,130-hp (843-kW) Sakae 21; from the fourth aircraft 20-mm cannon ammunition was increased, and later aircraft had square-tipped wings of 36 ft 1-in (11.00-m) span compared with the **A6M3 Model 22**'s rounded tips of 39 ft 4½ in (12.00 m); normal take-off weight 5,609 lb (2254 kg)
Mitsubishi A6M4: unsuccessful experimental variant with turbocharged Sakae engine.
Mitsubishi A6M5 Model 52: improved A6M3 with thicker wing skins, rounded wingtips and thrust-augmenting exhaust stacks; normal take-off weight 6,025 lb (2733 kg)
Mitsubishi A6M5a Model 52A: derivative of the A6M5 with thicker skin and improved Type 99 Model 2

Mark 3 cannon
Mitsubishi A6M5 Model 52B: improved A6M5a with extra protection, fire extinguishing system for the fuel tanks, and one 0.303-in (7.7-mm) machine-gun replaced by a 0.57-in (13.2-mm) Type 3 weapon
Mitsubishi A6M5c Model 52C: yet further improved model, with two 0.52-in (13.2-mm) Type 3 machine-guns added outboard of the cannon, armour behind the pilot, extra fuel capacity, and racks for eight 22-lb (10-kg) unguided air-to-air rockets
Mitsubishi A6M6c Model 53C: improved A6M5c with 1,210-hp (903-kW) Sakae 31 plus methanol/water boost, and self-sealing wing tanks
Mitsubishi A6M7 Model 63: dive-bomber version of the A6M6c intended for use from small carriers; centreline provision for one 551-lb (250-kg) bomb and underwing points for two 77-Imp gal (350-litre) drop tanks
Mitsubishi A6M8 Model 64: uprated model with 1,560-hp (1164-kW) Kinsei 62 engine, no fuselage guns, better protection, and normal take-off weight 6,945 lb
Mitsubishi A6M2-K: dual-control trainer version of the A6M2
Mitsubishi A6M5-K: d/c version of the A6M5
Nakajima A6M2-N: floatplane version of the A6M2 with single main float and two underwing stabilizing floats; normal take-off weight 5,423 lb (2460 kg)

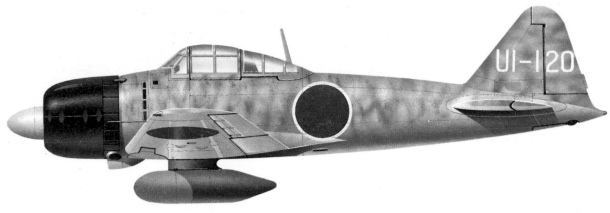

The A6M3 not only had a reduced span but also reduced fuselage fuel necessitated by the installation of the Sakae 21 engine, with two-speed supercharger, which pushed the firewall 8 in (20 cm) further aft. This A6M3 served on Kyushu, Japan, with the 251st Kokutai in late 1942. It is shown with the 72.6-Imp gal (330-litre) drop tank.

85 Plexiglass panels
86 Canopy lock/release
87 Windscreen
88 Fuselage starboard 0.303-in (7.7-mm) machine gun
89 Control column
90 Radio control box
91 Radio tuner
92 Elevator control linkage
93 Rudder pedal bar assembly
94 Cockpit underfloor fuel
95 Wing front spar/fuselage attachment
96 Fuselage forward main double frame
97 Ammunition magazine
98 Ammunition feed
99 Blast tube
100 Cooling louvres
101 Fuselage fuel tank, capacity 34 Imp gal (155 litres)
102 Firewall bulkhead
103 Engine bearer lower attachment
104 Engine bearer upper attachment
105 Oil tank, capacity 12.7 Imp gal (58 litres)
106 Bearer support struts
107 Cowling gill adjustment control
108 Machine gun muzzle trough
109 Barrel fairing
110 Oil filler cap
111 Fuselage fuel tank filler cap
112 Port flap profile
113 Port fuselage machine gun
114 Port wing gun access panels
115 Port inner wing identification light
116 Port wing flotation bag inner wall
117 Wing spar joins
118 Aileron control rods
119 Port aileron (fabric-covered)
120 Aileron tab (ground adjustable)
121 Aileron external counter-balance
122 Control linkage
123 Wing skinning
124 Port outer wing identification light
125 Port navigation light lead conduit
126 Wingtip hinge
127 Wing end rib
128 Port wing flotation bag outer wall
129 Wingtip structure
130 Port wingtip (folded)
131 Port navigation light
132 Port wingtip hinge release catch
133 Pitot head
134 Wing leading-edge skinning
135 Wing front spar
136 Port wing gun muzzle
137 Port undercarriage visual indicator
138 Undercarriage hydraulics access
139 Nacelle gun troughs

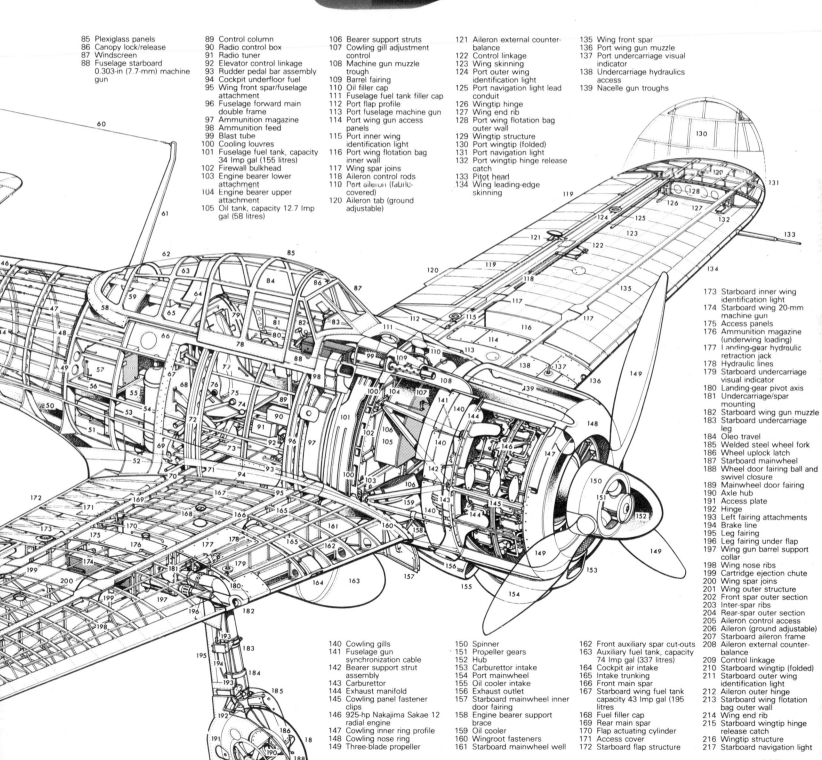

173 Starboard inner wing identification light
174 Starboard wing 20-mm machine gun
175 Access panels
176 Ammunition magazine (underwing loading)
177 Landing-gear hydraulic retraction jack
178 Hydraulic lines
179 Starboard undercarriage visual indicator
180 Landing-gear pivot axis
181 Undercarriage/spar mounting
182 Starboard wing gun muzzle
183 Starboard undercarriage leg
184 Oleo travel
185 Welded steel wheel fork
186 Wheel uplock latch
187 Starboard mainwheel
188 Wheel door fairing ball and swivel closure
189 Mainwheel door fairing
190 Axle hub
191 Access plate
192 Hinge
193 Left fairing attachments
194 Brake line
195 Leg fairing
196 Leg fairing under flap
197 Wing gun barrel support collar
198 Wing nose ribs
199 Cartridge ejection chute
200 Wing spar joins
201 Wing outer structure
202 Front spar outer section
203 Inter-spar ribs
204 Rear-spar outer section
205 Aileron control access
206 Aileron (ground adjustable)
207 Starboard aileron frame
208 Aileron external counter-balance
209 Control linkage
210 Starboard wingtip (folded)
211 Starboard outer wing identification light
212 Aileron outer hinge
213 Starboard wing flotation bag outer wall
214 Wing end rib
215 Starboard wingtip hinge release catch
216 Wingtip structure
217 Starboard navigation light

140 Cowling gills
141 Fuselage gun synchronization cable
142 Bearer support strut assembly
143 Carburettor
144 Exhaust manifold
145 Cowling panel fastener clips
146 925-hp Nakajima Sakae 12 radial engine
147 Cowling inner ring profile
148 Cowling nose ring
149 Three-blade propeller
150 Spinner
151 Propeller gears
152 Hub
153 Carburettor intake
154 Port mainwheel
155 Oil cooler intake
156 Exhaust outlet
157 Starboard mainwheel inner door fairing
158 Engine bearer support brace
159 Oil cooler
160 Wingroot fasteners
161 Starboard mainwheel well
162 Front auxiliary spar cut-outs
163 Auxiliary fuel tank, capacity 74 Imp gal (337 litres)
164 Cockpit air intake
165 Intake trunking
166 Front main spar
167 Starboard wing fuel tank capacity 43 Imp gal (195 litres)
168 Fuel filler cap
169 Rear main spar
170 Flap actuating cylinder
171 Access cover
172 Starboard flap structure

One of the best wartime photographs of Japanese Reisen operations, this scene shows A6M5c or A6M6c fighters of the Genzan Kokutai at Wonsan in the final weeks of the war. The 5c and 6c were the ultimate members of the Reisen family to see combat duty; they were crippled by being forced to use a low-powered engine.

These A6M2-N fighter seaplanes appear to be on the catapult of a surface warship, but this is a false impression. They are on the slipway of a surface base, perhaps at Tulagi, heavily lashed down and with control locks in place. Fighter seaplanes were generally outclassed and had little impact on operations in World War 2.

at Yokosuka fitted two A6M2s with turbocharged Sakae engines, but these were gravely unreliable. Nothing could be done but hastily to contrive an interim improved version, the A6M5; and, like so many hasty interim fighters, such as the Spitfire Mk IX, it was made in greater numbers than all the others. The chief modification was a new wing, with fixed rounded tips of 36 ft 1 in (11.00 m) span and thicker skins to enable the new version to dive at much higher speeds; previously limitations in diving speed had made the Zero easy to catch. This added 416 lb (189 kg) to the weight, and did nothing for manoeuvrability, but a slight improvement in performance resulted from fitting individual or paired exhaust pipes to the 14 cylinders with nozzles arranged to give forward thrust at full power. Together with a careful detail refinement all this added up to a significantly better fighter, and when it reached combat units in numbers in the autumn of 1943, the A6M5 did something to redress the balance which had rather quickly tilted towards the US Navy with the entry to combat duty of the F6F Hellcat.

If any one aircraft can be said to have destroyed the myth of Japanese invincibility in the air, that aircraft was the F6F. In fact, in a pure test of turn radius, the F6F would be hard-pressed to hold any A6M that was skilfully flown, but that was not the end of the story. Sheer lack of power in the Japanese fighter meant that it was far behind its opponent in armour and firepower, and in its ability to withstand battle damage. Lack of power was also the reason for the rate of climb falling off, compared with the lighter earlier versions, to levels below that of the heavyweight F6F. Even with thicker wing skins the A6M could not escape by diving away; in fact faced with an F6F, F4U or Spitfire Mk VIII there was no way an A6M pilot could survive except by exceptional flying, amazing luck or shooting down his opponent. And, as 1943 proceeded, this became more and more difficult.

Fortune turns

For one thing, the Allied fighters were not only getting dramatically superior but they were arriving in floods that completely overwhelmed the Japanese. Even in 1941–2 the Zeros had been outnumbered, but they had been deployed in concentrated groups that gained total local control and inflicted catastrophic losses, while the motley collections of Allied machines were scattered and often under no central direction. By 1943 the US Navy, US Marines, US Army Air Force and British Commonwealth forces were all co-ordinated and enjoyed numerical superiority everywhere. Not least of the Imperial Navy's problems was its rapid attrition in aircraft-carriers. Even as early as the Battle of Midway in June 1942 – often regarded as the start of the turnaround in fortunes in the Pacific war – the great carriers *Akagi*, *Hiryu*, *Kaga* and *Soryu* were all sunk; the light carrier *Shoho* had been sunk a month earlier, and *Ryujo* went to the bottom in August 1942. These crippling losses in seagoing air power gravely restricted the Imperial Navy's ability ever again to achieve command of the sky, at any place or at any time.

There was yet a further serious problem which had as much effect as all other factors combined. In air combat the man is every bit as important as the machine. Even flying an inferior aircraft, in the rather primitive days of World War 2, a brilliant and courageous pilot could often run up strings of victories over opponents flying faster or better-armed aircraft. In 1941 the Imperial Navy pilots had been well trained, and were aggressive and in most cases experienced. Many had seen a year or more of actual fighting in China or against the USSR, and in their hands a Zero was deadly. By 1943 hardly any of these pilots were still alive, and their replacements were by comparison ineffectual. The home-based training programme was wholly inadequate, and by autumn 1944 the once-dominant Sentais were being re-organized into kamikaze (suicide) squads in a desperate attempt to stem the tide of Allied advance.

Improved armament

Throughout the war the need for long range had been manifest, but whereas at the start the A6M had been supreme in this regard, especially after its experienced pilots had learned correct long-range cruise techniques at high boost pressure but low crankshaft revolutions, by 1943 the Sakae 21 had resulted in smaller fuselage tankage (in part rectified by adding two small 9.9-Imp gal/45-litre tanks in the outer wings) and appreciably higher fuel consumption. Crucial need to keep weight down precluded heavier armament, though the Type 99 cannon was improved through several versions with a longer barrel and higher muzzle velocity, rate of fire increased from 490 to an eventual 750 rounds per

The most important of all Imperial Navy fighters in the final year of the war, the A6M5 was identifiable by its ejector exhaust stacks and fixed rounded wingtips. This colourful example served as a combat trainer with the Genzan Kokutai at Wonsan, Korea (later to be in North Korea and scene of bitter fighting a decade later).

minute, and a 125-round belt in place of the original 100-round drum. The greater muzzle velocity had the possibly important effect of extending the effective range (typically from 2,624 ft/800 m to 3,281 ft/1000 m). This was one factor where the A6M could have scored over the US fighters that relied on the 0.5-in (12.7-mm) Browning. In practice, Japanese pilots lacked the shooting skill to open fire accurately at long ranges, and at normal air-combat distances the much more rapid rate of strikes from the typical US armament of six 0.5-in (12.7-mm) guns proved decisive.

When fitted with the long-barrel belt-fed cannon the A6M5 became the A6M5a, available from production in the spring of 1944. Within weeks the A6M5b was coming off the line, and this partly rectified one of the type's gravest shortcomings, lack of protection. The A6M5b had improved armour, automatic fire-extinguishers in the main fuel tanks and a slab of bullet-proof glass behind the windscreen. A small increase in firepower resulted from substituting the 0.52-in (13.2-mm) Type 3 heavy machine-gun for one of the rifle-calibre weapons ahead of the windscreen. Hundreds of A6M5a and A6M5b fighters took part in the great battles around the Marianas and Philippines in the summer of 1944, but the first major engagement of the A6M5b was such a slaughter at the hands of F6Fs that US pilots called it 'The Marianas Turkey Shoot'. To a considerable degree this was because of the superior skill of the American pilots.

Two of the aircraft in this line-up are A6M2 Reisen fighters; the rest are A6M2-K dual trainers, 515 of which were delivered from the end of 1943 onwards. Their unit appears to be the Kasumigaura Kokutai, and the colour dark green, with black cowls. The small strakes on the rear fuselage improved spin recovery.

This debacle spurred the Imperial Navy into a further desperate attempt to improve the A6M, a requirement being issued for racks for underwing rockets, extra 0.52-in (13.2-mm) guns outboard of the cannon, a large additional fuel tank behind the cockpit and a fully armoured pilot seat. If the A6M had needed extra power beforehand, it doubly needed it now, but permission to fit a larger engine was not granted. After building 93 with the improvements demanded Mitsubishi did receive some Sakae 31 engines, with extra power gained by injecting water/methanol to prevent detonation at full throttle, but most of these engines were retained by the maker, Nakajima, which went into production with the resulting A6M6c at the end of 1944. This was the final model of Reisen to see action, and it could not do more than earlier models to hold back the overwhelming advance of the Allied land, sea and air forces towards Japan.

The A6M7 was equipped to carry a 551-lb (250-kg) bomb as well as outer-wing drop tanks. The A6M8 at last had a more powerful engine, the 1,560-hp (1164-kW) Mitsubishi Kinsei 62, resulting in a slightly larger cowling and removal of the machine-guns previously fitted above it. This did not fly until May 1945 and no production aircraft could be completed. There were many experimental forms of armament and special equipment fits, but by far the most important were the kamikaze lash-ups with, usually, a 551-lb (250-kg) bomb hung on the rack normally used for the centreline drop tank.

Total production of the A6M was about 10,449 (3,879 by Mitsubishi and 6,570 by Nakajima), and these were complemented by 327 Nakajima-built A6M2-Ns, and 515 A6M2-Ks and A6M5-Ks (236 by Dai-Nijuichi Kaigun Kokusho and 279 by Hitachi Kokuki KK).

Messerschmitt Me 262

The Me 262 was not just a revolutionary engine in a conventional airframe. The design of its wings, tail unit and firepower was years ahead of its time; it was a winner and, unlike some predecessors it was a joy to fly.

Young German gunners, huddled around their light 20-mm and 37-mm Flak weapons, could be excused for a slight lack of attention to their task at their first sight of the Messerschmitt Me 262s on the snow-covered expanses of Rheine-Hopstein air base in the autumnal sleet of 1944. In every sense the sleek shark-like fuselages, mottled ochre and olive green, and beset with razor wings from which hung the huge turbojets, were a portent of the future. The noise, the high-pitched whine and howl, of the Jumo 004B-1 turbines, the swirls of snow, the hot paraffin-tainted blast: all were of a different time. But this was the present: beset by Allied

Messerschmitt Me 262B-1a/U1 under test with the USAAF coding of FE-610 (Foreign Evaluation) at Wright Field in 1946. The aircraft was captured by the British following possible service with the 10./NJG 11. The armament installed was two 30-mm MK 108A-3s and two 20-mm MG 151/20 cannon: AI radar was an FuG 218 (Neptun V).

air superiority on all sides, the skies over Westphalia were dangerous elements for operations of the Luftwaffe's dwindling strength. Black-helmeted pilots, crouched forward in the narrow cockpits of their Messerschmitt Me 262A-2a fighter-bombers, anxiously scanned the overcast for the first signs of the diving Hawker Tempests, North American P-51s or Supermarine Spitfires, as they coaxed throttles and jabbed brakes prior to take-off. Flak gunners trained their pieces along the approach paths, watched for the red Very lights that would bring them to instant action, and heard the

thunder of the departing jets. With such machines, how could Germany lose the war in the air? Such a thought must have raced through minds. But the job of a Flak gunner is humble, and he and his comrades could have had no insight into the extraordinary train of events and decisions that were instrumental in the denial in quantity of Germany's most potent air weapon of World War 2. In the heady days of 1941, when the Messerschmitt Me 262 series was born, no one person in the Third Reich could foresee the need, the desperate need, for an outstanding aircraft with which to wrest air supremacy from the hands of the enemy.

The Heinkel concern

was already deeply involved in the development of a fighter powered by the new reaction-turbine engines when, on 4 January 1939, the Augsburg-based Messerschmitt AG received orders from the German air ministry (RLM, or Reichsluftfahrtministerium) to produce specifications for a similar type of aircraft. Two plans were drawn up by a team led by Dipl.Ing. Waldemar Voigt, one for a twin-boom configuration and the other for a pod-and-boom design. Neither of the two existing turbojet designs was considered to be powerful enough for a single-engine fighter, and as a result Voigt was forced to turn to the design of a twin-engine aircraft.

Heinkel had already turned to twin engines with the development of the promising He 280 series powered by the six-stage axial-flow BMW P 3302 engines, and Germany's first definitive jet fighter, the Heinkel He 280 V2 prototype, lifted off from Rostock-Marienehe's runway at 15.18 on 30

March 1941 with Fritz Schafer at the controls. And within six weeks of this maiden flight the UK too flew her first jet aircraft: powered by a Whittle-designed W1X centrifugal-type turbojet of 860-lb (390-kg) thrust, the Gloster E.28/39 took to the air on 15 May. Back at Augsburg work had proceeded slowly on the design of what at first bore none of the hallmarks that graced the Heinkel product, or gave any hint of the fineness of line that was a characteristic of Messerschmitt's piston-engine fighters. The design was termed the Messerschmitt P 1065 VI and, in the absence of its twin jet engines, was fitted with a 730-hp (545-kW) Junkers Jumo 210G driving a two-blade propeller. This ugly duckling was then renamed the Messerschmitt Me 262 V1, and was taken into the air for the first time on 18 April 1941. Test pilots Karl Baur and Fritz Wendel reported no vices on subsequent flight programmes: no urgency was attached

Messerschmitt Me 262A-1a cutaway drawing key

1 Flettner-type geared trim tab
2 Mass-balanced rudder
3 Rudder post
4 Tail fin structure
5 Tailplane structure
6 Rudder tab mechanism
7 Flettner-type servo tab
8 Starboard elevator
9 Rear navigation light
10 Rudder linkage
11 Elevator linkage
12 Tailplane adjustment mechanism
13 Fuselage break point
14 Fuselage construction
15 Control runs
16 FuG 25a loop antenna (IFF)
17 Automatic compass
18 Aft auxiliary self-sealing fuel tank (132 Imp gal/600 litre capacity)

19 FuG 16zyR/T
20 Fuel filler cap
21 Aft cockpit glazing
22 Armoured aft main fuel tank (198 Imp gal/900 litre capacity)
23 Inner cockpit shell
24 Pilot's seat
25 Canopy jettison lever
26 Armoured (15-mm) head rest
27 Canopy (hinged to starboard)
28 Canopy lock
29 Bar-mounted Revi 16B sight (for both cannon and R4M missiles)
30 Armourglass windscreen (90-mm)
31 Instrument panel
32 Rudder pedal
33 Armoured forward main fuel tank (198 Imp gal/900 litre capacity)

34 Fuel filler cap
35 Underwing wooden rack for 12 R4M 55-mm rockets
36 Port outer flap section
37 Frise-type aileron
38 Aileron control linkage
39 Port navigation light
40 Pitot head
41 Automatic leading-edge slats
42 Port engine cowling

43 Electrical firing mechanism
44 Firewall
45 Spent cartridge ejector chutes
46 Four 30-mm Rheinmetall Borsig MK 108 cannon (100 rpg belt-fed ammunition for upper pair and 80 rpg for lower pair)
47 Cannon muzzles
48 Combat camera
49 Camera aperture
50 Nosewheel fairing
51 Nosewheel leg
52 Nosewheel
53 Torque scissors
54 Retraction jack

55 Hydraulic lines
56 Main nosewheel door (starboard)
57 Compressed air bottles
58 Forward auxiliary fuel tank (37 Imp gal/170 litre capacity)
59 Mainwheel well
60 Torque box
61 Main spar
62 Mainwheel leg pivot point
63 Mainwheel door
64 Mainwheel retraction rod
65 Engine support arch
66 Leading-edge slat structure
67 Auxiliaries gearbox
68 Annular oil tank
69 Riedel starter motor housing
70 Engine air intake
71 Hinged cowling section
72 Junkers Jumo 004B-2 axial-flow turbojet
73 Starboard mainwheel
74 Wing structure
75 Automatic leading-edge slats
76 Mainspar
77 Starboard navigation light
78 Frise-type ailerons
79 Trim tab
80 Flettner-type geared tab
81 Starboard outer flap section
82 Engine exhaust orifice
83 Engine support bearer
84 Starboard inner flap structure
85 Faired wing root

to the flight development of the Me 262 V1 during that summer, for indeed little priority was deemed necessary. Of far greater import for the Messerschmitt concern were the improvements to the Bf 109 and Bf 110 combat types, and the development of their replacements.

The engines for the Me 262 V1 eventually arrived from Spandau in mid-November 1941: these were BMW 003s each of 1,213-lb (550-kg) static thrust. But on this first flight with the BMW 003s Wendel suffered a double flame-out shortly after take-off, and was forced to put PC + UA down

---

Messerschmitt Me 262 variants

Me 262 V1: first prototype (PC + UA) with single Junkers Jumo 210G piston engine; later fitted with two BMW 003 turbojets
Me 262 V2: test airframe for fitment of two BMW 003 turbojets
Me 262 V3: test airframe (PC + UC) with two Junkers Jumo 004 turbojets; first prototype to be flown by service test pilots; fourth prototype
Me 262 V4: (PC + UD) of similar configuration
Me 262 V5: fitted with two Jumo 004s, this PC + UE differed in having a fixed nosewheel, whereas previous prototypes have conventional tail wheels
Me 262 V6: definitive prototype (VI + AA) with lighter Jumo 004B-1 turbojets, and retractable tricycle landing gear; the **Me 262 V7** (VI + AB) was similar but with redesigned cockpit canopy and cockpit pressurization; many subsequent *Versuchs* prototypes evolved for testing of engines, radio, radar, and weapons systems
Me 262A-0: pre-production airframes based on the Me 262 V7 configuration; 23 units produced, and passed to test-centre at Rechlin and to service trials detachment (EKdo 262) in late April 1944
Me 262A-1a: standard interceptor fighter configuration with twin Jumo 004B-1 turbojets, four Rheinmetall-Borsig MK 108A-3 30-mm cannon, Revi 16.B gunsight, and FuG 16zY radio; the **Me 262A-1a/U1** designation covered three trials units with two MG 151, two MK 103 and two Mk 108 cannon
Me 262A-2a: standard fighter-bomber configuration, similar to Me 262A-1a but with two Schloss 503A-1 bomb

racks for two 551-lb (250-kg) bombs, and armament normally reduced to two 30-mm MK 108 cannon; the **Me 262A-2a/U2** was a trials development with Lotfe 7H bomb-sight, glazed nose, and accommodation for prone bomb-aimer
Me 262A-3a: trials models intended for close-support role
Me 262A-5a: reconnaissance-fighter with either twin nose-mounted Rb 50/30 oblique cameras, or single Rb 20/30 or Rb 75/30; adapted to the reconnaissance role
Me 262A-1a/U3 was used by a number of units
Me 262B-1a: conversion trainer with dual flight controls under redesigned canopy; deletion of rear main fuel tank necessitated carriage of two 66-Imp gal (300-litre) drop-tanks on Schloss 503A-1 Wikingschiff racks
Me 262B-1a/U1: interim two-seat night-fighter with FuG 218 *Neptun V* airborne interception radar and FuG 350 ZC (*Naxos*) passive homer; fewer than a dozen in service by 1945
Me 262B-2a: definitive night-fighter with lengthened fuselage to contain additional fuel tanks; two produced
Me 262C-1a: point-defence interceptor fighter with twin Jumo 004B-1s supplemented by tail-mounted Walter RII-211/3 (HWK 509) bi-fuel rocket motor to give outstanding rates of climb; one trials aircraft produced
Me 262C-2b: point-defence interceptor; twin BMW 003R power units, each consisting of a BMW 003A turbojet and a BMW 718 bi-fuel rocket, fitted in place of conventional motors; one produced

---

with some damage. Fortunately, an alternative to the touchy BMWs was available. This was the Junkers Jumo 004 which had been developed by Dr Anselm Franz's team since its award of a contract as far back as July 1939 for a development specification. In their adherence to axial compressors, German engine designers showed much courage and foresight: this type of compressor was difficult to construct and balance, and was susceptible to vibration and could be damaged far more easily than the tough centrifugal type of compressor. But it became apparent that the acceleration rates, fuel efficiency, power output, and drag coefficients of axial-flow turbojets far exceeded the figures produced by the tougher, and sometimes more reliable, centrifugal types. By August 1941 the Jumo 004 was giving 1,323-lb (600-kg) static thrust, and many of the earlier problems had been cured.

Jumo 004s were installed on the Messerschmitt Me 262 V3 (PC + UC), and this aircraft, bereft of the piston engine and still with tailwheel landing gear, left Leipheim's runway on the morning of 18 July 1942 in Wendel's experienced hands. It looked correct in every way, and it flew beautifully, and henceforth the fortunes of the Messerschmitt Me 262 were to rise at the expense of its nearest rival, the Heinkel He 280, which suffered a series of setbacks until its eventual cancellation in March 1943.

In the Luftwaffe's interest

Service test pilots of the Erprobungsstelle (test establishment) at Rechlin showed interest in the Me 262 from its earliest days. It was largely at their instigation that Messerschmitt received contracts to produce a number of prototypes for weapons and engine tests. The experienced Major Wolfgang Späte had already reported his enthusiastic findings when the General der Jagdflieger, Adolf Galland, flew the Me 262 V4 on 22 May 1943, to become unequivocal in his constant praise for this revolutionary aircraft. At a conference in Berlin on 25 May it was suggested that the piston-engine Messerschmitt Me 209A be cancelled, and that all efforts be directed to the production of the Me 262: three days later a

production order for 100 was made. But other events now took a hand. On 17 August 1943 the US 8th Air Force's attack on Regensburg destroyed much of the embryonic Me 262 production lines, forcing Messerschmitt AG to move its jet development centres to Oberammergau, near the Bavarian Alps. The delay occasioned by the move was increased by a chronic shortage in the supply of skilled labour and production slipped by many months.

In the meantime the Me 262 V5 introduced the tricycle landing gear that was to become standard, only on this prototype the nose-gear was fixed. The definitive Me 262 V6 (Jumo 004Bs) flew on 17 October 1943: the VI + AA featured a retractable tricycle landing gear, gun bays and blast ports, the electrically operated tailplane, and the beautiful high-speed wing with automatic leading-edge slats and trailing-edge flaps.

Can it carry bombs?

By the autumn of 1943 Germany was on the defensive in the USSR and Italy, and was being subjected to furious aerial assault by day and by night: not least of Hitler's concerns was when and where the Allies would strike in north west Europe. During the amphibious invasions in North Africa, on Sicily, and recently of Italy at Salerno and Reggio, Allied air power had kept the Luftwaffe and the German naval forces at bay, and had thus prevented the loss of shipping that could have jeopardized the entire extent of these operations. Therefore nobody could have been surprised when

Aerial photograph of an Me 262A-1a of III Gruppe of Ergänzungs-Jagdgeschwader Nr 2 (III/EJG 2). This powerful conversion unit, based at Lechfeld, flew many sorties against Allied aircraft in the spring of 1945, with Leutnant Bell downing a P-38 Lightning with this particular aircraft on 21 March 1945. The EJG 2 was formed on 2 November 1944.

Messerschmitt Me 262A-2a Jagdbomber (Jabo) of 1./KG 51, based at Achmer in March 1945. By the spring of 1945 the Me 262s of I and II/KG 51 were operating energetically from airfields in the Rheine complex, with a predeliction for low-level skip-bombing attacks at dawn and dusk on the Allied front line.

many senior commanders, including Hitler himself, mooted the concept of the Messerschmitt Me 262 as a fighter-bomber as opposed to an interceptor: the idea was tactically sound. It was at Insterberg, in East Prussia, on 26 November 1943 that Hitler watched the dove-grey VI + AA being put through its party tricks by the able Gerd Linder. Present was Professor Willy Messerschmitt to answer the inevitable query from the fascinated Hitler: yes, indeed, the Me 262 could carry up to

In the quest for maximum rates of climb for point-defence work some Messerschmitt Me 262s were modified for development programmes with liquid-fuelled Walter rockets. Illustrated is the Me 262C-1a first flown by Gerd Linder on 27 February 1945. The type arrived too late to enter service, although Major Heinz Bär of III/EJG 2 claimed a P-47 in this Me 262C-1a in the spring of 1945.

2,205-lb (1,000-kg) of bombs with uncomplicated conversion work completed within two weeks per unit! So from this day the Messerschmitt Me 262 was destined to play a dual role: that of a fighter-bomber and that of a pure air-superiority fighter. Neither the role nor the aircraft could by now have had any influence on the outcome of the war. It was too late to start a major production scheme: oil and aviation kerosene, precious alloys, and skilled airframe and engine specialists were at a premium. The Messerschmitt Me 262 had been recognized in its full potential, but too late in the war.

In service

Service conversion of the Me 262 was placed under Hauptmann Werner Thierfelder's Erprobungskommando 262 at Lechfeld, to where the unit moved on 21 December 1943: pilots were drawn from 8. and 9./ZG 26. The EKdo 262 was given a batch of pre-production Me 262A-0 aircraft, and finally got into the swim of operations in the early summer of 1944. Thierfelder was killed in combat with 15th Air Force Mustangs over Bavaria on 18 July, and his place was taken by Hauptmann Neumeyer. The RAF brought back its first confirmation of the Me 262's existence on 25 July, when a de Havilland Mosquito of No. 544 (PR) Squadron was intercepted near Munich.

Messerschmitt Me 262A-2a of 1./KG 51, the 9K + FH (Nr 111625). Command of Kampfgeschwader Nr 51 came under Major Wolfgang Schenk in November 1944: during the summer of that year Schenk took his Kommando into action with Me 262s on the Normandy war front.

Equipped with Messerschmitt Me 262A-2a fighter-bombers, the Einsatzkommando Schenk (Major Wolfgang Schenk) was formed at Lechfeld in July, before posting to the Normandy invasion front: the unit was based at Châteaudun, Etampes and Creil, before pulling back to Juvincourt, near Reims, in late August. It was on 28 August 1944 that Allied fighter pilots downed the first ME 262 to be lost in combat. Operations by Einsatzkommando Schenk continued in a desultory manner until its incorporation into the I Gruppe of Kampfgeschwader Nr 51, which began combat operations from

Messerschmitt Me 262A-2a/U1 fighter-bomber of Erprobungskommando Schenk in the summer of 1944: this was the first Luftwaffe unit to take the Me 262 fighter-bomber into action. Normal bomb load was two SC250 (551-lb) bombs, but for attacks on troop positions and transports the Me 262 carried two AB250 containers.

Messerschmitt ME 262

Specification

Messerschmitt Me 262A-1a

Type: single seat air-superiority fighter

Powerplant: two Junkers Jumo 004B-1, -2, or -3 axial-flow turbojets each rated at 1,984-lb (900-kg) static thrust

Performance: maximum speed 514 mph (827 km/h) at sea level, 530 mph (852 km/h) at 9,845 ft (3000 m), 540 mph (869 km/h) at 19,685 ft (6000 m) and 532 mph (856 km/h) at 26,245 ft (8000 m); initial climb rate 3,937 ft (1200 m) per minute; service ceiling above 40,000 ft (12190 m); range 652 miles (1050 km) at 29,530 ft (9000 m)

Weights: empty 8,378 lb (3795 kg); empty equipped 9,742 lb (4413 kg); maximum take-off 14,080 lb (6387 kg)

Dimensions: span 40 ft 11½ in (12.50 m); length 34 ft 9½ in (10.58 m); height 12 ft 7 in (3.83 m); wing area 234 sq ft (21.73 m²)

Armament: four 30-mm Rheinmetall-Borsig MK 108A-3 cannon with 100 rounds per gun for the upper pair and 80 rounds per gun for the lower pair, and aimed with Revi 16.B gunsight or EZ.42 gyro-stabilized sight, plus provision for 12 R4M air-to-air rockets under each wing

Messerschmitt Me 262A-1a fighter in the colours of the 9.Staffel Jagdgeschwader Nr 7, based at Parchim in early 1945 under 1.Jagddivision of I Jagdkorps in the defence of the Reich. After capture at the end of the war this particular aircraft, Nr 500491, was given the code FE-111 by the technical branch of the USAAF for evaluation. In the course of 1979 the aircraft was stripped down, refurbished and rebuilt in over 6,000 hours of work, and placed on display at the National Air and Space Museum, Washington DC, where it remains to this day. The illustration accentuates the Me 262's sleek lines: the airframe alone, in particular the wing design, was considered by the Allies to be far ahead of their own attainments in the field of high-speed flight.

Rheine-Hopsten under Major Umrau in October 1944. The value of the Me 262 as a reconnaissance aircraft was soon recognized, and a few went to the Einsatzkommando Braunegg, and to Nahaufklärungsgruppen 1 and 6.

Hitler's firm insistence on the Messerschmitt Me 262 being the property of the General der Kampfflieger (Marienfeld) denied Galland the opportunity of forming the first fighter unit until September 1944. One of Germany's finest fighter pilots, Major Walter Nowotny, formed the Kommando Nowotny based at Achmer and Hesepe near Osnabrück, to fly its first mission against Allied bombers and fighters on 3 October 1944. The Messerschmitt Me 262A-1a (two Jumo

III Gruppe was formed from the survivors of Kommando Nowotny, while the I/JG 7 was later formed at Parchim. Four additional bomber units were formed on 30 January 1945: these were KG(J)6, KG(J)27, KG(J)54 and KG(J)55. Of these only I/KG(J)54 at Giebelstadt, II/KG (J) 54 at Kitzingen and III/KG(J)6 at Prague-Ruzyne played any part in operations. The only occasions on which Jagdgeschwader Nr 7 made any impact were during the battles of 18–21 March 1945 when, using Oranienburg and Parchim, a daily average of some 40

Many Messerschmitt Me 262s were captured by Soviet forces in Prague airfield complex in May 1945. Alias an Me 262A-1a, this Czechoslovakian Avia-assembled S-92 Turbina was operated by the 5th Fighter Squadron (5.stihaci letka) of the Czech air force in 1950–1. One Avia S-92, coded V-34, is now on display at the Narodni Technical Museum in Prague.

Third Messerschmitt Me 262 prototype. The Me 262V3 was the first prototype to fly on turbojet power alone, the date being 18 July 1942. It was transferred to the German Aviation Experimental Establishment (DVL) in April 1944 for high-speed flight testing, and written off on 12 September 1944 following damage in an air attack.

004B-1 turbojets) formed the establishment of around 30. The armament was exceptionally potent and consisted of four Rheinmetall-Borsig MK 108A-3 30-mm cannon; the pilot was protected by 9-mm back armour, and a 90-mm armour-glass windscreen. With a maximum speed of 531 mph (855 km/h) at 26,245 ft (8000 m), the Me 262A-1a could outrun anything that the Allies had in their inventory.

Kommando Nowotny disbanded shortly after the death of its leader on 8 November 1944. The potent jet, the presence of which thoroughly alarmed Allied intelligence in the West, continued to be used in penny packets on bombing attacks (with AB250 containers) on Allied front lines, reconnaissance missions, and an occasional foray against enemy fighters. In mid-November Oberst Johannes Steinhoff formed the nucleus of Jagdgeschwader Nr 7 at Brandenburg-Briest:

or more sorties was put up against American bombers. A new unguided air-to-air weapon, the R4M rocket, was used on Me 262A-1a fighters for the first time during these encounters. Final day operations fell to Generalleutnant Galland's Jagdverband 44 (JV 44) at München-Riem, to the aforementioned units, and to the night-fighting Messerschmitt Me 262B-1a/U1 aircraft of 10./NJG 11 at Burg.

Over the period March 1944 to 20 April 1945 the Luftwaffe took delivery of 1,433 Me 262s, but for the Allies the impact of this fine aircraft was largely psychological. After the war they acknowledged that in design the Messerschmitt Me 262 was years ahead of those of other nations, and its secrets permitted the Russians and the Anglo-Americans to accelerate development of jet fighter and bomber aircraft to the magic of Mach 1.0 and beyond over the ensuing years.

Boeing B-29 Superfortress

No other aircraft ever combined so many technological advances as the B-29. Designed for a specific strategic task, it later spawned the double-deck Stratocruiser airliner, the KC-97 tanker/cargo aircraft, the swollen Guppies and the entire lineage of modern heavy aircraft from the Soviet Tupolev bureau.

It is probable that a detailed analysis of the Soviet 'Blackjack' swing-wing bomber of the 1980s would unearth design features that can be traced right back to the B-29. And the Boeing B-29 Superfortress was started more than three years before the USA entered World War 2, in October 1938. In one of his last acts before he was killed in a crash at Burbank the US Army Air Corps Chief of Staff, General Oscar Westover, had officially established a requirement for a new super-bomber to succeed the Boeing B-17, at a time when the B-17 itself was being denied funds by the Congress. Despite totally negative reaction from the War Department, procurement chief General Oliver Echols never gave up in his fight to keep the super-bomber alive, and it had the backing of 'Hap' Arnold, Westover's successor. The bomber was to be pressurized to fly very fast at high altitude: the figures for

speed (390 mph/628 km/h), range (5,333 miles/8582 km) and military load were staggering.

At the Boeing Airplane Company in Seattle they did at least have experience of large pressurized aircraft, unlike all other companies, but there seemed no way to reconcile the conflicting factors. For most of 1939 the answer seemed to be to fit Pratt & Whitney's slim sleeve-valve liquid-cooled engines inside the wing, but newly hired George Schairer soon pointed out that as the biggest drag item was the wing, the best course was to make the wing as small as possible and not try to put engines inside it. (Thus began a basic philosophy which saw sharp contrast between the Boeing B-47 and the British V-bombers, and has continued to today's Boeing Models 757 and 767.) How does one pressurize a fuselage containing enormous bomb doors? The answer here was to make the colossal bomb bays unpressurized and link the front and rear pressure cabins by a sealed tunnel. Chief engineer Wellwood Beall was first to crawl through the mock-up tunnel in January 1940.

By March 1940 the demands had increased, including 16,000 lb (7258 kg) of bombs for short-range missions,

Dave's Dream was built as B-29-40-MO 44-27354, but it is pictured here with Major W. P. Swancutt in command heading for Bikini atoll on 1 July 1946, where the modified aircraft dropped the first post-war nuclear weapon. The 509th Composite Group named the aircraft for bombardier Dave Semple, killed in a B-29.

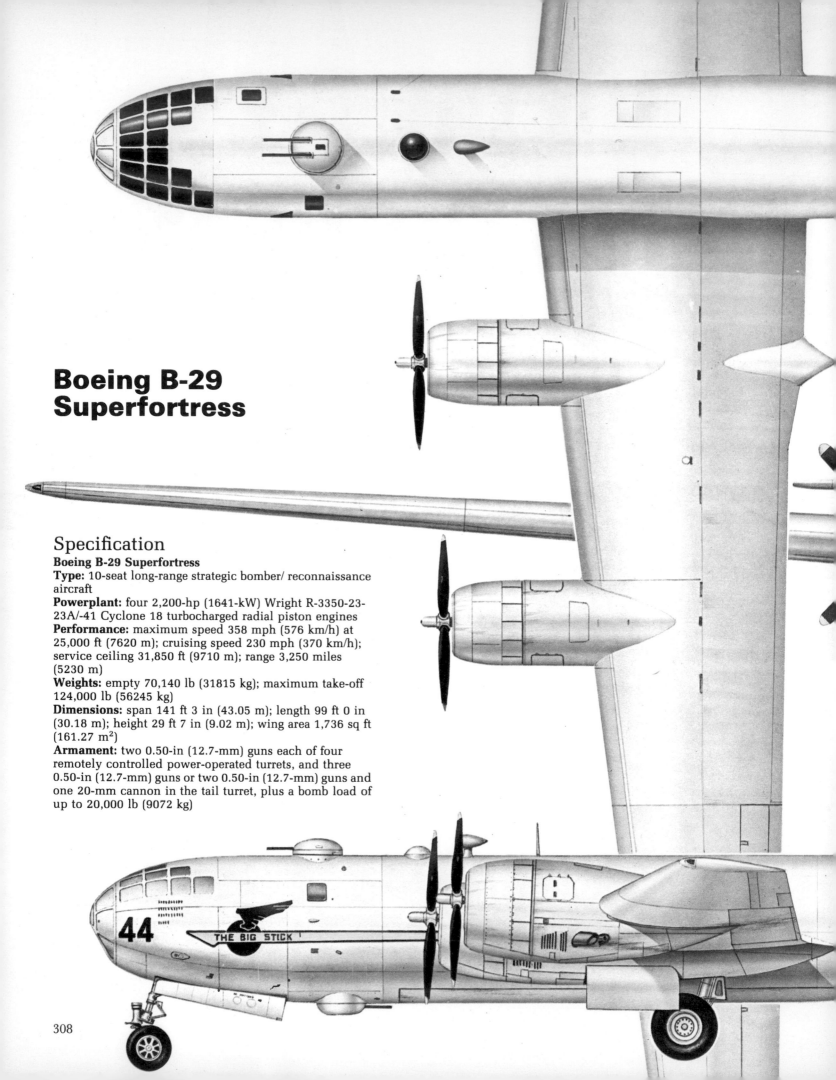

Boeing B-29 Superfortress

Specification

Boeing B-29 Superfortress

Type: 10-seat long-range strategic bomber/ reconnaissance aircraft

Powerplant: four 2,200-hp (1641-kW) Wright R-3350-23-23A/-41 Cyclone 18 turbocharged radial piston engines

Performance: maximum speed 358 mph (576 km/h) at 25,000 ft (7620 m); cruising speed 230 mph (370 km/h); service ceiling 31,850 ft (9710 m); range 3,250 miles (5230 m)

Weights: empty 70,140 lb (31815 kg); maximum take-off 124,000 lb (56245 kg)

Dimensions: span 141 ft 3 in (43.05 m); length 99 ft 0 in (30.18 m); height 29 ft 7 in (9.02 m); wing area 1,736 sq ft (161.27 m²)

Armament: two 0.50-in (12.7-mm) guns each of four remotely controlled power-operated turrets, and three 0.50-in (12.7-mm) guns or two 0.50-in (12.7-mm) guns and one 20-mm cannon in the tail turret, plus a bomb load of up to 20,000 lb (9072 kg)

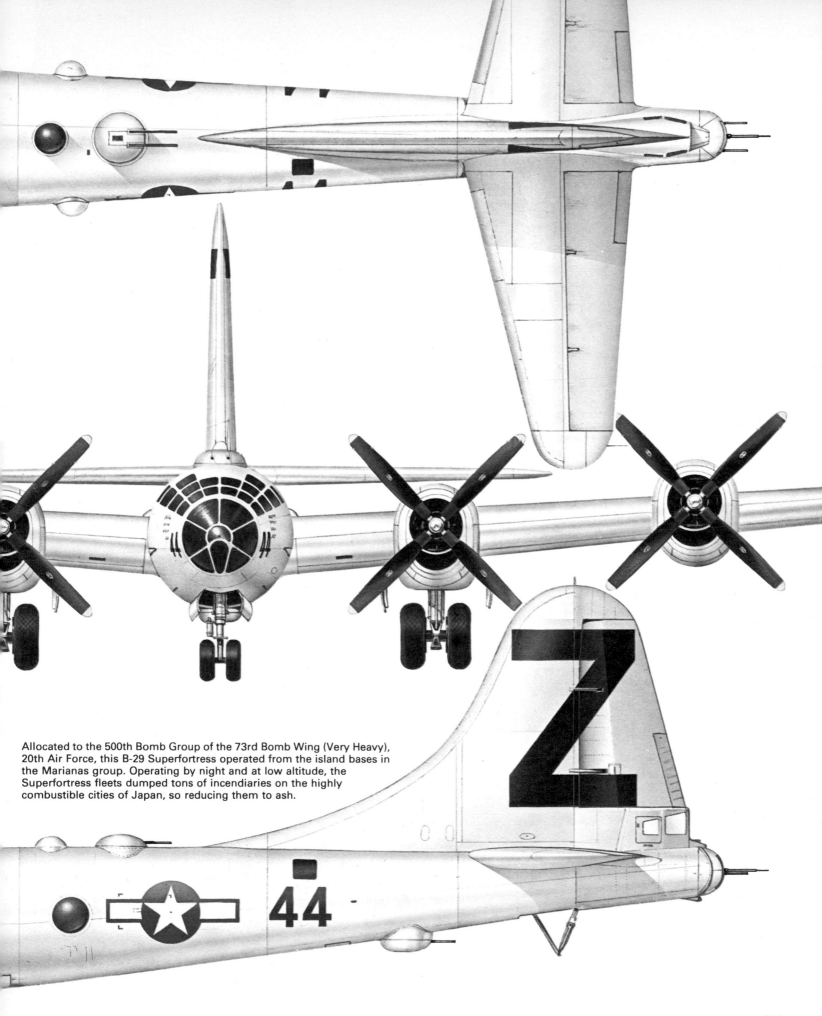

Allocated to the 500th Bomb Group of the 73rd Bomb Wing (Very Heavy), 20th Air Force, this B-29 Superfortress operated from the island bases in the Marianas group. Operating by night and at low altitude, the Superfortress fleets dumped tons of incendiaries on the highly combustible cities of Japan, so reducing them to ash.

Boeing B-29 Superfortress

The very first Superfortress was XB-29 no. 41-002, design of which took place in 1939-40, ready for a first flight on 21 September 1942. Olive-drab and grey, it had three-blade propellers, no defensive turret system and numerous details which were later altered, yet the basic airframe was almost identical to production B-29s.

powered turrets, and far more protection including armour and self-sealing tanks. Weight had already leapt in stages from 48,000 to 85,000 lb (21773 to 38556 kg), and with the fresh demands the design finally rounded out at a daunting 120,000 lb (54432 kg). With just 1,739 sq ft (161.55 m²) of wing, the wing loading was going to be 69 lb/sq ft (336.9 kg/m²), about double the figure universally taken in 1940 as the desirable limit. Test pilot Eddie Allen was happy that the Boeing Model 345 would be flyable (just) if it had the biggest and most powerful high-lift flaps ever thought of, to reduce take-off and landing speeds to about 160 mph (257 km/h), which was about double the equivalent speed of such familiar machines as the B-17 and Supermarine Spitfire. Structurally it meant the wing skins were going to be more than three times as thick as any seen before. Precision bolts

were going to be needed instead of rivets, yet every part of the exterior had to be smooth as glass, with no projections. Nobody knew yet how to make the remote-control gun turrets, or even the multi-ply tyres.

Funds from USAAC

As the BEF was rescued from the beaches at Dunkirk the new bomber was designated the B-29, and in August the US Army Air Corps provided funds for two (later three) prototypes. Work was rushed ahead, but nobody knew how to stop guns and propeller mechanisms from freezing at far over 30,000 ft (9145 m), which Boeing was confident the aircraft could reach. The intense wing loading was all

Boeing B-29 Superfortress cutaway drawing key

1. Temperature probe
2. Nose glazing
3. Optically flat bomb aiming panel
4. Bombsight
5. Windscreen panels
6. Forward gunsight
7. Bombardier's seat
8. Pilot's instrument console
9. Control column
10. Co-pilot's seat
11. Pilot's seat
12. Side console panel
13. Cockpit heating duct
14. Nose undercarriage leg strut
15. Steering control
16. Twin nosewheels
17. Retraction struts
18. Nosewheel doors
19. Underfloor control cable runs
20. Pilot's back armour
21. Flight engineers station
22. Forward upper gun turret, four 0.5-in (12.7-mm) machine-guns 500-rpg
23. Radio operator's station
24. Chart table
25. Navigator's instrument rack
26. Fire extinguisher bottle
27. Forward lower gun turret, two 0.5-in (12.7-mm) machine-guns, 500-rpg
28. Ventral aerial
29. Navigator's seat
30. Hydraulic system servicing point
31. Access ladder
32. Forward cabin rear pressure bulkhead

33. Armoured bulkhead
34. Pressurized tunnel connecting front and rear cabins
35. Astrodome observation hatch
36. Forward bomb racks
37. Bomb hoisting winches
38. Catwalk
39. Bomb rack mounting beam
40. Pressurized tunnel internal crawlway
41. D/F loop aerial
42. Radio communications aerials
43. Starboard main undercarriage wheel bay
44. Wing inboard fuel tanks, 1,415-US gal (5356 litres)
45. Starboard inner engine nacelle
46. Intercooler exhaust flap

Boeing B-29 variants

XB-29: Boeing Model 345 prototypes (41-002, 41-003 and 41-18335)
YB-29: service-test aircraft with armament (41-36954/36967); total 14
B-29: main production by BW (Boeing Wichita), BA (Bell Airplane) and MO (Martin Omaha); total 1,620 BW, 357 BA and 204 MO
B-29A: span 142 ft 3 in (43.36 m), R-3350-57 or -59 engines, and four-gun forward upper turret; built at Boeing Renton (BN); total 1,119
F-13A: conversions as strategic reconnaissance aircraft with large camera installations and long-range tanks; total 117
RB-29A: redesignation in 1948 of F-13A
TB-29A: conversions as crew trainers
ETB-29A: TB-29A modified for parasite attachments of F-84 jet fighters at wingtips (44-62093)
B-29B: R-3350-51 engines, defensive armament removed except tail turret; built by Bell (BA); total 311
EB-29B: conversion to launch XF-85 Goblin parasite jet from trapeze (44-84111)
B-29D: ex-XB-44, later became B-50
XB-29E: conversion to test different electronic defensive fire-control
B-29F: Arctic conversions of six aircraft
XB-29G: conversion (44-84043) to test experimental turbojets in pod extended below bomb bay
XB-29H: conversion of B-29A for different defensive armament
YB-29J: conversions (six) to test commercial R-3350 powerplants
RB-29J: conversions (two YB-29J) as multi-sensor reconnaissance aircraft; also called **FB-29J**
YKB-29J: conversions (two YB-29J) for tests of Boeing Flying Boom inflight-refuelling system
CB-29K: conversion to military cargo aircraft
B-29L: original designation of B-29MR
KB-29M: major programme of rebuilds as inflight-refuelling tankers (92) with British looped hose method
B-29MR: conversions (74) as receivers to link with inflight-refuelling hose
KB-29P: major programme of conversions (116) as inflight-refuelling tankers with Flying Boom for SAC
YKB-29T: single conversion of KB-29M (45-21734) as triple-point tanker
DB-29: various conversions as drone and target directors
GB-29: conversions to launch the XS-1, X-1, X-2 and X-3 supersonic research aircraft

QB-29: conversions to remotely piloted target vehicles
SB-29: conversions as ASR (air/sea rescue) platforms with British airborne lifeboat
WB-29: weather reconnaissance aircraft with various air sampling systems
XB-39: conversion of YB-29 with four Allison V-3420 double liquid-cooled engines
XB-44: conversion with 3,000-hp (2238-kW) Wasp Major R-4360-33 engines; became B-29D
P2B-1: conversions (four) for US Navy patrol duty, later rebuilt as **P2B-1S** radar picket (AEW) platforms
P2B-2S carrier aircraft for D-558-II Skyrocket, with one transferred to NACA for research
B-50A: production version of B-29D with new wing material, tall vertical tail and reversible propellers; total 79
TB-50A: conversions (11) as crew trainers
B-50B: increased gross weight and modified systems; total 45
EB-50B: conversion to test tandem ('bicycle') landing gear for B-47
RB-50B: conversions as strategic reconnaissance aircraft with 583-Imp gal (2650-litre) underwing tanks; total 44
YB-50C: planned prototype of next generation **B-54**; not completed
B-50D: definitive bomber with frameless nose, 583-Imp gal (2650-litre) underwing tanks, new forward upper turret etc; total 222
DB-50D: conversion to launch vehicles in Bell XB-63 Rascal programme
KB-50D: conversion as prototype of later tankers
TB-50D: conversions (11) as unarmed crew trainers
WB-50D: conversions (36) as weather reconnaissance platforms
RB-50E: conversions of RB-50B, new sensors; total 14
RB-50F: conversions (a different 14) with SHORAN navigation radar
RG-50G: conversions (15) with air/ground mapping radar, new navaids and B-50D-type radar
TB-50H: new-build programme of unarmed crew trainers; total 24
WB-50H: weather conversion of TB-50H
KB-50J: major conversion programme for inflight-refuelling tankers with Flight Refuelling A-12B hose drum unit at wingtips and in rear fuselage, plus extra tankage and new observation stations; rebuilds by Hayes Aircraft which then added 5,800-lb (2631-kg) thrust General Electric J47-23 booster jet pods under the outer wings; conversions of all RB-50E, RB-50F and RB-50G plus seven B-50D aircraft
KB-50K: conversions to KB-50J standard of all TB-50Hs

against the designers, but using four monster Wright R-3350 Duplex Cyclones, each with not one but two of General Electric's best turbochargers and driving 16 ft 7 in (5.05 m) Hamilton Standard four-blade propellers, the propulsion was equal to the task. The crew finally rounded out at 10, with the pilot and co-pilot riding in the extreme nose surrounded by Plexiglas windows with the bombardier between them, the navigator facing ahead behind the pilot, the flight engineer (often two) facing aft behind the co-pilot and the radio operator farther aft.

Behind this nose section were two giant bomb bays, from which an electric sequencing system released bombs alternately from front and rear to preserve the centre of gravity position. Between the two bays was a ring forming the structural heart of the aircraft and integral with the main wing box, the strongest aircraft part built up to that time.

On the wing were four monster nacelles, which Schairer showed to have less drag than engines buried in a bigger wing. After four main gears had been studied, a way was found to fold simple two-wheel gears into the inboard nacelles. Fowler flaps were screwed out electrically to add 21 per cent to area of the wing, fighting a wing loading which by September 1940 reached 71.9 lb/sq ft (351.1 kg/m²) and climbed to a frightening 81.1 lb/sq ft (396.0 kg/m²) by the time of the first combat mission.

Behind the wing the rear pressure cabin had three sighting stations linked to two upper and two lower turrets, each with twin 0.5-in (12.7-mm) machine-guns. The electric fire control was normally set so that the top station controlled either or both the upper turrets, the side stations the lower rear turret, and the bomardier the forward lower turret, but control could be overridden or switched (because gunners

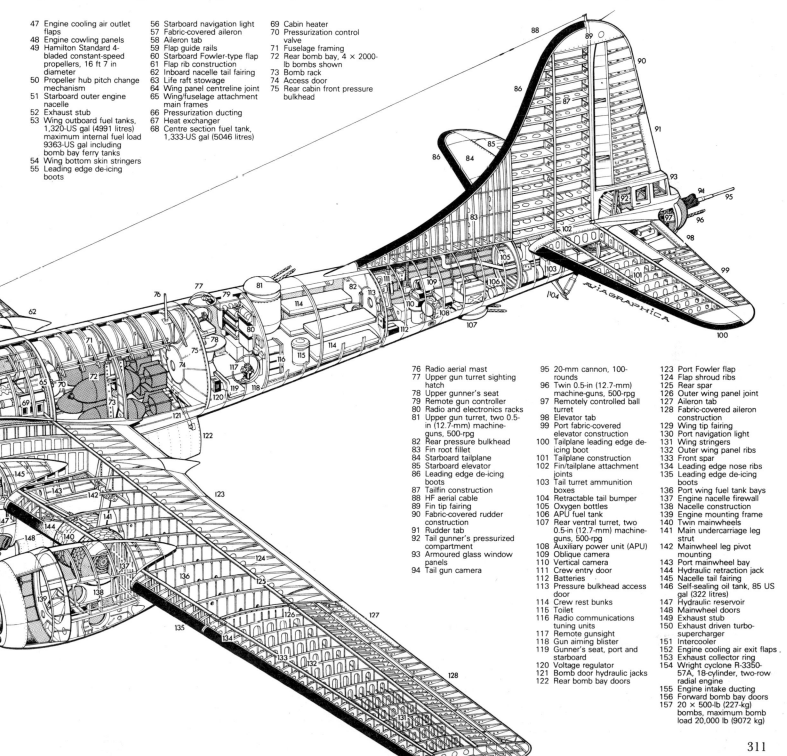

47 Engine cooling air outlet flaps
48 Engine cowling panels
49 Hamilton Standard 4-bladed constant-speed propellers, 16 ft 7 in diameter
50 Propeller hub pitch change mechanism
51 Starboard outer engine nacelle
52 Exhaust stub
53 Wing outboard fuel tanks, 1,320-US gal (4991 litres) maximum internal fuel load 9363-US gal including bomb bay ferry tanks
54 Wing bottom skin stringers
55 Leading edge de-icing boots
56 Starboard navigation light
57 Fabric-covered aileron
58 Aileron tab
59 Flap guide rails
60 Starboard Fowler-type flap
61 Flap rib construction
62 Inboard nacelle tail fairing
63 Life raft stowage
64 Wing panel centreline joint
65 Wing/fuselage attachment main frames
66 Pressurization ducting
67 Heat exchanger
68 Centre section fuel tank, 1,333-US gal (5046 litres)
69 Cabin heater
70 Pressurization control valve
71 Fuselage framing
72 Rear bomb bay, 4 × 2000-lb bombs shown
73 Bomb rack
74 Access door
75 Rear cabin front pressure bulkhead

76 Radio aerial mast
77 Upper gun turret sighting hatch
78 Upper gunner's seat
79 Remote gun controller
80 Radio and electronics racks
81 Upper gun turret, two 0.5-in (12.7-mm) machine-guns, 500-rpg
82 Rear pressure bulkhead
83 Fin root fillet
84 Starboard tailplane
85 Starboard elevator
86 Leading edge de-icing boots
87 Tailfin construction
88 HF aerial cable
89 Fin tip fairing
90 Fabric-covered rudder construction
91 Rudder tab
92 Tail gunner's pressurized compartment
93 Armoured glass window panels
94 Tail gun camera
95 20-mm cannon, 100-rounds
96 Twin 0.5-in (12.7-mm) machine-guns, 500-rpg
97 Remotely controlled ball turret
98 Elevator tab
99 Port fabric-covered elevator construction
100 Tailplane leading edge de-icing boot
101 Tailplane construction
102 Fin/tailplane attachment joints
103 Tail turret ammunition boxes
104 Retractable tail bumper
105 Oxygen bottles
106 APU fuel tank
107 Rear ventral turret, two 0.5-in (12.7-mm) machine-guns, 500-rpg
108 Auxiliary power unit (APU)
109 Oblique camera
110 Vertical camera
111 Crew entry door
112 Batteries
113 Pressure bulkhead access door
114 Crew rest bunks
115 Toilet
116 Radio communications tuning units
117 Remote gunsight
118 Gun aiming blister
119 Gunner's seat, port and starboard
120 Voltage regulator
121 Bomb door hydraulic jacks
122 Rear bomb bay doors
123 Port Fowler flap
124 Flap shroud ribs
125 Rear spar
126 Outer wing panel joint
127 Aileron tab
128 Fabric-covered aileron construction
129 Wing tip fairing
130 Port navigation light
131 Wing stringers
132 Outer wing panel ribs
133 Front spar
134 Leading edge nose ribs
135 Leading edge de-icing boots
136 Port wing fuel tank bays
137 Engine nacelle firewall
138 Nacelle construction
139 Engine mounting frame
140 Twin mainwheels
141 Main undercarriage leg strut
142 Mainwheel leg pivot mounting
143 Port mainwheel bay
144 Hydraulic retraction jack
145 Nacelle tail fairing
146 Self-sealing oil tank, 85 US gal (322 litres)
147 Hydraulic reservoir
148 Mainwheel doors
149 Exhaust stub
150 Exhaust driven turbo-supercharger
151 Intercooler
152 Engine cooling air exit flaps
153 Exhaust collector ring
154 Wright cyclone R-3350-57A, 18-cylinder, two-row radial engine
155 Engine intake ducting
156 Forward bomb bay doors
157 20 × 500-lb (227-kg) bombs, maximum bomb load 20,000 lb (9072 kg)

Boeing B-29 Superfortress

could be knocked out in action). In the extreme tail was another gunner driving a turret with two 0.5-in (12.7-mm) guns and a 20-mm cannon. Combat experience with B-17s in 1942 showed the need for more forward firepower and the upper forward turret was later replaced by a four-gun model, but this required a larger magazine which obstructed the interior.

In any case over 2,000 B-29s were to be built before this turret could come on production, because immediately after Pearl Harbor a colossal manufacturing programme was organized, involving vast new plants across the nation. Major parts were made in over 60 new factories, the enormous nacelles, each as big as a P-47, coming from a new Cleveland facility operated by the Fisher Body Division of General Motors. Final assembly was organized at three of the world's largest buildings, Boeing at Wichita, Martin at Omaha and Bell at Marietta (today the same building houses the Lockheed-Georgia Company). Later yet another line was set up at Boeing Renton. All this had been organized before the olive-drab XB-29 (41-002) had even flown, but from the first flight, on 21 September 1942 (initially using three-blade propellers), it was clear that the B-29 was going to be a winner. It could so easily have been what test pilots then called 'a dog'; and one of the firms delegated to build B-29s was convinced Boeing's figures were far too optimistic and that the whole programme was a giant mistake. What made the B-29, by 1942 named Superfortress, now vitally important was that it was obviously going to be the only aircraft with the range to attack Japan.

Incorporating the Boeing-designed 'flying boom' refuelling unit, the KB-29P was first delivered to SAC in March 1950. With it is shown a North American RB-45C Tornado. As can be seen, the air-refuelling tanker version had its armament removed, but an extra observation station was added at the rear.

Externally indistinguishable from the B-29, the Tupolev Tu-4 made its public debut at the 1947 Soviet Aviation Day held at Tushino, Moscow. This photograph of the original aircraft was taken in 1983 at Monino, which was closed to the public shortly afterwards.

To say that the good results of ship 41-002 were a relief would be an understatement. Far more money (three billion dollars) had been invested in the B-29 programme long before its wheels left the ground than in any other project in the history of any nation. At the same time the technical snags were severe, and multiplied. Many, such as power-plant fires and runaway propellers, were highly dangerous, and three months into the flight programme the prototypes had logged just 31 of the 180 hours scheduled. The low point in the programme was 18 February 1943 when Eddie Allen and his crew of 11, plus 19 meat-packers on the ground, were killed when blazing 41-002 just failed to make it to the runway. Underlying it all was the certain knowledge that the lost B-29 had ushered in a new capability in aviation.

Even when the Superfortresses trickled and then poured off the lines, they were so complex that nobody in uniform fully understood them. All went to a modification centre at Salina, Kansas, where over 9,900 faults in the first 175, urgently needed for the new 20th Bomb Wing, were bull-dozed right by a task force of 600 men in 'The Battle of Kansas'. Sheer manpower and the USA's mighty industrial power forced the obstacles out of the way, and the B-29s not only began racking up the hours but their baffled crews gradually learned how to manage them, how to fly straight and level in a goldfish bowl without continuously using instruments, and above all how to get something faintly resembling the published range with heavy bombloads. Air miles per pound of fuel were improved by exactly 100 per cent between January and March 1944. And the complex systems grew reliable in the ultra-cold of 33,000 ft (10060 m).

On 5 June 1944 the first combat mission was flown from Kharagpur, India, to Bangkok; the worst problem was an unexpected tropical storm. On 15 June the first of the raids on Japan was mounted, from Chengtu (one of many newly bulldozed B-29 strips in China) to the Yawata steelworks. The specially created 20th Air Force grew in muscle, and in October 1944 the first B-29s arrived on newly laid runways on the Marianas islands of Tinian, Saipan and Guam, just taken from the enemy. Swiftly the numbers grew as the mighty plants back home poured out B-29s and B-29As with 12 in (0.30 m) more span and the four-gun front turret, while Bell added 311 B-29Bs with all armament stripped except that in the tail, making a great difference in reduced weight

One of very few surviving pictures of 'parasiting', this photograph was taken during trials in 1949–51 to see if a bomber really could tow fighters over long ranges. ETB-29A-60 44-62093 was much more modified for Project Tom Tom, towing F-84D-1 Thunderjets 48-641 and 48-661. Another B-29 carried the XF-85 Goblin.

and complexity. The B-29B was made possible by the patchy fighter opposition, and many Superfortresses were similarly stripped in the field.

Moreover, the commander of the XXI Bomber Command, Major General Curtis LeMay, boldly decided to bomb Tokyo by night from low level, with a full load of incendiaries. There were many reasons for this, but the chief ones were that it promised much greater bombloads and the elimination of bombing errors attributable to jetstream winds. This policy, totally at variance with the idea of high-altitude day formations, resulted in the greatest firestorms the world has ever seen, and the biggest casualties ever caused by air attack. They were far greater than the 75,000 of Hiroshima, hit by the 20-kiloton 'Little Boy' atom bomb dropped on 6 August 1945 from Colonel Paul Tibbetts' B-29 *Enola Gay*, or the 35,000 of Nagasaki hit by the 20-kiloton 'Fat Man' dropped

with 583-Imp gal (2650-litre) underwing tanks), 222 of the definitive B-50D and finally 24 TB-50H crew trainers.

In the 1950s hundreds of B-29s kept flying, almost all modified for different roles but including 88 ordinary B-29 bombers handed to the RAF and used as the Boeing Washington by Bomber Command's Nos 15, 35, 44, 57, 90, 115, 149, and 207 Squadrons. In the USAF the jet-assisted KB-50J went on tanking until the last pair were struck off charge in Vietnam in 1963. But this is not really the end of the story.

Back in 1943 Josef Stalin began a major campaign to get B-29s. He never succeeded, and work began on a Soviet copy, though smaller and without the complex armament. Then out of the blue, on 29 July 1944, a B-29 made an emergency landing in the Soviet Union near Vladivostok after bombing Japan. Two more arrived later (one of them was the *General H. H. Arnold Special*, the 175th to be built

Together with Consolidated C-87s and other modified B-24s, the B-29 was pressed into service as a tanker to bring to Chinese B-29 airbases the fuel needed for the missions over Japan. Many were permanently modified as tankers, an example being B-29-1-BW 42-6242, one of the first production block, which served with the 486th BG.

Eighty-eight ex-USAAF B-29As were supplied to the RAF to meet the UK's long-range bombing requirements of the 1950s; the aircraft were known as 'Washingtons'. An aircraft of No. 90 Sqn based at Marham, Norfolk, is shown. This squadron won the Sassoon and Laurence Minot trophies for visual bombing and gunnery in 1952.

on 9 August from *Bock's Car*. The war ended five days later. Only by the incredibly bold decision to go into the biggest multi-company production programme ever organized long before the first flight did the B-29 manage to make so large a contribution to World War 2. By VJ-Day more than 2,000 were actually with combat crews, and though 5,000-plus were cancelled days later the manufacturing programme was slowed progressively, and did not close until May 1946, by which time 3,960 B-29s had been built. Hundreds were modified for different tasks, and many were launched on new careers as air/sea rescue aircraft, turbojet test-beds or tankers, which kept them busy for another decade or more. Back in 1942 Boeing had begun to work on the Model 367 transport version with a much larger upper lobe to a 'double bubble' fuselage, the first XC-97 flying on 15 November 1944. Various improved bomber versions were cancelled but the B-29D, with new engines, was continued and became the B-50.

A B-29A (42093845) was flown with the 28-cylinder Pratt & Whitney R-4360 Wasp Major engine in early 1944 as the XB-44 and the 3,000-hp (2238-kW) engine made such a difference that other changes were made, including a wing made of 75ST aluminium alloy giving much greater strength with 650 lb (295 kg) less weight, and a taller vertical tail. There were many systems changes, and the propellers were made reversible. The new bomber, the B-29D, went into production at Renton in July 1945. Manufacture continued, at a reduced pace, with the changed designation B-50. The first production B-50A finally emerged in June 1947, and Boeing built 79, followed by 45 strengthened B-50Bs (all but one being rebuilt as unarmed RB-50B reconnaissance aircraft

and picked out on the Wichita line by the USAAF chief of staff, who said 'This is the one I want as soon as you can build it; it will complete our first Bomb Group'), and within weeks they were all being carefully taken apart. In an operation without parallel, the Russian technicians studied every part of the B-29 to the extent of preparing their own production drawings, establishing material specifications, manufacturing tolerances and production procedures. The vast Tupolev bureau finally went into production, trying to short-cut some areas by buying tyres and brakes in the USA. These purchases did not succeed, but they did make the US government believe the previously incredible rumours of what the Soviets were doing.

First the Tupolev bureau built much simpler aircraft, the big-bodied Tu-70 and Tu-75 transports, both of which incorporated the complete wing and many other parts of the 'captured' B-29s. The Tu-70 flew on 27 November 1946. On Aviation Day, 3 August 1947, three Soviet copies of the B-29, designated Tu-4 by the VVS (air force), thundered over Moscow. They were followed by over 300 others. Like the B-29 four years earlier, the Tu-4 test programme in 1947-9 was marked by plenty of problems, but the Tu-4 eventually matured and not only comprised the core of a formidable nuclear strike force but, to a far greater extent than the B-29 itself, led to versions of much greater power and capability including the Tu-80 and Tu-85 which represented the all-time pinnacle of piston-engine bomber development to the traditional formula. Very considerable amounts of B-29 technology were carried straight across to the Tu-88 (Tu-16 'Badger') and Tu-95 (Tu-20 'Bear'), and small features can no doubt be distinguished in today's Tu-22M 'Backfire'.

This EC-121D, derived from the Super Constellation, is shown here patrolling over the Gulf of Tonkin in November 1969. It was used to monitor the skies over Vietnam and was intended as an early warning aircraft against Russian MiGs *(Photo: US Air Force)*.

Lockheed Constellation

Though it initially suffered from protracted technical problems, the 'Connie' became the best-loved piston-engine airliner of all, and, in its maker's words, was 'Queen of the Skies'. Finally, while commercial Connies were slowly rotting away, military examples of a dozen species were working unnoticed around the clock.

In its day the Lockheed Constellation was the biggest, most powerful and most expensive of all airliners. But it avoided joining the list of unsuccessful giants, because at first its capacity was not so great as to frighten the airlines. The 'Connie', as it was affectionately known, was made possible by the development of engines of great power, and this power was used for speed, and to lift fuel for long range while cruising in pressurized comfort at high altitude. Once the basic type was established, Lockheed met the demand for greater capacity by introducing one of the first and greatest of all 'stretching' programmes to yield the 'Super Connie', seating up to 100 or more.

But in 1938 this could not be foreseen. On 23 June of that year the McCarran Act had transformed US commercial aviation, and the manufacturing industry had rationalized into the same three names that dominate it today, Boeing, Douglas and Lockheed. The first two had already built the big four-engine DC-4 and pressurized Model 307 Stratoliner, but Lockheed was overloaded with small twins and the military Hudson and P-38, and its promising Excalibur remained a succession of mock-ups. This was tough, because Lockheed had a strong leaning towards powerful, fast aircraft, and had pioneered pressure cabins with the XC-35 flown in May 1937. Nothing much could be done until

suddenly on 9 June 1939 the company was visited by the famed Howard Hughes, who had secretly bought most of the stock of TWA, and Jack Frye, whom he had appointed president.

Hughes had lately given Lockheed a giant boost by flying a Model 14 airliner around the world in record time. TWA was in severe trouble with money and route competition, and Hughes urged the development of a new super-luxury transport that could fly nonstop coast-to-coast across the continental USA. The specifications sounded out of this world (empty weight 52,300 lb/24132 kg, four 2,200-hp/1641-kW engines, cruising speed over 300 mph/483 km/h and the ability to fly from New York to London nonstop), and all Lockheed's rivals gave Hughes a thumbs-down. But Lockheed's Bob Gross called in his top designers, Hall L. Hibbard and Clarence L. 'Kelly' Johnson, and said 'Come up with something'. Long meetings were held at a secret Hughes place on Romaine Street, Hollywood, and before the end of

Known to Lockheed as the Model 749-79-38, the C-121A was a properly designed military transport, the C-69s having mainly been converted airliners. USAF No. 48-616 is seen here in MATS (Military Air Transport Service) markings, flying as a PC-121A passenger aircraft. Engines were 2,500-hp (1864-kW) R-3350-75 Duplex Cyclones.

US Army Air Force no. 42-94553 was a Model 049-39-10, ordered pre-war by TWA but built as a C-69-5. It is shown in May 1946 finish without olive-drab paint, and with the 'buzz number' CM-553. Later it was struck off the Army strength and sold to TWA, with civil registration N52414. All early models had circular porthole-type windows.

HI-328, registered to Aerolineas Argo SA of the Dominican Republic. An L-749A, she served with several operators before going to Dominica, which was a final stronghold of old Connies until Argo – an all-cargo airline – ceased flying in 1983.

the year a formal meeting took place at which Hughes asked the price and was told $425,000. He rocked back and forth like an Indian at a pow-wow and said 'Hell, TWA can't pay, the damn airline's broke. Go ahead and build 40, I'll have to pay for them myself.'

C-69 for the US Army

Wartime pressures delayed the Model 49 Constellation, but eventually Lockheed hired pilot Eddie Allen to take the first one aloft on 9 January 1943. No commercial production was allowed after Pearl Harbor, and TWA's idea of a commercial lead with a super dream-ship evaporated as PanAm came in alongside; and in the event all production went to the US Army. But even in olive drab the C-69, as it was now called, was quite something. Its wing was a scaled-up version of the wing of the P-38, with giant area-increasing Fowler flaps. The fuselage was curved like the body of a fish and ended in a triple tail. The circular-section cabin seated 64 passengers, though Hughes was bemused that the US Army could take out all the luxury and still contrive to make the C-69 heavier than the Model 49. All flight-control surfaces were hydraulically boosted. Not least, the height of the Constellation off the ground was unprecedented. In two respects, however, the civil registered NX67900, or Lockheed ship no. 1961, was conventional: it had normal cockpit windows instead of once-planned perfectly streamlined nose, and the engines were also fairly conventional instead of being in perfectly streamlined nacelles with reverse-flow cooling from inlets in the leading edges.

During the war the USAAF received 22 Constellations, comprising nine ex-TWA and 13 of a contract for 180 signed in 1942. At VJ-Day the military contract was cancelled. Lockheed shut down the Burbank plant for five days to plan its future. It almost decided to start again with an even newer Constellation, but finally elected to buy back surplus govern-ment tooling, parts, materials and unfinished C-69s. This resulted in the commercial Model 049 having an 18-month lead over the DC-6 and Stratocruiser, and even more over the Republic Rainbow, and within nine days 103 Constellations valued at $75.5 million had been ordered by eight airlines. TWA at last got the first of 27 Model 049s in November 1945. CAA certification followed on 11 December. Commercial services followed in early February 1946, TWA flying the New York–Paris and PanAm the New York–Bermuda routes.

The USAAF sold its surplus C-69s to airlines in 1946, and the in-service record built up so fast that by July 1946 over 200 million passenger miles had been flown without anyone suffering injury. This was despite numerous engine fires and both engine and propeller failures, but on 11 July 1946 a TWA training flight crashed at Reading, Pennsylvania, because the pilots could not see from the smoke-filled cockpit. A six-week grounding followed, in which 95 modi-fications were made to the powerplant and systems. There was light at the end of the tunnel (and the DC-6 and other rivals were grounded too): on 19 October 1946 the first definitive post-war Model 649 took the air, so luxurious and with such good air-conditioning and soundproofing it was called the 'Gold Plate Connie'. Eastern worked on the speci-fication and was first to use it, one of its features being a Speedpak external cargo pod under the belly.

Post-war civil success

Ten airlines then bought nearly 100 Model 749s in which 2,700-hp (2014-kW) engines enabled gross weight to rise to 102,000 lb (46267 kg), with a long-range tank in each outer wing to give an extension of range of 1,000 miles (1609 km) without any reduction in payload. Payload/range was further enhanced by the Model 749A at 107,000 lb (48535 kg), with Curtiss paddle-blade propellers. The USAAF (now the USAF) again adopted the Constellation, buying 10 Model

This historic photograph was taken at Burbank on 9 January 1943 when the very first Constellation, painted in US Army olive drab, took off for the first time. It was to suffer its fair share of technical problems, but it opened up a new plateau in air transport range, speed and comfort.

The final variant of the Super Constellation was the L-1049H, which featured a mixed passenger/cargo configuration. The speed and ease of conversion from one role to the other was a prime requirement of this last variant of the 'Queen of the Skies'.

KLM Royal Dutch Airlines was one of the first operators of the Turbo-Compound engined L-1049C, which was placed in use on the North Atlantic in August 1953. Just a year later KLM took delivery of this tip-tanked L-1049G, PH-LKE, which could fly the Amsterdam–New York route much better with less frequent stops for refuelling.

With a maximum range of 4020 miles (6469 km), uprated Wright TC-18-DA3 Turbo-Compound engines and an increased cabin length of 56 ft (17.06 m), the L-1049G proved the most successful Super Constellation model in sales terms. Shown here is Lufthansa's D-ALUB. The airline flew its first intercontinental service from Hamburg to New York on 8 June 1955.

749s as C-121s of various sub-types, two of which were General MacArthur's *Bataan* and General Eisenhower's *Columbine*. Later another of this batch (48-610) was used as *Columbine II* when Eisenhower became President. The US Navy, which in 1945 had used two R7O-1 transports off the US Army line, purchased two Model 749s as its first dedicated radar picket (AEW) aircraft, initially designated PO-1W and later WV-1. Initially flown in June 1949, these were the first aircraft in the world bought from the start as high-flying radar stations, if one discounts modified single-engine Grumman TBM-3 Avengers. Their giant radars were served by aerials (antennae) above and below, but despite the grotesque appearance the addition of extra height to the fins resulted in a very tractable aircraft, and the success of these first two examples led to massive orders of no fewer than 27 distinct subsequent versions for various electronic purposes.

The unexpected USAF and USN sales helped carry the commercial line through a bad patch, and spurred Lockheed into the striking 'stretch' which turned the Constellation into the Model 1049 Super Constellation. By 1950 the whole programme, under Carl M. Haddon, was poised for its second generation, backed by Lockheed Aircraft Service which had begun at Idlewild in 1949 spurred by the Berlin Airlift, in which C-121s flew almost six million passenger miles from Westover AFB to Rhein-Main. But the big news was the L-1049, in which Hibberd injected rational sense with a straight passenger tube of constant section, it having been realized that an airliner in which the body section varied continuously was a mistake.

The first L-1049, the old no. 1961 rebuilt, flew on 13 October 1950. There were many minor changes, but the most obvious one apart from the 18 ft 4 in (5.59 m) extra length was the switch from port-holes to rounded square windows, removing what had become another outdated feature despite the better fatigue resistance of rings to squares. TWA was behind the Super Constellation, though it was pipped to the post by Eastern which got the new transport, able to seat 99, on the Miami run on 15 December 1951. The largely new engine installations worked well, as did the improved de-icing systems and the larger cockpit windows, integrally stiffened wing skins machined in the newly opened 'Hall of Giants' at Burbank, and better environmental systems.

The L-1049B was a cargo model with integrally stiffened floor and two large loading doors. Lockheed was requested by the US Navy to switch to the complex new Wright Turbo-Compound engine derived from the existing R-3350 used in all previous Constellations, and the 3,250 hp (2425 kW) available from each engine not only promised more speed but also a jump in gross weight to 133,000 lb (60329 kg), representing a further great advance in payload/range. Though the Turbo-Compound engine predictably took a long time to mature, it also totally removed the slight sluggishness which

One of the last European airlines to continue flying the Super-G was Iberia, the national airline of Spain (though it withdrew them long before its last cargo DC-4!). EC-AMP is shown on test near Burbank prior to delivery in 1956. One can almost imagine the deep rumble of those Turbo-Compound engines and mighty propellers!

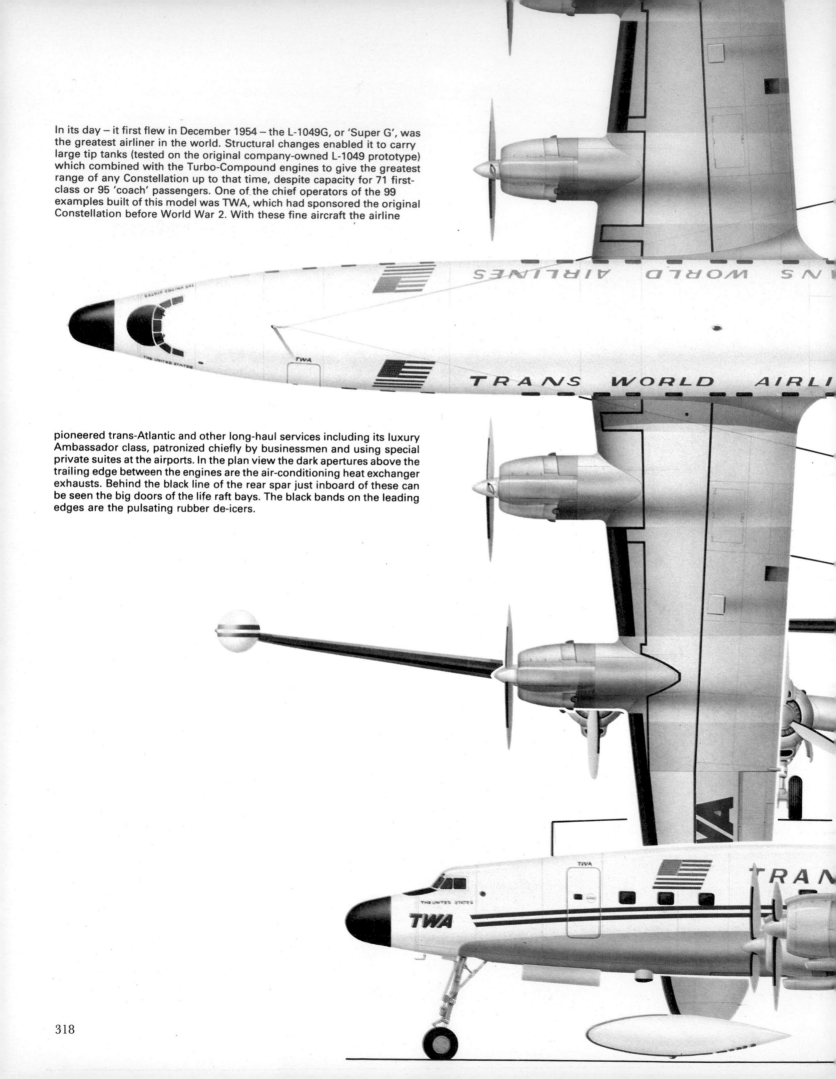

In its day – it first flew in December 1954 – the L-1049G, or 'Super G', was the greatest airliner in the world. Structural changes enabled it to carry large tip tanks (tested on the original company-owned L-1049 prototype) which combined with the Turbo-Compound engines to give the greatest range of any Constellation up to that time, despite capacity for 71 first-class or 95 'coach' passengers. One of the chief operators of the 99 examples built of this model was TWA, which had sponsored the original Constellation before World War 2. With these fine aircraft the airline

pioneered trans-Atlantic and other long-haul services including its luxury Ambassador class, patronized chiefly by businessmen and using special private suites at the airports. In the plan view the dark apertures above the trailing edge between the engines are the air-conditioning heat exchanger exhausts. Behind the black line of the rear spar just inboard of these can be seen the big doors of the life raft bays. The black bands on the leading edges are the pulsating rubber de-icers.

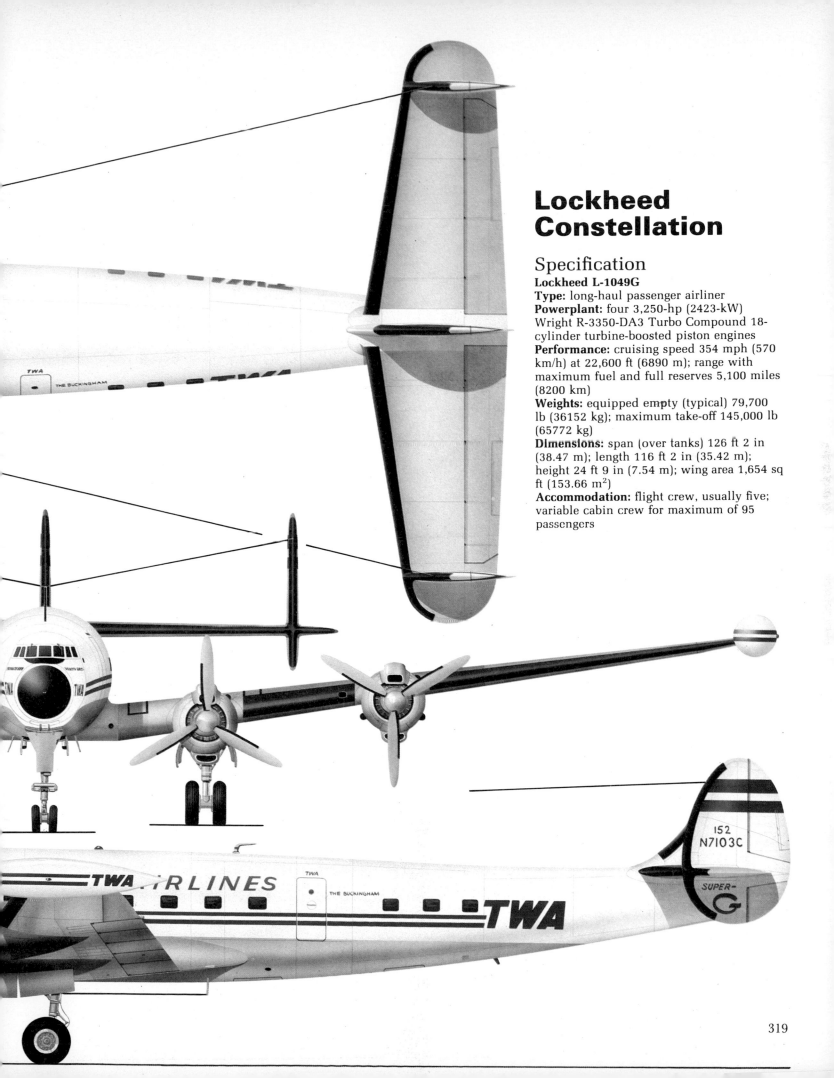

Lockheed Constellation

Specification

Lockheed L-1049G

Type: long-haul passenger airliner

Powerplant: four 3,250-hp (2423-kW) Wright R-3350-DA3 Turbo Compound 18-cylinder turbine-boosted piston engines

Performance: cruising speed 354 mph (570 km/h) at 22,600 ft (6890 m); range with maximum fuel and full reserves 5,100 miles (8200 km)

Weights: equipped empty (typical) 79,700 lb (36152 kg); maximum take-off 145,000 lb (65772 kg)

Dimensions: span (over tanks) 126 ft 2 in (38.47 m); length 116 ft 2 in (35.42 m); height 24 ft 9 in (7.54 m); wing area 1,654 sq ft (153.66 m²)

Accommodation: flight crew, usually five; variable cabin crew for maximum of 95 passengers

had crept into the original Model 1049, which cruised at barely 300 mph (483 km/h). In addition to 57 US Navy R7V-1s, of which 32 were transferred to the USAF as C-121Gs, Lockheed sold 33 C-121Cs to the USAF. The C121C was cleared to 135,000 lb (61236 kg), and the others introduced the uprated 3,500-hp (2611-kW) R-3350-34 engine and could take off at 145,000 lb (65772 kg). Subsequently the USAF and US Navy variants of the Model 1049 far outnumbered the commercial versions, as the variants list shows.

Comfort and capability

Seaboard & Western bought a commercial version of the Model 1049B, but the passenger version was the Model 1049C, first put into service by KLM on the New York–Amsterdam route in August 1953. Increasingly the airliner models were fitted with weather radar, which added 3 ft (0.91 m) to the length, as in the military variants. This helped improve passenger comfort, especially on US coast-to-coast trips, and such was the capability of the Model 1049C that from 19 October 1953 TWA at last opened a nonstop service between Los Angeles and New York, rival-ling that opened by American with the similarly powered DC-7. This was a time when the British de Havilland Comet was blazing the trail of the airline jet. The Constellation's Mach 0.58 was less impressive, but history was to show that the US industry, greatly aided by the unfortunate collapse of the original Comet programme, was able to fend off this new competition with its fundamentally old generation piston-engine machines, with the Model 1049 in the forefront. Unit price, typically $1 million for a Model 749, rose to $1.25m with the first Model 1049s, and more than doubled with later Model 1049 versions.

The Model 1049D was an improved cargo aircraft, and the Model 1049E a corresponding passenger version, but most Model 1049E aircraft were actually completed as Model 1049Gs, which were among the most important of all commercial versions. Improved climb ratings from the R-3350-DA3 Turbo-Compound enabled gross weight to reach 137,500 lb (62370 kg), which among other things enabled 600-US gal (2271-litre) tip tanks to be added. The Model 1049G entered service with Northwest in January 1955. A convertible passenger/cargo model was the Model 1049H, of which 54 were built. The very last Constellation was an L-1049H delivered in November 1958.

Piston-engine pinnacle

Before then, one final model had been designed, flown and built in quantity; but the quantity was small, and this was the only version to prove unprofitable to Lockheed, because its development cost over $60 million. The model 1649A Starliner was launched in 1954 to meet the severe comp-etition of the DC-7C Seven Seas on ultra-long routes, especially the nonstop North Atlantic services. No Model 1049 was really a nonstop Atlantic aircraft (certainly not westbound)

and TWA for the last time decided to push Lockheed into a further development of what had by this time become an old aeroplane. In going for long range Lockheed capitalized on the one thing the Super Constellation could offer in comp-etition with the new Comet 3: lower fuel consumption, though of course it was 115/145 grade gasoline. Fitting Turbo-Compounds had inevitably resulted in severe noise and vibration in an airframe originally planned for about half this power, and it was ultimately decided to out-do Douglas by designing a totally new wing, of great span and high aspect ratio, which would give unrivalled cruising efficiency, house more fuel and enable the engines to be moved well away from the fuselage to reduce noise and propeller vibration.

The Model 1649A first flew on 10 October 1956. It was a beautiful aircraft, and can be regarded as the final pinnacle

Acting as relay stations for signals from ground sensors in Project 'Igloo White', 30 ex-USN EC-121Ks and EC-121Ps proved invaluable to the US Air Force's intelligence operations during the Vietnam war.

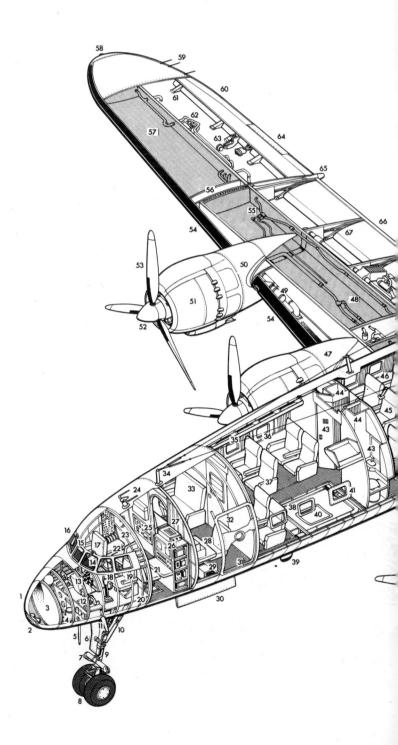

This Lockheed L-1049G served for 10 years from 1955 with Air India as VT-DJX on the airline's trunk routes. Eight Super-Gs were then passed on to the Indian Air Force, where for a further decade they flew not only transport but also maritime reconnaissance missions with No. 6 Sqn. Radar was retained, but the tip tanks were removed.

Lockheed L-1049C Super Constellation cutaway drawing key

1 Nose cone
2 Landing and taxiing lamps
3 Front pressure bulkhead
4 Hydraulic brake accumulator
5 Radio mast
6 Nosewheel leg door
7 Steering jacks
8 Twin nosewheels
9 Nosewheel leg strut
10 Retraction linkages
11 Pitot tube mast
12 Rudder pedals
13 Instrument panel
14 Instrument panel shroud
15 Windscreen wipers
16 Windscreen panels
17 Co-pilot's seat
18 Control column
19 Pilot's seat
20 Flight deck floor level
21 Radio operator's station
22 Flight engineer's station
23 Starboard crew door
24 VOR aerial
25 Engineer's instrument panel
26 Radio racks
27 Cockpit bulkhead
28 Navigator's chart table
29 Underfloor battery bay
30 Nosewheel doors
31 Forward entry door
32 Cabin bulkhead
33 Crew rest area

34 Radio aerial mast
35 Overhead luggage racks
36 Starboard emergency exit window
37 Forward cabin seating
38 Forward underfloor freight hold, total freight hold volume 728 cu ft (20.61 m³)
39 Radio altimeter
40 Ventral freight door
41 Port emergency exit windows
42 Ventral ADF sense aerial
43 Toilet compartments, port and starboard
44 Wardrobes
45 Main cabin four-abreast seating
46 Cabin wall trim panels
47 Starboard inner engine nacelle

48 Starboard wing integral fuel tank, total fuel capacity 6,550 US gal (24760 litres)
49 Supercharger oil cooler
50 Starboard outer engine nacelle
51 Detachable engine cowling panels
52 Spinner

53 Hamilton Standard three-bladed propeller
54 Leading edge de-icing boots
55 Fuel system piping
56 Outer wing panel joint rib
57 Outboard integral fuel tank
58 Starboard navigation light
59 Static dischargers
60 Starboard aileron
61 Aileron balance weights
62 Fuel venting system piping
63 Aileron control hydraulic booster
64 Aileron tab
65 Fuel jettison pipe
66 Starboard Fowler-type flap
67 Flap guide rails
68 Starboard air conditioning plant

69 Fuselage centre section construction
70 Wing/fuselage attachment main frames
71 Centre section bag-type fuel tanks
72 Central flap control motor
73 Cabin floor panels
74 Fresh-air distribution ducting

75 Air conditioning system overhead ducting
76 Heating system overhead ducting
77 Cabin roof air distribution duct
78 Cabin partition
79 Lounge area
80 VHF aerial
81 Galley
82 Wardrobe
83 Aft cabin seating
84 Fuselage frame and stringer construction
85 Cabin attendants' folding seats
86 Wardrobes, port and starboard
87 Port and starboard washrooms
88 Cabin pressurization valves
89 Rear pressure bulkhead
90 Tailcone construction
91 Elevator mass balance weight
92 Fin/tailplane fillets
93 Starboard tailplane
94 Rudder control rods
95 Leading edge de-icing boots
96 Starboard fin
97 Fabric-covered rudder

98 Rudder trim tab
99 Lower rudder segment
100 Starboard elevator
101 Elevator trim tab
102 Centre fin construction
103 Centre rudder
104 Tail navigation light
105 Port elevator construction
106 Elevator tab
107 Port fin construction
108 Static dischargers
109 Port rudder construction
110 Tailplane tip fairing
111 Leading edge de-icing boots
112 Tailplane construction
113 Rudder and elevator hydraulic boosters
114 Tailplane attachment frame
115 HF aerial cable
116 Aft toilet compartments port and starboard
117 Rear underfloor freight hold
118 Rear cabin emergency exit window
119 Ladder stowage
120 Passenger entry door
121 Entry lobby
122 Folding table
123 Wing root fillet construction
124 Cabin heater unit
125 Port flap shroud panels
126 Life raft stowage bays
127 Port air conditioning plant
128 Heat exchange air exhaust ducts
129 Port Fowler-type flap

130 Flap shroud ribs
131 Fuel jettison pipe
132 Aileron tab
133 Port aileron construction
134 Static dischargers
135 Wing tip construction
136 Port navigation light
137 Leading edge de-icing boots
138 Port outboard fuel tank bay
139 Outer wing panel main spar
140 Outer wing panel joint rib
141 Rear spar
142 Wing rib construction
143 Engine nacelle construction
144 Air conditioning system turbine
145 Oil cooler air duct
146 Oil cooler
147 Engine mounting ring
148 Carburettor intake duct fairing
149 Twin mainwheels
150 Leading edge nose ribs
151 Front spar
152 Wing stringer construction
153 Main undercarriage leg strut
154 Retraction linkage
155 Main undercarriage wheel well
156 Mainwheel doors
157 Engine firewall
158 Exhaust collector ring
159 Wright R-3350-DA1 Turbo-Compound, 18-cylinder two-row radial engine
160 Propeller hub pitch change mechanism
161 Hamilton Standard three-bladed propeller
162 Carburettor intake duct
163 Engine oil tank
164 Main undercarriage mounting ribs
165 Inner wing integral fuel tank
166 Leading edge construction
167 Hydraulic reservoir
168 Cabin fresh air intake

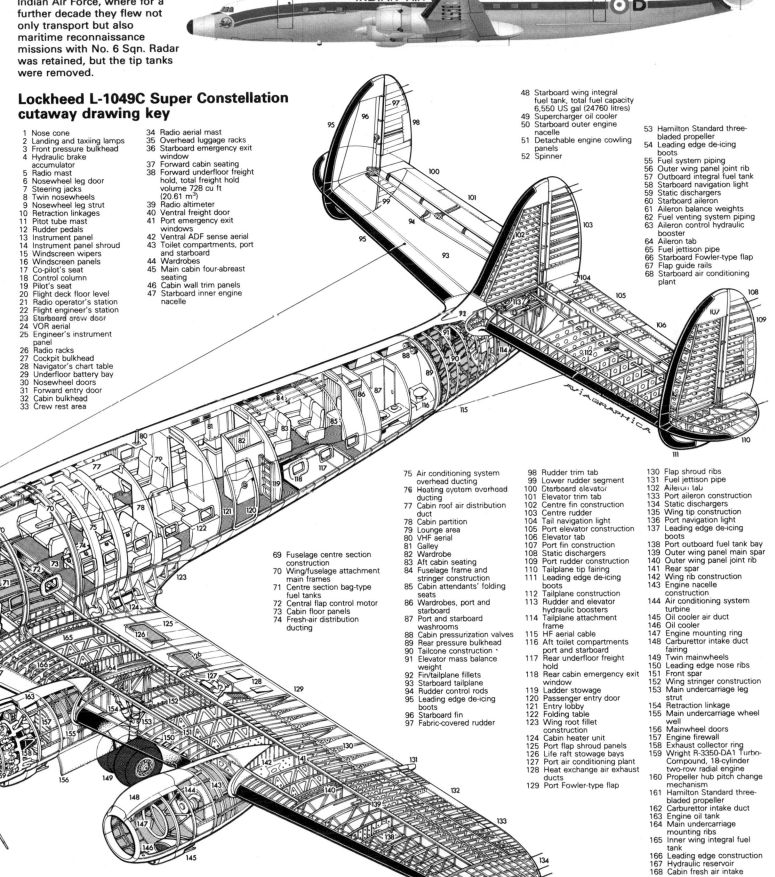

The first modern airborne early-warning aircraft to fly, with rotating rotodome-type aerial arrays, was this WV-2E of the US Navy first flown in 1956, with the new AN/APS-82 surveillance radar. In 1962 it was redesignated EC-121L, by which time several other rotodome-equipped C-121s were flying. They led to today's Boeing E-3A Sentry.

reached by the piston-engine airliner. The wing box, which had acute dihedral from the roots, was wholly skinned in gigantic machined planks. The body was slightly stretched, and the redesigned nacelles housed the most powerful civil piston engines ever used, driving Hamilton Standard three-blade propellers with synchrophasers to keep their speeds exactly synchronized. TWA, which called the Model 1649 the Jetstream, began services on the North Atlantic on 1 June 1957, but by then the jet era was only weeks away and at last the old Constellation had begun to lose its once powerful appeal. Only 44 of this vastly improved final version were sold, and all were withdrawn in the 1960s while basically older models kept at work, several occasionally trucking odd cargoes around the Caribbean and Dominica.

Far more important in the post-1960 era was the profusion of technically intriguing military versions, packed with unusual devices mainly of an electronic nature, which thundered faithfully all over the globe until 1980 despite concerted efforts made from 1975 to eliminate everything calling for 115/145 gasoline. In the 1960s Super Constellations of the USAF and the US Navy flew more than 600,000 hours, though by this time the basic type ceased to appear in books

on US military aircraft. Total production of all Constellation models was 856 (one XC-69, 233 Constellations, 578 Super Constellations and 44 Starliners).

On 15 April 1969 a US Navy Connie piloted by Lieutenant Commander James Overstreet was attacked by two North Korean MiG-17 fighters over the Sea of Japan and shot down. The loss of EC-121M no. 135749 from electronics squadron VQ-1, and of all 31 American crew members – the only loss in anger of a US military Constellation – highlights the special role of this aircraft type in reconnaissance, intelligence-gathering, and airborne early warning (AEW).

This role was first undertaken when the ubiquitous old 1961 was converted – again! – by Lockheed/Burbank for trials as an AEW platform. Modifications to accommodate radar and other gear gave the Connie a tall, narrow dorsal hump and a large under-fuselage bulge. This configuration was first seen operationally on the US Navy's PO-1W and PO-2W (later designated WV-1 and WV-2) weather-reconnaissance and AEW machines based respectively on the 749 and 1049 airliners.

Later, other duties were added to the AEW role, including electronic eavesdropping and countermeasures. The variety of humps, bumps and bulges protruding from various 'spook' Connies in the C-121 series became, itself, an encyclopedia-length subject. A one-off variant, the WV-2E, later called EC-121L, carried its antenna in a saucer-like disc evocative of today's Boeing E-3A Sentry.

In these Constellations, large crews could journey for up to 30 hours far from the Fleet or from shore, relief crews replacing each other while searching for air or sea threats. Initially, with the purpose of extending the range of ground and ship radars, USAF Constellations were used off American coasts by the Air Defense Command. In Vietnam, under the 'College Eye' programme, USAF Constellations stood off the enemy coast and reported MiG activity to endangered US combat pilots. In South Vietnam, the USAF's EC-121R, camouflaged and devoid of bulges, copied enemy radio transmissions for Intelligence. More than a dozen designations were eventually applied to 'spook' Connies (see Variants list), and today one of the most beautiful of these preserved machines is the US Navy's EC-121K no. 141292, from squadron VAQ-33, on display at the Air and Space Museum in Florence, South Carolina.

Lockheed Constellation variants

Model 049-39-10: pre-war TWA/PanAm aircraft with four 2,200-hp (1641-kW) R-3350-35 after being taken over by USAAF prior to completion; first aircraft (Lockheed no. 1961) completed as **XC-69** in olive drab, civil registration NX67900, later NX25600, later AAF 43-10309; remaining aircraft AAF **C-69-1** (43-10310/10317) and **C-69-5** (42-94549/94561); total 22
C-69C: conversion of 294550 as VIP transport, later **ZC-69C**
XC-69E: conversion of first prototype with 2,000-hp (1492-kW) R-2800 Double Wasp engines
Model 049 Constellation: initial new-build commercial model with 2,200-hp, later 2,500-hp R-3350-BA1 engines, gross weight 86,000 lb (39010 kg), later 90,000 lb (40824 kg) and later 96,000 lb (43546 kg); nos 2023/88, total 66
R70-1: initial US Navy counterpart of Model 049-46, used by VPB-101, BuAer nos not assigned
Model 649: commercial transport with 2,500-hp (1865-kW) R-3350-BD1 engines, gross weight 98,000 lb (44453 kg); total 14, later brought up to L-749 standard
Model 749: long-range tanks in outer wings; gross weight 105,000 lb (47628 kg); the **Model 749A** had stronger spars and main legs; gross weight 107,000 lb (48535 kg); total 9
C-121A (Model 749A-79-38): 2,500-hp (1865-kW) R-3350-75 engines as USAF passenger transports (48-609/617); at one time designated **PC-121A**, for passenger transport; total 9
VC-121A: VIP conversions, 48-610 as *Columbine II*, 48-613 as *Bataan* and 48-614 as *Columbine I*
VC-121B: special long-range VIP aircraft (48-608); total 1
Model 1049 Super Constellation: stretched version with 2,700-hp (2014-kW) R-3350-CA1 engines, gross weight 120,000 lb (54432 kg); prototype was conversion of no. 1961, redesignated N6201C; square windows retained but tip tanks deferred until the Model 1049G; total 24 (nos 4001/4024)

R7V-1: US Navy **Model 1049B**, first with 3,250-hp (2425-kW) R-3350-91 Turbo-Compound engines; weather radar lengthened nose 3 ft (0.91 m); total 51 (BuAer nos 128434/128444, 131621/131629, 131632/ 131659, 140311/140313); see C-121G and C-121J
PO-1W: see WV-1
WV-1: first AEW radar picket version, based on Model 749, height-finder radar above fuselage, plan surveillance radar below; crew 22; BuAer nos 124437/124438, total 2 and ordered as PO-1Ws
WV-2: production AEW model, later named **Warning Star;** based on Model 1049, 3,400-hp (2536-kW) R-3350-34 or -42 Turbo-Compounds, improved radars and data links, crew 26; BuAer nos 126512/126513, 128323/128326, 131387/131392, 135746/135761, 137887/137890, 141289/141333, 143184/143230, 145924/145941, total 142
WV-2E: conversion of BuAer no. 126512 with APS-82 radar using rotating dish 'rotodome'
WV-2Q: conversions (16-plus) as high-power ECM warning, D/F and jamming platforms
WV-3: weather reconnaissance variant, also called Warning Star, same basic airframe as WV-2 but totally different interior and equipment, no tip tanks, crew 8; BuAer nos 137891/137898, plus conversion of 141323, total 9; became WC-121N, but two to USAF as EC-121R
R7V-2: US Navy **Model 1249** high-speed transports to evaluate turboprop propulsion, restressed airframe for high speeds (437 mph/703 km/h); four P&W YT34-12A driving broad paddle-blade propellers; BuAer nos 131630/131631, 131660/131661, total 4
C-121C: standard USAF long-haul passenger transport for MATS derived from Model 1049, weather radar, 3,500-hp (2611-kW) R-3350-34 Turbo-Compounds; 54-151/183, total 33
EC-121C: see RC-121C

JC-121C: two C-121C (54-160, 54-178) and one RC-121C (51-3841) converted as systems (mainly electronics) test aircraft
RC-121C: first USAF AEW radar picket version, based on C-121C airframe with dorsal and ventral radars similar to WV-2; 51-3836/3845, total 10; in 1962 became EC-121C
TC-121C: nine RC-121Cs converted as AEW radar trainers; subsequently became EC-121C
VC-121C: conversions as VIP executive transports total 4 (54-167/168, 54-181/182)
EC-121D: see RC-121D
RC-121D Warning Star: improved long-range AEW&C (airborne early warning and control) version, tip tanks and other changes, equipped second AEW&C Wing (551st), basis for many other versions; 52-3411/3425, 53-533/556, 53-3398/3403, 54-2304/2308, 55-118/139, total 72; most became **EC-121D**
VC-121E: ex-USN R7V-1 (131650) transferred to USAF as 53-7885 as Presidential *Columbine III*
YC-121F: last two R7V-2 transferred to USAF as 53-8157/8158, later re-engined with T34-P-6
C-121G: transferred US R7V-1s to USAF for MATS use, renumbered 54-4048/4049; total 32
TC-121G: conversions as crew trainers; 54-4050/4052 and 4058, total 4
VC-121G: VIP conversion of 54-4051
EC-121H: rebuild of 551st AEW&C Wing EC-121Ds with SAGE data-links, large airborne computer, new navaids and other equipment; total 42
C-121J: transfer of C-121G (54-4079) back to USN as 140313; later became NC-121K
EC-121J: updates of EC-121Ds with extra equipment (classified); 52-3416 and 55-137, total 2
EC-121K: redesignation of WV-2
YEC-121K: conversion of WV-2 128324 for classified 'Ferret' Elint

JC-121K: conversion of EC-121K 143196 for classified Army test programme(s)
NC-121K: conversions (21-plus) for special tests, including C-121J and EC-121K 145925 for Project 'Magnet' mapping Earth's field
EC-121L: redesignation of WV-2E
EC-121M: redesignation of WV-2Q
WC-121N: redesignation of WV-3
EC-121P: conversions (13-plus) of EC-121K with ASW sensors and special overwater navaids; 143184, 143189, 143199, 143200 to USAF with numbers as before omitting initial 1
JEC-121P: four of above transfers (189/199/200) later on special USAF test
EC-121Q: conversions (unknown number) of EC-121Ds with augmented and updated AWACS systems
EC-121R: conversions (total 30) for Project 'Igloo White' in Vietnam, serving as airborne data-relay stations (67-21471/21500)
EC-121S: near-total rebuild of five C-121Cs (54-155, 159, 164, 170, 173) as Ec-121Q
EC-121T: classified conversions (25-plus) of EC-121D, H and J as Elint electronic intelligence platforms
Model 1049C: first commercial model with Turbo-Compounds (3,250-hp/2425-kW R-3350-DA1), strengthened wing, extra fuel; total 49
Model 1049D: cargo version of Model 1049C; total 4
Model 1049E: improved passenger model; total 18
Model 1049G: major upgrade of commercial aircraft with DA3 engines, tip tanks and other improvements; total 104
Model 1049H: corresponding long-range restressed cargo aircraft; total 53
Model 1649 Starliner: ultra-long-range model with new long span wing, slightly stretched body and many other improvements; total 44

Vickers Viscount

Between 1935 and 1965 American dominance of the world market for airliners encountered only one formidable competitor. This was the smooth Viscount, the first aircraft designed for turboprop propulsion.

With most aircraft, and no less so with engines, it takes a touch of genius to get the design right: too clever, and it takes too long to achieve reliability and the costs go through the roof; too crude, and it will be uncompetitive. With the Dart engine Rolls-Royce appeared to have erred on the side of crudity: in 1966 Rolls-Royce chief executive Sir Denning Pearson called the engine 'agricultural machinery', but he also commented that at that time nobody had ever junked a Dart-engined aeroplane. In fact mating four of these engines with the Viscount airframe proved so successful that in 1955 Convair, the immediate rival, tried to compete by offering the airlines a look-alike called the Convair Dart. It was never built, because the customers kept buying Viscounts.

Towards the end of World War 2 the UK tried hard to make up for lost ground by reconvening the Brabazon Committee to make specific proposals on which types of civil transport should be built when peace returned. It was rightly believed the nation had a world lead in gas-turbine engines, and though for the immediate future the industry had to make do with 'interim' airliners converted from bombers, for the longer term it was planned to design 'clean sheet of paper' aircraft which, where appropriate, would have turboprop or turbojet engines.

One of the most important requirements was the Brabazon Type II, intended to produce a major short-haul airliner for European routes, and clearly with global sales prospects. It was split into Type IIA (piston) and Type IIB (turboprop) concepts. The former category was filled by Arthur Hagg's aerodynamically outstanding Airspeed Ambassador, with two Centaurus engines. BEA bought 20, but for reasons not unconnected with de Havilland's takeover of the Airspeed company this remained the only order. The Type IIB clearly posed a higher technical risk, so the Ministry of Supply ordered prototypes of two rival types, the Armstrong Whitworth A.W.55 Apollo and Vickers-Armstrongs VC2. The latter appeared to be the result of careful studies at Weybridge started in mid-1944 to design a successor to the VC1 Viking, an interim DC-3 type machine derived from the Wellington bomber. First ideas centred on a stretched Viking with tricycle landing gear and stressed-skin wings carrying four 1,000-hp (745.7-kW) turboprops, but by January 1945 double-bubble pressurized drawings began to appear. In April 1946 the Type IIB specification (8/46) was published, calling for 24 seats, a 7,500-lb (3402-kg) payload and 1,000-mile (1609-

Stretching the V.630 into the V.700 did wonders for the Viscount's appearance. Here the first V.700, G-AMAV, is seen early in its career in 1950. It never belonged to BEA, though in 1953 it was named *Endeavour* as a member of the airline's 'Discovery' class, and with race number 23 on the tail took part in the race to Christchurch, New Zealand.

F-BGNK was the first Viscount to be built and the first to be exported, flying as a V.708 on 11 March 1953 and being delivered to Air France on 18 May. It was one of the very few Viscounts to crash fatally; during a crew training flight on 12 December 1956 it dived into the ground near Paris, killing the five Air France crew. The flight-deck windows were common to all early aircraft (though not quite the same as on the V.630 and 663); TCA asked for larger vertical windows with pull-in direct vision, and this became standard. Under the rear fuselage is the cabin air system ram inlet.

Vickers Viscount

Specification

Vickers Viscount V.708

Type: 49 (later 65) seat passenger airliner

Powerplant: four 1,400-shp (1044-kW) Rolls-Royce Dart 504 turboprops (later 700s: 1,600-shp/1193-kW Dart 510)

Performance: cruising speed 311 mph (501 km/h); take-off to 50 ft (15 m) at maximum weight 4,050 ft (1234 m); range with maximum 12,500 lb (5670 kg) payload, 940 miles (1513 km) (later versions up to 2,450 miles/3943 km).

Weights: empty 32,330 lb (14,665 kg); maximum 52,500 lb (23814 kg) (later versions up to 72,500 lb/32886 kg)

Dimensions: span 93 ft 8.5 in (28.56 m); length 81 ft 2 in (24.74 m) (later 700s: 81 ft 10 in, 24.94 m); height 26 ft 9 in (8.05 m); wing area 963 sq ft (89.47 m²)

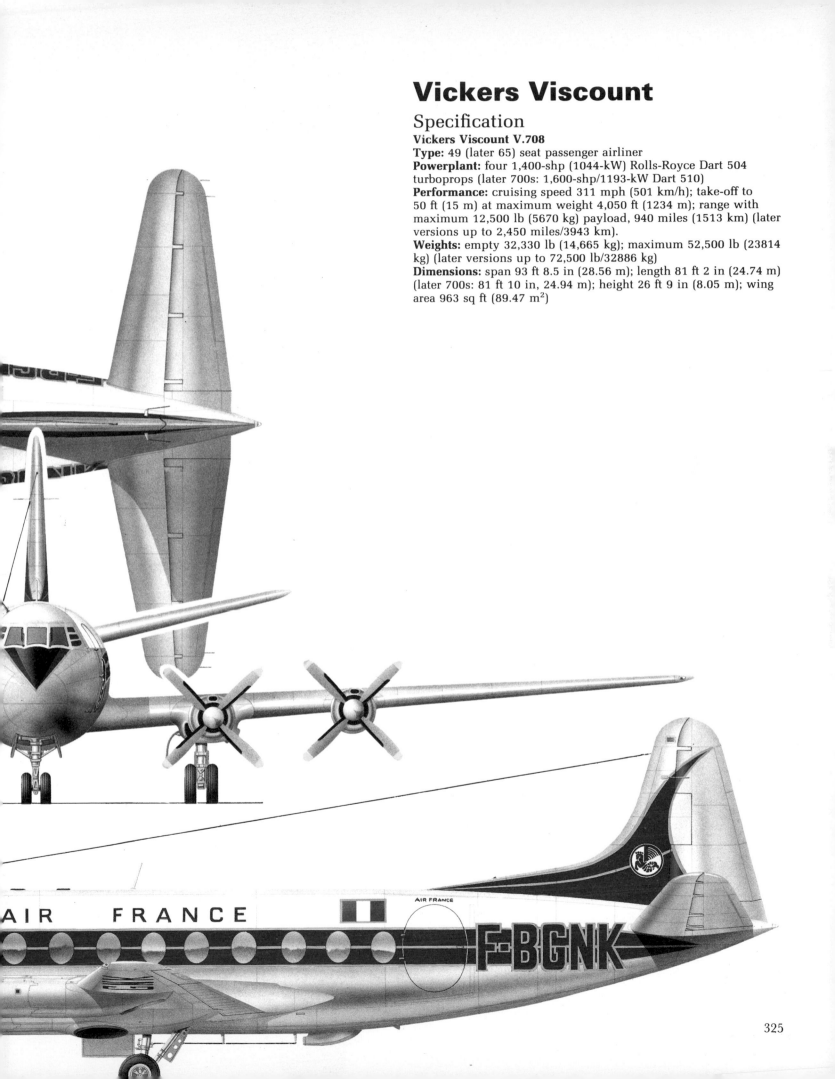

AIR FRANCE F-BGNK

Vickers Viscount

Originally the second Viscount 701 to be delivered to British European Airways in February 1953, G-ALWF flew as part of the airline's 'Discovery' class until transfer to Channel Airways. Subsequent operators were British Eagle and Cambrian Airways, the latter's colour scheme being shown here. The aircraft is now on show at the Imperial War Museum, Duxford.

TCA's order in November 1952 was most significant: for the first time a British company realized that an operator outside Britain might be able to improve the product and make it more acceptable in the world market. CF-TGK was no. 3 for TCA, delivered on 4 February 1955, and finally scrapped by Air Canada in July 1970.

km) range. In September Rex Pierson was promoted to be chief engineer, so his place as chief designer (Weybridge) was filled by G. R. Edwards. Sir George Edwards, as he became, was probably the most important leader the British aircraft industry has ever had, and he was to direct the Viscount, Valiant, Vanguard, VC10, TSR.2 and Concorde with the skill and confidence lacking from most other British companies but to be found in abundance in their American rivals. Without him the Viscount would almost certainly never have happened, because most British managements would have reacted differently at several crucial points in the programme.

For a start he decided to design for not 24 but 32 seats. He decided against a double-bubble and went for an almost circular fuselage, but with the cockpit roof added as an extra section built separately and attached on top. The wing was derived from that of the Wellington, via the Viking, with a single main spar but all stressed-skin structure, and with thermal de-icing and double-slotted flaps. The four engines were to be in pencil-slim nacelles, in turn calling for main gears each with two small wheels (which even then would be bulkier than the engines). Unlike de Havilland with the Comet, Vickers took great care to avoid any small-radius corners in the fuselage cut-outs, and both doors and windows were elliptical neutral holes. In later years the giant windows were to be highly popular with passengers, and Fokker adopted them for the F.27 Friendship along with many other Viscount parts including the engines and propellers.

At first the best engine seemed to be the Armstrong Siddeley Mamba, an advanced turboprop with an axial compressor. This was naturally picked for the rival Apollo, because both were Hawker Siddeley companies. When the Ministry placed its order on 9 March 1946 it specified two Mamba-powered VC2s (now the Vickers Type 609 and

named Viceroy, G-AHRF/RG), with Vickers to build a third at its own expense. The third was possibly to have the Rolls-Royce Dart engine, a seemingly more primitive turboprop with two centrifugal compressors derived from the Griffon supercharger and seven can-type combustion chambers around the outside. Edwards talked with Lionel Howorth, the Dart designer, and with Lord Hives, who assured him of Rolls-Royce's commitment to the engine. Because of the reliability of the centrifugal compressor and the fact that at that time the whole turbine experience had been with this type of engine, Edwards decided in March 1947 to pick the Dart. The designation with this engine was changed to V.630, and manufacture began at the secure experimental centre at Foxwarren of the two V.630s plus, to a later schedule, G-AJZW funded by Vickers, the V.640 with four 1,500-hp (1118.6-kW) Napier Naiads. In August 1947 India gained independence and the name Viceroy was changed to Viscount (names that hardly assist marketing, and in 1954 Capital Airlines was to print thousands of very necessary stickers saying 'Pronounced Vi-Count').

Success and failure

G-AHRF was flown by 'Mutt' Summers and 'Jock' Bryce from Wisley on 16 July 1948. The results could hardly have been better. The radical new engines ran like sewing machines, and the aircraft proved beautiful to fly. Edwards was just daring to believe that he might have a world-beater when, on 22 September 1948, BEA ordered its fleet of 20 Ambassadors. To say this was a body-blow is to understate the case; with loss of the prime customer there seemed little point in continuing. The third prototype was cancelled and work on the second slowed down. The existing machine was repainted in Ministry markings as VX211, but continued in low key to fly outstandingly well to gain a restricted certificate

The V.630 prototype appeared in numerous civil and Ministry colour schemes, and is seen here over Poole Harbour in January 1949 in Vickers house livery, with civil registration. A few months later it was VX211, but still in Vickers livery; then it carried a subdued BEA title, and by early 1950 had been repainted in full BEA airline livery.

One of the numerous ministerial nonsenses of the immediate post-war period was Britain's failure to use the world-beating Nene and Tay turbojets. The only British Tay-powered aircraft was the second Viscount, the V.663. Like its predecessor the Nene-Viking, it had four main landing gears, retracting on either side of the jetpipes.

of airworthiness on 19 August 1949. Meanwhile Edwards had been informed of the RDa.3 rating of 1,400 hp (1044 kW) compared with 990 hp (738.2 kW), and he then obtained from Peter Masefield and Bob Morgan of BEA an indication of renewed interest in the Viscount provided it continued to prove reliable and could be stretched to take advantage of the greater power. By this time the 32-passenger specification could be seen to be still too small, and in late 1948 Edwards cleared drawings for the RDa.3-powered V.700 version with a 47-seat fuselage lengthened by 88 in (2.23 m), and with 30 in (762 mm) added to the root of each wing, not only to increase lift but also to give larger propeller/fuselage clearance to reduce noise.

The second airframe had been diverted as a Ministry research aircraft powered by two Rolls-Royce Tay turbojets, each of 6,250-lb (2835-kg) thrust (it was the only British aircraft to use this engine). Serialled VX217, it was put on trials to support the Vickers Valiant bomber, being leased to Boulton Paul Aircraft for work on powered flight controls and then to Louis Newmark and Decca Navigator, overall spending eight years pioneering FBW (fly-by-wire) control systems. Its type number was V.663. As for the V.630, this

Lufthansa began using a number of Vickers Type 814s on its European routes in the late 50s and early 60s.

received clearance on 27 July 1950 for one month of scheduled airline operation, and on 29 July it took off from London Northolt in the hands of Captain H. R. 'Dickie' Rymer on a regular service to Paris Le Bourget. This was the first-ever airline service with any form of turbine power, and it was a revelation. G-AHRF made 35 further Paris trips, followed by eight to Edinburgh. The passenger reaction, and total reliability, confirmed BEA in its decision to buy the stretched version.

The prototype of the latter, the V.700 G-AMAV, was Ministry-funded and greatly speeded by using parts from the cancelled G-AJZW and bringing in other Vickers-Armstrongs factories such as Itchen (Southampton) for the wings and South Marston (Swindon) for the fuselage. Thus G-AMAV was able to fly from Weybridge on 28 August 1950, and it proved every bit as good as had been hoped. Despite the increase in size, and in gross weight from 40,000 to 50,000 lb (18144 to 22680 kg), performance was considerably enhanced and operating economics were much better. The turning

The VP-YNC was a version of the V.748 for CAA (Central African Airways) and the 100th Viscount to be built. It bore the name *Mlanje* and was delivered in 1956. After the Central African Federation was broken up on 1 January 1968 it was transferred to Air Rhodesia. Air Zimbabwe bought the aircraft in 1979.

This V.794 was one of the last short-bodied Viscounts. When it left the factory at Hurn it was numbered 431, and as TC-SES it was delivered to the Turkish airline THY in October 1958. Later it was transferred to the Turkish Air Force, where for a long time the three V.794s were used as troop transporters.

Typical of the smaller airlines that have recognized the value offered by the Viscount is Manx Airlines, an operator of relatively recent origin that leased this particular V.813 aircraft from British Midland Airways; the aircraft has seen over 25 years of operational flying.

point came on 3 August 1950 when at last BEA confirmed an order for 20 (later increased to 26) of the V.701 type with one class seating for 47 or 53 and augmented freight capacity both below and (at the rear) above the floor. The first V.701 (G-ALWE) flew on 20 August 1952. On 11 February 1953 Lady Douglas named it *Discovery*, all subsequent members of the class being named for famous explorers. By this time gross weight had been cleared at 56,000 lb (25402 kg), a full certificate of airworthiness was granted on 17 April 1953, and regular service started on the following day on the route from London Heathrow, via Rome and Athens, to Nicosia.

This was effectively the true start of the turbine age on the world's airlines (the jet Comet suffering a major hiccup), and orders began to come in as never before for a British airliner. First to sign were Air France and Aer Lingus, followed by TAA of Australia (which already used the immediate rival, the Convair-Liner). During 1952 Canada's TCA (now Air Canada) had begun discussions at Weybridge. The airline's list of engineering change orders soon exceeded 100 (one, for an on-board potable water dispenser, appearing in Weybridge documents as 'portable water'). A few years earlier a self-centred British industry might have declined to bother, but Edwards knew that to do the impossible and crack the North American market would demand a much more 'North American' aircraft, in many ways a better aircraft. It had much greater electrical power, two-pilot cockpit, new fuel system, provision for cold-weather operation and a revised interior, the specification being agreed as the V.724, and 15 were ordered in November 1952. This was just the start; TCA came back for V.757s of the V.700D family with 1,600-hp (1193-kW) Dart 510 engines and a gross weight of 60,000 lb (27216 kg), and altogether bought 51 Viscounts. In Washington Capital Airlines staked its whole operation on the British aircraft and took delivery of 60.

In October 1953 a race was flown from London to Christchurch, New Zealand. BEA considered that, though the Viscount was a short-hauler, it could get favourable publicity from entering. G-AMAV, still on Ministry charge, was fitted with a big rectangular fuel tank in the cabin, given the 'Discovery' name *Endeavour* and, under Captain W. Baillie and with chief executive Peter Masefield in the crew, averaged 290 mph (467 km/h) over the 11,795 miles (18982 km), which did nothing to harm either BEA or the Viscount. On the other hand Hughes Tool Company was one of the customers which flocked to Weybridge in 1953, Howard Hughes himself having a personal interest. The specification for the single V.763 was the longest ever drawn up, and a resident team of Hughes men inspected every part and

almost every rivet. Eventually the V.763 had to be shunted to one side, because it was getting in the way of the production line, and three years later it was re-registered YS-09C and sold to TACA of El Salvador, Hughes by this time being interested in Bristol Britannias and Boeing 707s.

The Dart 510 (RDa.6 rating) clearly made possible further increases in capability. Some V.700D aircraft had slipper tanks outboard of the outer engines for increased range, the first such being the fifth V.720 for TAA. More significant was

Vickers Viscount 810/840 Series cutaway drawing key

1 Radome
2 Weather radar scanner
3 Radar tracking mechanism
4 Front pressure bulkhead
5 Ranome hinge panel
6 Nose section construction
7 Pressurization relief valve
8 Control system linkage
9 Rudder pedals
10 Pneumatic system air bottle
11 Nosewheel doors
12 Forward retracting twin nosewheels
13 Nosewheel steering jack
14 Pitot head
15 Cockpit floor level
16 Seat mounting rails
17 Conditioned air delivery duct
18 Nosewheel steering control
19 Control column handwheel
20 Instrument panel
21 Weather radar display
22 Instrument panel shroud
23 Windscreen wipers
24 Windscreen panels
25 Overhead systems switch panels
26 Co-pilot's seat
27 Direct vision opening side window panel
28 Pilot's seat
29 Cockpit rear bulkhead
30 Cockpit pressure dome
31 Folding observer's seat
32 Cockpit doorway
33 Windscreen de-icing fluid reservoir
34 Wing and engine inspection floodlight
35 Radio and electronics equipment racks
36 Underfloor autopilot controllers
37 Cockpit section frame construction
38 Folding airstairs
39 Folding handrail
40 Entry lobby
41 Forward entry doorway
42 Starboard side baggage compartment

43 HF aerial mast
44 Hydraulic equipment compartment
45 Cabin front bulkhead
46 Cockpit pressure dome aft fairing
47 Forward passenger compartment
28 Four-abreast passenger seating
49 Forward entry door, open
50 Door latch
51 Door hinge link
52 Forward 'pull-out' emergency exit-window
53 Underfloor cargo hold, 250 cu ft (7.08 m³) capacity
54 Toilet compartments, port and starboard
55 Ventral cargo hold door, starboard side
56 Toilet compartment doors
57 Magazine rack
58 VHF aerial
59 Starboard engine nacelles
60 Engine cowling panels
61 Propeller spinner
62 Rotol four-bladed constant speed propeller
63 Propeller blade root de-icing
64 Starboard wing central fuel cells; total fuel system capacity 1,916 Imp gal (8710 litres)
65 Fuel system piping
66 Outboard fuel cells
67 Overwing fuel filler cap
68 De-icing air outlet louvres
69 Retractable landing taxiing lamp
70 Leading edge hot air de-icing
71 Starboard navigation light
72 Wing tip fairing with hot-air exhaust
73 Static dischargers
74 Starboard aileron
75 Aileron trim tab

76 Starboard double-slotted Fowler-type flap (down position)
77 Flap guide rails
78 Flap operating torque shaft and chain drive
79 D/F loop aerials
80 Fuselage frame and stringer construction
81 Floor beam construction
82 Main cabin passenger seating
83 Control rod runs
84 Front auxiliary spar attachment main frame
85 Main cabin 'pull-out' emergency exit windows
86 Main spar centre-section carry-through
87 Spar boom bolted joints
88 Cabin wall soundproof lining
89 Electrical system static inverters
90 Central flap drive motor
91 Main spar attachment double frame
92 Cabin trim panelling
93 VHF aerial
94 Overhead air conditioning ducting
95 Rear auxiliary spar attachment main frame
96 Cabin window panels
97 Main cabin four-abreast passenger seating, 52-seat layout (alternative 65-seat tourist or 75-seat coach class layouts)
98 Fresh air ducting
99 Individual passenger service units

100 Overhead coat/light luggage racks
101 Cabin rear bulkhead
102 Fin root fillet construction
103 Starboard tailplane
104 HF aerial cable
105 Starboard elevator
106 Elevator trim tab
107 Fin rib construction
108 Leading edge double skin de-icing air duct
109 VOR/ILS aerial
110 Fin tip fairing with hot-air exhaust
111 Rudder tab
112 Rudder construction
113 Tailcone
114 Tail navigation light
115 Spring tab
116 Anti-balance tab
117 Static dischargers

118 Port elevator construction
119 Tailplane rib construction
120 Leading edge de-icing air duct
121 Tailplane attachment main frame
122 Rudder and elevator control linkages
123 Rear pressure bulkhead
124 Wardrobe
125 Lounge compartment
126 Buffet/galley units, port and starboard
127 Rear entry/service door open

128 Cabin attendant's folding seat
129 Rear entry/service doorway, port and starboard
130 Fuselage skin panelling
131 Cabin floor panelling
132 Underfloor air conditioning plant
133 Wing trailing edge root fillet
134 Flap rib construction
135 Flap shroud ribs
136 Port double-slotted Fowler-type flap
137 Flap down position
138 Optional fuel jettison pipe
139 Port aileron rib construction

140 Aileron hinge control
141 Aileron tab
142 Static dischargers
143 Port wing tip fairing with hot-air exhaust
144 Port navigation light
145 Outer wing panel rib construction
146 Retractable landing/taxiing lamp
147 Leading edge de-icing hot air duct
148 Leading edge double skin panelling
149 Outer wing panel fuel tank bays
150 Rear auxiliary spar
151 Main spar
152 Outer wing panel spar joints
153 Petal-type engine cowlings, open position
154 Engine bearer struts
155 Main engine mounting ring frame
156 Engine annular air intake
157 Spinner
158 Intake lip de-icing

159 Oil cooler air intake
160 Forward retracting twin mainwheels
161 Main undercarriage leg strut
162 Rear drag strut
163 Central fuel tank bays
164 Inner wing panel rib construction
165 Main undercarriage hydraulic retraction jack
166 Mainwheel leg breaker joint
167 Engine nacelle mounting rib
168 Wheel bay door operating link
169 Engine fire extinguisher bottle
170 Mainwheel bay
171 Air ducting to conditioning system
172 Inboard fuel cells
173 Water/methanol tank, port and starboard, total capacity 75 Imp gal (340 litres)
174 Leading edge air ducting
175 Engine-driven cabin air compressor (three)
176 Engine accessory equipment gearbox
177 Jet pipe
178 Engine bearer struts
179 Fireproof bulkhead
180 Accessory gearbox drive shaft
181 Engine flame tubes
182 Oil cooler
183 Rolls-Royce Dart RDa.7/1 (Mk 525) turboprop engine
184 Propeller hub pitch change mechanism
185 Rotol or DH four-bladed constant speed propeller

G-AOYV was the prototype for the ultimate V.810 series, and was painted in the markings of the first customer (for the V.812). G-AOYV flew in December 1957 and spent over a year on company research from Wisley, in the course of which it was fitted with massive water spray rigs and a dummy Vanguard fin for de-icing certification trials.

ZS-CDT was no. 346 off the line and the first of seven V.813s for South Africa; SAA added a V.818 bought from Cubana. All had extremely long and successful careers, this particular machine, *Blesbok*, being sold eventually to BMA in 1972 as G-AZLP. All the British Midland fleet saw extensive prior service with other operators.

the decision to stretch the fuselage, in partnership with BEA. At first the V.801 was studied with a massive stretch, but it was then found that, by moving back the rear pressure bulkhead, a 111-in (2.82-m) internal stretch could be achieved with a fuselage only 46 in (1.17 m) longer. On 14 April 1954 BEA ordered 12 (later 24) of these longer V.802 aircraft, still sticking to names of discoverers. As before, many customers followed suit, but Rolls-Royce was by this time ardently developing the trusty Dart and kept offering increased power. In 1954 the 1,700-shp (1267.7-kW) Dart 520 (RDa.7) led to the V.806, with unchanged 320-mph (515-km/h) economical cruising speed but gross weight raised to 64,500 lb (29257 kg). In 1955 the Dart 525 (RDa.7/1) of 1,800-shp (1342.3 kW) led to the considerably revised V.810 series with structure restressed for greater weights and higher indicated airspeeds. The only visible change was a simpler rudder aerodynamic balance, but in fact gross weight was cleared to 72,500 lb (32885 kg) and cruising speed to 360 mph (579 km/h).

Healthy sales and production
The V.810 prototype flew on 23 December 1957, by which time Viscounts were flooding off the assembly lines, the V.800 series all being assembled at a newly established factory at Hurn. The V.700 was by this time in Vickers hands and it was re-engined with RDa.7s to speed Viscount V.810 series certification. At the end of this programme in 1963 it was unceremoniously given to the Fire School at Stansted, which was sad because the original V.630 prototype had been written off at Khartoum in 1952.

The plan in 1956 had been to offer a V.840 series with RDa.8 engines of 2,500 ehp (1864.3 kW), for a cruising speed of 400 mph (644 km/h). When Robert F. Six of Continental signed for 14 V.812s he intended to re-engine them later, and several other customers were interested in the '400-mph

Viscount', but it was never built. This was partly because with Boeing 707s in service 400 mph (644 km/h) was less impressive and partly because the engine-out certification would have required a substantial redesign of the rear fuselage and tail. As it was, the V.810 family kept selling very healthily, until the very last order was received from CAAC of the People's Republic of China (that country's first purchase from a Western source). The 444th and last Viscount was first flown on 2 January 1964, 438 of these being regular aircraft sold to customers. Several were bought new by executive owners (the first being the Canadian Department of Transport in 1954) and air forces (the first being the Indian Air Force, again in 1954). In 1955 United States Steel bought three, specially equipped for luxurious inflight conferences. When ex-airline Viscounts came on to the second-hand market every single example was snapped up by other customers, many of them being scheduled operators but including an increasing proportion of corporate customers.

Four aircraft with long lives in the UK included two ex-Capital V.745s used by the Empire Test Pilots School and two stretched examples (an ex-Ghana V.838 and ex-Austrian V.837) which did sterling work for the Royal Radar (now Royal Signals and Radar) Establishment. Several countries have used Viscounts as flying test-beds for radars and other systems, and in February 1982 a Canadian aircraft began flight testing the new PW100 turboprop (ironically a Dart replacement) with the new engine mounted far ahead of the original nose. In January 1985 at least 139 Viscounts were still active, including 93 with scheduled airline operators, the largest surviving fleet being that of British Air Ferries (14 plus two leased to Jersey). To the passenger the Viscount is still a very pleasant way to travel, in no way inferior to the short-haulers now being built. It will be some time before its distinctive sound disappears from the scene.

9G-AAU came very near the end of the line as no. 446, being delivered to Ghana Airways on 26 November 1961. Note the rectangular doors swinging aft on parallel arms which on the stretched 800-series replaced the original elliptical type to improve freight loading. Subsequently no. 446 was G-BCZR with Field, BMA, Southern International and Dan-Air. Viscount construction numbers included undelivered or unfinished aircraft, no. 446 being in practice no. 431.

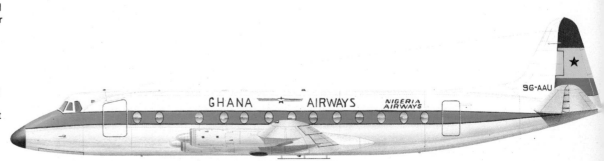

The Vickers Viscount was not greatly harmed by the jet age. Because it was so cheap to run there are still many machines like this V.806 in use. British Air Ferries used it for flights to Germany and Holland. (*Photo: Austin J. Brown/APL*)

Boeing B-52 Stratofortress

What is the greatest aircraft of all time? If one accepts a military type, few can rival the monster B-52 long-range bomber, which was designed to drop nuclear bombs from the stratosphere and is in service almost 30 years beyond its planned retirement date.

Today we are no longer amazed to find military aircrew flying aircraft older than they are themselves, but the B-52 (to later generations of its crews the Buff, politely translated as the Big Ugly Fat Fella) is one of the few aircraft that can properly be called a legend in its own time. Before it flew it was regarded as impossible to create, unless it had propellers. Unlike the other great bombers of USAF Strategic Air Command (SAC), its production was divided into eight versions, each significantly more capable than its predecessor. By the late 1950s the general view was that it was impossible to invent an externally carried load that would prove too much for it. By the 1960s it was being flown round the clock

on gruelling 'airborne alerts', while simultaneously forced down into the harsh turbulent air at the lowest safe levels at which so large an aircraft could be flown. By the 1970s sums far exceeding the original purchase price were being spent keeping the tired structures each in one piece and packing them with ever more extensive new avionic systems. Today,

An unidentified 'Big Belly' B-52D, probably of the 43rd BW, parked between missions at Andersen AB, Guam, in 1969. In these harsh trucking missions engines were invariably started at 452,000 lb (205023 kg) gross weight, 2,000 lb (907 kg) beyond the B-52D's safe structural limit. Note the stacked 750-lb (340-kg) bomb triplets on the left.

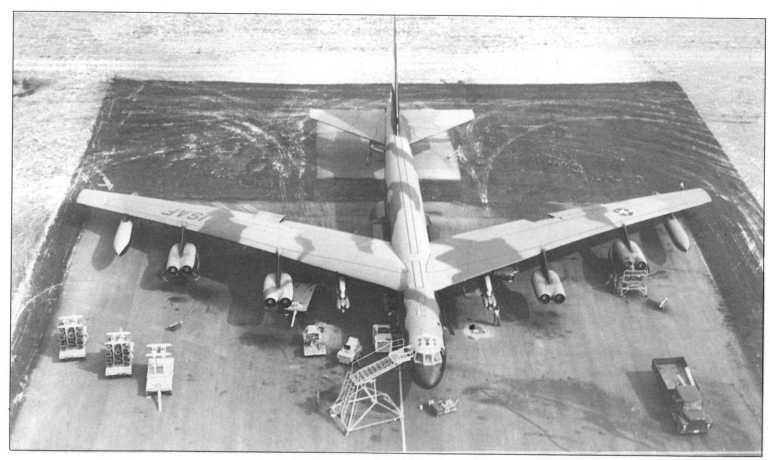

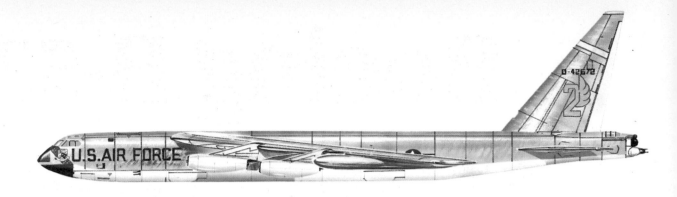

One of the last B-52Cs in service was 54-2672 (note 0-prefix denoting that the aircraft is over 10 years old) serving with the 7th BW at Carswell AFB, Fort Worth. The tail emblem is that of the 2nd Air Force, which no longer exists; today the 7th BW has been incorporated into the 19th Air Division within the 8th Air Force.

even though they have radar cross-sections bigger than the proverbial 'barn door', the tough old birds face many years of front-line duty, all much more severe than the serene stratospheric cruise for which they were intended.

The US Army Air Force set out its first specification for a turbine-engined (not necessarily jet) bomber to replace the B-36 in April 1945. There was then no prospect of achieving the required range with a jet, and there was no obvious turboprop (Northrop offered competition with its all-wing B-35 proposals powered by its own Hendy Turbodyne XT37 engine of 10,400 hp/7758 kW). The figures were refined in January 1946, and again all the jet projects failed by wide margins to meet the radius of 5,000 miles (8047 km) with a 10,000-lb (4536-kg) bombload. So when Boeing won the Phase I contract in June 1946 it was with the Model 462, which resembled an enlarged B-50 with six Wright XT35 Typhoon turboprops. By 1947 this had developed into a series of Model 464 studies which were even bigger and soon featured swept wings and tail. Inflight-refuelling then enabled size to be reduced, but there was plenty of opposition from the US Navy and even the commander of SAC, and the XB-52 was cancelled in January 1948.

On 24 June 1948 the Russians began their campaign to starve the Allies out of West Berlin, and just 24 hours later the B-52 was resurrected. Boeing received a Phase II award for two prototypes, serialled 49-230 and 49-231, to be ready

in 1951; but nobody liked the prospect of giant gearboxes and propellers, and few people believed they could be readied by 1951. On the other hand Pratt & Whitney, General Electric and Westinghouse were developing new turbojets offering more power with much lower specific fuel consumption. Boeing cut armament to tail guns only, pared the range and improved the aerodynamics, and armed themselves with truckloads of research data. Over 40,000 manhours had been devoted in early 1948 to a parallel study for a medium bomber with a bombload of 20,000 lb (9072 kg) and with four of the new turbojets each at an assumed rating of 8,500 lb (3856 kg); never built, it would have been broadly in the class of the Model 367-80 (prototype of the Model 707/717 series).

On 21 October 1948 six of Boeing's top engineers, led by Ed Wells, George Schairer and Maynard Pennell, arrived at Wright Field, Ohio, for a last presentation of the final design, the Model 464-350-0 turboprop. To their astonishment Colonel Pete Warden pre-empted their presentation by asking if they could let him have an updated proposal for a jet.

The team went back to their rooms in the Van Cleve Hotel in nearby Dayton and worked nonstop from the next day (Friday) until the morning of the following Monday, when at 8 a.m. they were back in Warden's office. They brought with them a total preliminary design of the B-52 as we know it today, with full performance specifications, weight breakdowns, costings and development schedules, plus a neatly finished desk-top model made in balsa from a nearby hobby shop and carrying USAF markings. To a large extent this staggering accomplishment was made possible by the existence of the medium-bomber study. To create the new jet B-52 the team scaled up the same design to have two engines in each pod instead of one.

A rare portrait of two B-52 prototypes flying together. Externally almost identical, they differed from later models in having tandem-pilot cockpits and no tail armament. The YB-52 (49-231) in the rear was the first to fly, in April 1952. It had flaperons and six spoiler sections above each wing for roll control.

A picture taken in February 1956 by the co-pilot of a B-52B of the 93rd BW, the original operator at Castle AFB, of an RB-52B (52-8715). This was one of the early B-52B/B-52D models with MD-5 rear fire control for two 20-mm cannon. By 1956 the A-3A with four 0.5-in (12.7-mm) guns had supplanted this installation.

The fifth B-52 ever built became *The High and Mighty One*, painted white, as an NB-52A at the AF Flight Test Center. It was the parent ship for the X-15 hypersonic aircraft, but is seen here on 4 October 1973 after release of the Martin Marietta X-24B lifting-body research aircraft.

The first flight

Maximum effort was immediately put behind this Model 464-49 project, and soon afterwards all turboprops were abandoned. By late 1950 the bomber had become the Model 464-67, and it was to this standard that the two prototypes were built. The second (49-231) had to be designated YB-52 because money was so tight that Logistics Command had to help pay for it, and that command is not empowered to fund experimental (X-prefix) aircraft! In the event, though the XB-52 was the first to leave the plant, on the night of 29 November 1951, it was the YB-52 that was the first to fly, on 15 April 1952. The colossal silver ship had already completed thunderous taxi runs, its eight YJ57 engines spewing black smoke and disturbing half Seattle. Now Tex Johnston, in leather wartime jacket, boarded through the small hatch under the whale-like nose and put on his yellow bonedome

Taken on 31 May 1956, this night scene shows a reconnaissance capsule being winched into an RB-52B. The capsule contained provisions for four to six cameras and/or various items of ECM and other electronics, as well as two human operators. The concept of convertible bomber/reconnaissance B-52s was dropped in the same year.

Boeing B-52G Stratofortress cutaway drawing key

1 Nose radome
2 ALT-28 ECM antenna
3 Electronic countermeasures (ECM) equipment bay
4 Front pressure bulkhead
5 Electronic cooling air intake
6 Bombing radar
7 Low-light television scanner turret (EVS system), infra-red on starboard side
8 Television camera unit
9 ALQ-117 radar warning antenna
10 Underfloor control runs
11 Control column
12 Rudder pedals
13 Windscreen wipers
14 Instrument panel shroud
15 Windscreen panels
16 Cockpit eyebrow windows
17 Cockpit roof escape/ejection hatches
18 Co-pilot's ejection seat
19 Drogue chute container
20 Pilot's ejection seat
21 Flight deck floor level
22 Navigator's instrument console
23 Ventral escape/ejection hatch, port and starboard

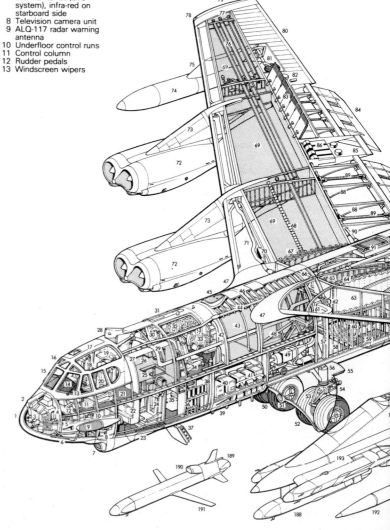

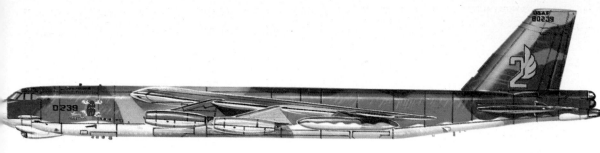

24 Radar navigator's downward ejection seat, navigator to starboard
25 Access ladder and hatch to flight deck
26 EWO instructor's folding seat
27 Electronics equipment rack
28 In-flight refuelling receptacle, open
29 Refuelling delivery line
30 Electronic warfare officer's (EWO) ejection seat
31 Rear crew members escape/ejection hatches
32 EWO's instrument panel
33 Gunner's remote control panel
34 Gunner's ejection seat
35 Navigation instructor's folding seat
36 Radio and electronics racks
37 Ventral entry hatch and ladder
38 Lower deck rear pressure bulkhead
39 ECM aerials
40 ECM equipment bay
41 Cooling air ducting
42 Upper deck rear pressure bulkhead
43 Water injection tank, capacity 1,200 US gal (4542 litres)
44 Fuselage upper longeron
45 Astro navigation antenna
46 Tank access hatches
47 Leading edge 'strakelets' fitted to identify cruise missile carriers
48 Forward fuselage fuel tank
49 Air conditioning plant
50 Forward starboard main undercarriage bogie
51 Landing lamp
52 Forward port main undercarriage bogie
53 Torque scissor links
54 Steering jacks

55 Main undercarriage door
56 Main undercarriage leg strut
57 Wing front spar/fuselage/main undercarriage attachment frame
58 Main undercarriage wheel bay
59 Doppler aerial
60 Central electronic equipment bay
61 Air conditioning intake duct
62 Front spar attachment joint
63 Wing root rib
64 Wing panel bolted attachment joint
65 Centre section fuel tank bay
66 Wing centre section carry-through
67 Starboard wing attachment joint
68 Vortex generators
69 Starboard wing integral fuel tank bays; total fuel system capacity (includes external tanks), 48,030 US gal (181813 litres)
70 Engine ignition control unit
71 Bleed air ducting
72 Starboard engine nacelles
73 Nacelle nylons
74 Fixed external fuel tank, capacity 700 US gal (2650 litres)
75 Tank pylon
76 Fuel venting channels
77 Tip surge tank
78 Starboard navigation light
79 Wing tip fairing
80 Fixed portion of trailing edge
81 Starboard outrigger wheel, stowed position
82 Hydraulic equipment bay
83 Roll control spoiler panels, open

84 Outboard single-slotted, Fowler-type flap, down position
85 Inboard fixed trailing edge segment
86 Chaff dispensers and flare launchers
87 Inboard single slotted flap, down position
88 Flap guide rails
89 Flap screw jacks
90 Flap drive torque shaft
91 Life raft stowage
92 Wing centre section/longeron ties
93 Central flap drive motor
94 Rear spar attachment joint
95 AGM-69 missile environmental control unit
96 Bomb bay rotary missile launcher

97 AGM-69 SRAM, air to ground missiles
98 Bomb bay rear bulkhead
99 Rear fuselage bag-type fuel tanks
100 Rear fuselage longeron
101 Fuel delivery and transfer piping
102 Fuselage skin panelling
103 Fuselage fuel system surge tank
104 Data link antenna
105 Rear fuselage frame construction
106 Rear equipment bay air conditioning plant
107 Ram air intake

108 Starboard tailplane
109 Vortex generators
110 Starboard elevator
111 Fin spar attachment joint: fin folds to starboard
112 Tailfin rib construction
113 VOR aerial
114 Lightning isolator
115 Fin tip aerial fairing
116 Rudder
117 Rudder tab
118 Hydraulic rudder control jack
119 Rudder aerodynamic balance
120 Rear ECM and fire control electronics pack
121 ECM aerial fairing
122 Brake parachute stowage
123 Parachute and door release mechanism
124 ALQ-117 retractable aerial fairing
125 AN-ASG-15 search radome
126 ALQ-117 and APR-25 ECM radome
127 Four 0.5-in (12.7-mm) machine-guns
128 AN-ASG-15 tracking radome
129 Remote control gun turret
130 Ammunition feed chutes
131 Ammunition tanks, 600 rounds per gun
132 Elevator tab
133 Port elevator
134 ALQ-153 tail warning radar
135 All-moving tailplane construction
136 Tailplane carry-through box section spar
137 Elevator aerodynamic balance
138 Centre section sealing plate

139 Tailplane trimming screw jack
140 Air conditioning ducting
141 Fuel system venting pipes
142 Ventral access hatch
143 Rear fuselage ECM equipment bay
144 ECM aerials
145 Strike camera compartment
146 Rear main undercarriage wheel bay
147 Bomb/wheel bay box section longeron
148 Main undercarriage mounting frame
149 Hydraulic retraction jack
150 Rear main undercarriage bogie units
151 Flap shroud ribs

152 ECM dispensers
153 Fixed portion of trailing edge
154 Port flaps, down position
155 Outboard single slotted flap
156 Port roll control spoiler panels
157 Hydraulic reservoir
158 Outrigger wheel bay
159 Fixed portion of trailing edge
160 Glass-fibre wing tip fairing
161 Port navigation light
162 Outer wing panel integral fuel tank
163 Port outrigger wheel
164 Fixed external fuel tank
165 Fuel tank pylon
166 Outrigger wheel retraction strut
167 Outer wing panel attachment joint
168 Engine pylon mounting rib
169 Pylon rear attachment strut
170 Engine pylon construction
171 Pratt & Whitney J57-P-43WB turbojet engine
172 Engine oil tank, capacity 8.5 US gal (32 litres)
173 Accessory equipment gearbox
174 Generator cooling air duct
175 Oil cooler ram air intakes
176 Engine air intakes
177 Detachable cowling panels
178 Leading edge rib construction
179 Front spar
180 Wing rib construction
181 Rear spar
182 Port wing integral fuel tank bays
183 Inboard pylon mounting rib
184 Leading edge bleed air and engine control runs
185 Weapons bay doors, open (loading) position
186 Bomb doors, open
187 Wing mounted cruise missile pylon
188 Boeing AGM-86B Air Launched Cruise Missiles (ALCM), six per wing pylon, stowed configuration
189 AGM-86B missile in flight configuration
190 Retractable engine air intake
191 Folding wings
192 AGM-69 SRAM, alternative load
193 Missile adaptors
194 Nacelle pylon
195 Port inboard engine nacelles
196 Central engine mounting bulkhead/firewall
197 Bleed air ducting
198 Generator cooling air ducting
199 Fuselage bomb mounting cradle
200 Free-fall 25-megaton nuclear weapons (four)

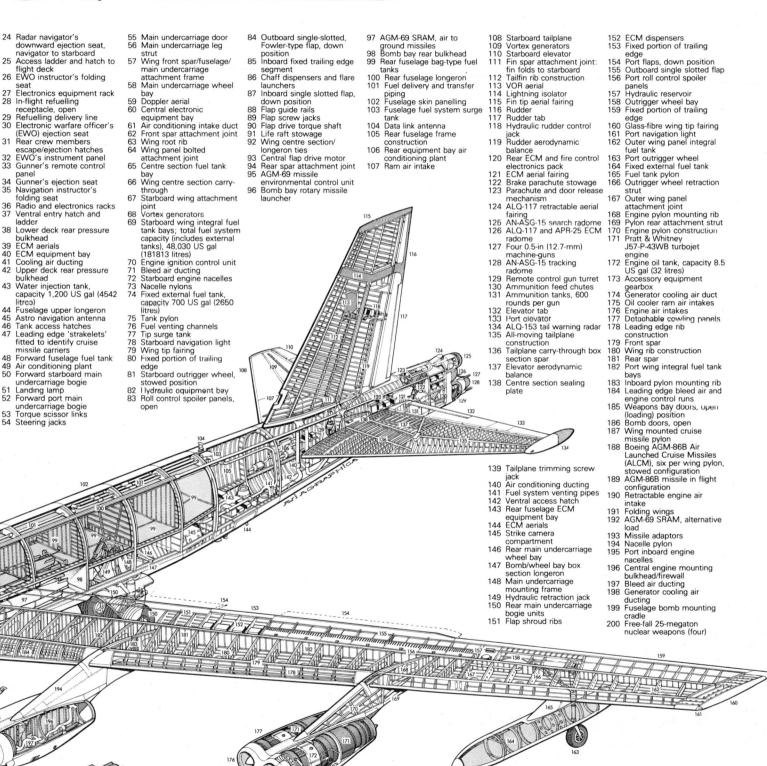

Boeing B-52 Stratofortress

USAF no. 55-0677 is a B-52D-25-BW, delivered from Wichita in 1958. It is pictured as it looked in 1972 during the gruelling 'Linebacker' missions in the face of intense SAM defences, with the standard load of 42 bombs each weighing 750 lb (340 kg) in the 'Big Belly' bomb bay and 24 weighing 500 lb (227 kg) on the wing pylons. Two years later it had been transferred from Guam's 43rd Strategic wing to the 2nd AF's 7th BW, 20th BS, with the winged '2' on the tail and the name *City of Fort Worth*, plus a map of Texas under the SAC badge on the nose.

Specification

Boeing B-52D-25-BW
Type: six-seat strategic bomber
Powerplant: eight 12,100-lb (5489-kg) thrust Pratt & Whitney J57-P29WA turbojets
Performance: maximum speed at low level about 415 mph (668 km/h); cruising speed at height 555 mph (893 km/h) or Mach 0.84; range 7,370 miles (11861 km); operating height from 500 to 45,000 ft (152 to 13716 m)
Weights: empty typically 189,000 lb (85730 kg); maximum 450,000 lb (204120 kg)
Dimensions: span 185 ft 0 in (56.39 m); length 156 ft 7 in (47.727 m); height 48 ft 3⅔ in (14.724 m); wing area 4,000 sq ft (371.6 m^2)
Armament: maximum 108 conventional bombs or four nuclear free-fall bombs (no SRAM, ALCM or MRASM) plus four 0.5-in (12.7-mm) tail guns

helmet in the front cockpit. Behind him at a higher level, a red bonedome denoted the presence of Lieutenant Colonel Guy M. Townsend. It was one of the most successful first flights ever, and instead of being a brief shakedown the YB-52 was put through three hours of intensive testing, clearing more than the first month's planned work on the first flight, before landing at flight-test base at Larson AFB, Moses Lake.

Nobody needs to have the B-52 described, but it is worth noting that the type abounded in novel features. Fuel capacity was greater than in any previous production aircraft at 38,865 US gal (147112 litres), compared with 21,000 US gal (79493 litres) for the B-36, giving a maximum take-off weight of 405,000 lb (183708 kg). On the ground the aircraft rested on four twin-wheel trucks, all of which were steerable and which could be slewed in unison to allow cross-wind landings to be made with the wings level and the aircraft crabbing diagonally on to the runway. Small outrigger wheels near the wingtips were pressed hard on the ground by a maximum fuel load, but at light weights the vast 35°-swept wings were arched upwards leaving these outrigger wheels high in the air. The gigantic fin, only the very trailing edge of which was hinged to form a rudder, could be power-folded to the right to allow the B-52 to enter standard USAF hangars. As not even the enormous power of the variable-incidence tailplane could be used to rotate the bomber on take-off the wing was set at an incidence of 8° for a fly-away with the fuselage horizontal. Thickness was mostly 8 to 10 per cent, but at the root the upper surface rose and was swept sharply forward to give a value of 15 per cent at the side of the body, where each wing was bolted to a bridge truss that was the strongest structural item ever built into any aircraft. Perhaps the most extraordinary of many odd features in the on-board systems was that all accessory power was taken from the engines in the form of high-pressure bleed air, ducted through stainless-steel pipes (under their thermal lagging these glowed cherry-red with the heat) to small high-speed turbines which screamed and hissed in every part of the aircraft driving alternators, hydraulic pumps, cabin-conditioning and everything else.

B-52G-105-BW no. 58-0231 looks rather tired, with numerous local patching and repainting after something like 12,000 hours of hard flying. It still lacks the OAS update and ALQ-153 pulse-doppler tail-warning radar. When cruise missiles are added these aircraft are given distinctive wing-root fairings.

Pre-flight orders

Even before first flight Boeing had a letter of intent for 500 B-52s and a vast nationwide production programme was organized. Many companies contributed major systems and equipment, while the airframe was assigned to Goodyear (centre fuselage, wing centre section, fuel tanks and internal floors and fuel decks), Aeronca (all bomb/wheel/crew doors and movable panels, rudder, elevators, spoilers and ailerons), Fairchild (outer wings, rear fuselage jointly with Temco, top panels, fin and tip-protection gears). Cessna (tailplane) and Rohr (aft fuselage, engine pods, pylon struts and external tanks). Aeronca also built the pressurized reconnaissance capsules, packed with cameras, other sensors and large ECM systems as well as two crew in downward-ejecting seats. The intention was that aircraft should fly with either the capsule or with maximum bombload depending on mission require-ments, but in fact no capsules were flown on combat missions.

In May 1951 the final mock-up review accepted a new cockpit with airline style side-by-side seating for the pilots, which offered many advantages. This was to be introduced at the 14th production aircraft, but in fact Boeing got it on the very first B-52A, flown on 5 August 1954. Subsequent versions are listed separately. Production built up rapidly, and in September 1953 Boeing Wichita was named as second-source producer, and eventually Wichita took over the whole programme to leave Seattle to churn out tankers and commercial Model 707s at rates which today seem astronomic.

The B-52B was cleared for combat duty on 29 June 1955 (more than six months earlier than the UK's Vickers Valiant, first of the V-bombers). The first units were both at Castle AFB, California: the 93rd Bomb Wing and the 4017th

Combat Crew Training Squadron. In its first year the B-52 had plenty of problems. Turbos exploded to cause fire or wreck sections of fuselage (they were shrouded in flak curtains), main-gear trucks tried to swivel left and right simultaneously or jammed at the maximum 20° slewed position, the pneumatic-system air ducts suffered high-frequency vibration and failed in fatigue to spew 750°F air, and the giant Fowler-type flaps cracked and broke under the intense sonic buffeting caused by repeated take-offs with the engines at full power with water injection. Indeed in February 1956 the 78 aircraft in service were grounded while the danger of exploding air turbos was removed. Much later the turbo system was abandoned (on the B-52F), it having finally been determined that conventional shaft drives resulted in more miles per gallon! The vast navigation/bombing and tail defence schemes were completely re-thought three times, while with the B-52G the entire aircraft was redesigned to have a lighter structure with less drag, six crew all grouped together in a much better pressurized compartment, with remote tail guns, and much greater internal fuel capacity (raised from 35,550 to 46,575 US gal/134571 to 176305 litres) with integral-tank wings. This model also introduced inboard-wing pylons (for the Hound Dog cruise missile), and on the unexpected extra version, the B-62H, these pylons were tailored to pairs of Skybolt missiles (later cancelled and replaced by Hound Dog or SRAM) while the engines were changed for TF33 turbofans giving much greater range and less noise. The 744th and last B-52 was delivered to Minot AFB on 26 October 1962.

Last of the B-52 variants, the B-52H model is powered by visibly larger TF33 turbofans derived from the original J57 turbojet, and offering much greater take-off thrust, without the need for water, with less noise and much reduced specific fuel consumption. The B-52H carried the Hound Dog missile until 1976.

By this time the B-52B had been withdrawn and the SAC bomb wings were feverishly learning low-flying while simultaneously maintaining an airborne alert with live nuclear weapons. Things were not helped by a succession of inflight structural failures, leading to extremely far-reaching and costly rebuild programmes, and to the Palomares incident of 17 January 1966 in which a B-52 and KC-135 collided fatally over a Spanish fishing village plunging four multi-megaton bombs on to land and sea (the search for the fourth bomb was an epic of deep-ocean technology). In January 1968 another B-52 with four H-bombs on board crashed on sea ice near Thule AFB, Greenland, and that was the end of airborne alerts with live thermonuclear weapons.

In its place came a totally different sort of mission: 9 or 10-hour 'trucking' with conventional 'iron' bombs from the slippery, algae-coated switchback runway at Guam to the featureless forests of Vietnam in which Viet Cong were thought to be lurking. The B-52 had been designed to carry nuclear bombs, and the limit for conventional weapons was 27 1,000-lb (454-kg) bombs. For the war in South East Asia Boeing-Wichita was awarded a 1966 contract for increased capability in the conventional role. The B-52F was given inner-wing pylons which, with long beams carrying four tandem triplets of bombs, added 24 bombs of up to 750-lb (340-kg) size (actual mass 825 lb/374 kg). The B-52D was given not only these wing racks but also the so-called Big Belly modification which, while not altering the volume of the internal bomb bays, rebuilt them structurally to house up to 84 bombs of nominal 500-lb (227-kg) size (actual mass 580 lb/263 kg), thus increasing total load from 27,000 lb the (12247 kg) to approximately 70,000 lb (31750 kg).

Today all B-52s have been retired except some of the B-52Ds and all of the B-52G and B-52H series, the newest and in most respects the best of all versions. A few major improvements, such as the totally new all-digital ASQ-48 nav/bomb system, are still being applied to the B-52D, some

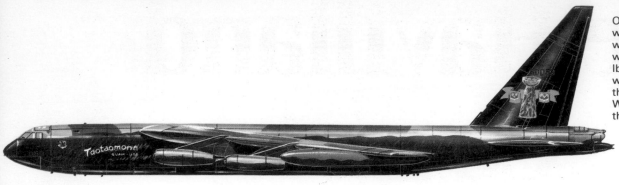

One of the first Wichita-built B-52s was B-52D no. 55-0069, seen as it was at the height of the Vietnam war when it was burdened by 400 lb (181 kg) of camouflage and black while operating from Guam with the 60th BS in the 43rd Strategic Wing. The 43rd was the last user of the B-52D, still at Guam.

Another early withdrawal from combat duty was the B-52F, one of which, Wichita-built 57-169, is seen when it was *Thunder Express* with 68 missions recorded with the 320th BW operating from Andersen AB, Guam. In 1986 320th still flew B-52s as part of the 15th AF's 14th Air Division at Mather AFB.

of which serve in the training role on Guam. The B-52G and B-52H, however, have already cost more than four times their extremely low original purchase price (about $6 million for a B-52D or B-52E and $9 million for a B-52G) on various update programmes, and plenty more are to come by mid-1990. Most of the modification funds in the 1960s went on the structure. In the 1970s the main effort was on adding SRAM (AGM-69A attack missile) of which two tandem triplets can be carried on each wing pylon plus another eight

on an internal rotary dispenser, the EVS (Electro-optical Viewing System) whose twin blisters can be seen under the nose, one for infra-red and the other for low-light TV), and quick-start capability to allow aircraft to scramble from air bases under attack by ICBMs or SLBMs. Many new avionic items are being added, and in December 1982 the first SAC unit became operational with the AGM-86B cruise missile, which by 1987 (as AGM-86C) equipped all 173 B-52Gs and possibly 96 of the B-52H version. Each aircraft carries 12 missiles on the wing pylons, and late in the 1980s may be modified internally to house a long eight-round dispenser. A 'strakelet' fairing on each leading edge, visible for treaty reasons to Soviet satellites, shows aircraft thus converted.

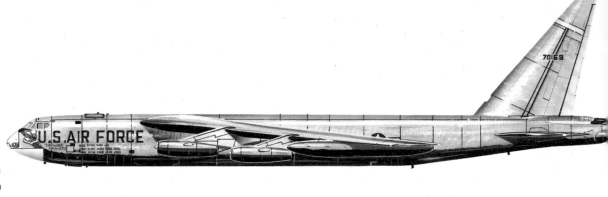

The Boeing B-52 was used for tactical bombing in Vietnam. This was a long way from the purpose the plane was originally designed for, but it proved to be extremely effective.

Boeing B-52 variants

XB-52 (Model 464-67): prototype (49-230); 8,700-lb (3946-kg) thrust YJ57-3 engines, crew five, 10,000-lb (4536-kg) bombload, no defensive guns, three spoilers per wing lus small servo-tab ailerons, water in 125-US gal (473-litre) tank under fin

YB-52: prototype (49-231), as XB-52 but six spoilers per wing plus flaperons, later rear turret with gunner and two 20-mm guns

B-52A (Model 464-201-0): three aircraft (52-001/003), side-by-side pilots, 9,000-lb (4082-kg) thrust J57-1W or J57-9W engines, internal fuel reduced to 35,550 US gal (134571 litres) plus 2,000 US gal (7571 litres) externally, operative inflight-refuelling receptacle and cross-wind landing gear

NB-52A: third aircraft rebuilt as parent aircraft of X-15 aircraft

B-52B (Model 464-201-1/3/4): total 50, comprising 23 **B-52B-35** bombers (53-373/376 and 380/398), first 10 initially with J57-1W engines, all later with 12,100-lb (5489-kg) thrust J57-19W or J57-29W engines, full combat equipment; 27 additional (52-004/013, 52-8710/8716, 53-366/372 and 377/379) ordered as **XR-16** reconnaissance aircraft, redesignated **RB-52B** and converted to bomber

NB-52B: aircraft 52-008 rebuilt as parent aircraft of X-15

B-52C (Model 464-201-6): total 35(53-399/408 and 54-2664/2688), cleared from 420,000 lb (190512 kg) up to 450,000 lb (204120 kg) external fuel up from 2,000 to 6,000 US gal (7571 to 22712 litres) in giant underwing

tanks, water moved to 125-US gal (473-litre) tank in each wing root, tail guns four 0.5-in (12.7-mm) with MD-9 fire control

B-52D (Model 464-201-7): total 170 (101 Seattle-built, 55-068/117 and 56-580/630; 69 Wichita-built, 55-049/067, 55-673/680 and 56-657/698), J57-29W engines; basically as B-52C but provision for reconnaissance capsule deleted

B-52E (Model 464-259): total 100 (42 Seattle-built, 56-631/656 and 57-014/029; 58 Wichita-built, 56-699/712 and 57-095/138), ASQ-38 nav/bomb system

B-52F (Model 464-260): total 89 (44 Seattle-built, 57-030/073; 45 Wichita-built, 57-139/183), 13,750-lb (6237-kg) thrust J57-43W, WA or WB engines, water in four tanks in leading edge next to pylon struts

B-52G (Model 464-253): total 193, all built at Wichita (57-6468/6520, 58-158/258 and 59-2564/2602), new integral-tank wing, fuel 46,575 US gal (176305 litres) internally plus 1,400 US gal (5300 litres) externally, weight 488,000 lb (221357 kg), J57-43WB engines, ASG-15 rear defence with gunner relocated in main crew compartment, short fin and complete structural redesign, ailerons eliminated, ully powered elevator/rudder; weapon bay configured for launching two ADM-20 Quail ECM decoy missiles, inner-wing pylons for two AGM-28 Hound Dog missiles; subsequently modifed to carry up to 20 SRAM or ALCM

B-52H (Model 464-261): total 102, all built at Wichita (60-001/062 and 61-001/040), 17,000-lb (7711-kg) thrust P & W TF33-1 or -3 turbofan engines, water eliminated, gross weight 505,000 lb (229068 kg) for take off and 566,000 lb (256738 kg) after maximum inflight-refuel, ASG-21 rear defence with 20-mm T-171 gun

de Havilland Comet

In May 1952 a de Havilland Comet left London for Johannesburg to open the jet age for the world's airlines. So far ahead of all competition was the Comet at this time that no rival even had any firm idea what to build. Amazingly, this lead was later completely lost, but the Comet was developed out of all recognition and was also used as the basis for today's Nimrod sub-hunter and AWACS-type platform.

At the height of World War 2, in late 1941, the UK took the farsighted step of appointing a special group of experts to study what commercial transport aircraft should be planned for use after final victory. In May 1943 the Second Brabazon Committee had its first meeting, and towards the end of that year issued a series of recommendations, one of which, called Type IV, was for a jet-propelled transport. It is paradoxical that, whereas in the USA several large jet bombers were then being planned, without the slightest thought of a jet airliner, in the wartime UK the reverse was true. A major factor was that in the pre-war era the United States had come to dominate the world airliner market, and it was rightly felt that the only way to compete after the war would be to take bold technological leaps.

The various Brabazon recommendations quickly became associated with particular companies, and Type IV went to de Havilland. This enterprise had both an Aircraft company, with a design team led by R. E. Bishop and R. M. Clarkson, and an Engine company whose top engineers were F. B. Halford and J. S. Moult. In early 1944 both de Havilland teams studied the Type IV, and after many possibilities had been examined they were given authority to go ahead with the D.H.106 in February 1945. Even then the design remained fluid, ranging from a twin-boom Vampire-like machine with three Goblin engines, via a canard to a tailless swept-wing machine scaled up from the D.H.108. British Overseas Airways Corporation (BOAC) found it hard to make up its mind what was wanted, and the D.H.106 hovered between a 14-passenger short-hauler and a nonstop North Atlantic mailplane carrying a few sacks of letters plus two VIP passengers.

Fortunately de Havilland managed to persuade BOAC and the government that a more conventional transport would be more useful; the company also recognized that trans-Atlantic range was unattainable. The design at last went ahead in September 1946, when the Ministry of Supply ordered two prototypes. BOAC had said in 1944 it would need 25, but it had second thoughts and the first production order, in January 1947, was for eight. British South American Airways then ordered six, but this airline was merged into BOAC who cancelled the BSAA order but increased its own purchase to nine. The name Comet was announced in December 1947.

Because of the dramatically advanced nature of the new Comet, parallel research programmes were launched to provide a basis of proven hardware. The new Ghost engine was tested in the outer nacelles of Avro Lancastrian VM703 and in a special high-altitude de Havilland Vampire TG278. The Lockheed Servodyne powered flight controls were exhaustively tested at Farnborough on Lancaster PP755, while control components were flown on a D.H.108 and a Hornet.

RAF Comet C. Mk.2 aircraft served No. 216 Sqn flawlessly from 1956 until April 1967, fully modified with reskinned fuselages, oval windows and many other changes for military operations. XK697, the 32nd Comet and intended to be G-AMXJ, was named *Cygnus* from October 1959. The legend later read Air Support Command.

de Havilland Comet

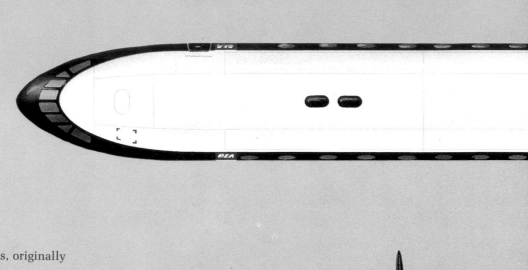

Specification

D.H.106 Comet 4B

Type: medium-range passenger transport

Powerplant: four Rolls-Royce Avon turbojets, originally 10,500-lb (4763-kg) Mk 542; later Mk 525B

Performance: maximum cruising speed 532 mph (856 km/h); typical field length 7,000 ft (2134 m); range with maximum payload (initial weight) 2,300 miles (3701 km), (final weight) 3,350 miles (5391 km)

Weights; empty 73,816 lb (33483 kg); maximum (initial) 152,500 lb (69174 kg) subsequently 156,000 lb (70762 kg) and finally 162,000 lb (73483 kg)

Dimensions: span 107 ft 10 in (32.87 m); length 118 ft 0 in (35.97 m); height 28 ft 6 in (8.69 m); wing area 2,059 sq ft (191.28 m²)

Accommodation: flight crew of three or four and normal seating for (initially) 101 passengers; (Dan-Air) 119 passengers

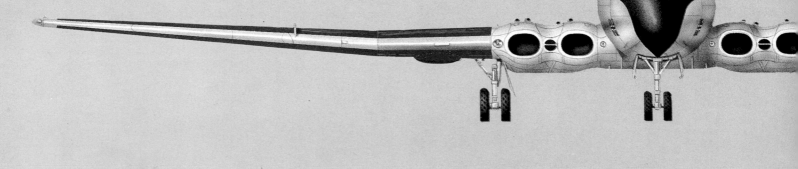

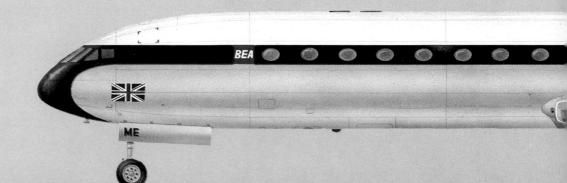

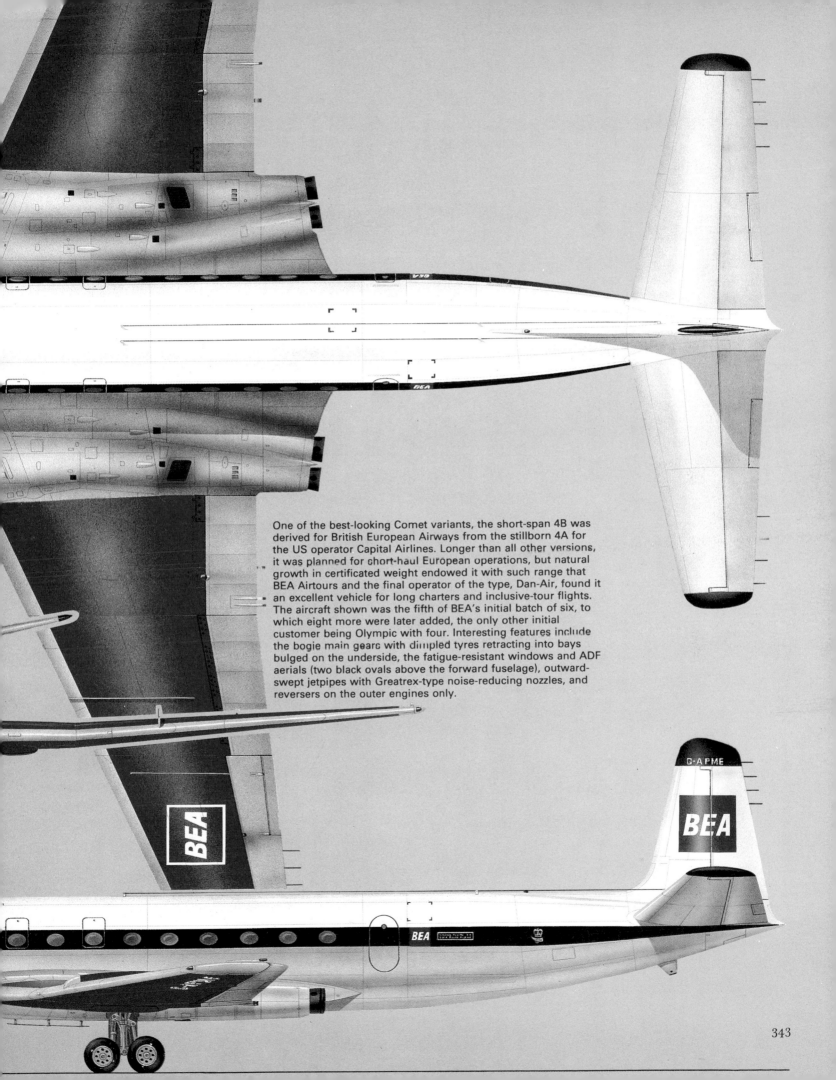

One of the best-looking Comet variants, the short-span 4B was derived for British European Airways from the stillborn 4A for the US operator Capital Airlines. Longer than all other versions, it was planned for short-haul European operations, but natural growth in certificated weight endowed it with such range that BEA Airtours and the final operator of the type, Dan-Air, found it an excellent vehicle for long charters and inclusive-tour flights. The aircraft shown was the fifth of BEA's initial batch of six, to which eight more were later added, the only other initial customer being Olympic with four. Interesting features include the bogie main gears with dimpled tyres retracting into bays bulged on the underside, the fatigue-resistant windows and ADF aerials (two black ovals above the forward fuselage), outward-swept jetpipes with Greatrex-type noise-reducing nozzles, and reversers on the outer engines only.

de Havilland Comet

G-ALYP – *Yoke Peter* – was the first production Comet I (roman numerals were used originally) and the third Comet built. She first flew on 9 January 1951 and on 2 May 1952 operated the world's first scheduled jet service. She piled up the hours, cracking insidiously until she burst open near Elba on 10 January 1954.

Even the streamlined nose was tested on an Airspeed Horsa glider, mainly to verify pilot vision in rain. Construction of the prototypes moved rapidly, and the first, unpainted and bearing Class B registration G-5-1, was rolled out at Hatfield on 25 July 1949 and flown by John Cunningham two days later.

A revolution in design

Though the Comet was less radical than it might have been, it nevertheless broke new ground in almost every part of its aerodynamics, structure, propulsion and systems. Basically, it had a low wing of substantial area whose 20° sweep resulted mainly from taper; the tail was unswept. The three widely separated spars passed through the fuselage under the floor, the inboard part of the wing on each side being bulged to house the 5,050-lb (2291-kg) thrust Ghost 50

One of the first air-to-air photographs ever taken of a Comet, G-ALVG is here seen in late 1949 after the addition of BOAC's Speedbird badge and a Union Jack on the fin. Later, G-ALVG had the full BOAC white-top livery then current, though it never served with the airline. It was scrapped after fatigue testing.

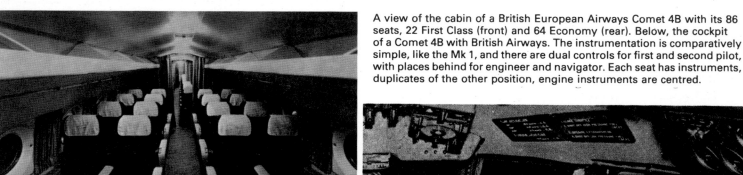

A view of the cabin of a British European Airways Comet 4B with its 86 seats, 22 First Class (front) and 64 Economy (rear). Below, the cockpit of a Comet 4B with British Airways. The instrumentation is comparatively simple, like the Mk 1, and there are dual controls for first and second pilot, with places behind for engineer and navigator. Each seat has instruments, duplicates of the other position, engine instruments are centred.

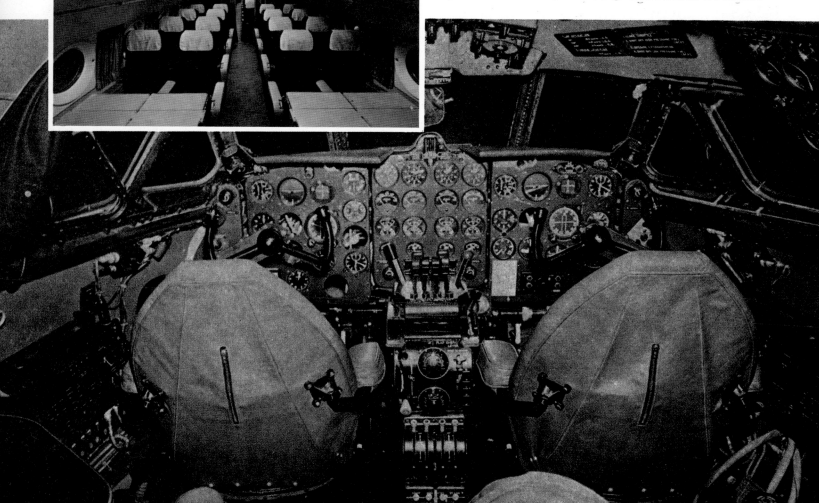

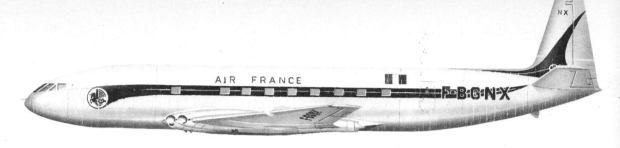

F-BGNX was the first of three Series 1A Comets for Air France (they were preceded by two for another French carrier, UAT), making its first flight on 6 May 1953. The airline opened Paris–Rome–Beirut services on 26 August 1953, but after the Certificate of Airworthiness was withdrawn in April 1954 Air France never again used Comets.

First of two Series 1A aircraft for CPA, CF-CUM had 7,000 gal (31823 litres) of fuel and water-methanol injection for full-load take-offs. After the destruction of her sister in a take-off crash she was passed to BOAC, where she served as G-ANAV. Photographed on 15 August 1952, she was the 13th Comet to be built.

turbojets, with plain oval inlets in the leading edge and long jetpipes projecting just behind the trailing edge. Large plain flaps were fitted, with split flaps under the jetpipes. The leading edge was fixed, with a small fence well outboard, ahead of the inner end of the powered aileron. Narrow perforated airbrakes could be raised ahead of the outer flap sections. Thickness ratio was 11 per cent, and the first Comet had a lower stalling speed and was easier to fly than most contemporary airliners with piston engines!

With a diameter of 10 ft (3.05 m), the circular tube fuselage was pressurized to 8.25 lb/sq in (0.58 kg/cm²), to give an 8,000-ft (2440-m) interior when flying at 40,000-ft (12190 m). This was double the pressure of any previous airliner, and a further factor was that outside temperatures of minus 70°C had a profound effect on materials throughout the aircraft. Not least of the innovations was the use of Redux metal-to-metal bonding throughout the structure. In effect a glueing

process, Redux had never before been used on such a scale or on such highly stressed parts. The de Havilland engineers conducted extensive tests to prove the strength of many critical parts, and also pressure-tested large fuselage sections. One of the latter exploded, the shattered pieces making it hard to pinpoint the source of the original crack, a fact that was later to be very significant. Its main result was to cause the company to switch to underwater pressure testing, where failures did not cause such explosive release of stored energy.

Secrecy worthy of a military project was maintained throughout. This applied especially to the quite simple engine installations, which were backed up by a neat stored-liquid rocket motor, a 5,000-lb (2268-kg) thrust de Havilland Sprite, between the jetpipes on each side to maintain take-off thrust in hot or high conditions. In sharp contrast with previous British aircraft, the Comet was planned to house all the fuel that could be packed in, virtually the whole wing apart from the engine and landing-gear bays forming a giant sealed integral tank with a capacity of 6,050 Imp gal (27503 litres), some three times that of a Lancaster. Another new feature was pressure fuelling, the large hose being attached in the underside of the wing to feed at the rate of one ton per minute. The cabin pressurization boldly took bleed air from the engines, while other bleed air was used to de-ice the wings and tail.

Overall technical risk was very great, and it is greatly to the credit of de Havilland that the company went ahead on the basis of an order for eight aircraft at a fixed price of £250,000 each. It rightly judged there would be many more orders once this revolutionary airliner had entered service. Passenger accommodation was on the basis of pairs of seats on each side of the aisle, and at the initial gross weight of 105,000 lb (47627 kg) it was possible to carry 36 passengers, eight in facing pairs in a 'smoking room' forward and 28 in the main cabin at what today seems the princely seat pitch of 45 in (1.14 m), the rearmost seats being in line with the jet nozzles. The limited underfloor space resulted in the main

G-APYC was the 37th of the 'New Comets' and was originally flown from Chester as SX-DAK of Olympic Airways, the only customer for the short-span 4B version other than BEA. She is depicted in Channel livery (1970–2), and finally found her way (like most surviving Comets) to Dan-Air in April 1972.

SU-ALC was the 39th of the 4/4B/4C series, being delivered as the first of nine 4Cs for Misrair. She is shown after repainting in the livery of UAA, Misrair's successor, with whom she was lost after 10 years of use in an accident near Tripoli on the second day of 1971. (Biggest export buyer was Aerolineas.)

Originally planned for 58 passengers, the Comet 4 was late in life regularly seating 106. G-APDR was the 18th of 19 Series 4 aircraft ordered by BOAC. She is seen here on pre-delivery testing in July 1958. Later she was sold to Mexicana and ended her days somewhat ignominiously – but usefully – in 1972 at the Standard Fire School.

The 45th Comet 4 series was this 4C for Middle East Airlines of the Lebanon. OD-ADR, along with sisters ADQ (no. 46) and ADS (no. 48), was destroyed in the Israeli attack on Beirut Airport on 28 December 1968. Altogether Comet 4, 4B and 4C aircraft flew almost exactly 2,000,000 hours, ending in December 1979.

baggage bay being above the floor, aft of the capacious flight deck laid out for two pilots, an engineer and a navigator.

Inevitably, every overseas trip by the prototype broke records, and it was established that full payload could be carried over a range of 1,750 miles (2816 km) cruising at 490 mph (788 km/h). The top of the fuselage was painted white, BOAC livery applied and civil registration G-ALVG bestowed, the certificate of airworthiness being issued as early as 21 April 1950. In December of that year the ungainly single-wheel main gears were replaced by neat four-wheel bogies (which could not retract in G-ALVG), and these were standard on the production machines. The latter also did not have the take-off rockets, though provision for them was retained.

The first production aircraft flew on 9 January 1951, and an unrestricted passenger-carrying certificate of airworthiness was awarded on 22 January 1952, ready for the start of regular service on 9 May. The initial route was from London to Johannesburg via Rome, Beirut, Khartoum, Entebbe and Livingstone, the end-to-end time being just under 24 hours. Thus, as Concorde was to do 25 years later, the Comet halved the effective size of the world; but in addition it utterly transformed air travel, the traditional thumping and lurching progress through bad weather being replaced by a totally effortless and virtually silent progress far above any turbulence, vibration or any kind of unpleasant environment. The world airline industry was naturally cautious, but could not overlook the fact that passengers who had flown in BOAC's Comet disliked any other kind of air travel.

Thus other customers slowly began to emerge, and de Havilland upgraded the basic aircraft to Comet 1A standard with weight raised to 115,000 lb (52163 kg), with extra fuel, 44 seats and water/methanol injection to maintain hot/high engine thrust. The first sale was to Canadian Pacific Airlines, followed by Air France, UAT and the Royal Canadian Air Force. For the next generation de Havilland switched to the Rolls-Royce Avon engine in the Comet 2, and early Avons flew the Comet 2X prototype on 16 February 1952. BOAC asked for 11 Comet 2s, using almost the same airframe as the Series 1 but with a 3-ft (0.91-m) stretch giving an extra passenger window on each side. After them came British Commonwealth Pacific, Japan Air Lines, LAV and Panair do Brasil, as well as the Comet 1A customers Air France, UAT and CPA. Suddenly de Havilland ran out of available capacity, because every inch of floorspace was already bursting with production on many other types, and Shorts at Belfast were brought in with a duplicate Comet 2 assembly line.

Developments and setbacks

At the 1952 Farnborough air show de Havilland announced the Comet 3. The power of later Avon engines enabled gross weight to jump to 145,000 lb (65772 kg), transforming the 44-seat 1,750-mile (2816-km) Comet 1 into a really capable and efficient airliner that could carry 76 passengers 2,700 miles (4345 km), and at slightly higher speed. With a fuselage stretch of 18 ft 6 in (5.639 m), the Comet 3 also looked a truly modern jetliner, and the Hatfield company was deluged with

enquiries. Sales were quickly made to BOAC, Air India and Pan Am, and plans were drawn up for a third Comet assembly line at the company's Chester factory. The Comet 3 prototype flew on 19 July 1954, by which time six BOAC Comet 2s had been completed, and shown their capability by flying nonstop to Khartoum, 3,064 miles (4930 km) in $6\frac{1}{2}$

de Havilland Comet 4 cutaway drawing key

1 Radome
2 Radar scanner
3 Front pressure bulkhead
4 Windscreen framing
5 Windscreen wipers
6 Instrument panel coaming
7 DME aerial
8 Rudder pedals
9 Cockpit roof construction
10 Co-pilot's seat
11 Control column
12 Pilot's seat
13 Engineer's control panel
14 Emergency escape hatch
15 Radio rack
16 Engineer's work table
17 Engineer's swivelling seat
18 Navigator's seats
19 Navigator's worktable
20 Nosewheel bay construction
21 Nosewheel leg strut
22 Twin nosewheels
23 Nosewheel door
24 Crew entry door
25 Crew's wardrobe
26 Forward galley
27 Galley supplies stowage boxes
28 Radio and electrical equipment bay
29 Forward starboard toilet compartment
30 Forward port toilet compartment
31 Wash basin
32 Air conditioning duct
33 Toilet servicing panel
34 Cabin window panel
35 First class cabin seats
36 Twin ADF loop aerials
37 Air conditioning grilles
38 Floor beams
39 Forward freight and luggage hold
40 Freight hold door
41 Control cable runs
42 Fuselage keel construction
43 Overhead hat rack
44 Cabin dividing bulkhead
45 Air distribution duct
46 Emergency escape window
47 Air conditioning plant
48 Hydraulics bay

49 Starboard wing integral fuel tanks
50 Flow spoilers
51 External fuel tank
52 Tank bumper
53 Fixed slot
54 Outer wing fuel tanks
55 Navigation light
56 Wing tip fuel vent
57 Static dischargers
58 Starboard aileron
59 Aileron tab
60 Flap outer section
61 Airbrake (upper and lower surfaces)
62 Fuel dump pipes
63 Fuel vent
64 Flap inboard section
65 Inboard airbrake (upper surface only)
66 Fuselage frame and stringer construction
67 Wing centre section fuel cells
68 Emergency escape hatch
69 Aileron servo controls
70 Main fuselage frame
71 Aft tourist class cabin
72 Rear freight hold/luggage compartment
73 Floor beam construction
74 HF aerial cable (port and starboard)
75 Overhead hat rack
76 Tourist class cabin seats
77 Aft galley
78 Starboard service door
79 Aft starboard toilet compartment
80 Aft radio rack
81 Rear pressure bulkhead
82 Anti collision light
83 Dorsal fin fairing

84 Starboard tailplane
85 ILS aerial
86 Starboard elevator
87 Leading edge de-icing ducts
88 Fin construction
89 HF blade aerial
90 Rudder balance weight
91 Rudder
92 Elevator hinge controls
93 Elevator tab
94 Port elevator
95 Tailplane construction
96 ILS aerial
97 Leading edge de-icing
98 Tailplane attachment
99 Fuselage fin frame
100 Tail bumper/fuselage vent
101 Rudder and elevator control rods
102 Access hatch to control bay
103 De-icing air supply duct
104 Rear freight hold

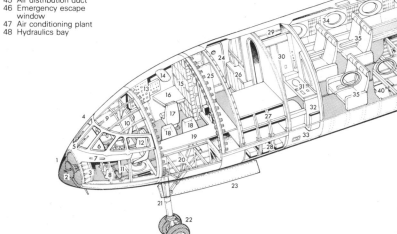

hours. But other things had happened by this time that crippled the programme.

The first accident came on 26 October 1952 when G-ALYZ failed to become airborne at Rome and was damaged beyond repair, though without injury to the 42 passengers and crew. On 3 March 1953 exactly the same thing happened to CF-CUN of CPA making a maximum-weight take-off in hot air at Karachi, and on this occasion all on board were killed. The cause was hauling back on the yoke too early, causing the aircraft to proceed down the runway with the wing stalled, the high drag preventing acceleration and the inlet angle reducing thrust. The answer was to droop the leading edge and refrain from hauling the aircraft off until a proper rotation speed had been reached.

More serious was the inflight destruction of G-ALYV while climbing out of Calcutta on the first anniversary of BOAC services on 2 May 1953. Tragically there was plenty of monsoon turbulence, and no enquiry was made to see whether or not the structural break-up might have been due to a weakness in the aircraft. But when the famed G-ALYP,

de Havilland Comet variants

D.H.106 Comet: two prototypes (G-ALVG and G-ALZK) with Ghost 50 engines and large single mainwheels; provision for Sprite rockets
Comet 1: nine production aircraft for BOAC with bogie main gears, Ghost 50-1 engines and no rockets (G-ALYP/S and G-ALYU/Z)
Comet 1A: 10 aircraft with more fuel (6,906 Imp gal/31395 litres) and water/methanol injection, for CPA, AF, UTA and RCAF
Comet 1XB: two RCAF (later CAF) Series 1As (nos 5301/5302) after structural rework in 1957
Comet 2X: one aircraft (G-ALYT), test-bed with Avon 501 engines
Comet 2: planned production civil transport with slightly longer fuselage (96 ft/29.26 m instead of 93 ft/28.35 m) and Avon 503 engines; 36 intended for BOAC and seven other operators; none delivered
Comet 2E: two ex-Comet 2s (G-AMXD and G-AMXK) used by BOAC for route-proving with modified airframes and Avon 524s in the outer positions; G-AMXD later rebuilt as radar and navaid laboratory for use by RAE as XN453
Comet 2(RAF): three aircraft (G-AMXA, G-AMXC and G-AMXE) transferred to RAF as XK655, 659 and 663; later designated **Comet E.Mk 2** for use as Elint platforms

Comet C.Mk 2: 10 aircraft begun as BOAC Series 2 but rebuilt for RAF; XK669 *Taurus*, XK670 *Corvus*, XK671 *Aquila*, XK695 *Perseus*, XK696 *Orion*, XK697 *Cygnus*, XK698 *Pegasus*, XK699 *Sagittarius*, SK715 *Columba* and XK716 *Cepheus*; XK669 and XK670 were initially **Comet T.Mk 2** trainers
Comet 3: one prototype (G-ANLO) with stretched fuselage and Avon 522 engines; later Avon 523, then (1958) rebuilt as Series 3B
Comet 3B: rebuild of G-ANLO as prototype of Series 4B with clipped wing, Avon 525 and other changes, finally rebuilt as blind-landing and avionics laboratory for RAE/BLEU with serial XP915
Comet 4: production fleet for BOAC, total 19 (G-APDA/DT) with revised airframe, Avon 524 engines and increased fuel
Comet 4A: planned short-haul version for Capital, not delivered
Comet 4B: short-haul version for BEA (14, G-APMA/MG, G-ARCO/CP, G-ARGM, G-ARJK/JN) and Olympic (SX-DAK/DAL/DAN/DAO) with Avon 525B engines and clipped wing
Comet 4C: final production model with long fuselage and large wing, total 30; last two completed as XV147 Nimrod with Avons and XV148 Nimrod with Speys, XV148 finally being avionics test-bed at Pershore/Bedford

105 Tailplane servo controls
106 Mail locker
107 Aft port toilet compartment
108 Passenger entry door
109 Door frame construction
110 Steward's seat
111 Tourist class passenger seating
112 Wing fillet construction
113 Life raft stowage
114 Inboard tailpipe duct
115 Exhaust silencer nozzles
116 Outboard tailpipe
117 Thrust reverser (outboard only)
118 Inboard flap section
119 Fuel vent
120 Fuel dump pipes
121 Flap jack
122 Flap connecting links
123 Port airbrake (upper and lower surfaces)
124 Outboard flap section
125 Flap construction
126 Aileron tab
127 Port aileron
128 Aileron hinge controls
129 Aileron construction
130 Static dischargers
131 Wing tip fuel vent
132 Port navigation light
133 Outer wing construction
134 Outboard fuel tank bays
135 Fuel tank access panels
136 Wing stringer construction
137 External fuel tank
138 Tank bumper
139 Fixed slot
140 Wing rib construction

141 Leading edge de-icing ducts
142 Four wheel bogie unit
143 Wing skin joint strap
144 Undercarriage well
145 Main undercarriage leg mechanism
146 Wing integral fuel tank
147 Rolls-Royce Avon R.A.29 engine
148 Inboard engine bay (engine omitted)
149 Engine mounting frame
150 Intake duct construction
151 Landing lamp
152 Engine intakes
153 Ram air intake
154 Heat exchangers
155 Taxi lamp

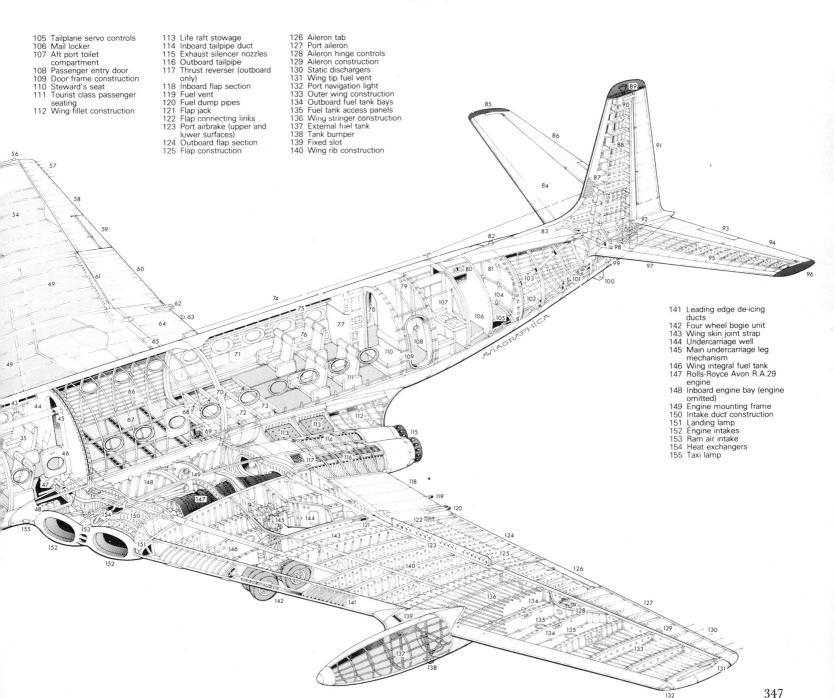

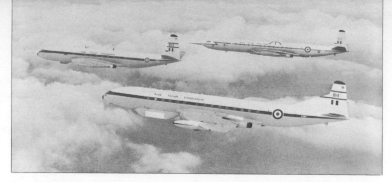

which had flown the first scheduled service, disappeared on 10 January 1954 outward bound from Rome, with no radio transmission from the crew, the Comet 1 was grounded and all available aircraft were subject to a detailed examination. Nobody knew what flaw to look for, but a month later a Royal Navy salvage team found the wreckage near Elba and began the laborious process of recovering every fragment. There were many theories as to what had happened, and after various small modifications the Comet 1s resumed services, but on 8 April G-ALYY disappeared while climbing out of Rome in the opposite direction. This time the Comets stayed grounded, causing great difficulties to BOAC, Air France, UAT and the RCAF.

There followed the biggest technical investigation up to that time, culminating in the certain knowledge that G-ALYP's fuselage had ripped open from a fatigue crack started at the corner of one of the rectangular cut-outs for the ADF aerials in the top skin. Another fuselage, that of G-ALYU, was tested in a giant water tank and after 1,830 simulated flights also ripped open, from the corner of a passenger window. Why de Havilland should have used straight-sided cut-outs in the most highly pressurized fuselage then attempted remained a mystery. For many months the whole Comet project hung in the balance. All export orders were terminated, and all Comet 1As were returned, except for those of the RCAF which without fuss were suitably modified with stronger skins and oval cut-outs and served with No. 412 Squadron until late 1964. The other Comet 1s and Comet 1As were used up in test programmes or simply scrapped. The Comet 2s were rebuilt with oval cut-outs in thicker skins and delivered from June 1956 to RAF Transport Command, whose 216 Sqn achieved a perfect record in intensive operation until April 1967. The assembly lines at Belfast and Chester were abandoned.

Two Comet 2s were passed to Rolls-Royce for use in developing the more powerful Avons being used in France's Sud Caravelle, and for BOAC route-proving, while three others with the original fuselage and with pressurization removed served as electronic-warfare 'ferret' platforms with RAF No. 51 Squadron at Wyton. But the big question was whether de Havilland could ever succeed in selling a completely redesigned derivative of the Comet 3, or whether the image was so damaged that the Comet had become unsaleable to the airlines and to the public. The answer came in February 1955 when BOAC announced it would buy 19 Comet 4s, similar to the Series 3 (which from the start had oval windows) but with even greater fuel capacity and range, with a weight up to 156,000 lb (70762 kg), which later grew to 162,000 lb (73483 kg). This at last resulted in a capable mainliner, but it was clear the new model would emerge into a world dominated by the Boeing 707 and Douglas DC-8. Thus, for narrow competitive reasons, the Comet 4's service life began on the North Atlantic on 4 October 1958, beating Pan Am's Model 707s into service by 22 days, though the type had never been intended for this route. BOAC's own Model 707-420s replaced the Comet on the Atlantic after little over a year.

The BOAC fleet of 19 Comet 4s demonstrated that at last de Havilland had created a safe airliner, and none were sold until 1965, and even then there were plenty of customers for the second-hand airliners. The first export order, in 1956, was for four Series 4 and 10 of a new clipped-wing long-body short-haul model, the Series 4A, for Capital Airlines of Washington DC. The Series 4A was specially strengthened for high speed at low levels, and it was a major blow when Capital was taken over by mighty United, which cancelled the order. But by this time BEA had become interested, and (to the disgust of the French, who said the Caravelle did the same job on two of the identical engines instead of four) in April 1958 the British airline ordered six Comet 4Bs, later increased to 14. Olympic ordered four. This version had clipped wings and even better payload, and without effort could carry over 100 passengers for 3,350 miles (5390 km), which a Caravelle certainly could not do. They put up a fine record, and de Havilland ended the programme by merging the long body with the large pinion-tanked wing to produce the Comet 4C.

The Comet 4C was the most successful model of all, being bought initially by Mexicana, Misrair (Egyptair), Aerolineas Argentinas, MEA, Sudan and Kuwait. Altogether 30 of this series were made, 23 of them at Chester, bringing total production to 113, the final examples being made speculatively and finally going to King Ibn Saud of Saudi Arabia, five for No. 216 Squadron RAF, one for the A&AEE at Boscombe Down and the last two being passed to Hawker Siddeley Manchester for use as starting points for the first Nimrods.

Some ex-BOAC Comet 4s were snapped up by the British Ministry of Aviation for research and trials purposes, notable examples being G-APDF which became the much-modified XV814, and G-APDS which grew a Nimrod AEW radome. Most, however, went to other airlines, all over the world. Malaysia Singapore purchased seven, but by far the most important operator after 1966 was the UK's Dan-Air. Having no doubts of the reliability and practicability of the now ageing Comet, the British independent purchased no fewer than 47 of various (Series 4, 4B and 4C) types, though never more than one-third were in use at any one time. Dan-Air really showed what Comets could do, even after the 1973 fuel crises trebled the price of kerosene, and it put 106 seats in its Series 4s and 119 into the Series 4Bs and 4Cs. Its scheduled and inclusive-tour Comet services finally ceased on 3 November 1980.

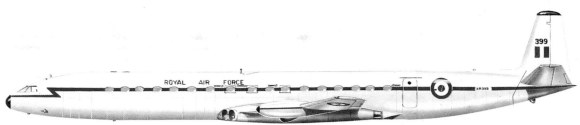

XR399 was built as a Comet C.Mk 4 for the RAF, almost at the end of the Chester line and first flown in March 1962. Usually fitted with 94 aft-facing seats, XR399 was the last of the five C.Mk 4s (basically 4Cs) which operated without any problems with No. 216 Sqn from RAF Lyneham. In 1975, with commendably few hours, she was sold to Dan-Air, being re-registered as G-BDIX.

Boeing 707

In 1954 Boeing risked more than the company's net worth to build the first Boeing 707. It seemed a desperate gamble, and possible sales were counted on the fingers. Nobody guessed that the same airframe would still be in production in 1983.

Though the British de Havilland Comet was the pioneer jetliner, it paid the penalty of being first. It remained an attractive exception to the mainstream of civil air transport, and its main effect was to show the enormous passenger appeal of a vehicle that got there in half the time after a trip that, in comparison with the noisy, vibrating piston-engined machines, was like being wafted by an angel. Could this rather small and supposedly uneconomic machine threaten the almost total grip of US industry on the world transport-aircraft market? The answer was clearly to meet the competition with an American jet, but how could it be financed? The only way seemed to be with federal aid, but after arguing the matter throughout 1949 the US Congress eventually in 1950 threw out a bill to fund a US jet prototype.

Douglas and Lockheed studied the problem intently and published a few brochures, but only Boeing (very much an also-ran in the civil transport aircraft business) had actually built large modern jets. By the autumn of 1950 the Seattle-based company could see that to meet its global range needs, the US Air Force would have to use inflight-refuelling not

only with its Boeing B-47 bombers but also with the giant new Boeing B-52. Boeing was building the tankers as well, in the form of KC-97s; but these were piston-engined, and to hook up with them the bombers had to slow down and lose almost half their altitude. Surely, reasoned Boeing, the answer was a jet tanker?

Boeing began by proposing a swept wing, jet-propelled KC-97 in March 1951. After much argument the idea was rejected by the USAF on 17 August 1951. Yet Boeing were convinced both the airlines and the US Air Force would eventually buy jet transports, and that the tanker and the civil liner could be basically the same design. But in the absence of airline orders, government prototype funds or even US Air Force interest, Boeing had to do it the hard way. It had to tighten its belt and produce a prototype with its own money. After the

Seen here at Mauritius, this Boeing 707-465 typifies hundreds of the type that will carry on flying with third-world operators well into the 1990s. By that time many may have logged 100,000 hours, setting new records for longevity, despite the unmatched light weight of the original airframe.

Boeing 707

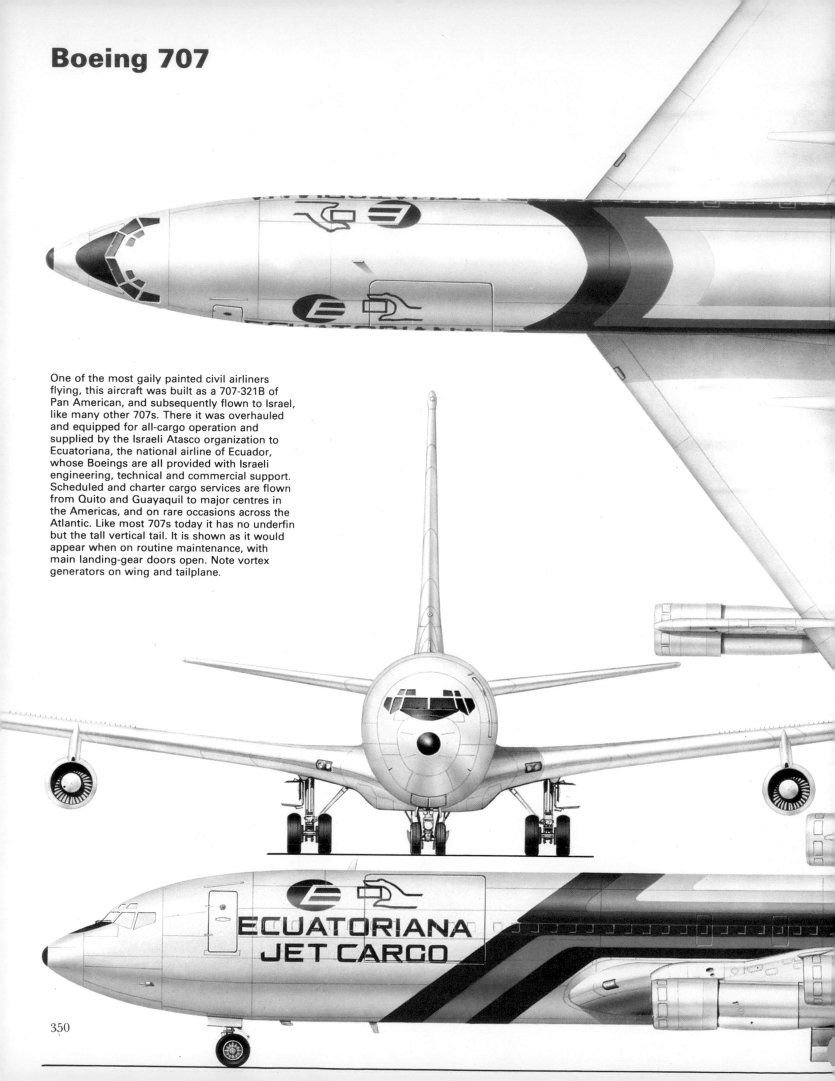

One of the most gaily painted civil airliners
flying, this aircraft was built as a 707-321B of
Pan American, and subsequently flown to Israel,
like many other 707s. There it was overhauled
and equipped for all-cargo operation and
supplied by the Israeli Atasco organization to
Ecuatoriana, the national airline of Ecuador,
whose Boeings are all provided with Israeli
engineering, technical and commercial support.
Scheduled and charter cargo services are flown
from Quito and Guayaquil to major centres in
the Americas, and on rare occasions across the
Atlantic. Like most 707s today it has no underfin
but the tall vertical tail. It is shown as it would
appear when on routine maintenance, with
main landing-gear doors open. Note vortex
generators on wing and tailplane.

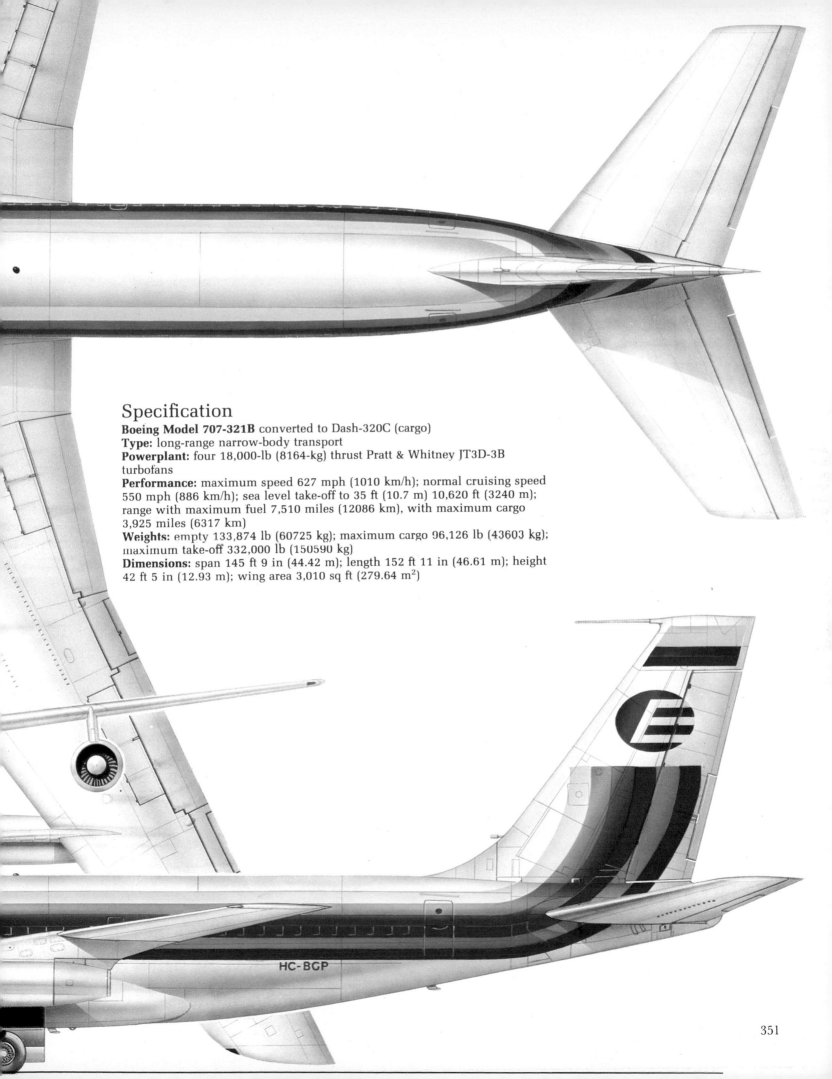

Specification

Boeing Model 707-321B converted to Dash-320C (cargo)
Type: long-range narrow-body transport
Powerplant: four 18,000-lb (8164-kg) thrust Pratt & Whitney JT3D-3B turbofans
Performance: maximum speed 627 mph (1010 km/h); normal cruising speed 550 mph (886 km/h); sea level take-off to 35 ft (10.7 m) 10,620 ft (3240 m); range with maximum fuel 7,510 miles (12086 km), with maximum cargo 3,925 miles (6317 km)
Weights: empty 133,874 lb (60725 kg); maximum cargo 96,126 lb (43603 kg); maximum take-off 332,000 lb (150590 kg)
Dimensions: span 145 ft 9 in (44.42 m); length 152 ft 11 in (46.61 m); height 42 ft 5 in (12.93 m); wing area 3,010 sq ft (279.64 m²)

HC-BGP

Boeing Model 707 variants

Model 367-80: company prototype; first flown 15 July 1954 and subsequently used in numerous research programmes

Model 707-102: four 13,500-lb (6124-kg) JT3C-6 engines; initial production version, with fuselage increased in width and length, gross weight raised to 225,000 lb (102060 kg) and finally 257,000 lb (116575 kg)

Model 707-120B: four 17,000-lb (7711-kg) JT3D-1 engines, aerodynamic improvements for Mach 0.91 cruise

Model 707-138: short-body model for Qantas, 10 ft (3,048 m) shorter

Model 707-220: as model 707-120 but four 15,800-lb (7167-kg) JT4A-3 engines

Model 707-320: first intercontinental version; all-round increase in size; four JT4A engines (various ratings); gross weight 312,000 lb (141520 kg)

Model 707-320B: aerodynamic improvements, four 18,000-lb (8165-kg) JT3D-3 engines; includes **VC-137C**; optional gross weight 333,600 lb (151321 kg)

Model 707-320C: as Model 707-320B but equipped for passengers (up to 202) or cargo

Model 707-420: as Model 707-320 (not Model 707-320B) but with 17,500 lb (7945-kg) or 18,000 lb (8165-kg) Rolls-Royce Conway 508 or 508A turbofans

Model 720: derivative of Model 707 series with lightweight structure and shorter fuselage tailored to short/medium-range operations

Model 720B: turbofan-engined version of Model 720

VC-137A: USAF version of Model 707-120 for VIP transport

VC-137B: designation of VC-137A after re-engining with JT3D; gross weight 258,000 lb (117025 kg)

VC-137C: Presidential (often 'Air Force One') aircraft, as Model 707-320B with various special equipment; gross weight 322,000 lb (146055 kg)

E-3A Sentry: AWACS platform; 21,000 lb (9525-kg) TF33-100/100A engines; gross weight 325,000 lb (147400 kg)

Cathay Pacific's colourful livery adorns Boeing airframe no. 18888, delivered in May 1965 as a 707-351C to Northwest Orient and sold in August 1974 to the Hong Kong carrier, with registration VR-HHE.

most searching evaluation, the company's board met on 22 April 1952 (exactly one week after the successful first flight of the B-52) and took the big decision. It would cost not less than $15 million.

Essential ingredient

One essential ingredient was the Pratt & Whitney JT3 engine, the lightweight commercial verson of the fuel-efficient J57 used in the B-52. But, whereas the giant bomber used eight of the 10,000-lb (4536-kg) thrust engines, the transport would need just four, hung in single pods below and ahead of the 35°-swept wing. The fuselage would not be that of the C-97 but larger, and with a more streamlined nose tipped by radar. (Even creating the radome would mean solving a completely new set of technical problems.) Gross weight worked out to 190,000 lb (86184 kg), and though the military model would have an interior configured for cargo and fuel, the commercial passenger aircraft could seat 130. Because it could fly at 600 mph (966 km/h), the jetliner promised to do three times the work of either the military KC-97 or a commercial type such as the Douglas DC-7 or Lockheed Super Constellation. But the airlines and US Air Force never showed more than polite interest as the prototype took shape at the Renton (Seattle) plant.

In fact the correct Boeing model number for the prototype was 367-80, and the company-owned prototype was to become popularly known as the Dash-80, but that was because the years of study had been numbered as suffixes to the same Model 367 number of the original piston-engined C-97. Numbers in the 500 series were reserved for gas turbine engines and in the 600 series for Boeing missiles, and aircraft numbers began again at 700. When the Model 367-80 finally became a flyable aircraft it was given the new designation Model 707. Subsequently Boeing deliberately capitalized on this memorable sequence by making their subsequent jet transports the Models 717, 727, 737, 747, 757 and 767.

Boeing E-3A Sentry cutaway drawing key

1 Weather radar scanner
2 Glide-slope aerial
3 Forward pressure bulkhead
4 Pilot's station
5 Central control console
6 Co-pilot's station
7 Flight engineer's station
8 Observer's supernumerary
9 Navigator's table
10 Navigator's overhead panel
11 Flight deck door
12 In-flight refuelling receptacle
13 Communication consoles (one unmanned TAC)
14 Forward entry door
15 Nosewheel hydraulic actuator
16 Nosewheel box
17 Twin nosewheels
18 Nosewheel doors
19 Forward cargo hold equipment bay
20 Flight essential avionics
21 Communications
22 Data processor functional group
23 Computer operator console
24 Bailout jettison mechanism
25 Bailout chute
26 DC power
27 Power distribution
28 Multi-purpose consoles (nine-off)
29 VHF aerial
30 Engine intakes
31 Secondary inlet doors
32 Turbocompressor intakes
33 Turbocompressor outlets
34 Nacelle pylons
35 Leading-edge wing flap
36 Main tank No. 3 (4,069 US gal/15400 litres each wing)
37 Fuel system dry bay
38 Main tank No. 4 (2,323 US gal/8791 litres each wing)
39 Reserve tank (439 US gal/1660 litres each wing)
40 Vent surge tank
41 HF antenna
42 Starboard outboard aileron
43 Tab
44 Starboard outboard spoiler (extended)

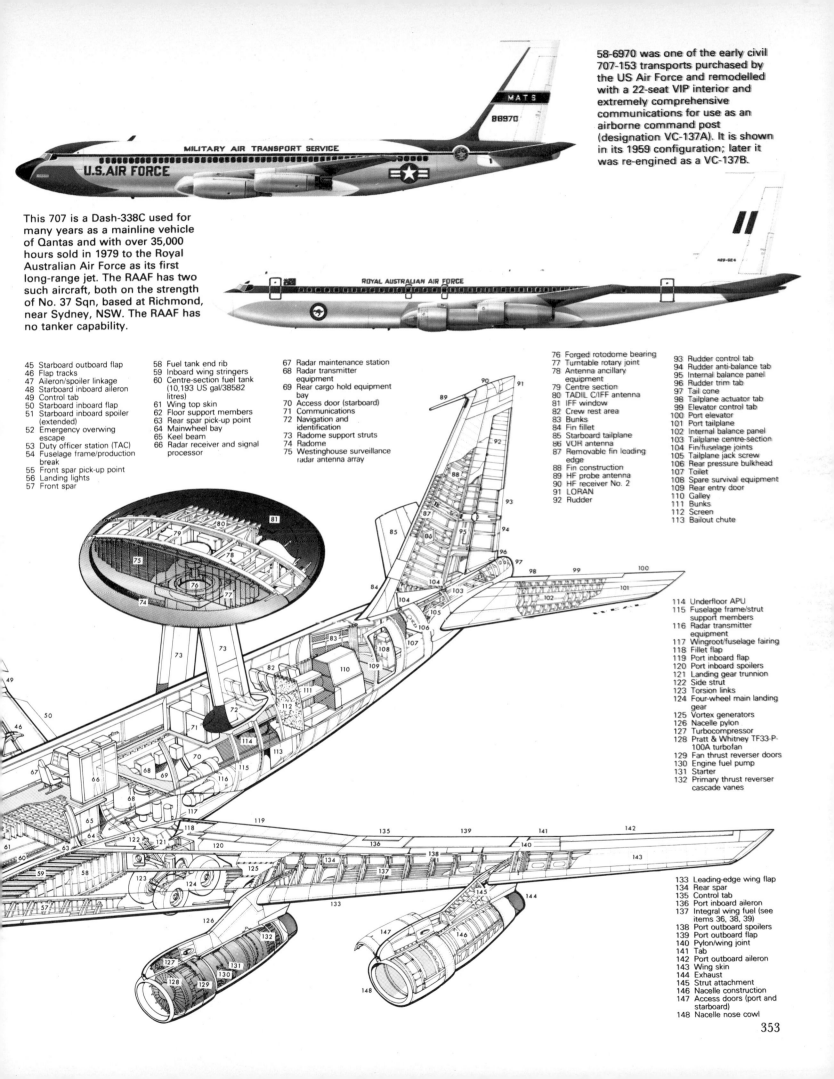

58-6970 was one of the early civil 707-153 transports purchased by the US Air Force and remodelled with a 22-seat VIP interior and extremely comprehensive communications for use as an airborne command post (designation VC-137A). It is shown in its 1959 configuration; later it was re-engined as a VC-137B.

MILITARY AIR TRANSPORT SERVICE

MATS
86970

U.S. AIR FORCE

This 707 is a Dash-338C used for many years as a mainline vehicle of Qantas and with over 35,000 hours sold in 1979 to the Royal Australian Air Force as its first long-range jet. The RAAF has two such aircraft, both on the strength of No. 37 Sqn, based at Richmond, near Sydney, NSW. The RAAF has no tanker capability.

ROYAL AUSTRALIAN AIR FORCE

45 Starboard outboard flap
46 Flap tracks
47 Aileron/spoiler linkage
48 Starboard inboard aileron
49 Control tab
50 Starboard inboard flap
51 Starboard inboard spoiler (extended)
52 Emergency overwing escape
53 Duty officer station (TAC)
54 Fuselage frame/production break
55 Front spar pick-up point
56 Landing lights
57 Front spar

58 Fuel tank end rib
59 Inboard wing stringers
60 Centre-section fuel tank (10,193 US gal/38582 litres)
61 Wing top skin
62 Floor support members
63 Rear spar pick-up point
64 Mainwheel bay
65 Keel beam
66 Radar receiver and signal processor

67 Radar maintenance station
68 Radar transmitter equipment
69 Rear cargo hold equipment bay
70 Access door (starboard)
71 Communications
72 Navigation and identification
73 Radome support struts
74 Radome
75 Westinghouse surveillance radar antenna array

76 Forged rotodome bearing
77 Turntable rotary joint
78 Antenna ancillary equipment
79 Centre section
80 TADIL C/IFF antenna
81 IFF window
82 Crew rest area
83 Bunks
84 Fin fillet
85 Starboard tailplane
86 VOH antenna
87 Removable fin leading edge
88 Fin construction
89 HF probe antenna
90 HF receiver No. 2
91 LORAN
92 Rudder

93 Rudder control tab
94 Rudder anti-balance tab
95 Internal balance panel
96 Rudder trim tab
97 Tail cone
98 Tailplane actuator tab
99 Elevator control tab
100 Port elevator
101 Port tailplane
102 Internal balance panel
103 Tailplane centre-section
104 Fin/fuselage joints
105 Tailplane jack screw
106 Rear pressure bulkhead
107 Toilet
108 Spare survival equipment
109 Rear entry door
110 Galley
111 Bunks
112 Screen
113 Bailout chute

114 Underfloor APU
115 Fuselage frame/strut support members
116 Radar transmitter equipment
117 Wingroot/fuselage fairing
118 Fillet flap
119 Port inboard flap
120 Port inboard spoilers
121 Landing gear trunnion
122 Side strut
123 Torsion links
124 Four-wheel main landing gear
125 Vortex generators
126 Nacelle pylon
127 Turbocompressor
128 Pratt & Whitney TF33-P-100A turbofan
129 Fan thrust reverser doors
130 Engine fuel pump
131 Starter
132 Primary thrust reverser cascade vanes

133 Leading-edge wing flap
134 Rear spar
135 Control tab
136 Port inboard aileron
137 Integral wing fuel (see items 36, 38, 39)
138 Port outboard spoilers
139 Port outboard flap
140 Pylon/wing joint
141 Tab
142 Port outboard aileron
143 Wing skin
144 Exhaust
145 Strut attachment
146 Nacelle construction
147 Access doors (port and starboard)
148 Nacelle nose cowl

Boeing 707

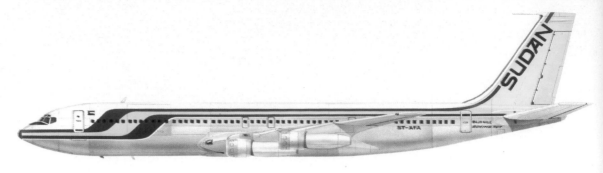

This Boeing 707-358C was one of the last of the type to be built (though beaten in this respect by the IIAF tanker shown on p. 157). With Boeing hull number 20897 and registration ST-AFA, it was delivered new on 17 June 1974 to Sudan Airways, with whom it has since operated on the trunk route to London with the individual name *Blue Nile*. Its partner, ST-AFB, is *White Nile*.

Question marks

The designation Model 717 was assigned to the proposed USAF tanker, but by 1954 the Korean War had ended, money was tight, and strong forces favoured a cheaper turboprop tanker, or even modified Convair B-36s or B-47s. There was still nothing certain about the programme when the Dash-80, painted in a rich company livery of chocolate-brown and chrome yellow, rolled out in a ceremony on 15 May 1954. The question marks loomed larger when, during taxi tests six days later, the left main gear smashed its way up through the wing and left the vital prototype lying crippled on its left outer engine pod. It was not until 15 July 1954 that Tex Johnston and Dix Loesch were able to fly the aircraft that was to keep the United States the world leader in civil transports.

By this time the USAF had told Boeing it wanted a new-build jet tanker, a great relief after the company had already spent not only $15 million on the prototype but half as much again on design and tooling for production machines. In October 1954 the first tanker order came through, for 29 aircraft, launching a gigantic programme of KC-135 and C-135 versions. This underpinned the commercial Model 707, but in 1954 Boeing did not enjoy the same clout with the airlines as mighty Douglas, and the announcement of the DC-8 on 5 June 1955 meant Boeing was going to have to fight every inch of the way. Moreover, on a run of 50 aircraft Boeing could see no way of pricing the 707 below $5.5 million, far above what the airlines would pay.

Nor was this all. To meet the competition of the DC-8, Boeing decided to do one of the costliest modifications possible: change the body cross section. It remained a figure-8 with smoothly faired sides but the upper lobe was increased in width by 4 in (10.16 cm) to 140 in (3.556 m), beating Douglas by 2 in (5.08 cm) and enabling a triple seat unit to be installed on each side of the aisle, for up to 150 passengers. A new form of fatigue-proof window structure was devised, with two small windows per seat row and chemically machined panels running the whole length of each side of the fuselage to double up on the original skin

This aircraft, one of the hardest-worked of all 707s, was built as a Dash-330C for Lufthansa, and registered D-ABUA. Delivered in 1965 it logged over 35,000 hours before being handed in April 1977 to German Cargo, a Lufthansa subsidiary, after complete gutting and conversion as a windowless freighter. It has since operated with high utilization on long-haul cargo charters throughout the world.

and frames. Boeing learned a great deal from the British investigation into Comet fatigue problems, as did other US builders. Fuel capacity was increased, with various arrangements of flexible cells inboard and integral tanks outboard, and the first models offered were the Model 707-120 series with a length of 144 ft 6 in (44.04 m) and the special Model 707-138 which was 10 ft (3.048 m) shorter. The standard launch engine was the JT3C-6, rated at 13,500-lb (6124-kg) thrust with water injection, and fitted with a large noise-suppressing nozzle with 20 separate tubes (which soon became covered with soot from wet take-offs).

Predictably the first airline customer was Pan American, which bought 20 Model 707-121s; but, to Boeing's consternation, it also signed for 25 DC-8s on the same day (13 October 1955) in a $296 million deal. Later in the same month United chose 30 DC-8s, and Douglas announced a longer-ranged DC-8 with the big JT4A engine. Boeing had to respond with a long-range Model 707, and unlike Douglas

N70700 lifted off from Renton on 15 July 1954 to open the world-wide era of jet transportation. After many years of valued research by Boeing, which involved several startling modifications, this historic aircraft was rebuilt in its original form for permanent preservation.

History was made when the Boeing 707-121 of Pan American World Airways opened the 'Big Jet' era on 26 October 1958 with a scheduled service from New York to Paris. Since that time the US grip on the air-transport industry has been almost total.

The Boeing 707-384B, *Mycenae*, belonging to Olympic Airways, has four Pratt & Whitney JT3D-3B engines. It was built in 1968 and was still in use in 1986. International noise regulations mean that all Boeing 707s now have to be fitted with sound absorbers.

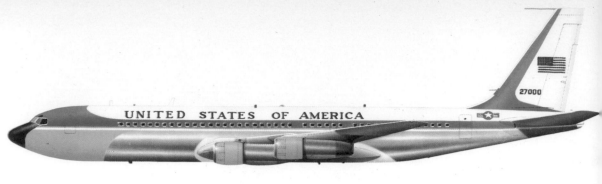

27000

Aircraft 72-7000 is perhaps the most senior aircraft in the US Air Force, because when the President is aboard it becomes Air Force One. Basically a civil 707-320C, it lacks the latter's underfin, and of course has a custom-built interior and very special navigation and communication installations for global self-sufficiency.

The first of many military 707s was this 707-153, delivered on 4 May 1959 to the USAF as a VC-137A, operated by the 1298th Air Transport Squadron with a 22-seat VIP interior convertible as an airborne command post. The engine pods with multi-pipe nozzles were typical of early JT3C aircraft. Later the three VC-137As were converted to VC-137B standard with JT3D (TF33) engines, for the 89th Military Airlift Wing.

(whose aircraft were all the same size) decided to make it larger. Braniff, in fact, was odd man out in buying the Model 707-220, which was the original size but had the JT4A, rated at 15,800-lb (7167-kg) thrust, for sprightly take-off at hot-and-high airports on routes to South America. But it was American's order for 30 Model 707-123s on 8 November 1955 that clinched the go-ahead and took Boeing to the 50 mark. Subsequently Boeing at least level-pegged Douglas. In the UK BOAC, having said it had no interest in jets and so getting the Vickers VC 7 cancelled, began talking with Boeing only four months later.

Rolls-Royce power

BOAC, like PanAm, was interested in Boeing's bigger longer-range model, the Model 707-320 Intercontinental. This had a new high-efficiency wing of 11 ft 7 in (3.53 m) greater span, a fuselage 8 ft 5 in (2.57 m) longer seating up to 189 passengers, much greater fuel capacity, and an initial gross weight of 312,000 lb (141520 kg). Launch engine was the JT4A at the increased rating of 16,800 lb (7620 kg), but Rolls-Royce's Conway bypass turbojet (a turbofan of very low 0.3:1 bypass ratio) fitted perfectly and offered greater power, lower installed weight and much better fuel consumption, and was selected by a small minority of airlines including BOAC and Lufthansa. The considerably greater capability of the Intercontinental quickly made this the standard type of Model 707, while the original size was developed into a new shorter-range family initially marketed with the same Model 717 number as the tanker but in 1959 renumbered as the Model 720.

The first production Model 707, Boeing no. 17586, was flown at Renton on 20 December 1957, but was actually numbered as the second of the initial batch of 20 Model 707-121s for PanAm, N708PA, the second production machine having the specially chosen registration N707PA. Flight development was generally trouble-free, and FAA certification was awarded on 23 September 1958. The world airline industry was poised on the brink of a new era. Some thought the prospect disastrous; one important expert said it was 'an industry gone mad'. Bristol, trying to sell Britannia turboprops, had insisted the Model 707 was technically impossible, and would need six engines. Even jet enthusiasts admitted that the Boeing monster was almost impossibly big, heavy, capacious, expensive to buy, needed runways longer than those available, could gobble up passenger-miles at a rate that seemed astronomic, and might indeed bankrupt the airlines (either those that bought it or those that stayed with propellers). The voices which predicted that what had become known as The Big Jets would result in a gigantic expansion of the air-transport business were muted and uncertain. Those that predicted an era of unknown profitability, and freedom from reliance on government subsidies, were hardly heard at all.

PanAm opened scheduled services between New York and Paris on 26 October 1958. New York and London and other European capitals soon followed. On these routes the Model 707-121 was marginal. It had not been designed for the North Atlantic, and the flight crews had to learn fast about correct take-off procedures and how to get the most air-miles per pound of fuel. Had noise certification been in force the operations would have been impossible. As it was,

The main display and control interfaces with the human crew of the E-3A are provided by these nine MPCs (multi-purpose consoles), plus three auxiliary display units. The normal mission crew comprises 13 AWAC (airborne warning and control) specialists, plus a flight crew of four to fly the aircraft. Up front are communications and data-processing, and at the rear the navigation units and crew-rest bunks.

Right at the very end of 707 production, in 1976–7, came a batch of 14 extremely well equipped 707-3J9C aircraft for the Imperial Iranian Air Force. They combined special communications for global operation with triple-point air refuelling, with tip-mounted hose/drogue installations and a Boeing high-speed boom driven by an operator in the rear fuselage. All were delivered before late 1977.

on westbound flights a refuelling stop was invariably needed at Iceland or one of the other wartime-built fields farther west. But these were the first halting steps of a revolution in global travel. On 25 January 1959 American began services with the Model 707-123 between New York and Los Angeles, and here there was no real problem.

Spurred by competition from the DC-8, CV-880 and European types, Boeing had been forced to embark on a programme of building ever-better jetliners. The original risk of $15 million had been left far behind. Now the risks were beginning to approach $100 million. What was still uncertain was whether or not the company would survive. The Model 707 was selling in dozens, but would it ever sell in hundreds? Pratt & Whitney met the competition of the Conway with a startlingly simple modification to the JT3C which replaced the first three stages of the compressor with two stages of enormous blades called a fan; and they coined the name turbofan, more descriptive than 'bypass turbojet' and easier to sell. Called the JT3D, the new engine began life at 18,000-lb (8172-kg) thrust and offered much better fuel economy and dramatically reduced noise as well as release from water injection. The result was a second generation of Model 707s characterized by a B suffix.

Before these were available, the big Model 707-320 Intercontinental flew as the 16th off the Renton line on 11 January 1959. It was certificated on 15 July the same year and entered service with PanAm a month later, sweeping away the Model 707-121 from trans-Atlantic routes with a replacement aircraft designed for the job, and able to carry a considerably greater payload non-stop even westbound. The UK's certification was held up while the ARB (today the CAA) studied the handling and stability in adverse circumstances and finally insisted on greater fin area. At first an underfin was added, with a tail bumper incorporated, but later this was

replaced by a much taller vertical tail which was retrofitted on almost all Model 707s and related military models. This cleared the way for the Conway-engined Model 707-420 family, which was approved in February 1960.

Boeing's bargain

In fact the first model to have the JT3D fan engine was the Model 707-120B. This stemmed from the Model 720, first flown on 23 November 1959, which looked like a Model 707-120 but in fact had a completely revised lightweight airframe matched to reduced weights for short/medium hauls, as well as aerodynamic improvements to the wing which resulted in better take-off and higher cruising speed. Sold at what was called a 'bargain basement' price, the Model 720 killed Convair's CV-880 stone dead even with JT3C engines, and 154 were quickly sold, most having the JT3D engine (either when built or as a retrofit) and styled Model 720B. When the extended-chord wing with high-lift leading-edge flaps was fitted to the Model 707-120 the result was the Model 707-120B, with fan engines, which needed less than half the runway length of the original Model 707-120, besides being quieter and making no visible smoke. American was first of many customers for this model which first flew on 22 June 1960. One oddball customer was Qantas, which bought the short-body Model 707-138 and later fitted fan engines to result in the Model 707-138B.

Last of the major variants was the Model 707-320C. Boeing had already fitted the fan engine to the Intercontinental to produce the Model 707-320B, and with it came a host of aerodynamic improvements including longer-span curved wingtips giving lower drag, and a high-lift leading edge with full-span flaps similar to those of the Model 707-120B and Model 720B. The Model 707-320B entered service with PanAm in June 1962, and a year later the same pioneer airline began using the Model 707-320C mixed-traffic version certificated for up to 202 passengers or 96,126 lb (43603 kg) of cargo, with special provisions for loading and positioning very large or heavy items. The Model 707-320C quickly became the standard model, and the customers kept coming.

In the 1950s the Model 707 and DC-8 had fought a pretty even battle. In the 1960s Boeing began to draw ahead, and when a DC-8 operator, Northwest Orient, bought a much bigger fleet of 26 Model 707-351Cs it looked as if the DC-8

Though the general level of serviceability in the Islamic Iranian Air Force is believed to be very low, the 707-3J9C is a very useful long-range aircraft and at least some of the original force of 14 are kept in operation. Since 1980 efforts have been made to maintain their capability as tankers, especially for the Grumman F-14As.

Boeing 707

This profile shows the first production Boeing E-3A Sentry, USAF 73-1674, which was preceded by two special test aircraft designated EC-137D (numbers 71-1407 and 71-1408). The latter were converted 707-320B airframes, with the JT3D (TF33-7) engine, whereas the production Sentry incorporates many refinements and is powered by the TF33-100A of 21,000 lb (9525 kg) thrust with large generators.

was finished. Douglas fought back with the stretched DC-8 Super Sixty series, but finally closed the DC-8 line at aircraft no. 556 in May 1972. But the Model 707 kept on selling, in slowly diminishing numbers. Many late customers were air forces, starting with the USAF which applied the designation C-137 (see variants). Canada and Iran were among customers for military models with inflight-refuelling capability by wing-tip hosereels and drogues. The total for all regular transport variants was 970, completed in 1986.

The remaining current aircraft using the Model 707 airframe is the E-3A Sentry, or AWACS (Airborne Warning and Control System). This impressive aircraft was planned with eight TF34 engines for greater endurance, but to save money was finally built with four TF33-100/100A engines, military versions of the JT3D. Packed with electronics, the E-3A's purpose is surveillance of the entire airspace within a radius of some 250 miles (402 km), with a Westinghouse APY-1 radar whose main aerial rotates with a 30-ft (9.14-m) roto-dome rotating six times per minute. The USAF has since 1977 been building up a force of 34 E-3As, and NATO is deploying an additional 18 paid for by most NATO European nations, registered in Luxembourg, completed with a special avionic fit by Dornier at Oberpfaffenhofen and based at Geilenkirchen. Last is the E-8A, a platform for the Joint STARS attack radar.

Distinguished by a communications probe aerial at both wingtips, the NATO E-3A Sentries have been flown from Boeing Aerospace to the Dornier plant at Oberpfaffenhofen for final fitting-out with a third HF radio, a new data analysis and programming group and underwing hardpoints for self-defence weapons which initially include AIM-9L Sidewinders.

Starfighter:
manned missile

'Missile with a man in it': such was Lockheed's slogan describing the F-104 Starfighter, visually perhaps the 'hottest' aircraft ever built. Its wing looks too small to be believable, and for just this reason it was never a good air-combat fighter. Large numbers were built, however, to fly attack, reconnaissance and stand-off intercept missions.

In the early 1950s the swept-wing North American F-86 Sabres of the US Air Force were having a hard time in combat with the unexpected Mikoyan-Gurevich MiG-15. The Soviet fighter was as good as the F-86 in almost all aspects of flight performance and in climb and ceiling it was definitely superior. Lockheed's C. L. 'Kelly' Johnson, then chief engineer and soon to be vice-president, visited the F-86 squadrons and listened to their plea for more speed, more climb, and more altitude. Back at the plant in Burbank, Los Angeles, he was well along with planning a new fighter to

Above Sidewinders are particularly prominent on this Royal Netherlands air force F-104G, with tanks instead of Sidewinders on the wingtips. The unit is No. 323 Sqn at Leeuwarden. Today the Starfighter, once the foremost Netherlands type, is becoming rare.

Above These Starfighters are two of the original F-104As (the more distant of the pair is the no. 2 production aircraft) photographed in the late 1960s after their return to active status with the very powerful J79-19 engine. They were briefly again used by Aerospace Defense Command after having previously been in the Air National Guard.

Left Seen here flying in the vicinity of Palmdale, California, USAF no. 53-7786 was the original Model 83, the first XF-104 prototype. It was lighter and less powerful than the F-104A, but the main recognition feature was the use of plain engine inlets. The engine was one of the rare afterburning J65 Sapphires.

Lockheed F-104-6

Specification

Lockheed F-104G
Type: single-seat fighter and attack aircraft
Powerplant: one General Electric J79-11A turbojet engine rated 15,800 lb (7167 kg) with full afterburner
Performance: maximum speed (clean) at 40,000 ft (12192 m) 1,300 mph (2092 km/h); service ceiling (clean) 55,000 ft (16764 m); mission radius (typical lo-lo conventional attack) 315 miles (507 km), (no bombs but four external tanks) 690 miles (1110 km)

Weights: empty 14,082 lb (6390 kg); maximum 28,779 lb (13054 kg)
Dimensions: span (no tanks or missile shoes) 21 ft 11 in (6.68 m); length 54 ft 9 in (16.69 m); height 13 ft 6 in (4.15 m); wing area 196.1 sq ft (18.22 m²)
Armament: usually one 20-mm M61A-1 gun; four underwing pylons for total load of 4,000 lb (1814 kg); pairs of Sidewinder AAMs may be carried on wingtips or fuselage pylons

Now replaced by a Panavia Tornado, this Lockheed F-104G served until early 1982 with Federal German Marineflieger wing MFG 1 based at Schleswig in northern Germany. MFG 1 is tasked in the anti-ship attack role, with secondary photo-reconnaissance duties. This aircraft is depicted with a centreline practice bomb carrier and two Kormoran anti-ship missiles under the wings. The plan view shows the access doors above the 'piccolo' power units for the ailerons, just 1 in (25.4 mm) deep. In the front view the single

M61 gun can be seen, as well as the levered-suspension main landing gears with Dowty-licensed Liquid Spring shock struts and landing lights inside the doors. The side elevation shows the airfield arrester hook and electrically de-iced engine inlets.

Lockheed F-104

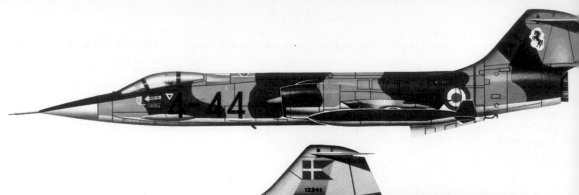

Until 1967 the Aeronautica Militare Italiano was organized into large *aerobrigate* (air brigades) each with several *gruppi* (squadrons). This European-built F-104G served with the 4ª Aerobrigata's 9° Gruppo throughout the 1960s (note Ferrari-style prancing horse badge). The 9° Gruppo is now an F-104S fighter unit.

USAF no. 12341 (actually 62-12341) was one of a batch of 48 F-104Gs built by Canadair on MAP instructions and in this case allocated to the Royal Danish air force. It is shown in the light grey overall finish originally applied in 1964 when serving with Esk 723 at Aalborg in the interceptor role.

succeed the F-80 Shooting Star. What the front-line pilots told him convinced him to go for performance at all cost. The result was one of the most startling aeroplanes ever built. At times it has been the centre of furious controversy, and as a fighter for close combat it was never outstanding. But for moving at high speed in a straight line it has few rivals, and late in its life it blossomed forth as an exceptionally good attack machine.

Johnson did not just sit down and design the F-104: he was surrounded by parametric studies for fighters of all shapes and sizes, and until early 1952 had leaned heavily towards substantial aircraft powered by the new J57 or J67 (Olympus-derived) engines. To try to meet the demand for still greater performance he took one of the best J67-powered fighters, weighing 31,849 lb (14447 kg), and stripped it of everything removable. The weight came down to 28,100 lb (12746 kg) but the improvement in performance was hardly noticeable and as a fighter the stripped-down machine was inferior. After further study Johnson and his team decided to build a much smaller fighter, the Model 83, to meet the USAF requirement for Weapon System 303A (a supersonic day fighter). The Mach number chosen was 2.2, the practical limit for an airframe made of conventional aluminium alloys.

Aerodynamically the Model 83 was almost unique in having wings tailored purely to the supersonic regime, only 3 per cent thick and of extraordinarily small span and area, without sweep. Almost everything was packaged in the long circular-section body, tailored closely to the chosen engine, the superb new X-24A by General Electric, fed by lateral inlets leaving a long needle nose for radar if necessary. To reduce weight the canopy was made non-jettisonable and the seat was designed to fire downwards. One of the factors contributing to this potentially dangerous idea was that, after studying no fewer than 285 different tail arrangements, it was decided to use a powered slab tailplane at the very top of the fin in what has since become known as the T-tail

The Japan Air Self-Defense Force operates the F-104J single-seater in the interceptor role and also the F-104DJ trainer, built by Lockheed but assembled, like the F-104Js, by Mitsubishi. In the foreground is the fifth production aircraft parked next to a F-104DJ two-seater and with the fin and canopies of a Mitsubishi T-2 visible beyond.

Taiwan is another of the refuges of surviving Starfighters, though for several years a replacement (the F-16 has been favoured) has been unsuccessfully sought. These four F-104Gs serve with the 5th Wing, each carrying Sidewinders in the interceptor role. They carry nose numbers 4303, 4311, 4313 and (rear) 4354 plus buzz number FG-792.

configuration. It was considered that ejecting over this tail might be even more of a problem at the speeds to be reached by this aircraft.

Other novel engineering was found throughout the aircraft. Because the wing was so small, the maximum depth at the root being a mere 4.2 in (107 mm), it was difficult to fit anything inside it. All fuel had to be in flexible cells in the overcrowded fuselage. To drive the outboard ailerons Lockheed and the Bertea company devised so-called piccolo actuators containing a row of 10 small hydraulic rams in a solid block of aluminium fitting within the available depth

Below USAF no. 63-8455 was one of the fifth production block of TF-104G two-seaters made by Lockheed. Known as the Lockheed Model 583D-10-20, they usually had no gun but retained the NASARR radar and weapon delivery boxes. TF-104Gs used by the Luftwaffe at Luke AFB look identical except for red/white/blue tank fins.

of 1.1 in (28 mm). To enable the tiny wing to generate sufficient lift at reasonable take-off speeds, the leading edge was hinged to pivot downwards under electric actuation, in one of the world's first 'droop snoot' configurations. For landing, even more radical measures were necessary, and the F-104 was the first production application of the boundary-layer controlled blown flap which had just been devised by John D. Attinello: high-pressure air bled from the engine is blown at supersonic speed through narrow slits ahead of the upper surface of the flap, to prevent flow separation and generate powerful lift. The British Dowty company provided Liquid Spring shock struts (made under licence by H.M. Loud) small enough to cushion the shock of landing in small main landing gears pivoted to the fuselage and re-tracted forwards and inwards. Armament comprised the revolutionary new gun developed by General Electric as Project Vulcan, spewing out 6,000 shells a minute from six 20-mm barrels (and even today the standard gun of US fighters). Another new weapon, the simple Sidewinder air-to-air missile, could be carried on each wingtip in place of drop tanks.

The USAF liked the Model 83, and in March 1953 placed a contract for two prototypes, designated XF-104, numbers 53-7786/7787. Lockheed's name, Starfighter, was officially adopted. The General Electric engine was not even run on the test-bench until 8 June 1954, so Johnson planned the two XF-104s to have the lower-powered Wright XJ65-W-6, an afterburner-equipped derivative of the British Sapphire rated at 10,200-lb (4627-kg) maximum thrust. Plain sharp-lipped fixed inlets were used, and the nose gear retracted to the rear. Design and manufacture at Johnson's famed 'Skunk Works' were rapid, and Tony LeVier began taxi tests with the first aircraft at Edwards AFB in February 1954. On 28 February LeVier made a 300-ft (91-m) hop and on the morning of 4 March he accomplished a flawless first flight, with a non-afterburning J65 rated at 7,200-lb (3266-kg) thrust. With Herman 'Fish' Salmon and Joe Ozier also handling the test flights, LeVier explored the limits of handling and soon found severe pitch-up problems which took a long time to cure. Meanwhile Lockheed's main plant, especially Burbank's shop B-1, was busy with the revised design and manufacture of a pre-production run of 17 YF-104As, with significant changes.

Prototype roll-out

Called Lockheed Model 183, and with USAF numbers 55-2955/2971, all were powered by the YJ79-GE-3, rated with afterburner at 14,800-lb (6713-kg) thrust. For the first time in any aircraft the engine was combined with a fully variable duct system that could adapt itself to all the contrasting conditions from take-off to Mach 2.2 at high altitude. The inlets were greatly enlarged and fitted with half-cones to position the oblique shockwave formed at supersonic speeds. Instead of a series of auxiliary inlets and overboard bleeds, a very large secondary airflow was ducted around the

Below Canada was one of the chief participants in the F-104G production programme, the Canadian Armed Forces calling the type the CF-104. Aircraft no. 12854 was originally operated unpainted by the RCAF's (as the CAF air branch was then called) No. 441 Sqn at Marville, France. It is shown with the Vicom camera pod under the fuselage.

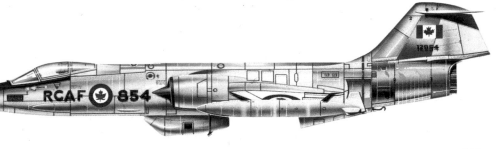

FX-31 was one of the 18 F-104Gs (plus two two-seat TF-104s) flown from 1963 until 1980 by the FAB's (Belgian air force) No. 350 Sqn at Beauvechain. With similarly based No. 349 Sqn they operated in the all-weather interceptor role, though the Starfighter was not really adequate for the job in European weather.

engine and discharged around the primary nozzle, and the nozzle itself was composed of fully variable ejector-profiled petals driven by hydraulic (lubricating oil) actuators to match nozzle area and shape to the flight Mach number and altitude. The fuselage was lengthened to accommodate five fuel cells, the nose gear was redesigned to retract forwards, the electrical system was more than doubled in power, and later modifications included the incorporation of operative flap-blowing and a ventral underfin at the tail.

The first YF-104A, still lacking numerous non-vital items, was rolled out on 23 December 1955, and on 17 February 1956 Salmon took it aloft. It was the first aircraft, apart from General Electric's XF4D-1 test aircraft, to fly on the power of a J79. Subsequent testing was exciting, punctuated by various incidents, and it took very much longer to clear the aircraft as an operational fighter than it had taken to design and build in the first place. The second XF-104 and three YF-104As were lost, but another YF-104A was saved when LeVier managed a dead-stick landing after the engine had been drenched in kerosene from a tank pierced by a shell-case that entered one of the engine inlets. General Electric introduced the J79-3A engine with a modulated afterburner, the gun (then designated T-171) became available, and Lockheed finally turned to the manufacture of 153 production F-104As for the USAF inventory.

On 17 April 1956 Lockheed organized a giant press ceremony at which the previously classified F-104 was unveiled by General Otto P. Weyland, commander of Tactical Air Command. The inlet geometry was still secret, so the inlets were covered by large streamlined fairings. Ten days later Mach 2 was exceeded, and later in 1956 there was added the MA-10 avionic system, comprising an ASG-14 gunsight ranging radar and a small infra-red detector for sighting at night. Basically the F-104A was a visual day fighter, with the gun and either two tanks or Sidewinders. Service clearance was received on 26 January 1958, and deliveries began to the 83rd Fighter Interceptor Squadron at Hamilton AFB, near San Francisco. Engine reliability was poor, and though dead-stick landings were accomplished at 275 mph (442 km/h) most pilots ejected, when the downward-fired seat proved deadly at low level. By April 1958 the F-104A was grounded, but aircraft still with the maker kept flying and USAF pilots set numerous world records including absolute speed at 1,404.19 mph (2259.83 km/h), zoom altitude at 91,249 ft (27813 m) and a series of time-to-height records up to 82,021 ft (25000 m).

Subsequently many F-104As were converted into other sub-types as shown in the variants list. This model was withdrawn from USAF duty in 1959, though many continued with the Air National Guard and a few were given the powerful J79-19 engine in 1968. Surplus aircraft were supplied to Taiwan (25), Jordan (36), Pakistan (12) and Canada (1).

The RF-104A was cancelled, so Lockheed next built 26 F-104B tandem trainers (Model 283) with reduced fuel, no gun and various other changes including a larger fin and

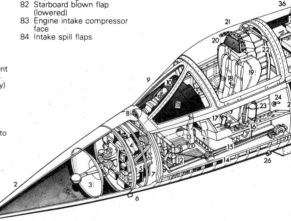

Though the Aeritalia F-104S is the most important Italian Starfighter variant the Aeronautica Militare Italiano also uses the RF-104G and, as seen here, the TF-104G two-seater. The aircraft illustrated is one of 28 supplied to the 20° Gruppo which shares Grosseto with an operational squadron, the 9° Gruppo (F-104S).

Lockheed (Aeritalia) F-104S Starfighter cutaway drawing key

1 Pitot tube
2 Radome
3 Radar scanner dish
4 R21G/H multi-mode radar equipment
5 Radome withdrawal rails
6 Communications aerial
7 Cockpit front bulkhead
8 Infra-red sight
9 Windscreen panels
10 Reflector gunsight
11 Instrument panel shroud
12 Rudder pedals
13 Control column
14 Nose section frame construction
15 Control cable runs
16 Pilot's side console panel
17 Throttle control
18 Safety harness
19 Martin-Baker IQ-7A ejection seat
20 Face blind seat firing handle
21 Cockpit canopy cover
22 Canopy bracing struts
23 Seat rail support box
24 Angle of attack probe
25 Cockpit rear bulkhead
26 Temperature probe
27 Nosewheel doors
28 Taxiing lamp
29 Nosewheel/leg strut
30 Nosewheel
31 Steering linkage
32 AIM-7 Sparrow avionics (replacing M-61 gun installation of strike model)
33 Inertial platform
34 Avionics compartment
35 Avionics compartment shroud cover
36 Cockpit aft glazing
37 Ram-air turbine
38 Emergency generator
39 Avionics compartment access cover
40 Fuselage frame construction
41 Pressure bulkhead
42 Ammunition compartment auxiliary fuel tank (101.5 Imp gal/462 litre capacity)
43 Fuel feed pipes
44 Flush-fitting UHF aerial panel
45 Anti-collision light
46 Starboard intake
47 Engine bleed air supply to air conditioning
48 Gravity fuel fillers
49 Fuselage main fuel tanks (total internal capacity 746 Imp gal/3391 litres)
50 Pressure refuelling adaptor
51 Intake shock cone centre body
52 De-iced intake lip
53 Port intake
54 Shock cone boundary layer bleed
55 Boundary layer bleed air duct
56 Auxiliary intake
57 Hinged auxiliary intake door
58 Navigation light
59 Leading edge flap jack
60 Intake trunking
61 Fuselage main longeron
62 Wing root attaching members
63 Intake flank fuel tanks
64 Wing-mounting fuselage mainframes
65 Control cable runs
66 Electrical junction box
67 Dorsal spine fairing
68 Starboard inboard pylon
69 Leading edge flap (lowered)
70 AIM-7 Sparrow AAM
71 Missile launch rail
72 Starboard outer pylon
73 Tip tank vane
74 Tip tank latching unit
75 Starboard wingtip tank
76 Fuel filler caps
77 Starboard aileron
78 Aileron power control jacks
79 Power control servo valves
80 Fuel lines to auxiliary tanks
81 Flap blowing duct
82 Starboard blown flap (lowered)
83 Engine intake compressor face
84 Intake spill flaps
85 Aileron torque shaft
86 Hydraulic reservoir
87 Air conditioning bleed air supply pipe
88 General Electric J79-GE-19 turbojet
89 Engine withdrawal rail
90 Starboard airbrake (open)
91 Fin root fillet
92 Elevator servo controls
93 Elevator/all moving tailplane hydraulic jacks
94 Push-pull control rods
95 Tailfin construction
96 Fin tip fairing
97 Tailplane rocking control arm
98 Starboard tailplane
99 One-piece tailplane construction
100 Tailplane spar
101 Tailplane spar central pivot
102 Fin trailing-edge construction

powered rudder. Next came 77 F-104C single-seat fighter-bombers for Tactical Air Command, with the more powerful J79-7 engine, operative flap-blowing, a removable inflight-refuelling probe and underwing and belly pylons for tanks, Sidewinder missiles or 1,000-lb (454-kg) bombs. These equipped the 479th TFW at George AFB from 16 October 1958 until 1965; subsequently many were camouflaged and sent to Vietnam where they operated with some success in the day-attack role. Production for the USAF was completed by 21 F-104D (Model 283) two-seaters based on the F-104C but without the gun. The two-seaters had two separate canopies, each hinged to the left, though downward-ejection seats were retained.

By mid-1957 Lockheed was left in no doubt the F-104 programme was going to be about one-tenth as large as it had expected, unless the company carried out extensive internal redesign and, moreover, found new customers. The key to further sales was West Germany's Luftwaffe, which not only required about 1,000 supersonic fighter-bombers, but also wanted to build them under licence to restore its once

mighty aviation industry. As early as 1956 Lockheed had begun the redesign process with a project designated F-104-7, but in late 1958 this was redesignated F-104G (for Germany). In a total about-face from the concept of a small, light and simple day fighter built solely for performance, the F-104G was planned as a heavy, complex and extremely effective attack aircraft, and in particular as a carrier of tactical nuclear weapons to point targets using advanced all-weather navigation and weapon-delivery systems.

The airframe was totally redesigned, with 36 large heavy-press forgings, 60 no-draft close-tolerance forgings, numerous machined and composite skin panels, Spraymat electrically

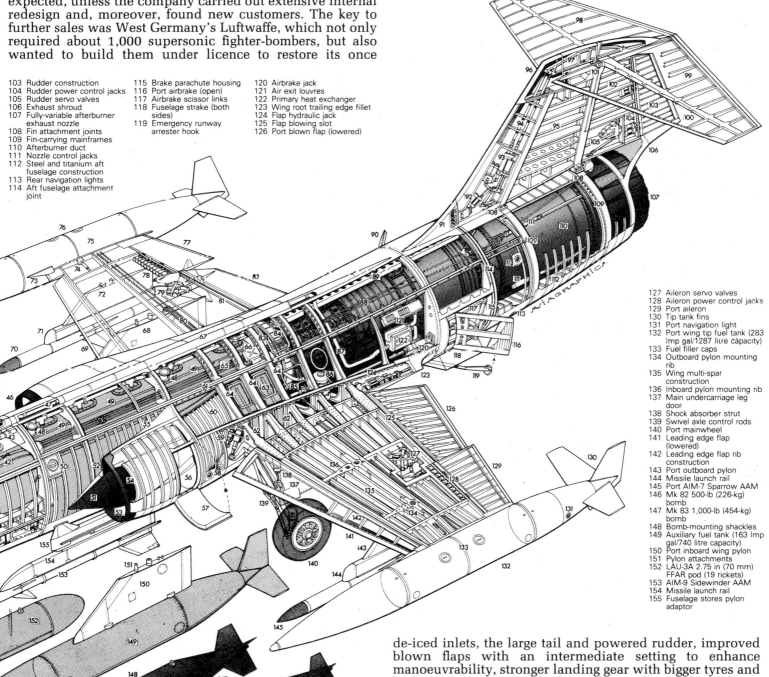

103 Rudder construction
104 Rudder power control jacks
105 Rudder servo valves
106 Exhaust shroud
107 Fully-variable afterburner exhaust nozzle
108 Fin attachment joints
109 Fin-carrying mainframes
110 Afterburner duct
111 Nozzle control jacks
112 Steel and titanium aft fuselage construction
113 Rear navigation lights
114 Aft fuselage attachment joint
115 Brake parachute housing
116 Port airbrake (open)
117 Airbrake scissor links
118 Fuselage strake (both sides)
119 Emergency runway arrester hook
120 Airbrake jack
121 Air exit louvres
122 Primary heat exchanger
123 Wing root trailing edge fillet
124 Flap hydraulic jack
125 Flap blowing slot
126 Port blown flap (lowered)
127 Aileron servo valves
128 Aileron power control jacks
129 Port aileron
130 Tip tank fins
131 Port navigation light
132 Port wing tip fuel tank (283 Imp gal/1287 litre capacity)
133 Fuel filler caps
134 Outboard pylon mounting rib
135 Wing multi-spar construction
136 Inboard pylon mounting rib
137 Main undercarriage leg door
138 Shock absorber strut
139 Swivel axle control rods
140 Port mainwheel
141 Leading edge flap (lowered)
142 Leading edge flap rib construction
143 Port outboard pylon
144 Missile launch rail
145 Port AIM-7 Sparrow AAM
146 Mk 82 500-lb (226-kg) bomb
147 Mk 83 1,000-lb (454-kg) bomb
148 Bomb-mounting shackles
149 Auxiliary fuel tank (163 Imp gal/740 litre capacity)
150 Port inboard wing pylon
151 Pylon attachments
152 LAU-3A 2.75 in (70 mm) FFAR pod (19 rockets)
153 AIM-9 Sidewinder AAM
154 Missile launch rail
155 Fuselage stores pylon adaptor

de-iced inlets, the large tail and powered rudder, improved blown flaps with an intermediate setting to enhance manoeuvrability, stronger landing gear with bigger tyres and high-capacity anti-skid brakes, a larger drag chute and, not least, the J79-11A engine. In the nose was the Autonetics F15A NASARR multi-mode radar, amidships was the first inertial navigation system ever to go into operational service in any aircraft (Litton LN-3) as well as various advanced

Looking distinctly tired after long service, and due for imminent replacement by a General Dynamics F-16, no. 17754 of the Danish air force was one of the last batch of F-104Gs built by Canadair on MAP (Military Assistance Program) account. Full USAF serial is 64-17754. Note the prominent fuselage pylons, added to take Sidewinders.

weapon-aiming subsystems, and in the cockpit Lockheed finally bowed to pressure and fitted the C-2 seat which ejected upwards. A total of 3,000 lb (1361 kg) of external weapons could be carried, including a 2,000-lb (907-kg) special store (nuclear weapon) under the fuselage.

Success with the Luftwaffe

There was plenty of competition, but Lockheed's F-104G (otherwise the Model 683-10-19) Super Starfighter beat the lot, because, even though it did not exist, it promised to fly all the missions the Luftwaffe wanted. Federal Germany signed on 18 March 1959; this triggered off Canada, Japan, the Netherlands, Belgium, the USAF for MAP customers, Italy and an additional USAF MAP buy, in that order. A gigantic European manufacturing programme was created, made up of Arge Nord (Hamburger, Weser, Focke-Wulf, Fokker and Aviolanda), Arge Süd (Messerschmitt, Heinkel, Dornier and Siebel) and a West Group (Avions Fairey and SABCA). Together these built respectively 350, 210 and 188 aircraft. Initially the Belgians were teamed with Italy, but finally the Italian group was separate (Fiat, Aerfer, Macchi, SIAI-Marchetti, Piaggio and SACA) and it assembled 229 F-104Gs. The Canadians made 200 Canadair CL-90 (CF-104) ground-attack and reconnaissance aircraft, and also shipped 121 sets of wings, aft fuselages and tails to Europe, 40 sets to Lockheed and 40 sets to Japan, and also delivered a further 110 MAP aircraft built to F-104G standard. In contrast the Japanese F-104J is configured for the air-to-air role, with the gun fitted and external armament of four Sidewinders; Mitsubishi, assisted by Kawasaki, built 207 of this model. The Japanese also received 20 Lockheed-built F-104DJ trainers. There are many sub-variants, as listed.

The first F-104G flew in Lockheed hands at Palmdale on 5 October 1960, as the first of 96 supplied by Lockheed to the Luftwaffe. The first Arge Süd aircraft flew on 10 August 1961, followed by the first Arge Nord aircraft on 11 November 1961. The first CF-104 was airlifted to Palmdale and flew on 26 May 1961, the first West Group aircraft on 4 December 1961 and the first Italian machine on 9 June 1962. The only major problem with this otherwise extremely potent attack aircraft was that the Luftwaffe pilots often lacked experience to cope with a mount that was totally unforgiving, and suffered a loss-rate which in 1963 reached 139 per 100,000 flight hours. The Luftwaffe had fought strongly for the Martin-Baker seat, having refitted its Republic F-84F and Canadair Sabre fighters with the British seat and noted the major improvement in reliability and pilot survival. But West Germany had no means of qualifying the alternative seat, and placed a contract with the USAF. The latter did all it could to prevent the British seat being fitted, and after 23 months of argument the Germans gave in and accepted the Lockheed C-2 seat, which at least ejected upwards. Fatalities continued at a serious level, despite urgent seat-modification programmes. The crafty Danes quietly fitted Martin-Baker

During the heyday of the Luftwaffe's F-104G, each *Geschwader* (wing) was assigned eight tandem dual TF-104G trainers, able to undertake conversion and continuation training as well as fly operational sorties. This TF-104G flew with JG 32, based at Lechfeld during the 1970s.

seats to their Canadair-built MAP aircraft, but it was not until 8 March 1967 that the US campaign to keep Martin-Baker out collapsed, and in 12 months the entire German and Italian F-104 inventories had the British GQ-7 seat. Martin-Baker made no announcement.

More than 25 F-104G developments never came to pass, among them V/STOL models, Spey-powered interdictors and the next-generation CL-1200 Lancer (USAF X-27). But the 1966 German/Italian proposal for the F-104S (S for Spey engine and also for Sparrow missile) did lead to a new sub-type. Planned as an all-weather interceptor, and thus marking a return to air fighting, the F-104S incorporates many large and small improvements including a new R21G/H multi-mode radar and radar-guided AAMs, either Sparrow or Italy's own Aspide. The US Defense Department managed to keep out the British engine, and the F-104S has the uprated J79-19. The main external distinguishing feature is the pair of small canted ventral fins, one on each side of the main ventral fin. Lockheed and Aeritalia shared development, but all production took place in Italy. Lockheed flew a pattern aircraft in December 1966 and Turin-assembled aircraft followed from 1969 until March 1979, when production was completed at 206 for Italy and 40 for Turkey. Since 1982 some Aeronautica Militare Italiano aircraft have been recycled for updating to improve look-down shoot-down capability, to enhance electronic-warfare capability and to enable attack missions to be flown accurately against ground targets at low level, in all weather.

Lockheed F-104 variants

XF-104: YJ65 engine, short fuselage, plain inlets (2 prototypes)

YF-104A: YJ79 engine, long fuselage, advanced inlet/nozzle system (17 service-test aircraft)

F-104A: J79-3A, fitted with gun, tip attachments and retrofitted with ventral fin (153 production aircraft)

NF-104A: rocket-boosted conversion for NASA Astronaut training, also designated **F-104N** (3F-104A conversions)

QF-104A: target-drone conversions (24YF-104A/F-104A conversions in various sub-types)

RF-104A: unarmed photo-reconnaissance version of F-104A (projected)

F-104B: tandem trainer with larger vertical tail (26 production aircraft)

F-104C: J79-7 engine, extra underwing and centreline pylons, inflight-refuelling probe, blown flaps (77 production aircraft)

F-104D: two-seat version of F-104C (21 production aircraft)

F-104DJ: Japanese version of F-104D with J79-IHI-11A made in Japan (20 production aircraft)

F-104F: two-seat trainer based on F-104D structurally but with F-104G avionics and C-2 seat (30 production aircraft)

F-104G: redesigned attack aircraft with new airframe, J79-11A engine, NASARR radar and five stores attachments; most retrofitted with Martin-Baker seats (1,127 production aircraft)

CF-104: Canadian derivative for attack and (with multi-sensor pack fitted) reconnaissance (200 production aircraft)

CF-104D: Canadian two-seat derivative of CF-104 (38 production aircraft)

RF-104G: five sub-types all configured for tactical reconnaissance, with NASARR and either an external multi-sensor pod or camera pod, or with the gun removed and an internal pod (189 production aircraft)

TF-104G: two-seat version of F-104G with no gun or centreline pylon but retaining full avionics (220 production aircraft)

RTF-104G: two-seat multi-sensor reconnaissance aircraft, some configured for electronic warfare missions (projected)

F-104H: export version with simplified equipment, optical gunsight but no NASARR (projected)

TF-104H: two-seat version of F-104H (projected)

F-104J: J79-IHI-11A, Japanese fighter version (210 production aircraft)

F-104S: Italian all-weather interceptor, J79-19 engine, gun/AAM fit (245 production aircraft)

Sukhoi's Super-strikers

The Sukhoi Su-7 'Fitter' has for more than 20 years been one of the world's leading ground-attack aircraft. It could carry either bombs or adequate fuel, but not both at the same time, so was regarded as obsolescent by 1970. Today advanced swing-wing derivatives are still in production.

One of the fundamental features of Soviet procurement is that nothing is thrown away it if can be used (there are always masses of air and ground crews familiar with established hardware), and aircraft are kept in production in progressively improved versions to avoid the need to introduce completely new designs. Nothing better exemplifies this than the long series of tactical attack aircraft developed by the Sukhoi OKB (experimental design bureau), which remain in production despite the fact that almost 10 years ago they were joined by a totally new aircraft of greatly

A striking US Navy photo of a 'Fitter-J', one of the latest export variants of the Tumansky-powered Sukhoi swing-wing family, of the Libyan Arab air force in late summer 1981. This one is carrying two tanks and two 'Advanced Atoll' AAMs. The Libyans have received well over 100 swing-wing Su-17 and Su-77 aircraft.

increased capability, the formidable Su-24 'Fencer'. Transformed by swing-wings, new engines and improved sensor and weapon-delivery systems, the new members of the family, known by the reporting name 'Fitter' to NATO

Sukhoi Su-20 'Fitter'

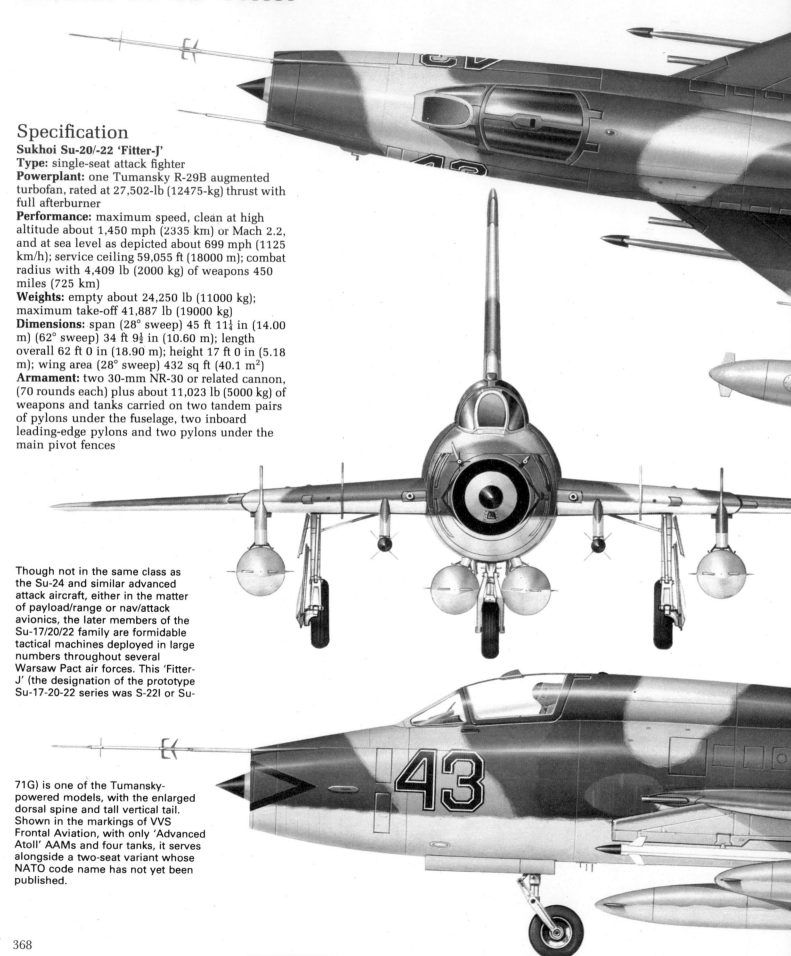

Specification

Sukhoi Su-20/-22 'Fitter-J'
Type: single-seat attack fighter
Powerplant: one Tumansky R-29B augmented turbofan, rated at 27,502-lb (12475-kg) thrust with full afterburner
Performance: maximum speed, clean at high altitude about 1,450 mph (2335 km) or Mach 2.2, and at sea level as depicted about 699 mph (1125 km/h); service ceiling 59,055 ft (18000 m); combat radius with 4,409 lb (2000 kg) of weapons 450 miles (725 km)
Weights: empty about 24,250 lb (11000 kg); maximum take-off 41,887 lb (19000 kg)
Dimensions: span (28° sweep) 45 ft 11¼ in (14.00 m) (62° sweep) 34 ft 9½ in (10.60 m); length overall 62 ft 0 in (18.90 m); height 17 ft 0 in (5.18 m); wing area (28° sweep) 432 sq ft (40.1 m²)
Armament: two 30-mm NR-30 or related cannon, (70 rounds each) plus about 11,023 lb (5000 kg) of weapons and tanks carried on two tandem pairs of pylons under the fuselage, two inboard leading-edge pylons and two pylons under the main pivot fences

Though not in the same class as the Su-24 and similar advanced attack aircraft, either in the matter of payload/range or nav/attack avionics, the later members of the Su-17/20/22 family are formidable tactical machines deployed in large numbers throughout several Warsaw Pact air forces. This 'Fitter-J' (the designation of the prototype Su-17-20-22 series was S-22I or Su-71G) is one of the Tumansky-powered models, with the enlarged dorsal spine and tall vertical tail. Shown in the markings of VVS Frontal Aviation, with only 'Advanced Atoll' AAMs and four tanks, it serves alongside a two-seat variant whose NATO code name has not yet been published.

Sukhoi Su-7

This ageing Su-7BMK is shown in the livery in which it was painted in 1978 when it was serving with a Frontal Aviation regiment in the Trans-Baikal Military District in eastern Siberia. Substantial numbers of older Sukhoi attack aircraft are still serving in advanced training units in less-sensitive Soviet regions.

personnel, make this the most prolific dedicated attack family since World War 2.

In World War 2 Pavel Osipovich Sukhoi had few successes, and his run of bad luck continued until his OKB was summarily shut by Stalin's order in 1949. After Stalin's death in 1953 Sukhoi applied for permission to reopen, and this was quickly granted. Lavochkin's OKB was unsuccessful and a strong rival was needed to offer competition to the Mikoyan/Gurevich team. The two latter designers and Sukhoi were all invited to the Kremlin later in 1953 and appraised of the two new shapes for future supersonic combat aircraft being refined at TsAGI, the national aerodynamics centre. One was a sharply swept (leading edge 62°) machine with a swept tailplane; the other was a pure delta, of just under 60° leading-edge sweep, also with a swept tailplane.

Two configurations

Furious efforts to apply the lessons of Korea to a new generation of warplanes were centred on these shapes, the Sukhoi OKB quickly confirming that while the delta showed lower drag and seemed better for an interceptor, the long swept wing gave better lift at low speeds and was clearly superior for attack aircraft. Sukhoi was authorized to expand his bureau rapidly and build prototypes for both missions. The first prototypes of both configurations flew in the spring and summer of 1955. The T-1 (T for *treoogol*, or three-angled) eventually led to numerous other types, including a long series of production interceptors with VVS (air force) designations Su-9, Su-11 and Su-15. The S-1 (S for *strelovidnosti*, or arrowed or sweptback) was first flown by Andrei Kochetkov in about May 1955 and led to the family of attack aircraft.

Even before the 1949 closure Sukhoi had worked closely with Arkhip L. Lyulka's turbojet OKB, and it was Lyulka who furnished the engine for all the first generation of new Sukhois. The Type 31 engine, designated AL-7 in VVS service, was a large and impressive single-shaft axial with initially eight and later nine compressor stages with supersonic flow, and variable stators, on the first two rows of blades. In the same size and thrust class as the American JT4 (J75) it was developed from 1952 and had an afterburner added by 1954. It was ideal for the Sukhoi aircraft, which were relatively large machines, much bigger than the rival MiG-21 and in the size class of the American Republic F-105 attack bomber and Convair F-106 interceptor.

From the start the S-1 handled extremely well, the OKB pilots Kochetkov, Korovushkin and Mikhailin releasing the prototype for preliminary NII (State scientific research institute) testing before the end of 1955 even though it had a primitive engine with two-position nozzle and fixed nose inlet. In 1956 pre-production prototypes began to appear, designated Su-7 by the VVS, and these incorporated the definitive AL-7F engine with fully variable afterburner and what may have been the first variable inlet in the Soviet Union, with a translating centrebody and various bleed and auxiliary inlet doors. With this powerplant installation the level Mach number rose to 2.05, compared with the figure of

1.71 demanded by the 1953 specification. It is also almost certain that even the very first S-1 had a single powered 'slab' tailplane, the first in the USSR and ahead of the introduction of such a tail to the well-established MiG-19.

By the time several S and T prototypes had briefly flashed over Tushino at the 1956 Aviation Day display, both had been selected for mass production at factories far from the Sukhoi bureau at distant Komsomolsk in eastern Siberia.

Sukhoi Su-7MBK 'Fitter-A' cutaway drawing key

1 Pitot tube
2 Pinch vanes
3 Yaw vanes
4 Engine air intake
5 Fixed intake centre-body
6 Radome
7 Ranging radar scanner
8 ILS aerial
9 Radar controller
10 Weapon release ballistic computer
11 Retractable taxiing lamp
12 SRO-2M 'Odd-rods' IFF aerials
13 Intake suction relief doors
14 Intake duct divider
15 Instrument access panel
16 Su-7U 'Moujik' two-seat operational training variant
17 Armoured glass windscreen
18 Reflector sight
19 Instrument panel shroud
20 Control column
21 Rudder pedals
22 Control linkages
23 Nose undercarriage wheel well
24 Nosewheel doors
25 Torque scissor links
26 Steerable nosewheel
27 Low pressure 'rough-field' tyre
28 Hydraulic retraction jack
29 Cockpit pressure floor
30 Engine throttle
31 Pilot's side console panel
32 Ejection seat
33 Canopy release handle
34 Parachute pack headrest
35 Rear view mirror
36 Sliding cockpit canopy cover
37 Instrument venturi
38 Radio and electronics equipment bay
39 Intake ducting
40 Air conditioning plant
41 Electrical and pneumatic systems ground connections
42 Cannon muzzle
43 Skin doubler/blast shield
44 Fuel system components access
45 Main fuel pumps
46 Fuel system accumulator
47 Filler cap
48 External piping ducts
49 Starboard main undercarriage leg pivot fixing
50 Shock absorber pressurization charging valve
51 Gun camera
52 Starboard wing integral fuel tank
53 Starboard wing fence
54 Outer wing panel dry bay
55 Wing tip fence
56 Static discharger
57 Starboard aileron
58 Flap guide rail
59 Starboard Fowler flap
60 Flap jack
61 Fuselage skin plating
62 Fuselage fuel tank
63 Wing/fuselage attachment double frame
64 Engine compressor face
65 Ram air intake
66 Engine oil tank
67 Bleed air system 'blow-off' valve
68 Fuselage break point, engine removal
69 Lyulka AL-7F-1 turbojet
70 Afterburner duct
71 Fin root fillet
72 Autopilot controller
73 Starboard upper airbrake, open
74 Rudder power control unit
75 Artificial feel unit
76 Tailfin construction
77 VHF/UHF aerial fairing
78 RSIU (very short wave fighter radio) aerial
79 Tail navigation light
80 Sirena-3 tail warning radar
81 Rudder
82 Brake parachute release tank
83 Brake parachute housing
84 Parachute doors

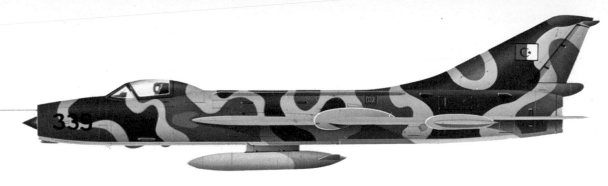

This rather attractive three-colour camouflage is used on most front-line aircraft of the Force Aérienne Algérienne (Algerian air force), which among other Soviet-supplied equipment has two squadrons dedicated to ground-attack operations using these Su-7BMs. The air-bleed port outside the engine is outlined in red.

85 Engine exhaust nozzle
86 Port all-moving tailplane
87 Static discharger
88 Tailplane anti-flutter weight
89 Tailplane construction
90 Pivot mounting
91 Tailplane limit stops
92 Variable area exhaust nozzle flaps
93 Nozzle control jacks
94 Fin/tailplane attachment fuselage frame
95 Afterburner cooling air intake
96 Rear fuselage frame and stringer construction
97 Insulated tailplane
98 Airbrake housing
99 Hydraulic jack

100 Tailplane power control unit
101 'Odd rods' IFF aerials
102 Port lower airbrake, open
103 Engine accessories
104 Jettisonable JATO bottle
105 Port Fowler flap
106 Port wing integral fuel tanks
107 Aileron control rod
108 Port aileron construction
109 Static discharger
110 Wing tip fairing
111 Port navigation light
112 Wing tip fence
113 Pitot tube
114 Wing rib and stringer construction
115 Port outer stores pylon

116 UV-16-57 rocket launcher pack
117 Auxiliary fuel tank, inner pylon
118 Port mainwheel
119 Low-pressure 'rough-field' main undercarriage
120 Inner stores pylon
121 Port wing fence
122 Mainwheel doors
123 Main undercarriage leg strut
124 Leg shortening link
125 Hydraulic retraction jack
126 Wing fuel tank filler cap
127 Port mainwheel bay
128 Main undercarriage up-lock
129 Aileron power control unit
130 Retractable landing lamp
131 Ammunition tank (70 rounds per gun)
132 30-mm NR-30 cannon

133 Cannon pressurization bottle
134 Ventral gun gas venting intake
135 Radar altimeter
136 Fuselage pylon, port and starboard
137 Twin fuselage mounted auxiliary fuel tanks
138 551-lb (250-kg) concrete piercing bomb
139 1,102-lb (500-kg) HE bomb

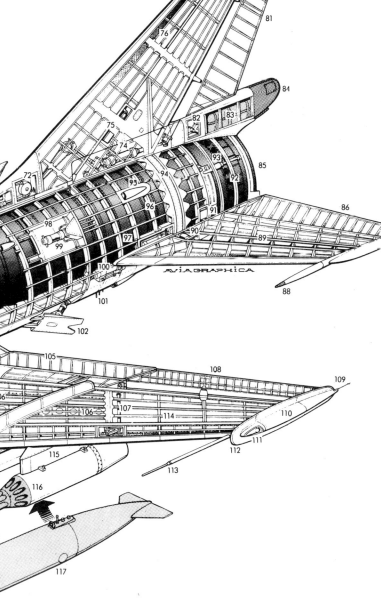

The original pre-production batch of Su-7s had been warmly received, and by 1957 numerous suggestions from the user had been added to improvements recognized as desirable by the OKB in the second batch of development aircraft designated S-2, S-21, S-22 etc. Unlike the delta interceptor, which worked its way through many further generations of development, the S-2 sub-family led straight to a production run of several hundred identical attack aircraft designated Su-7B. These entered service with the FA (*Frontovaya Aviatsiya*, or frontal aviation) before March 1959.

The aircraft were typically Russian, with the maximum design simplicity and robustness for troublefree service with minimal servicing in the harshest environments. The wing has no dihedral, a fixed leading edge with no dogtooth or slot, and only very modest fences at the inner and outer ends of the powered ailerons. Large flaps of modified Fowler type make a great difference at low speeds, and the all-round good handling has always made these aircraft perhaps more popular than their capability warrants. The cockpit is pressurized and air-conditioned, and offers an excellent all-round view thanks to the raised aft-sliding canopy. The levered-suspension landing gear cushions the roughest airstrips, and powerful multi-disc brakes, quadruple airbrakes on the removable rear fuselage and a ribbon parachute in a ventral box all assist quick stopping. The inbuilt punch comprised two of the extremely powerful NR-30 guns in the roots of the wing, fed by curved magazines between the engine duct and fuselage wall holding 70 (maximum 73) rounds per gun.

The wing was designed for four pylons, two rated at 1,653 lb (750 kg) ahead of the main gears and two at 1,102 lb (500 kg) just inboard of the inner fences. But on almost every mission the internal fuel capacity of 7,011 lb (3180 kg) was insufficient, and with the two side-by-side ventral drop tanks adding the necessary extra 2,094 lb (950 kg) the total weapon load had to be limited to an unimpressive 2,205 lb (1000 kg). To put this in perspective, it is no better than that of small fighters of World War 2, and much less than the bomb load of any modern respectable basic jet trainer.

Dual trainer

In 1961, when 21 Su-7Bs took part in the Tushino parade, the Su-7BKL entered service with numerous small changes including a nose pitot boom mounted on the upper right of the nose instead of at the top ahead of the windshield, and two prominent duct fairings along the upper sides of the centre fuselage. A tandem dual trainer, the Su-7U, went into production at about this time, with a rather clumsy arrangement of tandem clamshell canopies and a dorsal spine joining the rear canopy and fin. This was not positively identified in the West until 1967, when it was given the name 'Moujik'.

By 1966, if not earlier, deliveries had switched to the Su-7BM with the uprated (24,250-lb/11000-kg rather than 22,046-lb/10000-kg thrust) AL-7F-1 engine, larger blast panels in the fuselage skin beside the gun muzzles, twin braking parachutes repacked in a long box under the

Starting the Lyulka engine of an early Su-7BMK close-support aircraft of the CL (Czech air force). Czechoslovakia at one time had 70 of these in front-line duty, with as many in reserve, but most have now been relegated to operational training. The twin drop tanks are an essential fit for most missions.

rudder and other changes including the first ECM (electronic countermeasures) suite. The new braking parachutes were for pulling up on short strips, and rough-field capability was further improved in the mass-produced Su-7BMK by fitting larger tyres of lower inflation pressure (also done to other VVS-FA types at this time), the nosewheel doors being blistered to clear the new tyre. Two large solid take-off assistance rockets could be clipped under the rear fuselage. In parallel the trainer moved into Su-7UM and Su-7UMK versions.

Well over 1,000 of the Su-7BM and Su-7BMK models were exported. Some 600 of these saw war service, suffering heavy losses in Egypt, Syria and India, the total of losses in action in these three countries in 1967–73 exceeding 240. A lot of blame can probably be attributed to inexperience and bad tactics, and the Egyptians never lost their high regard for even these primitive Sukhois. Production of these variants cannot have been less than 2,000, completed in about 1972.

During the early 1960s V/STOL was intensively studied by Soviet designers, and the rival merits of fuselage jet-lift engines and variable-sweep wings were evaluated. Jet lift was flown on an early Su-15 twin-jet interceptor, but not on a member of the Su-7 family where the problems were almost insuperable. But swing wings looked promising, and in partnership with TsAGI a scheme was drawn up for fitting pivoting outer panels to the existing airframe, though with a new wing centre section (much the same was done to other aircraft including the much larger Tupolev Tu-22). The S-22I (I for *Izmenyaemaya strelovidnostyu*, or variable-sweep) flew very successfully in 1966 and was displayed at the Aviation Day show in 1967. Though flown impressively at that show, and called 'Fitter-B' by NATO, the half-span pivot location and general air of improvization resulted in the Western assessment being a dismissal of the S-22I (also called Su-7IG, the suffix meaning variable-geometry) as an unimportant one-off of which nothing more would be heard.

Though some of the CL (Czech air force) tactical aircraft are uncamouflaged, most are now finished in the standard Warsaw Pact scheme for aircraft in this category, including this Su-7BMK, illustrated with tanks under the wings as well as the usual twin belly pair. No bombs can be carried in these circumstances.

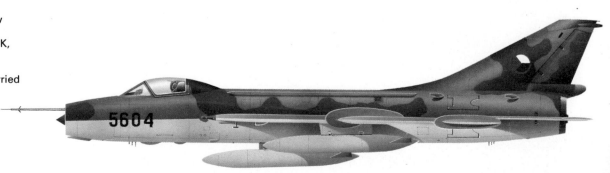

Despite its remarkable age, the Polish air force still owed around 50 Su-7 'Fitter A's in combat service in the mid-1980s. Here the aircraft are being fitted with brake parachutes. (Photo: M. Taylor)

Sukhoi Su-7

This Lyulka-powered Su-20 of the Egyptian air force was originally assigned in 1977 to the 55th Strike Squadron. On the nose is the individual aircraft number 3536 in

Arabic numerals. Note the clamshell canopy with rear-view mirror, and the four tanks yet vacant inboard wing pylons for bombs or other stores of 1,000 lb (454 kg) each.

٣٥٣٦

A totally different species from earlier Sukhois, the final sub-family have many of the features of late-model MiG-21s with deep fuselage spines giving reduced drag yet increased internal fuel. This Su-20 'Fitter-J' of the Libyan Arab air force is one of the Tumansky-powered single-seaters which may represent the final development.

Single enormous fences were noted at the pivot location, their lower edges incorporating weapon or tank pylons. Small changes were seen in the ailerons, flaps and landing gear, and the new outer wings were fitted with full-span slats and inboard slotted flaps usable at minimum sweep only. There was some disagreement among Western analysts over the capability of the Su-7IG and the pessimists won, claiming it was not worth studying.

It was thus no small surprise when from 1971 production swing-wing 'Fitters' began to appear in the VVS and also in the Polish air force; less than two years later versions were in squadron strength in a growing number of Arab air forces. This prompted an urgent reappraisal which disclosed that the swing-wingers had the much more powerful AL-21F-3 engine (which in fact has a lower specific fuel consumption than the AL-7 and extends range) and a very much refined airframe, the most obvious change being the dorsal spine from the new clamshell canopy to the modified fin. Called 'Fitter-C', this machine, which is actually the basic Su-17 in VVS service, carries twice the bomb load of the Su-7BMK a distance 30 per cent farther from airstrips little more than half as long! The original appraisal had erred by more than 150 per cent.

By 1975 export versions were known to have the designation Su-20, and by 1977 Peru announced receipt of the Su-22, showing that the basic type was now regarded primarily as a bomber rather than a fighter (only fighters have odd service numbers). By 1980 it was realized that the VVS itself uses the Su-20 designation (attention to this may have been drawn by the correction of the supposed designation of Su-19 for the other and much larger Sukhoi bomber to the correct one of Su-24).

By 1975 the production Su-20 had improved air-data sensors on its pitot boom, with front and rear seats of cruciform relative-wind vanes. A year later a laser ranger and marked-target seeker began to look through a window cut in the underside of the inlet centre-body, and a small terrain-avoidance radar looked ahead from a new pod added along the underside of the nose. This version was dubbed 'Fitter-D' by NATO. About a year later the dorsal fin was enlarged to counter the degraded yaw stability of the under-nose fairing, though the original tails were not modified. Progressive advances in ECM fit occurred approximately each year, the overall fit reaching a very high standard by

1980. The first-generation swing-wing family included dual trainers, generally called Su-22U or 'Fitter-E' (instead of 'Moujik').

In the late 1970s it was suddenly noticed that production aircraft had a bulged rear fuselage, detailed study revealing the odd fact that this bulge is vertically asymmetric. Though full information is lacking, and much of what follows is partly speculative, it is known that most Su-20 and -22 aircraft built since 1978 have the Tumansky R-29B engine, the same as that used by the MiG-27, which offers a much more modern propulsion system with more thrust and reduced fuel consumption, lower installed weight and less smoke. In 1986, the Su-21 ('Fitter-F') and Su-22 ('Fitter-G' and 'J') had appeared, the 'Atoll'-armed 'J' going to the Libyan air force.

As the current production 'Fitter-H' has a new wing, new tail, new fuselage and new engine, not much remains of the Su-7 but the maker's name. Nevertheless, it has the advantage, much appreciated in the Soviet Union, of being a derivative instead of a new type. For this reason some 650–850 of the chief swing-wing versions are in front-line VVS service and the best part of another 100 with AVMF (naval aviation) regiments near the Baltic, despite the parallel production of the Su-24. The swing-wing variants have probably roughly doubled the total production from 2,000 to 4,000. Export customers include Algeria, Czechoslovakia, Egypt, India, Iraq, Libya, Peru, Poland, Somalia, Syria, Vietnam and North and South Yemen.

Sukhoi attack fighter variants

S-1: original swept-wing prototype, flown spring 1955
Su-7: pre-production series for VVS evaluation
S-2: first of series prototypes
Su-7B: series derivative of S-22, AL-7F engine rated at 19,840-lb (9000-kg) thrust with full afterburner
Su-7BKL: relocated instrument boom, fuselage duct fairings
Su-7BM: twin brake chutes at base of rudder, AL-7F-1 engine rated at 22,046-lb (10000-kg) thrust with full afterburner, larger gun blast panels
Su-7BMK: short rough airstrip model with low-pressure tyres and RATO rockets
Su-7U: first tandem dual trainer
Su-7UM, UMK: trainers corresponding to BM, BMK
Su-7IG, S-221: prototype with pivoted outer wings
Su-17 (SU020) 'Fitter-C': first swing-wing production version, AL-21F-3 rated at 24,700-lb (11200-kg) thrust with full afterburner, extra fuel and weapons, dorsal spine behind clamshell canopy, better sensors
'Fitter-D': lengthened nose, terrain-following radar in undernose pod, laser receiver in inlet centrebody

'Fitter-E': trainer version of 'Fitter-C' with right gun only and downward-drooped nose to improve view from rear cockpit ('Moujik' name dropped)
'Fitter-F': Tumansky R-29B engine rated at 25,350-lb (11500-kg) thrust with full afterburner in bulged rear fuselage; improved sensors and avionics, two guns
'Fitter-G': completely redesigned tandem two-seater, some dual trainers and others with combat pilot and systems operator, usually Lyulka engine; very deep dorsal spine, down-sloping nose, extra fuel, tall clean-cut fin with narrow square top and small ventral fin; right gun only; laser receiver but no TFR
'Fitter-H': corresponding single-seater, with deep dorsal spine behind down-sloped clamshell canopy and tail fin; small ventral fin, both guns, eight pylons and enhanced avionics
'Fitter-J': corresponding single-seater with R-29B engine
'Fitter-?': the reporting name has not been published for the R-29B two-seater, though this was first seen in early 1980

McDonnell Douglas Phantom

A name to strike terror into the heart of an enemy and inspire confidence in the minds of its pilots; an aviation trump card which for two decades assured victory in the air. And yet this multi-record-breaking fighter started life as a loser, rejected by service experts who eventually came to depend on it as the backbone of their airpower.

From the very outset, the F-4 Phantom II with its roaring engines and twin vapour trails was the greatest and most powerful American fighter plane, but it was also the fastest, with the highest operating ceiling and the longest range. Although the Soviet Union had bigger, heavier and more powerful fighters, they were, like all other machines of this class, inferior to the Phantom in terms of manoeuvrability and weapons capacity.

Fighters are supposed to seem small, sleek and agile; and many would say a great fighter has to be beautiful. In 1958 a new fighter thundered off the runway at Lambert Field, the St Louis Municipal Airport, that was none of these things. It was a great jagged-looking juggernaut, as big as a World War 2 bomber and with two seats, two engines and the bulkiest midriff in any plane of its size. One of its first users, an officer of the US Navy, described it as 'awkward as a goose with drooping tail feathers and middle-aged spread'. A pilot from the US Air Force thought it 'so ugly I wondered if it had been delivered upside down'. This fighter was the F-4 Phantom II. It was to smash every record open to a fighter to break, outperforming its many rivals in speed, climb, weapon load, radar power and even safe slow flying, to the extent that it became the yardstick against which every other contemporary and even later fighter was to be judged.

Phantoms poured off the St Louis assembly line for 23 years. In financial terms it was the top fighter in all history,

in any country. And it all happened because the McDonnell Aircraft Company (MAC) lost out to a rival in May 1953 in the seemingly vital contract for the US Navy's first supersonic fighter.

MAC's exceptionally talented engineers did not give up, but instead set about planning a better fighter. Picking up every scrap of information about the US Navy's thinking and possible future requirements, MAC in 1954 produced a mock-up of the F3H-G, with two Wright J65 engines, four cannon and no fewer than 11 weapon pylons for heavy and varied military loads. In November 1954 MAC's persistence paid off in a US Navy contract for two prototypes, designated AH-1, similar to the F3H-G but with two of the outstanding new General Electric J79 engines when these were ready. This much more powerful engine opened up exciting possibilities in higher performance, and MAC's team redesigned the inlets and nozzles so that they could be reshaped and controlled to match the airflow exactly to different speeds and Mach numbers up to and beyond Mach 2.

So impressive was the potential of the AH-1 multi-role

An RAF Phantom FGR.2 from No. 43 Sqn, 'The Fighting Cocks' from Leuchars, intercepts a Soviet long range reconnaissance Tu-95 'Bear' away from UK airspace. It is just one of the many tasks this versatile aircraft carries out for the nations that fly it.

McDonnell Douglas F-4E Phantom II

Specification

Type: two-seat multi-role fighter

Powerplant: two 17,900-lb (8119-kg) thrust General Electric J79-GE-17 afterburning turbojets

Performance: maximum speed (clean) 1,432 mph (2304 km/h) or Mach 2.17; initial climb (clean) 49,800 ft (15180 m) per minute; service ceiling 62,250 ft (18975 m); operating radius (four AIM-7F Sparrows, one Mk 28 and two tanks) hi-lo-hi 422 miles (680 km); ferry range 1,611 miles (2593 km)

Weights: empty 30,328 lb (13770 kg); maximum loaded 61,795 lb (28055 kg)

Dimensions: span 38 ft 4 in (11.68 m); length 63 ft 0 in (19.2 m); height 16 ft 5 in (5.00 m); wing area 530 sq ft (49.24 m²)

Armament: one M61A-1 20-mm gun with 639/640 rounds; four AIM-7E2 or -7F Sparrow III missiles recessed under fuselage; centreline pylon for any tactical store including 3,020-lb (1370-kg) M118 HE, nuclear, fire, cluster or other bombs, SUU-16/A or -23/A gun pods, spray tank, tow target or air-to-ground rockets; four wing pylons for Shrike, Standard ARM, Walleye, Harm or other missiles (inner pylons only can carry one Sparrow, or twin Falcon, or twin Sidewinder or other missiles); wide variety of ECM pods and tanks

The Phantom II is now nearly 35 years old, aged for a fighter. And yet its performance makes it still a front-line combat plane, able to handle contemporary missions in both ground attack and air-to-air combat. JV308 was an F-4E-35-MC, serial 67-308, delivered in late September 1968, and soon thereafter sent to South East Asia to help equip the 388th Tactical Fighter Wing, based at Korat Air Base, Thailand. It fought in that war from then on, subsequently being transferred to the 432nd TFW at Udorn before returning to the United States in 1973.

attack aircraft that the US Navy examined it in detail. In April 1955 a US Navy delegation came to St Louis and told MAC to replan it as a pure fleet defence fighter, the F4H-1. Ten of the 11 pylons were removed, leaving just the centre-line position to carry a large jettisonable fuel tank; the guns were removed and replaced by four of the new Sparrow II air-to-air missiles, carried semi-submerged on the flat underside of the amazingly broad fuselage; and the nose was given an even more powerful and versatile radar, specially designed by the Air Arm Division of Westinghouse, managed by a second crew-member.

The AH-1 contract was switched to two F4H-1 Phantom II fighters in May 1955, and the first of these, with Bureau of Aeronautics number 142259, made its maiden flight at St Louis on 27 May 1958. From the start it was clearly a fighter of extraordinary potential, and it quickly won over the XF8U-3 – an excellent aircraft built by Vought, the company that had beaten MAC in 1953 – and went into full production. The complex wing and flap-blowing system was operative on the sixth F4H-1, and other additions included a more bulged and pointed radome housing a radar with a larger scanner dish, an infra-red detector in a streamlined pod just beneath the radome, underwing pylons to carry a Sparrow or two close-range Sidewinder missiles on each side, and an inflight-refuelling probe. As for measured flight performance, this so consistently exceeded the guaranteed figures that the sum of all the plus and minus percentages where the actual figures differed from the calculated guarantees added up to an unprecedented +75 per cent!

By 1959 Phantoms had begun to set the greatest collection of world records ever gained by a single aircraft type. The first was the absolute height record, on 6 December 1959, at 98,557 ft (30040 m). Next came the 310.7-mile (500-km) closed-circuit record, set by the US Marine Corps on 5 September 1960 (the pilot was the famed Col. Tom Miller). This record fell at 15 minutes 19.2 seconds, officially 1,216.76 mph (1958.19 km/h) but actually – taking into account the distance round the large-radius turns – closer to about 1,315 mph (2116 km/h). This run meant almost half an hour in full afterburner mode, far beyond the capability of any other Western fighter. Three weeks later the 62.1-mile (100-km) circuit fell at a time of 2 minutes 40.9 seconds, or 1,390.24 mph (2237.4 km/h); actually the tightly banked circle was 65.2 miles (104.9 km) long, giving a true speed over 1,459 mph (2348 km/h). Records across the USA followed, for which air-refuelling was used. On 28 August 1961 the US Navy took the low-level speed record at 902.769 mph (1452.87 km/h) in the hot and turbulent air just above the desert. On 22 November 1961 the king of records fell to the Phantom: the high-altitude straight-line speed record was captured, the mean of two runs in opposite directions being 1,606.3 mph (2585 km/h), almost Mach 2.6; this was achieved by the second prototype, modified to have water injection to cool the air entering the engines. Many other records followed, including time-to-height records that no other aircraft could approach: the 10,000-ft (3048-m) level was

This historic photograph shows the first F4H-1 prototype tucking up its wheels on its first take-off on 27 May 1958 from St Louis Municipal Airport. No major modification was needed, and with 23 development aircraft (later styled F-4A) the new fighter was cleared for carrier service by 1960.

McDonnell Douglas F-4E Phantom II cutaway drawing key

1 Starboard tailplane
2 Static discharger
3 Honeycomb trailing edge panels
4 Tailplane mass balance weight
5 Tailplane spar construction
6 Drag chute housing
7 Tailcone/drag chute hinged door
8 Fuselage fuel tanks vent pipe
9 Honeycomb rudder construction
10 Rudder balance
11 Tail warning radar fairing
12 Tail navigation light
13 Fin tip antenna fairing
14 Communications antenna
15 Fin rear spar
16 Variable intensity formation lighting strip
17 Rudder control jack
18 Tailplane pivot mounting
19 Tailplane pivot seal
20 Fixed leading edge slat
21 Tailplane hydraulic jack
22 Fin front spar
23 Stabilator feel system pressure probe
24 Anti-collision light
25 Stabilator feel system balance mechanism
26 Tailcone cooling air duct
27 Heat resistant tailcone skinning
28 Arresting hook housing
29 Arresting hook, lowered
30 Starboard fully variable exhaust nozzle

31 Rudder artificial feel system bellows
32 Fin leading edge
33 Ram air intake
34 Fuselage No. 7 fuel cell, capacity 84 US gal (318 l)
35 Engine bay cooling air outlet louvres
36 Arresting hook actuator and damper
37 Fuel vent piping
38 Fuselage No. 6 fuel cell, capacity 213 US gal (806 l)
39 Jet pipe shroud construction
40 Engine bay hinged access doors
41 Rear AIM-7E-2 Sparrow air-to-air missile
42 Semi-recessed missile housing

43 Jet pipe nozzle actuators
44 Afterburner jet pipe
45 Fuselage No. 5 fuel cell, capacity 180 US gal (681 l)
46 Fuel tank access panels
47 Fuel system piping
48 Tailplane control cable duct
49 Fuselage No. 4 fuel cell, capacity 201 US gal (761 l)
50 Starboard engine bay construction
51 TACAN aerial
52 Fuselage No. 3 fuel cell, capacity 147 US gal (556 l)
53 Engine oil tank
54 General Electric J79-GE-17A turbojet engine
55 Engine accessories
56 Wing rear spar attachment
57 Mainwheel door
58 Main undercarriage wheel well
59 Lateral control servo actuator
60 Hydraulic accumulator
61 Lower surface airbrake jack
62 Flap hydraulic jack
63 Starboard flap
64 Honeycomb control surface construction
65 Starboard aileron
66 Aileron power control unit
67 Flutter damper
68 Spoiler housing

69 Wing tank fuel vent
70 Dihedral outer wing panel
71 Rear identification light
72 Wing tip formation lighting
73 Starboard navigation light
74 Radar warning antenna
75 Outer wing panel construction
76 Outboard leading edge slat
77 Slat control linkage
78 Slat hydraulic jack
79 Outer wing panel attachment
80 Starboard wing fence
81 Fuel vent system shut-off valves
82 Top of main undercarriage leg
83 Outboard pylon attachment housing
84 Inboard slat hydraulic jack
85 Starboard outer pylon
86 Mainwheel leg door
87 Mainwheel brake discs
88 Starboard mainwheel
89 Starboard external fuel tank capacity 370 US gal (1400 l)
90 Inboard leading edge slat, open
91 Slat hinge linkages
92 Main undercarriage retraction jack
93 Undercarriage uplock
94 Starboard wing fuel tank, capacity 315 US gal (1192 !)
95 Integral fuel tank construction
96 Inboard pylon fixing
97 Leading edge ranging antenna
98 Starboard inboard pylon
99 Twin missile launcher
100 AIM-9 Sidewinder
101 Hinged leading edge access panel
102 Wing front spar
103 Hydraulic reservoir
104 Centre fuselage formation lighting
105 Fuselage main frame
106 Engine intake compressor face
107 Intake duct construction
108 Fuselage No. 2 fuel cell, capacity 185 US gal (700 l)
109 Air-to-air refuelling receptacle, open
110 Port main undercarriage leg
111 Aileron power control unit
112 Port aileron
113 Aileron flutter damper

114 Port spoiler
115 Spoiler hydraulic jack
116 Wing fuel tank vent pipe
117 Port outer wing panel
118 Rearward identification light
119 Wing tip formation lighting
120 Port navigation light
121 Radar warning antenna
122 Port outboard leading edge slat
123 Slat hydraulic jack
124 Wing fence
125 Leading edge dog tooth
126 Inboard leading edge slat, open
127 Port external fuel tank, capacity 370 US gal (1400 l)
128 Inboard slat hydraulic jack
129 Port wing fuel tank, capacity 315 US gal (1192 l)
130 Upper fuselage light
131 IFF antenna
132 Avionics equipment bay
133 Gyro stabiliser platform
134 Fuselage No. 1 fuel cell, capacity 215 US gal (814 l)
135 Intake duct
136 Hydraulic connections
137 Starter cartridge container
138 Pneumatic system air bottle
139 Engine bleed air supply pipe
140 Forward AIM-7 missile housing
141 Ventral fuel tank, capacity 600 US gal (2271 l)
142 Bleed air louvre assembly lower
143 Avionics equipment bay
144 Variable intake ramp jack
145 Bleed air louvre assembly, upper

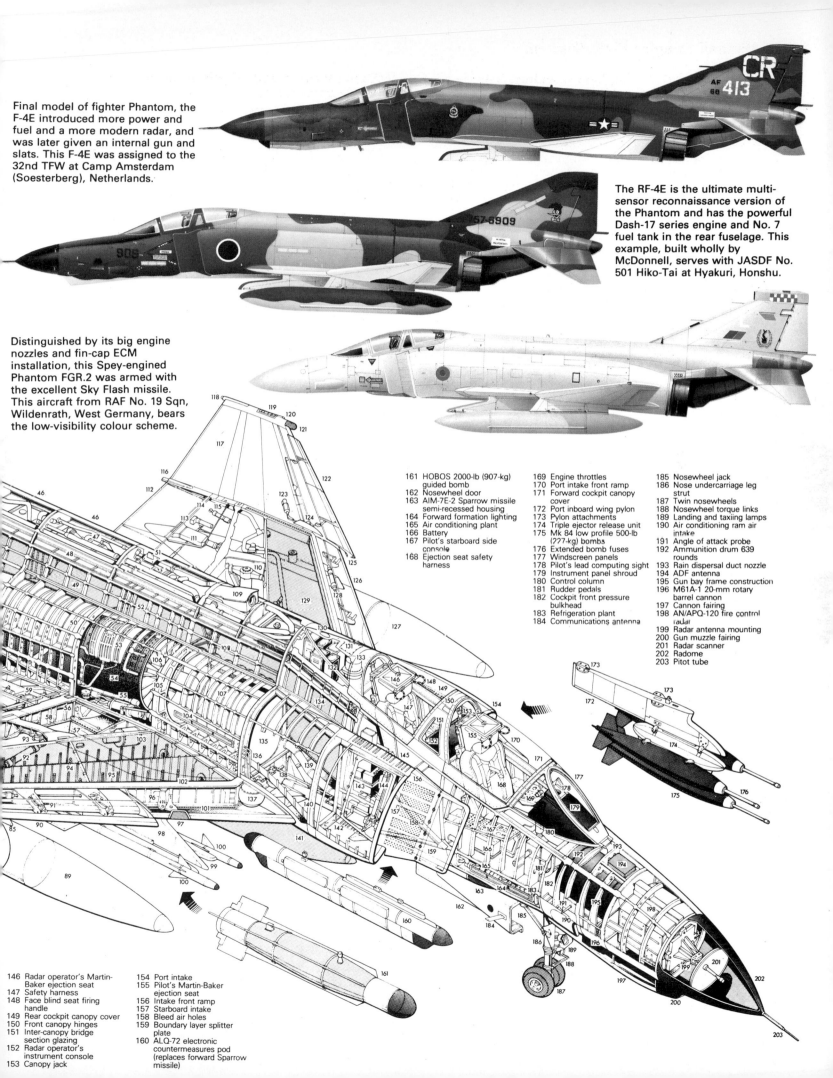

Final model of fighter Phantom, the F-4E introduced more power and fuel and a more modern radar, and was later given an internal gun and slats. This F-4E was assigned to the 32nd TFW at Camp Amsterdam (Soesterberg), Netherlands.

The RF-4E is the ultimate multi-sensor reconnaissance version of the Phantom and has the powerful Dash-17 series engine and No. 7 fuel tank in the rear fuselage. This example, built wholly by McDonnell, serves with JASDF No. 501 Hiko-Tai at Hyakuri, Honshu.

Distinguished by its big engine nozzles and fin-cap ECM installation, this Spey-engined Phantom FGR.2 was armed with the excellent Sky Flash missile. This aircraft from RAF No. 19 Sqn, Wildenrath, West Germany, bears the low-visibility colour scheme.

161 HOBOS 2000-lb (907-kg) guided bomb
162 Nosewheel door
163 AIM-7E-2 Sparrow missile semi-recessed housing
164 Forward formation lighting
165 Air conditioning plant
166 Battery
167 Pilot's starboard side console
168 Ejection seat safety harness
169 Engine throttles
170 Port intake front ramp
171 Forward cockpit canopy cover
172 Port inboard wing pylon
173 Pylon attachments
174 Triple ejector release unit
175 Mk 84 low profile 500-lb (227-kg) bombs
176 Extended bomb fuses
177 Windscreen panels
178 Pilot's lead computing sight
179 Instrument panel shroud
180 Control column
181 Rudder pedals
182 Cockpit front pressure bulkhead
183 Refrigeration plant
184 Communications antenna
185 Nosewheel jack
186 Nose undercarriage leg strut
187 Twin nosewheels
188 Nosewheel torque links
189 Landing and taxiing lamps
190 Air conditioning ram air intake
191 Angle of attack probe
192 Ammunition drum 639 rounds
193 Rain dispersal duct nozzle
194 ADF antenna
195 Gun bay frame construction
196 M61A-1 20-mm rotary barrel cannon
197 Cannon fairing
198 AN/APQ-120 fire control radar
199 Radar antenna mounting
200 Gun muzzle fairing
201 Radar scanner
202 Radome
203 Pitot tube

146 Radar operator's Martin-Baker ejection seat
147 Safety harness
148 Face blind seat firing handle
149 Rear cockpit canopy cover
150 Front canopy hinges
151 Inter-canopy bridge section glazing
152 Radar operator's instrument console
153 Canopy jack
154 Port intake
155 Pilot's Martin-Baker ejection seat
156 Intake front ramp
157 Starboard intake
158 Bleed air holes
159 Boundary layer splitter plate
160 ALQ-72 electronic countermeasures pod (replaces forward Sparrow missile)

passed on each climb roughly 30 seconds after the start of the take-off run. Perhaps the most impressive new record was that for the 98,425-ft (30-km) level that in fact went on to top 100,000 ft (30480 m).

Phantoms joined the US Navy and US Marine Corps in December 1960, having set wholly new standards in almost all aspects of mission capability. The designations were changed in 1962 and the original F4H-1F model, of which 45 were built, became the F-4A. It was identified by a straight top line from the canopy to the fin, and a small radome with 24-in (0.61-m) scanner. The first quantity-production model was the F-4B, with a raised canopy, improved inlets and larger ducts feeding J79-8 engines rated at 17,000-lb (7711-kg) thrust, and a larger radome housing the APQ-72 radar with a 32-in (0.81-in) dish. Tests proved this model could carry eight short tons (16,000 lb/7258 kg) of weapons on five pylons, far more than the US Navy's heaviest bomber and much more than any tactical fighter then in service with the US Air Force. MAC built 637 of this model, and hundreds served in Vietnam flying carrier-based attack, land-based bombing with the US Marines, air-combat sorties (such as MiG-CAP – MiG combat air patrol) and even FAC (forward air control) directing strikes from a position next to surface targets.

So impressed was the US Air Force that, after prolonged tests, it decided in March 1962 to buy the Phantom as the standard weapon system of most wings in TAC (Tactical Air Command). At first designated F-110, the US Air Force model was almost at once restyled F-4C. It was a minimum-change aircraft, though the US Air Force felt it had to have larger lower-pressure tyres, self-contained cartridge/pneumatic starters for J79-15 (Dash-15) engines, anti-skid brakes, a receptacle for the 'flying boom' refuelling system, dual controls and various avionics changes. MAC delivered 583 between 1963 and 1966, and these too played a major role in the South East Asia war.

So successful was the F-4C that it led immediately to two new models. One was the RF-4C, a dedicated reconnaissance platform for the most advanced tactical reconnaissance of its era. The APQ-72 radar was replaced by a small APQ-99 set for mapping, terrain-following and collision-avoidance, with the rest of the re-shaped nose filled with forward-oblique, lateral and panoramic cameras. In the underside was installed a large SLAR (sideways-looking airborne radar) giving a high-definition picture strip along the flight-path.

Further back was placed an IR (infra-red, or heat) line-scan system giving a clear thermal-image film picture of the same area. Masses of special communications and electronics were installed from nose to tail. The US Air Force bought 505 of these, and the US Marines converted 46 F-4B fighters into RF-4B models similar in equipment to the RF-4C.

Outwardly not easy to distinguish from the more common fighter version, the RF-4C carries no armament yet costs more because of its sophisticated reconnaissance sensors and communications systems. Here a pair of RFs from the USAF 363 TRW leave Nellis AFB during the 1981 Red Flag exercise.

Land-based variant

The other new model triggered off by the F-4C was the F-4D, the result of a relaxation of the law that the US Air Force had to accept the F-4B with minimal changes. The folding wing and some other naval features were retained, but the F-4D introduced many avionic items tailored specifically for land-based missions against ground targets. An inertial navigation system was installed, together with improved radar, a lead-computing optical sight, weapon-release computer and an impressive suite of EW (electronic warfare) equipment. More powerful electric generators were installed, and the F-4D was made compatible with 'smart' bombs, the Maverick air-to-surface missile, the Falcon air-to-air missile and, later, many other new ordnance items. Many F-4D models lacked the undernose pod for an IR sensor. MAC delivered a useful 825 of this series, and they flew more hours in Vietnam than any other fighter except the F-100.

As the ultimate US Air Force model the F-4E was planned with improved avionics; and in the course of design in 1966 it was decided to fit the most powerful J79, the 17,900-lb (8119-kg) Dash-17A, and use the extra thrust to handle an added seventh fuel tank at the tail. The main change was planned to be a new radar, and Westinghouse finally came up with the all-solid-state APQ-120 offering much more capability in a smaller and lighter package in a slimmer nose. New Martin-Baker seats with zero/zero (at rest on the airfield) capability were fitted, and the tailplanes were given the inverted leading-edge slat previously seen on other models (F-4J, K and M). Deliveries of the F-4E began in 1967, but five years later frequent stall/spin accidents in Vietnam – caused by pulling tight turns at very low level with many

Wearing the camouflage now standard on Japanese (JASDF) tactical combat aircraft, this RF-4EJ is one of the multi-sensor reconnaissance version supplied to Japan from St Louis, initially for No. 501 Sqn. The JASDF fighter Phantoms, styled F-4EJ, were manufactured under licence in Japan.

In conformity with modern ideas about low-visibility insignia, this RF-4B is painted in the current low-contrast markings of Navy and Marine Corps combat aircraft. This RF-4B also bears the muted insignia of VMFP-3 photo-recon squadron, based at El Toro, California.

West German industry gained an important slice of the overall F-4 production programme, a proportion which increased with Phantoms built for the Luftwaffe. Two wings are equipped with the RF-4E, a version slightly simpler than the RF-4C; this one is in the markings of AG (Aufklärungs Geschwäder) 52 at Leck, in 2nd ATAF.

The F-4C was the original 'minimum-change' model for the US Air Force. This 1963-funded example, with infra-red seeker under the nose, was in 1980 serving with the 171st FIS of the Michigan ANG

The F-4D was the first land-based model designed specifically for US Air Force requirements, with emphasis on attack on surface targets. This example, without the prominent infra-red seeker under the nose, was flying in 1970 with the Imperial Iranian AF's 306th Fighter Sqn.

tons of ordnance on board, something never asked for in the original design – led to a new wing leading edge with giant slats instead of the blown droop flaps. The slatted wing not only dramatically cut the number of fatal accidents but also significantly reduced the turn radius and thus made the F-4E a better dogfighter. After much argument another change rectified what had been the Phantom's chief shortcoming: lack of an internal gun. Cannon could previously be carried in external pods, but in 1967 an M61 multi-barrel 20-mm cannon was fitted under the nose, fed by a drum of 640 rounds. This was a godsend to the Phantom pilots in Vietnam who had previously had to throw away their long-distance kill capability while closing to positive visual identification range, at which distance they had no gun with which to shoot down enemies.

Phantoms join the Royal Navy

In 1964 the Royal Navy decided to buy the Phantom and, after long development, the F-4K became operational in 1968–9. This is powered by Rolls-Royce Spey afterburning

turbofans, fed by enlarged ducts and with shorter but larger nozzles. Despite giving 20,350-lb (9231-kg) thrust, these engines actually resulted in a deterioration in performance except in range. Called Phantom FG.1 by the Fleet Air Arm, the F-4K model also introduced folding nose radar, a double-extending nose leg for British catapult take-offs, an inverted slat on the tailplanes and British avionics and equipment. The RN took 24, and 28 more went to the RAF which also bought 118 of an uprated version designated F-4M and with the British title Phantom FGR.2. This has increased-capacity landing gears and anti-skid brakes, as well as a completely new nav/attack system and many other updated avionic items which from 1975 included an analog-controlled radar warning system with aerials in a long flat-topped extension added to the top of the fin. External loads could include a giant EMI multi-sensor reconnaissance pod carried on the centreline.

In 1963 the US Navy and US Marines planned a second-generation Phantom based as closely as possible on the F-4B, and this matured as the F-4J. It has 17,900-lb (8119-kg) Dash-10 engines, an integrated missile/weapons control system with new radar, a seventh fuel tank, the slatted tail, Martin-Baker zero/zero seats, stronger landing gears, drooping ailerons and uprated electric generation. MAC built 522 of this version, completing in 1972. The F-4N is a remanufactured

Outside the United States the largest user of the Phantom II is Israel, whose Heyl Ha'Avir received 204 F-4Es, similar to this example, plus 12 of the RF-4E reconnaissance version. They have seen prolonged combat duty, extending over south Lebanon and Syria up to the present day.

McDonnell Douglas F-4E Phantom

The F-4N is the remanufactured and updated F-4B, in many respects equal to the F-4J but not incorporating the wing slats now flying on the F-4S (rebuilt F-4J). This F-4N flew with one of the most famous Navy fighter outfits, VF-111 'The Sundowners'.

Most costly of all versions of the Phantom, the F-4G is the Wild Weasel II electronic-warfare platform, 116 of which were produced in 1975–81 by rebuilding F-4Es. This example served with 81 TFS, 52 TFW, at Spangdahlem AB, West Germany.

F-4B with extensive new equipment, 227 of these being produced. Likewise the F-4S is a remanufactured F-4J with stronger fatigue-resistant airframe, leading-edge slats and inboard leading-edge flaps, totally new outer wings and updated fire-control avionics. By 1981 there were 300.

Wild Weasel

An even larger rebuild, the F-4G Advanced Wild Weasel, is the US Air Force's standard tactical platform for suppressing hostile radars, especially those for guiding surface-to-air missiles. The F-4G can be produced by rebuilding an F-4D or F-4E, but most in 1981 were F-4Es. The main new subsystem is the APR-38 RHAWS (radar homing and warning system) with 57 aerials all over the aircraft, including new emitters and passive receivers in a pod on top of the fin. Apart from AAMs (air-to-air missiles) for its own defence, the F-4G can carry such anti-radar missiles as the Shrike (all versions), Standard ARM (anti-radar missile) and Harm (high-speed Arm). A force of 116 aircraft was rebuilt, starting in 1978.

This massive sustained manufacturing programme has been boosted by numerous exports. One of the first was a loan of 24 F-4Es to Australia pending delayed delivery to the RAAF of the F-111C. The West German Luftwaffe purchased 88 of a simplified and slightly different unarmed reconnaissance version called EF-4E, which opened the way to useful participation by German companies in all subsequent Phantom manufacture. After 1970 the West German government signed contracts for a further 175 of a dedicated fighter model, the F-4F, which at one time was expected to be a single-seater but finally crystallized as a somewhat simplified F-4E. Another F-4E variant was made in Japan. The first two F-4EJ fighters were made by MAC and flown to Japan. These were followed by eight sent out in kit form, and after successfully assembling and testing these, Mitsubishi made a further 130 F-4EJ Phantoms at Nagoya.

Other planes went to Greece (56), Iran (177), Israel (216), South Korea (19), and Turkey (40). 14 RF-4Es were flown from St Louis to Japan, and 16 Phantoms of the same type ordered by Iran stayed on the tarmac in St Louis because of the Iranian Revolution.

The Israeli Air Force was upgrading its F4s in 1986. First prototypes were fitted with Kfir-type canard surfaces and new avionics include Elta pulse-Doppler radar and other sophisticated combat gadgetry.

McDonnell Douglas Phantom II variants

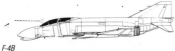

XF4H-1: two prototypes

F-4A: two 15,000-lb (6804-kg) J79-GE-2 engines (later GE-2A), Westinghouse APQ-50 radar, four recessed Sparrow III missiles (21 pre-production and 24 production)
TF-4A: trainer conversion of F-4A without arrester hook or combat equipment (small number of conversions)
F-4B: two 17,000-lb (7711-kg) J79-GE-8A/8B engines, raised cockpits with higher canopy, Westinghouse APQ-72 radar (637 built)

RF-4B: unarmed reconnaissance derivative of F-4B with basically same equipment and systems as RF-4C (12 built for US Marine Corps)

RF-4B of US Marine Corps

DF-4B: RPV control aircraft (drone mother ship), rebuild of F-4B
QF-4B: pilotless RPV drone (44 converted from F-4B)
F-4C: two 17,000-lb (7711-kg) J79-GE-15 engines with cartridge starters, wider low-pressure main tyres, completely revised avionics with APQ-100 radar, ASN-48

inertial system, AJB-7 bombing system, LADD timer and AGM-12B Bullpup control panel, dual flight controls and inflight-refuelling boom receptacle instead of probe (583 built for USAF, but 36 passed to Spain)

RF-4C: multi-sensor reconnaissance derivate of F-4C with longer nose housing cameras, APQ-99 forward-looking radar, APQ-102 SLAR and (in fuselage underside) AAS-18A IR linescan, with augmented EW subsystems and communications including HF with flush shunt aerial in sides of fin (505 built)

RF-4C Nose Section

F-4D: developed from F-4C to meet full requirements of USAF with APQ-109 radar fire-control, ASG-22 servoed sight, ASN-63 inertial system, ASQ-91 weapon release computer, and uprated generators; IR seeker under nose often removed (793 built for USAF and 32 for Iran; 36 USAF aircraft transferred to South Korea)

F-4E: two 17,900-lb (8119-kg) J79-GE-17 engines, seventh fuel cell, longer but slimmer nose with APQ-120 radar fire-control; later fitted with M61 20-mm gun under nose and later still with leading-edge slats in place of blown droop flaps and Tiseo electro-optical target viewing system on left wing (831 built for USAF, plus 538

for export to West Germany, Israel, Iran, Greece, Turkey, Japan and South Korea)

F-4EJ: variant of F-4E for JASDF (Japan) with tail-warning radar and interfaces with AAM-2 missiles (140 built, including 138 assembled or manufactured in Japan)
RF-4E: reconnaissance variant of F-4E with equipment generally as RF-4C (130 built for export customers West Germany, Japan, Israel, Iran, Greece and Turkey)
F-4F: two 17,900-lb (8119-kg) J79-MTU-17A engines and generally as F-4E but without seventh tank, stabilator slat and certain classified equipment items (175 built for West Germany, with German-supplied airframe sections)
TF-4F: small number of dual trainer conversions of F-4F
F-4G: defunct designation of 12 F-4Bs fitted with ASW-21 digital data-link, subsequently modified to F-4B standard but not included in F-4B total
F-4G: currently active designation of F-4D (2) and F-4E (116) rebuilt as Wild Weasel II EW aircraft with APR-38 system and various missile provisions
F-4H: not used, to avoid confusion with original F4H-1
F-4J: two 17,900-lb (8119-kg) J79-GE-10 engines; updated US Navy/Marine aircraft with Westinghouse AWG-10 pulse-doppler fire control, slatted stabilator and drooping (16½°) ailerons, AJB-7 bombing system, uprated generators (522 built)

F-4K: two 20,350-lb (9231-kg) Rolls-Royce Spey 202/203 engines, with AWG-11 fire-control with double-hinged folding radome, drooping ailerons, slatted stabilator, fuselage and ducts widened to handle increased engine airflow, strengthened main gears and double-extending nose leg, much British avionic equipment (52 built for UK)

Royal Navy F-4Ks (Phantom FG.1s)

F-4M: development of F-4K for RAF with F-4C wheels/tyres/brakes, no stabilator slat, AWF-12 fire control, Ferranti nav/attack system, British airframe sections; later updated with ECM fin-cap installation and Sky Flash missiles (118 built for UK)

Royal Air Force F-4M (Phantom FGR.2) showing Sky Flash missiles

F-4N: updated F-4B with remanufactured structure and avionic updating (228 rebuilt)
F-4S: updated F-4J with F-4N improvements plus manoeuvring slats on outer wings only (302 rebuilt)
F-4CCV: experimental research CCV (control-configured vehicle) aircraft with fly-by-wire controls, canard foreplanes and outboard flaperons (single aircraft rebuilt)

North-American X-15: the black bullet

More than 16 years after its last flight, the North American X-15 remains the world's fastest and highest-flying aircraft. Remarkably, this brilliant feat of engineering was obtained at the cost of only one fatal accident. In the course of 199 flights between June 1959 and October 1968, the X-15 made exceptionally valuable contributions to many scientific fields.

Midway through World War 2, a number of piston-engined aircraft broke the sound barrier when diving. But there were serious aerodynamic problems involved in doing so, because at speeds above Mach 0.8 the laws of hydrodynamics no longer apply. If the flow velocity of air exceeds the speed at which sound is transmitted, the basic laws affecting the compressibility of gases start to change, and localised disturbances such as compression shock occur. It was obvious that the turbojet and rocket engines under development at the time would soon be attaining even higher speeds and thus creating even bigger problems. So scientists all over the

world were agreed that the problems with compressibility needed to be solved.

In the United States, this quest was spearheaded by the National Advisory Committee for Aeronautics (NACA, the forebear of today's National Aeronautics & Space Administration), with Dr William F. Durand, its chairman of the Special Committee for Jet Propulsion, suggesting on 18 December 1943 that the US Army, US Navy, NACA, and the

The three X-15s were used for research purposes by the American Air Force the Navy and NASA.

North American X-15

Specification

North American X-15 (with large rocket engine)
Type: single-seat research aircraft
Powerplant: one Thiokol (Reaction Motors) XLR99-RM-2 single-chamber throttlable liquid-propellant rocket engine, with a thrust rating of 57,000 lb (25855 kg) at 45,000 ft (13716 m)
Performance: maximum speed 4,104 mph (6605 km/h); maximum altitude 354,200 ft (107960 m); typical range 275 miles (440 km)
Weights: empty 15,000 lb (6804 kg); maximum launch 33,300 lb (15105 kg)
Dimensions: span 22 ft 4 in (6.81 m); length 50 ft 9 in (15.47 m); height 13 ft 0 in (3.96 m); wing area 200 sq ft (18.58 m^2)

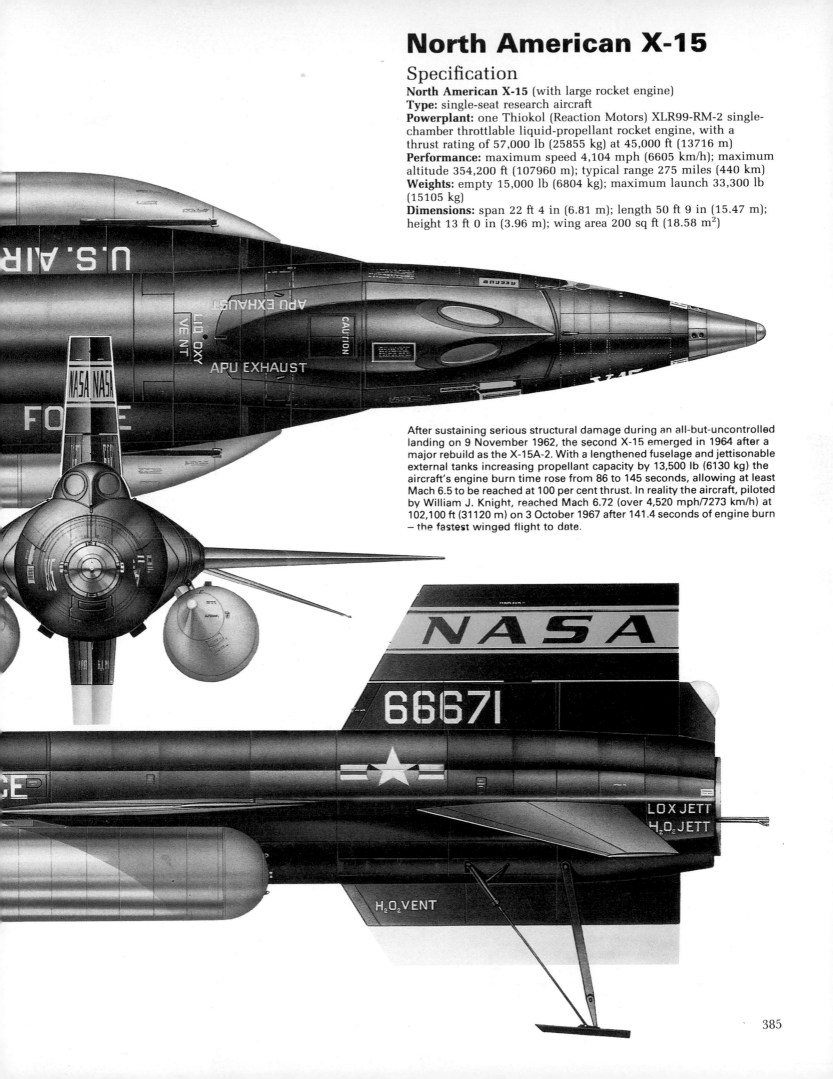

After sustaining serious structural damage during an all-but-uncontrolled landing on 9 November 1962, the second X-15 emerged in 1964 after a major rebuild as the X-15A-2. With a lengthened fuselage and jettisonable external tanks increasing propellant capacity by 13,500 lb (6130 kg) the aircraft's engine burn time rose from 86 to 145 seconds, allowing at least Mach 6.5 to be reached at 100 per cent thrust. In reality the aircraft, piloted by William J. Knight, reached Mach 6.72 (over 4,520 mph/7273 km/h) at 102,100 ft (31120 m) on 3 October 1967 after 141.4 seconds of engine burn – the fastest winged flight to date.

In lieu of the Reaction Motors-designed XLR99-RM-1 powerplant, the first X-15 was fitted with two uprated XLR11 rocket engines for the initial test flights. With a modest 8,000-lb (3632-kg) thrust per engine, the first powered flight on 17 September 1959 saw Mach 2.11 easily attained.

Neil Armstrong, Forrest Peterson, Joe Walker and John McKay were all X-15 test pilots. Armstrong became world-famous as an astronaut.

aircraft industry define jointly the specification for a research aircraft to explore high transonic and low supersonic speeds. Subsequently, inter-service rivalries scuttled this joint effort and the USAAF funded the Bell X-1 and X-2 programmes while the USN sponsored the Douglas D-558-1 and D-558-2 series, with NACA co-operating in both projects.

The USAAF and Bell were first out of the gate as the X-1, dropped at 27,000 ft (8230 m) from the belly of a Boeing B-29 flying over Pinecastle Field in Florida, made its first un-powered flight on 19 January 1946. The X-1 first fired its XLR-11-RM-3 rocket engine during its twelfth flight on 11 April 1947; three days later the turbo-jet-powered Douglas D-558-1 of the US Navy was first flown. Of the two, it was the X-1 which rightfully gained the greater fame as, during the aircraft's 31st flight on 14 October 1947, Captain Charles E. Yeager became the first pilot to fly supersonically when he reached Mach 1.06 at 43,000 ft (13106 m) over Muroc Field, the future Edwards AFB in California's Mojave Desert. (Contrary to the story in the popular movie *The Right Stuff*, this was Yeager's 12th flight in the X-1, not his first!)

These two types of pioneering research aircraft were followed in February 1948 by the D-558-2 (first flown with a turbojet, then from October 1949 with a turbojet and rocket, and finally from September 1950 without a turbojet but with a more powerful rocket), in July 1951 by the X-1D, in June 1952 by the Bell X-2, in February 1953 by the X-1A, in September 1954 by the X-1B, and in December 1955 by the

X-1E. With the availability of these more capable aircraft, military and NACA pilots were able to reach greater and greater speeds: Mach 1.45 with the X-1 on 26 March 1948, Mach 1.88 on 7 August 1951 and Mach 2.005 (the world's first Mach 2+ flight) on 20 November 1953 both with the D-558-2, Mach 2.44 with the X-1A on 12 December 1953, and Mach 2.87 with the X-2 on 23 July 1956. Finally, the first Mach 3+ (Mach 3.196) flight was made on 27 September 1956 by Captain Milburn Apt in the ill-fated X-2. Like-wise, higher altitudes were progressively obtained until 7 September 1956 when the Bell X-2 reached 125,907 ft (38376 m). However, a high price had been paid for these results as, in addition to Captain Apt, two test pilots were killed while six of the 14 research aircraft (six X-1s, two X-2s, and six D-558s) were destroyed.

In June 1952, 10 months after acquiring the modified second prototype of the D-558-2 (then the fastest aircraft but still 17 months away from flying at twice the speed of

This is the view from the B-52 motherplane prior to launch of the X-15. Extensive wind tunnel tests were carried out by NACA to ensure an effective X-15/B-52 launch procedure from the special launch pylon once sufficient height had been obtained. For the X-15 pilot, an ejection seat was provided for use up to Mach 4.

sound), NACA had urged that the research programme be expanded to explore flight characteristics at speeds of Mach 4 to 10 and altitudes of 12 to 50 miles (19.3 to 80.5 km). This ambitious programme was beyond the financial reach of a single agency, however, and following numerous research studies representatives of NACA, the US Air Force and the US Navy met on 9 July 1954 to discuss the need for a hypersonic research vehicle and the eventual joint sponsoring of its acquisition and testing. More discussions followed until late 1954 when NACA and the two services were ready to request proposals from the industry. The gestation period for the highly successful X-15 had begun.

Four manufacturers responded to this invitation: Bell submitted its D-171 design, Douglas its Model 684 D-558-3, North American its NA-240, and Republic its Model AP-76. Initially the US Air Force representatives favoured the North American entry while their US Navy colleagues, pleased with the results so far achieved with the D-558-2, leaned towards the Douglas Model 684. In the end, however, the joint selection team agreed in September 1955 that the NA-240 was 'the most suitable for research and potentially the simplest to make safe for the mission'. Contract AF-(600)-31693, calling for three X-15 research aircraft, was awarded to North American Aviation, Inc. by the USAF in June 1956.

Following contract award, design of the NA-240 was refined: the all-moving upper portion of the vertical tail surfaces were revised to improve directional control at high speeds, and the originally planned split trailing-edge speed brakes constituting the rear portion of the upper vertical tail surfaces were replaced by large surfaces at the base of the dorsal and ventral fins. The landing gear, which at first was to be comprised of twin nosewheel and retractable metal skids beneath the centre fuselage, was modified by relocating the landing skids to the aft end of the fuselage. Another design change initiated during this phase was the replacement of the encapsulated emergency escape system by a conventional ejector seat of advanced design usable by the pilot for emergency egress at speeds up to Mach 4.

To withstand temperatures of up to 1,200°F (649°C) caused by aerodynamically induced friction, the North American design team, under the direction of Harrison Storms and Charles Feltz, planned from the outset to use titanium and stainless steel for most of the internal structure, while Inconel X nickel alloy sheets were to be used as skin coverings. Other noteworthy design features included the selection of small trapezoidal wing surfaces of thin section

The relatively small size of the X-15 is apparent as it is carried aloft under the mother plane. On this, the first flight, the X-15 carried not rocket fuel but hydrogen peroxide for control system operation. Trouble was encountered during the approach, but a safe landing was just possible at Edwards AFB.

(5 per cent, or 2 in/5.08 cm at the root and 0.375 in/0.95 cm at the tip), the use of the all-moving tailplane for roll control, and provision for a three-stick control system. A conventional central stick was to be used to control the aircraft in pitch and roll during low-speed atmospheric flight, a side-mounted stick was for use during acceleration and re-entry, and another side stick actuated reaction jets during exo-atmospheric flight. The cockpit, with dualpane heat resistant glass panels and Inconel X construction, was pressurized and refrigerated; in addition, the pilot was to wear an MC-2 full-pressure suit.

Like previous US supersonic research aircraft, with the notable exception of the D-558-2 in its original configuration, the X-15 was to be powered by a rocket engine and air-launched. Its weight and size, however, precluded the launch of the X-15 by existing Boeing B-29 and B-50 mother aircraft. After briefly considering the modification of a Convair B-36 for this role, the contractor and the government selected the Boeing B-52 as the X-15 launch aircraft. Accordingly, a B-52A (serial number 52-003) and a B-52B (52-008) were delivered to North American to be modified as an

The first X-15 streaks upwards towards the boundary of the atmosphere and beyond. Such was the aircraft's performance that a new NACA/USAF tracking network was created, a 485-mile (780-km) corridor 50 miles (80 km) wide over California and Nevada with emergency landing sites on various dry lakes.

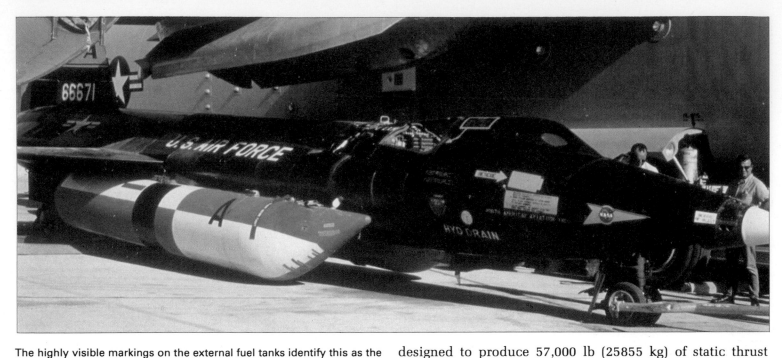

The highly visible markings on the external fuel tanks identify this as the X-15A-2 following rebuild and conversion by North American. Here the aircraft has left its ground pulley device and is about to be hoisted and attached to the underwing pylon visible immediately above.

NB-52A and an NB-52B respectively by installation of a launch pylon beneath the starboard wing, rocket fuel top-off tanks in the bomb bays, and observation and recording domes on the right fuselage side.

As originally proposed in 1955, the NA-240 was to have been powered by a Thiokol XLR30-RM-2 rocket, but during the detail design phase it was decided to replace this engine with a more powerful XLR99-RM-1. Burning a mixture of liquid oxygen and anhydrous ammonia, the XLR99 was

designed to produce 57,000 lb (25855 kg) of static thrust and to be throttled between 40 and 100 per cent. Its development, however, lagged behind that of the airframe. To avoid delaying the programme, North American proposed to start flight trials with two Reaction Motors XLR11s (improved versions of the rocket engine first used on the Bell X-1 in 1946). Even though the two XLR11s could generate a combined thrust of only 16,000 lb (7257 kg), only 28 per cent of that of the XLR99, the aircraft was still expected to reach a top speed of Mach 3.0. As this represented a worthwhile improvement over the then maximum speed of Mach 2.44 attained on 12 December 1953 by the Bell X-2, the contractor's proposal was endorsed by NACA and the two services.

Roll-out and flight trials
Component manufacturing for the first X-15 (US Air Force serial number 56-6670, constructor number 240-1) started in September 1956, and the aircraft was rolled out at the Inglewood plant 25 months later. Bearing US Air Force markings as this service was the contracting agency, the X-15 was trucked to Edwards AFB where preparations were made for the flight trials. To initiate these trials, North American

North American X-15A-2 cutaway drawing key

1 Hypersonic flow sensor
2 Nose cone
3 Power supply amplifier
4 Pitch control reaction jets
5 Yaw control reaction jets
6 Front equipment bay
7 Inconel-X skin plating
8 Heat insulating lining
9 Nosewheel bay
10 Undercarriage leg pivot
11 Nose undercarriage leg (shortens on retraction)
12 Free-fall nose undercarriage member
13 Twin nosewheels
14 Nosewheel door
15 Door air scoop
16 Pitot tube
17 Instrument panel shroud
18 Back of instrument panel
19 Rudder pedals
20 Antenna
21 Engine throttle control
22 Ballistic control column
23 Pilot's seat
24 Aerodynamic control column
25 Knife-edge cockpit canopy
26 Fused silica elliptical windows
27 Pilot's starboard side console
28 Safety harness
29 Port side console
30 Telescopic strut for ejection seat blast shield
31 Folded stabilizing vanes
32 Headrest
33 Cockpit canopy open position
34 Rocket powered ejection seat
35 Instrumentation inertia platform
36 Liquid nitrogen cooling system
37 Ventral antenna
38 Canopy insulation
39 Canopy hinge
40 Forward connecting link to NB-52 launcher pylon
41 Sprung doors to connectors
42 Stellar camera platform
43 Two oblique astronomical cameras
44 Two vertical astronomical cameras
45 Camera platform gimballed mounting
46 Systems equipment compartment
47 Control runs
48 Twin General Electric auxiliary power units
49 APU exhausts
50 Cooling system vent
51 Two APU generators
52 Starboard external fuel tank, anhydrous ammonia, 6,006 lb (2724 kg)
53 Starboard side fairing
54 Liquid oxygen vent
55 Liquid oxygen tank pressure bulkhead
56 Equipment cooling system liquid nitrogen tank
57 Reaction control jet HTP fuel tanks, port and starboard
58 Port external tank nose fairing
59 External tank front attachment
60 Recovery parachute
61 Parachute release link
62 Fuel tank pressurizing helium reservoir
63 Pipe runs in side fairing
64 Side fairing frames
65 Test and recording equipment
66 Liquid oxygen fuel tank
67 Fuel tank compartment bulkheads
68 Tank baffles
69 Welded Inconel-X fuel tank skins
70 Internal stiffeners
71 Liquid oxygen filler cap
72 Welded external tank stiffeners
73 Liquid oxygen supply pipe to engine
74 Liquid oxygen tank rear pressure bulkhead
75 Fuel pipes to roll control reaction jets
76 Liquid hydrogen fuel tank for ramjet engine
77 Access panels
78 Starboard wing panel
79 Roll control reaction jets
80 Interchangeable starboard wing tip
81 Wing tip instrumentation
82 Fixed trailing edge section
83 Starboard landing flap
84 Aft attaching links to NB-52 launcher pylon
85 Anhydrous ammonia main fuel tank
86 Tank dividing bulkheads
87 A-frame wing mounting struts
88 Flap jack attachment
89 Ammonia filler point
90 Ammonia fuel feed pipe
91 Inconel-X welded tank skins
92 Ammonia tank rear pressure bulkhead
93 Welded external tank stiffeners
94 Liquid oxygen feed pipe
95 Access panels
96 Turbopump HTP fuel tank, 64 US gal (242 litres)

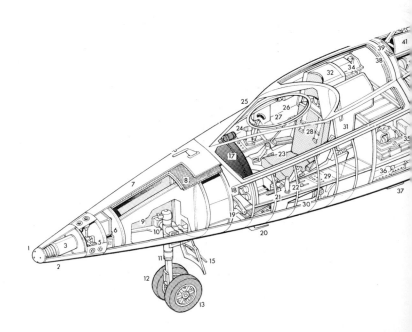

Lock
'B

The SR-71 began life on
service at incredible eff
Command's few SR-71s a

The story of Lockheed's Blackbird seri
altitude reconnaissance planes goes ba
the CIA declared that it could no longe
U-2 for its overflights of the Soviet Un
cruising altitude of around 70,000 ft
longer safe from fighters and ground-

Whether or not this story is true n
but the CIA could well have originate
replacement. In the event, Gary Powe
near Sverdlovsk by an SA-2 on 1 May
have been only on Powers' release tha
he had fallen asleep during his fi
allowed the aircraft to descend to 47,0
it came within the reach of ground o
reconnaissance may have been in
onward.

However, Clarence ('Kelly') Johnso
Lockheed's Advanced Development
less formally as 'The Skunk Works
lectures that the project began as a
Sources within the USAF have been
the original requirement called for a
at least 106,000 ft (32310 m). It is
development contract was awarded 1
1959, following competitive biddin
Dynamics and North American.

Whatever the original basis for the
quite possible that the USAF and CI
ing an aircraft that would form the
ceptor and a high-altitude reconnai

One of the first photographs released for pu
YF-12A revealed nothing whatever of the ai
planform. The full serial was 60–6934, and it
YF-12A by the cut-back chine at the nose an
centre one folded to the side.

North American X-15 variants

X-15 (initial configuration): for initial flight trials the first two X-15s (56-6670 and 56-6671) were powered by two four-chamber XLR11 rocket engines, each producing 8,000-lb (3629-kg) thrust

X-15 (final configuration): identical to the earlier configuration but with the XLR11 engines replaced by a 57,000-lb (25855-kg) thrust XLR99 engine; the first two X-15s were retrofitted with this engine while the third (56-6672, c/n 240-3) was originally fitted with the XLR99; for most of the later flights the ventral fin was removed to improve lateral stability during high angle-of-attack re-entry

X-15A-2: designation given to the second X-15 after it had been modified in 1963 to investigate higher speeds; two external propellant tanks were attached beneath the fuselage and the windshield design was improved; to withstand the higher temperatures caused by aerodynamically-induced friction, the X-15A-2 could be finished with M25S ablative coating

X-15 (with delta wing): proposed modification of the third X-15, which was to have had its straight trapezoidal wing replaced by a slender delta wing and scramjet engine mounted on its fin; this project was abandoned following the loss of the aircraft before modification

X-15 (satellite launcher): the use of the X-15 to launch a Scout satellite was considered briefly but rejected as being more expensive than conventional launch methods

Booster-launched X-15: North American proposed an **'X-15B'** as an alternative for the Project Mercury manned space programme; the 'X-15B' was to have used a Navaho missile booster for launch; the company later proposed the use of the X-15 as an expendable spacecraft to be launched into space by four Martin Titan rockets; neither project was realized

had already retained the services of A. Scott Crossfield, an experienced NACA test pilot who had flown the X-1, D-558-1, and D-558-2, and who on 20 November 1953 had made the world's first Mach 2+ flight. With Scott Crossfield strapped in the cockpit, the first X-15 was mated to the NB-52A launch aircraft for its initial unpowered flight on 8 June 1959. Control oversensitivity, noted during this flight, forced a postponement of powered flights until appropriate modifications had been made.

Powered flight trials began on 17 September 1959 when Scott Crossfield reached Mach 2.11 at an altitude of 52,341 ft

(15954 m) in the XLR11-powered second X-15 (56-6671, c/n 240-2). A near repeat flight was made one month later without problems, but the fourth flight on 5 November was marred by an engine fire and an emergency landing at Rosamund Dry Lake, during which fuselage structural failure occurred. Fortunately, Crossfield was not injured and 55-6671 was repaired to fly again on 11 February 1960 (the programme's sixth flight). NACA having been reorganized into the National Aeronautics & Space Administration during 1958, it was for NASA that Joe Walker made the X-15's ninth flight on 25 March 1960 to become the first government pilot to fly the type. Walker also became the first pilot to fly the X-15 at more than Mach 3.0 when he reached Mach 3.19 with the XLR11-powered first prototype on 12 May. Other agencies soon joined the flight trials: on 13 April 1960 Captain Robert White made the first USAF flight, and on 23 September 1960 Commander Forrest Peterson first flew the X-15 for the US Navy. Flown by the contractor's pilot and by government pilots, the X-15 made a total of 29 flights with the XLR11 engines, reaching a top speed of Mach 3.50 (2,275

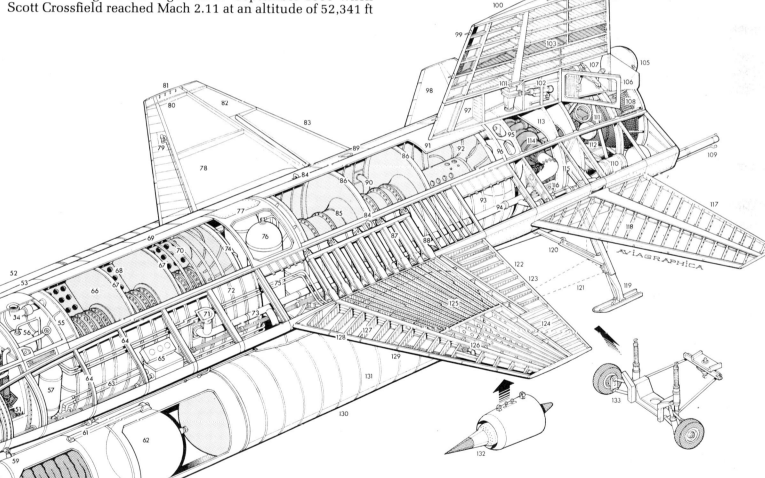

97 Vertical stabilizer fixed stub section	100 Vertical stabilizer upper rudder section	105 Helium tank to pressurize liquid nitrogen	111 Engine mounting struts
98 Starboard all-moving tailplane	101 Rudder spar pivot	106 Airbrake	112 Thiokol XLR99 rocket engine
99 Instrumented leading wedge	102 Rudder jack	107 Airbrake jack mechanism	113 Rear fuselage frames
	103 Communications aerial	108 Rocket chamber nozzle	114 Rocket engine turbopumps
	104 Wedge section rudder	109 Liquid oxygen jettison pipe	115 Tailplane spar pivot
		110 Turbopump lubrication tank	116 Tailplane jack

117 Port all-moving tailplane	126 Roll control reaction jets
118 Inconel-X tailplane construction	127 Leading edge construction
119 Port main landing skid	128 Inconel-X leading edge heat sink strip
120 Skid lowering hydraulic jack strut	129 Thermal expansion slots in leading edge
121 Position of wedge section ventral rudder, jettisonable for landing	130 Port external fuel tank, liquid oxygen, 7,494 lb (3399 kg)
122 Port landing flap	131 Mylar-type wrapped insulated tank skins
123 Square section trailing edge	132 Auxiliary ramjet engine (replaces ventral rudder)
124 Fixed trailing edge section	133 Ground handling wheeled dolly
125 Inconel-X multi-spar wing construction	

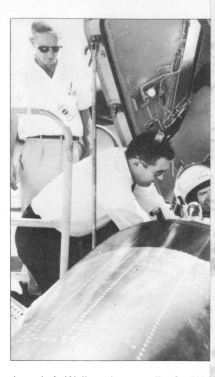

Joseph A. Walker, the test pilot for NAS[...]
prepares for another flight during 1964. [...]
Walker made the government's first X-1[...]
22 August 1963 flew X-15A-2 to 345,200[...]
altitude record.

mph/3661 km/h) on 7 February [...]
made the last XLR11-powered fl[...]

By then the second X-15 had al[...]
the XLR99 and had been flown th[...]
its first flight in the hands of a go[...]
reached Mach 4.43 on 7 March [...]
then progressively increased unt[...]
piloted by Captain White, the [...]
achieve its original design spe[...]
exceeded only once when on 5 D[...]
Rushworth took the first X-15 (n[...]
Mach 6.06 (4,018 mph/6466 km/[...]
at a slightly lower Mach (Mach [...]
favouring true air speed, Joe Wa[...]
record of 4,104 mph (6605 km/h)[...]
altitude flights took the X-15 abo[...]
mark on 11 October 1961, to a r[...]
m) on 22 August 1963.

On 9 November 1962, followi[...]
56-6671 made an emergency lan[...]
Lake and rebounded; the left sl[...]
aircraft ended on its back. The N[...]
hospitalized for surgery to crush[...]
was returned to the factory. F[...]
aircraft to its original configura[...]
advantage of the forced progra[...]
several modifications which wou[...]
even greater speeds. On the ba[...]
known that this was achievable [...]
without undue risks by increasin[...]
carried and thus increasing the r[...]
from 86 to 145 seconds, by m[...]
eliminate the critical point of hi[...]
by making use of an ablative c[...]
aerodynamic heating problems ([...]
to reach locally over 3,000°F/1[...]
obtained by adding two large e[...]
containing liquid oxygen, and[...]

Many of the Lockheed SR-71 Blackbird's technical details are still strictly secret. With its maximum speed of more than three times the speed of sound, and a cruising height of about 82,000 ft (25,000 m), it is still the fastest and highest-flying aircraft in the world. (*Photo: Lockheed*)

ments. Low drag at Mach 3 implied a highly swept delta wing. Since the engines and the long fuselage (needed to house a vast amount of fuel and to bring the centre of gravity forward) projected ahead of the wing, they were given 'chines' to make them act as lifting surfaces and to improve directional stability. The fuselage was canted up relative to the thrust line, to make it act as a fixed lifting canard.

One of the disadvantages of the delta wing is that the vertical tail tends to be ineffective at high angles of attack (AOA). Lockheed therefore replaced the conventional single fin over the rear fuselage with two vertical tails on the engine nacelles. The customary wind tunnel tests were run to measure drag and predict handling characteristics, but in some respects the latter objective proved difficult to attain, since the fuselage flexes appreciably under inertia and aerodynamic loads, and since it is distorted by the cooling effect of the fuel in contact with the undersurface.

Fortunately, the very high temperatures created by kinetic heating from the surrounding air were predicable with accuracy. These structural temperatures range at cruise speed from 800°F (425°C, hotter than a soldering iron) – around the leading edges and intakes to 450–500°F (230–260°C, hotter than the maximum temperature in a household oven) for most of the wings and fuselage. The outside skin temperatures around the rear of the engine nacelles reach 900–1,100°F (480–595°C). The jetpipes glow white hot, even with the minimum afterburner setting required in cruise, so bright that they can be used as a reference in night-time formation flying.

High temperature problems

To cope with these extremely high temperatures for lengthy periods, approximately 93 per cent of the structure was designed in titanium alloy, although this involved extremely high costs and required the development of new fabrication techniques. Likewise, conventional fuels could not be used. These aircraft use JP-7, which has a very low vapour pressure and is fully compatible with high temperature operation, although it is contained in integral tanks with no insulation between the fuel and the aircraft skin. Conventional lubricants (oils and greases) are likewise unusable in such aircraft: the specially developed oil used in the Pratt & Whitney J58 engines has to be preheated to 86°F (30°C) before each flight. Hydraulic fluid and seals, electrical connectors, windscreen transparencies, radomes and wiring were other problem areas resulting from the high temperatures encountered in flight.

Lockheed SR-71A serial 64–17955 shortly after touchdown, with braking parachute deployed. Note the parachute housing on top of the rear fuselage, the upward angle on the elevons, the unique three-abreast mainwheel arrangement (unusually for an American aircraft, the doors are left open), and the forebody chine.

In order to reduce the problems of structural expansion caused by the heat, chordwise corrugations were incorporated in the wing skin. To minimize the heat problems of the main landing gear, the wheels are retracted into the fuselage, where they can be cooled more easily than in the wing. The wing fuel is used first (during the climb) because of the heating problem caused by the disproportionately large surface area of these thin, flat tanks. The whole aircraft is painted in a special high-emissivity dark blue paint (visually indistinguishable from black), which emits heat at 2103 times the rate of unpainted titanium, and gives a surface temperature reduction of 25–50°F (14–28°C) during cruise.

The J58 engine (manufacturer's designation JT11D-20B) is a single-spool afterburning turbojet with a high titanium content. In order to minimize the probability of surging at high speeds, air is bled continuously from the fourth compressor stage and ducted to the afterburner, where it reduces operating temperatures and improves thrust augmentation. As stated above, the JP-7 fuel has little tendency to vaporize at normal temperatures, and it has been reported that a lighted match can safely be dropped into a pool of JP-7 without the fuel catching fire! Because of this characteristic, engine and afterburner ignition have to be achieved chemically, rather than electrically: triethyl borane (TEB) is injected, producing instant combustion on coming into contact with the JP-7. For inflight-refuelling, the JP-7 is carried in special tanker aircraft, designated KC-135Qs.

The engine is fed with air through a conical multi-shock intake with a translating spike, which is automatically angled to compensate for AOA and sideslip. It exhausts via an ejector nozzle with blow-in doors. According to Lockheed, the hardest design problem was to make the engine inlet and exhaust work correctly. The inlet cone translates through a distance of almost 3 ft (91.4 cm) to keep the shock wave pattern in the optimum position, the force required from the hydraulic actuator being almost equal to the maximum static thrust of the engine.

To revert to the history of the 'Blackbird' series, the first A-11 had its maiden flight in great secrecy on 26 April 1962, some 32 months from signature of contract, an incredibly short gestation period for such an advanced aircraft. The

Lockheed SR-71

Specification

Lockheed SR-71A 'Blackbird'
Type: tandem-seat strategic reconnaissance aircraft
Powerplant: two afterburning Pratt & Whitney J58 turbojets, each of 29,750-lb (13494-kg) static thrust (Mks B, C. Pratt & Whitney J 58-1 (JT) 11D-20B continuous bleed after burning turbojets of 32,500 lb (14.742 kg))
Performance: maximum speed 2,189 mph (3523 km/h); operational ceiling approximately 85,000 ft (25908 m); range at least 3,300 miles (5311 km) without flight refuelling
Weights: (estimated) empty 60,000 lb (27215 kg); maximum take-off weight 145,000 lb (65770 kg) (later 170,000 lb (77.112 kg))
Dimensions: span 55 ft 7 in (16.95 m); length 107 ft 5 in (32.74 m); height 18 ft 6 in (5.64 m); wing area 1,800 sq ft (167.3 m²)

All the external design features of the Lockheed SR-71A are to be seen in this illustration which also shows the fact that the 'Blackbird' is really painted a very dark blue. The wing planform is basically a delta, although there is considerable taper on the trailing edge, rounded tips, and cut-outs for the engine exhausts. Despite the long inboard chords, the wing is relatively thin, as shown by the head-on view. This also brings out the wing-body blending and the camber of the outboard leading edge, which in some photographs makes the wing appear to be kinked. Immediately aft of the two-seat cockpit is a window for the Northrop astro-inertial navigation system, and the flight refuelling receptacle.

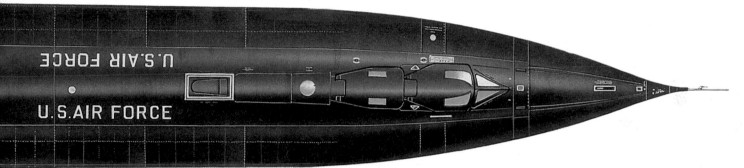

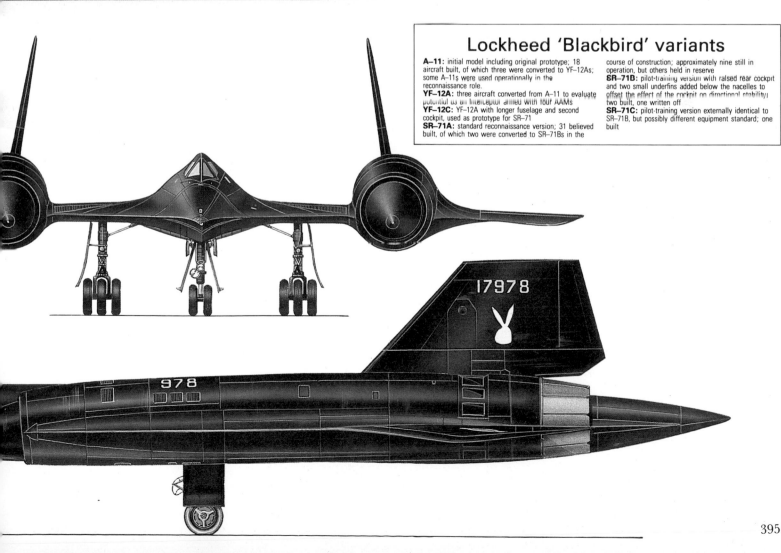

Lockheed 'Blackbird' variants

A–11: initial model including original prototype; 18 aircraft built, of which three were converted to YF–12As; some A–11s were used operationally in the reconnaissance role.
YF–12A: three aircraft converted from A–11 to evaluate potential as an interceptor armed with four AAMs
YF–12C: YF–12A with longer fuselage and second cockpit, used as prototype for SR–71
SR–71A: standard reconnaissance version; 31 believed built, of which two were converted to SR–71Bs in the

course of construction; approximately nine still in operation, but others held in reserve
SR–71B: pilot-training version with raised rear cockpit and two small underfins added below the nacelles to offset the effect of the cockpit on directional stability; two built, one written off
SR–71C: pilot-training version externally identical to SR–71B, but possibly different equipment standard; one built

flight took place at a location often referred to simply as 'The Ranch', and more formally known as Watertown Strip at Groom Dry Lake, Nevada. How the aircraft came to be designated A-11 has never been explained; the preceding Lockheed F-104 began life as the Model 83. However, the company appears to refer to the latest of its more secret designs merely as 'The Article', hence it is possible that the design that went ahead in 1959 was simply the 11th drawing in that series of 'Articles'.

The number of A-11s built has never been declared officially, but some sources put the number as high as 18, with serials running from 60–6924 to 60–6941. Of these, three (60–6934, 60–6935 and 60–6936) were built to a modified standard to become interceptor prototypes under the USAF designation YF-12A (possibly also designated A-12). One aircraft (66–6937) was built with a longer fuselage providing for a second cockpit and extra fuel, and increasing overall length from 101 ft (30.78 m) to 107 ft 5in (32.74m). It was designated YF-12C, and served as the prototype for the SR-71 reconnaissance aircraft. In the original A-11 and the SR-71 the fuselage chines were extended right to the nose of the aircraft. In the case of the YF-12A the chines were cut back to clear the nose radome, and this (combined with the fatter nose) reduced directional stability, so a folding centre-line underfin was added, together with two fixed stub-fins under the nacelles.

Announcement of project

The large tracts of land owned by the US Department of Defense made possible flight tests in complete secrecy (they are being used today to test 'Stealth' prototypes), and it was only on 29 February 1964 that the existence of the basic A-11 was disclosed, when President Lyndon B. Johnson made a brief statement on the project. At that time the only photographs released were side-views of the aircraft (60–6934, buzz number FX-934) on the ground, giving no clue to its wing planform. However, on 24 July 1964 the existence of the SR-71 project was revealed by President Johnson, and on 30 September a YF-12A was shown to the public at Edwards AFB, and its wing planform and chine configuration were finally unveiled.

The original role of the SR-71 is still something of a mystery, since its designation does not fit into any established series. The most widely accepted explanation is that the aircraft was really designated RS-71, following the North American RS-70 Mach 3 strike aircraft project (which sparked off development of the MiG 25), and that the President simply mixed up the two letters. Rather than admit his mistake, his staff then explained the 'SR' designation as meaning strategic reconnaissance.

This aircraft (serial 64–17956) was originally built as a standard SR-71A, but was later converted (along with 64–17951) to a SR-71B trainer. After one of these aircraft crashed, a further SR-71A (64–17981) was converted for pilot training and designated SR-71C, although the distinction from the SR-71B is not clear.

On the other hand, if the SR-71 began life as a strike aircraft with a secondary reconnaissance capability, how was it to deliver its warload? The YF-12A had had four relatively small Hughes XAIM-47 air-to-air missiles buried in the front fuselage chines (to be guided by a Hughes ASG-18 radar), but this method of stowage was not suitable for a multi-megaton warhead. Perhaps the obvious solution was to house the warhead in an external pod, as was done in the case of the Convair B-58A Hustler, which first flew in 1956.

Lockheed SR–71 'Blackbird' cutaway drawing key

1 Pitot tube
2 Nose mission equipment bay
3 Detachable nose cone joint frame
4 Cockpit front pressure bulkhead
5 Rudder pedals
6 Control column
7 Instrument panel
8 Instrument panel shroud
9 Knife edged windscreen panels
10 Engine throttle levers
11 Oxygen cylinder
12 Pilot's ejection seat
13 Upward hinged cockpit canopy cover
14 SR–71B dual control trainer variant
15 Raised instructor's rear cockpit
16 Reconnaissance systems officer's (RSO) canopy cover
17 RSO's zero-zero ejection seat
18 Side console panel
19 Cockpit environmental system equipment bay
20 Rear pressure bulkhead
21 Canopy hinge joint
22 Astro-navigation star tracker
23 Navigation and communications systems electronics
24 Nosewheel bay
25 Landing and taxiing lamps
26 Twin nosewheels
27 Torque scissor links
28 Nosewheel steering control jack
29 Nose undercarriage pivot fixing
30 Palletized reconnaissance equipment packages, interchangeable

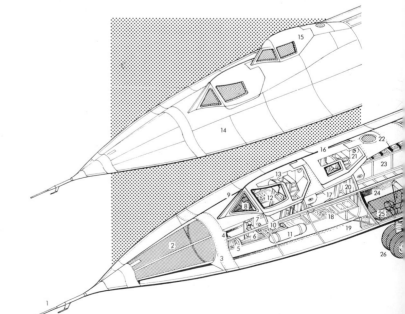

The SR-71As are inflight-refuelled through receptacles in the upper fuselage from the booms of Boeing KC-135Qs. These are the only tankers equipped to deliver the Blackbird's JP-7 fuel, which was developed specifically to withstand the high structural temperatures generated in Mach 3 cruise.

31 Forward fuselage longeron
32 Air refuelling receptacle
33 Forward fuselage integral fuel tanks
34 Titanium skin plating
35 Fuselage chine member
36 Close-pitched fuselage frame construction
37 Forward fuselage production joint
38 Blended wing/fuselage main integral fuel tanks (JP–7 fuel)
39 Main undercarriage wheel bay
40 Three-wheel main undercarriage bogie
41 Hydraulic retraction jack
42 Starboard main undercarriage, stowed position

43 Corrugated titanium wing skin panelling
44 Moveable intake, conical centre-body
45 Centre-body retracted (high speed) position
46 Engine air intake
47 Automatic intake control air data probe
48 Intake suction relief doors
49 Variable suction relief doors
50 Hinged engine cowling panel

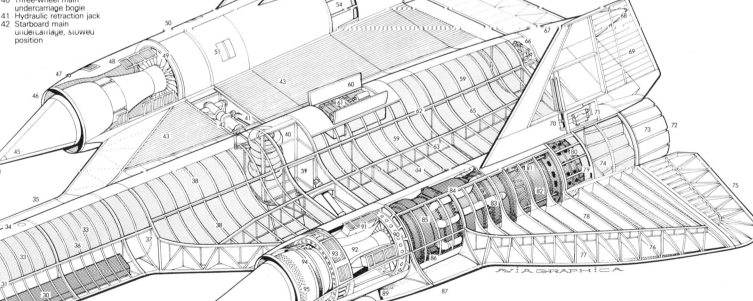

51 By-pass duct blow-in doors
52 Starboard outer wing panel
53 Outboard, roll control, elevon
54 Engine bay, tertiary air flaps
55 Tailfin fixed root section
56 All-moving starboard fin
57 Exhaust nozzle ejector flaps
58 Inboard, pitch control, elevon

59 Aft, fuselage integral fuel tanks
60 Brake parachute doors
61 Ribbon parachute stowage
62 Rear fuselage longeron
63 Wing root rib
64 Inboard wing panel integral fuel tank
65 Close-pitched wing/fuselage frame construction
66 Elevon mixer unit

67 Tailcone
68 Fuel jettison
69 Port all-moving tailfin
70 Fin pivot fixing
71 All-moving fin hydraulic jack
72 Port engine exhaust nozzle
73 Ejection flaps
74 Ejector mixer duct
75 Port outer elevon titanium rib construction
76 Outer leading-edge rib

77 Under-cambered leading edge
78 Outer wing panel construction
79 Exhaust duct tertiary doors
80 Afterburner nozzle
81 Variable-area afterburner nozzle control jacks
82 Afterburner duct
83 Compressor bleed air by-pass ducts

84 Outer wing panel/engine cowling hinge axis
85 Pratt & Whitney JT11D–20B (J58) single spool turbo-ramjet engine
86 Engine accessory equipment bay
87 Outer wing panel/nacelle chine
88 Port main undercarriage three-wheel
89 Main undercarriage leg door
90 Intake duct secondary by-pass annular louvres

91 Centre-body bleed air louvres
92 Diffuser chamber
93 By-pass duct suction relief louvres
94 Intake annular by-pass duct
95 Centre-body boundary layer bleed air holes
96 Port engine intake
97 Intake moveable centre-body

construction

What is known for sure is that at least two of the A-11s had a dorsal pylon to carry a small D-21 drone aircraft, powered by a Marquardt ramjet. The drone is sometimes referred to as the GTD-21, and is believed to have been codenamed 'Oxcart'. It is 40 ft (12.19 m) long, has a span of 17 ft (5.18 m), and is essentially similar to the engine pod of the parent aircraft, but fitted with its own delta wing and chines. At least 38 are said to have been built in the period 1964–9, and it might be conjectured that the drone could carry either a nuclear weapon or reconnaissance sensors.

Reports suggest that two A-11s were fitted with the pylon, and were each given a second cockpit in place of a camera bay, so that a man would be carried to check the functioning of the drone's equipment and to launch it. Launching was achieved by ejecting the drone forcibly upward. It is believed that this was attempted only once, on 5 January 1967, when the drone separated but came down and struck the launch aircraft. Both crashed. The drone was then equipped with a rocket booster to permit launches from much slower aircraft, and was fitted under the wing of a small number of B-52s for reconnaissance tests codenamed 'Tagboard' over South East Asia. Some 19 D-21s were returned to Davis-Monthan AFB, and 17 are still there. Several A-11s were lost in accidents, and it is said that the remainder were held in reserve for possible use in the reconnaissance role from 1968 to October 1976, when they were finally retired.

The YF-12A established nine performance records in the course of a single day, 1 May 1965. These included a sustained altitude of 80,275 ft (24462 m), a speed of 2,070 mph (3331 km/h) and a speed over a closed circuit of 1,689 mph (2718 km/h). The type was evaluated in 1969 by the USAF under the Improved Manned Interceptor programme, but no production order resulted, probably because of the high cost of operating these hand-made aircraft and the dwindling threat of the manned supersonic bomber. Two YF-12As (60–6935 and 60–6936) were used in a joint USAF/NASA high-Mach, high-altitude Advanced Supersonic Technology research programme from 1970 to 1974. The remaining A-11s and YF-12As (a total of at least nine) are now stored under guard at the Lockheed facility at Palmdale, California.

The first SR-71A had its maiden flight at Palmdale on 22 December 1964. The number built is still classified, but it is generally believed that there were three batches, totalling 31 aircraft, with serials running from 64–17950 to 64–17980, all delivered in the period 1966–9. Two (64–17951 and 64–17956) were converted to SR-71B trainers, with raised rear cockpits and the YF-12A's two fixed underfins restored to improve weathercock stability. Following the loss of one trainer, a further aircraft (64–17981) was built and given the designation SR-71C, although the difference from SR-71B has not been revealed.

Deliveries to SAC's Beale AFB in northern California began in January 1966, to the 9th Strategic Reconnaissance Wing, part of the 14th Air Division of the 15th Air Force. It is believed that nine SR-71s were operated by the 1st SRS, although the two training aircraft may now be flown by the 5th SRTS. Detachments of SR-71s fly routinely from Mildenhall in England and Kadena in Okinawa. The aircraft has been used operationally over the Middle East on several occasions, over South East Asia, and over North Korea.

The SR-71s of the 9th SRW have established numerous records. On 26 April 1971 an aircraft piloted by Lieutenant Colonel Estes covered 15,000 miles (24140 km) in approximately 10 hours 30 minutes, cruising at Mach 3 when not refuelling. For this flight the crew was awarded the USAF Mackay Trophy. On 1 September 1974 an SR-71 (64–1792) flew the 3,490 miles (5616 km) from New York to London in 1 hour 56 minutes, piloted by Major Sullivan, and on 8 September the aircraft established a new record from London to Los Angeles, a distance of 5,645 miles (9084 km) covered in 3 hours 47 minutes, arriving (in terms of local time) roughly four hours before take-off!

In July 1976 a number of records were established, including two which were still world records in 1982. On 27th July, an SR-71A flown by Major Adolphus Bledsoe Jr flew a 621-mile (1,000-km) circular course at an average speed of 2,092.33 mph (3367.13 km/h). On the following day, an SR-71A flown by Captain Robert Holt flew a horizontal endurance flight at 85,073 ft (25929 m). On the very same day, an SR-71A flown by Captain Eldon Joersz flew a straight 9.3–15.5 mile (15/25 km) straight course at an average speed of 2,193.21 mph (3529.47 km/h). Depending on the air temperature at the time, this could have been equivalent to Mach 3.3. Whether we still need such a costly aircraft in the age of the spy satellite is very much open to question.

Small wonder, therefore, that when General David Jones, USAF, was Chairman of the Joint Chiefs of Staff, he described the SR-71 as 'the most survivable US platform for manned overflights of heavily defended areas'.

Boeing 727

What makes a winner in the cut-and-thrust of commercial aviation design? The answer is much hard work, adequate research funding, and a keen eye on the demands of a difficult market. Boeing gambled much on its neat Model 727, and were rewarded when sales exceeded the most sanguine hopes.

Long before the introduction of the successful 707 and 720 series, Boeing's headquarters in Seattle was carrying out a preliminary study for a medium-capacity airliner of short-to-medium range to supply the demand for domestic flights in the USA. A high-performance jet aircraft suitable for short runways and with a low landing speed was required, to take a place in the market which was not being filled by the long-haul Douglas DC-8, Convair 880 and Boeing 707/720, which were rather too large, and the shorter-range Sud-Aviation S210 Caravelle and Douglas DC-9 which were still at an early stage of development. There was no doubt that there was a market for such an aircraft. But as always, Boeing needed buyers for the plane before they could start producing it. This meant that, apart from the USA, there had to be good prospects of selling high-performance medium-range airliners abroad as well. Boeing was also afraid that the new British de Havilland D.H. 121 Trident, with its unique three-jet configuration, would be a strong rival which might be hard to overtake. At the end of the 1950s, the outlook for the commercial aircraft industry was a very bright one. There was a pressing need for larger passenger capacity on the busy US and European routes. The old Douglas DC-3, Douglas DC-6 and Lockheed L-749, which were piston-engined, and the relatively new Lockheed L-188 Electra turboprop were cheap to run, but too slow, and the new Caravelle had too small a capacity.

The design of the Boeing Model 727, as the new type was named, started in February 1956, and the parameters laid before Boeing's preliminary design group were exacting. Whereas other companies, notably de Havilland (later merged with the Hawker Siddeley group), were vying for high cruise Mach numbers to reduce seat-air mile costs, Boeing wanted this factor on its Model 727, but combined with field operating characteristics that, in such a large aircraft, at first seemed impossible to attain. Put basically, this meant a high power/weight ratio for sprightly acceleration and take-off and, of course, a highly adaptable and efficient wing. The wing design of the Model 727 broached new horizons, and its unique system of lift-augmentation flaps and slats allied with spoilers was to become the format in the mighty Model 747. By the time that design work had been finalized, on 18 September 1959, the wing structure had developed into a low-wing format of 3° dihedral, a thickness chord-ratio of between 8 and 9 per cent, with 2° incidence and special Boeing aerofoil sections: sweepback at quarter-chord was 32° and was less than that of the Model 707. But if the basic wing was of routine design, then the high-lift and lift-dump devices most certainly were not: on the trailing edge of the wing massive triple-slotted flaps, totalling 388 sq ft (36.04 m²) with 40° setting, were combined with four leading-edge slats on the outer two-thirds of the wing, and three Krueger leading-edge flaps on the inner one-third portion. These were joined by seven spoilers on each upper wing surface (0–40°) which doubled as airbrakes and/

This Boeing 727-256, construction no. 20595, first flew on 23 October 1972 and was delivered to Iberia on 11 May the following year. Named *Vascongadas*, it is currently in service with a further 36 of the same type on Iberia's European and North African services.

Boeing 727-277 (construction no. 22641) of Ansett Airlines, Australia, in the new livery adopted in 1981. The aircraft was first flown as N8278V and was the 1753rd example of 1832 built. It entered service with Ansett on 20 June 1981 and is one of 16 Boeing 727-277s currently operated.

A Boeing 727-200 of Alaska Airlines, which uses the type largely for
services within Alaska and to Seattle. The company has four such aircraft,
plus four of the shorter-fuselage Model 727-100s.

This Boeing 727-81 was the 124th to be built and was delivered to All Nippon Airways on 18 March 1965. Alaska Airlines subsequently leased it, on 22 June 1972, and bought it on 14 December 1974 as N124AS. The aircraft was written off in a landing accident at Ketchikan on 5 April 1976.

Boeing 727-113C of Ariana Afghan Airlines. The aircraft first flew on 30 December 1969 and was delivered to Ariana on 15 January 1970, enabling the airline to commence jet services to London and Moscow. Ariana operates two Boeing 727s.

or roll augmentation spoilers. This beautiful wing was the key behind what was to be the phenomenal success story of the Boeing 727: it gave the aircraft immense utility. Clean, the aircraft was as fast and efficient as the best; dump the flaps and the Kruegers and even at maximum landing weight the pilot could land on any small municipal or rural field in the United States.

Taking shape

Allied with the excellent field performance, the new Model 727 had lively performance and good fuel economy with the adoption of the 14,000-lb (6350-kg) thrust Pratt & Whitney JT8D-1 turbofan in August 1960. The fuselage upper portion was identical to that of the Model 707/720 series: this saved some $3 million in jig and tool costing, standardized the flight deck layouts and gave the aircraft intercontinental six-abreast cabin accommodation for the passengers. In addition much stress was laid upon independence of operation: the Model 727 needed nothing on the ground if a stop-go transit was required, having a Garrett Ai Research GTC 85 auxiliary

power unit for electrics, pneumatic-starting and cabin conditioning, an airstar on Door 1 Left and a ventral staircase to the rear. With a very high maximum landing weight, as a result of wing stressing and landing gear strength, the Model 727 could take on fuel at the originating station, fly several transits, and gain quick turn-arounds. All these facets were built in during the course of very thorough research and design, entailing 150 studies of which 68 underwent some 1,500 hours of tunnel-testing. Construction go-ahead was given in August 1960, with Boeing acting on the good faith of Eastern Air Lines and United Air Lines. Actually, it was not until 5 December 1960 that these operators placed their orders: 20 for United with another 20 on option, and 40 for Eastern. By February 1963 four Model 727s were on the lines at Renton.

At 11.33 on 9 February 1963 the first flight was made from Renton when Lew Wallick, Boeing's senior experimental test pilot, lifted N7001U off after a run of 3,000 ft (914 m); the co-pilot was Dick Loesch and the engineer M. K. Shulenberger. N7001U weighed in at 130,000 lb (58968 kg), carried 5,500 US gal (20200 litres) of fuel and 16,000 lb (7258 kg) of test equipment, and flew for 2 hours 1 minute before Wallick put her down in 2,000 ft (610 m) on Paine Field's limited concrete. To the assembled Press, Wallick said that 'She

Thirty-seven Boeing 727-256 aircraft provide the mainstay of Iberia's short/medium-haul operations. Each aircraft is able to carry up to 189 passengers over a range of 2,465 miles (3965 km).

Boeing 727

CS-TBW

CS-TBW

AIR PORTUGAL

CS-TBW is the 13th Boeing 727 supplied to TAP, Transportes Aereos Portugueses, the national airline of Portugal. TAP's early 727s were short-bodied 082s, or convertible 727-172C aircraft, but the latest are of the current standard model, the precise series being 727-282. Altogether these advanced 727s are fast, capable and extremely trouble-free aircraft, their most serious faults being relatively old engines which result in noise and fuel consumption that compares unfavourably with today's aircraft, such as the Boeing 757 or Airbus Industrie A310. The dark grills on all three engines are the outlets for the thrust-reversers. On the trailing edge of the 32°-swept wing are inboard high-speed ailerons (between the inboard and outboard sections of triple-slotted flap) and outboard ailerons used at low speeds only, all operating in conjunction with the spoilers seen on the upper surface. Just visible in the side view under the no. 1 engine nozzle is the hydraulically operated aft stairway; many airlines sealed this stairway shut after a hijacker with over a million US dollars parachuted through it!

Specification

Boeing 727-200

Type: medium-range passenger or mixed-traffic airliner

Powerplant: three Pratt & Whitney JT8D-9A (14,500 lb/6577 kg thrust), JT8D-15 (15,500 lb/7031 kg) or JT8D-17 (17,400 lb/7893 kg) turbofans

Performance: maximum cruising speed 599 mph (964 km/h); range at long-range cruise speed of 542 mph (872 km/h) with maximum fuel 2,729 miles (4392 km)

Weights: empty equipped 102,000 lb (46675 kg); maximum take-off 209,500 lb (95027 kg)

Dimensions: span 108 ft 0 in (32.92 m); length 153 ft 2 in (46.69m); height 34 ft 0 in (10.36 m); wing area 1,700 sq ft (157.9 m²)

Accommodation: flight crew of three, variable cabin crew for up to 189 passengers, typical mixed-class seating, 14 first and 131 tourist

Boeing Model 727 variants

Model 727-100: first production model, there being no prototypes; fuselage length 133 ft 2 in (40.59 m); standard transport for up to 131 passengers with three Pratt & Whitney JT8D-1 or D-7 turbofans, with later models having JT8D-9s; maximum take-off weight of 160,000 lb (72576 kg), with later variants certified to 169,000 lb (76668 kg)

Model 727-100C: convertible passenger/cargo model with freight door, strengthened floor and floor beams, but otherwise identical to Model 727-100; optional payloads of 94 mixed-class passengers, or of 52 passengers and baggage plus 22,700 lb (10297 kg) of cargo on four pallets, or of 38,000 lb (17237 kg) on eight pallets

Model 727-100QC: installation of roller-bearing floors for palletized galley and seating and/or palletized freight; conversion from cargo to all-passenger achievable within 30 minutes; freighter conversion with increased ramp weight to 170,000 lb (77112 kg, maximum take-off weight of 169,000 lb (76658 kg), and maximum landing weight of 142,000 lb (64411 kg)

Model 727 100 Business Jet: optional fittings for luxury or business travel; extra fuel tanks in lower cargo compartments to provide a range with 10,700 US gal (40504 litres) of about 4,150 miles (6680 km) with a 4,000-lb (1814-kg) payload; option for dual Carousel IV or Litton LTN501 INS and long-range weather radar

Model 727-200: stretched version with fuselage length of 136 ft 2 in (41.50 m), andk basic accommodation for 163 passengers and a maximum capacity of 189; structurally strengthened; revised centre engine air inlet; three JT9D-9 turbofans, each rated at 14,500-lb (6577-kg) thrust to 84°F, standard with JT8D-11s or JT8D-15s

Advanced Model 727-200: increased ramp weight to 191,000 lb (86638 kg) and fitted with sound-suppression; improved avionics with options for INS. Flight Management, dual FD-108 flight directors or Collins FD-110, or Sperry Z-15 flight directors, and Sperry SP-150 Model 5 auto-pilot

Advanced Model 727-200F: pure freighter model with JT8D-17A turbofans; no windows, and up to 11 pallets can be loaded through a port-side hatch; the first customer was Federal Express

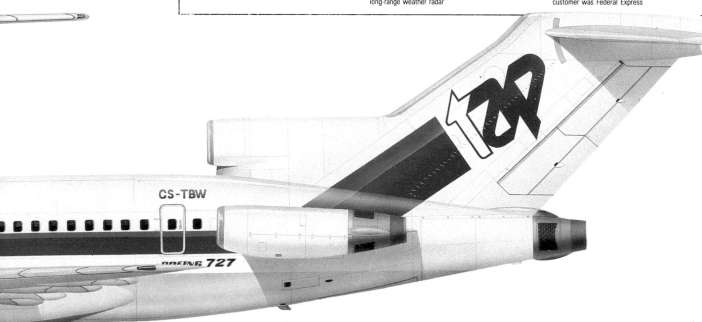

Supplementing the Lockheed C-130 Hercules in the long-range transport role, the Royal New Zealand Air Force operates three ex-United Air Lines Boeing 727-100Cs, one of which is being cannibalized for spares.

Air Charter International of France operates two Boeing 727-2X3 aircraft powered by three Pratt & Whitney JTD-15 turbofans. The airline leases additional aircraft from Air France, Air Inter and EAS when required.

behaved as expected, even better than expected in many respects.' And indeed few problems cropped up during subsequent testing. The second Model 727 (N72700) flew on 12 March, and by the end of the month four Model 727s were undergoing thorough flight trials from Paine, Seattle, Edwards AFB, Denver and Albuquerque. By mid-May N7001U had completed 430 hours on flutter and structural damping tests up to Mach 0.9; 320 hours had been completed by N72700 on systems and braking; 180 hours on Model 727 no. 3, including handling high-g pull-ups, side-slipping and even barrel-rolls; while 313 hours had been completed in furnishing and air-conditioning on Model 727 no. 4. The order book was filling: 25 to American Air Lines, 40 to United, 10 to TWA, 12 to Lufthansa, and four to the Australian TAA and Ansett-ANA.

FAA certification for the production Model 727-100 was signed on 20 December 1963. Analyses of performance showed that the Model 727-100's parameters were 10 per cent in excess of Boeing's original guarantees: it was faster with better specific fuel consumption offered by the JT8D-1s, slower on the approach, and used reduced field lengths, being quite capable of operations from 5,000-ft (1525-m) runways at maximum weights. In the 1,100 hours of tests since 9 February 1963, dives in excess of Mach 0.95, take-offs at 160,000 lb (72576 kg), take-offs on two engines, and maximum-energy stops in less than 900 ft (274 m) had been made. Significantly, it was at this juncture that the Model 727's arch rival was being readied; on 19 December 1963 the Trident 1 (G-ARPF) completed crew training to be scheduled for its first service with BEA in April.

Already a battle royal was in progress between Boeing with its Model 727 and Hawker Siddley with the Trident 1C and 1E for the lucrative foreign export markets. In November 1963 Boeing 727 N7003U completed its world tour started on 17 September of that year: out-bound from Montreal it plied the route to Tokyo via the Azores, Rome, Beirut, Karachi (where an uneasy meeting with Trident 1 G-ARPE took place), Calcutta, Bangkok and Manila. Thence the route went via Manila to Australia, followed by visits to Johannesburg and Nairobi, and back via Europe to the States. At home Eastern Air Lines signed up its first Model 727-100 on 22 October 1963 with the intention of starting scheduled services between Miami and New York (La Guardia) in January. The airline flew its first service with the Model 727-100 on 1 February 1964 from Miami to Philadelphia with a Washington (National) transit. Five days later United Air Lines started its schedules: daily Denver/San Francisco shuttles were started, with the line commencing operations on the high-intensity New York-Los Angeles-San Francisco-Seattle routes. In the meantime the salesmen were busy.

Boeing Advanced 727-200 cutaway drawing key

1 Radome
2 Radar dish
3 Radar scanner mounting
4 Pressure bulkhead
5 Windscreen panels
6 Instrument panel shroud
7 Back of instrument panel
8 Rudder pedals
9 Radar transmitter and receiver
10 Pitot tube
11 Cockpit floor control ducting
12 Control column
13 Pilot's seat
14 Cockpit eyebrow windows
15 Co-pilot's seat
16 Engineer's control panel
17 Flight engineer's seat
18 Cockpit door
19 Observer's seat
20 Nosewheel bay
21 Nosewheel doors
22 Twin nosewheels
23 Retractable airstairs (optional)
24 Handrail
25 Escape chute pack
26 Front entry door
27 Front toilet
28 Galley
29 Starboard galley service door
30 Cabin bulkhead
31 Closet
32 Window frame panel
33 Radio and electronics bay
34 First class passenger cabin, 18 seats in mixed layout
35 Cabin roof construction
36 Seat rails
37 Cabin floor beams
38 Cargo door
39 Anti-collision light
40 Air conditioning supply ducting
41 Forward cargo hold
42 Cargo hold floor
43 Baggage pallet container
44 Tourist class passenger cabin, 119 seats in mixed layout

45 Communications antenna
46 Fuselage frame and stringer construction
47 Cabin window frame panels
48 Air conditioning system intake
49 Air conditioning plant
50 Overhead air ducting
51 Main fuselage frames
52 Escape hatches, port and starboard
53 Wing centre section no. 2 fuel tank
54 Centre section stringer construction
55 Cabin floor construction
56 Starboard wing no 3 fuel tank
57 Inboard Krueger flaps
58 Krueger flap hydraulic jack
59 Leading edge fence
60 Outboard leading edge slat segments
61 Slat hydraulic jacks
62 Fuel vent surge tank
63 Navigation lights
64 Starboard wing tip
65 Fuel jettison pipe
66 Static dischargers
67 Outboard, low speed, aileron
68 Aileron balance tab
69 Outboard spoilers
70 Outboard slotted flap
71 Flap screw jack mechanism
72 Inboard, high speed, aileron
73 Trim tab
74 Inboard spoilers
75 Inboard slotted flap
76 Fuselage centre section construction
77 Pressurized floor over starboard main undercarriage bay

78 Auxiliary power unit (APU)
79 Port main undercarriage bay
80 Tourist class, six-abreast, passenger seating
81 Overhead hand baggage stowage bins
82 Cabin trim panels
83 Rear cargo door
84 Aft cargo compartment floor
85 Passenger overhead service panels
86 Starboard service door/rear emergency exit
87 Aft galleys
88 Closet
89 Toilets, port and starboard
90 Cabin rear entry door
91 Starboard engine cowling
92 Centre engine intake
93 Noise attenuating intake lining
94 Intake S-duct
95 Duct de-icing
96 Fin root fairing construction
97 Fin construction
98 VOR aerial
99 Elevator control cables

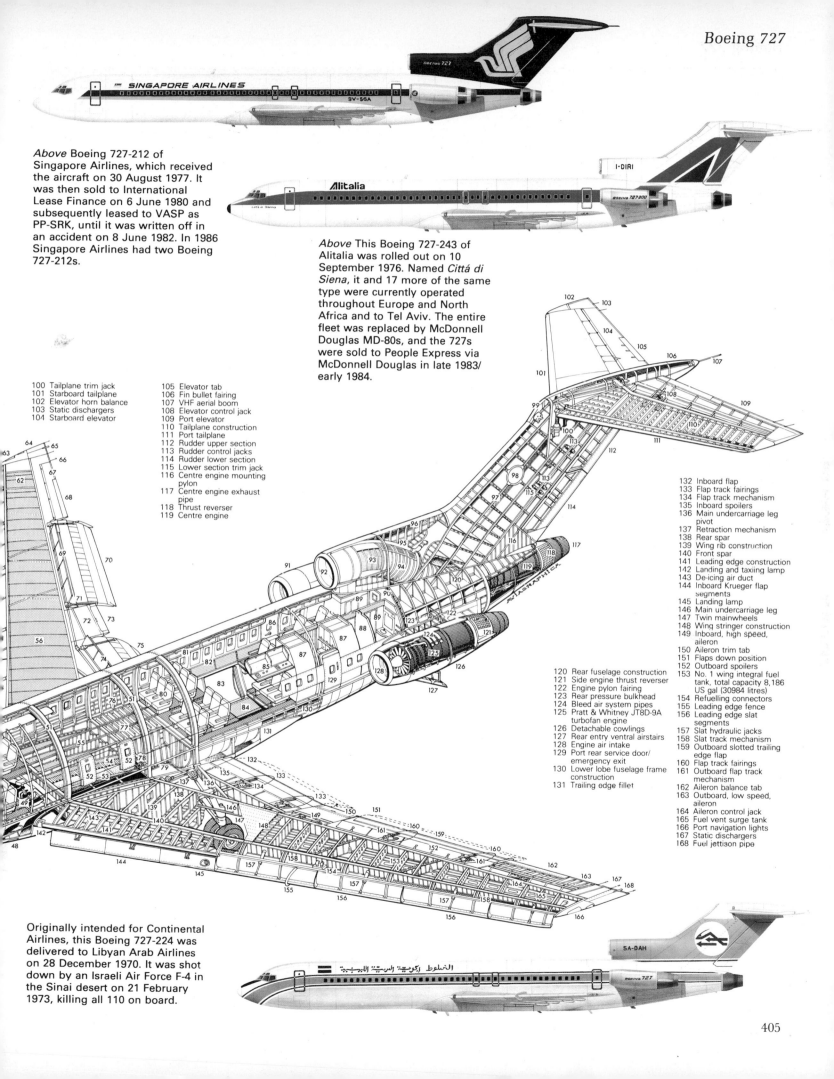

Above Boeing 727-212 of Singapore Airlines, which received the aircraft on 30 August 1977. It was then sold to International Lease Finance on 6 June 1980 and subsequently leased to VASP as PP-SRK, until it was written off in an accident on 8 June 1982. In 1986 Singapore Airlines had two Boeing 727-212s.

Above This Boeing 727-243 of Alitalia was rolled out on 10 September 1976. Named *Cittá di Siena*, it and 17 more of the same type were currently operated throughout Europe and North Africa and to Tel Aviv. The entire fleet was replaced by McDonnell Douglas MD-80s, and the 727s were sold to People Express via McDonnell Douglas in late 1983/ early 1984.

100 Tailplane trim jack
101 Starboard tailplane
102 Elevator horn balance
103 Static dischargers
104 Starboard elevator

105 Elevator tab
106 Fin bullet fairing
107 VHF aerial boom
108 Elevator control jack
109 Port elevator
110 Tailplane construction
111 Port tailplane
112 Rudder upper section
113 Rudder control jacks
114 Rudder lower section
115 Lower section trim jack
116 Centre engine mounting pylon
117 Centre engine exhaust pipe
118 Thrust reverser
119 Centre engine

120 Rear fuselage construction
121 Side engine thrust reverser
122 Engine pylon fairing
123 Rear pressure bulkhead
124 Bleed air system pipes
125 Pratt & Whitney JT8D-9A turbofan engine
126 Detachable cowlings
127 Rear entry ventral airstairs
128 Engine air intake
129 Port rear service door/ emergency exit
130 Lower lobe fuselage frame construction
131 Trailing edge fillet

132 Inboard flap
133 Flap track fairings
134 Flap track mechanism
135 Inboard spoilers
136 Main undercarriage leg pivot
137 Retraction mechanism
138 Rear spar
139 Wing rib construction
140 Front spar
141 Leading edge construction
142 Landing and taxiing lamp
143 De-icing air duct
144 Inboard Krueger flap segments
145 Landing lamp
146 Main undercarriage leg
147 Twin mainwheels
148 Wing stringer construction
149 Inboard, high speed, aileron
150 Aileron trim tab
151 Flaps down position
152 Outboard spoilers
153 No. 1 wing integral fuel tank, total capacity 8,186 US gal (30984 litres)
154 Refuelling connectors
155 Leading edge fence
156 Leading edge slat segments
157 Slat hydraulic jacks
158 Slat track mechanism
159 Outboard slotted trailing edge flap
160 Flap track fairings
161 Outboard flap track mechanism
162 Aileron balance tab
163 Outboard, low speed, aileron
164 Aileron control jack
165 Fuel vent surge tank
166 Port navigation lights
167 Static dischargers
168 Fuel jettison pipe

Originally intended for Continental Airlines, this Boeing 727-224 was delivered to Libyan Arab Airlines on 28 December 1970. It was shot down by an Israeli Air Force F-4 in the Sinai desert on 21 February 1973, killing all 110 on board.

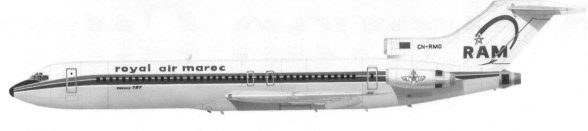

Boeing 727-2B6 of Royal Air Maroc, who took delivery of this 1236th example on 9 December 1970. Eight further Boeing727-2B6s were used by the airline from its base at Anfa Airport, Casablanca, to points in North Africa and Europe.

Lufthansa's first Model 727-100 (D-ABIB) was rolled out in January 1964, the first of 12 for crew training and the start of the Europa-Jet schedules intended for a start in April (first operation on 16 April 1964); on 10 May the German operator flew its first Frankfurt-Heathrow service, and by July 1964 six of its Model 727-100s were serving the European and Middle Eastern network.

The announcement of the decision taken by Japan Air Lines and All Nippon to choose the Model 727-100 instead of the Trident came as a bitter blow to Hawker Siddeley. Both airlines looked upon the Trident 1C and 1E with favour, but wanted the stretched Trident 1F. But the latter was not due for certification until the spring of 1966, and JAL and All Nippon's intention was to start internal services by April of that year: the Model 727-100 was for them the obvious choice with deliveries promised for October 1965. All Nippon was swung by the decision of its big brother, and no doubt by the poor showing of the Trident from Osaka's 6,200-ft (1890-m) runway in hot weather: in July and August when seasonal temperatures approached 40°C the Trident's poor field operating characteristics would have precluded break-even loads. On 15 May 1964 JAL signed a purchase and loan agreement for six Model 727-100s, the deal being worth $37.5 million with spares. The basic price of the aircraft was $4.5 million, with Boeing promising the first in August 1965.

As if to underline the Model 727-100's first-rate field operating abilities, Boeing's Jack Waddell took one into Bolivia's La Paz airport (field elevation 13,358 ft/4072 m) on 23 May 1964: the first jet commercial transport ever to land at La Paz took off within 7,400 ft (2256 m) in 44°F at a weight of 129,000 lb (58514 kg). And as if to bring it home, Waddell demonstrated an engine failure on take-off. Standard Boeing 727-100s were by now certified for up to 131 passengers, with maximum take-off weights of either 160,000 lb (72576 kg), or up to 169,000 lb (76658 kg); 14,000-lb (6530-kg) thrust Pratt & Whitney JT8D-7s were standard, with the option of the 14,500-lb (6577-kg) thrust JT8D-9s.

A diversity of options

Despite the sales success of the Model 727, the deliveries and options of some 200 were still about 100 short of the break-even figure. On 22 July 1964 Boeing announced its promotion of the Model 727-100C convertible cargo/passenger model: brochures gave operation from a 5,000-ft (1525-m) runway with carriage of 30,000-lb (13608-kg) payloads over a distance of 1,900 miles (3058 km), or the carriage of eight pallets (36,750 lb/16670 kg) over 1,500 miles (2414 km). The St Paul-Minneapolis-based Northwest Orient signed for three as the first customer. Identical to the Model 727-100 except for heavier flooring and floor beams and the cargo-door of the Model 707-320C, the Model 727-100C gave operators the option of flying passengers by day and freight by night, thus enhancing utilization: galleys and seats

were quickly removable, hatracks could be stowed, and the aircraft could be changed to passenger/cargo or all-cargo configuration within two hours.

By April 1967 the Model 727 was the most widely used commercial jet airliner in service: in that month Sabena took delivery of the 400th aircraft while a total of 586 was on order, in comparison with 564 Model 707s. In June 1967 Pan American placed an order for the milestone 600th, and the aircraft was on option or in service with 32 carriers. On 27 July 1967 Wallick took the first Model 727-200 (N7270C) off Renton's runway and, after a flight of 2 hours 10 minutes, landed at Paine Field for FAA inspection. Certification followed on 30 November 1967 after 457 hours of test flying. Announced on 5 August 1965, the Model 727-200 was the stretched version offering 163 seats, up to a maximum of 189: the fuselage was lengthened by 10 ft (3.05 m) both forward and aft of the main landing gear wheel-well, with localized structural strengthening. Three JT8D-9s powered the Model 727-200, with options for 15,000-lb (6804-kg) thrust JT8D-11s, or 15,500-lb (7031-kg) thrust Pratt & Whitney JT8D-15s. In the meantime Boeing had given the market the Model 727-100QC with palletized passenger seats and galleys, and advanced cargo-loading techniques; ramp weight was increased to 170,000 lb (77,112 kg). Luxurious furnishings and advanced communications were also available on the Model 727-100 Business Jet, the first being ordered by International Telephone and Telegraph on 13 November 1970. The Advanced Boeing 727-200 was announced on 12 May 1971, with a ramp weight of 209,000 lb (86638 kg), and deliveries started in June of the next year. With increased fuel capacity and JT8D-15s, the aircraft offered a range 800 miles (1287 km) greater than that of earlier models.

The Boeing 727 has long been the most successful commercial jet airliner with a production run of more than 1,500. The number of aircraft sold exceeded the wildest dreams of Boeing's builders and managers. Finally, after 1,832 machines had been built, production ceased in 1984.

Lufthansa was one of the first airlines to buy the 727, and later exchanged it for the more modern 727-200. The picture shows a 727-230 Adv., of which Lufthansa still owned 34 in 1986.

Mikoyan-Gurevich MiG-23 & MiG 27

Since World War 2 the military world has welcomed half a dozen classic fighter aircraft which were built in thousands. One of them is still being built and developed after 20 years of production – the Mikoyan-Gurevich swing-wing fighter family known to NATO as 'Flogger'.

Work on the Mikoyan-Gurevich 'Flogger' began in the early 1960s after a large number of MiG-21s and Sukhoi Su-7s had been supplied to Soviet front-line air forces and tactical air defence units. At the time these types compared very favourably with Western aircraft in terms of speed and manoeuvrability, but so far as weaponry, range, and navigation and combat equipment they left a great deal to be desired from the very outset. As there was little prospect of correcting these shortcomings, it was no surprise that when they issued specifications for the next generation of fighter-bombers to come into use in 1970, Frontal Aviation, the Soviet tactical air defence/strike force, placed great emphasis on firepower, range and sophistication.

The requirement was issued before April 1965, when the first engagement between USAF and North Vietnamese fighters heralded a new era in air warfare. The requirement did not call for greatly improved agility in air combat; the standards set by the MiG-21 would be quite adequate. Instead, the new fighter was to have greater endurance, a heavier armament and a much more powerful radar than its predecessor, and the air-to-ground strike mission was at least as important as air combat. Field performance was to

be comparable with that of the smaller and lighter MiG-21.

The MiG bureau produced two prototype aircraft to the FA's specification, apparently sharing some common design features. One of these resembled an enlarged MiG-21, with the same mid-set delta wing and conventional tail, but to reduce the field length within reasonable bounds it was fitted with two lift-jet engines in the centre-section. The other, designated Ye-231, was a straightforward application of the then-fashionable variable-sweep, or variable-geometry (VG) formula. It is probable that both prototypes made their first flights in late 1966 or early 1967; by the time they appeared at the air show held at Domodedovo, near Moscow, in July 1967, the weight penalties and control complications inherent in the lift-jet design had led to its abandonment in favour of the swing-wing Ye-231. Following the show, the delta received the NATO codename 'Faithless' and the Ye-231 was labelled 'Flogger'.

These MiG-23BNs, here shown flying in formation, belong to the Indian Air Force. The model is something of a hybrid, with the nose, the pylons and main engines of the MiG-27 and the air intakes, thrust nozzles and cannons of the MiG-23.

A Libyan MiG-23 'Flogger-E', armed with K-13A missiles. In its first major action in the Middle East, in 1982, the MiG-23 proved no match for the IAI Kfir or General Dynamics F-16, though this was largely because of great disparity in pilot tactics and skill. Israeli pilots consider the 'Flogger'

inferior to the MiG-21 as a dogfighter, while the export version shown here has a similar radar and weapons.

Mikoyan-Gurevich MiG-23

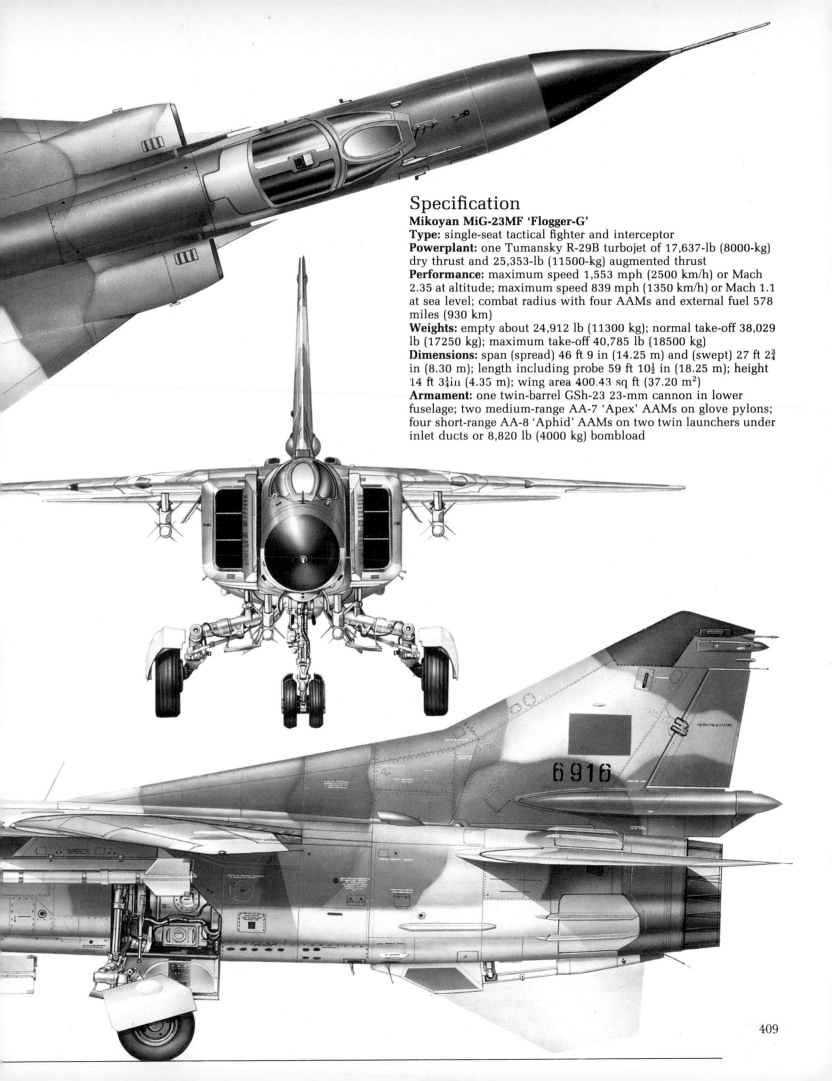

Specification

Mikoyan MiG-23MF 'Flogger-G'

Type: single-seat tactical fighter and interceptor

Powerplant: one Tumansky R-29B turbojet of 17,637-lb (8000-kg) dry thrust and 25,353-lb (11500-kg) augmented thrust

Performance: maximum speed 1,553 mph (2500 km/h) or Mach 2.35 at altitude; maximum speed 839 mph (1350 km/h) or Mach 1.1 at sea level; combat radius with four AAMs and external fuel 578 miles (930 km)

Weights: empty about 24,912 lb (11300 kg); normal take-off 38,029 lb (17250 kg); maximum take-off 40,785 lb (18500 kg)

Dimensions: span (spread) 46 ft 9 in (14.25 m) and (swept) 27 ft 2¾ in (8.30 m); length including probe 59 ft 10½ in (18.25 m); height 14 ft 3¼in (4.35 m); wing area 400.43 sq ft (37.20 m²)

Armament: one twin-barrel GSh-23 23-mm cannon in lower fuselage; two medium-range AA-7 'Apex' AAMs on glove pylons; four short-range AA-8 'Aphid' AAMs on two twin launchers under inlet ducts or 8,820 lb (4000 kg) bombload

Western intelligence continued to track the development of the Ye-231, including the construction and deployment of a small pilot batch of 'Flogger-A' aircraft closely resembling the prototype. It was not until early 1973, though, that the US Department of Defense could publicly confirm that the type was entering service in quantity and that its service designation was MiG-23; this designation has previously been attributed to the MiG-25 'Foxbat'. Later in that year, the true production MiG-23 entered service with Soviet units in East Germany, and photographs were leaked to Western magazines, revealing the design philosophy.

Variable geometry

The MiG-23 falls squarely into the group of VG aircraft conceived in the 1960s. All of them followed NASA's discovery that the fundamental problem of VG (the wings move aft as they are swept, creating a massive trim imbalance) could be solved without physically sliding the wing root through the fuselage as had been done on earlier VG designs. By moving the pivots outboard, twisting and tapering the outer wing panels and fitting a large and powerful all-moving tailplane, the trim problem could be kept under control without sacrificing the many advantages of VG. Maximum sweep could be sharper than was practical with a fixed wing, allowing high speeds at low level and good transonic acceleration, while the spread configuration was efficient in subsonic cruise and provided good field performance at high weights.

VG made a particularly good match for the newly developed augmented turbofan engine. The turbofan's excellent thrust/weight ratio in reheat could drive a VG aircraft well above Mach 2. Without reheat, its miserly fuel consumption put previously unattainable range performance within reach of the fighter aircraft. All the VG aircraft designed in the early 1960s had augmented turbofan powerplants, including the MiG-23; designated R-27, its engine was designed by the Tumansky bureau, which had powered the MiG-19, the MiG-21 and most of Mikoyan's prototypes.

The basic Ye-231 was a typically clean, straightforward design. The nose inlet featured on earlier MiGs gave way to side inlets, to make room for a useful search radar; the inlets were very like those of the F-4, with vertical moving ramps and wide boundary-layer ducts, and were efficient over a wide speed range without excessive weight or complexity. Thanks to the elimination of the full-length nose inlet ducts, the lean fuselage could hold a respectable amount of internal fuel in addition to the pilot, gun and avionics.

Early MiG-23 'Flogger-B' of a Soviet Frontal Aviation unit. Noteworthy points include the chin housing for an infra-red detection system or, possibly, a laser-ranging device – eliminated from later aircraft – and armament of four K-13A (AA-2 'Atoll') infra-red-homing missiles.

MiG-23 'Flogger' variants

Ye-231 'Flogger-A': bureau designation for prototype aircraft, flown in 1966–7
MiG-23 'Flogger-A': small batch of service-test aircraft, similar to prototype, produced in 1969–70
MiG-23MF 'Flogger-B': much modified standard fighter variant, in service since 1973: steadily improved with R-29B engine, provision for external fuel and other modifications
MiG-23U 'Flogger-C': two-seat conversion/proficiency trainer based on MiG-23MF
MiG-27 'Flogger-D': dedicated ground-attack aircraft based on MiG-23MF airframe with new forward fuselage, relocated pylons, six-barrel cannon and other changes
MiG-23 'Flogger-E': export fighter development of

MiG-23MF with R-27 engine, 'Jay Bird' radar and AA-2 'Atoll' missiles
MiG-23BN 'Flogger-F': export ground-attack type with MiG-27 forward fuselage and MiG-23-type inlets and nozzle
MiG-23MF 'Flogger-G': further improved fighter with shorter dorsal fin extension and new nose landing gear; recent versions have six-missile armament
MiG-23BN 'Flogger-H': similar to 'Flogger-F', but with additional antennae
MiG-27 'Flogger-J': recent MiG-27 variant with modified nose and wing leading-edge root extensions; has been seen with underwing gun pods as primary armament

Mikoyan MiG-23MF 'Flogger-G' cutaway drawing key

1 Pitot tube
2 Radome
3 'High Lark' radar scanner dish
4 Radar dish tracking mechanism
5 ILS antenna
6 Avionics cooling air scoop
7 Radar and avionics equipment bay
8 Ventral doppler antenna
9 Yaw vane
10 Air data probe
11 SRO-2 'Odd-Rods' IFF antenna
12 Armoured windscreen panel
13 Head-up display
14 Instrument panel shroud
15 Radar 'head-down' display
16 Instrument panel
17 Rudder pedals
18 Angle of attack transmitter
19 Laser rangefinder housing
20 Nosewheel steering unit
21 Torque scissor links
22 Pivoted axle beam
23 Twin aft-retracting nosewheels
24 Nosewheel spray/debris guard
25 Shock absorber strut
26 Nosewheel doors
27 Hydraulic retraction jack
28 Control column
29 Ejection seat firing handles
30 Wing sweep control lever
31 Engine throttle control lever
32 Pilot's ejection seat
33 Electrically heated rear view mirror

34 Ejection seat headrest
35 Upward hingeing cockpit canopy cover
36 Canopy jack
37 Starboard air intake
38 Canopy hinge point
39 Boundary layer splitter plate
40 Boundary layer bleed air holes

41 Port engine air intake
42 Intake internal flow fences
43 Retractable landing/taxiing lamp, port and starboard
44 Temperature probe
45 Variable area intake ramp doors
46 Boundary layer bleed air ejector
47 Avionics equipment bay
48 ADF sense aerial
49 Boundary layer air duct
50 Forward fuselage fuel tank
51 Ventral cannon ammunition magazines
52 Ground power connections

53 Intake suction relief doors
54 Weapons system electronic control units
55 SO-69 Sirena 3 radar warning antennae
56 Fuselage flank fuel tanks
57 Wing glove fairing
58 Starboard Sirena 3 radar warning antennae
59 176-gal (800-litre) jettisonable fuel tank
60 Nose section of MiG-23U 'Flogger-C' two-seat tandem trainer variant
61 Student pilot's cockpit
62 Folding blind-flying hood
63 Rear seat periscope, extended
64 Instructor's cockpit
65 MiG-23BN 'Flogger-F' dedicated ground attack variant
66 Ventral radar ranging antenna

67 Laser ranger nose fairing
68 Raised cockpit section
69 Armoured fuselage side panels
70 Wing leading edge flap, lowered
71 Starboard navigation light
72 Wing fully forward (16-deg sweep) position
73 Port wing integral fuel tank, total internal fuel capacity 1,265 gal (5750 litres)
74 Full span plain flap, lowered
75 Starboard wing intermediate (45-deg sweep) position
76 Starboard wing full (72-deg sweep) position
77 Two-segment spoilers/lift dumpers
78 Non-swivelling, jettisonable wing pylon

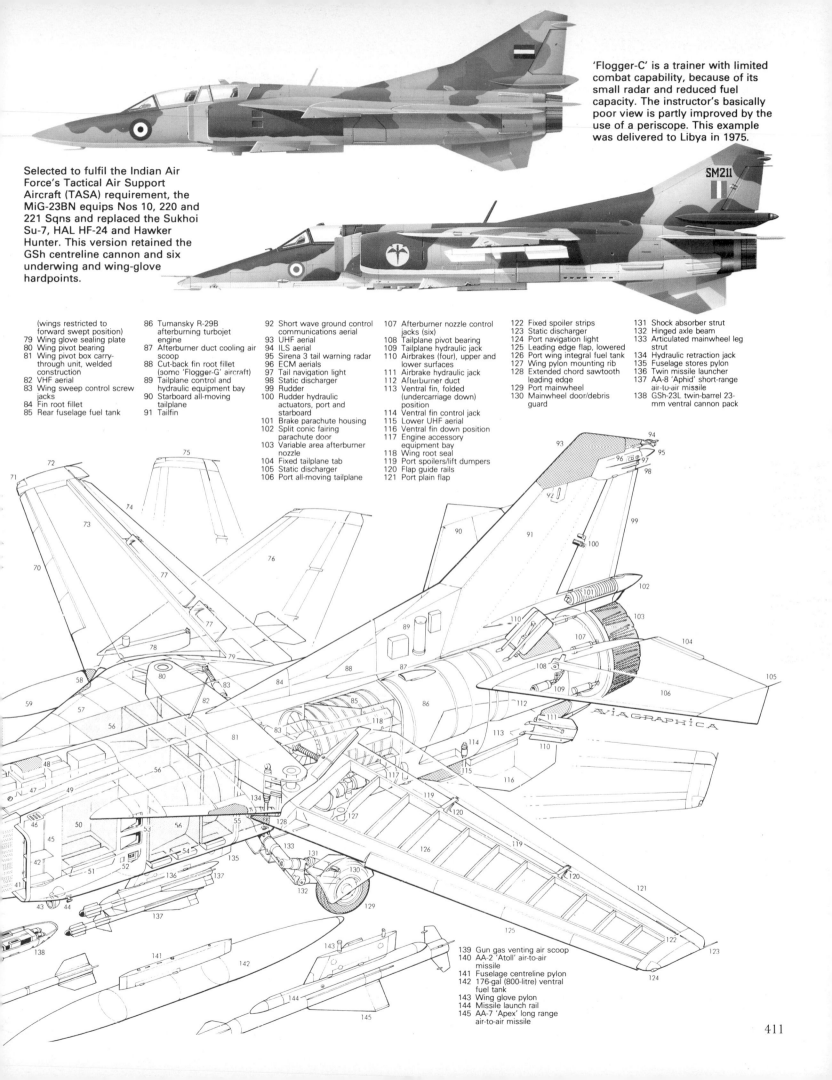

'Flogger-C' is a trainer with limited combat capability, because of its small radar and reduced fuel capacity. The instructor's basically poor view is partly improved by the use of a periscope. This example was delivered to Libya in 1975.

Selected to fulfil the Indian Air Force's Tactical Air Support Aircraft (TASA) requirement, the MiG-23BN equips Nos 10, 220 and 221 Sqns and replaced the Sukhoi Su-7, HAL HF-24 and Hawker Hunter. This version retained the GSh centreline cannon and six underwing and wing-glove hardpoints.

(wings restricted to forward swept position)
79 Wing glove sealing plate
80 Wing pivot bearing
81 Wing pivot box carry-through unit, welded construction
82 VHF aerial
83 Wing sweep control screw jacks
84 Fin root fillet
85 Rear fuselage fuel tank

86 Tumansky R-29B afterburning turbojet engine
87 Afterburner duct cooling air scoop
88 Cut-back fin root fillet (some 'Flogger-G' aircraft)
89 Tailplane control and hydraulic equipment bay
90 Starboard all-moving tailplane
91 Tailfin

92 Short wave ground control communications aerial
93 UHF aerial
94 ILS aerial
95 Sirena 3 tail warning radar
96 ECM aerials
97 Tail navigation light
98 Static discharger
99 Rudder
100 Rudder hydraulic actuators, port and starboard
101 Brake parachute housing
102 Split conic fairing parachute door
103 Variable area afterburner nozzle
104 Fixed tailplane tab
105 Static discharger
106 Port all-moving tailplane

107 Afterburner nozzle control jacks (six)
108 Tailplane pivot bearing
109 Tailplane hydraulic jack
110 Airbrakes (four), upper and lower surfaces
111 Airbrake hydraulic jack
112 Afterburner duct
113 Ventral fin, folded (undercarriage down) position
114 Ventral fin control jack
115 Lower UHF aerial
116 Ventral fin down position
117 Engine accessory equipment bay
118 Wing root seal
119 Port spoilers/lift dumpers
120 Flap guide rails
121 Port plain flap

122 Fixed spoiler strips
123 Static discharger
124 Port navigation light
125 Leading edge flap, lowered
126 Port wing integral fuel tank
127 Wing pylon mounting rib
128 Extended chord sawtooth leading edge
129 Port mainwheel
130 Mainwheel door/debris guard

131 Shock absorber strut
132 Hinged axle beam
133 Articulated mainwheel leg strut
134 Hydraulic retraction jack
135 Fuselage stores pylon
136 Twin missile launcher
137 AA-8 'Aphid' short-range air-to-air missile
138 GSh-23L twin-barrel 23-mm ventral cannon pack

139 Gun gas venting air scoop
140 AA-2 'Atoll' air-to-air missile
141 Fuselage centreline pylon
142 176-gal (800-litre) ventral fuel tank
143 Wing glove pylon
144 Missile launch rail
145 AA-7 'Apex' long range air-to-air missile

Something of an oddity, this 'export model' Flogger-E is marked as a PVO (national air defence) interceptor. It has been suggested that such aircraft have been supplied to Soviet forces because production of the advanced systems fitted to the 'Flogger-G' cannot match the output of airframes.

The outer wings were hydraulically driven from 16° to 72° sweep (an intermediate 45° position could be selected, but full-range, automatic control was not provided) and were attached to the ends of a heavy structural box passing through the upper fuselage above the inlet ducts. The swing-wing geometry of the original Ye-231 was not unlike that of the General Dynamics F-111, with outboard pivots, sizable fixed gloves and the tailerons (tailplane halves capable of collective and differential movement) located close behind the wings at the same high position. In the interests of simplicity, there were no swivelling wing pylons, and the wing high-lift devices were confined to full-span three-section plain flaps and drooped outboard leading edges. Overwing spoilers and the large tailerons were used for roll control.

One of the problems of a VG aircraft is the landing gear, banished from its usual place in the wings. The MiG team arrived at a unique main gear design: the mainwheels were suspended from two rigid beams, L-shaped in front view, which were pivoted at the fuselage keel and swung upwards into the fuselage sides. This gave the aircraft a wide track, but a pronounced nose-up sit which left no room for conventional ventral fins. Instead, a single large ventral fin was fitted, and this folded right and upwards as the main gear was extended. Four separate airbrakes were grouped around the tail; this provided ample deceleration with minimal trim change.

Design problems

Flight tests of the Ye-231 soon revealed serious stability and control problems in high-speed manoeuvring flight, and full production was postponed while some drastic modifications were made to the basic design. The tailerons and dorsal fin were moved some 3 ft 3.37 in (1.0 m) rearwards, and the wings were redesigned: the new outer wings featured large leading-edge extensions, terminating in dogteeth at the junction with the fixed glove. The new wings were more sharply tapered, shifting the aerodynamic centre forwards, while the claws served the same purpose as dog-teeth or fences, shedding a vortex across the upper wing and inhibiting the spanwise-and-rearwards flow which causes tip-stalling The effect of the modifications was to reduce pitch-up in high-speed turns, reduce the shift of the aerodynamic centre with increasing sweep, and increase the effectiveness of the tail surfaces at all speeds.

The modifications were incorporated in the first major production version, the MiG-23MF 'Flogger-B', which entered service in 1973.

The MiG-23MF was also designed to carry the new weapons and avionics which had been developed for the type. Glove pylons carried a pair of large air-to-air R-32R missiles, codenamed AA-7 'Apex' by NATO, while belly pylons were fitted for two very small, highly manoeuvrable R-60 AA-8 'Aphid' missiles. (Up to 1976, however, MiG-23MFs were often seen with launch rails for the older K-13A AA-2 'Atoll' and AA-2-2 Advanced Atoll). In the lower fuselage, between the intakes, the MiG-23MF carried the newly developed GSh-23 cannon, a remarkable weapon with two ultra-short barrels and an effective range of about 1,000 yards (915 m), firing at a rate of 3,000 rounds per minute. A large nose radome housed the Soviet Union's first pulse-Doppler fire-control radar, named 'High Lark' by NATO, and a laser rangefinder, probably for use in air-to-air gunnery, was mounted under the nose. More antennae, housed in the tip of the fin, the ends of the claws and the forward fuselage, betrayed the presence of comprehensive electronic countermeasures and surveillance equipment.

As the MiG-23 entered service, another new version of the type was completing its trials. While the MiG-23MF was designed to replace the MiG-21 in the tactical air-defence role, the new version was intended to supersede the Su-7 ground-attack fighter, and was extensively modified for the strike role. Designated MiG-27, the new version appeared in East Germany in 1975, and was code-named 'Flogger-D'.

The MiG-27 used the basic airframe of the MiG-23, but had a completely new forward fuselage. Shorter than the fighter's nose, it sloped more steeply ahead of the cockpit and offered a better downward view. Its sides were armoured, and it housed a laser rangefinder, a small ranging radar and Doppler navigation equipment. The variable-area inlets and nozzle of the MiG-23 were replaced by lighter fixed inlets and a simpler exhaust, reducing speed at high altitude but saving weight. The glove pylons were retained, but the ventral pylons were moved out to the inlet ducts to make room for larger stores. Another pair of smaller pylons was provided on the sides of the rear fuselage, possibly for counter-measures equipment or rocket-assisted take-off gear.

The MiG-27 is armed with a range of guided air-to-surface missiles (ASMs). Very little is known about these missiles (it appears that they are seldom carried outside secure areas of the Soviet Union, and certainly not in East Germany) but the US Department of Defense has stated that the Soviet Union has developed seven new tactical ASMs since the mid-

Both the MiG-27 and MiG-23BN appear to be in Soviet service in some numbers; this is an example of the latter. The location of the pylons under the belly rather than the inlet ducts reduces the external load, and the aircraft carries a less powerful gun than the MiG-27.

The cut-back dorsal fin of the 'Flogger-G' is a ready identification mark; other changes include the redesigned nosewheel leg and bulged doors. The centreline drop tank is almost invariably carried. The finish is a standard Frontal Aviation/Warsaw Pact scheme.

Algeria was an early export recipient of the MiG-23BN 'Flogger-F' strike fighter. Three squadrons of the type, totalling some 40 aircraft, were reported to be in service in early 1984. Most were delivered in 1975-6; they have not been used in action.

1970s. They included the radio-commanded AS-7 'Kerry', the long-range anti-radar AS-9 (although this weapon is more usually associated with the larger Su-24), the laser-guided AS-10 and guided glide bombs.

Other improvements applied to the MiG-27 were also incorporated on the MiG-23 in the course of production. These included the more powerful Tumansky R-29B engine and provision for fuel tanks under the outer wings. These were carried on fixed pylons, and were designed to be jettisoned before the wings were swept back.

With these two versions established in production, the Soviet Union's output of 'Floggers' reached a peak rate of nearly 500 aircraft per year in the mid-1970s. By the end of 1982, it was estimated that some 3,500 of the type had been built. The result has been that Soviet and allied air forces have been able to re-equip very fully and quickly with the MiG-23 family, and it would be fair to say that the MiG fighter was the main element in a rapid improvement in Warsaw Pact airpower in the late 1970s.

All the other members of the 'Flogger' family stem from the MiG-27. The first of these to appear was the MiG-23U 'Flogger-C', a two-seat trainer version of the MiG-23MF with a slightly raised rear cockpit and a smaller radar. The MiG-23U is used as the trainer for the MiG-27 and other attack variants as well as for the MiG-23 fighters, and some sources have suggested that similar two-seat aircraft may be used in the ECM and defence-suppression roles.

Middle Eastern allies of the Soviet Union were the first export customers for the MiG-23; Egypt, Libya and Syria took delivery of their first batches in the course of 1975. All of them, however, received deliberately downgraded export models of the type. The first of these was the 'Flogger-E' fighter, which differed from the MiG-23MF in having a much smaller radar (probably related to the 'Jay Bird' system fitted to later MiG-21s) and in being armed with AA-2 'Atoll' missiles. More recently, however, export customers appear to have received the more potent MiG-23MF.

A hybrid version of the family, combining MiG-23 and MiG-27 features, was first seen in 1975 and was at first thought to be a MiG-27 development aircraft. It soon became apparent, however, that it was an attack aircraft for non-Soviet forces, and it is designated MiG-23BN. It has the nose of the MiG-27, and the same duct-mounted pylons and enlarged mainwheels. However, it has the inlets, exhaust and gun of the MiG-23. The initial version was code-named 'Flogger-F' by NATO; the version supplied to Eastern European air forces, with additional antennae, is identified as 'Flogger-H'. This version is also being built under licence in India, alongside the 'Flogger-C' trainer.

The first-line fighter version of the MiG-23 has been continuously refined. NATO applies the designation 'Flogger-G' to MiG-23s produced since 1978; these are distinguished by a shorter dorsal fin and a modified nose landing gear housed under bulged doors. Recent improve-

Late-model 'Flogger-G' in landing configuration. Note the slender external tank, designed to be retained at supersonic speeds. The type is more festooned with antennae than any other fighter aircraft, indicating the type's comprehensive electronics suite.

Standard MiG-23U 'Flogger-C' trainers of Soviet Frontal Aviation. MiG-23 pilots are trained according to a precise manual of tactics, designed to suit their fast but unmanoeuvrable aircraft. As in the West, two-seaters are attached to each unit for refresher training and check-outs.

ments are reported to include improved head-up displays; new MiG-23s, like modern Western fighters, dispense with a full-time radar scope in the cockpit. Since 1982, 'Flogger-G' has also been seen in a six-missile configuration, with duct-mounted twin pylons for four AA-8 missiles. The 'High Lark'/AA-7 combination has also been improved; the MiG-23MF is believed to have 'some ability to engage low-flying targets' according to the Department of Defense, and the type is now used alongside the Su-15 by Soviet PVO air-defence units as well as by Frontal Aviation.

The latest MiG-27 version is known as 'Flogger-J', and is distinguished by changes to the nose and small leading-edge root extensions (LERXs). These seem too small to have any great aerodynamic effect, and may house antennae for an improved ECM suite. The type has also been seen with a pair of gun pods under the wing gloves, with barrels which can be depressed for attacking ground targets. The MiG-27 is still used mainly by the Soviet air forces.

MiG-23s have seen action in the war between Iraq and Iran, and between Syria and Israel. Syria's 'Flogger-Es' suffered heavy losses in action against the Israeli IAI Kfirs and General Dynamics F-16s in June 1982, but this was ascribed to tactics rather more than technology. Generally, the MiG-23 is regarded as a well equipped and capable aircraft, much less agile than the F-16 but somewhat faster and,

currently, carrying a heavier, longer-range armament; this imbalance exists largely because the USAF has elected to wait for the new AIM-120 instead of integrating the earlier Sparrow missile with the F-16. So far, the MiG-23 and MiG-27 have been available in greater numbers than the F-16.

An unexpected operator of the MiG-23 is the US Air Force, which is known to maintain one or two of the type at a base in Nevada. Obtained from Egypt after its rift with the Soviet Union, they are used for the development of air combat tactics. In late 1983, Atlanta-based aviation services company Flight International proposed to acquire and support more ex-Egyptian MiG-23s for the US Navy.

It seems that production of the MiG-23/27 has been slowed down during recent years and the Soviet Union is now concentrating more on the MiG-29 'Fulcrum', the MiG-31 'Foxhound' and other very sophisticated types. It is possible that the MiG-29 is intended to replace the MiG-23. The US Defense Ministry regards the 'Fulcrum' as a proper multi-purpose fighter aircraft like the American McDonnell Douglas F-18 or F-16: an aircraft which can be used both as a fighter and an attack aircraft without any modifications being needed. The MiG-23 will doubtless go on being built and used for another few years before being replaced by the new types. The success of the 'Flogger' lies mainly in its well-balanced specifications, flexible and advanced design and unique serial production. The result is an aircraft which stands up well under any kind of use.

By 1986, sources in the West estimated that some 450 'Flogger B/G' interceptors were operational with the Soviet strategic air defence arm, with about 3,000 marks in other offensive/defense roles.

A rare view of MiG-23BN 'Flogger-H' strike fighters in service with the Indian Air Force. The type is being produced under licence by Hindustan Aeronautics Limited (HAL) and it is expected that some 200 domestically built aircraft will join the current force of 90 MiG-23BNs. The IAF also has the 'Flogger-G.'

Boeing 747
'Jumbo Jet'

While Douglas merely stretched the DC-8, Boeing went back to a clean sheet of paper to create a civil airliner much larger than any previously built. Immediately dubbed 'The Jumbo Jet', it revolutionized today's air-transport world in which two great advances, the wide-body airliner and the high bypass ratio fan engine, move more traffic with less noise and at much lower unit cost.

Ever since it came into being, the Boeing Company (formerly Boeing Airplane Company) has repeatedly made daring decisions to develop new transport or bomber aircraft which have shown to be in the forefront of technology. This has often been despite the fact that they have had no advance orders for an aircraft when they have begun planning it, and often also despite putting the company's entire assets on the line to develop the aircraft. The greatest risk Boeing ever took was the Boeing 747, even though it had one order from PanAm. In fact, this was probably the greatest risk any manufacturing company has ever taken. But it paid off, and once again Boeing established a milestone in the history of aviation.

This single type of aircraft, even today the most powerful, the heaviest and most capable ever constructed (not forgetting the old airships and giant flying boats of the past), transformed air transport by more than doubling the load of passengers or cargo that could be carried, by more than quadrupling the available payload volume, and not least by introducing a wholly new form of propulsion giving jet speed but with much reduced fuel consumption and less than one-tenth as much noise.

New generation jetliners
Boeing Commercial Airplane Company, the subsidiary responsible for civil transport aircraft, began to study a new-generation jetliner in the early 1960s for long-range high-traffic routes. Rival Douglas was in the throes of eking out DC-8 production by a dramatic process of stretching in the Super Sixty series. Boeing eventually chose not to reply with a super-stretched 707 but to build a totally new and much larger aircraft with a wider fuselage; it was to usher in a new era of so-called wide-body transports. Such an aircraft was possible because, at the same time, General Electric and Pratt & Whitney were developing completely new large turbofan engines for the US Air Force CX-HLS competition for a giant military freighter (won by Lockheed with its C-5A).

With aircraft of this size, new configurations of fuselage became possible. Boeing engineers exhaustively studied double-bubble schemes with two pressurized tubes full of passengers, either side-by-side or superimposed, as well as a single giant tube with two decks inside. In the event the decision was taken to use a single tube but with only one enormous passenger floor, extending right to the nose. Underneath there was room for the capacious bays for electronics, electrics, air-conditioning and hydraulics, as well as cargo holds of unprecedented size. If necessary, galleys and other passenger-service items could be at the lower level. The flight deck was placed above the ceiling of

Named *City of Esch-sur-Alzette* (written in English), this 747-200F is one of a pair operated on intensive all-cargo services, mainly to the USA, by Cargolux Airlines International of Luxembourg. This windowless front-loading variant is far more capable than any other airline freighter, carrying 254,640 lb (115500 kg).

Probably the most costly production aircraft in history, the E-4 AABNCP (Advanced Airborne National Command Post) would in time of crisis become the seat of government of the United States. This drawing shows the first E-4A as built with JT9D engines. Later it was fitted with F103 engines and became an E-4B.

the passenger deck, forming a slight blister above the nose and extended to the rear in an upper deck for typically 32 passengers. The main deck could seat up to 500 passengers in high-density 10-abreast seating (3 + 4 + 3), but 350 was judged a more likely number with an ultra-luxurious first-class section (seating passengers in pairs along the sides of the nose) extending right up to the radar filling the tip of the nose.

Boeing went for a high cruising speed with the model 747, adopting an advanced design of wing with the exceptional sweep-back angle of $37\frac{1}{2}°$ at 25 per cent chord (one-quarter of the way back from the leading edge). The leading edge was given a typically ambitious high-lift system, with three sections of Krueger flap hinged down from the under surface of the wing inboard of the inner engines, five sections of novel variable-camber flap between the engines, and five more sections between the outer engines and the tip on each side. The variable-camber flaps resembled traditional slats but comprised flexible skins carried on pivoted links in such a way that as they were hydraulically extended ahead of and below the leading edge they arched into a curve to give maximum control of the airflow at high angles. On the trailing edge were placed enormous triple-slotted flaps, with each section running on steel tracks with prominent fairings projecting behind the trailing edge. Above the wing on each side were added six sections of aluminium honeycomb spoiler, four outboard for control in flight (augmenting the roll power of the conventional trailing-edge low-speed ailerons) and two ground spoilers inboard to destroy lift after landing and thus increase braking power. High-speed ailerons were added at the trailing edge behind the inboard engines where the flaps could not be used.

Though the engine installation looked conventional, being arranged on four widely separated wing pylons as in the model 707 of 15 years earlier, they were on a scale never before seen except on the military C-5A. In fact Boeing picked the loser in the C-5A engine competition. Pratt &

Left Up to the end of 1985, more than 670 Boeing 747s of all versions had been ordered. In the Everett hangars, aircraft are being completed for Air France and Alitalia, as well as a shortened SP version for the Australian airline, Qantas.

N7470 was the very first Jumbo, seen here on its maiden flight (on which the landing gear was not retracted) on 9 February 1969. Even at that time there was a very healthy customer-list, as shown by the 28 airline symbols on the forward fuselage. Retained by Boeing, and later fitted with a tanker boom, this 747 is now N1352B.

Whitney, whose JT9D was offered as a robust and reliable turbofan of the new high-bypass-ratio type with a thrust of 41,000 lb (18598 kg). Extremely difficult engineering problems had to be solved in hanging the engines, in arranging a fan-duct reverse and hot-stream spoiler, and in reducing drag. Another tough engineering problem was the landing gear, eventually solved by using four main gear four-wheel bogies, two of them on tall inwards-retracting legs pivoted to the wings and the other pair on forward-retracting units pivoted to the fuselage, the four retracted bogies lying together in a large bay amidships under the floor. All flight controls are hydraulically powered, the rudder and elevators being divided into equal-size halves, no tabs being used anywhere. The APU (auxiliary power unit) for ground air conditioning and electric power was placed in the extreme tail of the fuselage.

Not only did Boeing have to build the 747: the company also had to build a new factory to make it, and the new plant at Everett, swiftly created in a 780-acre clearing in a forest, is the largest building (in cubic capacity) in the world. Together with many other programmes Boeing's commitments were awesome, and employment in 1968 peaked at 105,000, compared with 60,000 at the peak in World War 2. The risk on the model 747 easily topped one billion dollars, but thankfully orders kept rolling in, and when the first aircraft off the production line (Ship RA001) emerged from the new plant on 30 September 1968 a total of 158 orders had been gained from 26 airlines.

Engine snags

With so new and complex an aircraft it would have been surprising if there had been no snags, but in fact the difficulties, mainly centred on the engines, were prolonged. In crosswinds the engines were difficult to start and ran roughly, and distortion (so-called ovalization) of the casings caused blades to rub in a way that had not been apparent in more than two years of ground testing and flight development using a B-52. Pratt & Whitney had to devise a Y-shaped frame to hang the engine differently, and eventually produced a new version of JT9D that avoided the problem. But the first flight was delayed until 9 February 1969. This aircraft was retained by Boeing for many development purposes. The first to be delivered was handed to Pan American on 12 December 1969, and that airline – after an unprecedented amount of engineering and training effort and investment in new ground facilities – finally got the model 747 into service on the New York–London service on 22 January 1970.

Popularly called the 'Jumbo Jet', the model 747 hit the headlines as well as the pockets of its customers and the world's airport authorities. For a while it appeared almost to be premature, because traffic did not grow as expected and load factor (proportion of seats filled) was often low. With great courage, Boeing continued production at maximum rate, and both the orders and the variants continued to grow. From the outset Boeing had organized a vast manufacturing programme with major sections of airframe made by sub-contractors: Northrop make the main fuselage sections, for example; and Fairchild Republic build the flaps, ailerons, slats and spoilers. With such large structures, exceptional

Boeing 747-127

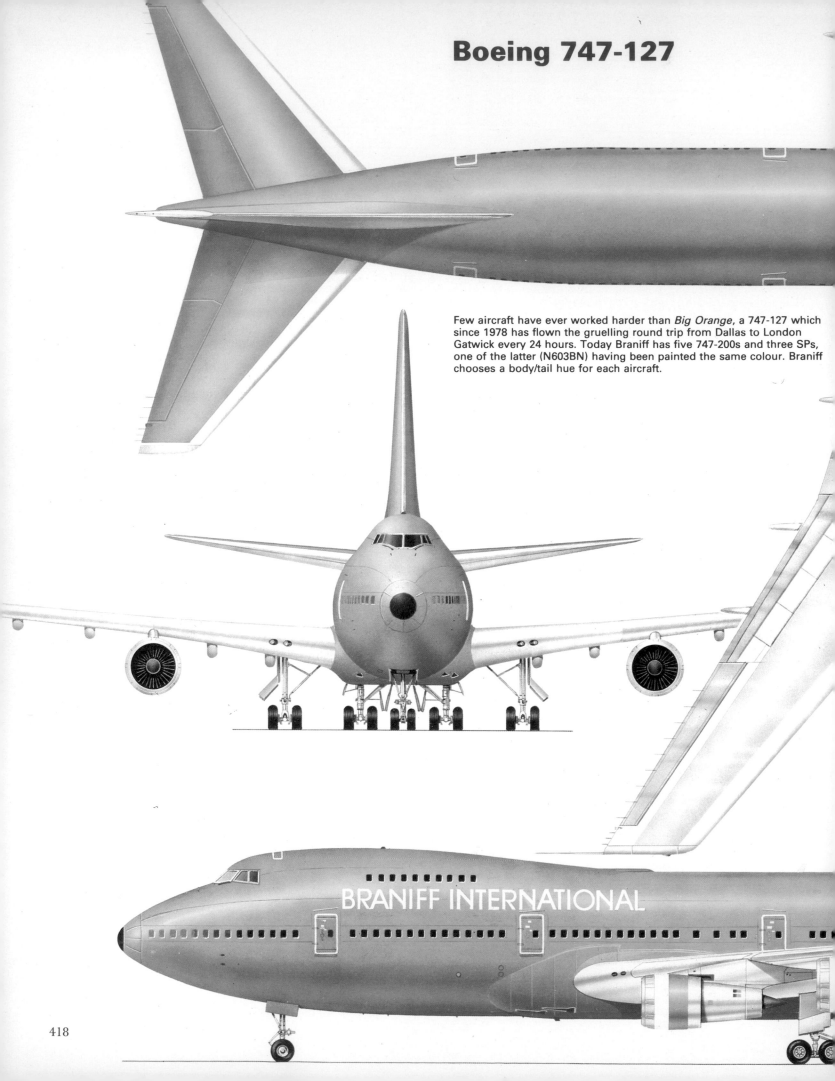

Few aircraft have ever worked harder than *Big Orange*, a 747-127 which since 1978 has flown the gruelling round trip from Dallas to London Gatwick every 24 hours. Today Braniff has five 747-200s and three SPs, one of the latter (N603BN) having been painted the same colour. Braniff chooses a body/tail hue for each aircraft.

BRANIFF INTERNATIONAL

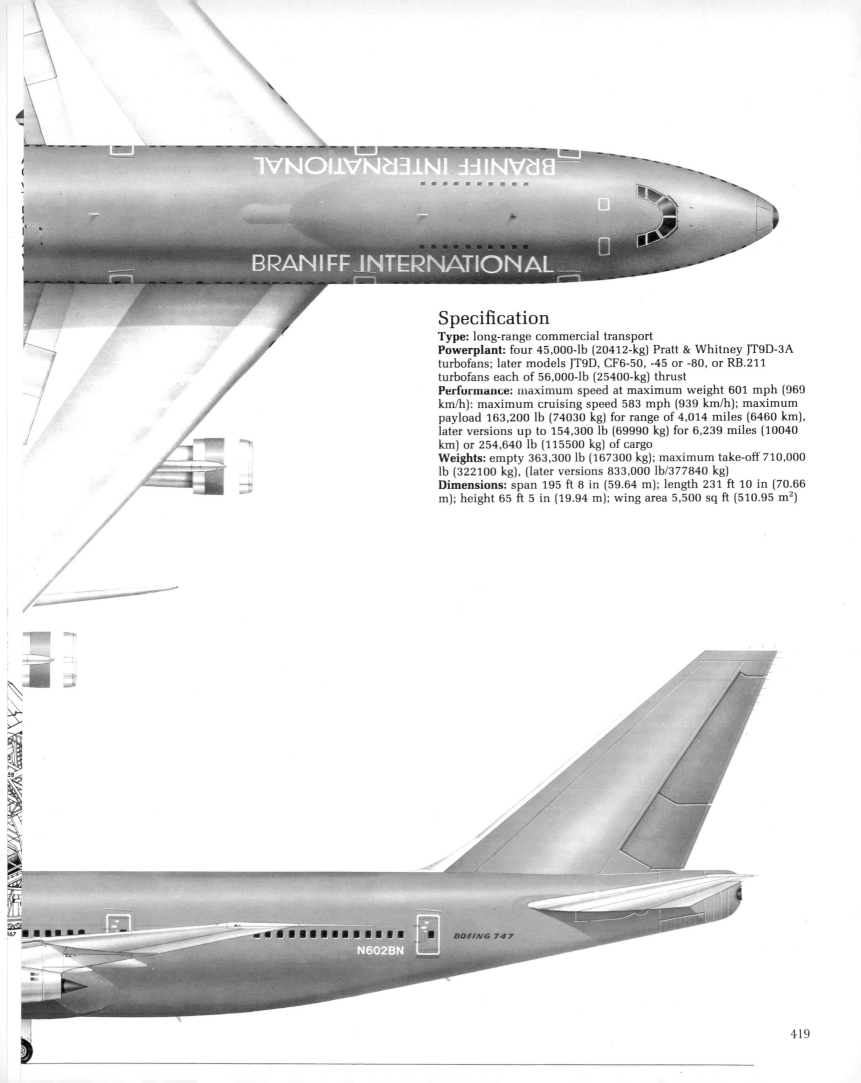

Specification

Type: long-range commercial transport

Powerplant: four 45,000-lb (20412-kg) Pratt & Whitney JT9D-3A turbofans; later models JT9D, CF6-50, -45 or -80, or RB.211 turbofans each of 56,000-lb (25400-kg) thrust

Performance: maximum speed at maximum weight 601 mph (969 km/h): maximum cruising speed 583 mph (939 km/h); maximum payload 163,200 lb (74030 kg) for range of 4,014 miles (6460 km), later versions up to 154,300 lb (69990 kg) for 6,239 miles (10040 km) or 254,640 lb (115500 kg) of cargo

Weights: empty 363,300 lb (167300 kg); maximum take-off 710,000 lb (322100 kg), (later versions 833,000 lb/377840 kg)

Dimensions: span 195 ft 8 in (59.64 m); length 231 ft 10 in (70.66 m); height 65 ft 5 in (19.94 m); wing area 5,500 sq ft (510.95 m²)

The four Rolls-Royce/SNECMA Olympus 593 engines allow the Concorde to travel at twice the speed of sound. Because of the aircraft's steep take-off and landing angles, the nose tilts downwards slightly to give a better view from the cockpit.

The STAC embraced not only government technologists, top men from engine and airframe companies and numerous officials, but also nominees from civil airlines. Nobody then could possibly foresee that opposition to such a project would assume the proportions of a national crusade, or that for political reasons the USA and many other countries would delay for years admitting such an aircraft to its airports or even permit it to fly overhead, and certainly the price of fuel was not expected to be multiplied tenfold. All that could be seen clearly was that the technical problems were of an order of magnitude greater than those of other aircraft. Just one immutable problem was that, for any given amount of wing lift, the drag is more than doubled as the vehicle accelerates from Mach 0.9 to beyond Mach 1.

Three options

It was obvious that a supersonic airliner would need a novel configuration, with a wing of very low aspect ratio and an extremely long body of minimal cross-section. The STAC studied three main answers. One was an area-ruled aircraft with a curious M-wing, initially swept forward and then back to the tips, cruising at Mach 1.2 (800 mph/1285 km/h) for 1,500 miles (2414 km). Second was a slender delta, very much like the eventual Concorde, but cruising at Mach 1.8 (1,200 mph/1930 km/h) for 3,500 miles (5635 km). Third was a steel/titanium monster cruising at Mach 3 (2,000 mph/3220 km/h) for 3,500 miles (5635 km). The third idea was deemed technically too difficult and costly, though for a further 14 years it consumed over $2,000 million in the USA. In March 1959 the STAC recommended Mach 1.2 short-range or Mach 1.8 transAtlantic, and the Ministry of Aviation awarded contracts for detailed studies of the latter aircraft. By late 1960 it was clear not only that the slender delta, with an ogival (curved) leading edge, was the best shape but also that its aerodynamic efficiency improved up to about Mach 2.2. This not only reduced journey time but improved propulsion efficiency, because the latter depends on the ram pressure generated in the engine inlet and this rises rapidly with increasing Mach number.

By 1960 Bristol Aircraft, then in the process of merging into the British Aircraft Corporation (BAC), had schemed the Type 198, a 130-passenger transAtlantic SST looking much like today's Concorde but powered by six Bristol Siddeley Olympus engines.

In the summer of 1961 the aviation ministry decided a 380,000-lb (172368-kg) six-engine aircraft was too ambitious, and asked for a 100-seater weighing 250,000 lb (113400 kg) with four engines. By this time Sud-Aviation in France, likewise in the throes of becoming part of a giant group (SNIAS or Aérospatiale), had studied Mach 2 SSTs and decided on a very similar configuration but aimed at short ranges as a 70/80-seat successor to the company's Caravelle. At the Paris Air Show in June 1961 Sud displayed a model of its idea, named Super Caravelle. Some months previously BAC had, on government insistence, put out feelers to possible foreign partners, and Sud-Aviation was the only positive response. The first formal meetings were held during the Paris Air Show, and a month later at Weybridge.

British Airways' third Concorde sits on the tarmac at Melbourne, Australia. The airline and manufacturers spent much time and trouble proving the route to Australia, but met with much opposition from overflown countries and residents local to destination airports. Concorde was banned from landing at the airport at Sydney.

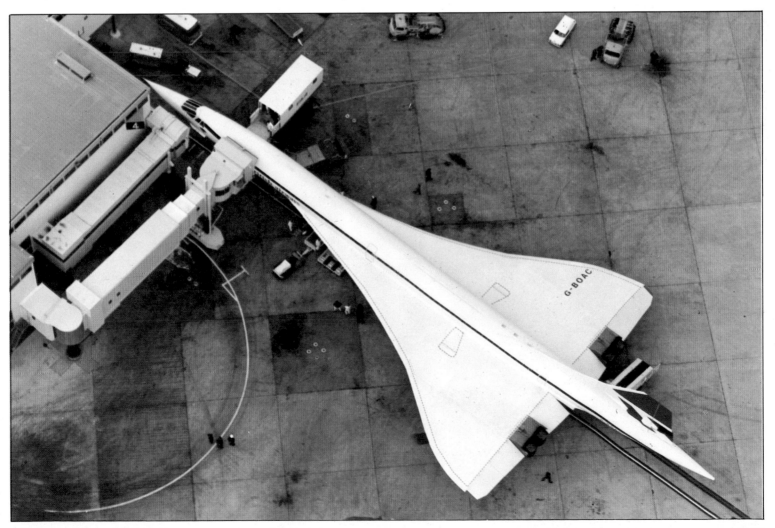

Concorde

The similarity between the British and French proposals was amazing, almost the only difference apart from size, weight and range being that Sud thought it could get away without using a hinged 'droop snoot' nose, while BAC considered such a feature essential for adequate forward view during the nose-high landing. After many further talks, an inter-government agreement of 29 November 1962 formally launched the project, with government funding on a 50/50 basis and the main effort shared between BAC and Aérospatiale on the airframe and Bristol Siddeley (from 1966 Rolls-Royce) and SNECMA on propulsion, using as a basis an enlarged Olympus called the Olympus 593. The British partner was charged with developing a transAtlantic version, while the French adhered to a short-haul model with a ventral stairway instead of fuel in the rear fuselage. A Committee of Directors was appointed to run the airframe, and another to manage the engine, and there were separate British and French government contracts to each national industrial group.

Suffice to say that such an arrangement will never be repeated, but it was made to work by the goodwill and towering stature of the main engineers involved. Sir George Edwards, who when head of Vickers-Armstrongs (Aircraft) in 1958 had predicted the entire future course of events with extreme accuracy, was the architect of the whole project. Top designers at Bristol were Sir Archibald Russell and Dr Bill Strang, while leaders at Aérospatiale were Pierre Satre and Lucien Servanty. Collaboration extended down through the main airframe and engine teams to the hundreds of major suppliers of systems and equipment.

Gradually the French accepted the idea of a transAtlantic SST, especially after a large meeting of possible airline customers had shown in 1963 that the feeling of the market was that the proposal was not bold enough. A powerful body of opinion held that the Anglo-French SST would be outmoded by the promised later American SST to carry some 250 passengers at Mach 3. It needed steady nerves to stick to the belief that 100 passengers at about Mach 2 was right.

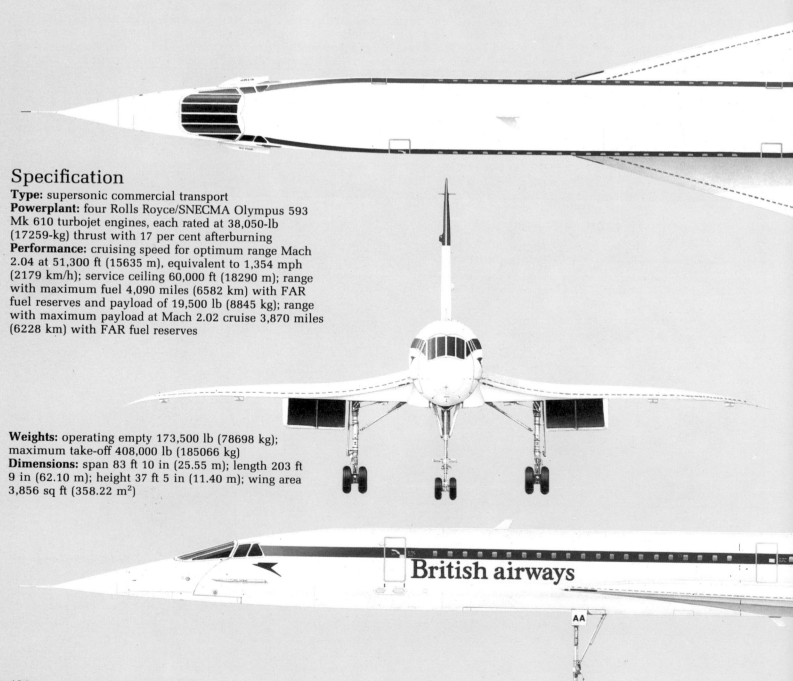

Specification

Type: supersonic commercial transport
Powerplant: four Rolls Royce/SNECMA Olympus 593 Mk 610 turbojet engines, each rated at 38,050-lb (17259-kg) thrust with 17 per cent afterburning
Performance: cruising speed for optimum range Mach 2.04 at 51,300 ft (15635 m), equivalent to 1,354 mph (2179 km/h); service ceiling 60,000 ft (18290 m); range with maximum fuel 4,090 miles (6582 km) with FAR fuel reserves and payload of 19,500 lb (8845 kg); range with maximum payload at Mach 2.02 cruise 3,870 miles (6228 km) with FAR fuel reserves

Weights: operating empty 173,500 lb (78698 kg); maximum take-off 408,000 lb (185066 kg)
Dimensions: span 83 ft 10 in (25.55 m); length 203 ft 9 in (62.10 m); height 37 ft 5 in (11.40 m); wing area 3,856 sq ft (358.22 m²)

Aérospatiale/British Aerospace Concorde

The sixth production Concorde, which first flew on 5 November 1975 and entered service with British Airways on 21 January 1976 when it flew a service from London to Bahrain. The elegantly simple lines of the Concorde, optimized for an economical cruising speed of just over Mach 2, tend to disguise the extreme complexity, in both aerodynamics and systems, of this pioneering SST. Some indication of the sophisticated aerodynamic factors is indeed given by the modified ogival wing planform with its cambered leading edges, but the intricacies of the powerplant/fuel and electronics systems are not even suggested. The latter are the key to the effective operation of the aircraft, controlling the trim of the machine and the performance of the engines to suit exactly the relevant flight conditions. Though the nose is shown in the raised position, the visor is not extended.

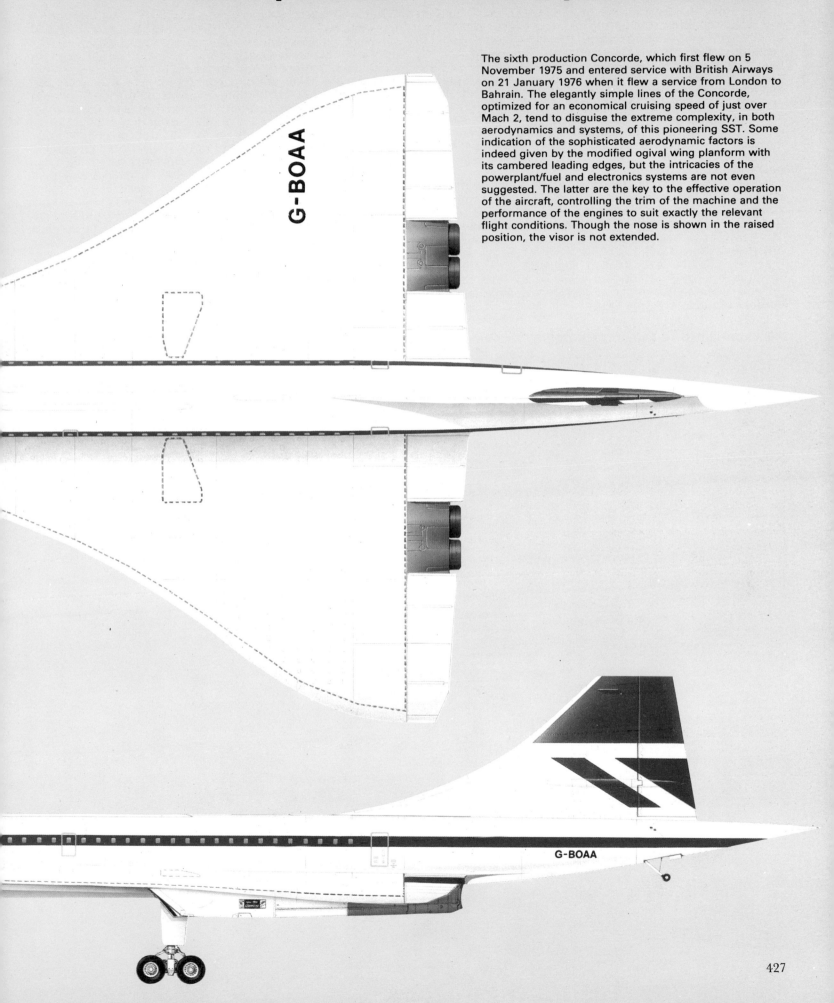

Concorde

Named Concorde in 1963, the Anglo-French machine grew from 262,000 lb to 286,000 lb (118843 kg to 129730 kg), increasing the seating for the full range from 90 to 100, but the engine team then redesigned the Olympus, as the Mk 593B, to give much greater power, and this allowed the Concorde to follow the pressures of the market and grow to 326,000 lb (147874 kg) with 118 seats. In early 1965 design was brought to a halt, and construction of prototypes 001 and 002 began. In parallel a colossal research programme was funded, including a complete airframe thermal rig at Farnborough and the Handley Page H.P.115 and BAC.221 research aircraft were put to use flight-testing many of the new systems.

Though part of the agreement was that there should be an assembly line in both countries, producing odd-numbered aircraft at Toulouse St Martin and even-numbered at Filton (Bristol), there was no duplication in actual manufacture. Thus BAC was assigned the nose, tail and engine installations, and Aérospatiale the wings, centre fuselage and landing gears. France actually had about 60 per cent of the airframe because the UK had most of the engine, while systems were shared more or less evenly and included a number of items from the USA.

Aerodynamically the design is a tailless ogival delta. The wing has continuous subtle curvatures, with strong conical camber giving pronounced leading-edge droop outboard, but the basic thickness is extremely low, only 3 per cent inboard and 2.15 per cent outboard of the engines. Wing sections were made at Bouguenais, Toulouse, St Nazaire and Marignane, and the section outboard of the engines was made by Dassault at Bourges. Flight control is by six elevons, two of them inboard of the engines, each driven by a Dowty Boulton Paul tandem jack in the 4,000-lb/sq in (281.2-kg/cm²) hydraulic system. One of the drawbacks is that at take-off and landing these surfaces cannot be used to increase wing camber and thus lift and drag, but the problem of trimming out the change in centre of pressure (the point through which the resultant lift force acts) was solved very neatly without causing any drag. Most of the 26,330 Imp gal (119695 litres) of fuel is housed in integral tanks in the thin wing and under the passenger floor, but by using extra tanks at the extreme front of the wing and in the tail of the fuselage it was found possible to shift the centre of gravity of the aircraft to match the shift in the centre of pressure. During transonic acceleration the contents of the forward tanks are pumped into the rear trim tank and main tankage. At the end

Aérospatiale/BAe Concorde cutaway drawing key

1 Variable geometry drooping nose
2 Weather radar
3 Spring pot
4 Visor jack
5 'A'-frame
6 Visor uplock
7 Visor guide rails and carriage
8 Droop nose jacks
9 Droop nose guide rails
10 Droop nose hinge
11 Rudder pedals
12 Captain's seat
13 Instrument panel shroud
14 Forward pressure bulkhead
15 Retracting visor
16 Multi-layer windscreen
17 Windscreen fluid rain clearance and wipers
18 Second pilot's seat
19 Roof panel
20 Flight-deck air duct
21 3rd crew member's seat
22 Control relay jacks
23 1st supernumerary's seat
24 2nd supernumerary's folding seat (optional)
25 Radio and electronics racks (Channel 2)
26 Radio and electronics racks (Channel 1)
27 Plug-type forward passenger door
28 Slide/life-raft pack stowage
29 Cabin staff tip-up seat
30 Forward galley units (port and starboard)
31 Toilets (2)
32 Coats (crew and passengers)
33 Twelve 26-man life-rafts
34 VHF 1 antenna
35 Overhead baggage racks (with doors)
36 Cabin furnishing (heat and sound insulated)
37 4-abreast one-class passenger accommodation
38 Seat rails
39 Metal-faced floor panels
40 Nosewheel well
41 Nosewheel main doors
42 Nosewheel leg
43 Shock absorber
44 Twin nosewheels
45 Torque links

46 Steering mechanism
47 Telescopic strut
48 Lateral bracing struts
49 Nosewheel actuating jacks
50 Underfloor air-conditioning ducts
51 Nosewheel door actuator
52 Nosewheel secondary (aft) doors
53 Fuselage frame (single flange)
54 Machined window panel
55 Underfloor forward baggage compartment (237 cu ft/6.72 m³)
56 Fuel lines
57 Lattice ribs
58 No. 9 (port forward) trim tank
59 Single-web spar
60 No. 10 (port forward) trim tank
61 Middle passenger doors (port and starboard)
62 Cabin staff tip-up seat
63 Toilets
64 Emergency radio stowage
65 Provision for VHF3
66 Overhead baggage racks (with doors)
67 Cabin aft section
68 Fuselage frame
69 Tank vent gallery
70 No. 1 forward collector tank
71 Lattice ribs
72 Engine-feed pumps
73 Accumulator
74 No. 5 fuel tank
75 Trim transfer gallery
76 Leading-edge machined ribs
77 Removable leading-edge sections with:
78 Expansion joints between sections
79 Contents unit
80 Inlet control valve
81 Transfer pumps
82 Flight-deck air duct
83 No. 8 fuselage tank

84 Vapour seal above tank
85 Pressure-floor curved membranes
86 Pre-stretched integrally machined wing skin panels
87 No. 8 wing tank
88 No. 4 forward collector tank
89 No. 10 starboard forward trim tank
90 No. 9 starboard forward trim tank
91 Quick-lock removable inspection panels
92 Spraymat leading-edge de-icing panels
93 Leading-edge anti-icing strip
94 Spar-box machined girder side pieces
95 No. 7 fuel tank
96 No. 7a fuel tank
97 Static dischargers
98 Elevon
99 Inter-elevon flexible joint nozzles/reverser buckets
100 Combined secondary nozzles/reverser buckets
101 Nozzle-mounting spigots
102 Cabin air delivery/distribution
103 Inspection panels
104 Cold-air unit
105 Fuel-cooled heat exchanger
106 Fuel/hydraulic oil heat exchanger
107 Fire-suppression bottles
108 Main spar frame
109 Accumulator
110 No. 3 aft collector tank
111 Control linkage
112 'Z'-section spot-welded stringers

113 Riser to distribution duct
114 Anti-surge bulkheads
115 No. 6 (underfloor) fuel tank
116 Machined pressurised keel box
117 Fuselage frame
118 Double-flange frame/floor join
119 Machined pressure-floor support beams
120 Port undercarriage well
121 Mainwheel door
122 Fuselage/wing attachments
123 Main spar frame
124 Mainwheel retraction link
125 Mainwheel actuating jack
126 Cross beam
127 Forked link
128 Drag strut
129 Mainwheel leg
130 Shock absorber
131 Pitch dampers
132 Four-wheel main undercarriage
133 Bogie beam
134 Torque links
135 Intake boundary layer splitter
136 Honeycomb intake nose section
137 Spraymat intake lip de-icing
138 Ramp motor and gearbox
139 Forward ramp
140 Aft ramp
141 Inlet flap

142 Spill door actuator
143 Intake duct
144 Tank vent gallery
145 Engine front support links
146 Engine-mounting transverse equalizers
147 Oil tank
148 Primary heat exchanger
149 Secondary heat exchanger
150 Heat-exchanger exhaust air
151 Rolls-Royce/SNECMA Olympus 593 Mk 610 turbojet
152 Outer wing fixing (340 high-tensile steel bolts)
153 Engine main mounting
154 Power control unit mounting
155 No. 5a fuel tank
156 Tank vent
157 Transfer pump
158 Port outer elevon control unit fairing
159 Static dischargers
160 Honeycomb elevon structure
161 Flexible joint

162 Port middle elevon control hinge/fairing
163 Power control unit twin output
164 Control rod linkage
165 Nacelle aft support link
166 Reverse-bucket actuating screw jack
167 Retractable silencer lobes ('spades')
168 Primary (inner) variable nozzle
169 Pneumatic nozzle actuators
170 Nozzle-mounting spigots
171 Port inner elevon control hinge/fairing
172 Control rod linkage
173 Location of ram-air turbine (RAT) in production aircraft
174 Accumulator
175 Vent and pressurisation system

Singapore Airlines were an enthusiastic potential partner on the British Airways far eastern route, and for a time some Concordes were painted in Singapore colours on one side of the fuselage. But, once again, overflying rights became a drag on the costs and benefits of the operation and Singapore was forced to withdraw.

of supersonic cruise the contents of the rear trim tank are pumped forward into the front trim and main tanks.

Ruling structural material is an aluminium alloy developed in the UK as RR.58 and produced in France under the designation AU2GN. The engines, however, are almost entirely of ferrous alloys, titanium alloys, Waspaloy or high-nickel alloys, and they are fed by extremely large ducts leading from fully variable sharp-edged inlets with electric anti-icing, and with front and rear variable upper wall ramps and controllable doors in the underside through which air can be admitted or expelled. In the course of development the engine was further increased in power, given a new jetpipe combining afterburner, variable nozzle and reverser, and also vaporizing combustors which eliminated visible

176 Forged wing/fuselage main frames
177 Ground-supply air-conditioning connection
178 Control mixing unit
179 Control rod (elevon) linkage
180 Aft galley unit
181 Rear emergency doors (port and starboard)
182 Wingroot fillet

183 Air-conditioning manual discharge valve
184 Automatic discharge/relief valve
185 First-aid oxygen cylinders
186 Rear baggage compartment (door to starboard)
187 Rear pressure bulkhead
188 Fin support frames

189 No. 11 aft trim tank
190 Machined centre posts
191 Shock absorber
192 Retractable tail bumper
193 Tail bumper door
194 Tank overflow and pressure relief lines
195 Tail cone bulkhead

196 Fuel jettison
197 Monergol-powered emergency power unit (pre-production aircraft only)
198 Tail cone
199 Rear navigation light
200 Rudder lower section
201 Servo control unit fairing (manual stand-by)
202 Fixed rubber stub
203 Multi-bolt fin-spar attachment
204 Fin construction
205 Fin spar
206 Air-conditioning ducting
207 HF antennae
208 Finroot fairing
209 Leading-edge structure
210 Servo unit threshold bellcrank
211 Servo control unit fairing
212 VOR antenna
213 Rudder upper section
214 Static dischargers

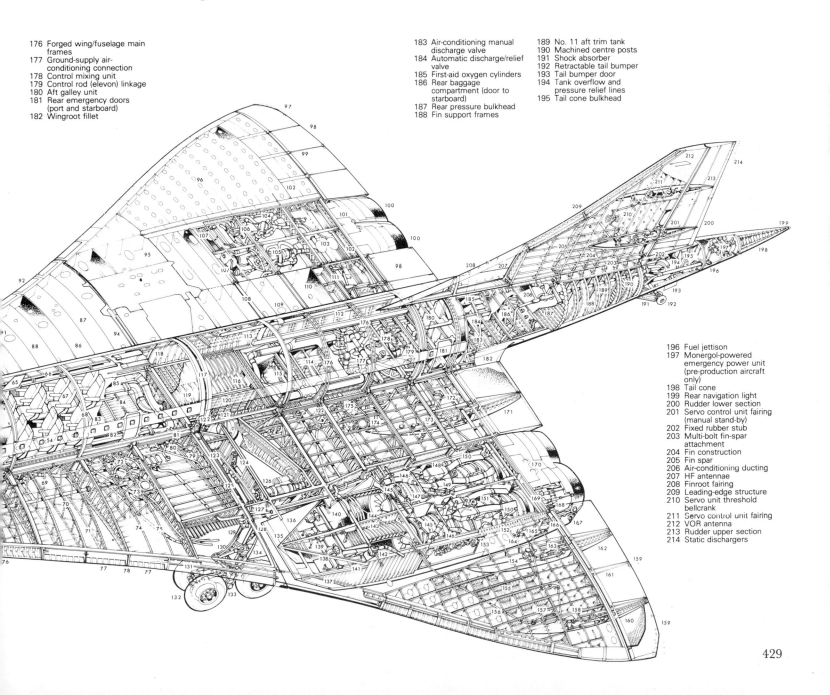

smoke. The four-wheel main gears fold inward and have Dunlop carbon/carbon brakes, the first service application of such brakes in the world and indicative of the unprecedented severity of the rejected take-off of the fully loaded aircraft. There is no braking parachute or airbrake, and leading edges are fixed. Systems, however, are advanced and complex, though the hydraulic pressure had been used on the Bristol Britannia. The system marking the biggest jump in complexity was undoubtedly the engine inlets, followed by environmental control, with the high cabin pressure-differential of 10.7 lb/sq in (0.75 kg/cm^2) and the fuel used as a heat-sink.

By 1966 major pieces of structure were on thermal/fatigue test, the engine was running with its variable exhaust system and the main flight simulator was in use. Prototype 001 was rolled out at Toulouse on 11 December 1967, but it was the following August before it taxied and the first flight was delayed until 2 March 1969, the pilot being André Turcat. No. 002 flew in command of Brian Trubshaw from Filton a month later. Airline pilots first flew the prototypes in November 1969, and from the first there were no major problems connected with the aircraft. The problems stemmed from protesters, who considered SST a menace to the environment (apparently on the grounds mainly of noise), and from soaring increase in development cost, half of which was the result of the childishly low initial estimate, which made no allowance for the progressive increases in size and capability of the aircraft, and half of inflation, for which no allowance at all had been made.

Contracts signed

By 1971 the prototypes were making long overseas trips, and in December that year the first pre-production aircraft, with visibly different vizor, longer forward fuselage and extended tail, made its first flight from Filton to the UK test base at Fairford. On 28 July 1972 British Airways signed with BAC for five aircraft and Air France signed with Aérospatiale for four. There had previously been options by PanAm and purchase agreements by China, but these were never taken up. Prototype 001 was retired to a museum at Le Bourget in October 1973, two months before the first flight by the first production aircraft. By 1975 there was hardly a major city that had not been visited by at least one Concorde, and very intensive route proving was showing a remarkable reliability even at this early date. Scheduled services began on 21 January 1976, British Airways flying London–Bahrain with aircraft 206 and Air France flying Paris–Dakar–Rio with 205. Services to Washington were begun by both airlines on 24 May 1976. Prototype 002 was retired to Yeovilton on 4 March 1976 and 01 to Duxford on 20 August 1977. Category III autoland was cleared in passenger operation on 1 September 1978.

Though passenger operations could not have been more successful, both in terms of passenger appeal and reliability

(to the extent that in 1981 Concorde was several times the most punctual type in British Airways service according to the monthly report to the airline board, averaging 94 per cent), political troubles and rising fuel costs crippled the global plans for using the aircraft properly and had by late 1982 reduced utilization to an extremely low figure. A joint British Airways/Braniff service from Washington on to Dallas was suspended in June 1980, and the British Airways service to Singapore followed five months later. In April 1982 Air France discontinued services to Caracas and Rio, and by summer 1982 the only scheduled services were (British Airways) twice daily to New York and thrice weekly to Washington, and (Air France) 11 a week to New York, to which two continue to Washington and two to Mexico City. A small amount of additional flying is made up by charters to business companies and enthusiast groups.

Certainly the main traffic routes are transAtlantic, and so far they have brought British Airways some 495,000 passengers and Air France about 360,000, out of a total of just over a million. The aircraft has sustained reliability in excess of 93 per cent on sectors up to 4,000 miles (6440 km) in length, total service flight time being over 67,000 hours on more than 20,000 scheduled departures. Small changes, for example to the inlet lips and rudder trailing edge, have had a significant good effect on operating economics, but profitability remains marginal. Both airlines have announced they believe they are entering an era of Concorde profitability. Indeed British Airways has been looking at ways to increase Concorde operations, including running a cargo service in partnership with Federal Express, opening passenger service to Miami and a nonstop route to Lagos, Nigeria.

At government level, a great deal has been done to minimize the costs of research projects, which are only really necessary if a new generation of Concordes is envisaged. In May 1982 the then British Trade and Industry Minister, Norman Lamont, held formal talks with the French Transport Minister, Charles Fitermann, to carry out a detailed review of the whole project. But even before this, it was established that giving up the project would cost more money than it would save. The discussions centred around the question whether it would be possible to spread the remaining costs more equitably. Although both British Aerospace and Aérospatiale envisage a new generation with an improved lift/drag ratio of 10 compared with the present Concorde's 7, as well as further improving the engines, there is little chance that these proposals will ever come to fruition. In the current environment, there is no long-term future for supersonic airliners.

Air France's routes to South America looked promising with little but the Sahara desert and the Atlantic Ocean to overfly. But crippling fuel costs ruined the route despite the exceptional appeal and reliability of the service. Air France now flies Concorde only to New York, Washington and Mexico City.

McDonnell Douglas F-15 Eagle

Spawned by the long-range air combat requirements of the Vietnam War, and proved by the Israelis in dogfights and strike escort missions, the McDonnell Douglas F-15 is without doubt the world's finest all-weather day/night air superiority fighter.

Although everyone hopes it will never happen, if there were military conflict between the two superpowers, the Soviet side would outnumber the Americans both on the ground and in the air. To win a conventional war, as demonstrated in the final stages of World War 2 against Germany and Japan, and in Korea at the beginning of the 1950s, the Americans would need air superiority. As today's fighting forces have to operate in almost every conceivable situation, this air superiority would have to apply to night-time flying and to every possible type of weather. In the Western world there is only one aircraft type that is superior to the best of the Soviet Union's military aircraft, even when outnumbered by the other side. This is the McDonnell Douglas F-15 Eagle.

It is an essential part of USAF doctrine that the first and highest priority of tactical air forces is to achieve air superiority, denying the opposing force the effective use of air space, while simultaneously accomplishing their own missions. In Korea, air superiority was evidenced by a kill ratio of better than 10:1 in favour of the North American F-86 Sabre, which shot down 810 enemy aircraft for 78 F-86s lost in the air. A crucial factor in this success was that the F-86 had bases reasonably close to the combat area: Suwon was only 270 miles (430 km) from where the MiGs patrolled, and Kimpo was even closer. At one stage (January 1951) the F-86s were forced to withdraw to Johnson AFB in Japan, which took them out of reach of the Korean action.

An F-15A of the 49th Tactical Fighter Wing, based at Holloman AFB, New Mexico. Note the massive dorsal airbrake, which has given rise to some criticism regarding its effect on rear view in combat. This photograph also illustrates the excellent all-round view that the canopy provides, and the wide spacing of the fins.

An F-15A of the 1st Tactical Fighter Wing (based at Langley AFB, Virginia) flying over the base, which is also the headquarters of Tactical Air Command, whose badge is painted on the fin. The 1st TFW is now part of the United States Rapid Deployment Joint Task Force, which would deploy to the Middle East in emergency.

No substitute for piston engines

Jet fighters were thus not true replacements for the long-range piston-engined fighters of World War 2, such as the North American P-51 Mustang, Republic P-47 Thunderbolt and Lockheed P-38 Lightning. This point was driven home in the 1960s, when the USAF attempted to win control of the air over North Vietnam. Some degree of control was eventually won, but at times the monthly kill ratio favoured the enemy's Mikoyan-Gurevich MiG-17s and MiG-21s, and the USAF prevailed only by the extensive use of inflight refuelling for its fighters.

It appears to be common practice after a war for air forces to decide that aerial dogfights are a thing of the past. Fighter speeds progress, and the air staffs judge that close combat is no longer possible: the opposing aircraft will be moving too fast to see one another or to manoeuvre to maintain contact, and (in any case) the pilots will be subjected to crushing g-loads. Whether for these or other reasons, the idea of an air superiority fighter was largely abandoned by the USAF after Korea. The service took little interest in the Lockheed F-104 Starfighter, funding instead nuclear strike aircraft such as the Republic F-105 and General Dynamics F-111, and all-weather interceptors such as the Convair F-102 and F-106.

The commitment of USAF aircraft to the Vietnam war in 1962 thus found the service with only a handful of F-104Cs

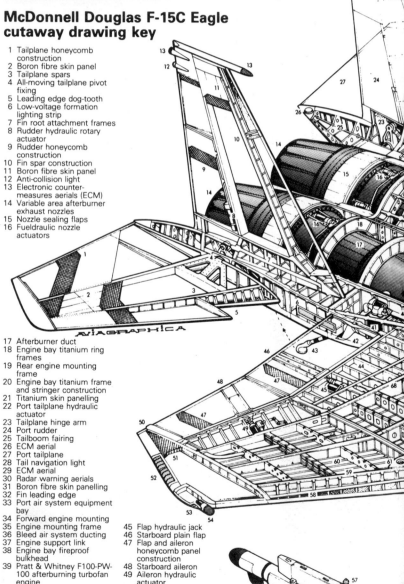

McDonnell Douglas F-15C Eagle cutaway drawing key

1 Tailplane honeycomb construction
2 Boron fibre skin panel
3 Tailplane spars
4 All-moving tailplane pivot fixing
5 Leading edge dog-tooth
6 Low-voltage formation lighting strip
7 Fin root attachment frames
8 Rudder hydraulic rotary actuator
9 Rudder honeycomb construction
10 Fin spar construction
11 Boron fibre skin panel
12 Anti-collision light
13 Electronic counter-measures aerials (ECM)
14 Variable area afterburner exhaust nozzles
15 Nozzle sealing flaps
16 Fueldraulic nozzle actuators
17 Afterburner duct
18 Engine bay titanium ring frames
19 Rear engine mounting frame
20 Engine bay titanium frame and stringer construction
21 Titanium skin panelling
22 Port tailplane hydraulic actuator
23 Tailplane hinge arm
24 Port rudder
25 Tailboom fairing
26 ECM aerial
27 Port tailplane
28 Tail navigation light
29 ECM aerial
30 Radar warning aerials
31 Boron fibre skin panelling
32 Fin leading edge
33 Port air system equipment bay
34 Forward engine mounting
35 Engine mounting frame
36 Bleed air system ducting
37 Engine support link
38 Engine bay fireproof bulkhead
39 Pratt & Whitney F100-PW-100 afterburning turbofan engine
40 Starboard air system equipment bay
41 Engine bleed air primary heat exchanger
42 Heat exchanger ventral exhaust duct
43 Retractable runway arrester hook
44 Wing trailing edge fuel tank
45 Flap hydraulic jack
46 Starboard plain flap
47 Flap and aileron honeycomb panel construction
48 Starboard aileron
49 Aileron hydraulic actuator
50 Fuel jettison pipe
51 Aluminium honeycomb wing tip fairing
52 Low-voltage formation lighting
53 Starboard navigation light
54 ECM aerial
55 Westinghouse ECM equipment pod

The first prototype of the F-15A Eagle was rolled out at St Louis in June 1972, and made its first flight on 27 July, being joined in the flight test programme by the first two-seat F-15B on 7 July 1973. Note the nose boom for test instrumentation (including yaw and angle of attack vanes), which was deleted on the production aircraft.

McDonnell Douglas F-15 Eagle

This F-15B or -15D lacks any national insignia, and appears to have been used for tests of a new camouflage scheme, reminiscent of the schemes that were applied to battleships during World War 1. This type of camouflage clearly breaks up the basic shape of the aircraft, and may be effective on the ground.

56 Outboard wing stores pylon
57 Pylon attachment spigot
58 Cambered leading edge ribs
59 Front spar
60 Machined wing skin/stringer panels
61 Outboard pylon fixing
62 HF flush aerial
63 Leading edge fuel tank
64 Inboard pylon fixing
65 Wing rib construction
66 Starboard wing integral fuel tank, total internal fuel load, 13,455-lb (6103-kg)
67 Wing root rib support struts
68 Titanium wing spars
69 Wing spar/fuselage attachment pin joints
70 Machined fuselage main bulkheads

71 Wing/fuselage fuel tank interconnections
72 Airframe mounted engine accessory gearbox
73 Standby hydraulic generator
74 Jet fuel starter (JFS)/auxiliary power unit (APU)
75 Engine intake compressor face
76 Cooling system intake bleed air spill duct
77 Port wing trailing edge fuel tank
78 Port plain flap
79 Flap hydraulic jack
80 Aileron control rod
81 Aileron hydraulic actuator
82 Port aileron

83 Fuel jettison pipe
84 Wing tip fairing
85 Low-voltage formation lighting
86 Port navigation light
87 ECM aerial
88 Cambered leading edge
89 Outboard pylon fixing
90 Port wing internal fuel tank
91 Fuel system piping
92 Inboard pylon fixing
93 Leading edge fuel tank
94 Anti-collision light
95 Boom-type air refuelling receptacle
96 Bleed air duct to air conditioning plant
97 Control rod runs

98 Dorsal airbrake, open
99 Airbrake glass-fibre honeycomb construction
100 Airbrake hydraulic jack
101 Centre fuselage fuel tanks
102 Intake ducting
103 Ammunition feed chute
104 M61A-1 Vulcan 20-mm cannon
105 Hydraulic rotary cannon drive unit
106 Starboard anti-collision light
107 Ventral main undercarriage wheel bay
108 Main undercarriage leg strut
109 Starboard mainwheel
110 Inboard stores pylon
111 Air-to-air missile adaptor
112 Bomb rack
113 Mk 82 low drag 500-lb (227-kg) HE bombs
114 Bomb triple ejector rack
115 Missile launch rail
116 AIM-9L Sidewinder air-to-air missile
117 AIM-7F Sparrow air-to-air missile

118 Sparrow missile launcher unit
119 Cannon muzzle aperture
120 Cannon barrels
121 Central ammunition drum 940-rounds
122 Airbrake hinges
123 Forward fuselage fuel tanks
124 UHF aerial
125 Intake duct bleed air louvres
126 Intake by-pass air spill duct
127 Variable area intake ramp hydraulic actuator
128 Air conditioning system cooling air exhaust duct
129 Canopy hinge point
130 Air conditioning plant
131 Intake incidence control jack
132 Intake duct variable area ramp doors
133 Intake pivot fixing
134 Starboard engine air intake
135 Nosewheel leg door
136 Nose undercarriage leg strut
137 Nosewheel
138 Landing/taxiing lamps
139 Nosewheel retraction strut

140 Rear underfloor equipment bay
141 Tactical electronic warfare system (TEWS) racks
142 Cockpit coaming
143 Rear pressure bulkhead
144 Canopy jack
145 Cockpit pressurization valves
146 Structural space provision for second crew member (F-15D)
147 Cockpit aft decking
148 Canopy arch
149 Port intake external compression lip
150 Fuel and sensor tactical (FAST) pack, conformal fuel pallet, capacity 5,000-lb (2268-kg)
151 600-US gal (2270-litre) external fuel tank
152 Cockpit canopy cover
153 Ejection seat headrest
154 Seat safety handle/arming lever
155 Canopy emergency jettison linkage
156 Ejection seat launch rails
157 Safety harness
158 McDonnell-Douglas ACES II 'zero-zero' ejection seat
159 Cockpit sloping bulkhead
160 Pilot's side console panel
161 Air conditioning ducting
162 Forward underfloor equipment bay, built-in test equipment (BITE) and liquid oxygen converter

163 Low-voltage formation lighting strip
164 Port side retractable boarding ladder
165 TACAN aerial
166 Angle of attack probe
167 Rudder pedals
168 Control column
169 Pilot's head-up display (HUD)
170 Instrument panel shroud
171 Frameless windscreen panel
172 ADF sense aerial
173 Radio and electronics equipment bay, port and starboard
174 Cockpit front pressure bulkhead

175 Pitot tube
176 UHF aerial
177 Radar mounting bulkhead
178 Radome hinge mounting
179 ILS aerial
180 Radar scanner mounting and tracking mechanism
181 Huges APG-63 pulse doppler radar scanner
182 Scanner mounted IFF aerial array
183 Glass-fibre radome

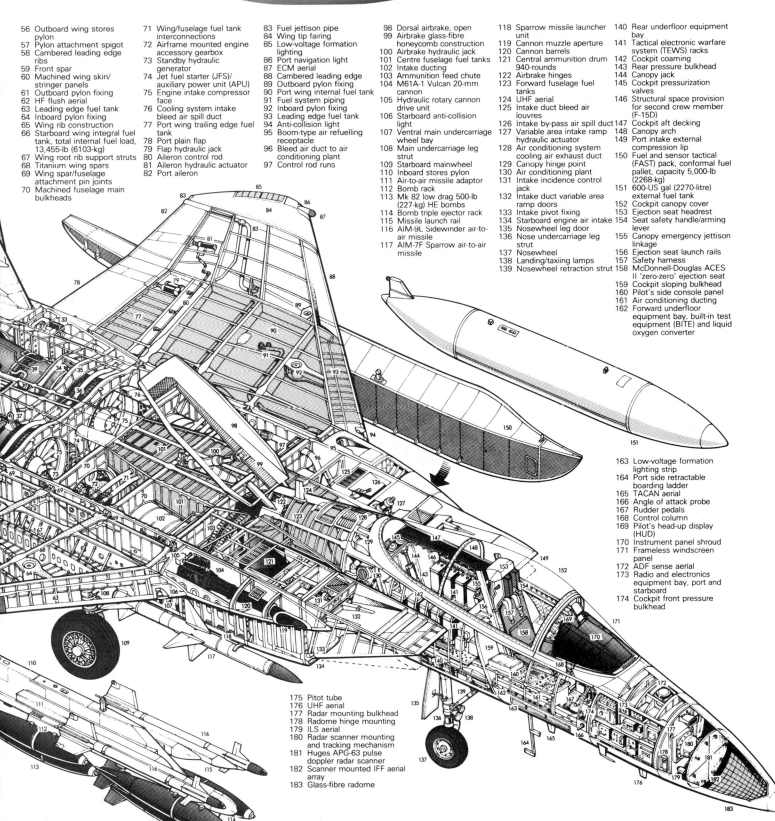

McDonnell Douglas
F-15A Eagle

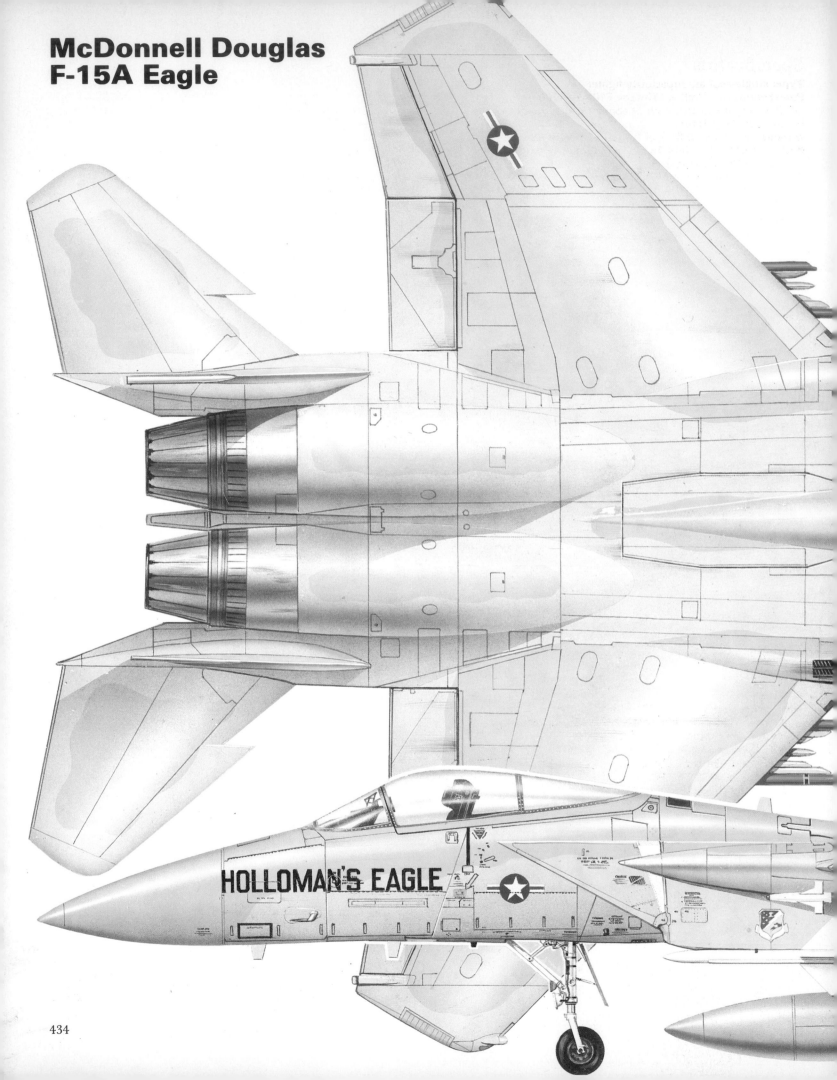

HOLLOMAN'S EAGLE

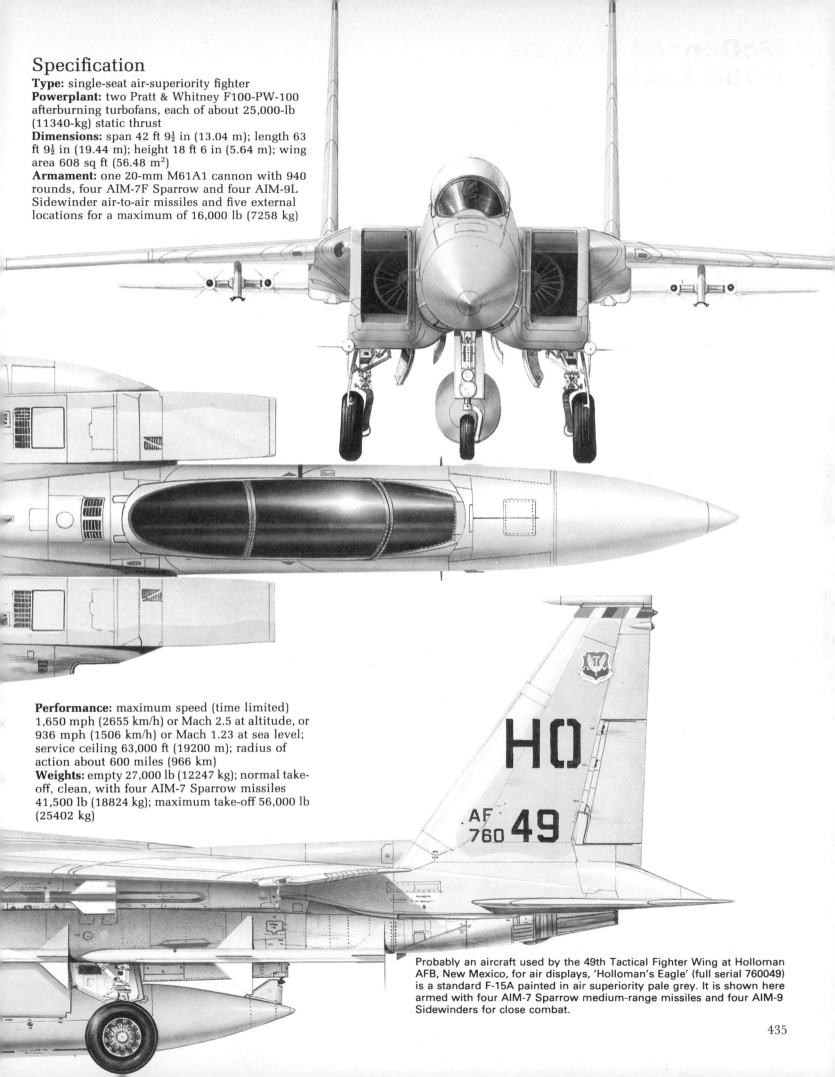

Specification

Type: single-seat air-superiority fighter
Powerplant: two Pratt & Whitney F100-PW-100 afterburning turbofans, each of about 25,000-lb (11340-kg) static thrust
Dimensions: span 42 ft 9½ in (13.04 m); length 63 ft 9½ in (19.44 m); height 18 ft 6 in (5.64 m); wing area 608 sq ft (56.48 m²)
Armament: one 20-mm M61A1 cannon with 940 rounds, four AIM-7F Sparrow and four AIM-9L Sidewinder air-to-air missiles and five external locations for a maximum of 16,000 lb (7258 kg)

Performance: maximum speed (time limited) 1,650 mph (2655 km/h) or Mach 2.5 at altitude, or 936 mph (1506 km/h) or Mach 1.23 at sea level; service ceiling 63,000 ft (19200 m); radius of action about 600 miles (966 km)
Weights: empty 27,000 lb (12247 kg); normal take-off, clean, with four AIM-7 Sparrow missiles 41,500 lb (18824 kg); maximum take-off 56,000 lb (25402 kg)

Probably an aircraft used by the 49th Tactical Fighter Wing at Holloman AFB, New Mexico, for air displays, 'Holloman's Eagle' (full serial 760049) is a standard F-15A painted in air superiority pale grey. It is shown here armed with four AIM-7 Sparrow medium-range missiles and four AIM-9 Sidewinders for close combat.

An F-15 being refuelled by a KC-135, the simple vee-form of the boom controls indicating that the tanker is not the more advanced KC-10. The refuelling receptacle of the F-15 is set in the port intake fairing, opposite the M61 cannon on the starboard side. It will be seen from the shadow that contact has not yet been made.

in the air-superiority category. This was initially of no great consequence, since it was a counter-insurgency war with no opposing aircraft, but when bombing missions were scheduled against North Vietnam late in 1964, the gap in the inventory gave rise to serious problems.

Following unsuccessful trials with various types of fighter (including the F-102 and F-104) in the air-superiority role, the USAF was forced to adopt the US Navy's McDonnell F-4 Phantom all-weather interceptor. This was first (F-4D) fitted with an external gunpod (the F-4's missile armament having limited value in a dogfight, especially in terms of g-capability and combat persistence), and later was given a nose cannon and leading-edge manoeuvring flaps. The resulting F-4E entered service in October 1967, and proved invaluable both for MiGCAP (MiG combat air patrol) duties and as a bomb-carrier.

However, the radius of action needed in Vietnam was far greater than that required in Korea, and the problem was compounded by the new fighter generation's fuel-guzzling afterburning engines. Missions to Hanoi and Haiphong had to be flown from remote, secure bases in South Vietnam and Thailand, over a radius of 400 miles (640 km) or more. Although the Phantom was designed for relatively long range and endurance, the only way that adequate combat time could be achieved at such distances was by inflight refuelling, which was generally used both into and out of the target.

Lavish use of aerial tankers (Boeing KC-135s) allowed the F-4E to protect USAF strike aircraft and go hunting for MiGs, but it was blindingly clear that in a 'hotter' scenario the tankers would not enjoy such a permissive operating environment, and that many more of them would be needed to support the strategic bombers, rather than tactical fighters. What was required was a new class of fighter that could beat anything the Russians put in the air, yet would have sufficient range and combat persistence significantly to reduce demands on tanker support.

In 1965 the USAF requested funding for feasibility studies of a new air-superiority fighter, designated F-X, and in due course an RFP (Request For Proposals) was issued in September 1968. The finalists in the competition were Fairchild-Republic, North American Rockwell, and the McDonnell Aircraft (McAir) division of the McDonnell Douglas Corporation (MDC). In December 1969 McAir was selected to proceed with the development of the F-15 under

the direction of Air Force Systems Command, with formal authorization in January 1970. This was the first completely new fighter developed specifically for the USAF since the F-101 Voodoo, also a McAir product, which first flew on 29 September 1954.

The initial contract covered the manufacture of 20 pre-series aircraft: 18 single-seat F-15As and two TF-15A (later redesignated F-15B) tandem-seat trainers. The F-X requirement had called for a single-seat, twin-engined aircraft to perform the fighter sweep, escort and CAP missions. Preliminary details suggested that the F-15 would be twice as good as the F-4E in rate of climb and acceleration.

To achieve this breakthorough in performance, the F-15 was given a relatively low wing loading and a thrust/weight ratio in excess of unity, the first time so much power had been installed in a non-V/STOL fighter. In broad terms, it would have a clean weight of 40,000 lb (18144 kg), and a total thrust of 50,000 lb (22680 kg). In terms of level flight speed, this thrust would give a sea-level capability of about Mach 1.2, a sustained level speed of Mach 2.2 at altitude, and a dash speed in excess of Mach 2.5.

The installation of so much thrust was possible by virtue of a new generation of engines, with a thrust/weight ratio of around 8:1, giving so light a powerplant weight that there was still plenty of scope for internal fuel. The engine chosen was the Pratt & Whitney F100 afterburning turbofan, selected in February 1970. A few months later the Hughes APG-63 radar was chosen, giving an all-aspect, look-down, shoot-down capability in combination with AIM-7F Sparrow and AIM-9L Sidewinder missiles.

First flight

The F-15 was also to have had the Philco-Ford GAU-7A 25-mm Gatling gun with caseless ammunition. In this concept the projectile is bonded to a solid block of propellant, to eliminate the weight of the normal case and the time needed to extract it after firing.

The Strike Eagle (serial 71291) in ground attack configuration, with clusters of Mk 82 bombs on wing pylons and on the conformal fuel tanks mounted on the sides of the fuselage, and Sidewinders on the sides of the wing pylons. Strike Eagle is a private venture by McDonnell Douglas.

An F-15A in USAF air superiority grey, the LA on the fin designating that it belongs to the 58th Tactical Fighter Training Wing at Luke AFB, Arizona. The badge on the fin is that of Tactical Air Command, and that on the side of the air intake is that of the unit. The F-15A is externally identical to the F-15C.

An F-15A of the Israeli air force. Both single- and two-seat Eagles were supplied to Israel from 1976 under the Peace Fox programme. The number exported were 51 and the F-15s fly with No. 133 Sqn. Saudi Arabia took 62 F-15Cs and 15 F-15Ds.

Unfortunately, development problems with the gun and its revolutionary ammunition led to its cancellation, and the F-15 reverted to the well-proven General Electric M61 Vulcan gun that arms most American fighters.

The first F-15A was formally rolled out in June 1972, and had its maiden flight on 27 July, being followed by the first two-seater on 7 July 1973. Funding for the first 30 production aircraft was released late in 1973, and for a further 77 aircraft (to complete the first wing) a year later. The first of 729 production F-15s then planned (one in seven being a two-seater) left the ground on 25 November 1974. Initial operational capability was declared in July 1975, following delivery of the 24th aircraft. The first wing was fully equipped by the end of 1976.

Having got the F-15 into service, this may be a convenient point to describe the aircraft that McAir had produced. In several respects the F-15 bears a strong family resemblance to the preceding F-4, despite being a completely new design. The highly tapered, moderately swept wing is broadly in line with F-4 practice, although it is set high on the fuselage and avoids the need for the steep outboard dihedral of its predecessor. A better clue to the F-15's ancestry comes from the semi-recessed Sparrow missiles and the way the jetpipes are cut short, with the tail mounted well aft. In the case of the F-4, there is a single fin mounted on what is effectively a vestigial fuselage or tail boom. for the F-15, the use of Vigilante-style intakes necessitated the use of twin vertical tails to avoid the destabilizing airflow from the flat upper surface of the cowlings, so the aircraft has been given twin tail-booms on either side of the afterburners, with half the vertical tail and half the tailplane mounted on each.

One of the most important considerations in the design of the F-15 was operation at high angles of attack (AOA). This led to the choice of horizontal-ramp two-dimensional intakes, rather than the vertical ramps used on the F-4. A feature unique to the F-15 is that the intakes are hinged about the lower lip, and rotated downward as AOA increases, which minimizes spillage drag and its adverse effect on the vertical tails. Another important consideration was all-round view: the F-15 provided the best rear view of any fighter since the F-86, with the pilot seated high in a bubble canopy. Combat effectiveness also benefits from the use of an advanced head-up display (HUD) and the fact that most of the control functions needed in combat can be carried out without the pilot removing his hands from the control column and throttles. This HOTAS (hands-on-throttle-and-stick) system has controls for radar and missiles, gun, airbrake, microphone button and weapons release.

The F-15 airframe is relatively conventional in construction, but the rear fuselage is largely built of titanium, which makes up 26.5 per cent of structure weight. Graphite composites are used in the airbrake and the tail surfaces, but represent only 1.0 per cent of the structure. Dash speeds of more than Mach 2.5 are permitted, as are indicated airspeeds of 936 mph (1506 km/h), and load factors of +9g and −3g. The aircraft has been flown to an AOA of +120° and −60°. In air-superiority configuration, the F-15 takes off in 900 ft (275 m) and lands in 2,500 ft (760 m).

Perhaps the most dramatic demonstration of the aircraft's performance was the USAF 'Strike Eagle' project of early 1975, in which an F-15 set new record times to eight altitudes, beating figures previously set by the F-4 for the lower five and the Soviet Union's E-266 (MiG-25 'Foxbat') for the upper three heights. The new times were: 27.57 sec to 9,845 ft (3000 m) 39.33 sec to 19,685 ft (6000 m), 48.86 sec to 29,530 ft (9000 m), 59.38 sec to 39,370 ft (12000 m), 77.04 sec to 49,215 ft (15000 m), 122.94 sec to 65,615 ft (20000 m), 161.02 sec to 82,020 ft (25000 m) and 207.8 sec to 98,425 ft (30000 m).

The F-15 thus made its mark even before the first unit was fully equipped. In 1986 the USAF had nine F-15 squadrons in the continental USA, four in Europe, and three in the Pacific. Aside from the 57th Tactical Training Wing (tail code WA) at Nellis AFB, Nevada and the 58th TTW at Luke AFB, Arizona (code LA), the F-15 equips the 1st Tactical Fighter Wing (code FF) at Langley AFB, Virginia, the 36th TFW (code BT) at Bitburg AB in Germany, the 49th TFW (code HO) at Holloman AFB, New Mexico, the 33rd TFW (code ED) at Eglin AFB, Florida, the 32nd Tactical Fighter Squadron (code CR) at Camp New Amsterdam in the Netherlands, and the 18th TFW at Kadena AB, Okinawa (code ZZ).

The USAF also had plans to buy a total of 240 additional F-15s to replace the F-106 in the air defence of the continental USA (CONUS). In July 1981 deliveries began to the 48th Fighter Interceptor Squadron at Langley.

Export customers

The F-15A and F-15B have also been sold to Israel under the 'Peace Fox' programme, which involved 51 aircraft, of which deliveries began in 1976. The F-15s are flown by No. 133 Sqn, apparently as escorts to strike and reconnaissance aircraft. They have been involved in several dogfights with Syrian MiG-21s and MiG-23s over Lebanon (with very satisfactory results), and escorted the F-16s making the strike against Iraq's Osirak nuclear powerplant on 7 June 1981, covering a radius of 600 miles (960 km).

On 26 February 1979 the first of the new F-15Cs took to the air, and deliveries began in the middle of 1980. This second single-seat model has its internal fuel increased from 11,635 lb (5278 kg) to 13,455 lb (6103 kg) under the PEP-2000 programme. The F-15C also has provision for FAST (Fuel And Sensor Tactical) packs on each side of the fuselage, each

giving an additional 5,000 lb (2268 kg) of fuel. With FAST packs in place and three 600-US gal (2271-litre) tanks on pylons, the F-15C's gross weight is increased to 66,700 lb (30255 kg). This gives an endurance of over five hours, and an unrefuelled ferry range of 3,080 miles (4957 km). The F-15C and the corresponding F-15D two-seater also have a programmable radar signal processor, giving a fourfold increase in computer capacity, and the ability to continue tracking one target while searching for others at the same time.

The Japanese Air Self-Defense Force (JASDF) acquired 88 F-15s to replace four squadrons of F-104Js and operate alongside six squadrons of F-4EJs, the latter apparently being tasked with the less difficult targets. Deliveries began in July 1980. This 'Peace Eagle' programme includes 12 F-15DJ two-seaters, which, like the first two F-15J single-seaters, will be built at St Louis by McAir. The remaining 86 F-15Js will be constructed by Mitsubishi Heavy Industries. The first F-15J, which is identical to the F-15C aside from some avionics changes, was handed over in July 1981, and the first operational squadron was activated at Nyutabaru AB in late 1982 or early 1983.

The third export customer for the F-15 is Saudi Arabia, which took 62 F-15Cs and 15 F-15Ds delivered between early 1982 and late 1984, with two further F-15Cs as attrition reserves. These aircraft replaced three BAe (BAC) Lightning squadrons based at Dharan, Taif and Khamis Mushayt. Their primary role is be air defence, but the Royal Saudi air force has also requested FAST packs, inflight refuelling provisions, multiple ejection racks (MERs), glide bombs and cluster bomb units (CBUs).

Eagle modifications

At the Farnborough Air Show in 1980 McAir displayed a modified F-15 termed Strike Eagle, a two-seater with FAST packs, provision for up to 12,000 lb (5443 kg) of external stores, and with its Hughes APG-63 modified to function

An F-15A of the 58th Tactical Fighter Training Wing, based at Luke AFB, Arizona. The 58th TFTW is the equivalent of an operational conversion unit in British terminology, and is composed of the 461st, 550th, and 551st Tactical Fighter Training Squadrons. Weapons training is performed by the 57th Tactical Training Wing.

as a synthetic aperture radar (SAR), giving extremely high resolution against ground targets, without loss of the normal air-to-air modes. It has been reported that with this modification the radar can distinguish between two points less than 10 ft (3 m) apart, from a range of 11 miles (18.5 km).

Deriving from the Strike Eagle demonstrations, the USAF is now to buy approximately 400 F-15E two-seaters for the all-weather ground-attack role. It is not known whether or not this new variant will have SAR, but it is expected to have some avionics changes, provisions for new types of weapon, and possibly a forward-looking infra-red (FLIR) sensor.

Other possible uses for the F-15 in the future are photo reconnaissance (with the RF-15 being used as a replacement for the FR-4E), and 'Wild Weasel', or defense suppression using non-heat-sensitive AGM-88A high-speed rockets (HARM) built by Texas Instruments. The F-15 is also currently being tested as a launch platform for Anti-Satellite Rockets (ASAT).

McDonnell Douglas F-15 Eagle variants

F-15A: Initial single-seat production version for USAF and Israeli Air Force, with internal fuel limited to 11,635 lb (5278 kg)

F-15B: Initial two-seat trainer version of F-15A, weighing approximately 800 lb (363 kg) more empty: overall dimensions unchanged but canopy shape revised to allow for second pilot

F-15C: Improved single-seater with 13,455 lb (6103 kg) of internal fuel, provision for FAST packs, and a programmable radar signal processor; ordered by USAF and Royal Saudi air force, and forms the basis for the F-15J

F-15D: two-seat equivalent of F-15C

F-15DJ: two-seater for Japan, based on F-15D

F-15E: two-seat operational aircraft for USAF with increased emphasis on ground attack; has larger HUD, higher capacity computer, improved equipment cooling, forward-looking infra-red (FLIR) and provision for Maverick and AMRAAM

F-15J: single-seater for Japan, based on F-15C, but with locally-developed electronic warfare equipment and GCI data-link; most of these aircraft to be built by Mitsubishi under licence

TF-15: original designation for F-15B; abandoned on 1 December 1977

Strike Eagle: McAir private-venture two-seater with all-weather ground attack capability based on synthetic aperture radar (modified APG-63)

Ascendant Airbus

The first wide-body twin-engined commercial aircraft to enter service, bringing new standards of quietness and fuel economy to regional routes around the world, the A300/310 family is outstanding proof of Europe's technological, industrial and financial capabilities, making Airbus Industrie the principal competitor to Boeing.

Since the first A300 made its maiden flight on 28 October 1972, Airbus Industrie has experienced a meteoric rise as one of the major manufacturers of large-capacity airliners, and has proved to be Boeing's most dangerous rival. This new form of joint venture, described in French law as a 'Groupement d'Interêt Economique', has attained its current share of the market by developing a totally new type of airliner used on a dense network of short and medium distance routes and combining financial benefits with reliability and safety.

What follows is the story of how a number of European companies combined their technological and industrial capabilities successfully to challenge the virtual monopoly of commercial transports enjoyed by US manufacturers throughout most of the post-war years.

Studies of wide-body airliners began on both sides of the Atlantic in the 1960s, with American manufacturers concentrating on larger, longer-range aircraft such as the four-engine Boeing 747, which flew in 1969, and the three-engine DC-10 and TriStar, which both flew in 1970. European manufacturers were meanwhile projecting smaller, short-range aircraft, and in 1965 French and West German manufacturers combined to establish a study group (Studiengruppe

Airbus). At that stage British European Airways was in the market for a 200-seater to replace the Vickers Vanguard and, in view of the impact of rising fuel prices on traffic growth in the 1970s, this would have been a very practical size of aircraft. However, the other major European airlines felt at that stage that a capacity of 250–300 seats would be more economical in terms of seat-mile costs, and was essential if aircraft movements at the main airports were to be controlled.

Competitive mix

An element of competition was introduced by the industrial groupings that developed. Sud-Aviation worked with Dassault on the Galion, while Hawker Siddeley Aviation combined efforts with Breguet and Nord-Aviation on the HBN-100, the latter eventually forming basis for the A300. The principal contractors for the three countries were to have been HSA, Sud-Aviation and Arbeitsgemeinschaft

Line-up of A300s at the flight test building at Toulouse. Garuda Indonesian Airways has ordered nine A300B4-200s, of which six have been delivered. Eastern Air Lines has two A300B2-200s and has received 23 of 32 A300B4s on order. Iberia has all six of its A300B4-100s, which, like Garuda's B4s, are Pratt & Whitney-powered.

Airbus Industrie A300

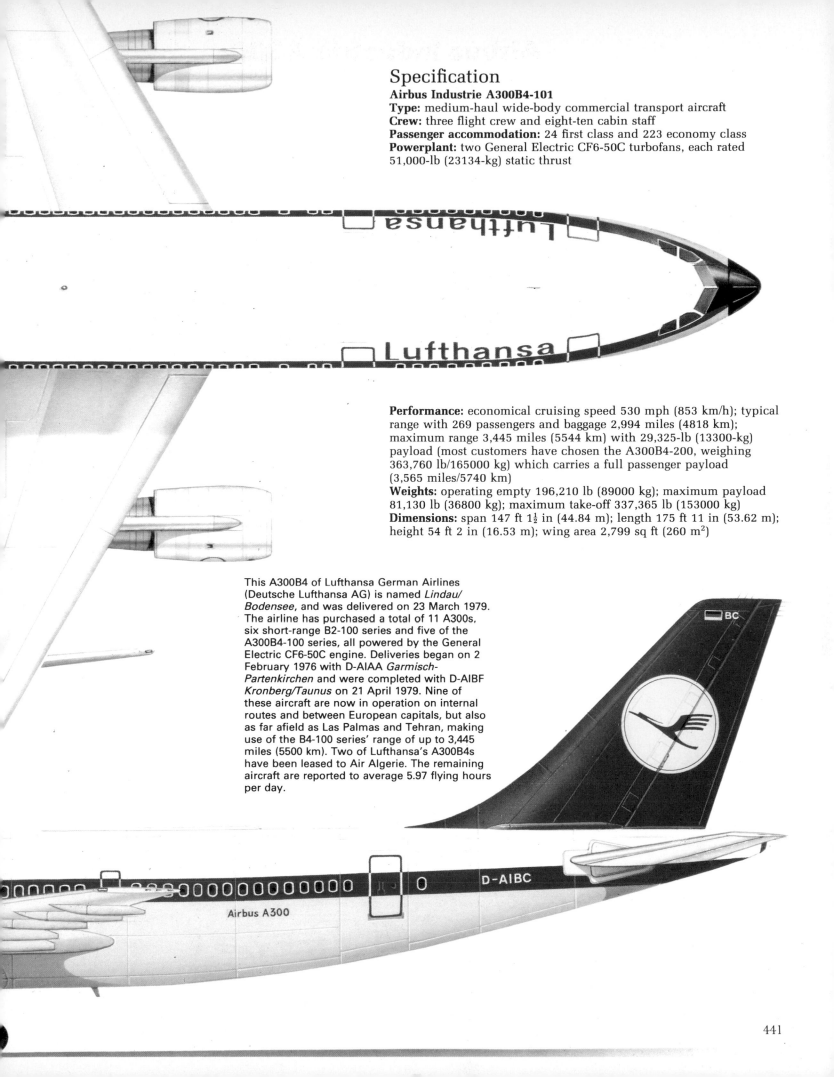

Specification
Airbus Industrie A300B4-101
Type: medium-haul wide-body commercial transport aircraft
Crew: three flight crew and eight-ten cabin staff
Passenger accommodation: 24 first class and 223 economy class
Powerplant: two General Electric CF6-50C turbofans, each rated 51,000-lb (23134-kg) static thrust

Performance: economical cruising speed 530 mph (853 km/h); typical range with 269 passengers and baggage 2,994 miles (4818 km); maximum range 3,445 miles (5544 km) with 29,325-lb (13300-kg) payload (most customers have chosen the A300B4-200, weighing 363,760 lb/165000 kg) which carries a full passenger payload (3,565 miles/5740 km)
Weights: operating empty 196,210 lb (89000 kg); maximum payload 81,130 lb (36800 kg); maximum take-off 337,365 lb (153000 kg)
Dimensions: span 147 ft 1½ in (44.84 m); length 175 ft 11 in (53.62 m); height 54 ft 2 in (16.53 m); wing area 2,799 sq ft (260 m²)

This A300B4 of Lufthansa German Airlines (Deutsche Lufthansa AG) is named *Lindau/Bodensee*, and was delivered on 23 March 1979. The airline has purchased a total of 11 A300s, six short-range B2-100 series and five of the A300B4-100 series, all powered by the General Electric CF6-50C engine. Deliveries began on 2 February 1976 with D-AIAA *Garmisch-Partenkirchen* and were completed with D-AIBF *Kronberg/Taunus* on 21 April 1979. Nine of these aircraft are now in operation on internal routes and between European capitals, but also as far afield as Las Palmas and Tehran, making use of the B4-100 series' range of up to 3,445 miles (5500 km). Two of Lufthansa's A300B4s have been leased to Air Algerie. The remaining aircraft are reported to average 5.97 flying hours per day.

The purchase of five A300B4-200s by Trans-Australia Airlines signalled a change in the country's two-airline policy of identical equipment for TAA and Ansett, the latter choosing the Boeing 767. TAA's A300s, the only wide-bodied airliners on Australia's domestic routes, link Brisbane, Sydney, Melbourne and Perth.

Airbus, which last in 1967 became Deutsche Airbus GmbH. The two engines were to have been Rolls-Royce RB.178-51s, later superseded by RB.207s. However, at that time the TriStar appeared to be moving ahead much more quickly and to have an assured future, so Rolls-Royce dropped development of the RB.207 to concentrate on the RB.211 for the Lockheed aircraft. (The engine was later found to require so much financial investment that Rolls-Royce had to be taken over by the British government.)

The UK role in what was to prove the most successsful European collaborative air transport venture of all time then suffered a further blow when the British government declined to join in funding development of the A300 because of lack of orders. Nevertheless, in May 1969 the French and German governments decided to go ahead, and construction of the first prototype A300B1 began in October of that year. The UK's only major part in the programme was that HSA acted as a subcontractor to Airbus Industrie, designing, developing and manufacturing the wings (although the leading and trailing edges were built by VFW-Fokker, later Fokker BV). This arrangement subsequently provided a great deal of 'tin-bashing' work for the UK, but the country's failure to seize the lead in the Airbus programme gave to France key areas such as the front fuselage, which was of far greater significance to equipment suppliers. The Airbus thus began on the basis of French and German funding, with Fokker-VFW of the Netherlands and CASA of Spain joining the industrial grouping, in December 1970/1971.

The aircraft that emerged was somewhat smaller than the 300-seater envisaged when the designation A300 had been chosen, hence the name A300 for the (approximate) 250-passenger redesign. The reason for this reduction in size was partly that potential customers had begun saying that the original concept would have had excessively high plane-mile costs, and partly that the high thrust of the RB.207 was no longer available. The A300B was designed so that in principle it could accept the General Electric CF6, or the Pratt & Whitney JT9D, or the RB.211, although all the initial aircraft used the CF6 in a standard McDonnell Douglas wingpod. Some later A300s have the JT9D, but in 1986 the RB.211 had not yet found an A300 launch customer.

Further co-operation

Airbus Industrie was formally constituted in December 1970 with Sud-Aviation and Deutsche Airbus as the principal industrial partners. As further countries joined in the programme, the work-split became more complex. Sud-Aviation (later part of Aérospatiale) was allocated the all-important nose fuselage, lower centre fuselage and engine

Airbus Industrie A310 cutaway drawing key

1 Radome
2 Weather radar scanner
3 Radar scanner mounting
4 VOR localizer aerial
5 Front pressure bulkhead
6 Windscreen panels
7 Windscreen wipers
8 Instrument panel shroud
9 Control column
10 Rudder pedals
11 Cockpit floor level
12 ILS aerial
13 Pitot tubes
14 Access ladder to lower deck
15 Captain's seat
16 Centre control pedestal
17 Opening side window panels
18 First Officer's seat
19 Overhead systems control panel
20 Maintenance side panel
21 Observer's seat
22 Folding fourth seat
23 Cockpit bulkhead
24 Air conditioning ducting
25 Crew wardrobe/locker
26 Nose undercarriage wheel bay
27 Hydraulic retraction jack
28 Taxiing lamp
29 Steering jacks
30 Nosewheel doors
31 Forward toilet
32 Wash hand basin
33 Galley
34 Starboard entry/service door
35 Door mounted escape chute
36 Cabin attendant's folding seat
37 Hand baggage locker/wardrobe
38 Port main entry door
39 Door latch
40 Door surround structure
41 Radio and electronics racks
42 Runway turn-off lights
43 Fuselage frame and stringer construction
44 Floor beam construction
45 Forward freight hold
46 Freight hold door
47 Cabin wall trim panels
48 VHF communications aerial
49 Overhead stowage bins
50 Curtained cabin divider
51 First-class passenger compartment, 18 seats
52 Air system ducting
53 Cabin window panels
54 Overhead baggage lockers
55 Galley unit
56 Air system circulation fan
57 Tourist-class seating, 193 seats
58 Air conditioning supply ducting
59 Water tank

442

One of eight A300B4-100s operated by Olympic Airways. Now entirely owned by the Greek government, Olympic was originally founded in 1957 by Aristotle Onassis, who bought TAE Greek National Airlines and thus gained a monopoly of internal routes and national designation for overseas services.

Airbus Industrie A300 and A310 variants

(Note: the following list deals only with the principal variants; the model number (A300) is followed by a function letter, B indicating basic passenger version, C convertible, and F freighter; the airframe designation number as set out below has its last two digits modified to show the type of powerplant, numbers 01 to 19 for General Electric engines, 20 to 39 for Pratt & Whitney engines, and 40 to 59 reserved for Rolls-Royce; it is followed by two digits indicating variations in design weights)

A300B1: designation allocated to the two prototype aircraft, of which only one is now flying (a/c SN2)
A300B2-100: initial production short-haul version with 'simple' wing leading edge, as used by Air France to introduce the series into regular service in May 1974
A300B2-200: similar to A300B2-100 series, but with wing-root leading-edge Krueger flaps (as developed for the A300B4 series) and with the A300B4's wheels and brakes, to give the aircraft the capability to operate from hot/high airfields (e.g. by South African Airways); examples of this series include the **A300B2-201** with CF6-50C and the **A300B2-220** with JT9D-59A engines
A300B2-300- similar to A300B2-200, but with increased zero-fuel and landing weights for improved payload and multi-stop flexibility; first operator was SAS
A300B2-600: based on A300B2-200, but stretched to provide two extra seat rows and space for two extra LD3 containers; it also has slightly uprated engines, the rear fuselage and tailplane of the A310, more composite materials, and slightly more range

A300B4-100: basic medium-haul version, with additional fuel tank in the centre wing box, slightly stronger structure, uprated wheels and brakes, and Krueger flaps at the wing leading-edge root, first operator was Germanair; this series includes the **A300B4-101** with CF6-50C and the **A300B4-120** with JT9D-59A engines
A300B4-200: similar to A300B4-100, but with increased take-off weight by virtue of strengthened wings, fuselage and landing gear, allowing a higher payload or a range up to 3,600 miles (5795 km) for transcontinental operations
A300B4-600: stretched version derived from A300B4-200, with modifications as for A300B2-600; first ordered by Saudi Arabian Airlines
A300C4: convertible freighter version with large upper-deck cargo door on port side of aircraft, a reinforced cabin floor, smoke detection system in the main cabin, and interior trim adaptable to the freighter role; first operated by Hapag-Lloyd
A300F4: all-freighter version similiar to A300C4, but with all passenger provisions removed and cabin windows blanked over
A310-200: short-fuselage derivative of A300, typically seating 237; has new, smaller and aerodynamically advanced wing, redesigned rear fuselage, two-man cockpit, and higher proportion of composite materials; sub-series include **A310-202** with CF6-80A1, **A310-221** with JT9D-7R4D1, and A310-241 with **RB.211-524D4** engines
A310-300: extended-range version with increased fuel capacity and higher take-off weight, and with fuel transfer between the main tanks and a tailplane tank to reduce trim drag
A310C: convertible freighter version

60 LD3 baggage container (eight in forward hold)
61 Slat drive shaft gearbox
62 Wing spar centre section carry-through
63 Ventral air conditioning packs (two)
64 Port overwing emergency exit door
65 Wing centre-box fuel tank, capacity 4,234 Imp gal (19250 litres)
66 Centre section floor beams
67 Wing spar attachment main frame
68 Fuselage centre section construction
69 Starboard overwing emergency exit door
70 Starboard wing inboard fuel tank, capacity 3,066 Imp gal (13937 litres)
71 Nacelle pylon
72 Starboard Pratt & Whitney JT9D engine nacelle
73 Alternative General Electric CF6-80A1 turbofan engine
74 Common nacelle pylon
75 Pylon attachment points
76 Pylon tail fairing
77 Pressure refuelling connections
78 Slat screw jacks
79 Screw jack drive shaft
80 Leading edge slat segments
81 Fuel tank divider rib
82 Fuel pumps
83 Outboard fuel tank, capacity 866 Imp gal (3938 litres)
84 Fuel system piping
85 Vent surge tank
86 Starboard navigation lights
87 Wing tip fairing
88 Tail navigation and strobe lights
89 Static discharge wicks
90 Fixed portion of trailing edge
91 Outboard spoilers
92 Spoiler hydraulic jacks
93 Flap screw jacks
94 Flap carriage mechanism
95 Outboard single-slotted Fowler-type flap
96 Fuel jettison pipe
97 Centre spoilers/airbrakes
98 Flap drive shaft
99 Aileron triplex hydraulic jacks
100 Starboard all-speed aileron
101 Inboard spoilers/lift dumpers
102 Inboard double slotted flap
103 Wing rear spar/fuselage main frame
104 Centre cabin air circulation fan
105 Pressure floor above wheel bay
106 Starboard main undercarriage, retracted position
107 Undercarriage door jack
108 Equipment bay walkway
109 Undercarriage bay pressure bulkhead
110 Flap drive motor
111 Eight-abreast tourist class seating
112 Fuselage frame and stringer construction
113 Rear freight hold door
114 LD3 baggage container (six in rear hold)
115 Freight hold bulkhead
116 Cabin floor panels
117 Seat attachments rails
118 Rear cabin air circulation fan
119 ADF aerials
120 Fuselage skin plating
121 Central overhead stowage bins
122 Ceiling lighting panels
123 Starboard rear entry door
124 Galley units
125 Fin root fairing
126 Fin attachment bolted joints
127 Fin spars
128 Starboard tailplane
129 Starboard elevator
130 Tailfin construction
131 Glass-fibre reinforced leading edge
132 Fin tip fairing
133 Static discharge wicks
134 Carbon fibre rudder skin panels
135 Honeycomb rudder construction

136 Rudder triplex hydraulic jacks
137 APU equipment bay
138 Garrett GTCP 331–250 auxiliary power unit
139 Tailcone fairing
140 APU exhaust duct
141 Port elevator construction
142 Elevator triplex hydraulic jacks
143 Static discharge wicks
144 Port tailplane construction
145 Leading edge nose ribs
146 Tailplane pivot fixing
147 Moving tailplane sealing plate
148 Tailplane centre section
149 Tailplane trim screw jack
150 Fin support structure
151 Rear pressure bulkhead
152 Rear toilet compartment
153 Cabin attendant's folding seat
154 Rear entry door
155 Cabin window panel
156 Eight-abreast rear cabin seating
157 Cabin side wall frames
158 Bulk cargo hold
159 Freight hold skin panelling
160 Wing trailing edge fillet
161 Port inboard double slotted flap
162 Spoiler/lift dumpers
163 Undercarriage side struts
164 Main undercarriage pivot fixing
165 Inboard flap track mechanism
166 Aileron triplex hydraulic jacks
167 Port all-speed aileron construction
168 Port spoiler/airbrakes
169 Flap down position
170 Flap guide rails
171 Fuel jettison pipe
172 Flap track fairings
173 Fixed portion of trailing edge
174 Static dischargers
175 Tail navigation and strobe lights
176 Wing tip fairing
177 Port navigation lights
178 Wing rear spar
179 Front spar
180 Port leading edge-slats
181 Slat screw jacks
182 Slat guide rails
183 Leading edge de-icing air piping
184 Telescopic de-icing air duct
185 Wing skin joint strap
186 Wing stringer construction
187 Port wing integral fuel tank bays
188 Wing rib construction
189 Main undercarriage leg strut
190 Hydraulic retraction jack
191 Port main undercarriage four-wheel bogie
192 Nacelle pylon attachment joint
193 Engine mounting pylon
194 Hot stream exhaust nozzle
195 Fan air exhaust duct
196 Reverser cascade, closed
197 Bleed air ducting
198 Pratt & Whitney JT9D-7R4D turbofan engine
199 Engine fan blades
200 Intake ducting
201 Detachable engine cowlings
202 Bleed air system pre-cooler
203 Inboard leading edge slat
204 Bleed air delivery ducting
205 Inner wing integral fuel tank
206 Leading edge wing root fairing
207 Wing root Krueger flap

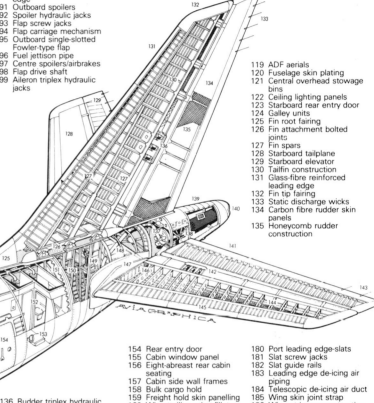

In 1986 only one of the three General Electric-powered A300B4-200s for Air Afrique had been delivered. Constituted in 1961 by agreement between 11 independent African states that were formerly French colonies, Air Afrique operates services linking 22 African countries to France, Italy, Switzerland and the USA.

One of three A300B4-100s currently operated by Philippine Airlines (PAL), which has two additional aircraft of the same type yet to be delivered. One of the older airlines in the Far East, PAL was formed in 1941, but soon had to terminate operations due to the war. The airline resumed its operations in February 1946.

pylons. Messerschmitt-Bölkow-Blohm (MBB) was given the rear fuselage, vertical tail, and upper centre fuselage, plus the flap guides. VFW-Fokker (more recently a subsidiary of MBB) builds the cylindrical fuselage section ahead of the wing. Fokker (as mentioned earlier) makes the wing leading and trailing edges, while HSA (now British Aerospace) was given responsibility for the main torsion box. CASA makes the horizontal tail and front fuselage door. Messier of France produces the landing gear. Both SNECMA in France and MTU in Germany make parts for the CF6 engine, which for the Airbus series is assembled by SNECMA. Major components of the A300 are flown between factories in Airbus Industrie's Super Guppies for assembly.

Behind the three-crew flight deck, the fuselage of 18 ft 6 in (5.64 m) diameter provides for six-abreast seating in first class, seven in business, eight in economy, or nine in charter, while the underfloor hold accommodates up to 20 LD3 containers in pairs abreast. All current models of the A300B take 220–345 seats, depending on cabin configuration, although 269 is typical of all-tourist (eight abreast) seating, and have a two-crew flight deck.

The wing is moderately swept, with a very advanced aerofoil section that permits a high cruise speed without significant compressibility effects, i.e. drag rise due to shock-induced separations. It is fitted with leading-edge flaps and two-slot Fowler trailing-edge flaps. Each wing has two ailerons, the inboard one functioning at all speeds and drooping in sympathy with the flaps, and the outboard one working only at low speeds. Four spoilers on each side act as airbrakes, and three as lift-dumpers. The flying controls are powered by triple hydraulic systems, with manual reversion. The landing gear has twin-wheel nose unit and four-wheel bogies on each main leg.

Reverting to the development history of the A300B, the first of two B1s (F-WUAB, later F-OCAZ) had its maiden flight on 28 October 1972, followed by the second (F-WUAC, now OO-TEF) on 5 February 1973. The first of the initial production series (F-WUAD the first A300B2 short-haul version) took to the air on 28 June 1973 and second A300B2 (F-WUAA) on 20 November 1973. The A300B2 was awarded Franco-German certification on 15 March 1973, and FAA certification on 30 May 1974. The A300B2 entered service with Air France on the Paris–London run on 23 May 1974.

Thus ended the first phase of the struggle to develop a major European commercial transport aircraft that could be sold successfully all over the world. However, some of the most difficult days for Airbus Industrie were yet to come. The critics who had claimed that the aircraft would be a technical flop now changed their argument to say that it would never be sold in economical numbers. In the mid-1970s sales were certainly slow to materialize (only one aircraft was sold in 1976). One of the keys to the success of Airbus was the launching of the A300B4 for medium-haul routes, a heavier version which offered a range of 3,000 miles (4825 km) and later 3,600-miles (5800 km) in comparison with the 1,845-mile (2970-km) range of the A300B2, all these figures relating to 269 passenger loads. Four of the A300B4s were taken by Eastern Air Lines on a six-month lease, beginning late in 1977. The following April, delighted with the results obtained with the A300B4s, Eastern bought them and ordered 25 more with options on a further nine. The acceptance of the aircraft by a major US operator was a turning point in sales of the A300B series and, although Airbus never succeeded in winning over other American airlines, orders started pouring in from the rest of the world, including certain areas (such as the Far East) that were enjoying a substantial growth in traffic. In 1978 Airbus (with 23 per cent of the market) was second only to Boeing in wide-body sales, and within three years had pushed Boeing out of the lead.

Efficiency, reliability and sales

As sales boomed, development continued on variants of the A300B theme. The A300C4 was produced as a convertible freighter version, which entered service with Hapag-Lloyd of Germany in 1980. An A300B equipped with Pratt & Whitney JT9D engines flew in May 1979, and in the following January the A300B2 with JT9D-59As entered service with Scandinavian Airlines. Garuda Indonesian Airways and Iberia also use the Airbus with JT9Ds. It may be added that Garuda was the first airline to take delivery of the A300 equipped with the two-crew 'forward-facing crew cockpit' (FFCC), as developed for the later A310, the delivery taking place in January 1982. Two months later, on 4 March, the A300B celebrated its millionth accident-free flying hour, a remarkable achievement by any standard. Since its introduction into service, the A300B has averaged a technical dispatch reliability of 98.5 per cent, higher than that of any other wide-body. Airbus Industrie is also rightly proud of the fact that US Civil Aeronautics Board figures show that the A300B's direct maintenance costs in the USA are the lowest for all wide-bodies currently in service.

Although chronologically out of step, since it comes after the short-fuselage A310, it is convenient to complete the current story of A300B development with mention of the A300-600, which Airbus decided to fund in December 1980.

Egyptair has ordered eight A300B4-200s, of which five have been delivered, and are operated alongside one B4-100 leased from Hapag Lloyd. Formed in 1932 as Misr Airwork (later Misrair), the airline became United Arab Airlines in 1960, and in 1971 was renamed Egyptair. The fleet includes seven Boeing 707-320Cs and seven Boeing 737s.

Toa Domestic Airlines has ordered nine A300B2-200s, of which six are so far in operation. This airline was formed in 1971 by the merger of Japan Domestic Airlines and Toa Airways. Services are provided over an extensive network of scheduled domestic routes, serving 35 Japanese cities.

The 'Dash-600' is a slightly stretched version, with two extra seat rows, typically seating 285 in all-tourist class, and providing space for two extra LD3 containers under the floor. It has uprated CF6-80C or JT9D-7R4H engines, the more sharply tapered rear fuselage and smaller horizontal tail developed for the A310, considerably more components made of composite materials, and slightly more range. The Dash-600 made its first flight around mid-1983, and entered service in the spring of 1984, following certification with Pratt & Whitney engines in the first half of that year.

In the longer term Airbus Industrie can only secure a major share of the overall commercial transport market (the aim appears to be around one-third) by developing aircraft across a broad spectrum, rather than exploiting one narrow slot. Market surveys have shown some demand for variants of the A300B offering longer range and for others offering higher seating capacity over short/medium stages, but these potential markets appear to be comparatively small and a

long way in the future. There were, however, strong indications of a much larger demand for a wide-body aircraft seating around 225, i.e. a short-fuselage A300. It was on this basis that development of the A310 was given the go-ahead in July 1978, leading to first flight of the aircraft (F-WZLH) on 3 April 1982, painted in Lufthansa colours on the port side, and Swissair to starboard. The A310 entered service in 1983, followed by the longer-range A310-300 in 1986.

The A310 fuselage is shortened by 11 frames in comparison with that of the A300, i.e. by 22 ft 10 in (6.96 m), to give a capacity of 211–289 seats. A typical mixed-class configuration would seat 237, with which payload the A310 has range of 3,530 miles (5680 km). The A310-300 will use a fuel

Formed in 1972 to succeed MSA (Malaysia-Singapore Airlines), Singapore Airlines (SIA) has ordered 12 A300B4-200s, of which five were in service in late 1982. Airbus Industrie has been extremely successful in its sales to the Far East.

In March 1983 the first three Airbus A310s were delivered to Lufthansa, which had ordered 25 in April 1979 as successors to the Boeing 727. The type A300 differs from the shorter A310 in having transsonic wings and the 'Forward Facing Crew Concept', with only two pilots and new computer screen and keyboard technology.

transfer system between the main tanks and a tank in the tailplane to reduce trim drag, extending this range to 4,055 miles (6525 km).

The A310 also has a new, smaller, and aerodynamically advanced wing, JT9D-7R4D-E1 or CF6-80A1 or Dash-80A3 engines, and (as mentioned above) a smaller and lighter horizontal tail, a redesigned rear fuselage, a two-man cockpit, and a higher percentage of composite materials. The British wing is so successful that no vortex generators or fences are required (making the A310 the only new-generation airliner with a completely 'clean' wing), yet optimum cruise Mach number has been increased from 0.78 to 0.805. In addition, buffet-limited coefficient has been increased by 10 per cent, with the result that the A310 can fly 2,000 ft (610 m) higher at the same weight, or can carry 11 tons (11.177 tonnes) more payload at a given height.

In the course of a remarkable route-proving programme through the Middle and Far East, the second A310 (F-WZLI), carrying a load equivalent to 210 passengers and their baggage, and flying in the face of headwinds averaging 52 mph (83.5 km/h), flew nonstop from Kuwait to Singapore, a distance of 4,625 miles (7445 km). Flying from Kuala Lumpur to Bangkok, the A310 reached 43,000 ft (13105 m), a remarkable altitude for an aircraft of its class. More significantly, it was found that at Mach 0.80 the aircraft burns 6.5 per cent less fuel than predicted — a remarkable saving.

In order primarily to share in the A310 programme, British Aerospace became a full partner in Airbus Industrie in January 1979. In the combined A300/310 programme, Aérospatiale (France) has a 37.9 per cent share, as does Deutsche Airbus (representing MBB of Germany), while British Aerospace has 20 per cent, and CASA (Spain) has 4.2 per cent. Fokker of the Netherlands and Belairbus of Belgium are both Airbus Industrie associates, the latter participating only in the A310.

In early 1984 it was decided that the small Airbus A320 would be built: a short- and medium-range aircraft for around 150 passengers and a narrow fuselage cross-section. This was the first subsonic airliner with full fly-by-wire steering and sidesticks instead of control rods. This type had received more than 250 orders and options by the beginning of 1986, and is planned to come into use in 1989. Around 400 Airbuses of other types had been ordered by that time. Airbus Industrie is also planning two totally new versions, the four-engined very long-range A340 and the twin-engined medium-range A330, carrying more than 300 passengers. A start to the programme was made in 1987.

This photograph of the A310 assembly line includes two aircraft approaching completion for Swissair.

Panavia Tornado Euro-defender

The first warplane to be designed to meet the needs of three nations — the UK, West Germany and Italy — the Panavia Tornado is now in production both as an attack aircraft and as an all-weather interceptor. Possessing capabilities much greater than those of any previous aircraft of its size, it can carry every weapon in the NATO tactical armoury.

The Panavia Tornado was born out of an international design programme shared by three companies who had been on opposite sides in World War 2: Messerschmitt, of Germany, Supermarine, of England, and Fiat of Italy. It is now one of the most powerful defence systems in the whole arsenal of the West, not least because it combines weaponry from all three countries and thus constitutes a real deterrent against potential attack.

The multi-national Tornado programme can be traced back to 1967, when many NATO countries were planning a new combat aircraft, and looking for partners to share development costs. The original leaders in this enterprise were West Germany and Canada, with Belgium, Italy and the Netherlands all showing interest in taking up smaller shares of the design and production workload. In that same year France withdrew from a proposed co-operation programme with the UK on a variable-sweep fighter, in order to concentrate on her own Dassault Mirage series. This left the UK to find other means to obtain what was primarily an English Electric Canberra bomber replacement.

Multi-nationalism under way

In the talks that followed, Canada and the four Continental nations placed emphasis on air superiority (their basic need was for a Lockheed F-104G Starfighter replacement), while the UK's interest centred on low-level strike. This diversity of roles made a variable-geometry aircraft virtually essential, and the would-be partners agreed that it should be a two-seat, twin-engined design. At that stage the project was designated MRCA-75 (Multi-Role Combat Aircraft for 1975), although in the event its development was to take rather longer than was envisaged in the late 1960s.

What might have become a six-nation transAtlantic programme then experienced a series of set-backs, when Canada's new Trudeau government pulled out, followed by the Belgians and the Dutch, all acting from a combination of political and economic motives. However, there remained the two most powerful nations, West Germany and the UK, who where ready to proceed as equal partners, and Italy as a relatively minor yet still important member of the team.

By pooling the requirements of the German air force (Luftwaffe) and navy (Marineflieger), the Royal Air Force, and the Italian air force (Aeronautica Militare Italiana), the new aircraft's basic roles were defined as: close air support for ground forces in the battle area; interdiction/strike against ground installations, airfields, supply depots, communications, etc; naval strike against shipping and coastal targets; air superiority above the battlefield; air defence/interception; tactical and long-range reconnaissance at both high and low levels; and aircrew training, while remaining operational.

To manage the development and production of the Tornado weapon system (including the powerplant and the special

The 16th and last of the Tornado prototypes is seen here in Marineflieger colours, with serial 9803 on the front fuselage, and the badge of MFG 1 (based at Schleswig) on the fin. It is carrying four MBB Kormoran anti-shipping missiles. The Tornado is replacing the F-104G Starfighter in German navy missions over the Baltic.

Panavia Tornado

Tornado 9805 is shown here in the paint scheme and markings of the Bundesmarine, having formerly flown with the test serial D9592. It is carrying four MBB Kormoran anti-shipping missiles. This aircraft was destroyed in an accident on 17 April 1980 while its crew were practising for the Hanover Air Show.

cannon), Panavia Aircraft was formed in Munich in 1969 by the three airframe participants, now designated Messerschmitt-Bölkow-Blohm (MBB), British Aerospace (BAe) and Aeritalia (AIT). In the same year Turbo-Union was formed in London by Rolls Royce, MTU and Fiat, to develop and manufacture the new RB.199 turbo-fan engine. Panavia now has as its principal subcontractors MBB, BAe, AIT, Turbo-Union, IWKA-Mauser (for the cannon) and Elliott's EASAMS division for avionics system integration. The Tornado project was given the formal go-ahead in 1970 by the tri-national government agency NAMMA, with costs to be split on a 42.5/42.5/15.0 per cent basis between the three countries.

Once the needs of the four services had been translated into practical terms, the Tornado had to possess five basic capabilities: to take off and land in very short distances, in order to continue operations from bomb-damaged runways; to fly at high speeds at low level for long distances, without excessive crew fatigue; to make low-level penetrations by day or night, regardless of weather conditions; to strike accurately with a heavy warload in a single-pass attack; and to fly at high supersonic speeds at altitude.

To achieve these capabilities, one of the main features of the aircraft was to be a variable-sweep wing. In the 'unswept' configuration this could generate high lift coefficients for take-off and landing, giving slow unstick and touchdown speeds. In the fully swept position, it would provide minimum gust response and hence a smooth ride during low-level penetrations, and low wave drag for supersonic flight at altitude.

In addition, the Tornado had to have engines of unusually low specific fuel consumption (SFC), yet with a high after-burning thrust to blast it off the runway in a short distance even with a heavy bombload, and to enable it to perform effectively in the air-to-air role. The engines also had to have thrust reversers, to stop the aircraft in a short distance when landing between bomb craters.

All-weather low-level penetration implied fully automatic terrain following, something never before achieved. First-pass attacks demanded highly accurate navigation, so that the crew could deliver their weapons without seeing the target, if necessary. Altogether, the Tornado was clearly going to be a large, complex aircraft, much more expensive than a single-role fighter, but infinitely more useful in stopping a Russian attack at night, or in the very limited visibility that is characteristic of European operations.

Design and development of the 'swing-wing' undoubtedly benefited from earlier experience at Warton (the BAe division concerned with Tornado). This dates back to wind-tunnel tests in 1964 on the P.45 project, and continued with work on the ill-fated Anglo-French VG fighter. The key to the design of this category of wing is the central carry-through structure box, which in this case is of electron-beam-welded construction (that of the earlier General Dynamics F-111 was of bolted steel), with Teflon-coated pivots.

The Tornado wing sweep varies from 25° in the fully forward position to 68° fully aft. On the interdiction/strike Tornado the wing is positioned manually, but in the air-

Panavia Tornado F Mk 2 cutaway drawing key

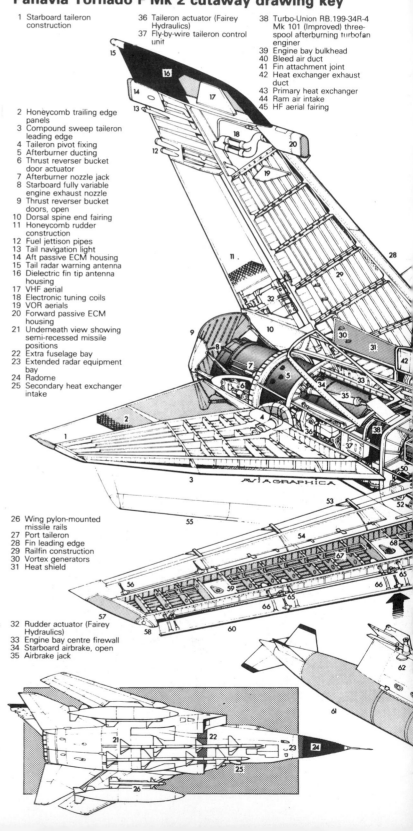

1 Starboard taileron construction
2 Honeycomb trailing edge panels
3 Compound sweep taileron leading edge
4 Taileron pivot fixing
5 Afterburner ducting
6 Thrust reverser bucket door actuator
7 Afterburner nozzle jack
8 Starboard fully variable engine exhaust nozzle
9 Thrust reverser bucket doors, open
10 Dorsal spine end fairing
11 Honeycomb rudder construction
12 Fuel jettison pipes
13 Tail navigation light
14 Aft passive ECM housing
15 Tail radar warning antenna
16 Dielectric fin tip antenna housing
17 VHF aerial
18 Electronic tuning coils
19 VOR aerials
20 Forward passive ECM housing
21 Underneath view showing semi-recessed missile positions
22 Extra fuselage bay
23 Extended radar equipment bay
24 Radome
25 Secondary heat exchanger intake

26 Wing pylon-mounted missile rails
27 Port taileron
28 Fin leading edge
29 Railfin construction
30 Vortex generators
31 Heat shield

32 Rudder actuator (Fairey Hydraulics)
33 Engine bay centre firewall
34 Starboard airbrake, open
35 Airbrake jack

36 Taileron actuator (Fairey Hydraulics)
37 Fly-by-wire taileron control unit
38 Turbo-Union RB.199-34R-4 Mk 101 (Improved) three-spool afterburning turbofan enginer
39 Engine bay bulkhead
40 Bleed air duct
41 Fin attachment joint
42 Heat exchanger exhaust duct
43 Primary heat exchanger
44 Ram air intake
45 HF aerial fairing

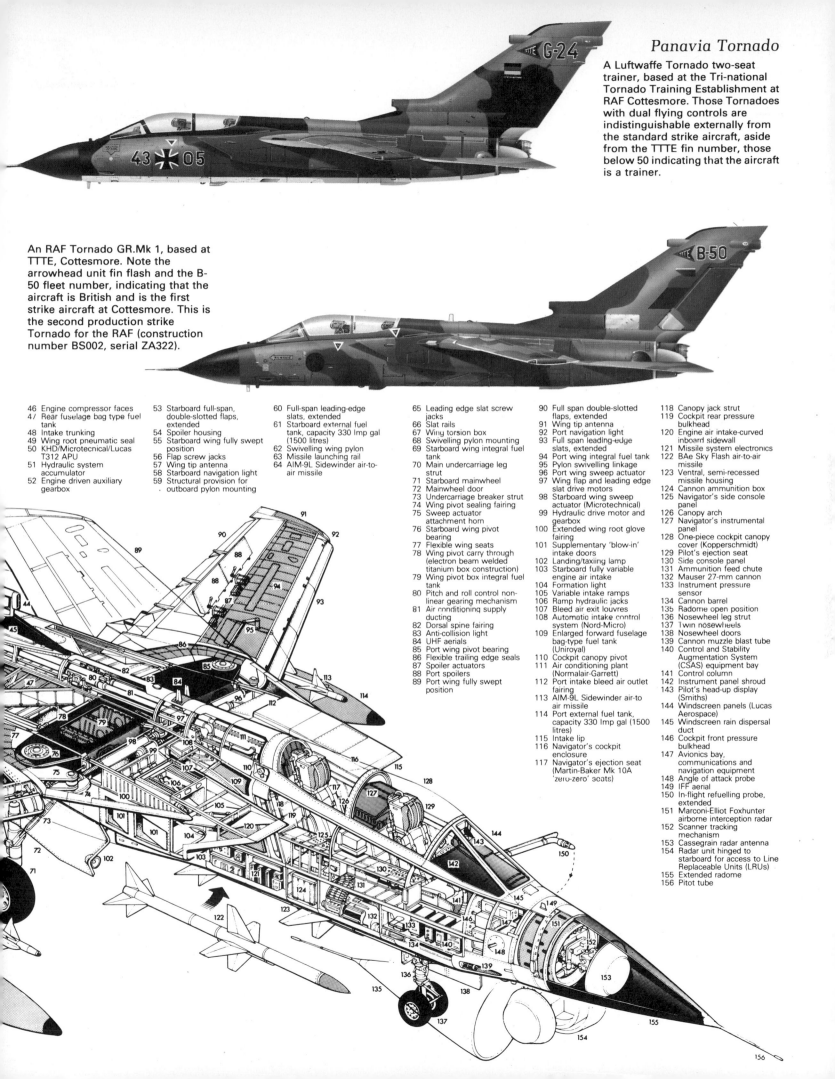

Panavia Tornado

A Luftwaffe Tornado two-seat trainer, based at the Tri-national Tornado Training Establishment at RAF Cottesmore. Those Tornadoes with dual flying controls are indistinguishable externally from the standard strike aircraft, aside from the TTTE fin number, those below 50 indicating that the aircraft is a trainer.

An RAF Tornado GR.Mk 1, based at TTTE, Cottesmore. Note the arrowhead unit fin flash and the B-50 fleet number, indicating that the aircraft is British and is the first strike aircraft at Cottesmore. This is the second production strike Tornado for the RAF (construction number BS002, serial ZA322).

46 Engine compressor faces
47 Rear fuselage bag type fuel tank
48 Intake trunking
49 Wing root pneumatic seal
50 KHD/Microtecnical/Lucas T312 APU
51 Hydraulic system accumulator
52 Engine driven auxiliary gearbox
53 Starboard full-span, double-slotted flaps, extended
54 Spoiler housing
55 Starboard wing fully swept position
56 Flap screw jacks
57 Wing tip antenna
58 Starboard navigation light
59 Structural provision for outboard pylon mounting
60 Full-span leading-edge slats, extended
61 Starboard external fuel tank, capacity 330 Imp gal (1500 litres)
62 Swivelling wing pylon
63 Missile launching rail
64 AIM-9L Sidewinder air-to-air missile
65 Leading edge slat screw jacks
66 Slat rails
67 Wing torsion box
68 Swivelling pylon mounting
69 Starboard wing integral fuel tank
70 Main undercarriage leg strut
71 Starboard mainwheel
72 Mainwheel door
73 Undercarriage breaker strut
74 Wing pivot sealing fairing
75 Sweep actuator attachment horn
76 Starboard wing pivot bearing
77 Flexible wing seats
78 Wing pivot carry through (electron beam welded titanium box construction)
79 Wing pivot box integral fuel tank
80 Pitch and roll control non-linear gearing mechanism
81 Air conditioning supply ducting
82 Dorsal spine fairing
83 Anti-collision light
84 UHF aerials
85 Port wing pivot bearing
86 Flexible trailing edge seals
87 Spoiler actuators
88 Port spoilers
89 Port wing fully swept position
90 Full span double-slotted flaps, extended
91 Wing tip antenna
92 Port navigation light
93 Full span leading-edge slats, extended
94 Port wing integral fuel tank
95 Pylon swivelling linkage
96 Port wing sweep actuator
97 Wing flap and leading edge slat drive motors
98 Starboard wing sweep actuator (Microtechnical)
99 Hydraulic drive motor and gearbox
100 Extended wing root glove fairing
101 Supplementary 'blow-in' intake doors
102 Landing/taxiing lamp
103 Starboard fully variable engine air intake
104 Formation light
105 Variable intake ramps
106 Ramp hydraulic jacks
107 Bleed air exit louvres
108 Automatic intake control system (Nord-Micro)
109 Enlarged forward fuselage bag-type fuel tank (Uniroyal)
110 Cockpit canopy pivot
111 Air conditioning plant (Normalair-Garrett)
112 Port intake bleed air outlet fairing
113 AIM-9L Sidewinder air-to air missile
114 Port external fuel tank, capacity 330 Imp gal (1500 litres)
115 Intake lip
116 Navigator's cockpit enclosure
117 Navigator's ejection seat (Martin-Baker Mk 10A 'zero-zero' seats)
118 Canopy jack strut
119 Cockpit rear pressure bulkhead
120 Engine air intake-curved inboard sidewall
121 Missile system electronics
122 BAe Sky Flash air-to-air missile
123 Ventral, semi-recessed missile housing
124 Cannon ammunition box
125 Navigator's side console panel
126 Canopy arch
127 Navigator's instrumental panel
128 One-piece cockpit canopy cover (Kopperschmidt)
129 Pilot's ejection seat
130 Side console panel
131 Ammunition feed chute
132 Mauser 27-mm cannon
133 Instrument pressure sensor
134 Cannon barrel
135 Radome open position
136 Nosewheel leg strut
137 Twin nosewheels
138 Nosewheel doors
139 Cannon muzzle blast tube
140 Control and Stability Augmentation System (CSAS) equipment bay
141 Control column
142 Instrument panel shroud
143 Pilot's head-up display (Smiths)
144 Windscreen panels (Lucas Aerospace)
145 Windscreen rain dispersal duct
146 Cockpit front pressure bulkhead
147 Avionics bay, communications and navigation equipment
148 Angle of attack probe
149 IFF aerial
150 In-flight refuelling probe, extended
151 Marconi-Elliot Foxhunter airborne interception radar
152 Scanner tracking mechanism
153 Cassegrain radar antenna
154 Radar unit hinged to starboard for access to Line Replaceable Units (LRUs)
155 Extended radome
156 Pitot tube

Three-view of an RAF Tornado GR.Mk 1 as it is expected to appear in production form with laser ranger and marked-target seeker under the front fuselage. It is shown armed with eight 1,000-lb (454-kg) bombs, and fitted with two 330 Imp gal (1500 litre) tanks and two ECM jamming pods. This is a typical configuration for long-range low-level strike.

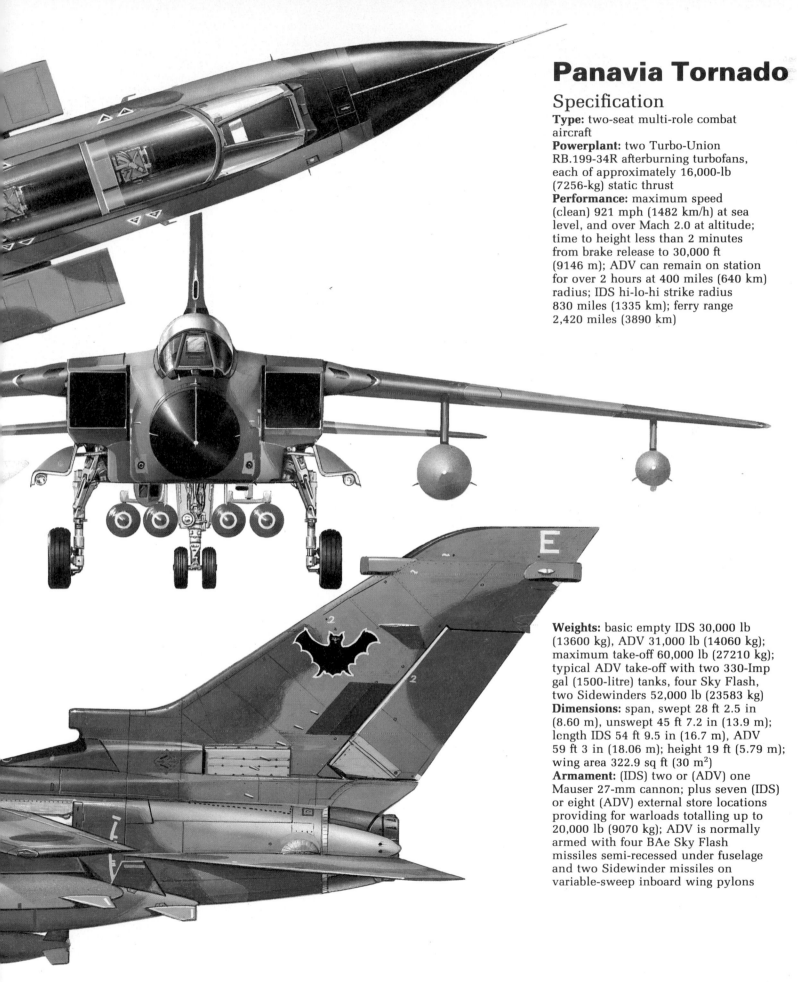

Panavia Tornado

Specification

Type: two-seat multi-role combat aircraft

Powerplant: two Turbo-Union RB.199-34R afterburning turbofans, each of approximately 16,000-lb (7256-kg) static thrust

Performance: maximum speed (clean) 921 mph (1482 km/h) at sea level, and over Mach 2.0 at altitude; time to height less than 2 minutes from brake release to 30,000 ft (9146 m); ADV can remain on station for over 2 hours at 400 miles (640 km) radius; IDS hi-lo-hi strike radius 830 miles (1335 km); ferry range 2,420 miles (3890 km)

Weights: basic empty IDS 30,000 lb (13600 kg), ADV 31,000 lb (14060 kg); maximum take-off 60,000 lb (27210 kg); typical ADV take-off with two 330-Imp gal (1500-litre) tanks, four Sky Flash, two Sidewinders 52,000 lb (23583 kg)

Dimensions: span, swept 28 ft 2.5 in (8.60 m), unswept 45 ft 7.2 in (13.9 m); length IDS 54 ft 9.5 in (16.7 m), ADV 59 ft 3 in (18.06 m); height 19 ft (5.79 m); wing area 322.9 sq ft (30 m²)

Armament: (IDS) two or (ADV) one Mauser 27-mm cannon; plus seven (IDS) or eight (ADV) external store locations providing for warloads totalling up to 20,000 lb (9070 kg); ADV is normally armed with four BAe Sky Flash missiles semi-recessed under fuselage and two Sidewinder missiles on variable-sweep inboard wing pylons

At Cottesmore in England, the Trinational Tornado Training Establishment converts pilots to a type which is new to them. In the foreground are Tornadoes in the colours of the Luftwaffe (left) and the Marineflieger with its white and grey colouring, as well as a mock-up in the 'house colours' of MBB.

defence variant (ADV) wing sweep is controlled automatically. The wing halves are moved by two separate hydraulic actuators, but if a discrepancy in wing sweep of 0.5° arises, the wings are automatically locked in place. If for any reason the wings should lock in the fully aft position (in which case the flaps cannot be used), the Tornado can still be landed safely, although the distance required is then similar to that for a conventional high performance aircraft, rather than a STOL design.

Most of the wing trailing edge is taken up with double-slotted flaps, while the leading edge is fitted with slats, with a Krueger flap on the inboard 'glove'. The slats and trailing-edge flaps can be used with the wing in the mid-swept position to enhance manoeuvrability. There are no ailerons, roll control being provided by differential tailplane movements (hence the name 'tailerons'), augmented by differential wing spoiler action at sweep angles below 45°. These spoilers also act as lift dumpers in the landing run, increasing the weight on the undercarriage and thus the aircraft's braking ability.

Fly-by-wire controls

All the flying controls are moved in response to electrical signals (i.e. 'fly-by-wire'), in which pilot demands from the control column and rudder bar are modulated by a CSAS (command stability augmentation system). However, in emergency the aircraft can be flown without the CSAS, and if the electrical signalling fails the Tornado can be flown by means of direct mechanical links to the tailerons.

The Turbo-Union RB.199 turbofan that was developed specifically to meet the Tornado's needs is noteworthy for its three-spool configuration, remarkably small size, short after-burner, and very low SFC. A three-spool layout was chosen to permit the highest possible pressure ratio (and hence the

lowest SFC) with minimum risk of engine surges. The RB.199 is only 34 in (86.4 cm) in maximum diameter and a mere 126 in (3.2 m) long. It weighs only 1,800 lb (816 kg).

To achieve the shortest possible landing run, the pilot can preselect thrust reverses before touchdown, and the buckets will then be deployed within one second of ground impact by microswitches on the undercarriage legs. To enhance directional stability while using thrust reversers, yaw damping is automatic via the nosewheel steering circuit.

Turning to the subject of the aircraft's avionics, Tornado has no fewer than five navigation modes. The principal mode employs a mix of data from the Ferranti inertial system and the Decca Doppler radar, giving less than half the position error of a pure inertial system. It also has a twin-gyro platform providing heading and altitude data, which can be used either with Doppler or air-data velocity inputs. Alternatively, the aircraft can be navigated in a pure inertial mode, and can combine inertial heading information with air data velocity.

Navigation data is supplied to the pilot in the form of Ferranti's optically projected moving map display, while the navigator has the same display combined with the returns from the ground mapping radar (GMR). In addition to the GMR antenna, the Tornado's nose houses that of the terrain-following radar (TFR), both of these radars being Texas Instruments products. The TFR enables the aircraft to be flown automatically via the CSAS at up to Mach 1.2 and at a pre-set clearance height above the ground, which the pilot can vary between 200 ft (60 m) and 1,500 ft (460 m). The TFR returns are also displayed to the pilot, so that he can monitor the functioning of the automatic system. He can also select the amount of g that the TF system can apply to the aircraft, thus controlling the roughness of ride. In the event of failure of the TFR, low level flight can be continued in a terrain-avoidance mode (i.e. making lateral manoeuvres, rather than in a vertical plane), using the contour mapping of the GMR.

In addition to the items of equipment listed above, the Tornado has an advanced Smiths head-up display (HUD), a radar altimeter, and a retractable laser ranger and marked-target seeker, developed by Ferranti.

The ninth prototype Tornado (and the second to be assembled in Italy) is seen here in the early paint scheme applied by all three countries. Its Italian air force serial is MM589, and it was based at Decimomannu in Sardinia for weapon trials, including external stores and tests of the autopilot.

The 11th prototype Tornado (9801) in Luftwaffe colour scheme and markings. This is possibly a minor variation on the standard colours, which consist of two shades of green and a somewhat darker grey than shown here. This aircraft was with Erprobungsstelle 61 at Manching, testing flying qualities.

Diversity of offensive armament

The Tornado will carry a wide range of external stores, including nuclear weapons, the 'Paveway' laser-guided bomb, Maverick air-to-ground missiles, the GBU-15 TV-guided glide bomb, Kormoran and P3T Sea Eagle anti-shipping missiles, the British BL755 cluster bomb, and JP233 airfield denial weapon, and West Germany's MW-1 (Mehrzweckwaffe, or multi-purpose weapon) bomblet dispenser, which will be used against tanks, aircraft hangars, runways, and aircraft parked in the open. The interdiction/strike (IDS) Tornado is also fitted with two Mauser 27-mm revolver cannon and 360 rounds of ammunition. Two rates of fire are available.

The IDS Tornado and the externally identical training aircraft represent the two initial production series. As described above, the IDS aircraft has an air-to-air capability, but UK requirements have now developed to place greater emphasis on long-endurance combat air patrol at considerable distance from any airfield. The RAF needed this capability to replace the McDonnell Douglas F-4 Phantom in providing air cover for convoys and Royal Navy units between the Arctic Circle and the English Channel, and in

The first prototype of the air defence variant of Tornado is seen here in standard configuration, with four BAe Sky Flash medium-range air-to-air missiles semi-recessed under the fuselage, two auxiliary fuel tanks on the wing pylons, and two AIM-9 Sidewinders mounted on the sides of the tank pylons.

One of seven Italian air force Tornadoes at Cottesmore, this is the first Italian-built trainer (IT001), which first flew on 25 September 1981. It is shown here bearing the TTTE fleet number I-40 and the Italian AF serial RS-01, presumably allocated by the Reparto Sperimentale for tests at Practica di Mare, near Rome.

Tornado F.Mk 2, as it is being operated by the RAF in the combat air patrol role over the waters surrounding the UK. Note the absence of a cannon on the port side, and the deletion of the laser unit under the front fuselage. The dark area at the fin tip is dielectric material, and those at the base of the fin are titanium panels to avoid scorching by hot air.

patrolling the Iceland-Faroes gap against incoming Soviet bombers and reconnaissance aircraft. These demands led to a major new derivative of the IDS Tornado, the air defence variant (ADV).

The ADV retains 80 per cent commonality with the IDS Tornado, but differs in various respects: the fuselage is extended by 53 in (1.34 m) to provide for ventral carriage of missiles, and more fuel and equipment space; the IDS radars are replaced by the Marconi-Elliott Foxhunter air intercept radar in a new nose shape; provision is made for four semi-recessed BAe Sky Flash radar-guided missiles under the fuselage. These are normally augmented by two Sidewinder IR-homing dogfight missiles on the sides of the inboard wing pylons; the left-hand Mauser cannon is removed to provide equipment space; the wing glove leading edge is swept 68°, rather than 60°; the avionics fit is revised to suit the new role; and visual target identification is assisted by a low-light TV camera mounted behind the windscreen, giving the pilot an enlarged and brightened view of the other aircraft. In daylight this TV facility will give positive identification in good time for a front-hemisphere firing of Sky Flash. In starlight conditions, it provides for shadowing and missile release.

The Foxhunter radar is a major advance, providing target acquisition at approximately 115 miles (185 km). It will be able to detect low-flying aircraft, and operate against multiple targets in a track-while-scan mode. The Sky Flash missiles will be effective against both aircraft and the larger cruise missiles, providing a firing range of over 28 miles (45 km), and the capability to destroy targets flying at less than 300 ft (90 m) above the ground.

Nine prototype and six pre-series IDS aircraft and three ADV prototypes have been built, and these are to be followed by 805 production aircraft, which will be augmented by four of the pre-series IDS Tornadoes being converted to full production standard. Of the 809 operational aircraft, 212 will serve with the German air force, 112 with the German navy, 385 with the RAF, and 100 with the Italian air force.

Tornado in service

It is envisaged that 165 of the RAF Tornadoes will be ADVs, but this number may be increased by at least 20 in the light of recent changes in UK defence plans. Three production contracts have so far been signed for 40, 110, and 164 aircraft, and manufacture of the fourth batch of 162 has now been authorized. Aircraft construction is split between the three countries (Germany making the centre fuselage, the UK the front and rear fuselage, and Italy the wings), but each country assembles aircraft for its own services. By mid-1981 over 60 Tornadoes had flown, and plans called for production to peak at 12 units monthly. To put these figures into perspective, the first prototype had flown in August 1974, and the first production aircraft only in July 1979, while the first ADV prototype made its maiden flight in October 1979.

Initial production deliveries took place in July 1980 to the Trinational Tornado Training Establishment at RAF Cottesmore. The first formal course began in January 1981, and at its peak Tornadoes will be used to produce up to 160 operational crews per year. From there, RAF crews will progress to the Weapons Conversion Units (WCU) at Honington, while German crews go to Jever for weapons training. The first RAF unit to receive the Tornado GR Mk 1 for operational use was No. 617 ('Dambusters') Sqn at Scampton, where it replaced the Vulcan B.2. The type also replaced the overland BAe (Blackburn) Buccaneers in No. 1 Group and RAF Germany, as well as reconnaissance Canberras and some SEPECAT Jaguars in RAF Germany. The first German unit was MFG1 at Schleswig, and the first Italian unit was the 6th Stormo at Ghedi.

The Royal Air Force has ordered 220 Tornado GR.Mk 1s, including trainer versions. The first delivery was to No. 9 Squadron in January 1982. A total of seven Strike/Attack Squadrons of the RAF are stationed in West Germany with their Tornadoes, which can also be equipped with tactical nuclear weapons, and there is also one squadron with reconnaissance planes. The RAF has a total of 165 Tornado F.Mk 2s defending its airspace.

In February 1986, eight F-3s were exported to Oman and 24 to the Saudi Arabian air force.

Panavia Tornado variants

GR MK 1: RAF designation for the IDS (interdiction/strike) aircraft that is standard in the four Tornado-user services (526 planned)

GR Mk 1 (T): RAF designation for the trainer version of the IDS aircraft, which is externally identical to the GR Mk 1 (118 planned) for four services

F Mk 2: RAF air defence variant (ADV) with longer fuselage, more fuel, revised avionics, a single cannon, increased sweep on the wing glove, and provision for four ventral Sky Flash missiles (165 planned)

Index

PICTURE CREDITS